UNLEASHING MICROSOFT® WINDOWS VISTA® MEDIA CENTER

Mark Edward Soper

que®
800 East 96th Street
Indianapolis, Indiana 46240

Unleashing Microsoft Windows Vista Media Center

ISBN-13: 978-0-7897-3671-0

ISBN-10: 0-7897-3671-3

Library of Congress Cataloging-in-Publication Data:

Soper, Mark Edward.
Unleashing Microsoft Windows Vista Media center / Mark Edward Soper.
p. cm.
ISBN 978-0-7897-3671-0
1. Microsoft Windows (Computer file) 2. Home entertainment systems. 3. Interactive multimedia. I. Title.
TK7881.3.S65 2008
006.7—dc22

2008036255

Printed in the United States of America

First Printing: October 2008

Trademarks

Warning and Disclaimer

Bulk Sales

Que Publishing offers excellent discounts on this book when ordered in quantity for bulk purchases or special sales. For more information, please contact

U.S. Corporate and Government Sales
1-800-382-3419
corpsales@pearsontechgroup.com

For sales outside of the U.S., please contact

International Sales
international@pearson.com

Associate Publisher
Greg Wiegand

Acquisitions Editor
Rick Kughen

Development Editor
Rick Kughen

Managing Editor
Kristy Hart

Project Editor
Jovana San Nicolas-Shirley

Copy Editor
Language Logistics, LLC

Indexer
Cheryl Lenser

Proofreaders
Jovana San Nicolas-Shirley
Karen Gill

Technical Editor
Mark Reddin

Reviewers
Will Schmied
Mark Reddin

Publishing Coordinator
Cindy Teeters

Book Designer
Anne Jones

Compositor
Nonie Ratcliff

Contents at a Glance

Table of Contents

Part V: Enhancing Windows Vista Media Center

Part VI: Appendices

About the Author

Mark Edward Soper has taught computer troubleshooting and other technical subjects to thousands of students from Maine to Hawaii since 1992. Mark is the author of nine books, most recently *Maximum PC Microsoft Windows Vista Exposed*, and coauthor of nine books, most recently *Upgrading and Repairing Networks, 5th Edition*. He is a longtime contributor to *Upgrading and Repairing PCs*, working on the 11th through 18th editions. He has contributed chapters to *Upgrading and Repairing Networks Second Edition, Special Edition Using Microsoft Windows Millennium Edition, Special Edition Using Microsoft Windows XP* (all editions) and *Special Edition Using Microsoft Windows Vista.* Mark is currently writing *Upgrading and Repairing PCs: A+ Certification Study Guide, 3rd Edition*. He is a regular contributor to *Maximum PC* magazine and website and has contributed chapters to *Maximum PC Guide to Building a Dream PC* and *Maximum PC Ultimate PC Performance Guide*.

Dedication

For the newest member of the family, Clara Louise Soper, who will grow up in a world of digital media without boundaries.

Acknowledgments

My name is on the cover of this book, but many, many others have made it possible.

First of all, I thank God for making it possible for me to meld my interests in history, photography, writing, current events, and technology into a career as a technology writer and trainer. He truly "directs my paths."

I also want to thank Cheryl, my wife, because her encouragement to start sharing my experiences made this book, and its many predecessors, possible.

My family continues to grow in size and technological scope, and I thank my children, their spouses, and their children for encouragement, inspiration, and the opportunity to troubleshoot their systems and discuss the industry.

Many thanks to the staff at Que Publishing for their work in bringing this book to life. In particular:

Paul Boger and Greg Wiegand, for building an outstanding production team.

Rick Kughen, for asking me to bring a new edition of a popular book to life and providing expert development.

Kristy Hart, for keeping everyone's efforts on track.

Jovana San Nicolas-Shirley, for keeping my author reviews on track.

Mark Reddin, for expert tech editing (as always).

Cindy Teeters, for keeping payments coming and working to improve the billing process.

...and the rest, including the graphics, design, and proofreading team members, for continuing to help produce outstanding technology books.

We Want to Hear from You!

As the reader of this book, *you* are our most important critic and commentator. We value your opinion and want to know what we're doing right, what we could do better, what areas you'd like to see us publish in, and any other words of wisdom you're willing to pass our way.

As an associate publisher for Que Publishing, I welcome your comments. You can email or write me directly to let me know what you did or didn't like about this book—as well as what we can do to make our books better.

Please note that I cannot help you with technical problems related to the topic of this book. We do have a User Services group, however, where I will forward specific technical questions related to the book.

When you write, please be sure to include this book's title and author as well as your name, email address, and phone number. I will carefully review your comments and share them with the author and editors who worked on the book.

Email: feedback@quepublishing.com

Mail: Greg Wiegand
Associate Publisher
Que Publishing
800 East 96th Street
Indianapolis, IN 46240 USA

Reader Services

Visit our website and register this book at informit.com/register for convenient access to any updates, downloads, or errata that might be available for this book.

Introduction

IN THIS INTRODUCTION

- Maximizing the Potential of Windows Vista's Multimedia Control Center
- How This Book Is Organized

One of the most significant, yet least used, features in Windows Vista Home Premium and Ultimate editions, is, ironically, so massive that it once required its own version of Windows XP. That feature is, of course, Windows Media Center (WMC).

WMC enables your PC to be the hub of your digital entertainment experience, and thanks to Windows Vista, you need not sacrifice basic Windows capabilities to enjoy the convergence of TV, movies, music, photography, and video. And to make it even more enjoyable, WMC is just as much at home in a media room with a big-screen HDTV as it is on your desktop. WMC enables you to sit back, relax with your favorite snacks and beverages, and surf your home media resources the same way you surf TV channels.

Maximizing the Potential of Windows Vista's Multimedia Control Center

Despite its capabilities, though, WMC is often overlooked by users looking to get more enjoyment and more usefulness out of Windows Vista. This book's Job 1 is to make sure you, the reader, understand what WMC can do, how it makes your life easier and more fun, and, not least, how you can build upon WMC to customize your digital media experience.

As you'll discover by reading this book, you can use portions of WMC without adding any special hardware to a typical PC. But, if you want to maximize what it can do, you'll also discover how to customize your existing system's hardware, which software components to add, and how to use other parts of Windows Vista to make WMC even more powerful and enjoyable.

As you read this book, you're sure to discover, just as I have, that WMC's simple interface conceals a very powerful, yet user-friendly, media hub. Helping you unleash that power is what this book is all about.

How This Book Is Organized

This book contains 16 chapters and two appendixes, covering every aspect of WMC from "What is WMC?" in Chapter 1 to "How do I solve problems with WMC?" in Chapter 16. Let's take a closer look at what you'll find between the covers of this book.

Part I, "Getting Started with Windows Vista Media Center," includes the following chapters:

Chapter 1, "Introducing Windows Vista Media Center," helps you understand the role that WMC plays in the Windows Vista experience, its Windows XP ancestors, and the WMC interface. It's the perfect way to introduce yourself to WMC, or as we often refer to it in these pages, WMC.

Chapter 2, "Equipping Your PC for Media Center," shows you the hardware that different components of WMC need to use. Whether you're building a PC from the ground up, remodeling an existing PC for use with WMC, or preparing to buy a computer for use with WMC, it's a must-read chapter.

Chapter 3, "Setting Up Windows Media Center," gives you a front-row seat as we set up a typical PC for use with WMC. From adjusting your picture to setting up your TV tuner, you'll understand the process from start to finish.

Once WMC is configured, it's time to enjoy it. That's what Part II, "Enjoying Media with WMC," is all about:

Chapter 4, "Viewing and Recording Live TV," shows you how to watch broadcast, cable, and Internet TV, how to deal with standard, digital, and HDTV, and how to record TV shows and series so you can enjoy them on your own schedule.

Chapter 5, "Watching and Recording Movies," shows you how to find out when your favorite movies will be broadcast on TV and how to enjoy your favorite films whether they're on TV, on DVD, or on your hard disk.

Chapter 6, "Importing and Playing Audio," guides you through the process of ripping your CD library to disk, creating playlists, enjoying Internet radio, and synchronizing the contents of a portable media player so you can take your music with you when you leave WMC.

Chapter 7, "Importing and Viewing Photos," helps you grab your photos from your digital camera, organize them, view them, fix common problems, and create impromptu slide shows with music.

WMC isn't just for enjoying media. You can also use it to explore the worlds of sports, news, gaming, and even use it to create your own media, as you'll discover in Part III, "Beyond the Basics of WMC," which includes:

Chapter 8, "Enjoying Sports with Windows Media Center," shows you how to enjoy the riches of sports news, TV, games, and fantasy sports from the comfort of your easy chair and media room.

Chapter 9, "Playing Games and Enjoying Online Content," helps you play the same family-friendly games included with Windows Vista from the comfort of the WMC interface, shows you how to turn WMC into a hardcore gaming launcher, and introduces you to third-party features that enable you to enjoy even more digital music, video, news, and other media without leaving the WMC interface.

Chapter 10, "Creating CDs and DVDs," is your step-by-step guide to creating CDs and DVDs of your favorite music, video, and photos right from the WMC interface.

WMC is powerful all by itself, but your home network makes it even more powerful, as you learn in Part IV, "Adding Windows Vista Media Center to Your Home Network," which includes:

Chapter 11, "Adding and Using Media Center Extenders," introduces you to a hidden side of your Xbox 360: the ability to access your PC's WMC interface via your home network. You'll also learn about other types of Media Center Extenders and how to improve their performance.

Chapter 12, "Connecting with Windows Home Server and Other PCs," helps you use WMC to enjoy media resources on PCs everywhere on your home network, including Microsoft's new Windows Home Server. You'll also learn how to fine-tune your home network for better performance, discover the best choices for Internet service, and learn how to tell when your router is slowing down your network.

Part V, "Enhancing Windows Vista Media Center," helps you learn to make Windows Vista Media Center more powerful by using it in conjunction with other Windows Vista components and third-party applications, and it helps you manage the most common issues you might encounter.

Chapter 13, "Using Windows Media Player with Windows Media Center," shows you how Windows Media Player works with WMC, how to configure its audio-ripping feature so you get the music quality and format you prefer, how to easily create playlists and rate audio, how to edit track and album information, and how to add visualizations so you can enjoy the full capabilities of your digital music collection within WMC.

Chapter 14, "Creating Photo and Video Content for Media Center," helps you explore how to import video, use Windows Live Photo Gallery to make your picture library more WMC-friendly, how to use Windows Movie Maker to shrink the size of your TV recordings, create custom videos, and create DVD slide shows you can enjoy in WMC and elsewhere.

Chapter 15, "Extending Media Center with Third-Party Apps," shows you an exciting world of programs you can use to customize WMC, make its built-in features more powerful, and add new features and capabilities. We've tracked down the software, so you can choose from a wealth of options to make WMC the media center you've always dreamed of.

Chapter 16, "Troubleshooting Media Center," provides expert advice on dealing with the most common problems you might run into and helps you protect your digital media collection.

This book also includes two appendices designed to help readers with specific questions:

Appendix A, "Using Windows Anytime Upgrade to Get WMC Features and More," is a must-read if you have a version of Windows Vista that doesn't include WMC (such as Windows Vista Basic or Business), or if you want to move up from Windows Vista Home Premium to the ultimate (Windows Vista Ultimate). This appendix helps you understand the process of using Windows Anytime Upgrade to move up to a better version of Windows Vista.

Appendix B, "Moving from Windows XP Media Center Editions to Windows Vista Media Center," helps users running PCs with Windows XP Media Center Edition to make the move to Windows Vista.

PART

I

Getting Started with Windows Vista Media Center

CHAPTER

1

Introducing Windows Vista Media Center

Windows Media Center (WMC) is an integral part of Windows Vista Home Premium and Ultimate editions. WMC provides a comfortable "10-foot user interface" (see Figure 1.1) for all of your digital media needs:

- Watch and record live TV on a PC display or a TV
- Listen to FM radio through your home theater system
- Select and play your favorite digital music tracks
- Enjoy special TV and video content brought to you by major producers
- Watch your favorite films from your DVD collection or from TV broadcasts
- Schedule TV recordings so you never miss an episode of your favorite shows, no matter when they're broadcast
- Create your own DVDs from TV recordings
- View, edit, and burn your favorite digital photos to CD or DVD

IN THIS CHAPTER

- Transfer playlists of your favorite digital media to a portable device
- Enjoy digital media stored on PCs throughout your home or office
- Create your own music mix CDs

You can run WMC with a remote control, so you can curl up on your favorite sofa and click your way through your digital media world.

FIGURE 1.1
Enjoying digital music with WMC.

A Brief History of Windows Media Center

Originally, WMC was developed as a special edition of Windows XP known as Windows XP Media Center Edition, which went through three major releases (original, Windows XP Media Center Edition 2004, and Windows XP Media Center Edition 2005) during its lifespan. From the beginning, Windows XP Media Center Edition (XP MCE) provided a full-screen interface control for enjoying movies, TV, video playback and recording, digital photos, and music playback and recording to the base features of Windows XP Professional (minus support for domain-based networks). Higher-quality TV recording, DVD recording, and other improvements were rolled out during the development of XP MCE.

Although XP MCE 2005 became a popular operating system choice for consumer-oriented systems in 2006, users of other Windows XP flavors never got the chance to try it unless they bought a system with XP MCE 2005 preinstalled or were brave enough to build their own, buying XP MCE 2005 from vendors specializing in component sales. XP MCE was never offered as an upgrade to Windows XP Home Edition or Windows XP Professional, in part because its hardware requirements were different from those for other XP editions.

Windows Vista and Windows Media Center

With the release of Windows Vista Home Premium and Ultimate editions, both of which include WMC, WMC is no longer an outsider to the world of Windows. WMC has arrived as a mainstream multimedia viewing and creation program.

WMC makes multimedia better and more fun, whether you use Windows Vista to play DVD movies or CD music, watch videos and live TV, record live TV, or enjoy your own video or photographic creations. WMC makes multimedia more fun because it enables you to integrate your home theater system with your PC. Thanks to WMC, you can enjoy digital media on the platform you prefer, anywhere from a 17-inch integrated widescreen and earbuds on your laptop to a 60-inch plasma HDTV and 7.1 digital surround audio. Thanks to WMC's support of mainstream home theater hardware, you can get the show off your tiny PC screen and tinny speakers and bring it to a crowd.

> **note** If you have other editions of Windows Vista, use the Windows Upgrade Anytime feature to upgrade to Home Premium or Ultimate editions. To learn more about pricing and the upgrade process, go to www.microsoft.com/windows/windows-vista/get/anytime-upgrade-overview.aspx.

WMC can be run on either your system's primary display or on a secondary display, which could be a conventional or HDTV as well as a CRT or LCD display. While the screenshots used in this book show WMC running on a conventional 1.33:1 (4:3) aspect ratio display, WMC is extremely well suited to 16:9 and 16:10 widescreen displays.

> **note** If you want to run WMC on a secondary display, enable the secondary display, switch WMC into windowed mode, and drag it to the display you want to use. Click the maximize button to run it in full-screen mode on the secondary display.

1

Where WMC Fits into Vista's Multimedia Experience

As I have written elsewhere (most notably in my book *Maximum PC Guide to Windows Vista Exposed*, available from Que Publishing), Microsoft Windows Vista is the most multimedia-friendly version of Windows yet released. Along with WMC, Windows Vista includes

- **Windows Media Player 11:** Plays DVD, audio, video, and music content; rips audio, and creates playlists and compilations.
- **Windows Movie Maker 6:** Edits movies and video using popular video, audio, and still image file formats, and supports widescreen and HD displays.
- **Windows Photo Gallery:** Organizes, previews, and edits still images in popular image formats.

As you can see, Windows Vista's multimedia features overlap each other in some significant ways. This is no accident: This overlapping design enables you to choose the best tool for enjoying or creating media. Table 1.1 lays out the major relationships.

Table 1.1 Interdependencies of Windows Vista Multimedia Utilities

Media Type	Windows Media Player	Windows Media Center	Windows Movie Maker	Windows Photo Gallery
Audio	Rips CD audio to WMA or MP3 formats; creates playlists; plays audio CDs; syncs WMA/MP3 to portable devices; rates audio; burns audio to CD/DVD	Plays WMA or MP3 audio tracks or playlists; burns audio to CD/DVD	Incorporates digital audio into movies; burns movies to CD/DVD	N/A
Photos	Plays photos; syncs photos to portable devices	Plays photos in full-screen; edits photos; burns photos to CD/DVD; plays photos based on ratings or tags	Creates movies from photos and other media sources; burns movies to CD/DVD	Edits, tags, rates photos; creates CD/DVD data disc or DVD slideshow for set-top players
Videos	Plays streaming, recorded or DVD video; syncs video to portable devices; creates playlist	Plays and records video; plays set-top DVDs and CDs; burns video to CD/DVD; plays movies created with Windows Movie Maker	Creates movies from WMC and other video sources; burns movies to CD/DVD	Tags, rates videos

Media Type	Windows Media Player	Windows Media Center	Windows Movie Maker	Windows Photo Gallery
Recorded TV	Plays recorded TV; syncs TV recordings to portable devices	Records live TV programs and series; burns TV programs and series to CD/DVD	Converts recorded TV into other formats; creates movies from recorded TV	Tags, rates TV recordings

As you can see from Table 1.1, WMC can use content created by other Windows Vista multimedia utilities and provides a convenient way to enjoy this media away from your computer.

➔ To learn more about using Windows Movie Maker and Windows Photo Gallery to create content, see Chapter 14, "Creating Photo and Video Content for Media Center," **p. 393**.

➔ To learn more about using Windows Media Player to rip music and create playlists, see Chapter 13, "Using Windows Media Player with Windows Media Center," **p. 375**.

Starting Windows Media Center

WMC can be started in two ways:

- From the Start orb's All Programs menu
- When Windows Vista starts

If you plan to run WMC on a system you use for other tasks, use the All Programs menu to start WMC. You can run WMC full-screen (refer to Figure 1.1) or in a window (see Figure 1.2).

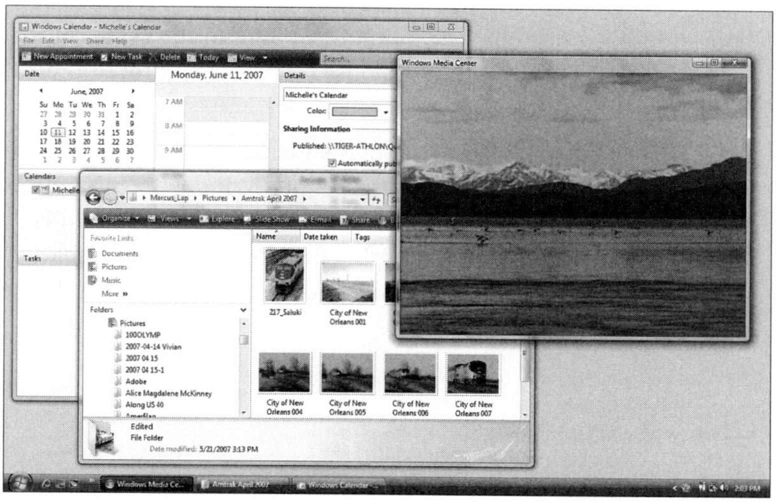

FIGURE 1.2

Playing video in a WMC window.

However, if you are using WMC on a dedicated media PC or a media server, you may prefer to boot directly into WMC. To start Windows Media Center when Windows Vista starts, use the Tasks menu in Windows Media Player. From the Tasks menu, select Settings, General, Startup and Window Behavior, Start Windows Media Center When Windows Starts (Figure 1.3 A). To keep WMC running in full-screen mode on a media PC or server, select the Media Only option from the Tasks menu (Figure 1.3 B).

➔ To learn more about setting up WMC, see Chapter 3, "Setting Up Windows Media Center," **p. 53**.

tip If you are running WMC at Windows startup, you probably don't want to be stopped by the Windows Vista logon dialog. If you set up only one user on the system running WMC and don't assign that user a password, you can boot directly into Windows Vista. However, if you use a password, you need to enable autologon.

To enable auto-logon in Windows Vista, you can use the same registry hack used by Windows XP. For details, go to http://support.microsoft.com and search for knowledge base article 315231, "How to Turn on Automatic Logon in Windows XP."

The WMC Interface

The WMC user interface takes full advantage of widescreen PC and HDTV displays, replacing text-heavy lists that were used in Windows XP Media Center Edition with easy-to-understand text/graphics menus. To switch between program categories (Pictures + Videos, Music, Now Playing, TV + Movies, Sports, Online Media, Tasks), scroll vertically with your mouse, your keyboard, or a WMC-compatible remote control. To select a particular item in a program category, use left and right arrows on your keyboard or remote control or move your mouse left or right. The highlighted item in the center of the screen starts as soon as you click it with the mouse or remote control or press Enter on your keyboard.

An IE7-like back arrow in the upper-left corner is used to return to the previous dialog. Window controls, as with any Windows Vista application, are found in the upper-right corner. Playback and channel controls are found along the bottom edge of the display (see Figure 1.4). To display these controls, move your mouse or press a key on your remote control. They auto-hide after a few seconds.

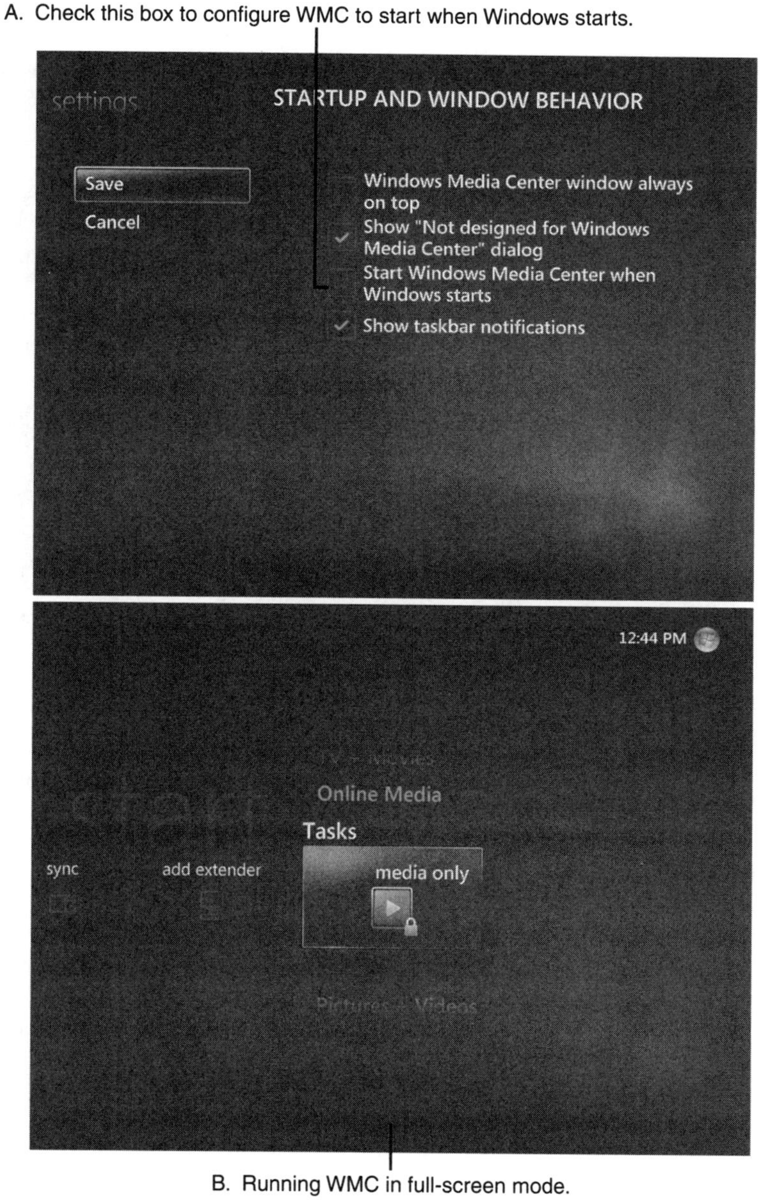

FIGURE 1.3

Options to use on a system dedicated to running WMC.
A. Configuring WMC to run automatically when Windows starts.
B. Running WMC in full-screen mode.

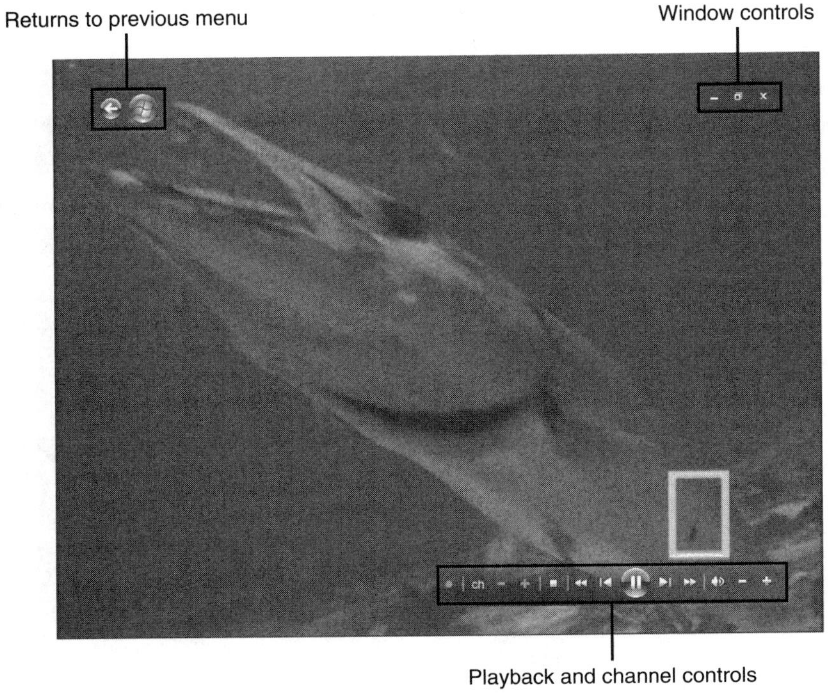

FIGURE 1.4

Playback and screen controls in WMC.

Features of WMC

WMC includes the following major features:

- **Pictures + Videos:** Play, edit, and burn still photos from Picture Library to disc; play and burn videos from Video Library to disc; access optional third-party services for editing, printing, sharing photos online, and other tasks. Can import photos from digital cameras or flash memory devices.
- **Music:** Play and burn digital music tracks and playlists from Music Library to disc; play FM radio (requires FM radio tuner); access optional third-party Internet radio and commercial music sources.
- **TV + Movies:** Play and record live TV programs; schedule recording of TV programs and series; play and record movies on TV; schedule recording of upcoming movies; access optional third-party TV and movie sources. (This feature requires a TV tuner.)

- **Sports:** Access real-time sports scores and updates; view player stats for NBA, NHL, and MLB fantasy league play; see live TV broadcasts and highlights (requires a TV tuner); access optional third-party sports and news sources (some require a TV tuner).
- **Online Media:** Access third-party media and services of all types, including optional services discussed in other chapters; run games and other programs optimized for the WMC interface from the Program Library.
- **Tasks:** Configure settings for various features of WMC and shutdown options; burn a CD or DVD; sync to a portable device; add a WMC extender; run WMC in full-screen "media only" view.

As you can see from this list, you may need to add some additional hardware to your system to optimize your WMC experience. Whether you're planning to buy a system that's already tricked out for WMC or want to transform an existing PC into a WMC powerhouse, you will learn what you need and how to install it in Chapter 2, "Equipping Your PC for Media Center."

CHAPTER

2

Equipping Your PC for Media Center

The incorporation of Windows Media Center (WMC) into Windows Vista's two most popular versions for home users, Home Premium and Ultimate, means that most Windows Vista users have the software they need to enjoy their favorite audio, video, and photo media from the comfort of their favorite couch, loveseat, or recliner. However, having WMC is only half the battle: If your computer doesn't include the right equipment to enjoy WMC, you'll need to upgrade it or replace it. This chapter shows you what you need to enjoy WMC's basic features, what your PC should include if you want to enjoy specific types of media, checklists you can use to assure that you build or buy the best PC for WMC, and how to upgrade your existing PC for better functionality with WMC.

IN THIS CHAPTER

Essential Components for Any Windows Media Center PC

Gertrude Stein said: "Rose is a rose is a rose." That simply isn't true about PCs. There's a reason that some PCs are just not suitable for Windows Vista Home Premium or Windows Vista Ultimate editions (both of which include WMC): They don't have enough horsepower "under the hood." So if you're wondering if your current PC is good enough for WMC, or if you're planning to buy, build, or upgrade your way to a WMC platform, what should you look for? The following tasks put the heaviest demands on the core components in a WMC PC:

- Watching live TV (broadcast or cable)
- Recording live TV (broadcast or cable)
- Displaying high-resolution (5MP or greater resolution) still photos
- Encoding video (to create a video DVD from digital video or still images)

If you plan to use WMC for any or all of these tasks, you will definitely want to make sure your PC has the performance needed in the following areas:

- Processor
- Memory (RAM) size
- Hard disk size
- DVD drive type
- Video card or integrated video type

These are among the most expensive parts of a system to upgrade, especially if upgrading requires replacing the motherboard, as it often does on a desktop system, or switching to a brand-new laptop, as is necessary if you are not satisfied with the processor or video type of your current laptop. The following sections help you weigh your current system—or the systems on your shopping list—in the balance to see if they measure up.

However, if you will be using WMC primarily to interact with digital music or web-quality video, system performance is less important.

WMC's Favorite Processors: Fast, Multi-Core, and 64-Bit!

The processor (also called the CPU) has a big role in determining how fast your system is. Everything you do with your computer is controlled by the processor, and most information sent to (or from) your computer goes through your processor. You're going to be happiest with the performance of WMC on local files if your computer contains one of the following processors:

Intel

Core 2 Duo, Core 2 Quad, Core i7 (fastest)

Pentium D, Pentium Dual-Core (slower, but acceptable)

AMD

Athlon 64 FX x2, Phenom (fastest)

Athlon 64 x2 (slower, but acceptable)

These processors come in many different models that feature different clock speeds (how fast the processor performs internally), external bus speeds (how fast the processor sends and retrieves information from other parts of the system), and L2 cache sizes (L2 cache stores the contents of recently read parts of main system memory, also known as RAM, for reuse). However, all models of these processors have the following common features:

- All run at fast clock speeds.
- All contain two or more processor cores.
- All contain a large amount of L2 cache.
- All support 32-bit or 64-bit operating systems.

Fast clock speeds enable the computer to perform tasks more quickly than with a slower processor of the same or similar type.

Two or more processor cores enable the processor to perform multiple tasks more quickly, such as encoding video or transferring pictures while you watch TV or a movie, or using a Media Center Extender to view WMC content on your PC while you're using your PC for other tasks.

➔ To learn more about Media Center Extenders, see Chapter 11, "Adding and Using Media Center Extenders," **p. 315**.

L2 cache enables the computer to perform similar tasks more quickly because the processor needs to fetch the contents of main memory less often.

32-bit operating systems have memory size limits that are becoming increasingly troublesome as image and media file sizes grow larger and larger. The ability to switch in the future to a 64-bit version of Windows Vista or future operating systems helps "future-proof" your PC.

TIME FOR 64-BIT NOW? MAYBE

The overwhelming majority of systems running Windows Vista Home Premium or Ultimate editions run the 32-bit version of these operating systems, even if the processor is designed for 64-bit operation. Until mid-2008, this made plenty of sense. It took a long time for vendors to develop 64-bit versions of drivers and application files, even though Windows Vista has been available since early 2007.

Starting in the summer of 2008, though, many vendors are now shipping systems running 64-bit versions of Windows Vista. If you're shopping for a new computer and you're planning to use it for working with digital SLR photos, home videos, HDTV or Blu-Ray HD movies, the ability of 64-bit Windows Vista to work with more than 4GB of RAM enables faster operation with large media files.

If you're already using a 32-bit version of Windows Vista, should you upgrade to a 64-bit version? Consider making the move if, and only if, your system meets these requirements. First, it must have a processor capable of running in 64-bit mode. If you're not using one of the processors listed in this section, check with your processor vendor to find out. Second, it must have provision for at least 4GB of RAM (and more, preferably). Third, application software as well as utility programs such as antivirus, firewall, antispyware, disc burning, and others must work properly in 64-bit mode (or must be upgraded to a 64-bit version).

To learn more about 64-bit Windows Vista, visit www.microsoft.com/windows/windows-vista/compare-editions/64-bit.aspx. To determine if a particular hardware device or program will run in 64-bit mode, visit the Windows Vista Compatibility Center at www.microsoft.com/windows/compatibility/, search for or browse for your device, and click the 64-bit tab on the device or program listing. In some cases, you might need to download an updated driver or upgrade to a newer version of a program.

If you decide to switch to a 64-bit version of Vista later, keep in mind that it requires a complete reinstall of your operating system. You will need to back up your media and other data first, as well. If you have only 32-bit install discs, you will need to order 64-bit install discs from Microsoft for a small fee. Go to www.microsoft.com/windowsvista/1033/ordermedia/default.mspx to place your order.

➔ To learn how to determine the hardware in your current system, see "Scoping Out Your Hardware," this chapter, **p. 49**.

If your system has one of the processors from the following list, it's running an older or an "economy" processor that lacks most or all of the features we've recommended. Keep in mind that depending on how you use WMC, it might be fine, but if you are planning to watch or record TV or encode digital video, a slow processor could be holding you back.

Intel

Celeron

Pentium 4

Pentium 4 Extreme Edition

Pentium Extreme Edition

AMD

Sempron

Athlon 64

Athlon 64 FX

Can you upgrade your processor? In the immortal words of yours truly, "It depends." Specifically, it depends on whether you have a desktop or a notebook computer. Most desktop computers have removable processors, but whether you can move to a faster processor (preferably a dual-core, tri-core, or quad-core model) depends upon the motherboard in the computer. Generally speaking, so-called "white-box" PCs built from standard components (either by the user or by a local or online dealer) are more likely to support a wide range of replacement processors than systems built by major vendors such as Dell, HP, Gateway, or Lenovo.

A new processor must not only fit into the existing motherboard, but its features (clock speed, multi-core function, voltage requirements, and so on) must also be supported by the existing motherboard. Processor upgrades are a favorite hobby of enthusiasts (and PC repair shops), but if you're an upgrade novice, it's not for you. However, some other upgrades are a lot easier to perform.

In some cases, you might need to replace the motherboard and the RAM to upgrade to a better processor. In that case, it's usually cheaper to shop for a new PC!

RAM-a-Rama: Bigger Is Better!

> **note** To determine if you have a 32-bit or 64-version of Windows Vista installed, view the System properties sheet (refer to Figure 2.2).

RAM (memory) is the workspace used by the processor to work with media and other information. If you want to make WMC work as well as possible, you'll want no less than 2GB of RAM in your system. Many recent systems include more than 2GB RAM, and systems running 64-bit versions of Windows Vista can use more than 4GB.

How much RAM can your system use? Again, in the immortal words of yours truly, "It depends." It depends on the design of your system, whether you're using a 32-bit or 64-bit version of Windows Vista, and the amount of memory you already have installed. Because memory modules contain different amounts of RAM, and systems have a limited number of slots for memory modules, it might be necessary to remove low-capacity memory to install more, larger-capacity memory.

Scanning Your System to Determine Memory Upgrade Options

There are several ways to find out how much memory your system contains and the available upgrades for your system. The easiest way is to visit a memory vendor's website and use its memory configuration scanning program, such as Crucial.com's Crucial System Scanner (see Figure 2.1).

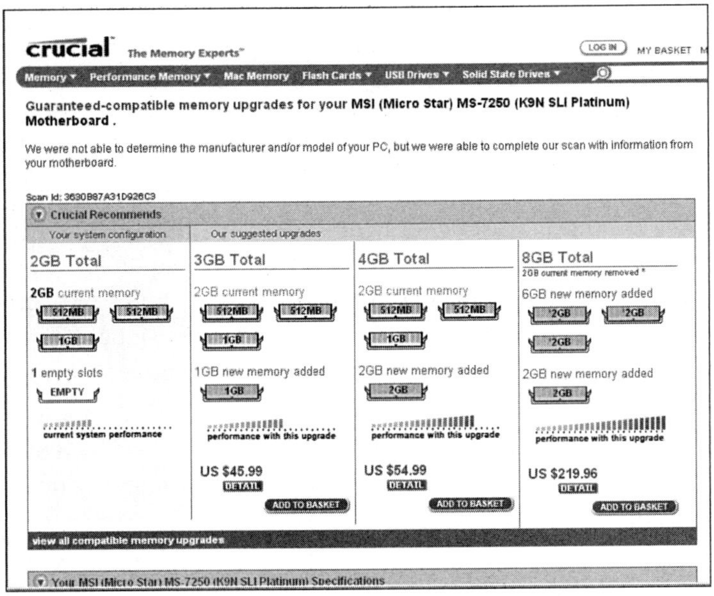

FIGURE 2.1

This system has 2GB of RAM installed, but it can handle more (and larger) memory modules.

If your system or motherboard is recognized by the scanner, you will find out how much memory (RAM) is already installed in your system, what upgrades fit in your system, and whether you need to remove lower-capacity modules to install higher-capacity modules.

Other Methods for Analyzing Your System's Memory

If your system is not recognized by a memory configuration program, or if you prefer to buy memory from a vendor that does not offer an online system scanner, you can use a two-step process:

1. Use Windows Vista's System properties sheet to determine how much memory your system has (see Figure 2.2).

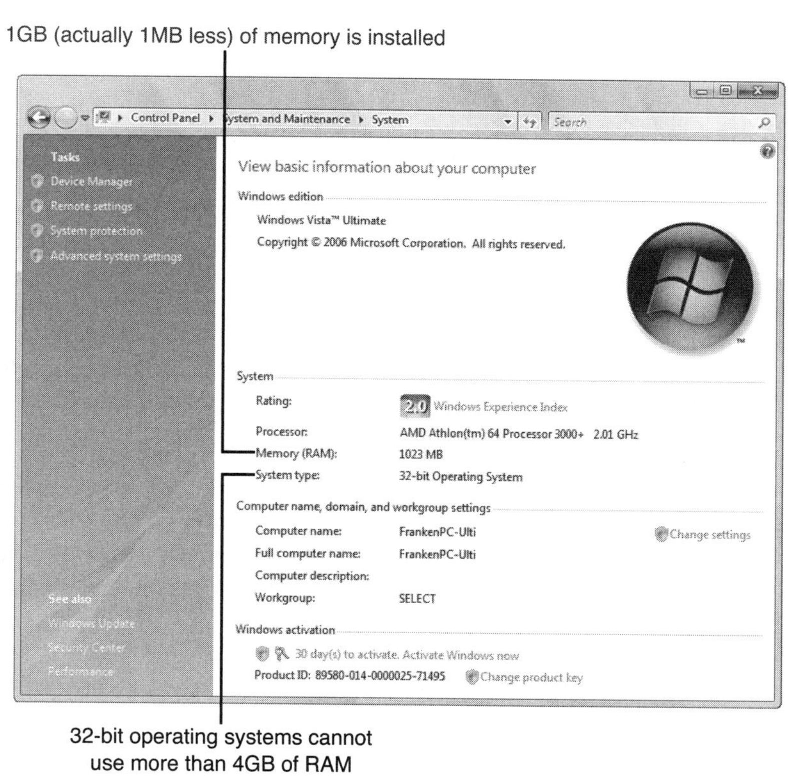

FIGURE 2.2

This system has 1GB (1023MB) of RAM; an upgrade to at least 2GB of RAM is highly recommended.

2. If you need to add more memory, visit a memory vendor's website and look up your system by brand and model number to determine possible memory upgrades. In Figure 2.3, I used the Kingston Memory

Search (www.kingston.com) to look up memory upgrades for my Micro-Star (MSI) K9AG Neo2-Digital motherboard.

System Info | Bank Schema | Upgrade Path | Warranty | Support | Show All

Standard Memory:	0 MB (Removable)
Maximum Memory:	4 GB using DDR2-800 8 GB using DDR2-533/667
Expansion:	4 Sockets
CPU & ChipSet:	AMD Athlon 64 (AM2) AMD 690G AMD Athlon 64 X2 (AM2) AMD 690G AMD Sempron (AM2) AMD 690G
Bus Architecture:	PCI; PCI Express; USB
Mfgr's System P/N's:	MS-7368-010
Comments	MODULES MUST BE ORDERED AND INSTALLED IN PAIRS for Dual Channel mode. Kingston offers "K2" Kit part numbers for Dual Channel mode. If 4GB is installed, the recognized memory may be reduced to 3.5GB or less (depending on system configuration and memory allocation). Maximum configurations require 64-bit operating system. AMD Sempron processors support DDR2-533 and DDR2-667 memory only. DDR2-800 modules are not supported with this processor.

FIGURE 2.3

This system can use up to 4GB or 8GB of RAM, depending on the speed of the memory modules installed.

MEMORY UPGRADE STRATEGIES

You will often have a choice between different sizes of modules to reach a desired memory size. For example, on a desktop computer, you can reach 2GB of RAM by installing one 2GB module, two 1GB modules, or four 512MB modules. If your system uses a dual-channel design (which accesses two identical memory modules as a single logical unit for faster memory access), you should buy memory in matched pairs and install them into the appropriate slots. (Most motherboards use color-coding to indicate the slots for each pair, so check the manual to determine the correct slots to use.) In such a case, a pair of 1GB modules provides faster performance than a single 2GB module.

The other rule of thumb for desktop computers is to install no more than 4GB on a system running a 32-bit version of Windows Vista. If you install 4GB of RAM, Vista will actually report only 3.25GB available for programs but will use the remaining memory for its own functions. 64-bit versions can use more than 4GB of RAM, so if you think you'll move to a 64-bit version of Vista in the future, buy two 2GB modules for a motherboard with four memory sockets, and leave two sockets empty for future use.

Memory installation strategies for notebook computers are different. Some notebook computers have only one socket for memory upgrades, and two is the maximum on most models. If the laptop has only one socket or user-replaceable memory module, install the largest module available for that model. If the laptop has two user-replaceable modules (or one installed and an empty socket), you might want to replace both modules with larger modules to maximize the memory in the system. For example, my HP Pavilion notebook shipped with 1GB of RAM in two 512MB modules. By replacing one module with a 1GB module, I increased system memory to 1.5GB. However, to reach 2GB, I would need to replace the other 512MB module with a second 1GB module.

Can you avoid the wasteful practice of swapping small modules for larger modules? If you can specify large modules when you buy a computer, you can. However, if all you can specify is the total amount of RAM in the system, count on most vendors to use smaller, less expensive modules to reach the desired size. If the amount of RAM in the system is not enough, you'll need to replace one or more modules to reach your target.

What if you don't know the brand and model number of your system? If you use an off-brand or "white box" PC built from standard components, or your system is using a different motherboard from the one originally installed, you might wind up in this category.

caution Can you reuse memory from one system in another system? In some cases, yes. However, there's much more to the process than seeing if the module will plug into the system. Memory chips on different modules run at different speeds and have different CAS Latency (CL) timings (CL refers to how quickly memory access changes locations in a memory module to find desired information). If you mix memory modules with different speeds and CL ratings in a system, many systems will crash or lock up, while others might run faster modules at the same speed as slower modules.

Unless you can determine that salvaged memory modules match your system's requirements, don't use them in your system. To try to find out if a memory module will work in your PC, check the brand and model number of the module on the vendor's website and see if that module is listed as a recommended module for your system.

2

If you cannot scan your system to determine memory upgrades, visit the Belarc website (www.belarc.com) and download the free Belarc Advisor program. This program can detect an enormous amount of information about your computer, but for our purposes, the most important information is the System Model, Main Circuit Board, and Memory Modules section of the report, which appears in your web browser (see Figure 2.4). Use this information when you visit a memory vendor's website to look up your system for memory upgrade options.

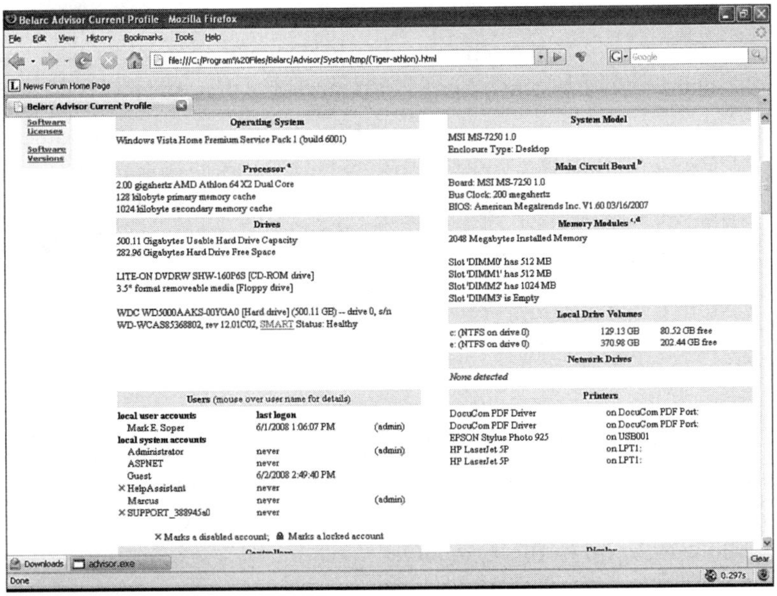

FIGURE 2.4

The right side of the Belarc Advisor report provides you with useful information for ordering memory for your system.

Hard Disks—Bigger, Better, More!

How do *you* plan to use WMC? If you're planning to record live TV, create a movie library on hard disk, or store a collection of pictures from today's high-megapixel-rated digital cameras, don't skimp on storage.

How much storage do you need? I'm tempted to tell you, "How much can you afford?" But, you'd probably prefer some hard numbers. OK, let's get to it.

Crunching the Numbers: TV Recording

If you're going to be recording live TV, a three-hour TV show recorded in high quality will use about 10GB of space. Thus, for every 30 hours of TV recorded in high quality, you'll need 100GB of space (figure less for lower-quality settings). Note that if you're using digital TV sources (digital cable, ATSC broadcast TV, or satellite TV), you must record in high quality. HDTV takes an even bigger chunk of hard disk space: only 15.5 hours of TV per 100GB of space.

Crunching the Numbers: Digital Photography

If digital photography's your game, expect to use between 2MB and 3MB per picture if your digital camera has a 6MP (megapixel) or higher rating and you shoot JPEG photos using maximum quality (variously called "Best," "Fine," "Superfine," and so on). Assuming 2.5MB per photo, you can store about 4,000 photos per 10GB or about 40,000 photos per 100GB.

However, if you're running a digital SLR camera like a Canon Rebel XTi, Nikon D40x, and so on and you're shooting RAW files, expect to use as much as 8–12MB per image. Assuming 9MB per file, you can store about 1,100 pictures per 10GB, or about 11,100 photos per 100GB.

If you shoot RAW+JPEG, add up the space for both file types to estimate how much disk space you need.

> **note** Unfortunately, WMC doesn't display RAW files. By shooting RAW+JPEG, or by converting RAW files to JPEG after shooting, you can view JPEG versions of your photos using WMC.
>
> If you want to view RAW files without leaving WMC, there's a way around the problem. By installing a Windows Vista-compatible codec from your digital camera vendor, you can view your files with Windows Photo Gallery or Windows Live Photo Gallery. And, by using a third-party program to start Windows Photo Gallery or Windows Live Photo Gallery from within WMC, you can enjoy your RAW files. For more information, see the section "Solving Codec Problems" in Chapter 16, "Troubleshooting Media Center," **p. 495**.

Crunching the Numbers: Digital Music

Like digital music? The quality and format you use for ripping music has a big impact on how much disk space you'll need for your digital music library. The highest quality you can get in digital conversion is to use a lossless conversion format, such as WAV or WMA Lossless. Because these formats do not use compression (which discards some information to reduce file size), the price you pay for lossless conversion is an enormous amount of space. For example, a 74-minute music CD takes over 700MB of disk space.

If you can afford the disk space required for lossless conversion, you can create a no-compromise digital music collection. Keep in mind, though, that if you are planning to create a digital music library that also works with portable media players, you would need to convert lossless formats into compressed formats that work with these players.

The most common compressed digital music formats include MP3 (which plays on practically any media player, including Apple's iPod series) and Windows Media Audio (WMA), which is widely supported by most third-party media players. MP3 files are generally larger than WMA files of comparable quality. However, the bit rate used to digitize music into compressed formats also has a big impact on file size. The higher the bit rate, the larger the file size, but the better the sound quality. The differences between lower bit rate and higher bit rate music is especially apparent if you have a high-quality home theater setup, speakers, and a room with good acoustics. My bias is toward converting music with the highest bit rate possible because you can always discard detail to shrink a song to fit on a portable player, but you can never get back quality lost during initial conversion if you use a lower bit rate. To compare the relative sizes you can obtain, I ripped a 41:48 album to CD with Windows Media Player 11 (included in Windows Vista and used by WMC for ripping audio) using four different settings, two for MP3 and two for Windows Media Audio (WMA). Table 2.1 lists the different formats, bit rates, and resulting sizes.

Table 2.1 Size Comparisons of MP3 and WMA Album Rips

WMA	File Sizes	Notes	MP3	File Sizes
64Kbps	19.4MB	Low Quality	128Kbps	38.2MB
128Kbps	38.6MB	Medium Quality	256Kbps	76.5MB
192Kbps	57.8MB	Best Quality	320Kbps	95.6MB

I recommend ripping audio in MP3 format if you have (or plan to buy) an Apple iPod or aren't sure whether you're going to add a portable media player to your technology collection.

> **note** Different WMA and MP3 ripping programs might achieve slightly different results.

Let's make the math simple. Assume each album in your collection has a duration of 41:48 (some are shorter and many are longer) and that you're going to use MP3 audio ripping at 320Kbps. You can store about 10.4 albums per GB, about 104 albums per 10GB, or about 1,040 albums per 100GB.

MP3 VERSUS WMA, OTHER DIGITAL MUSIC FORMATS

Why rip your music to the MP3 digital audio format? It's simple: MP3 works with practically every digital music player ever created. If you switch from a Microsoft Zune or Microsoft-based Plays For Sure player to an Apple iPod (or vice versa), your MP3 files will work just fine on your new player. Upgrade to a new PC, and your MP3s, because they're not encumbered with digital "rights" management (DRM), will work without a hitch.

By contrast, although Microsoft developed both the older Plays for Sure specifications and the Zune, the Zune can't play WMA files created for a Plays for Sure device. (Ironic name, isn't it?) Apple's iPod has never seen a WMA file it could play, and Plays for Sure and Zune alike turn up their noses at Apple's AAC digital music format.

Although you can convert digital files from one type to another, if you record in 256Kbps or higher bit rate MP3 format or buy DRM-free MP3 audio tracks, you'll never need to worry about whether your next PC or digital audio device will choke on your digital music collection, and you'll have high-quality music that is much easier on your hard disk than uncompressed WAV files.

Summing It All Up: How Much Space Do *You* Need?

If you're planning to record a lot of TV, rip a lot of digital music, and take a lot of digital photos, you'd better figure on at least a 500GB hard disk for your desktop PC—the "sweet spot" in the hard disk cost versus capacity calculation. You'll want to pick up an external hard disk of at least the same capacity for backups. Add 500GB internal and 500GB external, and you're looking at one terabyte! It's a lot of disk space, no matter how you slice it.

> **tip** With either desktop or laptop computers, keep in mind that you can configure Library Setup in WMC to point to external drives for storing all types of video, and you can configure TV recording to store recordings on an external drive. So if you're trying to use an existing system for WMC and don't want to (or can't) upgrade the internal hard disk, external drives plugged into USB 2.0, FireWire, or eSATA ports are a suitable substitute. Of course, you can also add external hard disks to a new system to avoid running out of space.

If you are using WMC on a laptop computer, look at a 320GB hard disk as a desirable size for heavy-duty media storage. Laptop computers use drives with smaller form factors, and these drives are more expensive per gigabyte than drives for desktop PCs.

➔ To learn more about using Library Setup to configure other hard disks for video recording, see "Optional Setup: Music, Pictures, and Videos Library" in Chapter 3, "Setting Up Windows Media Center," **p. 74**.

If you are planning to use an external hard disk as a dedicated storage device for a single PC or a backup device for several PCs, I recommend a USB 2.0, FireWire, or eSATA hard disk based on 3.5-inch hard disk mechanisms (see Figure 2.5). You can purchase drives in this form factor with capacities as high as 1TB, and the prices of these drives are not much more per gigabyte than for internal PATA or SATA hard disks. Keep in mind that these drives require an external AC power source.

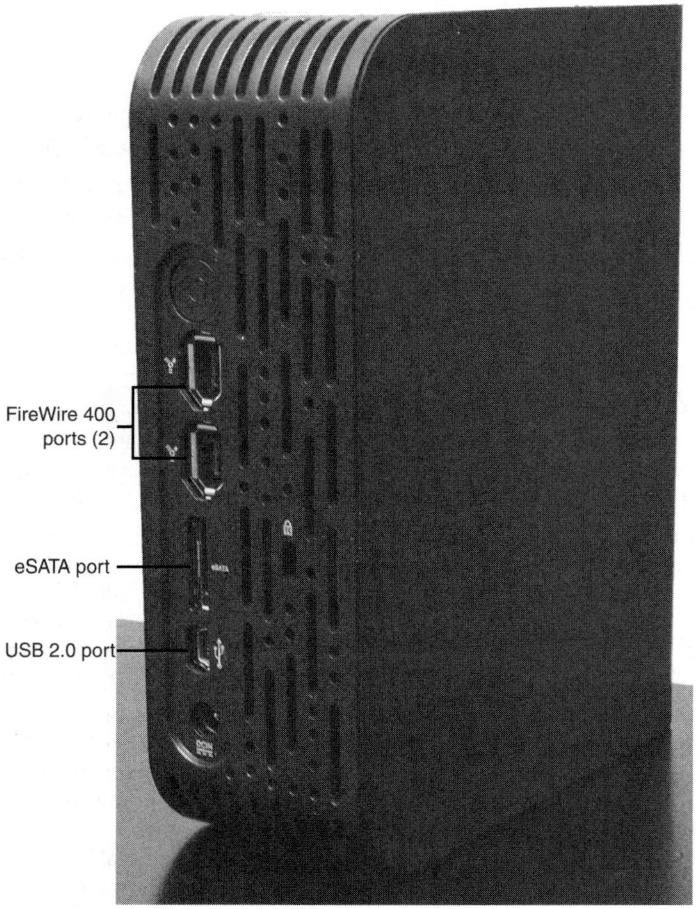

FIGURE 2.5

The rear of a Western Digital My Book Home Edition hard disk.

Smaller external hard disks based on 2.5-inch or 1.8-inch hard disk mechanisms can be powered from the host system's USB port, but their price per gigabyte is much higher because of the higher cost of the hard disk mechanisms they use. These drives are often much slower than external drives based on 3.5-inch hard disk mechanisms. I recommend these smaller drives for temporary storage or transferring of large amounts of data between systems.

Customizing Your WMC PC for Particular Tasks

Beyond the core components you need for using your WMC PC for any task, consider the following tasks you might want to perform:

- Want to use your WMC PC to browse the web or perform non-WMC tasks? The input devices (mouse and keyboard) are important considerations.
- Planning to watch and record live TV? Depending on the TV sources you prefer, the choice of TV tuner and even whether to buy a new PC or build one are affected.
- Whether you prefer digital music or surround-sound movies, the digital audio solution you choose is critical.
- If you work with DV video, you need to select hardware that helps you import and edit it.
- Prefer digital photography? You'll want to make sure you can easily import your favorite pictures.
- Whether you want to use your WMC PC to access digital media on other PCs, share digital media with a Media Center Extender device, or both, choosing the right network is essential.

The following sections help you choose the hardware you need to make your WMC PC work—and play—the ways you prefer.

Wireless Input Devices and Remote Controls

You can use either a Media Center Remote (Figure 2.6) or a keyboard and mouse to interact with WMC. The remote has the following advantages:

- Easy point-and-click operation of WMC menus
- Dedicated control buttons for TV, audio, and other tasks

FIGURE 2.6
A WMC remote control and USB receiver from Hauppauge.

The wireless keyboard and mouse have the following advantages:

- Easy text entry for naming albums, collections, and queues
- Enables WMC PC to work with standard Windows Vista desktop, web browser and other non-WMC applications when necessary

Which is better? Why not both! My WMC PC is equipped with a Logitech 2.4GHz wireless mouse and keyboard and a Media Center Remote, and I use each as appropriate.

When you use a mouse or compatible pointing device within WMC, a mouse control center appears in the lower-right corner of the screen (Figure 2.7). When you stop moving the mouse, the control center disappears after a few seconds.

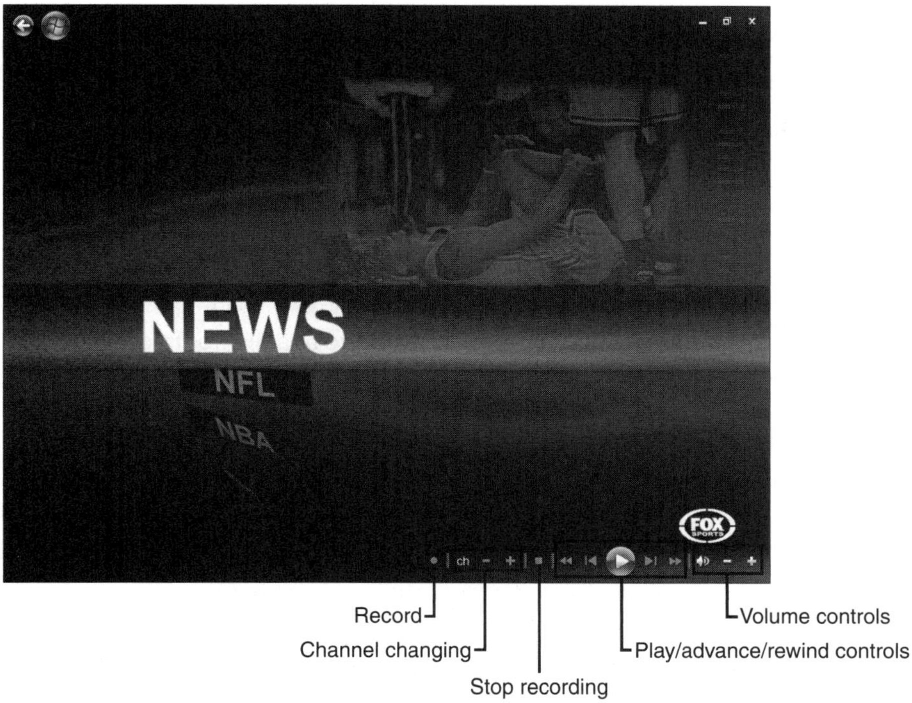

FIGURE 2.7

The mouse control center in WMC enables you to change channels, adjust volume, and record or play media.

CHOOSING A WIRELESS KEYBOARD AND MOUSE

If you're planning to run WMC "up close and personal," any wireless keyboard and mouse that works with Windows Vista (look for the Vista Premium Certified label or check the vendor's website) will work. However, if you're going to use WMC in a home theater room, check the specifications carefully.

Cordless mice and keyboards that use 2.4GHz frequencies enjoy a range of 20–30 feet, while Bluetooth-based devices feature a range of 30–60 feet, depending on the device. Older wireless mice and keyboards that use 27MHz radio frequencies have a maximum range of six feet, which means that you probably can't use them in your home theater room.

If your computer has a built-in Bluetooth transceiver, I recommend you buy a Bluetooth-based wireless mouse and keyboard, even if you don't need the range provided by Bluetooth. Using your system's built-in Bluetooth transceiver means that you don't need to use a USB port for a wireless keyboard/mouse transceiver. You can connect up to five other Bluetooth devices, and the connections between your PC and Bluetooth devices are encrypted for greater security.

However, if your computer doesn't have an integrated or add-on Bluetooth transceiver, you don't plan to add Bluetooth devices to your system in the future, and you need a range of no more than 20–30 feet between your WMC PC and your preferred location, get a 2.4GHz wireless mouse and keyboard. (These use a USB interface for the transceiver.) Most major mouse and keyboard vendors offer 2.4GHz devices. Note that wireless mice and keyboards that don't identify the frequency or connection type probably use the now-obsolete 27MHz frequency, which has a range of only six feet, or they might use the equally outdated IR (infrared) technology.

Whichever technology you use for wireless devices, do yourself a favor and change the batteries in both the mouse and the keyboard as soon as they start to weaken. Most wireless keyboard and mouse drivers display a warning in the Windows desktop's notification area when it's time to change batteries. If you spend all your time in WMC, though, there's another easy way to determine when to change batteries: when the keyboard or mouse stop working reliably. If your wireless mouse pointer seems to have a mind of its own or the wireless keyboard takes its own sweet time about typing characters, it's time to replace the batteries in both devices. Wireless mice and keyboards don't drain batteries very fast, so alkaline batteries are a good choice.

Watching and Recording Live TV and HDTV

If you want to watch or record TV on your WMC, you need a TV tuner—and there are plenty to choose from. Complicating matters is the looming February 18, 2009, deadline for the changeover from analog to digital broadcast TV and the issue of encrypted HDTV cable TV content.

The choices you need to make include the following:

- Which form factor? (add-on card or external)
- Which bus design? (PCI, PCI-Express, CardBus, ExpressCard, or USB 2.0)
- Which types of signals? (NTSC, analog cable, ATSC, digital cable, FM radio)
- Which type of tuner? (hybrid or dual)

Internal Versus External Tuners

External TV tuners using USB 2.0 interfaces are the best choice if you want some flexibility with the PC you're planning to use for WMC or if you're wanting to watch or record TV on your laptop and don't want to use a CardBus or ExpressCard tuner. Figure 2.8 illustrates a typical USB 2.0 TV tuner designed for use with HDTV, the Pinnacle HDPC Pro.

note Although the new ExpressCard slot provides laptops with PCI Express-compatible performance, don't assume that every ExpressCard-based TV tuner is a high-performance device. ExpressCard devices are in their infancy, and as with other new product families, the first designs in the marketplace are often best left on store shelves. Check reviews carefully *before* you buy.

FIGURE 2.8

The Pinnacle PCTV HD Pro USB 2.0 TV tuner includes connections for S-video and composite video. Photo courtesy Pinnacle Systems.

Although USB 2.0 is a good choice for standard broadcast or cable TV on a laptop, better choices exist if you are using a desktop PC. A PCI Express TV tuner card will typically provide better performance, assuming you have a recent PC with a PCI Express expansion slot. If you prefer an internal card but don't have PCI Express (aka PCIe) slots, you can use a PCI card. Figure 2.9 compares typical PCI and PCI Express TV tuners.

FIGURE 2.9

Typical PCI (top) and PCI-Express x1 (bottom) TV tuner cards.

Figure 2.10 compares PCI Express x1, PCI Express x16 (used for video cards), and PCI expansion slots on a typical desktop PC.

FIGURE 2.10

Typical PCI Express x1, PCI Express x16, and PCI expansion slots on a motherboard.

Internal Tuners—PCI Versus PCI Express

If you can use a PCI Express TV tuner, it's your best choice for a couple of reasons:

- Because PCI Express is replacing older expansion slot designs like PCI, PCI Express-based tuners usually include newer technologies, such as support for certain types of digital and HDTV signals or dual tuners to permit watching one channel while recording another.
- If you're planning to upgrade to a better PC or motherboard, a PCI Express card is easy to move to another system.
- PCI Express x1 slots have about two times the performance of PCI expansion slots, so they can better handle the bandwidth required for digital and HDTV signals.

However, if your existing desktop PC lacks PCI Express slots but is otherwise suitable for use with WMC, go with an up-to-date PCI TV tuner card.

NTSC TV and ATSC HDTV

TV tuner devices designed to work with NTSC or standard cable ought to be tagged with a label "For best flavor, use by February 17, 2009." Why? While standard cable TV is unaffected by the digital broadcast changeover scheduled for February 18, 2009, TV tuners that support only NTSC (analog) broadcast TV will become practically useless after that date unless they are connected to a digital-analog converter box. Starting February 18, 2009, all full-power broadcast TV in the U.S. will use digital signals. (Only a few repeater and low-power stations will continue to use analog signals after this date, and only until they convert to digital transmitters.)

If you're buying or building a PC for WMC, ignore any TV tuners that do not support ATSC, the term for over-the-air (broadcast) digital SDTV and HDTV digital signals. Tuners that support ATSC also support NTSC, so even if your area doesn't offer much in the way of ATSC TV now, you can still watch (and record) TV until the "big switch" takes place.

note If you're wondering whether you can use one of the digital TV converter boxes to enable an analog-only TV tuner to view digital TV broadcasts, you'll find the answer in Chapter 4, "Viewing and Recording Live TV."

➔ For details, see "Using a Converter Box with an NTSC TV Tuner," in Chapter 4, **p. 99**.

Digital Cable TV: QAM and OCUR

If you want to watch and record cable TV, you need to know another couple of terms: QAM (also called "clear QAM") and CableCARD.

QAM are unencrypted signals used by some cable TV providers for a few of their digital cable TV programs. Unfortunately, most digital cable TV channels on most cable TV networks are encrypted, which is why you must rent a cable box when you upgrade to digital cable. (It contains the decryption hardware needed to view the programs.)

What if you want to view all available digital cable TV on your PC, including HD and premium content like HBO, Showtime, and so on? Unfortunately, you're no longer in the DIY category: Thanks to the cable TV industry's fear of digital piracy, the only way you can equip a PC to view encrypted cable TV content is to buy a PC that is designed to support a feature known as OCUR (Open Cable Unidirectional Receiver) and is equipped with a digital cable TV tuner that supports OCUR.

tip Some vendors that sell OCUR-enabled PCs also sell the ATI TV Wonder Digital Cable Tuner separately, but it can be used only on PCs that are OCUR-ready.

To determine if your PC can use the ATI TV Wonder Digital Cable Tuner or any other OCUR-compatible TV tuner, use the OCUR BIOS Check Utility available from Doug Knox's WMC Edition utilities page at http://www.dougknox.com/xpmce/index.htm.

Because an OCUR-ready system has a specially designed BIOS that supports the DRM features demanded by premium HDTV cable TV content providers, you cannot retrofit an OCUR tuner to a PC that does not support OCUR. Essentially, then, your choices are limited to preconfigured PCs that include OCUR support. (Some might include the tuner, or you can add it afterwards.) The first and so far only digital TV tuner with OCUR support is AMD's ATI TV Wonder Digital Cable Tuner (Figure 2.11).

FIGURE 2.11

The ATI TV Wonder Digital Cable Tuner is the first OCUR-compatible TV tuner for PCs. Photo courtesy of Advanced Micro Devices.

However, having an OCUR-enabled tuner is only part of the answer to viewing full-quality HDTV from encrypted sources: You also need a display that supports the HDCP standard.

→ To learn more about HDCP, see "HDCP and Your Video Card or Integrated Video," this chapter, **p. 43**, and "HDCP and Your Display," this chapter, **p. 45**.

Hybrid and Dual Tuners

Low-end TV tuner devices often use a hybrid design to support broadcast TV (NTSC or ATSC) and cable TV. In a hybrid design, you can watch only one channel at a time. If your TV is no more than 30 inches wide, or if you're using a computer monitor, this might not be a major issue.

However, if you want to watch or record more than one channel at the same time (such as in picture-in-picture mode), get a TV tuner with true dual tuners. WMC can support multiple tuners, so if you're a real TV junkie, you can have two dual-tuner TV tuner cards! Systems that include the Media Center TV Pack for Windows Vista SP1 can use more tuners (up to six tuners for Home Premium; up to twelve tuners for Ultimate edition).

Video Card and Integrated Video

Whether you're planning to build or buy a new PC or convert an existing one for WMC, you don't need a powerhouse graphics card (unless you're also planning to use it for 3D gaming). However, if you want to use your WMC PC in conjunction with an HDTV, not just any video card will do.

For the very best results in HDTV viewing with WMC, look for a video card or integrated video that features a high definition multimedia interface (HDMI) or digital video interface (DVI)/HDMI port with high-bandwidth digital content protection (HDCP) support. That's a lot of acronyms, but understanding what they mean is very important if you're trying to assure the best video playback quality.

> **note** If you are building your own Media Center PC or are upgrading an existing PC to use with WMC, make sure the video card or integrated video port is supported by Windows Vista. Check the vendor's website to determine this information.
>
> To determine the video card or integrated video used in your system, use MSInfo32.

→ To learn more about MSInfo32, see "Using MSInfo32," this chapter, **p. 49**.

DVI and HDMI Ports

> **note** Most motherboards that include HDMI and DVI-D integrated video ports can use only one port at a time; jumper blocks on the motherboard are used to configure the port in use.
>
> An increasing number of video cards also include both HDMI and DVI ports.

The DVI port (Figure 2.12) has been a normal feature of most graphics cards for the last few years but has been slow to appear on laptop computers. DVI ports support digital video, and DVI-I versions can be retrofitted with a DVI-VGA adapter to enable them to connect to CRTs and older LCD panels.

The HDMI port (also shown in Figure 2.12) is completely compatible with DVI digital signals, enabling you to use a DVI-HDMI cable to connect your DVI-equipped PC to an HDTV equipped with an HDMI port. The difference between DVI and HDMI is that HDMI can also carry digital audio signals.

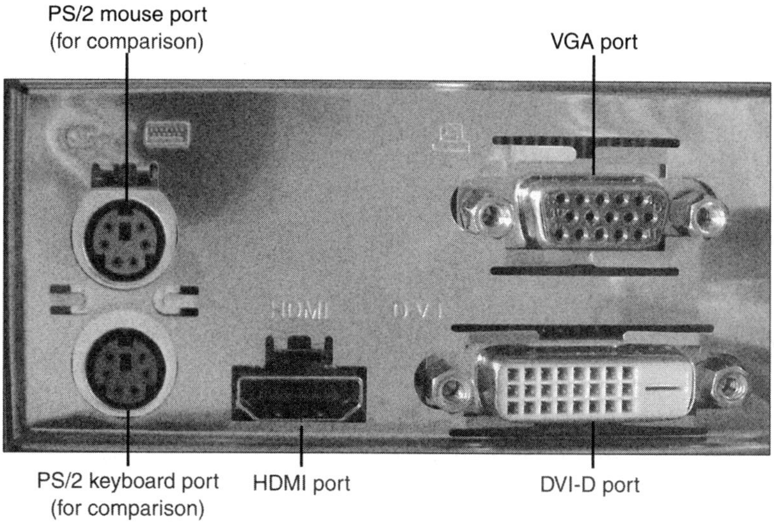

FIGURE 2.12
DVI, HDMI, and other ports on the port cluster of a typical desktop PC.

HDCP and Your Video Card or Integrated Video

If you want to enjoy Blu-Ray or other encrypted/DRM-enabled HD content at its full quality, you also need to make sure that your video card or integrated video port supports a standard called HDCP. HDCP displays Blu-Ray, the now-discontinued HD DVD and other encrypted HDTV content (such as premium HDTV channels) in full HD (up to 1080p) quality while also preventing copying of the video material. HDCP requires that the video source, digital interface, and display all support HDCP. If one or more of these devices does not support HDCP, you will see the content at a reduced quality level similar to DVD quality.

> **note** Although component video supports HDTV up to 1080p, component video cannot support HDCP.
>
> You will need a third-party program to play Blu-Ray or HD DVD movies in WMC. See the section "Watching Blu-Ray Movies in WMC," in Chapter 5, "Watching and Recording Movies," **p. 162**.

Video cards and integrated video solutions that include HDMI ports (refer to Figure 2.12) include HDCP support. What about DVI ports? Although HDMI is based on DVI, don't assume that a particular DVI-based video card or integrated video port includes HDCP support—check the spec sheet for the video card or the chipset used by the integrated video port.

> **note** You must check the spec sheet for each video card you are considering (rather than simply checking the spec sheet for the GPU used by the video card) because video cards require an additional hardware component to provide HDCP support. Although both ATI and Nvidia have claimed HDCP support in their GPUs for several years, very few video cards made before 2006 included the proper hardware support for HDCP.

Displays and Monitors

If you want to use WMC to view HDTV sources, it's time to leave behind 1280×1024 and lower-resolution CRT and LCD displays or standard TVs and connect your PC or Media Center Extender to an HDTV, HD-quality projector or flat-panel display that supports HDTV. Your digital photos and high-quality video sources look much better in HD than in standard resolutions.

> **note** If you want to display 720p HDTV on a computer monitor, you need a display with a native resolution of at least 1366×768. To display 1080p HDTV on a computer monitor, you need a display with a native resolution of at least 1920×1200.

HDCP and Your Display

If you want to use your WMC PC to display encrypted HD video sources, make sure your display supports HDCP. HDTVs with HDMI ports support HDCP, as do many (but not all) 22-inch and larger widescreen LCP displays with DVI ports. Before you buy, check the display's spec sheet to determine HDCP support.

Surround Sound

If you use a desktop PC for WMC, you might not need to add anything to your PC to have surround sound support. Many recent desktop PCs include support for 5.1 or 7.1 surround audio as part of their integrated audio. However, if you are planning to connect your PC to a home theater system, you will want to make sure that your PC has a digital audio output (also known as an SPDIF port). Some use a coaxial SPDIF output, while others use an optical SPDIF output. Figures 2.13 and 2.14 compare these ports and cables.

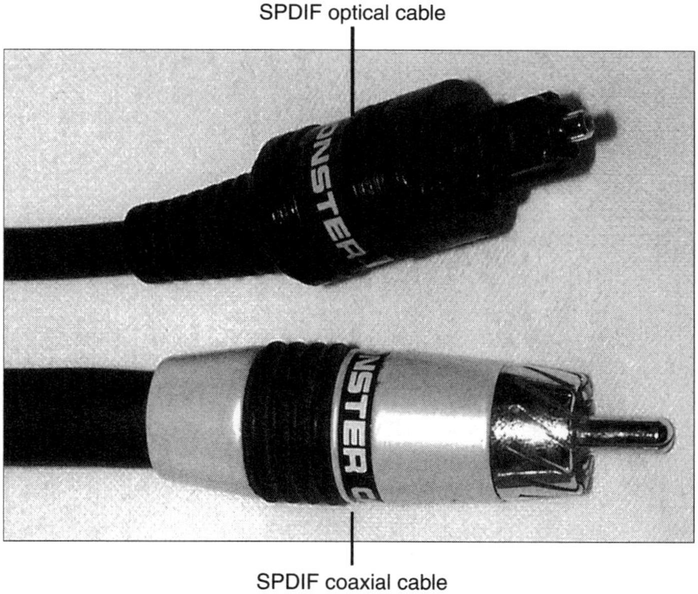

FIGURE 2.13
SPDIF cables.

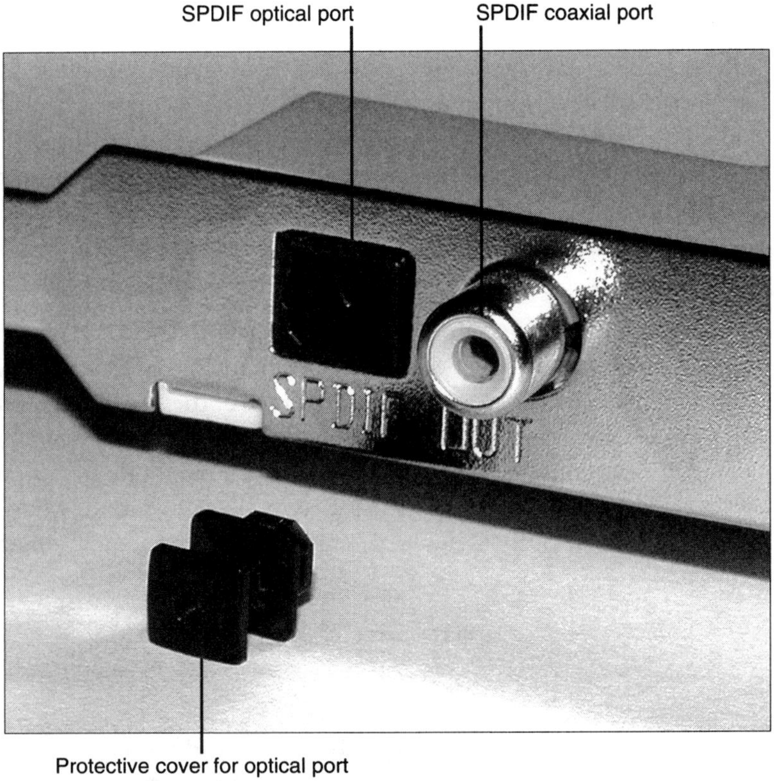

FIGURE 2.14
SPDIF ports on a slot bracket.

> **caution** Before you buy a replacement sound card or USB audio device, make sure you really need one. In some cases, your system or motherboard might have provision for an SPDIF port on a daughtercard or card bracket (like the one shown in Figure 2.14) that was not supplied with the system. (If you built your own system, you might not have installed it, so check your motherboard box.) Check with the system or motherboard vendor for details and to purchase the appropriate accessory if it's available for your system.
>
> If you decide that your onboard sound will not connect to a home theater system, make sure the sound card or USB device supports Windows Vista and provides 5.1 or 7.1 digital surround audio. Although Windows Vista has been available since early 2007, many sound card and device vendors have been slow to roll out Vista drivers or provide stereo-only output on Windows Vista.
>
> To improve stability and reliability, Windows Vista has a completely different audio subsystem than earlier versions of Windows, meaning that you must have native Vista drivers for your sound card or USB device. Check user reviews and check the vendor's website for Vista drivers before buying a replacement sound card or USB device.

If your onboard audio has multiple mini-jack ports designed for surround audio but does not have either type of SPDIF port, you can use computer speakers to achieve surround audio. However, if you want to connect your PC to a home theater system, you can replace your onboard audio with a sound card or external USB device that has an SPDIF port.

Working with Digital Video and Photos

If you bought a PC designed for use with WMC, you might already have the ports and connections you need to easily import digital video and photos. However, you can also purchase the components you need to upgrade an existing PC for WMC or to build a PC for WMC use.

FireWire (IEEE-1394) Ports

If you want to use your WMC PC to import video directly from a DV camcorder, you'll need a FireWire port (also known as an IEEE-1394 or i.Link port). Figure 2.15 illustrates these ports. Some motherboards include either a six-wire or four-wire FireWire port, but in many cases, you'll need to add a FireWire card to your system.

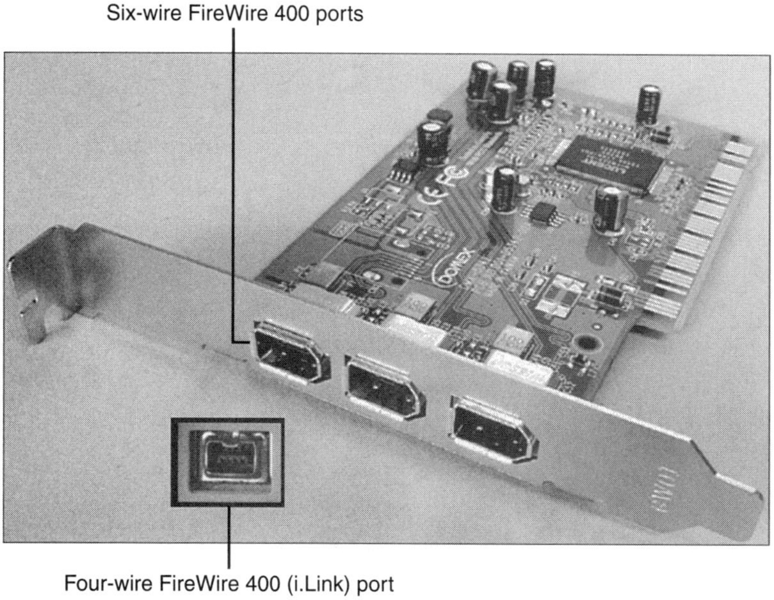

FIGURE 2.15

A FireWire card can be added to a system that needs FireWire ports.

Card Reader

You can import digital photos from your camera through its USB interface cable, but it's a clumsy method that also runs down your camera's batteries. Instead, I recommend using a card reader. Card readers are often included in desktop or laptop computers and photo printers.

2

caution Although many laptops made for WMC include integrated card readers, these card readers do not support Compact Flash. (Despite the name, CF is the largest flash memory card form factor in common use.)

If you are using a digital camera that uses Secure Digital (SD) flash cards, also note that the new SDHC cards (capacities of 4GB and above) cannot be read by card readers designed only for SD cards.

Thus, you might need to add a card reader to some systems that already have an onboard card reader.

If you need to add a card reader to your PC, you can plug it into a USB 2.0 port. However, the most elegant solution for a desktop PC is to use a card reader that slides into a drive bay (Figure 2.16).

note Before you buy an internal card reader, check to see how it connects to your computer. Some use a nine-pin connector that plugs into an unused USB 2.0 port header on your motherboard, while others must be plugged into a USB 2.0 port on the rear of the system.

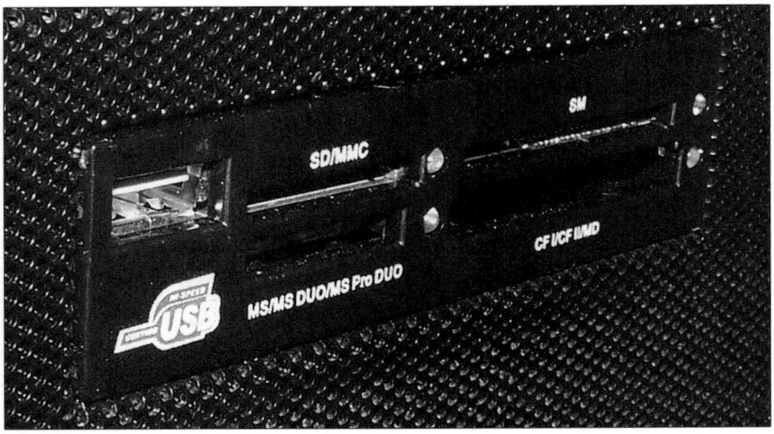

FIGURE 2.16

A multi-slot card reader.

Scoping Out Your Hardware

If you didn't build your PC, or if it's been upgraded from time to time, you might not know the exact details of the processor type and speed, memory size, hard disk size, and other details. Depending on the amount of information you need about your system, there are a variety of ways to find these things out.

Using MSInfo32

You might not need anything other than Windows itself to learn what you need to know about your system. With either Windows XP or Windows Vista, you can use the msinfo32 program to display a lot of hardware information (Figure 2.17).

> **tip** To run MSInfo32 in Windows Vista, click Start, click the Search box, and type in **msinfo32.exe**. When the program appears in the list of programs, click it to run it.
>
> To run MSInfo32.exe in Windows XP, click Start, click Run, type in **msinfo32.exe**, and click OK.

MSInfo32's System Summary Screen displays the essential information needed to answer the following questions:

- How much physical RAM (memory) is installed?
- How large is the hard disk?
- How much hard disk space is available?

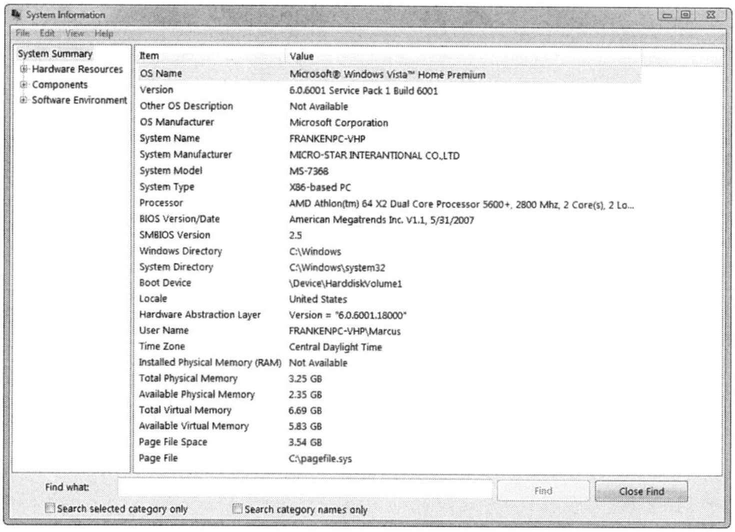

FIGURE 2.17
Using MSInfo32.

Using an Online System Scanner

The online system scanners discussed earlier in this chapter can be used to determine current memory size and available upgrades, and the Belarc Advisor displays other system information.

→ For details, see "RAM-a-Rama: Bigger Is Better!," this chapter, **p. 24**.

2

Building or Buying a Media Center PC

Whether you want to build or buy a new Media Center PC (or upgrade an existing PC for WMC), use the following checklist (Table 2.2) to make sure you get the features you need.

Table 2.2 Hardware Feature Checklist

Task	Category	Recommended Hardware	Notes
General WMC operation	Processor	Intel Core 2 Duo or Quad; AMD Athlon 64 x2; Turion 64 x2; Phenom	Upgrading the processor might also require replacing the existing motherboard and memory.
General WMC operation	RAM	2GB or more	Use up to 4GB with 32-bit versions of Vista; up to 8GB or more with 64-bit versions of Vista.
General WMC operation	Hard disk	500GB or larger (desktop); 320GB or larger (notebook) if you are planning to record live TV or work with digital video; 320GB or larger (desktop) or 250GB or larger (notebook) for digital music and photos only	Check system specifications to determine hard disk types supported; can be added externally.
General WMC operation	Wireless mouse and keyboard	2.4GHz RF or Bluetooth	Avoid 27MHz RF or all types of IR (infrared) devices.
Recording Live TV	TV tuner	ATSC, NTSC*, and ClearQAM or OCUR (CableCard) tuner	OCUR (CableCard) tuners are available only in new PCs made to support OCUR; the tuner might be bundled with the PC or be available as an extra-cost option.

Task	Category	Recommended Hardware	Notes
Watching TV, video, using WMC user interface, Vista desktop	Video card or integrated video port	DirectX 9 or greater support with native Vista (WDDM) drivers	Look for HDMI support for direct connection to HDTVs; look for HDCP support to view Blu-Ray and encrypted premium HD cable channels in full quality.
	HDTV or display	720p or 1080p HDTV or monitor supporting 720p or 1080p resolutions	Look for multiple HDMI connectors on HDTVs to enable various components to connect to TV; avoid old HDTVs that use component video instead of HDMI. (Component video doesn't support HDCP.)
Watching TV, video; listening to digital music	Sound card or onboard audio	5.1 or 7.1 surround sound; SPDIF port for connection to home theater system	7.1 surround sound is also known as Azalia or HD Audio; make sure the SPDIF port on the PC matches an available SPDIF port on the home theater system.
Importing digital video	I/O port	FireWire 400 or 800 port	Use adapter with FireWire 800 bilingual port to connect to a FireWire 400 device.
Importing digital photos	I/O port or device	USB 2.0 port	For direct connection to a camera via its USB 2.0 port and cable.
		Card Reader	Might be incorporated into photo printer or PC; verify that card reader works with current media type used in camera and displays drive letters in Windows Explorer.

2

CHAPTER

3

Setting Up Windows Media Center

IN THIS CHAPTER

- Making Sure Your PC Is Ready to Rumble
- Starting WMC and the Setup Process
- Custom Setup: Required Setup
- Custom Setup: Optional Setup
- Using Settings to Reconfigure Your System

Making Sure Your PC Is Ready to Rumble

Windows Media Center (WMC) automatically launches your choice of Express or Custom Setup when you start it for the first time, or you can start WMC and then set it up later. Although you *can* go back and set up missing pieces of your system later, you're probably better off making sure it has all of the pieces in place first.

So, how do you get started? First, make sure you've installed all of the hardware recommended in Chapter 2, "Equipping Your PC for Media Center," for the types of media you plan to use with WMC, including TV tuners, FM radio tuners, and so on.

→ For hardware recommendations and installation tips, see Chapter 2.

What's next? Drivers. Because WMC is designed to run on standard and HDTVs as well as traditional computer displays, make sure you're using the latest vendor-supplied drivers for your graphics card or integrated display adapter. If you're using the bare-bones graphics drivers provided by Microsoft, you're missing out on support for 3D configuration, HDTV configuration, and other options. If your display offers Vista-compatible drivers, be sure to download and install them as well.

Using a wireless mouse and keyboard? Check the range. If your system responds when you're in your usual easy chair, you're OK. However, if the system ignores your mouse and keyboard until you move closer, you may need a Bluetooth mouse and keyboard combo. Bluetooth input devices can work up to 30 feet away from the transceiver, compared to as little as 6 feet for old-school wireless devices. Windows Vista-certified non-Bluetooth input devices can have a range as far as 15 feet from the transceiver.

Worried about screen savers? If your system automatically boots into the Windows desktop (it will if you have set up only one user and not assigned a password), WMC disables the desktop screen saver when you're viewing TV or videos. However, if you are using a password, see http://support.microsoft.com/kb/929526 to learn how to disable the requirement to log back in after the screen saver kicks in.

note Bluetooth mouse and keyboard combos are available from Microsoft (Wireless Entertainment Desktop 8000 and 7000) and Logitech (diNovo Media Desktop Laser, Cordless Desktop MX 5000 Laser). These and other vendors also offer Bluetooth mice.

If you're using WMC with a standard monitor or with an HDTV that connects to your system via a VGA or DVI port on the display, you don't need to worry about display support. If you forgot to enable a port in the BIOS or need to run the Recovery Environment or startup menu in case you've hosed your system, no problem—you can see what you're doing in full widescreen glory. However, if you are using a TV (standard or HDTV) that connects via composite, S-Video, component, or HDMI connectors, keep in mind that you will not see anything onscreen until the friendly Windows Vista logon menu or desktop is

tip For emergency troubleshooting, keep a lightweight 14 or 15-inch LCD stashed away in a closet. You can plug it into your system in case of problems. Just make sure the unused connector on your dual-display graphics card matches the LCD display's connector type or use an adapter. You might be able to find a used display for under $100, as many companies are phasing out these sizes in favor of larger models.

displayed. Error or status messages that show up on a normal computer display during boot don't make it to the TV screen.

How's your network? Your Internet connection? Take a few moments with the Network and Sharing Center and Internet Explorer (IE) 7 to make sure your network is working. You must connect your WMC box to a working Internet connection if you are planning to use it to record live TV. The Internet provides the correct information needed to configure the tuner. And remember, if you want to enjoy everybody's music, video, and photo collections through WMC, their systems must be configured to allow network connections to their media folders. In Windows Vista, use the Network and Sharing Center, and turn on Media Sharing in the Sharing and Discovery portion of the dialog. With older Windows versions, make sure the folders you use for shared media, such as the Shared Documents folder on each system, are configured for sharing.

Once you've made sure your system is ready, it's time to set up WMC.

Starting WMC and the Setup Process

To start WMC for the first time, click the Start orb, click All Programs, and click Windows Media Center. The first time you run WMC, a Welcome dialog appears (Figure 3.1), prompting you to choose one of three options:

- Express setup
- Custom setup
- Run setup later

> **note** If you've already installed drivers for your remote control, you can use it to navigate through the setup program.

The Express setup option provides a shortcut to getting started with WMC. It downloads art and information for your media and puts you into the Customer Experience Information Program. Basically, Express setup is designed for users who plan to use WMC mainly for music, DVD, and photo playback.

If you're using WMC as a live TV and TV recording solution or want to fine-tune display colors or speaker configurations, you need a comprehensive setup program. Choose Custom setup, which is discussed in the following section.

Of course, if you're in too much of a hurry to set up anything, you can run setup later. Keep in mind that you must finish Custom Setup in a single setting. If you close Custom Setup, you must start over. Give yourself about 30 to 45 minutes to do everything, especially if you are planning to fine tune your display quality.

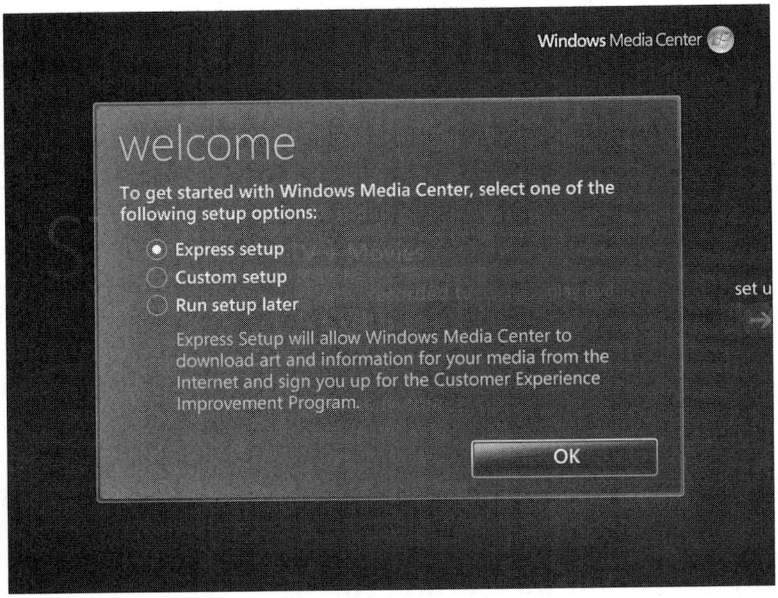

FIGURE 3.1
Selecting a setup option when starting WMC for the first time.

Custom Setup: Required Setup

When you select Custom setup, WMC displays a full-screen Welcome message and prompts you to click Next to continue. The Custom setup process is divided into two parts:

- Required Setup configures network and Internet settings.
- Optional Setup configures other features and advanced settings.

After reviewing these steps, click Next to continue setup. On the next screen, you will see the Windows Media Center Privacy Statement screen. Take a moment to review it now, or you can review it later.

1. On the next dialog, specify whether you'd like to join the Customer Experience Improvement Program. Select Yes, I'd Like to Join, and WMC configures your system to periodically send anonymous reports to Microsoft on how WMC is working. Feeling paranoid? Select No, Thank You. On the fence? Click the link to view the privacy statement online. Fortunately, the text is delivered using the easy-on-the-eyeballs WMC interface, not in a browser window. Make a selection, and click Next to continue.

2. On the next dialog, you are prompted to choose whether to let WMC download album art, movie and music information, and TV Program Guide listings. If you're planning to use WMC as a DVR or just want to make your digital life easier and more enjoyable, click Yes.
3. On the Required Components Have Been Set Up dialog, click Next. The Optional Setup dialog appears (refer to Figure 3.2).
4. If you don't need to configure TV tuners, optimize your display, set up speakers, or set up access to other users' and other systems' media libraries, click the I Am Finished button, click Next to finish setup, and get on with enjoying your media library.

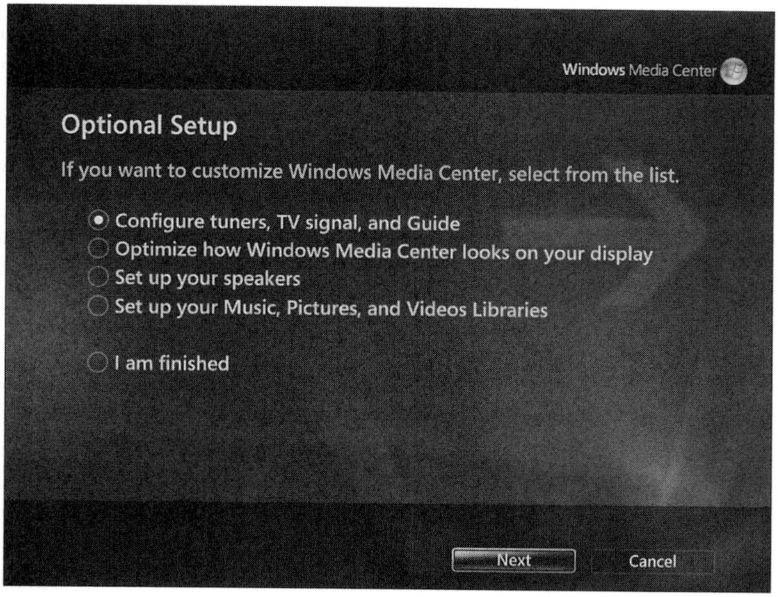

FIGURE 3.2
Preparing to run Optional Setup.

Custom Setup: Optional Setup

As you can see from the previous section, the required setup for WMC doesn't do much at all. While it assures that you get the online connections you need to make your media library easy to use, it doesn't touch the specifics of your hardware or home network configuration. That's the job of the Optional Setup menu (refer to Figure 3.2).

The Optional Setup menu can be used in any order, and you can stop at any time after you have completed a section. Just click I Am Finished after completing the portions that apply to your system, and WMC stores and uses your settings. However, in the following sections, I am assuming you have a "loaded for bear" WMC system that requires configuration of all features.

Optional Setup: TV

The first option on the Optional Setup menu configures TV tuners, TV signals, and the TV Program Guide (often referred to simply as "Guide"). Select it, click Next, and continue.

> **note** Why do you have an option to specify a different region? You can use this option to pick up over-the-air TV signals that Microsoft doesn't support in your country. For example, ATSC (over-the-air HDTV) can be picked up in Canada as well as the United States. However, Microsoft does not include ATSC support in the Canada region. The solution? Pretend you live in the U.S.! See the full write-up (which includes some Registry wizardry) at http://thenears.wordpress.com/2006/11/22/atsc-in-canada-with-media-center-vista-rtm/.

1. First, you must specify the region you are in. This enables you to receive the correct local TV program sources to choose from. If the default region is correct, click Yes then Next to continue. If you need to select a different region, click No, Next, and select the region.
2. After you select the region, WMC downloads the appropriate TV information for your region. On the following screen, you are prompted to set up TV signals. Click Configure My TV Signal Automatically, and click Next (see Figure 3.3).

> **note** If you select the option to configure your TV signal manually, you will need to specify your TV signal type. You can run this option later if auto-detection doesn't work.

3. During the scan process, WMC checks for signals from a set-top box, cable TV, and other supported TV signal types, including antenna signals. When the scan process is finished, WMC reports what it found (refer to Figure 3.4 for a typical example). Click Yes to accept the scan results, No, I Want to Try Again, or No, Proceed to Manual TV Signal Setup if you have problems. Selecting the scan results prompts you to accept the TV Program Guide ("Guide").

→ See "Activating the TV Program Guide," this chapter, **p. 62**, for details.

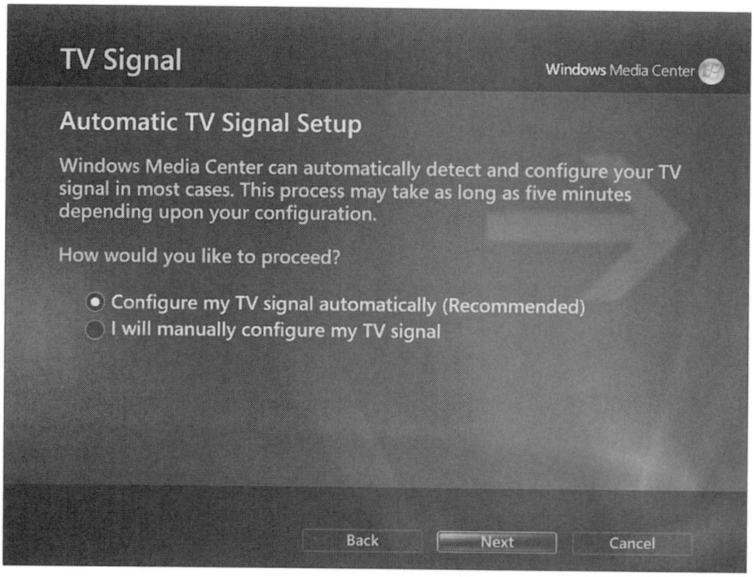

FIGURE 3.3

Preparing to detect TV signals.

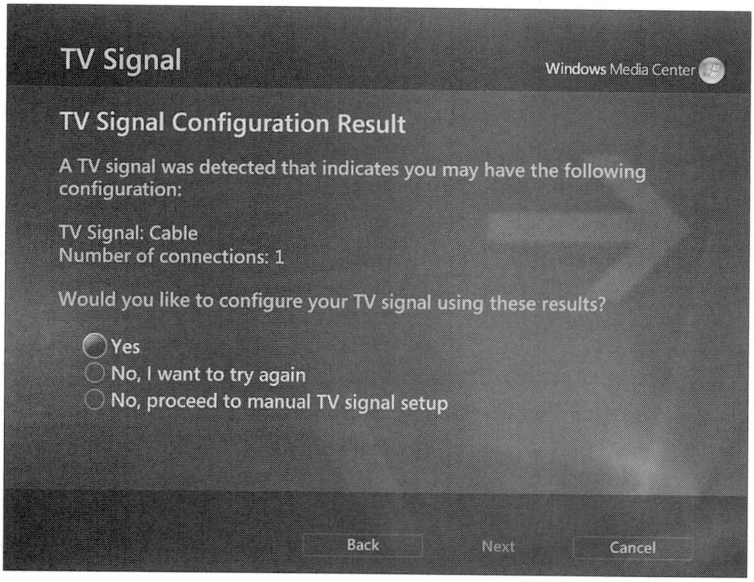

FIGURE 3.4

Preparing to set up the TV signals based on detected results.

SOLVING TV SIGNAL WOES

If you didn't get the results you expected during the scan for TV signals, check the following:

- **Make sure your TV tuner is working correctly.** Most TV tuner cards and USB devices include software that can be used outside of WMC. Exit WMC, and use the vendor's TV setup software to watch some TV. Granted, it might appear in a small window rather than the full-screen digital goodness of WMC, but if the vendor's TV software can't pick up any channels, WMC won't do any better.
- **Update your TV tuner's drivers.** Even if you received Vista-compatible drivers included with your TV tuner, you might find better drivers at the vendor's website.
- **Check your TV tuner setup.** Some TV tuner devices emulate two separate tuners, such as ATSC and cable TV, or standard and HDTV. Follow the manufacturer's recommendations for activating one tuner or the other before restarting a scan. Although WMC supports multiple tuners, it can have problems with a single device that emulates two tuners.
- **Check coaxial and data cables connecting to your TV tuner.** If you are using WMC as a complete replacement for TV, you may be using the same coaxial cable previously used for TV. However, if you are using a splitter to run WMC as well as your TV directly from a single connection or have added an extension to existing coaxial cable to connect your system to cable TV, check the connections on the additional components. Switch cables if possible to verify the cable works properly.
- **Check other components that could be interfering with the signal.** If you are using a broadband cable Internet connection for TV/WMC, make sure it is properly split and filtered. If you are using a surge suppressor with coaxial cable support, bypass it. If WMC can now pick up TV signals, the surge suppressor was either connected incorrectly to the coaxial cable or is defective. Replace the surge suppressor if it continues to give you grief.

- **Splitting your cable TV signal? Boost it!** If you are splitting a single incoming cable TV or external antenna signal to support two or more TVs as well as WMC, you may not be giving WMC a strong enough signal to work with. Pick up a TV signal booster, and solve the problem. Some good choices include Motorola's Signal Booster and the Electroline 8 port signal booster/amplifier. If a booster isn't feasible, consider switching to a low-loss splitter to reduce signal loss.

Manual TV Channel Setup

If an automatic channel scan isn't working for you, you can select No, Proceed to Manual TV Signal Setup and set up your TV signal manually. On the first dialog, you select the type of TV signal you use: Cable, Satellite, or Antenna.

If you select Satellite, the next dialog reminds you to verify that your satellite receiver is working correctly. Click Next to continue. Select from channels 2, 3, and 4, S-Video, or composite video to find a TV signal. A preview window displays the TV signal (refer to Figure 3.5). Click Scan Again if you need to rescan your TV after making adjustments. WMC detects the infrared (IR) hardware used by your set-top box and completes setup.

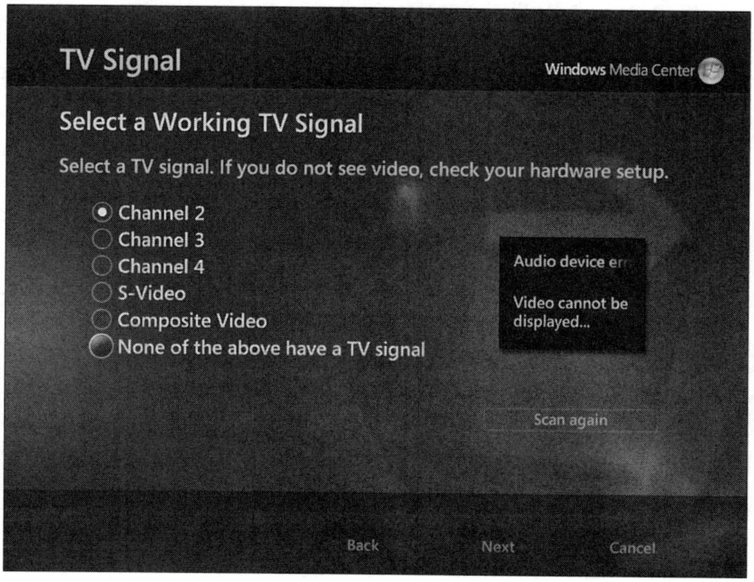

FIGURE 3.5

Searching for a working TV signal when setting up satellite TV manually.

If you select Antenna or Cable, you are prompted to use the TV Program Guide ("Guide"). See the next section for details.

Activating the TV Program Guide

Whether you are automatically or manually setting up your system for cable or antenna (over-the-air) TV, WMC asks you if you want to use the TV Program Guide ("Guide"). The Guide is a virtual necessity if you want to record live TV or movies automatically, but you can turn down the offer. (If you do, you will need to record manually or use another source for TV listings.) If you're feeling paranoid, you can view the Guide privacy statement before you answer the question, but be prepared for 68 screens of data (as delivered by the 10-foot WMC graphical user interface (GUI), so you don't need to squint).

After signing off on the Guide, U.S. residents are prompted to enter their zip codes. This information is used to find and download appropriate over-the-air (antenna) or cable TV providers to choose from. Select your TV signal provider from the list (see Figure 3.6 for a typical example), and the appropriate TV Program Guide downloads to your system, completing the TV portion of Optional Setup.

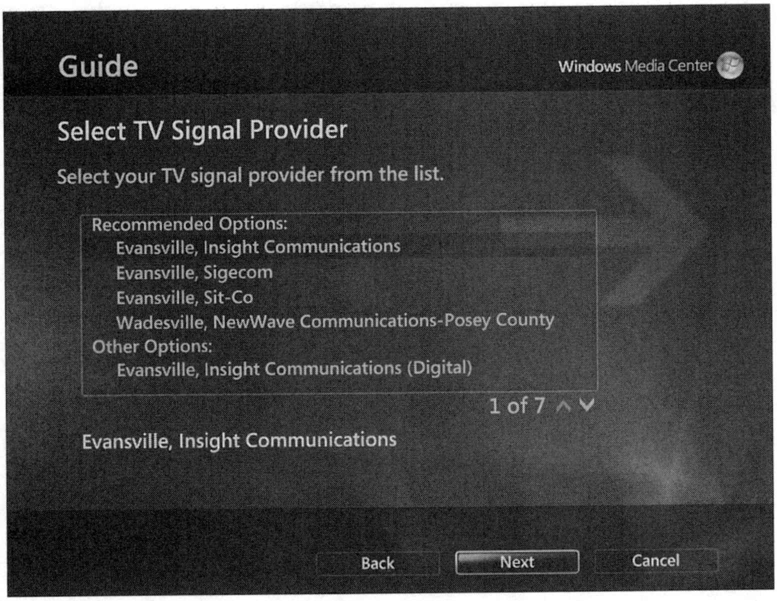

FIGURE 3.6
Selecting a TV signal provider.

Optional Setup: Optimize Display

After checking off TV tuner and signal configuration, the second step listed on the Optional Setup menu (refer to Figure 3.7) optimizes how WMC looks on your display.

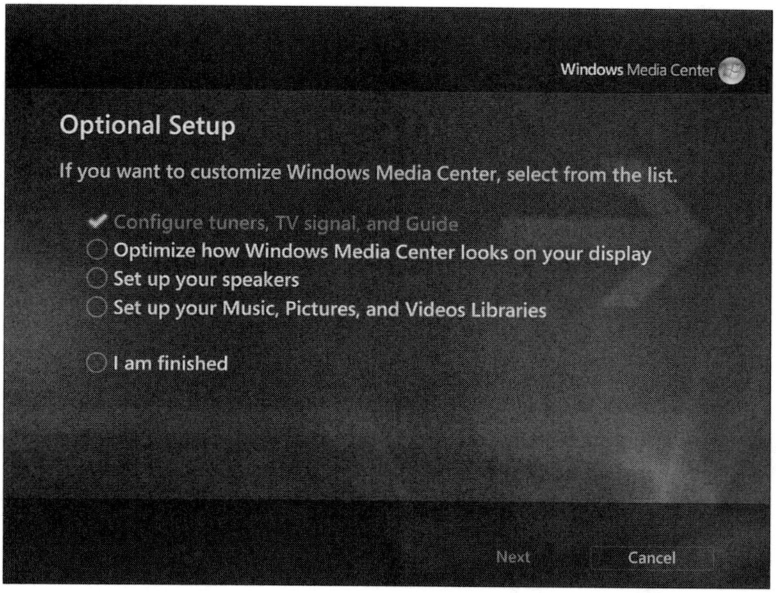

FIGURE 3.7
TV tuner and signal configuration—DONE!

On the first screen, WMC offers a video you can play to help you adjust color, contrast, aspect ratio, and brightness on your display. Click "Watch Video" to start the video, which features an attractive quartet of media-savvy yuppies playing pool, watching others play pool, and playing with projectors and displays while they explain how the display optimization process that follows will help you set up your display.

Adjusting the Preferred Display

On the next dialog, WMC asks if you are running the wizard on your preferred display. Click Yes if you are or No for instructions on rerunning the wizard on your preferred display later.

note If you want to run WMC on a secondary display, make sure you reduce it to a window and drag it to the secondary display before running this wizard.

On the next dialog, select your display type: monitor (CRT), built-in (laptop and all-in-one desktop units), flat panel (LCD monitor), television (all types), or projector.

tip Confused? Use this rule of thumb: If you connect to a VGA or DVI port on the display, it's a flat panel. If you connect to a HDMI or component port on the display, it's a TV.

Next, select your connection type from three families:

- Composite or S-Video
- DVI, VGA, or HDMI
- Component (YPbPr)

Move your mouse over each selection to see pictures of each connection type, or refer to Figure 3.8 (pictures of cable connectors).

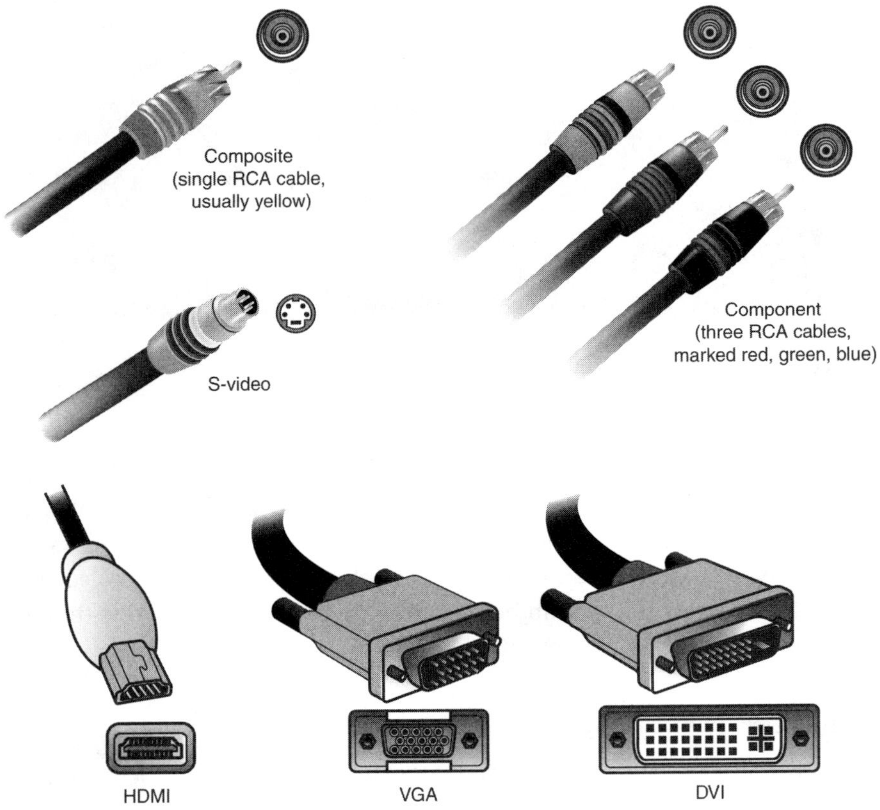

FIGURE 3.8
Video cable connector types.

Next, select the width (aspect ratio) of your display: traditional TV/monitor 4:3 ratio (also known elsewhere as 1.33:1) or widescreen 16:9 ratio.

note If you use an adapter to connect a DVI port on your PC to a component port on your display (refer to Figure 3.8), select Component.

Optimizing for Your Preferred Resolution

After you select the width of your screen, it's time to review your current display resolution. Click Yes to accept it or No if it is not correct.

note Don't get picky here: Some widescreen flat panel LCD displays actually use a 16:10 ratio in some resolutions. Put away your calculator, and select widescreen for any widescreen display.

If you answer No, a list of supported display resolutions appears (refer to Figure 3.9 A). Select the best one from the list. If you don't see the mode you want to use, click Select All Modes to see additional display resolutions along with the refresh rates they support (see Figure 3.9 B). Choose the mode you want to use.

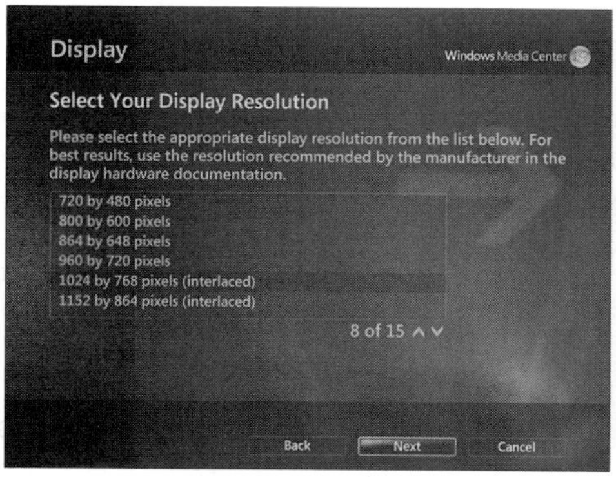

A. Supported list shows resolutions only.

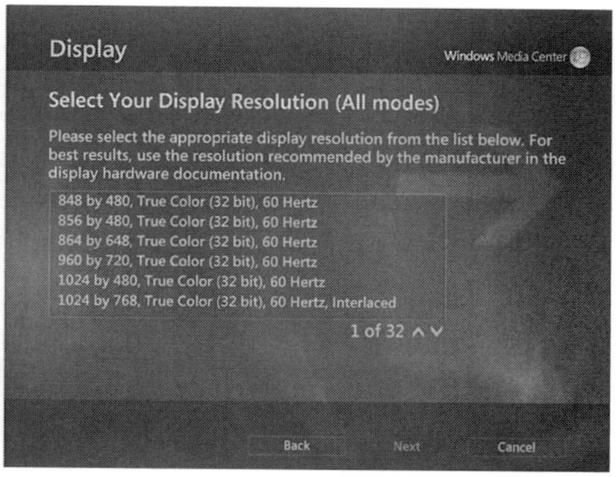

B. All modes also lists supported refresh rates.

FIGURE 3.9
Selecting a different display resolution.

When you select a different mode, WMC attempts to switch to the new resolution, apply an overscan correction, and optimize colors and fonts. Use the Preview option to see if the changes can be made. You will be notified if the resolution switch was successful. Click Yes to accept the changes. If you don't want to accept the changes or if the resolution changes didn't work, you are prompted to try a different resolution or stick with your current selection.

If you answer Yes, WMC applies overscan correction and optimizes the colors and fonts on your display. Use the Preview option to see the adjustments first. Click Yes to accept the changes.

Note that some resolutions might use interlaced video (refer to Figure 3.9). Interlaced video writes every other screen line with each pass of the electron gun that creates the picture inside the TV or CRT monitor. Although these resolutions look just as good within WMC as non-interlaced modes, interlacing makes the standard Windows desktop look jumpy. If you plan to switch between WMC and the standard Windows desktop, avoid interlaced resolutions if you can—your eyes will thank you!

tip If you are not using the best display resolution for WMC, but you cannot change it within WMC, you might need to change it through Control Panel's Personalization menu. Choose the Display Settings option.

If you are using an HDTV as your preferred WMC display, use the special HDTV support features of your graphics card driver's control center to change the resolution of your display. This might be available from the Advanced portion of the Display Settings dialog, or you might need to run a separate program.

Adjusting Display Settings

After you confirm (or adjust) your display resolution, it's time to adjust display settings. If you're satisfied with contrast, brightness, color, and other settings, click Finish This Wizard, and WMC checks off another task. However, if you want to fine-tune these settings, click Adjust Display Controls.

First, it's time to calibrate your display. Click Next to display a list of changes you can make. These include

- Onscreen centering and sizing
- Aspect ratio (shape)
- Brightness (black and shadow detail)
- Contrast (white)
- RGB color balance

Select the option you want to adjust, and click Next. You can run these tasks in any order and skip tasks you don't need to perform.

tip Make sure you know how to access the picture adjustment controls for your display before you start this process.

If you are using an HDTV, you will probably use an onscreen menu operated by your TV's remote control to make adjustments. Typical monitors, LCD flat panels, and standard TVs use adjustment knobs or onscreen menus operated by buttons on the display.

For built-in displays, such as those in laptop computers, see the computer's instruction manual. Many laptops include brightness and contrast controls on FN keys that are overlaid on the standard function keys F1-F12.

To adjust onscreen centering and sizing, watch the video (starring our old friends, the pool players), and use the centering and sizing controls to adjust the large picture so it matches the inset picture. Figure 3.10 shows you an example of an improperly and a properly adjusted display. Keep a careful eye on the edges of the display, which can be cut off if you don't adjust centering and sizing properly.

> **tip** If you are using HDTV via a DHCP connection or a monitor (CRT or flat panel), you probably don't need to run the Adjust Display Controls section of the wizard. However, if you are using a conventional TV using S-Video or composite or an HDTV that connects through component video, you should run the tests in this section to ensure that your display is in tip-top shape.

The video plays several times to allow you adequate time to make adjustments. However, if you are not satisfied (or just plain out of time to make adjustments), go back and run the test again. After the test is completed, it is checked off the Display Calibration list, and you can proceed to the Aspect Ratio adjustment.

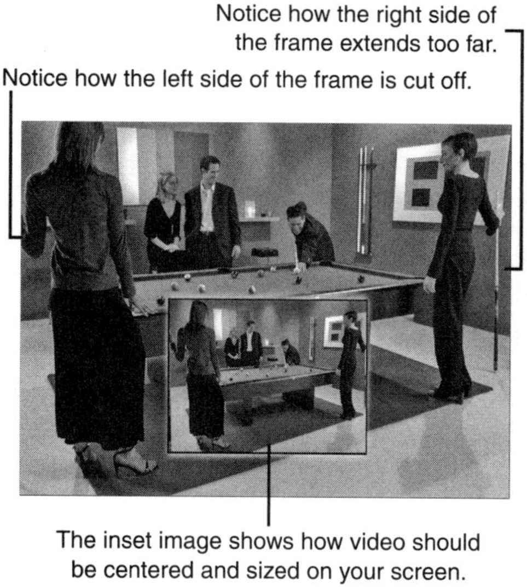

A. Improperly adjusted (cuts off left and top sides of image).

B. Properly adjusted to match inset.

FIGURE 3.10

Adjusting sizing and centering.

The Aspect Ratio (Shape) helps you fine-tune the screen geometry of your display. Even though you selected the aspect ratio of your display earlier in the setup process, you might still need to tweak the size and centering (screen geometry) of your display to ensure that squares are square, circles are circles, and so forth. During the video playback (which features the pool table seen in previous videos), adjust the display to make sure the billiard balls are round and the chalk block is square. Figure 3.11 shows you examples of incorrect and correct screen geometry.

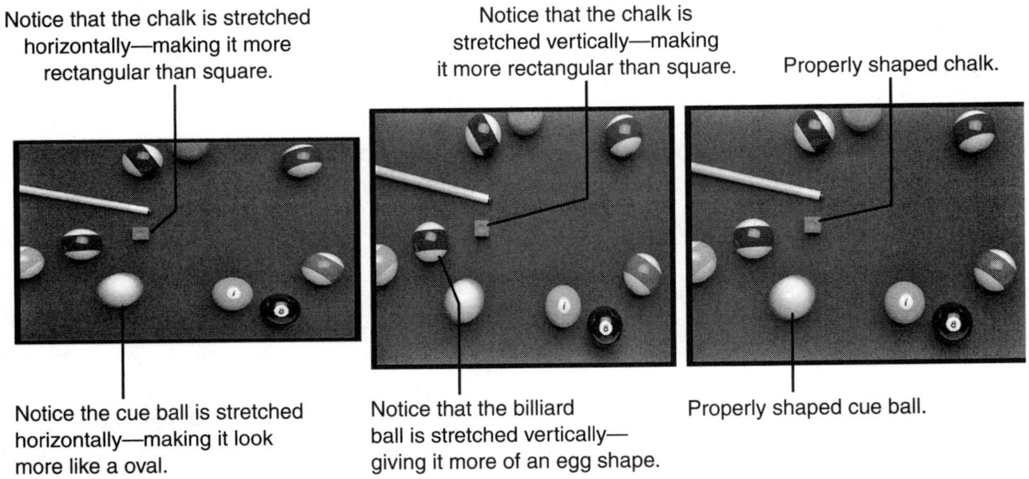

A. Shapes elongated horizontally: reduce horizontal size or increase vertical size to correct.

B. Shapes elongated vertically: increase horizontal size or decrease vertical size to correct.

C. Display properly adjusted.

FIGURE 3.11
Adjusting Aspect Ratio (Shape).

The video plays several times so you can make the necessary adjustments. At the end of playback, Aspect Ratio is checked off the Display Calibration list, and it's time to adjust Brightness.

Brightness calibration, despite the name, maybe ought to be called "black and shadow" calibration. It's designed to make sure you don't lose important details in the

> **tip** If you need to adjust display centering, see if your display includes a zoom feature that adjusts both horizontal and vertical settings at the same time to aid display centering. If your display is not properly configured to show shapes accurately, you will still need to adjust horizontal or vertical sizing individually.

shadows. Look for the brightness or "black level" control on your display, and while the video of the black-suited, gray-shirted pool player runs, adjust the controls if necessary so that the suit is black, and you can tell the difference between the suit and the shirt. Figure 3.12 shows an example of an incorrectly and correctly adjusted display.

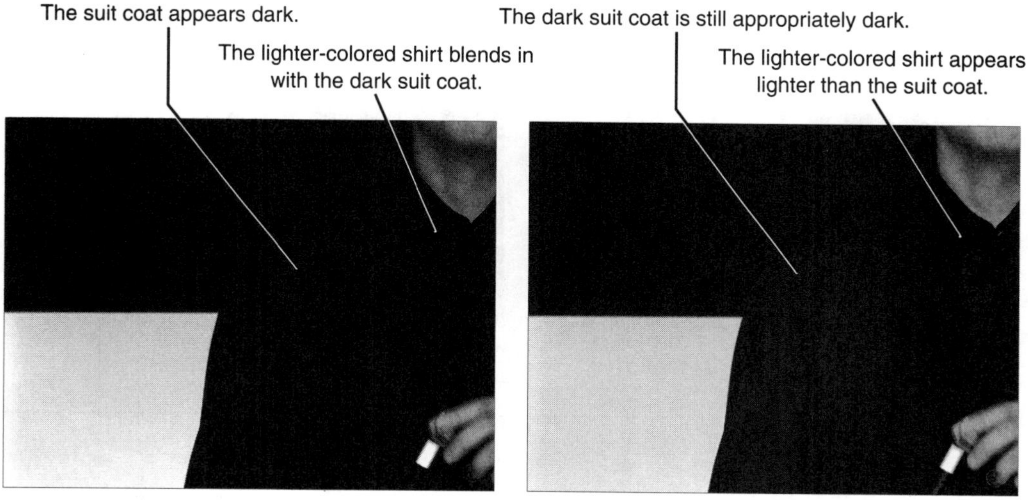

A. Incorrect brightness setting blends the black suit and gray shirt together.

B. Correct brightness setting shows the different colors of the suit and shirt.

FIGURE 3.12

Adjusting brightness (black and shadow).

The video plays several times so you can make the necessary adjustments. At the end of playback, Brightness is checked off the Display Calibration list, and it's time to adjust Contrast.

Contrast calibration is used to make sure bright areas don't lose detail. Look for the contrast or picture control on your display or display menu, and while the video of the white-shirted pool player runs, adjust the contrast if necessary to ensure that you can see the wrinkles and buttons on the shirt (see Figure 3.13).

As with other adjustments, you might get tired of watching the video play or be glad you have several chances to make the needed adjustments. At the end of playback, Contrast is checked off the Display Calibration list, and it's time to adjust your display's RGB color balance.

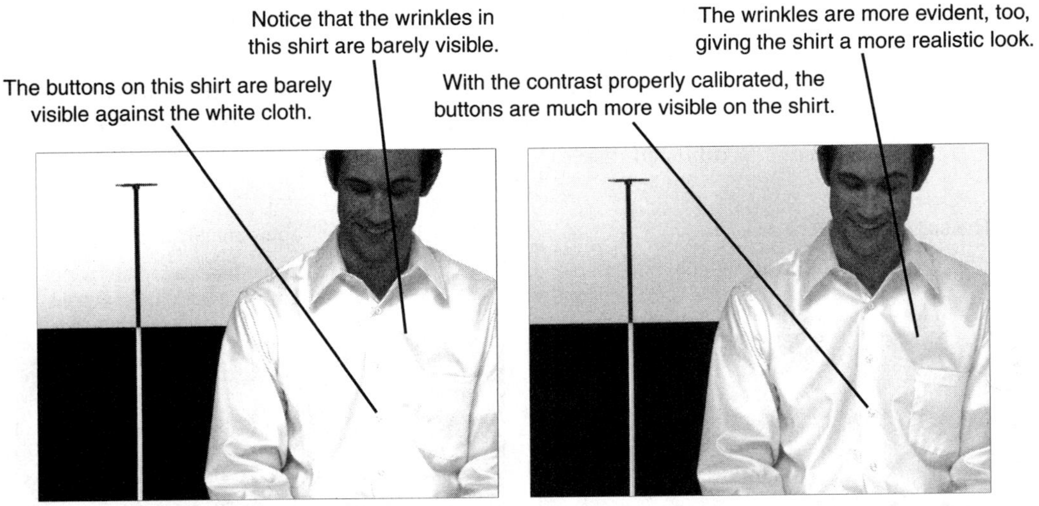

A. Incorrect contrast setting loses detail in the white shirt.

B. Correct contrast setting brings out detail in the white shirt.

FIGURE 3.13

Adjusting contrast.

RGB color balance calibration is designed to make sure your display produces accurate colors. If you can select a color temperature setting of 6500°K on your display's controls, use that setting, and you don't need to run this calibration. Otherwise, go to the next screen, and play the video. While the video plays, adjust color settings to remove any off-color appearance of the white and gray bars behind the pool player (Figure 3.14). The camera pans up from the table and zooms in on the bars.

At the end of playback, RGB Color Balance is checked off the list, and you're done with Display Calibration (Figure 3.15). Click Next to see a message that shows you're finished with Display setup. Click Next again to return to the Optional Setup menu.

FIGURE 3.14
Tweak the RGB color balance to make the bars look pure white and shades of gray.

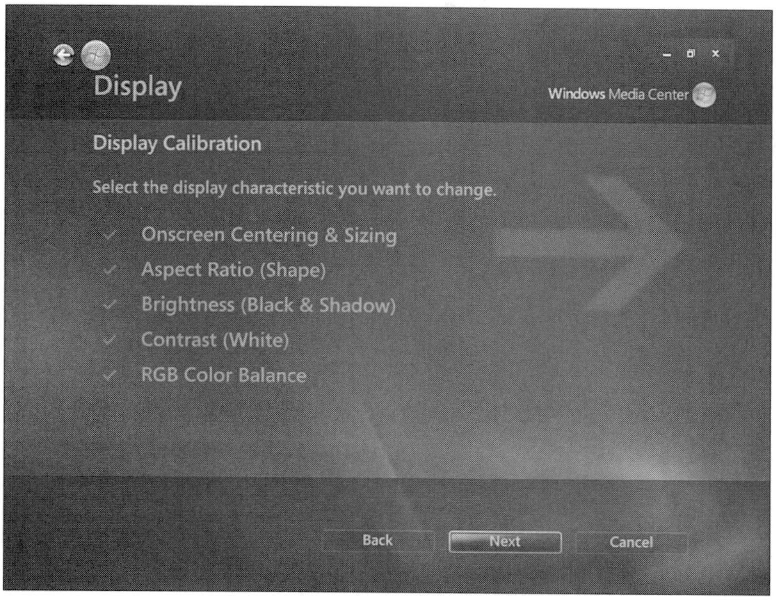

FIGURE 3.15
Finished with Display Calibration? The checkmarks say "Yes!"

Optional Setup: Speakers

With TV and display settings optimized, it's time to set up your speaker system. Select Set Up Your Speakers, and click Next to continue. The speaker setup dialogs are used to specify how many speakers you have and to test each speaker. From the Speaker Connection Type dialog, select from the following analog speaker connection types:

- Mini-plug
- Stereo RCA

Or from the following digital speaker connection types:

- Single RCA (coaxial SPDIF)
- Toslink (optical SPDIF)

Or built-in (for laptops and all-in-one units with integrated speakers).

As with the display connector type dialog, illustrations of each speaker cable type are shown. You can also refer to Figure 3.16 for help.

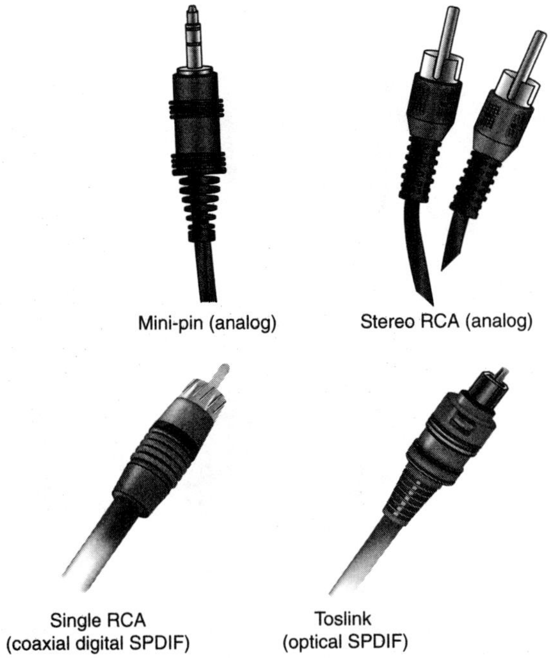

FIGURE 3.16

Audio cable connector types.

Next, specify your speaker configuration:

- 2 speakers (stereo)
- 5.1 surround (refer to Figure 3.17)
- 7.1 surround (refer to Figure 3.17)

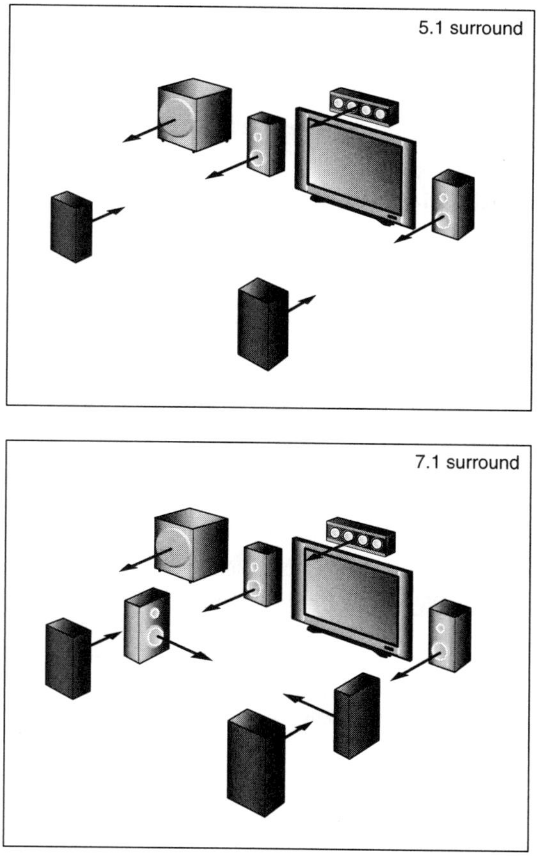

FIGURE 3.17

Surround audio configurations supported by Vista WMC.

Select your speaker type and on the next dialog, click Test. A different tone is played through each speaker. If all of your speakers are working, click I Heard Sound.... WMC displays the speaker setup you tested. Click Finish to wrap up this part of setup.

If some speakers didn't play, select I Did Not Hear Sound..., and a speaker troubleshooting guide is displayed on the next dialog. It reminds you to check speaker cable connections, audio/video codec installation, and to make sure Windows audio devices and drivers are properly configured. Click Back if you want to retry the test after making adjustments or Finish if you want to set up your audio later.

> **note** If you are sending audio to a home theater system's amplifier, make sure the home theater system is properly set up to play through all of its speakers. For example, on my 5.1 system, I can select two-channel output, which disables my rear and center speakers. Another possible gotcha is the audio source. Make sure you select the proper source for audio. For example, my system offers "Video" and "DVD" sources. You must select the source corresponding to the correct input jack(s), or you'll hear nothing from any speakers. Finally, check the volume control on your home theater system.
>
> If you are using speakers connected directly to your PC (or integrated speakers), make sure you haven't muted your audio or have the volume set so low you can't hear it. Some laptop computers include a mute/unmute button as part of the multimedia keys.

Optional Setup: Music, Pictures, and Videos Library

Library Setup is used to configure the folders that WMC uses for media it will play back. These folders can be located on your system or on other systems in your home network. By default, WMC watches the current user's Music, Pictures, and Videos folders for media files. However, you can configure WMC to watch other users' folders and folders on other systems, or you can prevent WMC from watching a particular folder.

➔ To learn how to add or remove folders later, see Chapter 12, "Connecting with Windows Home Server and Other PCs."

Adding Folders on Your System

> **note** To add folders from all users, open the C: drive, navigate to the Users folder, and select it. All media folders from all users will then be available to WMC.

To add a folder, click Add Folder to Watch. You can add folders on your computer, other computers, or both (refer to Figure 3.18). I recommend that you select the option to set up both local and network folders.

When you add folders on your computer, you see a list of folder locations, including your desktop, the current user's folders, Public Documents, the system hard disk, and CD/DVD drives (see Figure 3.19 A). To see subfolders of a particular location, click the plus (+) sign. To select a folder (and its subfolders), highlight it with your mouse or your remote, and click the checkbox or press the OK button on your remote. Use the scroll arrows to move to additional screens as needed. Click Next to continue.

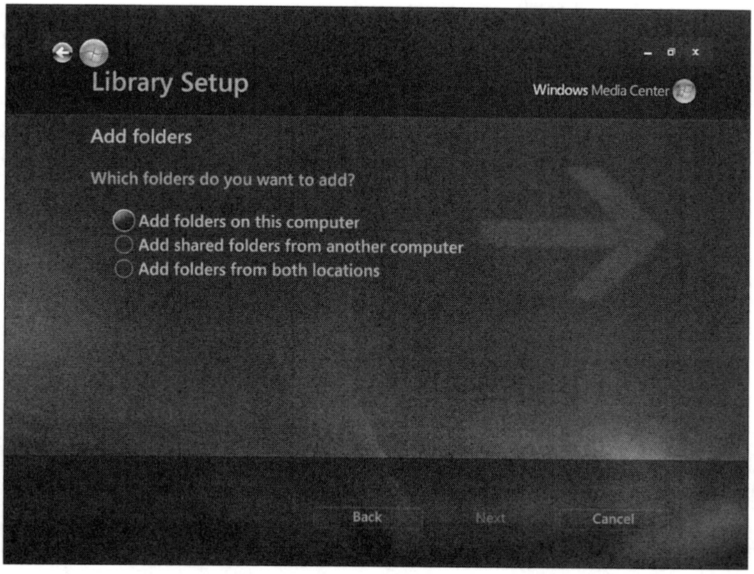

FIGURE 3.18

Library folder options.

Review the folders added, and click Finish to add those folders to WMC's watch list (refer to Figure 3.19 B). A pop-up dialog appears as folder contents are being added to WMC's libraries. Click OK to continue, or wait until the dialog is cleared away.

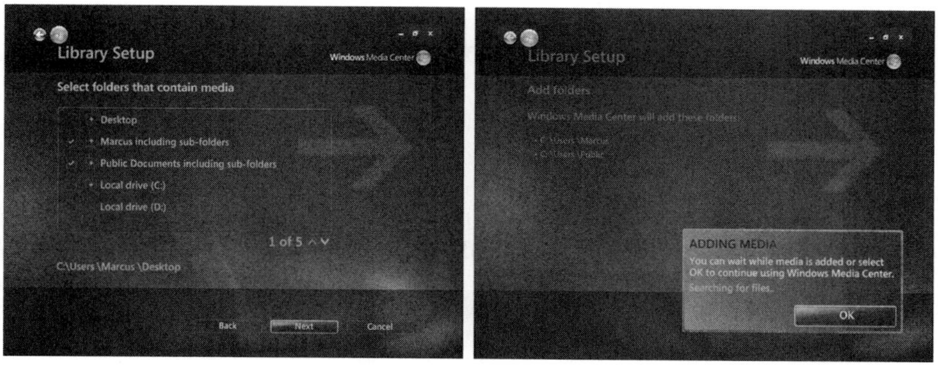

A. *Selecting local folders.*

B. *Folders being added to the media library.*

FIGURE 3.19

Adding local folders.

Adding Folders on Other Systems

When you add folders from other systems, a list of shared folders is displayed on your monitor (see Figure 3.20 A). Click the checkbox next to each folder that contains media files you want to play. Use the scroll arrows to move to additional screens as needed.

> **note** Some shared folders might not include data you can play with WMC. Before you start WMC setup, you might want to view the folders by using Network Explorer to make sure you select only folders that contain media files.

Review the folders added, and click Finish to add those folders to WMC's watch list. A pop-up dialog appears as folder contents are being added to WMC's libraries (see Figure 3.20 B). When you add folders from remote systems, it takes longer than adding folders on local systems. Click OK to continue, or wait until the dialog is cleared away.

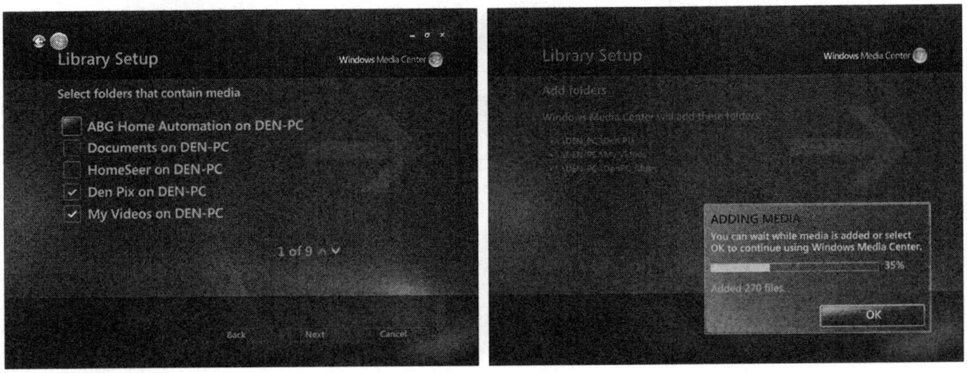

A. *Selecting network folders.*

B. *Folders being added to the media library.*

FIGURE 3.20
Adding network folders.

Wrapping It Up

After you complete Library Setup, the Optional Setup checklist is complete (see Figure 3.21). Click I Am Finished and then Next. Click Finish on the You Are Done! dialog, and you can start using WMC with a fully-configured system.

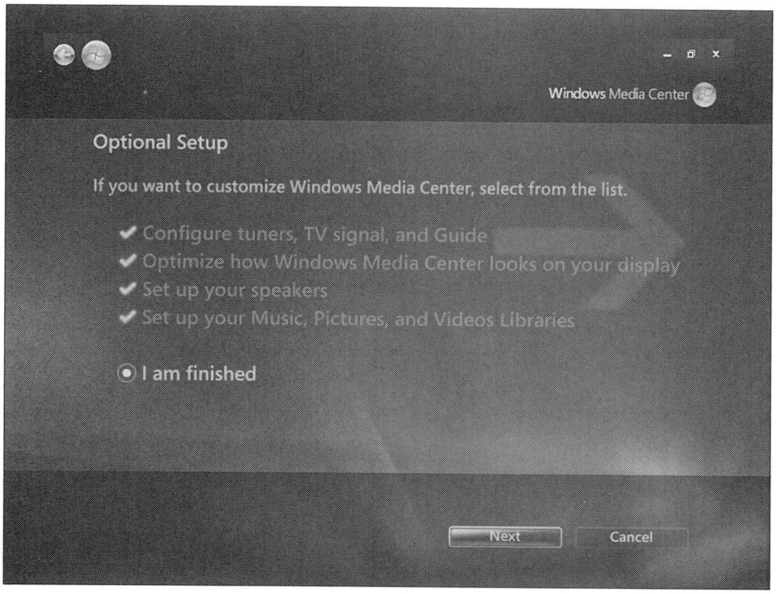

FIGURE 3.21
Optional setup is complete when all options are checked off.

Using Settings to Reconfigure Your System

OK, so you've configured WMC the way you want it—until you change your hardware. Maybe you're swapping your 25-inch conventional TV for a 42-inch HDTV, or you're ready to connect your PC audio to a new 7.1 surround home theater system. Whatever the change is you make to your WMC system, you don't need to run the entire setup process again. Instead, go to Tasks, and select Settings.

The Settings menu contains seven sections:

- General
- TV
- Pictures
- Music
- DVD
- Extender
- Library Setup

The following sections discuss how to use these menus to reconfigure your original setup options and to set up additional features.

Using the General Settings Menu

The General Settings menu includes nine different menu selections that govern the general operation of WMC:

- Startup and Window Behavior
- Visual and Sound Effects
- Program Library Options
- Windows Media Center Setup
- Parental Controls
- Automatic Download Options
- Optimization
- About Windows Media Center
- Privacy

Select the category, and a submenu with additional options appears.

Configuring Startup and Window Behavior

By default, WMC displays taskbar notifications, shows TV tips in the TV Program Guide, and displays a Not Designed for WMC dialog (if you try to run programs designed for the standard Windows GUI from within WMC). To change these options, to enable WMC to run on top at all times, or to run when Windows starts, check or uncheck the corresponding settings in the Startup and Window Behavior menu (see Figure 3.22). Click Save to save changes or Cancel to discard changes.

Configuring Visual and Sound Effects

By default, WMC produces various types of beeps, boops, and chimes as you navigate its features. To disable the sound effects or to disable the transition animations WMC uses, clear the appropriate checkboxes in the Visual and Sound Effects menu (refer to Figure 3.23).

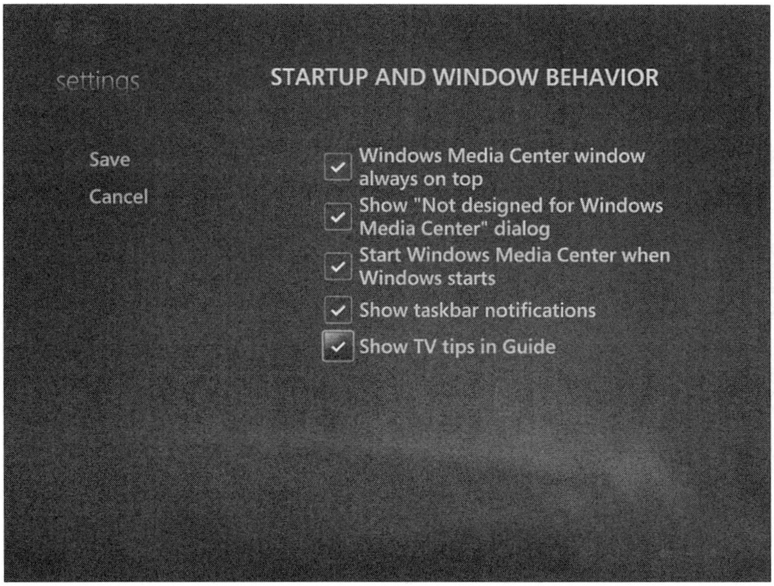

FIGURE 3.22

Suggested settings for optimizing WMC for full-screen, full-time use.

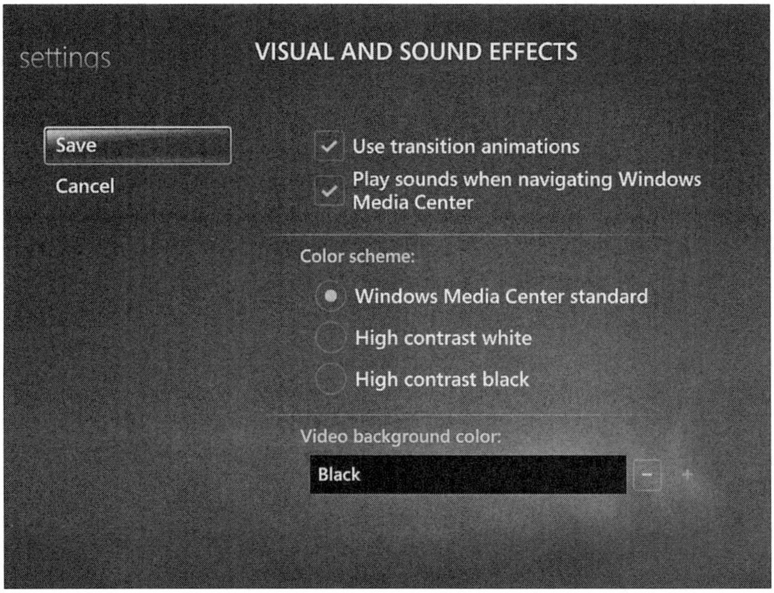

FIGURE 3.23

Adjusting sound effects and WMC screen display style.

You can also use this menu to switch to high-contrast white or high-contrast black menus (see Figure 3.24) or to change the background color used behind videos. Click Save to save changes or Cancel to discard changes.

A. High-contrast black. *B. High-contrast white.*

FIGURE 3.24
High-contrast WMC menus.

Configuring Program Library Options

WMC's Program Library includes any third-party applications optimized for Vista WMC that you might install, such as Adobe Photoshop Elements 5.0. Change how these programs work with the Program Library Options menu (see Figure 3.25).

Rerunning Windows Media Center Setup

If WMC's current setup is not working, you can rerun selected portions of setup or all of setup by selecting Windows Media Center Setup from the General menu and choosing the portions of setup to rerun (see Figure 3.26). If you change audio, display types, or add a TV tuner, you can rerun only the portions of setup affected by your change in hardware.

> **caution** If you choose Run Setup Again, WMC discards all of its current setup information and restarts Setup from the beginning.

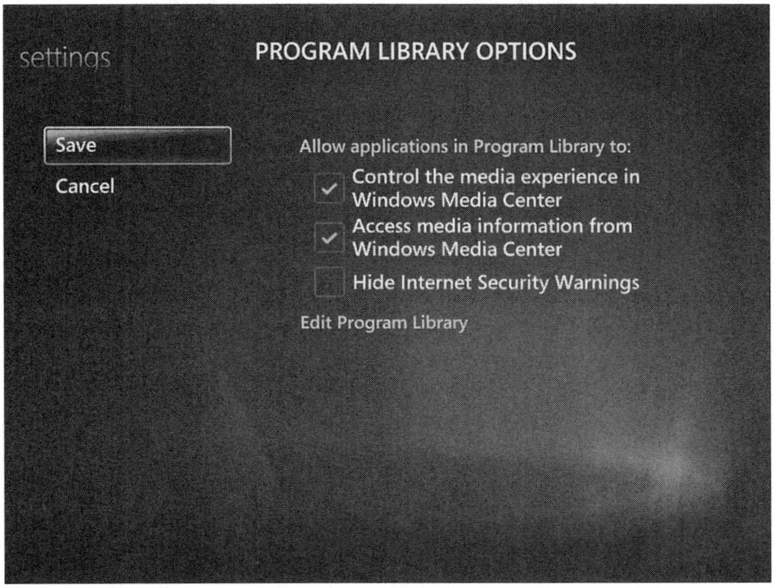

FIGURE 3.25

Adjusting how the Program Library works.

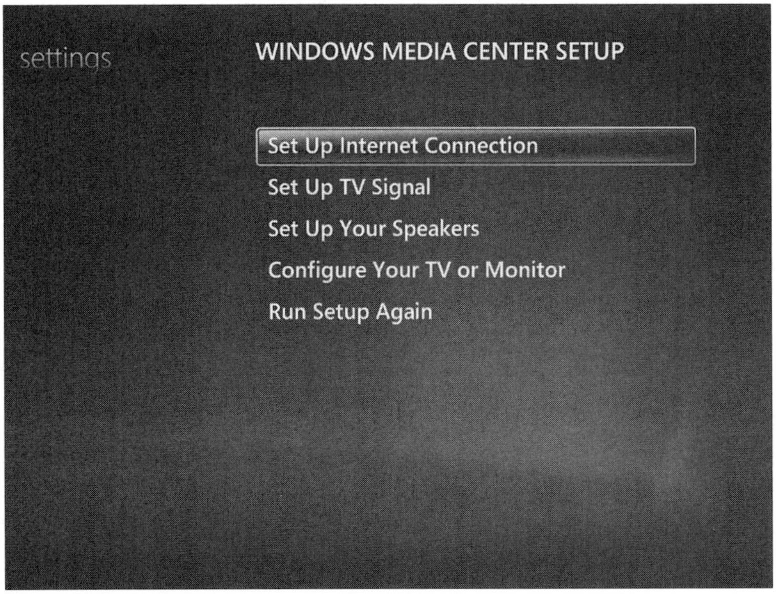

FIGURE 3.26

Use this menu to rerun portions or all of WMC setup.

Other General Settings Options

The Parental Controls menu is used to configure TV and movie viewing. Automatic Downloads is used to configure when WMC downloads the TV Program Guide. Optimization configures when WMC performs system optimizations. About WMC displays the current WMC version, the TV Program Guide Terms of Service, and the credits information for data providers. Privacy displays the current privacy statement and configures privacy and customer experience settings.

→ To learn more about the TV Program Guide and about Parental Controls for use with TV, see Chapter 4, "Viewing and Recording Live TV."

→ To learn more about Parental Controls for use with movies and DVDs, see Chapter 5, "Watching and Recording Movies."

Using Other Settings Menu Options

The TV Settings menu is used to configure TV signals, TV/monitor displays, audio, and closed captioning. The Pictures Settings menu adjusts how pictures are displayed. The Music Settings menu configures visualizations that play while music is being played. The DVD Settings menu configures language, closed captioning, and remote control options used during DVD playback. The Extenders Settings menu is used to configure WMC extenders, such as the Xbox 360. Library Setup is used to add or remove media folders from the watch list.

→ To learn more about the TV settings menu, see Chapter 4.

→ To learn more about the DVD Settings menu, see Chapter 5.

→ To learn more about the Music Settings menu, see Chapter 6, "Importing and Playing Audio."

→ To learn more about the Pictures Settings menu, see Chapter 7, "Importing and Viewing Photos."

→ To learn more about the Extenders Settings menu, see Chapter 11, "Adding and Using Media Center Extenders."

PART

II

Enjoying Media with Windows Media Center

CHAPTER

4

Viewing and Recording Live TV

Windows Media Center (WMC) can bring both broadcast and cable TV to your desktop, as well as the growing world of Internet TV. This chapter helps you understand your TV options, learn to equip your PC to tune in your preferred TV format, watch live TV, record live TV for enjoyment later, and enjoy Internet TV.

IN THIS CHAPTER

- Understanding Your TV Viewing Options
- Setting Up Your TV Signal
- Configuring the TV Program Guide
- Watching Live TV
- Recording Live TV
- Watching Recorded TV
- Watching Internet TV
- Parental Controls

Understanding Your TV Viewing Options

Even without the February 17, 2009, changeover from analog to digital broadcast TV in the U.S., understanding TV-watching options would be difficult enough. Although there's the risk you might have a bad attack of MEGO (my eyes glaze over) by reading this section, you need to understand what your viewing options are before you choose TV-tuner hardware for your PC. The choices you make will have a big influence on the TV signals you can watch on your PC—and what you can do with those TV signals.

Broadcast and Basic Cable TV

If you want to watch conventional broadcast or basic cable TV on your PC, any Vista-compatible TV tuner will work. Connect the coaxial lead from the cable TV service port (you don't need a tuner box) or from a TV antenna into the broadcast TV/cable TV connector on the TV tuner, as shown in Figure 4.1.

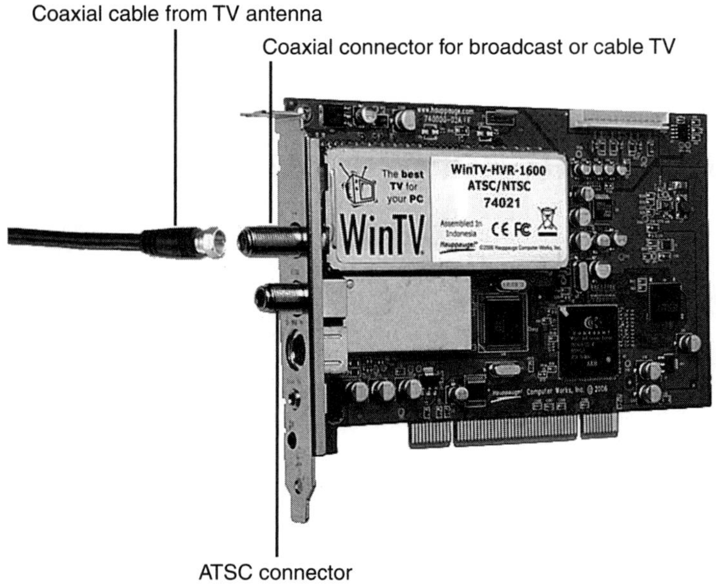

FIGURE 4.1

Connecting a TV antenna or cable TV coaxial cable to a typical TV tuner card.

However, after February 17, 2009, only low-power analog TV stations (basically repeaters and public-access channels) will remain on the air; today's local and network-affliate TV stations will be broadcasting digital TV signals. An analog broadcast (NTSC)/cable TV tuner will still be able to pick up basic cable TV signals after the changeover date but will no longer be able to pick up broadcast TV.

> **note** Some late-model TV tuners have two coaxial connectors, one for cable and NTSC (analog broadcast TV) and the other for ATSC (broadcast HDTV). Use the connector marked "TV" or "cable TV." Figure 4.2 shows an example of a TV tuner card with an ATSC connector.

What you need: standard TV tuner device (USB 2.0, PCI, PCI Express, or Express Card); antenna (for broadcast TV); cable TV input (for cable TV)

What changes after February 17, 2009: only cable TV can be received

Digital Broadcast TV (ATSC)

What's replacing NTSC analog broadcast TV? ATSC digital broadcast TV! In most U.S. broadcast TV markets, ATSC is already here, broadcasting side-by-side with conventional analog TV until the February 2009 changeover. ATSC digital TV comes in two flavors:

- **SDTV (standard definition TV):** SDTV is the same resolution as traditional analog broadcast TV but provides better picture quality because it uses a digital signal.
- **HDTV (high-definition TV):** HDTV supports 16:9 widescreen displays at 720p, 1080i, or 1080p resolutions, depending on the signal broadcast by the TV station.

Most 22-inch and larger widescreen computer displays are capable of displaying HDTV, or you can send your TV output to a true HDTV, but regardless of how you watch broadcast TV on your PC, you won't be watching *any* broadcast TV after the changeover unless your PC has an ATSC-compatible TV tuner device.

Connect the lead from the antenna to the ATSC connection on the TV tuner device, as shown in Figure 4.2.

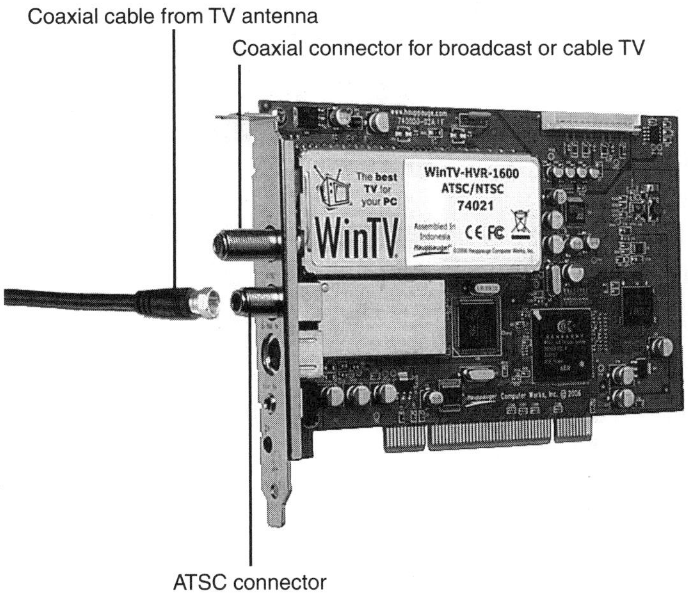

FIGURE 4.2

Connecting a TV antenna for ATSC broadcast TV to a TV tuner card equipped to pick up ATSC.

An ATSC-compatible TV tuner can also pick up analog broadcast TV (as long as it's around) as well as basic cable TV. However, for best results, you should use a directional powered TV antenna for picking up ATSC TV broadcasts instead of that cheap $10 set of rabbit ear antennas. Depending on where you live and how close you are to digital TV sources, you might even need a rooftop antenna for best results. Figure 4.3 illustrates a directional TV antenna you can use for picking up close-range HDTV broadcasts.

FIGURE 4.3

A powered antenna suitable for use with NTSC and ATSC signals. The remote control is used to aim the antenna and save configurations for each channel.

What you need: ATSC TV tuner device (USB 2.0, PCI, PCI Express, or Express Card); directional powered antenna

What changes after February 17, 2009: You might see higher-powered signals from existing ATSC stations, making it easier to pick them up; some stations might start broadcasting ATSC signals only after the changeover.

Digital Cable TV

An increasing number of consumers are opting for digital cable TV. Unlike standard cable TV, digital cable TV offers more channels (including music), on-demand TV, premium content, and current-movie networks such as HBO, Cinemax, and others. Unfortunately, it's a lot tougher to get your PC to work with digital cable TV.

Unlike standard cable TV, viewing digital cable TV with WMC almost always requires the use of a set-top box provided by the cable TV company. Here's why: Most digital cable TV is encrypted, and only the set-top box provided by the cable TV company can decrypt the signals transmitted so they can be used by your TV—or by your PC.

Ironically, this means that if your TV tuner has two connections, one for conventional broadcast and cable TV and another for digital signals (ATSC HDTV or clear QAM cable TV), you use the regular TV connection, not the digital connection!

What you need: Digital cable set-top box (provided by digital cable TV provider); WMC remote control with IR blaster cable (the IR blaster transmits control signals picked up the WMC remote to the set-top box); TV tuner device (USB 2.0, PCI, PCI Express, or Express Card). Figure 4.4 shows you how it all fits together.

What changes after February 17, 2009: Nothing.

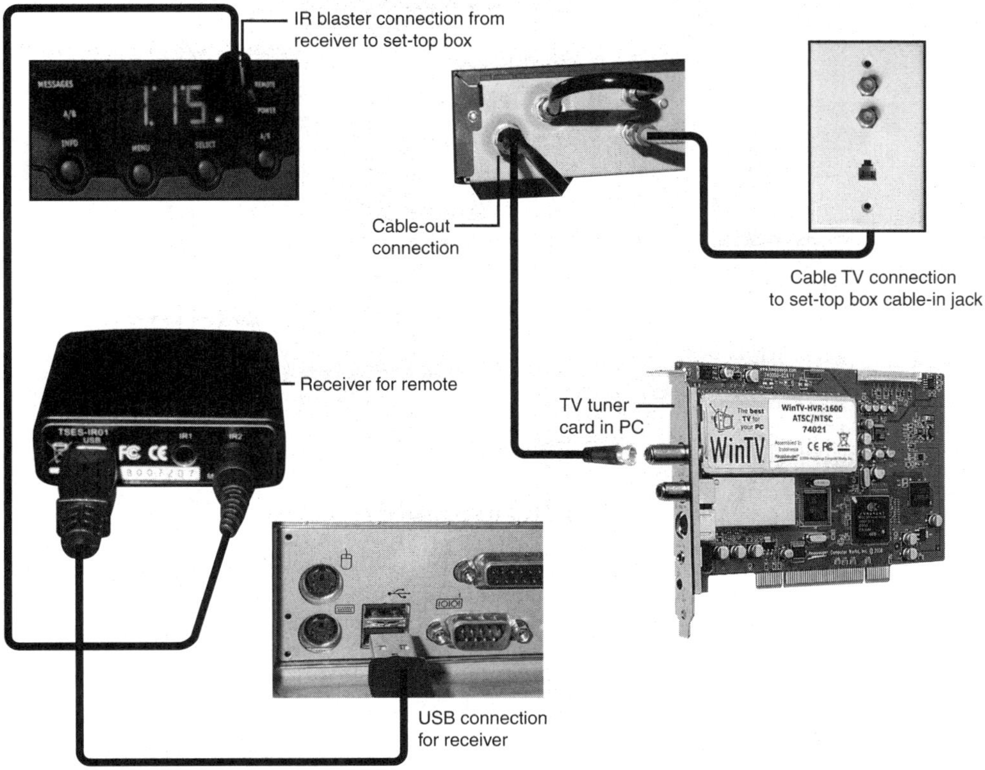

FIGURE 4.4

Connecting a digital cable TV set-top box to a TV tuner card and the IR blaster used by a WMC remote control.

Clearing Up the Confusion About Clear QAM

Although some late-model TV tuners now support unencrypted QAM (also known as "clear QAM") digital TV (typically by using the same connector as the one for ATSC broadcast HDTV), most installations of Windows Vista Media Center do not directly support Clear QAM digital cable TV. Although the Media Center TV Pack released to OEM suppliers in July 2008 adds support for Clear QAM digital cable TV channels, it is not known whether, or when, Media Center TV Pack will be available as an update for existing WMC users.

However, the lack of Clear QAM support might not be as great a disadvantage as it seems. To see if your digital cable TV provider offers Clear QAM channels, you can try the following experiment if you currently have digital cable TV service and a TV tuner that supports Clear QAM:

1. Disconnect the coaxial cable running to the digital cable TV box.
2. Connect this cable to the connection used for Clear QAM cable TV on your TV tuner.
3. Start the TV tuner application provided with your TV tuner hardware.
4. Use its search function to look for Clear QAM TV channels (see the software's documentation for details).
5. Compare the channels detected by the TV tuner with the channels available when you use the digital cable set-top box.

Prepare to be underwhelmed. When I tried this experiment, I discovered only two usable channels (a couple of local broadcast channels; the remainder were placeholders for pay-per-view sports channels) out of a dozen channels total, compared to over 150 via my digital cable TV set-top box. However, your mileage might vary; depending upon your cable TV supplier, you might find a lot of channels available.

If you discover that you can actually get a decent number of digital cable TV channels via Clear QAM, you can get WMC to "see" those channels by installing the Media Center TV Pack (if and when it becomes available), or by adding an HD HomeRun device from Silicon Dust (www.silicondust.com) to your Ethernet-based home network.

The HD HomeRun tuner from Silicon Dust enables all of the Windows Vista Media Center PCs on your Ethernet home network to view and record both ATSC and Clear QAM (unencypted digital TV) channels. (It also supports Windows XP Media Center and most third-party TV tuner applications, by the way.)

To learn more about using HD HomeRun with Windows Vista and to find a handy application for remapping channels, visit http://jarkhd.blogspot.com/2007/06/getting-hd-over-cable-with-vista-media.html.

HD Cable TV

The only way you can watch and record HD cable TV at present is by using an OCUR-compatible HDTV tuner, such as the ATI Digital Cable Tuner device from AMD.

➔ For physical setup and configuration details, see "Digital Cable Tuner," this chapter, **p. 97**.

> **note** If you connect an HD digital cable TV tuner to a standard TV tuner card as described in the previous section, only standard-definition signals will be passed to your computer.

Satellite TV

WMC will not directly support satellite TV until the release of "Fiji," the code name for the next release of WMC. In the meantime, though, you can use the method described in the section on Digital Cable TV to connect your satellite TV set-top box to your TV tuner.

➔ For physical setup details, see "Digital Cable TV," this chapter, **p. 88**.

➔ For software configuration details, see "Configuring Cable/Satellite TV Using a Set-Top Box," this chapter, **p. 93**.

Setting Up Your TV Signal

You can set up your TV signal either by running the Optional Setup: TV selection during the initial configuration of WMC or by selecting Tasks, Settings, TV, and Set Up TV Signal.

> **note** When you select this option, you will see a TV Signal Setup pop-up warning that using this option affects TV recording and may interrupt TV or radio on an MCE device. Click Yes to continue.

The Set Up Your TV Signal wizard appears. Click Next to continue.

On the next screen, WMC asks you to confirm your region, based on the locale settings used by Windows. Select Yes if the information is correct or No if it is not correct. If you select No, provide the correct locale information as prompted. Click Next to continue.

The Automatic TV Signal Setup dialog appears next. I recommend using the default setting (automatic) as shown in Figure 4.5.

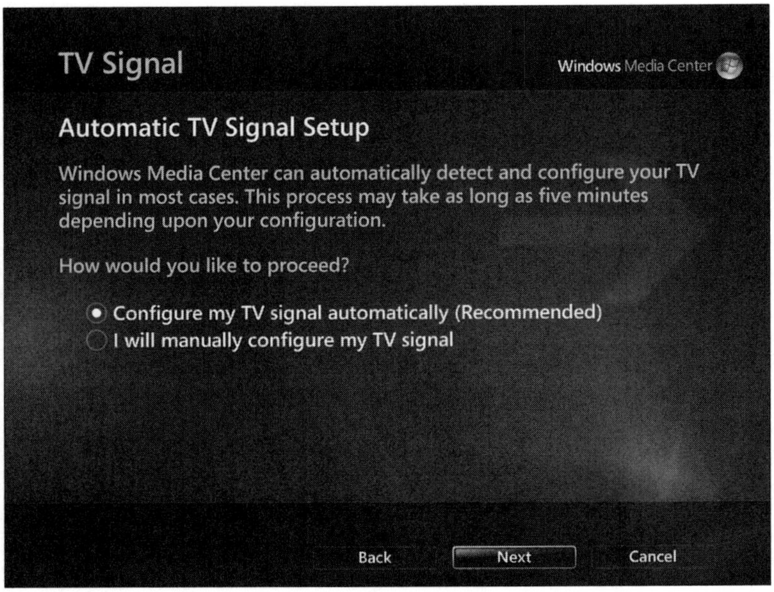

FIGURE 4.5
Selecting automatic TV signal setup.

4

During the next few minutes, the system scans for set-top box signals, cable signals, antenna, and digital antenna signals. It's a good time to take a break away from the PC. When finished, WMC displays the results. You should expect to see a message such as

- TV Signal: Cable (if you have standard cable TV without a set-top box)
- TV Signal: Set-top box (if you have cable or satellite TV routed through a set-top box)
- TV Signal: Broadcast (if you use only broadcast TV)

If your TV tuner also has an ATSC (broadcast HDTV) antenna lead connected to an antenna, you will see a reference to Digital TV Antenna connections. Figure 4.6 shows a system with both digital cable TV and ATSC (digital TV) connections.

What happens next depends on the type of connection you have. If you have standard cable (no set-top box) or broadcast (analog or digital) TV, WMC goes directly to the TV Program Guide setup. However, if you have a set-top box or a Digital Cable Tuner, there are more steps to perform first, as described in the next sections.

➔ For information on the TV Program Guide, see "Configuring the TV Program Guide," this chapter, **p. 100**.

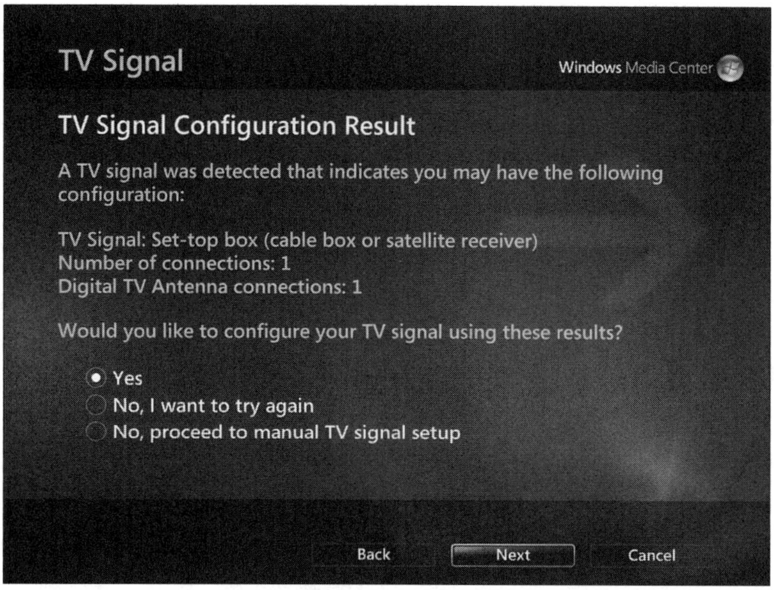

FIGURE 4.6

This system is connected to a set-top box and digital TV antenna (ATSC) signals.

4

Configuring Cable/Satellite TV Using a Set-Top Box

If you have a set-top box, you must next indicate whether you receive cable or satellite TV. After specifying your connection type, WMC checks to see if the IR control cable (also known as an IR blaster) is connected to your Media Center remote's receiver. If it isn't, you will see the dialog shown in Figure 4.7. Connect the IR control cable (refer back to Figure 4.4), and then click Try Again. When the cable is connected, you can continue.

TO REMOTE OR NOT TO REMOTE?

You don't actually *need* a WMC remote to watch TV or movies on WMC, but if you don't want to drag around a mouse and keyboard, you should buy one. You can use a WMC remote to enter text for naming recordings, controlling system volume, and even launching WMC from the Windows desktop with a single push of the green WMC logo button on the WMC remote.

The WMC remote includes a receiver that connects to a USB port on your computer. The receiver also includes one or more IR blaster ports to transfer signals received from the remote to the IR port on a set-top box, as well as an IR blaster cable. For semi-permanent installation, the IR blaster's IR emitter has a self-stick pad so you can place it over part of the window on the set-top box's IR receiver.

You can buy WMC-compatible remotes from Microsoft, Hauppauge, Logitech, and other vendors. Some WMC-compatible remotes can also be used in place of remotes for your TV and home theater equipment.

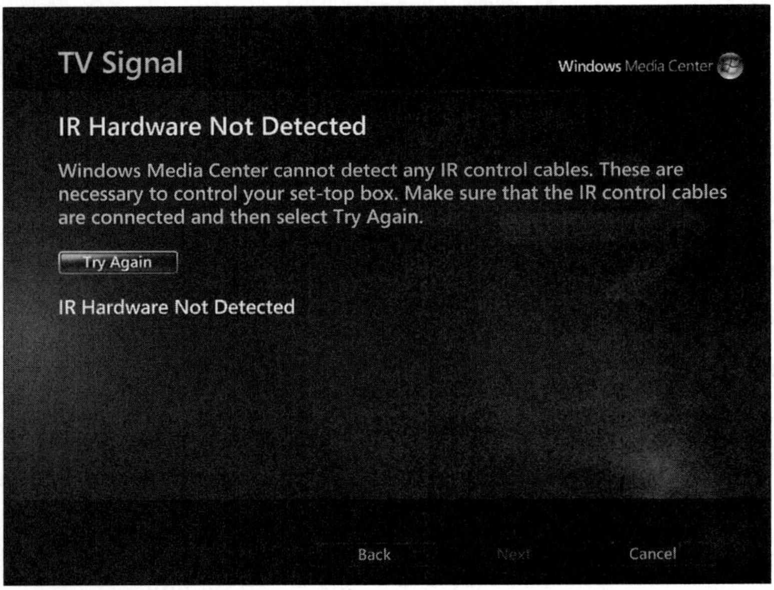

FIGURE 4.7

Confirming that the IR control cable (IR blaster) is connected to your WMC remote's receiver.

Next, WMC asks you if you have a remote for your set-top box. Answer Yes, and you are prompted to identify the codes used by your set-top box remote control so they can be duplicated by the WMC remote.

During the Identify Set-Top Box Remote process, you are asked to press and hold specified buttons (typically 0 and Enter) on your set-top box remote. Watch the screen for prompts. Figure 4.8 shows a typical example of this process.

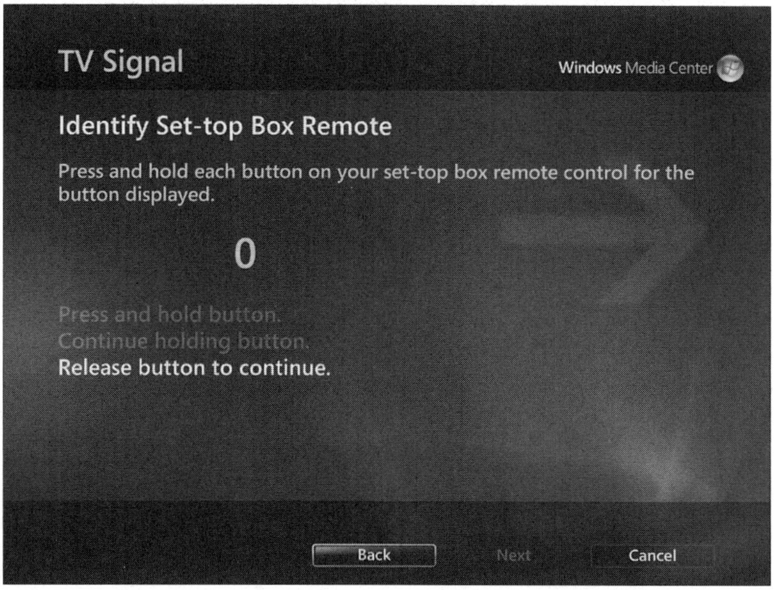

FIGURE 4.8
Identifying set-top box remote codes.

➔ If you have problems with WMC identifying your set-top box or remote, see "Troubleshooting Set-Top Box and Remote Not Recognized Problems," Chapter 16, "Troubleshooting Media Center," **p. 487**.

After you complete this process, pick up your WMC remote when prompted by the Set-Top Box Remote dialog and click Next to continue. To complete configuration of your remote, answer the following questions:

- **Select Number of Digits:** Choose the number of digits in the highest channel your set-top box receives.
- **How Do You Change Channels?:** Specify whether you press Enter (OK) or just enter the channel number.

Next, it's time to test channel changing. Enter the number of a channel you can

> **tip** If the channel didn't change properly, make sure the IR blaster cable is connected to the WMC receiver and make sure the IR blaster emitter is over the IR receiver window on the set-top box (refer to Figure 4.4). Rather than use the stick-on pad, I use easily removable tape, such as masking tape, to secure the emitter until I'm sure of the correct location. If you have problems with cats or curious toddlers who like to play with cables, consider using electrician's tape or duct tape to prevent the IR blaster from being pulled out of position.

pick up. (You can use either a keyboard or your WMC remote.) The WMC remote's receiver uses the IR blaster cable to transmit the channel-change code to the set-top box. Keep your eye on the small TV picture, and select whether the box changed channels correctly or not (Figure 4.9). Then click Next to continue.

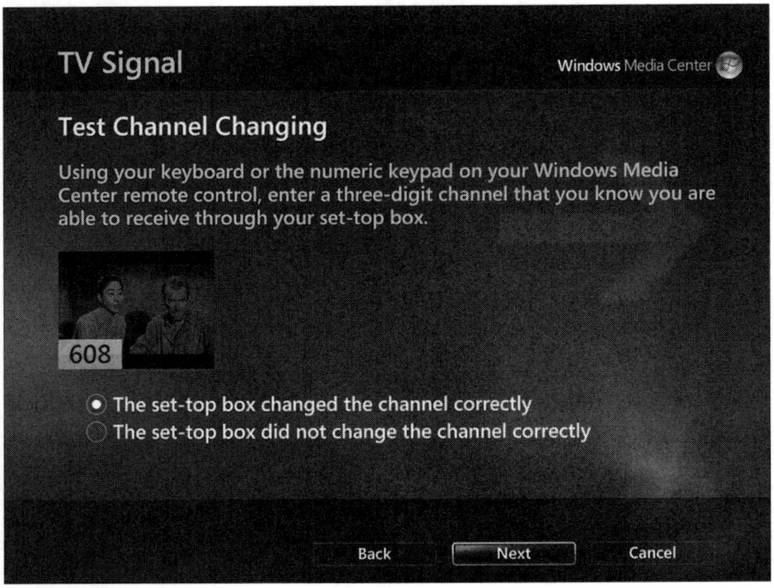

FIGURE 4.9

Testing channel changing.

Chances are you'll probably also want to use your WMC remote for some classic channel surfing, using the channel-change buttons. On the Set IR Signal Speed dialog (Figure 4.10), you are prompted to change channels using the channel up or down buttons on your remote at least six times. WMC starts out using Fast IR signal speed. If the channel did not change correctly, select The Channel Did Not Change Correctly, and WMC will use medium speed and then slow speed. When the test process is finished, WMC announces the selected speed on the next dialog.

Click Next, and you will continue to the TV Program Guide configuration wizard.

→ For details, see "Configuring the TV Program Guide," this chapter, **p. 100**.

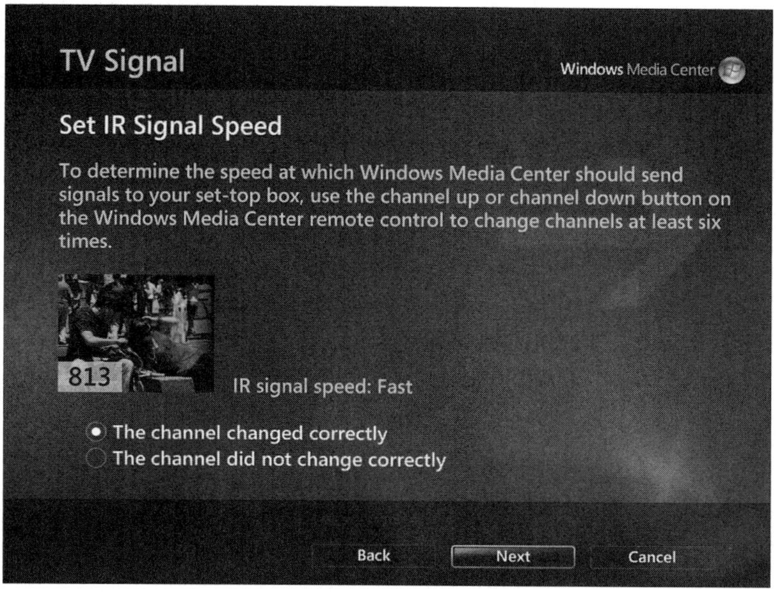

FIGURE 4.10
Configuring channel changing speed.

Digital Cable Tuner

As discussed in Chapter 2, "Equipping Your PC for Media Center," the Digital Cable Tuner (DCT) is the only way to receive and record cable-delivered encrypted HDTV, such as HBO, Showtime, and other premium channels, and it is only available for computers designed to support the Digital Cable Tuner with appropriate BIOS and other configurations. DCTs are available only in the U.S.

> **caution** If you are considering buying a PC that includes a DCT or adding a DCT to a PC that incorporates DCT support (these PCs are known as Premium Digital Cable Ready PCs), don't do it until you verify that your cable TV company supports CableCARD and DCTs. A DCT is a one-way device. However, if your cable TV provider uses switched digital video (SDV), a two-way service being developed to provide more HD content, you cannot use a DCT to receive HD cable TV signals.

Generally, the DCT is sold as part of a system that supports it, but additional tuners can be bought separately. WMC officially supports two DCTs, but registry modifications permit the use of up to four DCTs (or other TV tuners). By using multiple DCTs, you can enjoy picture-in-picture support or record one channel while watching another.

Although it's possible for the end user to configure a DCT, in most cases, configuration is performed by a technician sent out from the cable TV provider. The technician must install a special PC Card known as a CableCARD into the DCT and activate it. The CableCARD, like a digital cable set-top box, decrypts HD cable signals.

Many vendors recommend that you configure your TV setup before installing the CableCARD to verify that you can pick up basic cable TV. Follow this procedure:

1. Make sure the DCT is properly connected or installed in your PC.
2. Start WMC.
3. Start the Setting Up Your TV Signal process as described earlier in this chapter.
4. Digital Cable should be detected as the TV signal type.
5. When you continue, you see a dialog called Are You Digital Cable Ready? Select the option to continue without a CableCARD.
6. On the next dialog, enter the Digital Cable Product Key from the Certificate of Authenticity sticker on your PC. (It might also be found on your system DVD or in your documentation.)
7. When you set up the Guide, be sure to choose your cable TV provider's Digital service.
8. Record the serial number and ID numbers on the CableCARD. This information is needed to install it.
9. Shut down the PC. If the DCT is external, disconnect its power source.
10. Slide the CableCARD into the slot on the DCT.
11. If the DCT is an external unit, reconnect its power source.
12. Restart the computer.
13. Start WMC.
14. Go to Tasks, Settings, TV, and Set Up TV Signal.
15. The system will detect your CableCARD and prompt you to continue.
16. Enter the serial number for the CableCARD when prompted.
17. When prompted, call your cable TV provider and tell the representative you want to activate a CableCARD on a Windows Vista Media Center system. You might need to provide the serial and ID numbers for the CableCARD during this call.

18. After you activate the CableCARD, go to Set Up Guide Listings. Then verify that you can watch HD cable channels.

→ For details, see "Configuring the TV Program Guide," this chapter, **p. 100**.

note If you have more than one DCT, you must install each CableCARD separately. Once a CableCARD has been activated, it cannot be moved to a different DCT unless the cable TV company has been informed of the change and the CableCARD is reconfigured to an uninstalled configuration.

The DCT is a specific type of network device, and if you are unable to view TV channels with it or display some types of programs, you might need to adjust firewall settings, update firmware, or perform other diagnostic tasks. Contact your cable TV provider for assistance.

Using a Converter Box with an NTSC TV Tuner

You can buy a converter box to enable old-school NTSC TVs to pick up digital TV. Can you use the same box (the ones you can buy with the aid of a $40 voucher you get from https://www.dtv2009.gov/) to enable an analog-only TV tuner to pick up ATSC TV channels? After buying a couple of these boxes, I decided to find out.

For my experiment, I used the popular Magnavox TV100MW9 converter box along with an Hauppauge WinTV USB2 external TV tuner (29xxx) series and a Radio Shack directional powered antenna (the same one pictured earlier in this chapter). Could I get this combination to work? Not exactly.

After fiddling around with trying to run the automatic TV signal detection feature, which stubbornly insisted on seeing the converter box as a cable or satellite TV set-top box (and couldn't, therefore, see any ATSC channels), I was forced to set up the TV signal as a plain old antenna configuration. When I tuned into Channel 3, I was able to display the setup dialog for the converter box (the converter box sends signals to Channel 3 by default but can be configured to use Channel 4), but I couldn't switch to other channels to view ATSC TV.

The converter box supports digital TV channels like this: 7.1, 7.2, and so on. Unfortunately, WMC can't handle subchannels unless you use an ATSC TV tuner, and even then, it only recognizes the first subchannel (the one that carries the same content as the analog broadcast channel) and assigns each one a four-digit number well beyond the reach of even the most high-end cable TV service. Channel 14.1, for example, shows up on my ATSC TV tuner as 1141.

Trying to edit the Program Guide to let me select or change channels was equally useless. In the end, there was only one way to get WMC to see ATSC TV channels delivered via the converter box: I tuned WMC to Channel 3 and then used the remote control included with the converter box to manually select the channels I wanted to watch, using the converter box's own tuner. If this sounds like the way you used to connect your VCR to your TV, you're right. Not exactly 21st Century, is it?

In the end, I concluded that buying a digital converter box instead of a new TV tuner with ATSC support was a good way to waste $10-20 (plus tax) of your own money, not to mention $40 of the taxpayers' money (which, come to think of it, is your money, too!). If you want to watch over-the-air HDTV, you'll save plenty of time and headaches by using an up-to-date TV tuner with ATSC support. My converter boxes are now doing the job they were designed to do: bringing digital broadcast TV to TVs that don't have cable TV hookups.

Configuring the TV Program Guide

After WMC determines the type of TV signals you receive, it's time to set up the TV program guide, officially known as the Guide. This process can also be started manually from the Settings menu.

On the opening screen of the Set Up Your TV Program Guide process, click Next to continue. You must then agree to the Guide's privacy statement and terms of service before you can continue.

Next, you must enter your ZIP Code to continue. The ZIP Code is used to look up cable TV providers in your area. Select the appropriate provider from the list that is displayed on the next dialog (Figure 4.11).

> **note** If you select the option to view the privacy statement, your web browser opens and displays the privacy statement in a separate window. If you are running WMC on a system that makes using a web browser difficult, you can also access the Privacy Statement at http://www.microsoft.com/windowsxp/mediacenter/evaluation/privacy/mcevistaprivacy.mspx.

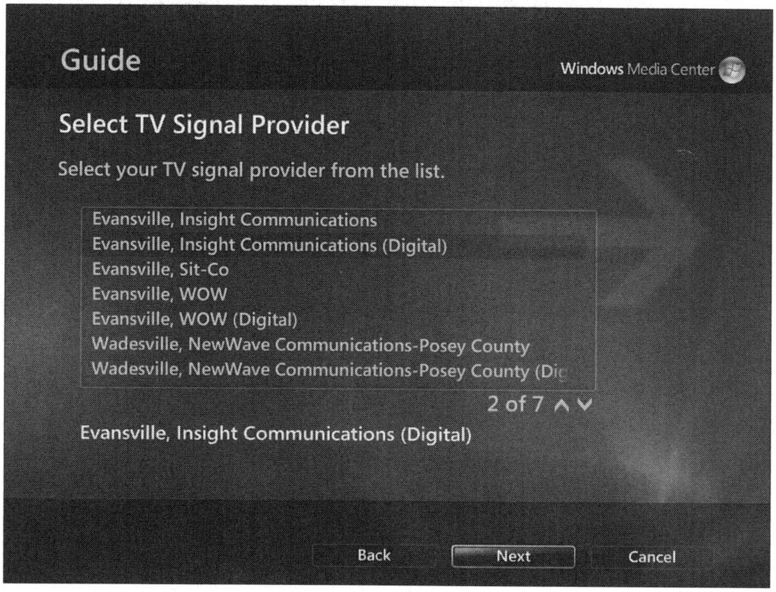

FIGURE 4.11
Selecting your cable TV provider.

caution There are three ways to foul up the TV signal selection process:

- Enter the wrong ZIP Code.
- Choose the wrong provider.
- Choose the wrong version of the provider's service.

If you don't see your cable TV provider, click Back and re-enter your Zip Code. Make sure you choose the Digital option for your provider if you use a digital set-top box or DCT. Otherwise, you won't see the digital channels you're paying for.

After you select your provider, WMC downloads the latest Guide information from the Internet. This can take a couple of minutes or more, even on a fast connection.

➔ If you have persistent problems with downloading Guide updates, see "Solving Network and Internet Problems," Chapter 16, **p. 480**.

note You might see a Guide Error pop-up message with a Cancel button during the process. This message is displayed if an error takes place. Click Cancel, select Yes on the Download Incomplete dialog, and click Next. Usually, the second try will work.

After the download is complete, click Finish or Next as prompted. If you're using cable or set-top box TV signals, you're ready to watch TV. However, if you're using ATSC signals, there's another step to complete.

Checking ATSC Channel Signal Strength

If your TV tuner picks up ATSC (digital HDTV), the next step is to check signal strength. Click Next when prompted to continue. You can also start this process manually by selecting Digital TV Antenna Signal Strength from the TV section of the Settings menu.

The ATSC providers in your area are listed, and WMC checks signal strength for each channel in turn. The process repeats until you click Next, enabling you to perform two tasks during the process:

- Adjusting the position of the antenna you use to pick up ATSC signals.
- Clearing the check box for channels that display minimal (none, one, or two bars) signal strength. When you clear the check box, the channel will be removed from the Guide.

The process is illustrated in Figure 4.12.

For best results, a rotating roof-mounted antenna is recommended. After you click Next, a You Are Done! dialog appears. Click Finish to exit.

If you're planning to install a roof-mounted antenna to help pick up ATSC channels, some useful web resources include

- The AntennaWeb site (www.antennaweb.org) helps you choose the best antenna for your location, based on your input, and provides a color-coded listing of nearby ATSC channels and the best type of antenna for each category of station.

tip Be sure to record the position of the antenna for each ATSC station you can pick up. If you use a powered rotating antenna, see if the remote control has a recall or memory function that can store antenna positions for reuse.

Note that some antennas don't rotate fast enough to the right position during the individual channel scan. To verify that you have the antenna in the best position for a particular channel, position the antenna, wait until WMC rescans the channel, and check the signal strength indicator. Green bars indicate the strongest signal, and orange bars indicate a weaker but still acceptable signal.

note You might have more ATSC channels listed than will fit on one screen. To see additional screens, click the down arrow icon below the signal strength bars. To return to the first screen, click the up arrow icon.

If you add a more powerful ATSC antenna later, repeat this process to determine if you can pick up more stations.

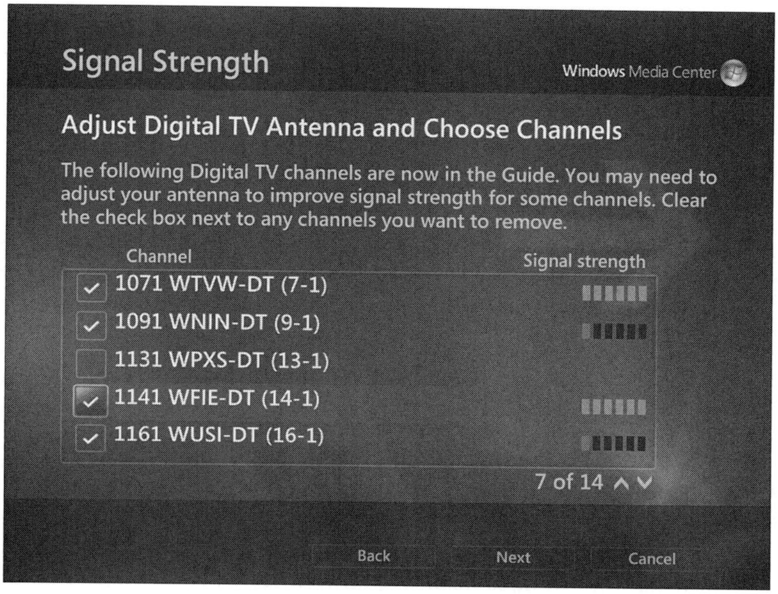

FIGURE 4.12
Scanning broadcast digital (ATSC) channels.

- How to Install a TV Antenna (www.terrestrial-digital.com/antenna_installation.html) provides basic tips on what you need, including when to use a pre-amp.
- Denny's Antenna Service (www.dennysatennaservice.com) offers lots of resources. Go to the Site Map to find specific recommendations by state and locality for antennas, pre-amps, and related equipment.
- Crutchfield's Choosing and Installing an Antenna for HDTV (www.crutchfield.com/Learn/learningcenter/home/antenna.html) provides a useful introduction to ATSC along with links to help rural users tune in distant ATSC (HDTV) signals.

Watching Live TV

To watch TV with WMC, you have three options:

- Go to the TV + Movies menu stripe and select Live TV. The current TV channel plays automatically. Use your WMC remote or your mouse to change channels.

- Go to the Guide and select a program.
- Go to Search and search for a program.

➔ For more information about Search, see "Using the Search Tool," Chapter 5, "Watching and Recording Movies," **p. 145**.

If you're a hard-core channel surfer, you might be OK with clicking the channel-changer on your remote or the channel change control on the mouse control panel, but if you're looking for a particular program that's on now (or later), check out the TV Program Guide.

Using the TV Program Guide

The Guide is the fast way to find out what's on TV now—and later. To access the Guide from the WMC desktop, scroll to the TV + Movies menu stripe and move across to the Guide. As Figure 4.13 shows, you can navigate to the Guide or other parts of the WMC desktop while continuing to watch TV. And even when the Guide is displayed, the current TV show continues to play behind it.

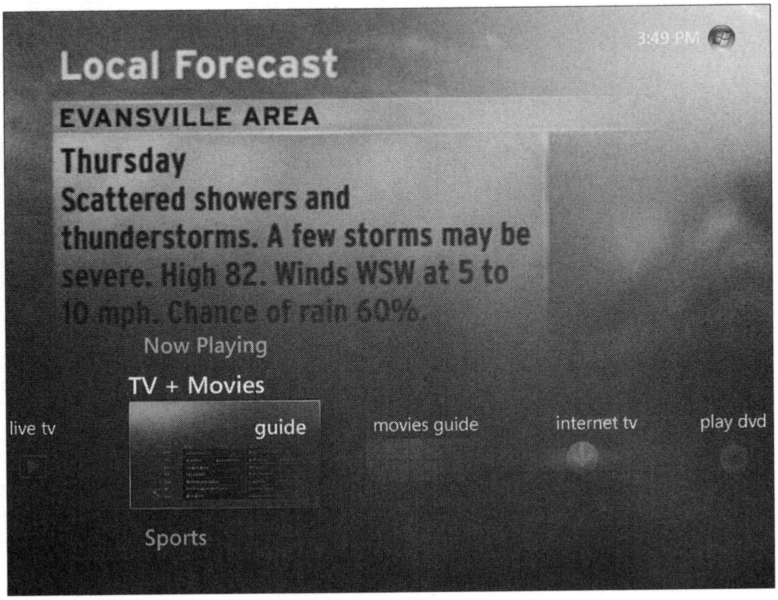

FIGURE 4.13
Navigating the WMC desktop while watching TV.

The basic Guide displays a range of channels (if you're watching TV, the current channel is shown at the top of the list) and the grid for the current block and subsequent blocks of time. Programs in the current time block are shown in white type; future programs are shown in blue type. The resolution and aspect ratio of your display determines how much of the grid you can see at a time. (With a widescreen display, you'll see more than you will see in standard mode.)

tip To switch quickly to the WMC desktop, click the WMC button on your WMC remote. If your WMC remote has a Guide button, you can use it to go directly to the Guide.

To use the Guide to find out the details of a particular show, highlight the show block. The series name, episode name, and other details appear. To watch a particular show, highlight the show block in the current time period and click OK on your WMC remote (or click the show with your mouse).

Viewing and Using Program Info for Current and Upcoming Shows

To see information about the show while you watch it, click the Info button on your remote or right-click your mouse; select Program Info from the menu (Figure 4.14).

FIGURE 4.14
Displaying the Info menu.

4

If you select a show in a future time period, you can record the show or see more information about the show. To see additional information about a forthcoming show, click its listing in the Guide.

Figure 4.15 compares Program Info listings for a TV show currently being broadcast and a forthcoming show.

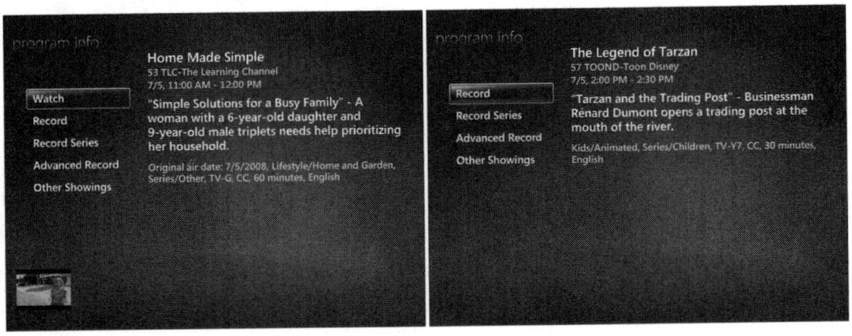

FIGURE 4.15

Program Info menus for a current show and a forthcoming show.

4

Options in the Program Info menu include

- **Watch:** Returns this program to full-screen for watching (applies only to a program currently being broadcast).
- **Record:** Records this episode only.
- **Record Series:** Records this and all future episodes of the show.
- **Advanced Record:** Configures recording quality and other settings.
- **Other Showings:** Displays other broadcast times for the series.

➔ For more information about recording TV, see "Recording Live TV," this chapter, **p. 110**.

Guide Tips and Tricks

To quickly move around in the Guide with your mouse, click the left/right/up/down arrows visible above the mouse control panel (Figure 4.16).

To see only the upcoming episodes on a single channel, highlight it, and the current and next two shows are listed below the guide. To see more upcoming episodes, click the channel, and a vertically scrolling list appears.

tip Want to surf the Guide even faster? Enter the channel number with your WMC remote or keyboard, and the Guide will display that channel (or the nearest channel if you enter a number not in your service package) at the top of the current listing.

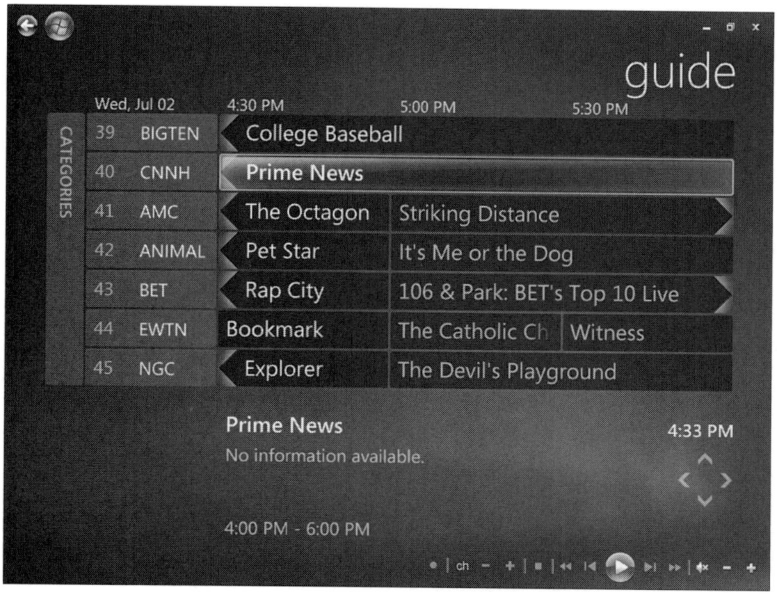

FIGURE 4.16

Click one of the directional arrows with your mouse to maneuver more quickly through the Guide.

Prefer to choose TV by categories? Click the Categories section at the left side of the Guide to expand it. From the expanded Categories list, move the selector over a category, and the Guide will display only the channels in the selected category (see Figure 4.17). Click the category, and you can then choose a channel from the list. To view all channels, click Categories again and select All.

> **note** When you return to the Guide after watching TV, the Guide automatically defaults to displaying all channels.

Editing Channel Listings

Unless you subscribe to every cable channel offered by your provider or are lucky enough to pick up every ATSC channel listed for your area, there are channels listed in the program guide that you can't pick up.

If you can't pick up an ATSC broadcast channel, you will see a No TV Signal message after you tune to it. (It can take a few seconds for this message to be displayed.)

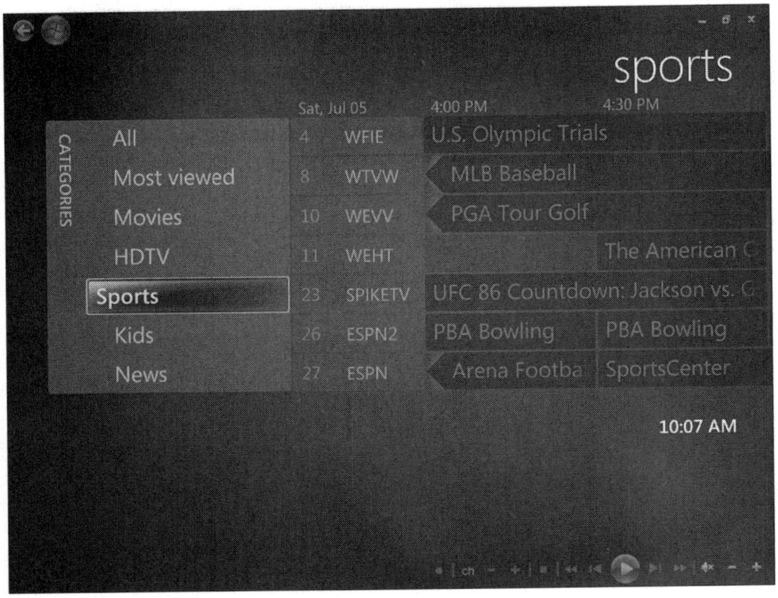

FIGURE 4.17

Choosing a channel category and selecting from channels in a particular category.

If you select a cable channel that's not in your package, you'll see a message from your cable operator encouraging you to place your order.

> **tip** If you upgrade your cable service or buy a better antenna for picking up ATSC signals, you can use the Restore Channel Defaults option shown in Figure 4.18 to restore all channels in the Guide. You can then re-edit your list.

Instead of trying to remember which channels are not available, use the Edit Channels option in the Guide section of the Settings menu (Figure 4.18). To get there from the WMC desktop, select Tasks, Settings, Guide.

To remove channels, select Edit Numbers, scroll through the Edit Channels listing, and clear check boxes for channels you can't pick up or don't have included. (Figure 4.19 shows a typical example.) After you're done editing channels, click Save to save your changes.

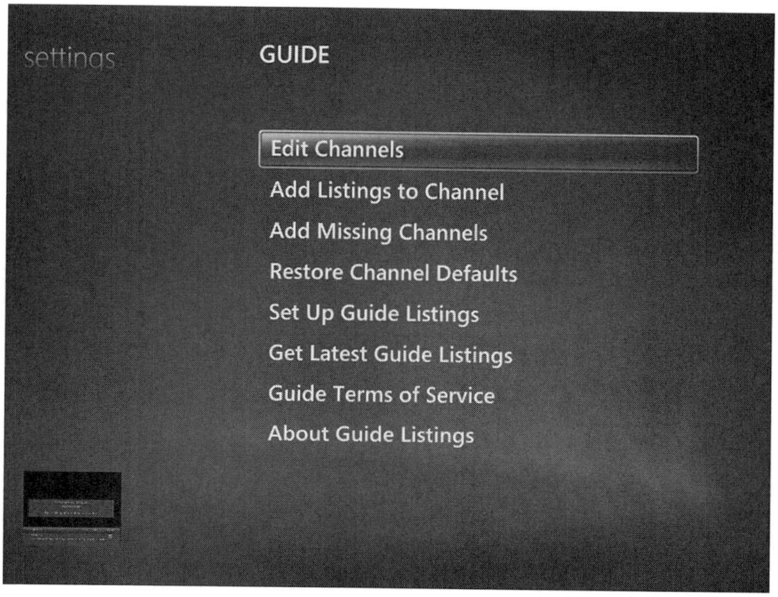

FIGURE 4.18

Starting the Edit Channels process.

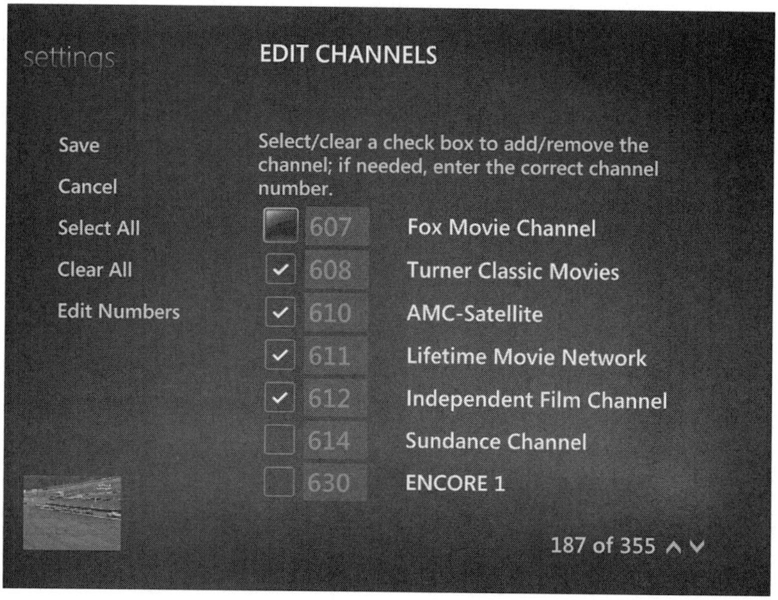

FIGURE 4.19

Editing channels.

Recording Live TV

WMC isn't just a way to watch TV—it can act as a DVR, enabling you to time-shift TV programs or create a long-term library of favorite TV shows. The following sections show you how to record TV and manage your TV recordings.

Configuring TV Recorder Settings

To configure TV recording defaults, open the TV settings menu and select Recorder. This opens the Recorder Settings menu.

The Recorder Settings menu has three sub menus:

- **Recorder Storage:** Specifies where to store TV recordings.
- **More TV Locations:** Selects where to look for TV recordings to view with WMC.
- **Recording Defaults:** Specifies quality, timing, and other settings used for recording TV and movies.

Recorder Storage

The Recorder Storage dialog provides a visual representation of available recording space at the current quality setting and offers options for changing where and how you record TV. The number of hours of TV you can record depend on three factors:

- Whether you're recording standard or HD video
- The amount of hard disk space available
- The quality setting used for recording standard video

Figure 4.20 compares the available recording space and time for a system hard disk with 60GB available for HDTV recording to an external hard disk with 200GB available for HDTV recording, both using Best recording quality. As you can see, using a larger hard disk, either as a system or an additional hard disk, permits much more TV to be recorded.

You can record even more standard-definition TV by reducing recording quality. Table 4.1 lists the possibilities for a system with 50, 100, and 200GB of space available for TV recording at available quality levels. Note that Better, Good, and Fair selections work only if you are recording analog TV, either from a broadcast source or from cable TV. Better, Good, and Fair options are ignored if you are recording standard digital or HDTV. ATSC standard-definition TV and digital cable TV is recorded in Best mode, and HDTV from either cable or ATSC sources is recorded in HD mode.

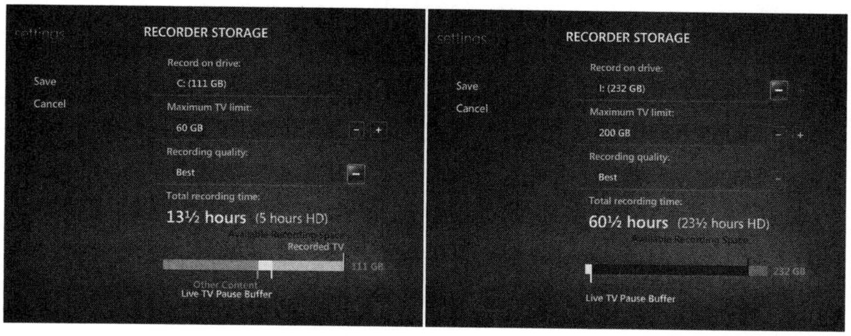

FIGURE 4.20

Less disk space means less recording time; more disk space means more recording time.

Table 4.1 TV Recording Time, Disk Space, and Quality Comparisons

	50GB	100GB	200GB
HD	5.5 hours	11.5 hours	23.5 hours
Best	15 hours	30 hours	60.5 hours
Better	24 hours	48.5 hours	97.5 hours
Good	35 hours	70.5 hours	141 hours
Fair	41 hours	82.5 hours	165 hours

The easiest way to increase available recording time without reducing recording quality is to connect or install an additional hard disk and use it strictly for TV recording.

HARD DISK EXPANSION STRATEGIES FOR TV RECORDING

Although you can add an internal SATA or PATA hard disk to your system to provide more room for TV recording, it's much easier to connect an external hard disk.

Of the most common external hard disk interface types, eSATA is the fastest, followed by FireWire 800, FireWire 400, and then USB 2.0. (You'll probably need to add an expansion card if you want to use FireWire or eSATA; however, if you have unused SATA ports on the motherboard, you can also get an SATA/eSATA adapter for about $10.)

If you plan to record HDTV programs, using an eSATA or FireWire 800 hard disk or an internal PATA or SATA hard disk is recommended. The slower FireWire 400 and USB 2.0 interfaces might occasionally cause dropped frames during recording. However, if you are recording standard TV, any of these interface types is satisfactory.

If you install an additional internal hard disk, you must prepare it using Disk Management before you can use it. However, if you attach an external hard disk, you can use it right away.

To switch to a different drive, click the plus (+) sign next to the current Record on Drive setting and choose another drive from the list.

tip You can record to only one drive, so choose the hard disk with the highest available capacity.

By default, the Maximum TV Limit setting shown in Figure 4.20, which specifies how much of your hard disk is available for recording TV, uses most of the available hard disk space on your system drive. Should you adjust it? I recommend that you change this amount only if you specify an additional drive for recording and use it only for TV recording. For example, I attached an external hard disk to my WMC PC and increased the Maximum TV limit from the default of 200GB to 225GB. (The drive was empty and has 232GB available/total space.) I don't recommend increasing the Maximum TV limit on your system drive, though, because Windows needs space for temporary files and for other types of data files.

After you change the Recorder Storage values, click Save to save your settings.

More TV Locations

Use the More TV Locations menu selection to select additional folders where TV recordings are stored so you can view them using WMC. Use this feature to specify various locations for Recorded TV on your computer.

Select Add Folder to Watch to search for other folders in which TV recordings are stored.

From the Select folders menu, click the check box for additional folders that contain (or might contain) TV recordings. By default, the Recorded TV folders on the system drive and on drives you add through the Recorder Storage menu are already checked. Click Next and then Finish to add specified folders. See Figure 4.21.

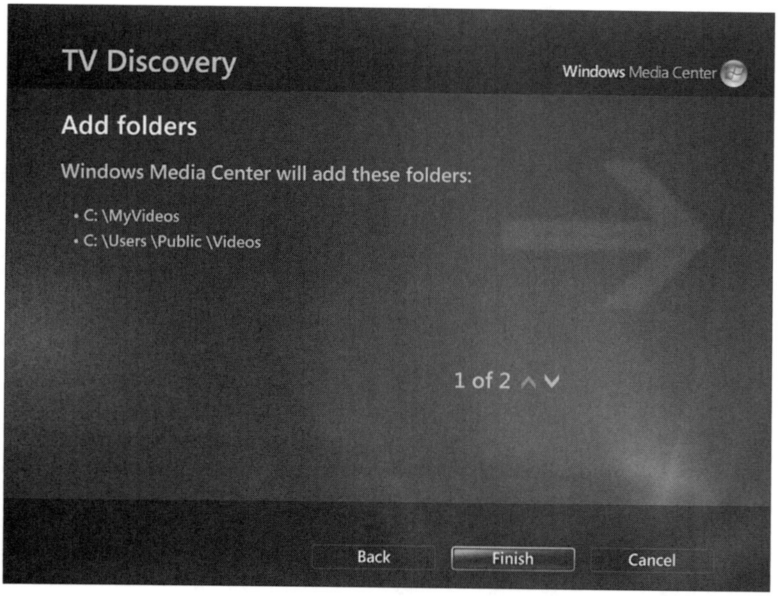

FIGURE 4.21
Adding folders that contain TV recordings.

Recording Defaults

The Recording Defaults menu (Figure 4.22) is used to configure general recording settings. These settings are used for all recordings, except when they are overridden by customized settings selected for particular recordings.

Recording defaults are split into two sections. (Defaults are shown in *italics*.) The General section includes

- **Keep:** *Until space needed*, For 1 week, Until I watch, Until I delete
- **Quality:** Best, better, good, fair (default is the setting chosen in Recorder Storage)
- **Start time:** 4 minutes before, 3 minutes before, *2 minutes before*, 1 minute before, on time
- **Stop time:** 2 minutes after, *3 minutes after*, 4 minutes after, on time

- **Preferred Audio Language:** *Installed language used by Windows*[1], any language

The Series Only section includes

- **Show type:** *First run and rerun*, first run, live
- **Channels:** *One channel only*, any channel
- **Airtime:** *Anytime*, specific time
- **Keep up to:** *As many as possible*, or a specified number of recordings (10, 7, 6, 5, 4, 3, 2, 1)

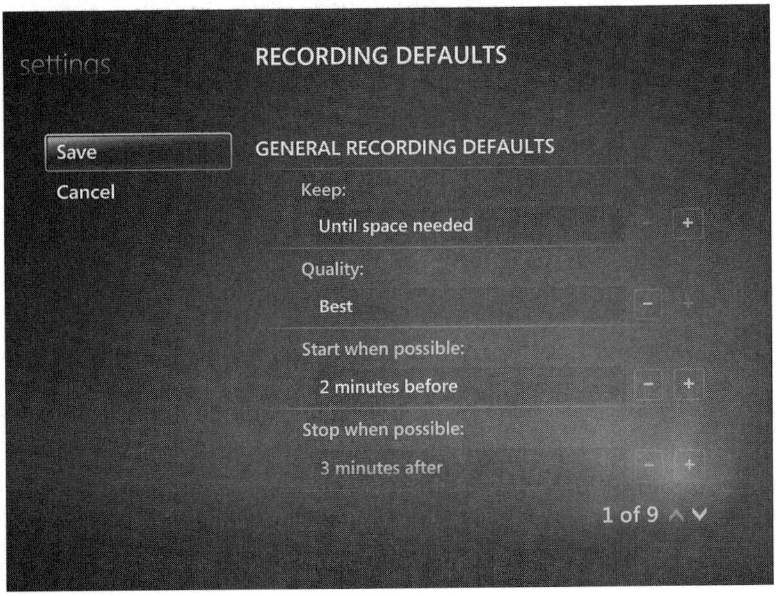

FIGURE 4.22

The Recording Defaults menu.

In most cases, the defaults are satisfactory, but consider the following reasons to make changes:

- If you want to build a permanent library of a particular TV series, use the Until I Delete option.
- If you want to minimize the likelihood of TV recording conflicts, choose the Any Channel option.

[1]For example, on a US-English installation, the preferred audio language is English.

- If you want to record only the first broadcast of the episodes in a particular series, choose the First Run option.

After making any desired changes, click Save.

Once you have configured your recording settings, it's time to start using WMC as your deluxe personal video recorder.

One-Touch Recording

To record a TV show while you're watching it, just press the Record button on your WMC remote or click the red dot on the mouse control panel (Figure 4.23). WMC will record the program from the current point to the end of the program.

FIGURE 4.23

Click the Record button in the mouse control panel to record the current program.

One-touch recording is great if you want to grab a copy of the interview you did for a local TV news program, but if you want to record complete TV shows, there are better ways to do it. Once again, it's time to use the Guide.

Scheduling Recordings Using the Guide

Thanks to WMC, you don't need to miss a program that will be playing while you're busy with the rest of your life.

To schedule a TV recording using the Guide, find the program you want to record and press the Record button on your WMC remote or click the red button on the mouse control panel. The program listing in the Guide displays a red dot to indicate it's being recorded or will be recorded (Figure 4.24).

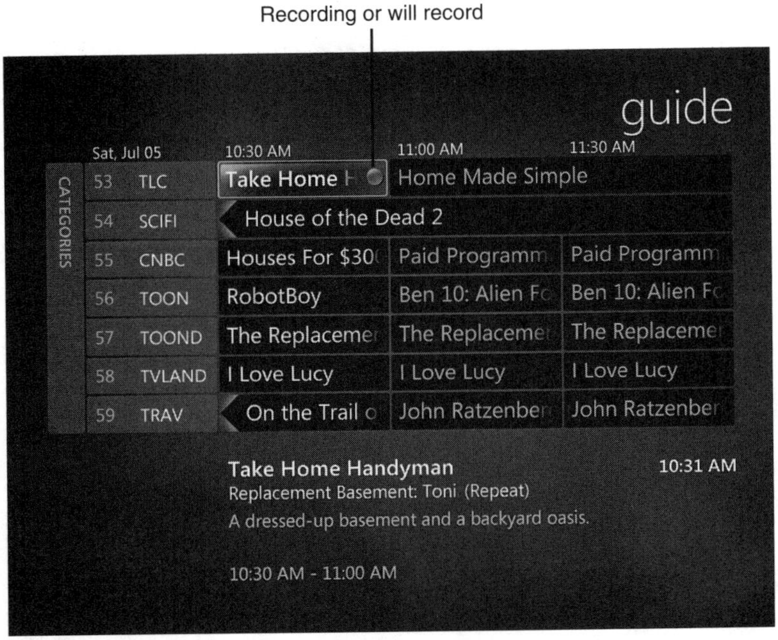

FIGURE 4.24

The red dot in the Guide tells you what is (or will be) recorded.

Recording a TV Series

If you're a fan of a particular TV series and you don't want to wait for the DVD set, you can use WMC to record all future episodes of your favorite series. Here's how.

To record a series directly from the Guide, right-click an episode of the series and select Record Series.

> **note** You can also use the Advanced Record (also known as Record Settings) dialog for an individual episode of a TV series to record the series. Change the Frequency setting from the default Record Single Show to Record Series. See Figure 4.29.

To record a series from the Program Info menu, open the episode's Program Info menu and click Record Series (Figure 4.25).

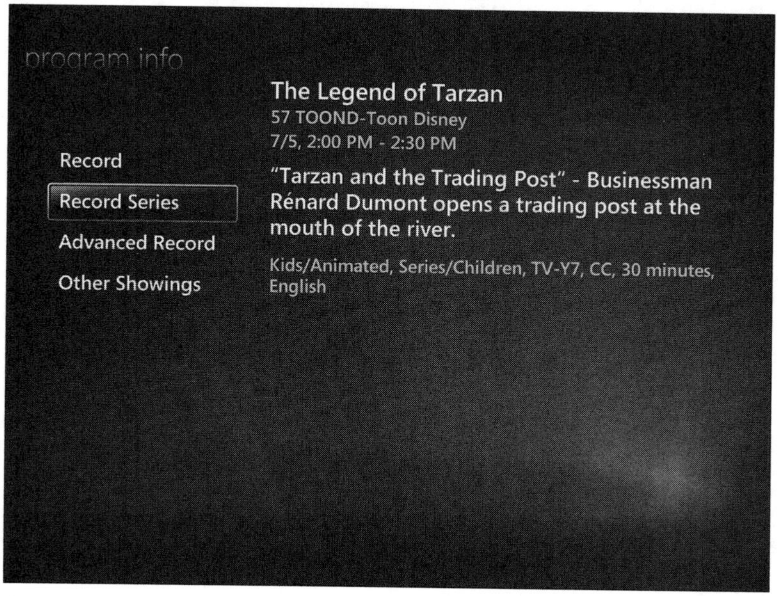

FIGURE 4.25
Recording a series from an episode's Program Info menu.

Dealing with Recording Conflicts

When you schedule a series to record, you might see a Conflict dialog. The Conflict dialog appears when some or all of the episodes of a series you want to record conflict with other scheduled recordings. (It also appears if you want to record a single show that conflicts with an already-scheduled recording.)

You have three options for resolving the conflict. You can record all episodes of the new series (conflicting series will not record), record only episodes of the new series that don't conflict with already-scheduled recordings, or select the instances to record. If you choose the last option, a Series Info dialog displays episode dates and show conflicts with the ! symbol (Figure 4.26). Look at the bottom of the screen to determine the conflict and for scroll up and scroll down buttons.

When you choose a conflicting episode, a special version of the Program Info dialog appears. Click Resolve Conflict to open the dialog shown in Figure 4.27. Choose the show you want to record and click Done.

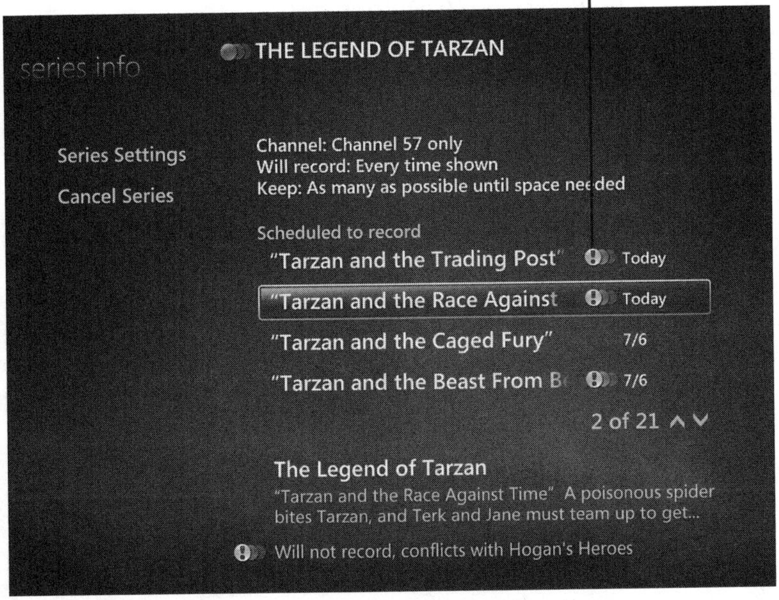

FIGURE 4.26
The Series Info dialog shows you the episodes that conflict with already-scheduled recordings.

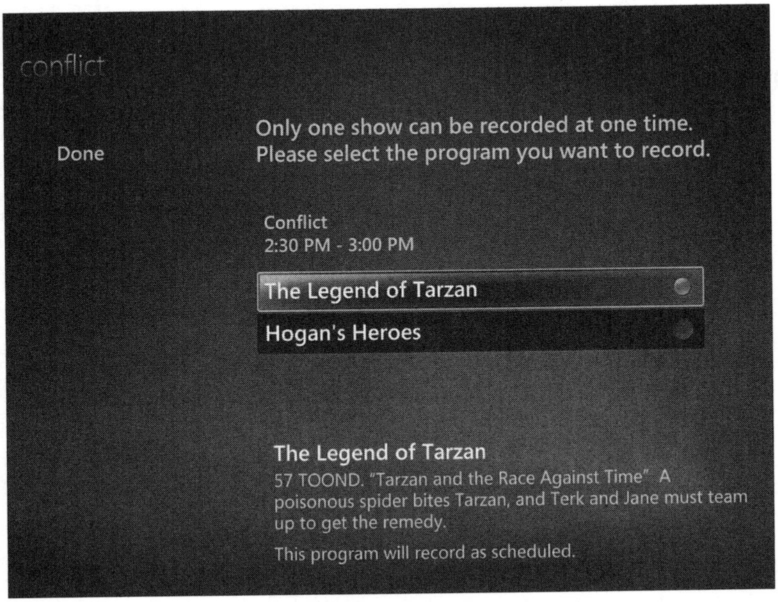

FIGURE 4.27
Who wins and loses in the recording conflict? You decide!

MORE TV TUNERS—FEWER CONFLICTS

To minimize recording conflicts, consider adding a second TV tuner card or Digital TV Tuner to your WMC PC. You can also buy cards with two cable TV tuners onboard, which is perfect if your system is short on expansion slots. With two TV tuners, you can record two shows at the same time or watch one show while recording another. Originally, Windows Vista Media Center officially supported only two TV tuner cards, but if your system includes (or you can install and download) the WMC TV Pack released to OEM supplier in July 2008, you can install up to six TV tuners on Windows Vista Home Premium or up to twelve TV tuners on Windows Vista Ultimate.

If you are unable to obtain the TV Pack, there are unofficial alternatives to enable WMC to use more than two tuners. If you don't mind mucking around in the Windows Registry, this tutorial at The Green Button will walk you through the steps: http://thegreenbutton.com/forums/post/129923.aspx. If you're a Registry newbie, though, be warned—this is not easy.

As an alternative to fiddling with the Windows Registry manually, you can download MCE Tuner Extender from http://mce.ramonvanbruggen.nl/ and use it to make the changes needed the easy way. It's freeware, but a donation to the developer would be greatly appreciated. If you value the ability to tell your children or spouse, "Hey, you can watch your favorite show while my James Bond marathon (or World Series game) is playing," without losing your sanity inside the Windows Registry, it's worth it!

Viewing the Episode List

To view a list of the episodes that will be recorded, open the Series Info menu. A typical list is shown in Figure 4.28.

➔ To resolve the conflict, see "Dealing with Recording Conflicts," this chapter, **p. 117**.

note If you see a (!) symbol next to an episode, it indicates the episode will not be recorded because of a conflict. Highlight the episode to determine the conflicting program.

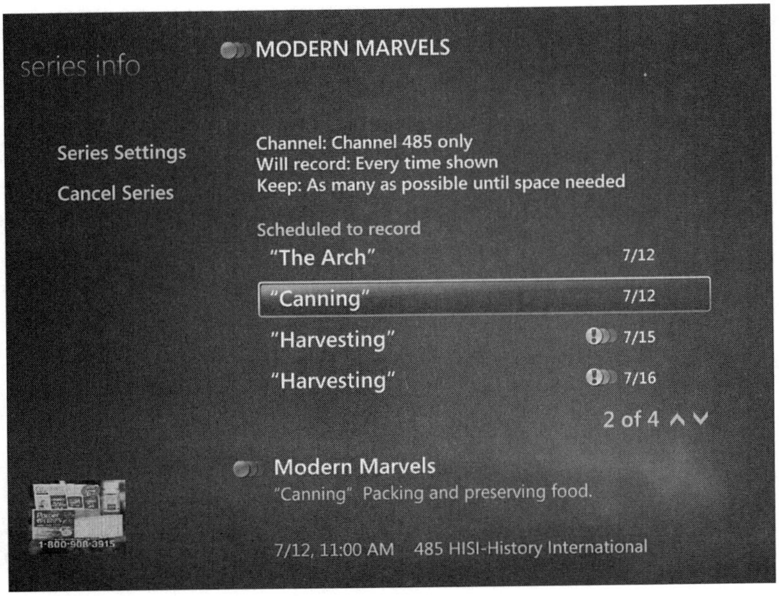

FIGURE 4.28

Check out the Series Info button to determine what will be recorded—and when.

Configuring Recording Quality and Other Settings

By default, TV recordings use the Recording Defaults configured through the TV Settings menu. However, if you want to change recording quality or other settings for a particular TV episode or series, you can override the Recording Defaults settings.

Recording Settings for an Individual Program

To change recording settings for an individual TV episode, open the Program Info menu and select Advanced Record. The Record Settings menu (Figure 4.29) includes four settings (Frequency, Stop, Quality, and Keep) that affect only the individual episode.

To record the episode with the settings shown, click Record. To cancel recording, click Do Not Record.

> **note** If you change frequency from the default Record Single Show to Record Series, the settings in Figure 4.29 are used to record the entire series.

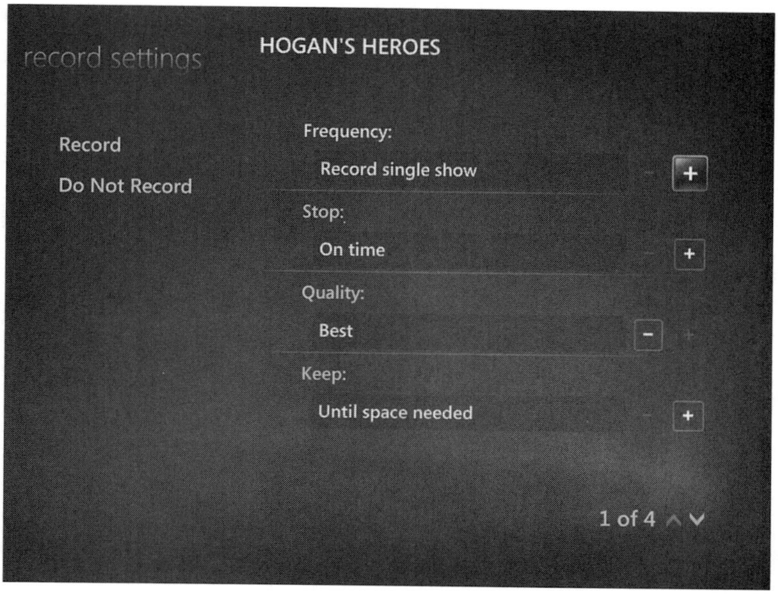

FIGURE 4.29

Use the Record Settings menu to select the settings to use for a single show.

Recording Settings for a TV Series

Once you have selected a TV series to record, you can access recording settings for a TV series in the following ways:

- Go to the listing for an episode of the series, open the Program Info menu, select Record Settings, and select Series Settings.
- Right-click an episode selected for recording, select Series Info, and select Series Settings.

Either method displays the seven-option Series Settings dialog shown in Figure 4.30.

Make the desired changes and click Save to save your changes.

→ To learn more about these options, see "Recording Defaults," this chapter, **p. 113**.

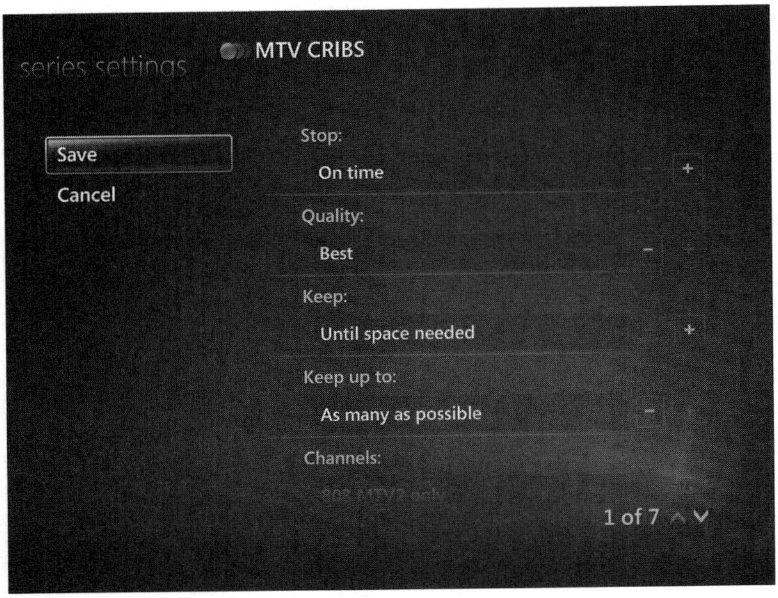

FIGURE 4.30
The Series Setting dialog.

Watching Recorded TV

Once you start clicking Record, you're going to accumulate a bunch of TV to watch whenever you want. Here's how to watch it and manage it.

The Recorded TV Menu

To open the Recorded TV menu, go back to the WMC desktop, scroll to the TV + Movies strip menu, and select Recorded TV.

By default, recordings are listed by date, with the current date's recordings listed first. To view programs by title, select Title. In the Title view, episodes of the same program are grouped together. Figure 4.31 shows the date view.

When you use the Title view, click the thumbnail for a particular series to display individual episodes. You can then select the episode you want to play.

To see details about a recording, such as the program name, episode name, channel number/name, date recorded, and duration, highlight it. The information is displayed below the program's thumbnail.

To play or manage a recording, click it, and the Program Info menu opens (Figure 4.32). From the Program Info menu, you can play the recording, delete it, specify how long to keep it, record the series, view other showings, or burn a CD or DVD.

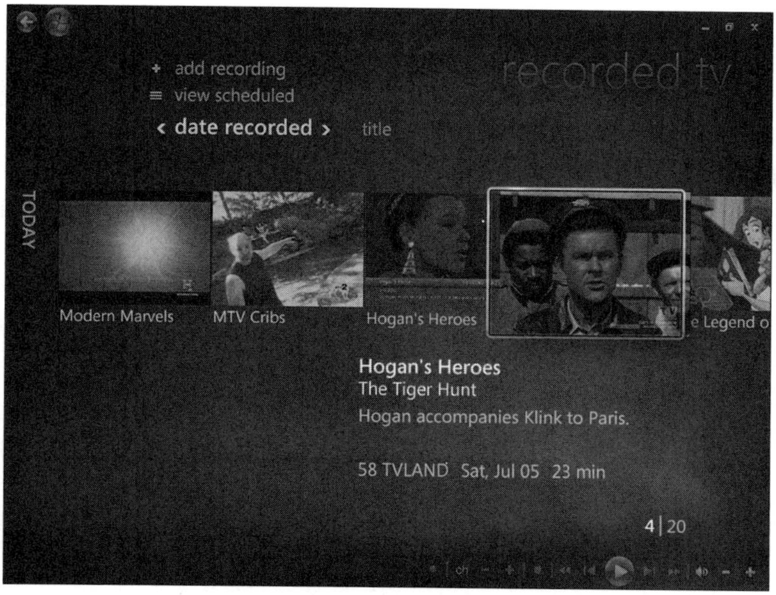

FIGURE 4.31

The Recorded TV menu's date view.

FIGURE 4.32

Use the Program Info menu to play or delete a recorded TV program.

➔ To learn more about burning a CD or DVD, see "Transferring TV Recordings to DVD" in Chapter 10, "Creating CDs and DVDs," **p. 295**.

tip You can also right-click the recording to display options for playing, deleting, or burning a recording.

Viewing Scheduled Recordings

To find out what TV shows or series you have scheduled for recording, click the View Scheduled icon. By default, programs are listed by date and time, but you can also sort them by title. Figure 4.33 shows the date/time view.

FIGURE 4.33
Viewing scheduled recordings by date/time.

At the bottom of the screen, WMC provides you with the total time and number of recordings scheduled.

To view more information for a particular episode, such as the episode title and plot outline, highlight it. To bring up the complete Program Info dialog, click the episode. You can view the information in brief form or in complete form, as shown in Figure 4.34.

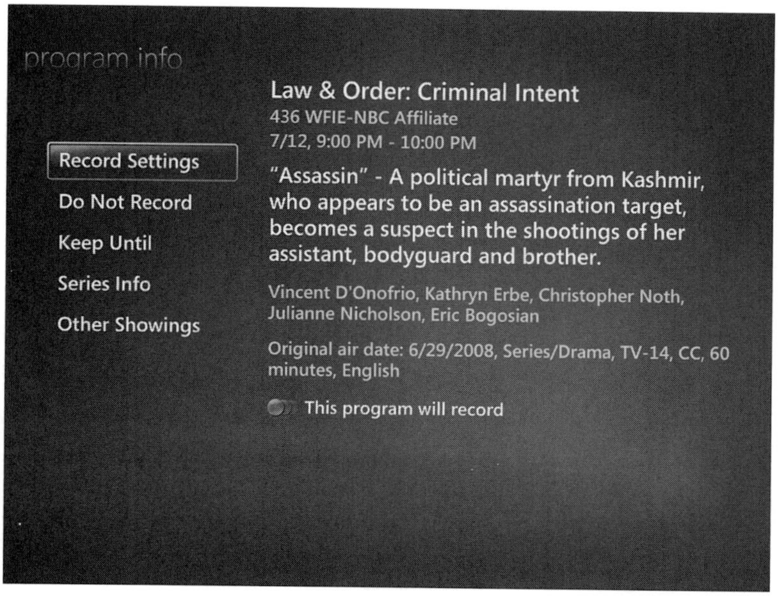

FIGURE 4.34

Viewing complete information for a TV episode to be recorded.

Using the Series View

The Series view shows TV series in order by priority. (You can also sort them by name and type.) If you have also used the Movies Guide's Record in Future option, you will also see movies listed here with Any Channel as the channel. Figure 4.35 shows the Type view, which is an easy way to distinguish series recordings from other types.

➔ To learn more about the Record in Future option, see "Recording Movies Not Listed in the Guide" in Chapter 5, **p. 148**.

To view more information about a series, click it. The Series Info display (Figure 4.36) lists the episodes scheduled to record, the channel, the recording frequency, and the Keep settings. To change these or other settings, click the Series Settings button, and the Series Settings dialog appears.

➔ To learn more about Series Settings, see "Recording Settings for a TV Series" in this chapter, **p. 121**.

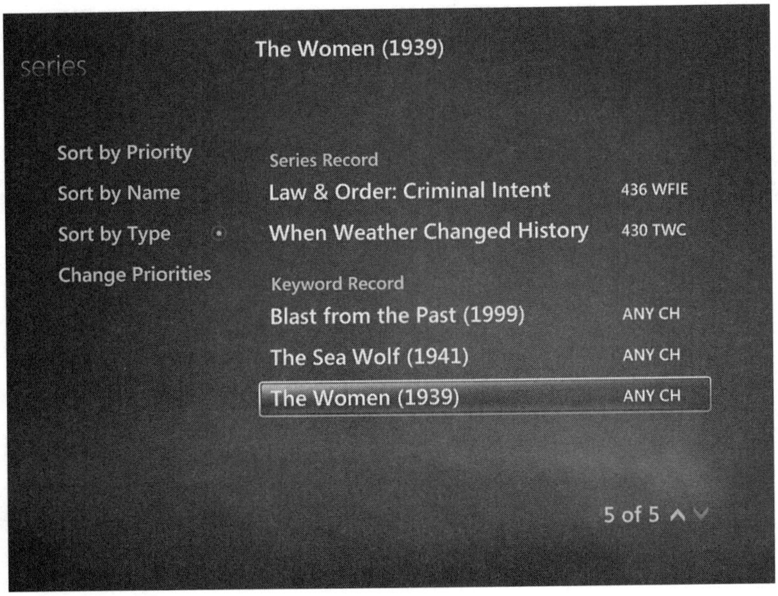

FIGURE 4.35

Viewing series to be recorded by type.

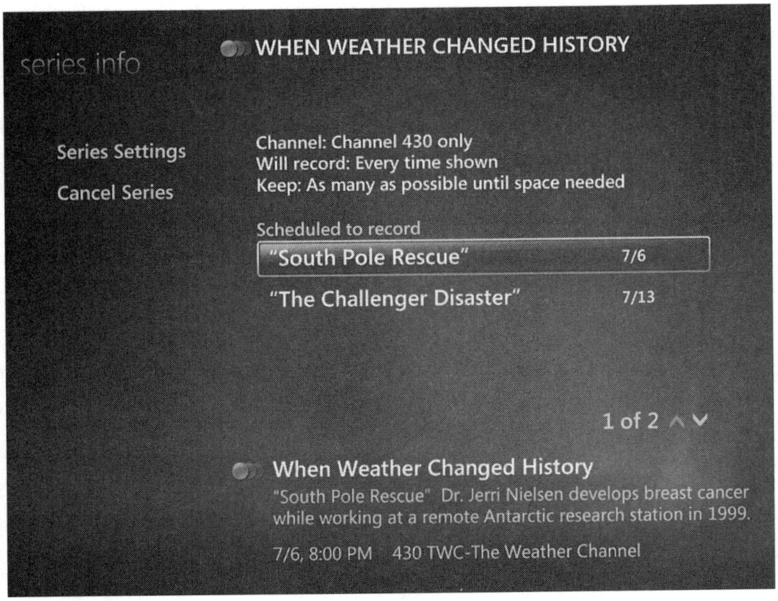

FIGURE 4.36

Using the Series Info menu to view details about a show to be recorded.

Deleting a Recording

When you're done with a recording, you can delete it from the main Recorded TV dialog or from the recording's Program Info dialog. When you select the option to delete the recording, you must click Yes on the confirming dialog to complete the operation.

Canceling Recording of a Series

If you decide you'd rather not record a series, select Cancel Series from the Series Info dialog shown in Figure 4.36 or right-click the series and select Cancel Series. Click Yes on the Cancel Series pop-up dialog.

> **note** Canceling series recordings has no effect on existing episodes' recordings. They remain on your system until they are deleted according to the Keep settings used when they were recorded or as changed later in the Series Settings or Record Settings menus, or when you delete them manually.

Add Recording

The Add Recording option in the Recorded TV dialog provides a quick way to choose your favorite recording method. You can choose to record an individual program or series from the Guide or by using Search, or you can create a custom recording using Channel and Time or Keyword.

→ To learn more about recording an individual TV program from the Guide, see "Scheduling Recordings Using the Guide," this chapter, **p. 116**.

→ To learn more about recording a TV series from the Guide, see "Recording a TV Series," this chapter, **p. 116**.

→ For more information about Search, see "Using the Search Tool," Chapter 5, **p. 145**.

Selecting the Channel option seems, at first glance, like a step backwards to the days of recording with a VCR. When you select the Channel option, the Manual Record dialog shown in Figure 4.37 appears. You must specify the channel, frequency, date, start and stop time, keep until setting, and recording quality. The main reason to use the Channel/Manual Record dialog is if you want to record a contiguous block of shows, such as a *Batman* marathon, without needing to select each and every show separately.

To name the recording, select Change Title, and the Rename dialog (Figure 4.38) appears. Enter the title of the recording using your WMC remote or keyboard. After you complete naming the recording, the recording name replaces the MANUAL RECORDING text at the top of the dialog. Click Record to save the recording. The recording will be displayed in your list of scheduled recordings.

FIGURE 4.37
The Manual Record dialog.

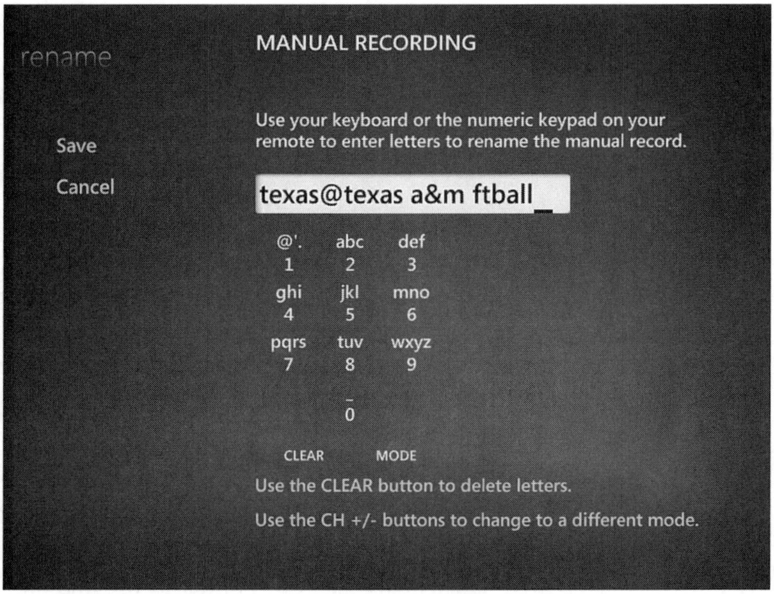

FIGURE 4.38
Entering a name for a manual recording.

If you have a recording conflict, the Conflict dialog appears. You must then select whether to keep the manual recording or go with the recording(s) you've already set up.

tip To avoid conflicts, check the dates and times of your scheduled recordings first.

➔ To learn more about handling recording conflicts, see "Dealing with Recording Conflicts," this chapter, **p. 117**.

Watching Internet TV

U.S. users of WMC can also watch TV content without using a TV tuner. As long as you have a broadband Internet connection, you can watch Internet TV.

To get started, select Internet TV from the TV + Movies strip menu. Internet TV includes the following categories: TV, movies, music, viral (videos), lifestyles, sports, tech, news, and top picks. Here's what to expect in each category:

- **TV:** Complete TV series, full episodes from other series, and clips from major broadcast and cable TV channels
- **Movies:** Trailers for current and forthcoming movies, new movies on DVD, cast interviews, and reviews
- **Music:** Concerts and most-watched movie trailers
- **Viral videos:** Wild and wacky news stories, TV show clips, and web sensations; as well as shorts from iFilm, VideoJug, and others; SuperBowl ads; and much more
- **Lifestyles:** Make your life better, from golf swings to cooking, from travel to new car models, and much more
- **Sports:** Current sports news—baseball, football, basketball, soccer, motorsports, and more
- **Tech:** The latest gadgets, trade shows, TechWatch, Microsoft news, and Media Center tips
- **News:** Current news stories, in-depth coverage, and celebrity news
- **Top Picks:** A grab bag of the most popular videos

The quality of the video featured on Internet TV varies from slightly below standard TV quality to near HD-quality. The faster your Internet connection, the better it looks.

To navigate through Internet TV, select a category at the top of the screen and then through the subcategories until you find your video. Highlight a video and click OK on your WMC remote (or click it with your mouse) to play the video full-screen.

> **note** To find more sources for web-based TV and video, such as TV Tonic, MSN TV Today, and more, check out Chapter 9, "Playing Games and Enjoying Online Resources."

Internet TV is best regarded as a way to sample what's on TV, rather than as a true replacement for a TV tuner. However, it's a useful way to stay up-to-date on what's happening if you have an Internet connection but no TV connection.

Parental Controls

WMC, like Windows Vista itself, includes a powerful parental controls system. However, it doesn't require that each user has his or her own account. Because people of different ages might be sharing a single computer running WMC, WMC uses an access code-based system to control access to TV programs, movies, and DVDs. The following sections show you how to use these features to make WMC family-friendly.

Enabling and Using Parental Controls

To enable the parental control feature, switch to the Tasks strip, select Settings, and select General from the Settings menu. In the Settings menu, select Parental Controls.

> **note** Once you create an access code, you will need to re-enter it every time you enter the Parental Controls menu.

When you open Parental Controls, the first task you must perform is to create an Access Code (Figure 4.39), which, like a PIN number, must contain four digits.

WMC then displays the Parental Controls menu.

The Parental Controls menu includes four selections:

- TV Ratings
- Movie/DVD Ratings
- Change Access Code
- Reset Parental Controls

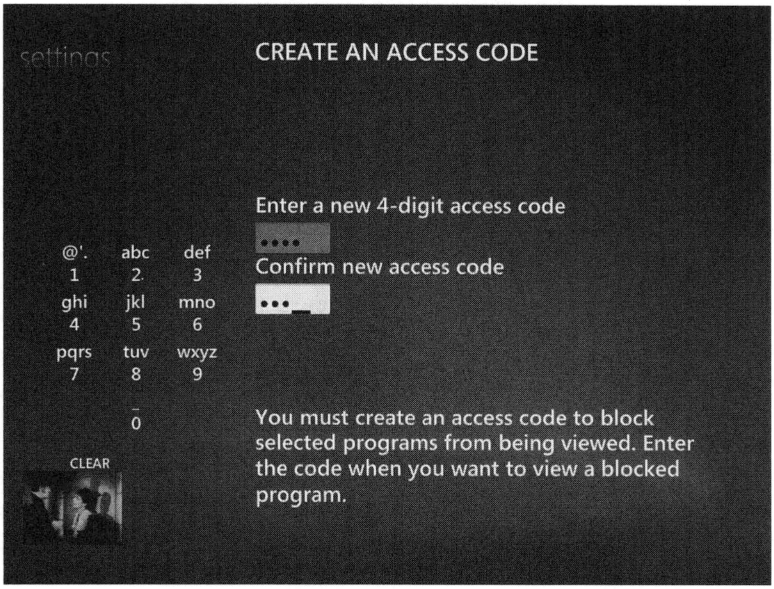

FIGURE 4.39
Creating an access code.

The following sections show you how to use each option.

Configuring and Using TV Ratings

Select TV Ratings from the Parental Controls menu to display the TV Ratings dialog. To enable TV blocking, click the Turn on TV Blocking check box. Select the maximum rating permitted. You also have the option to block unrated TV programs. Figure 4.40 shows the TV Ratings dialog as it appears after enabling TV blocking.

Understanding TV Ratings

The TV Ratings system used by WMC is the same one supported by the V-chip technology built into recent televisions. Because WMC doesn't use the TV tuner in your TV set, you must use the TV blocking feature in WMC if you want to use TV ratings to control access to undesirable TV programs.

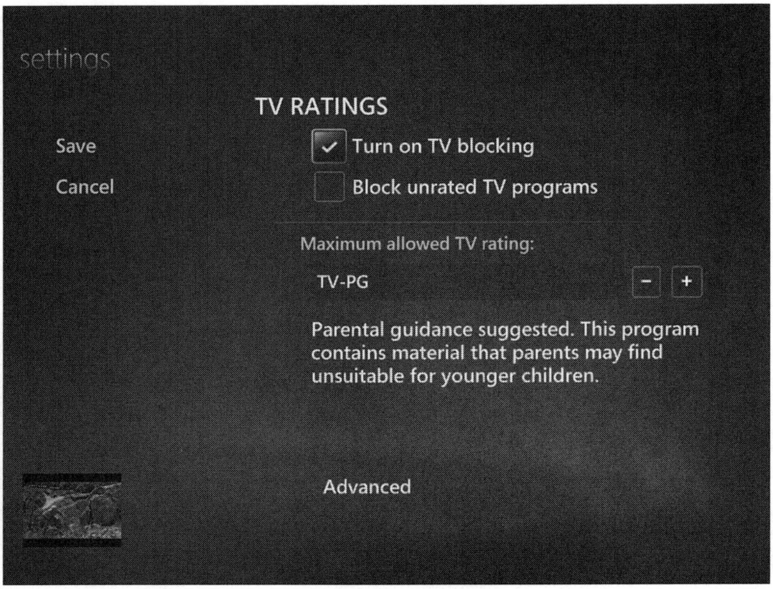

FIGURE 4.40
The TV Ratings dialog configured to block TV with ratings over TV-PG.

The TV ratings supported by WMC in the U.S. include

- TV-MA (Mature Audiences Only; similar to MPAA's R rating for movies)
- TV-14 (Parents Strongly Cautioned; similar to MPAA's PG-13 rating)
- TV-PG (Parental Guidance Suggested; similar to MPAA's PG rating)
- TV-G (General Audience; similar to MPAA's G rating)
- TV-Y7 (designed for children age 7 and older)
- TV-Y (all children)
- None (all TV programs with ratings are blocked)

Most networks add additional information to the basic TV ratings used by WMC to indicate content types. For example, TV-Y7 FV indicates a show for children ages 7 and above that contains fantasy violence.

To learn more about the TV Ratings system and additional rating codes, see http://www.timewarnercable.com/centralny/programming/tvrating.html. To learn more about the MPAA movie rating system, see http://www.mpaa.org/FlmRat_Ratings.asp.

When you select any TV rating other than None, a link to an Advanced dialog is provided. You are prompted to save the changes you have made to the

TV Ratings dialog before opening the Advanced dialog. The Advanced dialog (Figure 4.41) enables you to customize the basic restrictions for the TV rating you selected in the following areas:

- Fantasy Violence
- Suggestive Dialogue
- Offensive Language
- Sexual Content
- Violence

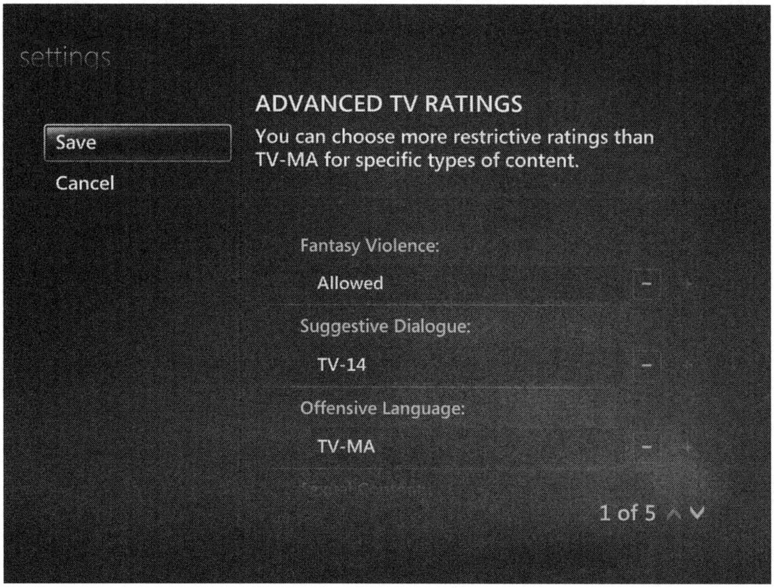

FIGURE 4.41
The Advanced TV Ratings dialog.

When you're finished customizing your changes, click Save to lock in your settings.

After you enable TV blocking, any attempt to watch a TV program that exceeds the rating brings up a "Program Blocked" screen. To override the block, press the OK button on your remote control and enter the access code.

> **tip** To assure that WMC starts using TV restriction settings right away, close it and restart it.

TV blocking doesn't affect your ability to record TV programs or movies that exceed the specified rating. However, the Recorded TV menu displays blocked programs with a distorted thumbnail (see Figure 4.42). When you attempt to view the recording, the Blocked Program dialog appears, and you are prompted to provide your access code before you can view the recording.

FIGURE 4.42
Blocked TV recordings are displayed with a blurred image in Recorded TV.

Configuring and Using Movie/DVD Ratings

To control movie and DVD access, select the Movie/DVD Ratings from the Parental Controls menu. The Movie/DVD Ratings dialog (Figure 4.43) works in a similar fashion to the TV ratings dialog. You have the option to turn on movie blocking, to specify a maximum allowed movie rating, and to block unrated movies.

When you enable Movie/DVD Ratings, any attempt to play a movie or DVD that exceeds the rating specified brings up the same Program Blocked dialog used by TV Ratings. And, as with TV Ratings, you must enter the access code to view the movie.

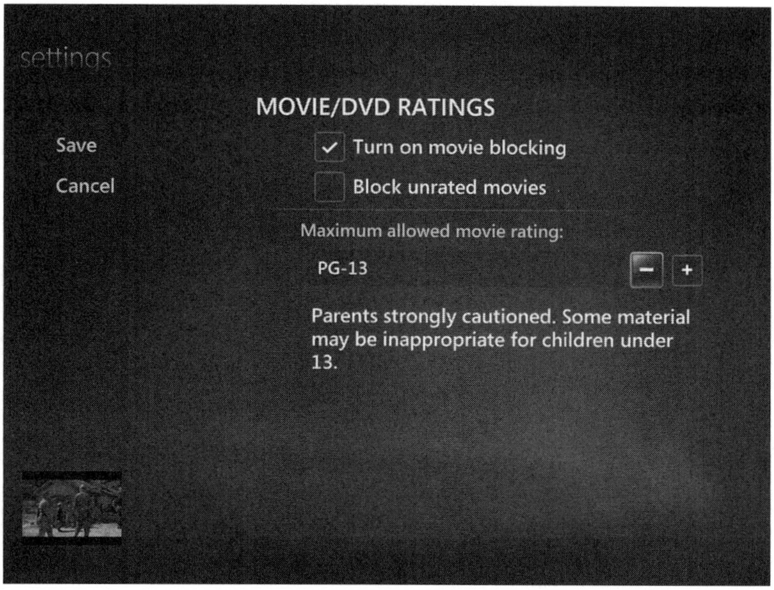

FIGURE 4.43

The Movie/DVD Rating dialog after enabling blocking.

Specifying a New Access Code

You might want to change your access code from time to time, especially if somebody's been paying a little too close attention whenever you enter your access code. To change the current access code, select Change Access Code. Enter a new four-digit access code and reenter it to confirm the change (Figure 4.44).

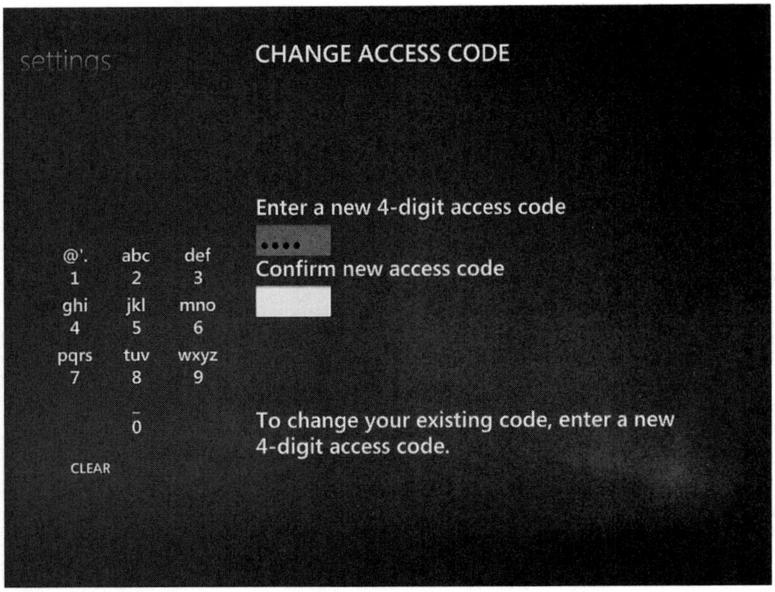

FIGURE 4.44
Changing your access code.

Resetting Parental Controls

You can reset parental control settings back to their defaults and clear out your access code by selecting Reset Parental Controls from the Parental Controls menu. Click Yes on the confirming dialog to reset all controls.

If you decide to re-enable Parental Controls later, follow the steps in the previous sections as needed.

CHAPTER

5

Watching and Recording Movies

IN THIS CHAPTER

Windows Media Center (WMC) can bring the magic of movies to your PC, whether you use it to watch or record movies on TV or to enjoy films from your DVD collection. By adding third-party software, you can also enjoy Blu-Ray discs in WMC.

How to Find Your Favorite Movies *Your* Way

WMC makes it very easy to find the films you want to watch live or record for future enjoyment. Choose your favorite method from the TV + Movies menu (Figure 5.1):

- To find movies by viewing time, genres, or top ratings, use the Movies Guide menu.
- To find movies by title, keyword, category, actor, or director, use the Search tool.
- To play movies on DVD, use the Play DVD menu.

Later in this chapter, I'll also show you how to add a plug-in that enables WMC to play movies you've stored on your hard disk and how to get support for Blu-Ray movies. However you like your movies (live, recorded, on DVD, on hard disk, or Blu-Ray), WMC has the best seats in the house ready for you.

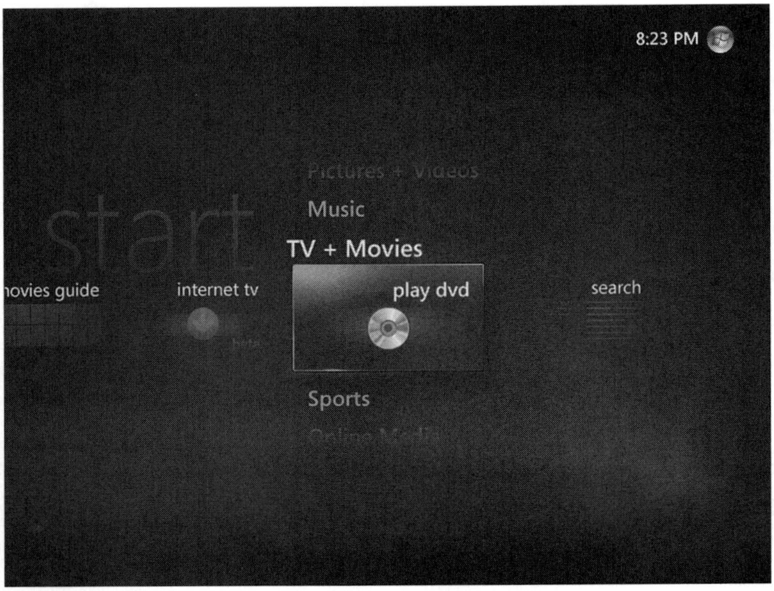

FIGURE 5.1
Movie-watching selections are found on the right side of the TV + Movies menu.

Introducing the Movies Guide

Unlike the Program Guide you learned about in Chapter 4, "Viewing and Recording Live TV," the Movies Guide has movies—and nothing but movies. The Movies Guide takes full advantage of today's widescreen displays to show movie titles by poster or packaging (Figure 5.2).

You can find your favorite films in a variety of ways:

> **caution** If your cable TV or satellite TV package includes adult-oriented content, keep in mind that these movies will show in the Movies Guide.
>
> To prevent access by users to undesirable movie or TV content, set up a separate account for each user in Windows Vista's Control Panel and use the Parental Controls feature in Windows Media Center.

- Want to watch a movie right now? Open the On Now menu (also shown in Figure 5.2); it lists films that are currently being broadcast on the movie-oriented TV channels in your program guide.
- Can't find a movie to watch right now? Check out the On Next menu: It lists films that will be broadcast right after the films listed in the On Now menu.

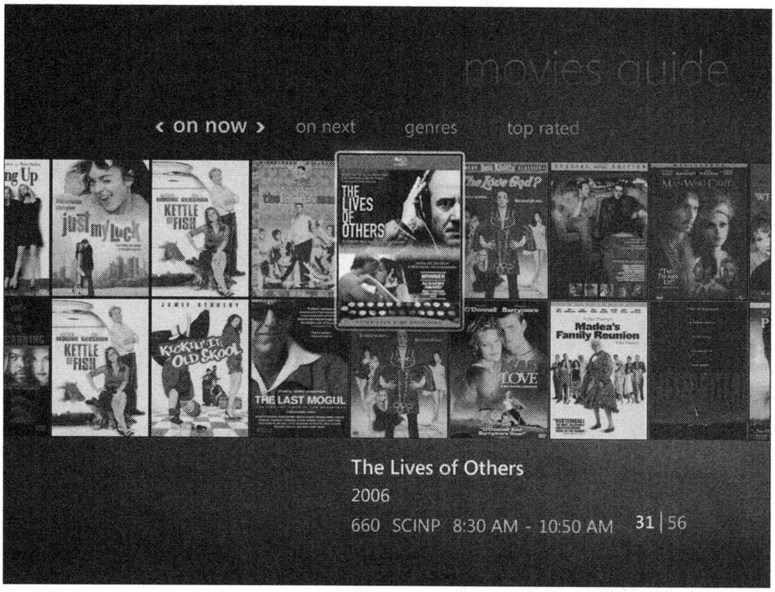

FIGURE 5.2

The Movies Guide's On Now menu.

➔ To learn how to use Parental Controls in Windows Media Center, see the "Parental Controls" section, Chapter 4, **p. 130**.

If you're more systematic in your movie watching, use one of the following menu options:

- Want to watch a western? Cuddle up with your sweetheart for a romantic evening? Relive history? Dive into the Genres menu (Figure 5.3) to start exploring.
- If you prefer the best in moviemaking, go straight to the Top Rated menu: It lists only three- and four-star movies (Figure 5.4).

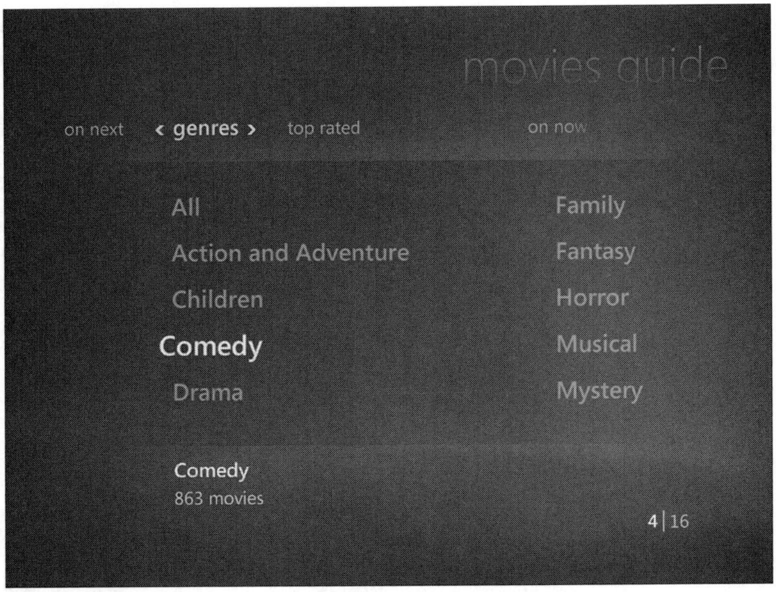

FIGURE 5.3

Some of the genres in the Genres menu.

FIGURE 5.4

Selecting a film from the Top Rated menu.

You can select a film as soon as you open the menu containing the film, but it does take a few moments (or longer) to display poster or package graphics. Some older or independent films might not have a suitable graphic, so only the title is shown.

When you click a film, the title, release date channel number and name, and broadcast date and time are shown below the thumbnail (refer to Figure 5.4). The numbers at the lower-right corner of the screen indicate the total number of films in the current menu or submenu and the current selection.

note The Movies Guide lists only films that are being broadcast now or up to 14 days from now. If you want to plan out your movie viewing in a longer timeframe, visit the websites of your favorite movie channels to see what films will be available later, and then look for them once they fall into the timeframe of the Movies Guide.

tip By default, different parts of the Movies Guide use different display options. Most menus use the small thumbnail view, while others use the list view. To change between these views or to switch to the optional large view, right-click a movie listing from any menu and select the view you want.

Watching a Movie from the On Now Menu

To watch a movie, select it from the On Now menu and click Watch from the Movie Details menu (Figure 5.5).

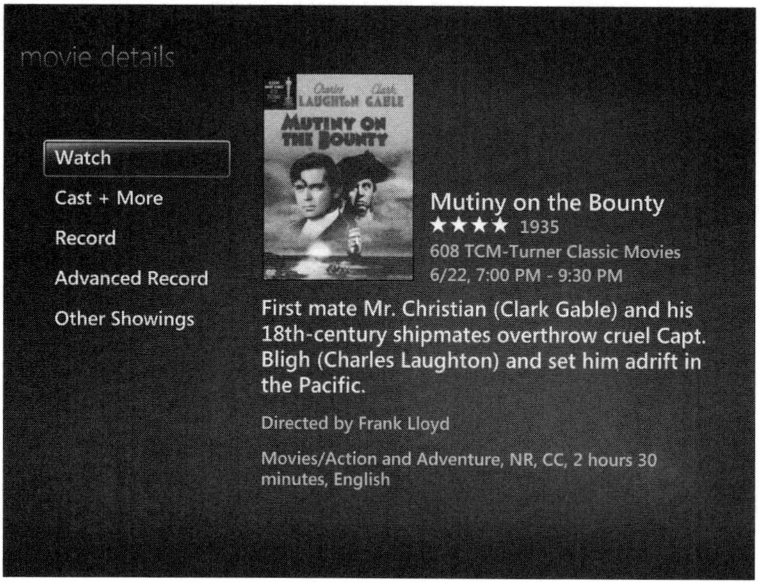

FIGURE 5.5

Preparing to watch Mutiny on the Bounty.

The Movie Details menu shown in Figure 5.5 lists the title, star rating, release date, channel, time, a brief synopsis with leading cast members, the director, and classification information (genre, MPAA rating, TV rating, whether the film has closed captioning, running time, and language).

Other options include Cast + More, which displays a scrolling list of cast information, reviews, and similar movies (Figure 5.6), as well as Record, Advanced Record, and Other Showings.

caution Although you can record a currently broadcast movie from the Movie Details menu, you've probably missed the beginning of the picture. If you want to record the entire film, check the Other Showings menu, and if the picture will be shown again, select the future showing for recording.

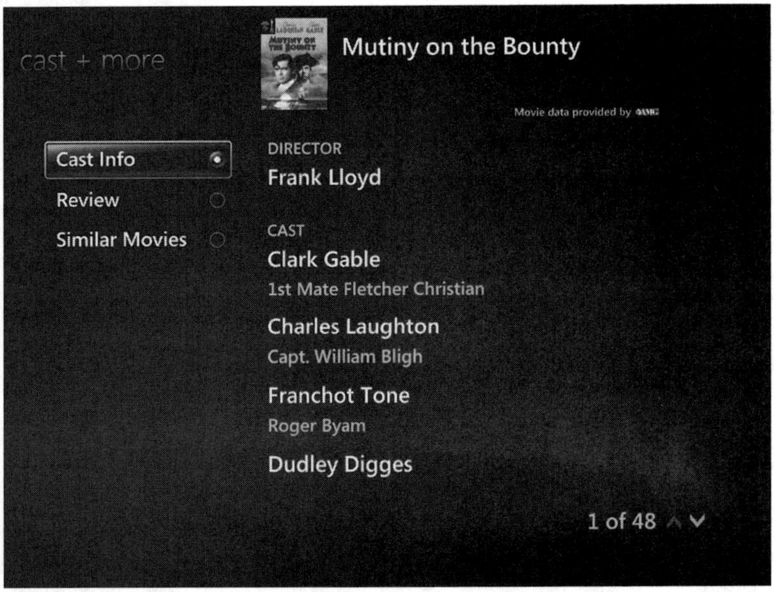

FIGURE 5.6

Use the Cast + More dialog to learn more about a movie.

Have time for a movie, right now? On Now is the place to go.

➔ To learn more about using Recording, Advanced Recording, and Other Showings to record a movie, see "Recording Movies," this chapter, **p. 147**.

➔ To learn how to record movies listed as "Not in Guide" when they are broadcast, select "Recording Movies Not Listed in the Guide," this chapter, **p. 148**.

5

Using the On Next Menu

The On Next menu lists the next film in the rotation on your TV provider's movie channels. When you select a movie from the On Next menu, the options offered on the Movie Details menu (Figure 5.7) are similar to those listed for movies on the On Now menu, except that the Watch option is missing.

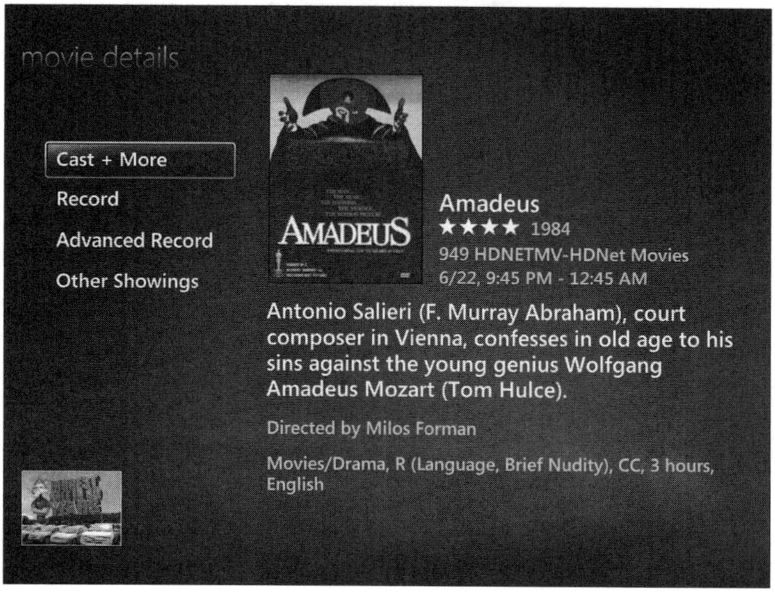

FIGURE 5.7
Movie Details for a movie selected from the On Next menu.

The On Next menu provides you with a convenient way to see what's next. However, if your movie tastes are more specific, there are better ways to use the Movies Guide to find what you prefer, such as the Genres and Top-Rated menus.

Using the Genres Menu

The Genres menu gives you a way to drill down through the movies in the Movies Guide by their genre to find your favorite. Choose your favorite type of film from the 18 genres listed, and you can then select by title, year, rating, or start date (see Figure 5.8).

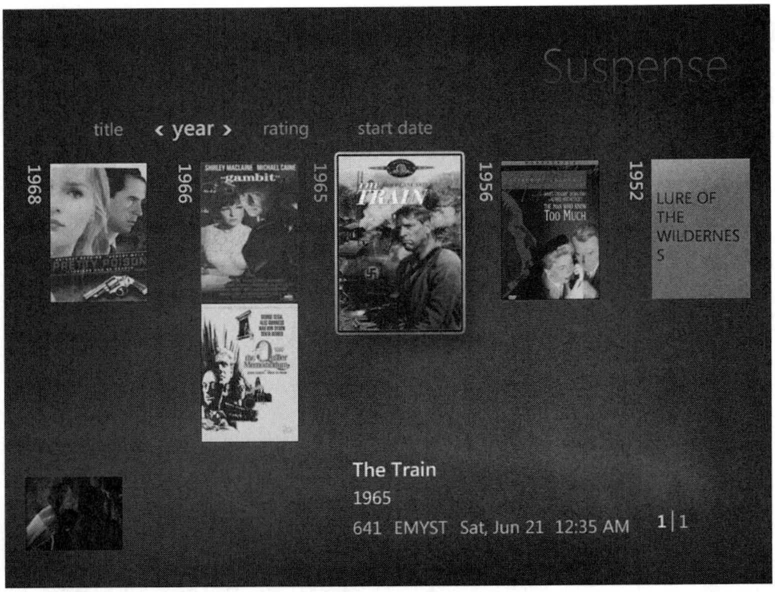

FIGURE 5.8
You can navigate the Genres menu by year, rating, and start date.

When you select by start date, today's films are listed first.

Using the Top-Rated Menu

There are plenty of one-star horrors and two-star mediocrities cluttering up the movie channels at any given time. If you prefer to watch only the best, open the Top Rated menu and choose from only four-star (listed first) and three-star movies in the current guide listings (Figure 5.9).

FIGURE 5.9

Prefer the classics? Use the Top Rated menu to find your favorites—fast.

Using the Search Tool

The Movies Guide is the perfect way to browse for movies, but if you're looking for a particular title, a particular actor, or a particular director, you'll spend a lot of time scrolling through listings. Save yourself time and frustration by leaving the Movies Guide and going to the Search tool.

You can search by Title, Keyword, Categories, Movie Actor, or Movie Director.

Select the search and then enter the search term(s) using either your remote control or a keyboard. To save time, names that match the letters entered show up in the middle of the screen (Figure 5.10).

> **tip** You can search for actor or director by first or last name.

When you see a match, highlight it, and click OK on your remote to see matching movies or TV shows (Figure 5.11).

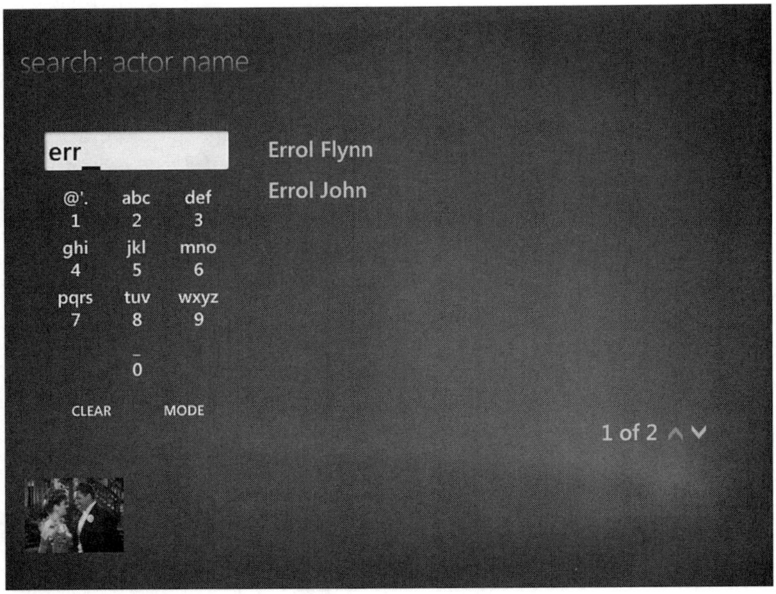

FIGURE 5.10
Searching for classic movie swashbuckler Errol Flynn.

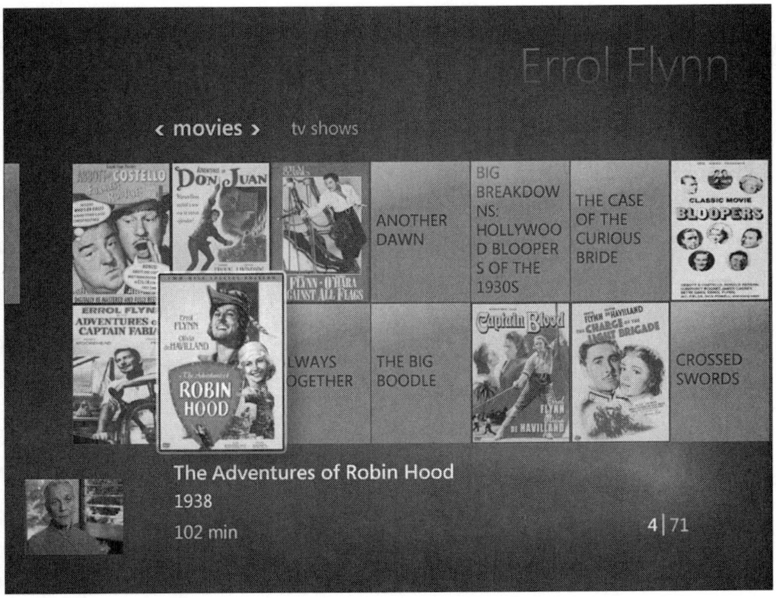

FIGURE 5.11
Using Search to track down movies featuring Errol Flynn.

> **note** If a movie or TV show currently listed in the Program Guide is selected, the channel and broadcast time are shown beneath the title and date. If a movie is not currently listed in the Program Guide, the year and running time are listed.

Keep in mind that searching by title can be tricky in a couple of ways. Although only one actor or actress can use a particular name (others with the same given name must use a different stage or onscreen name), there are no restrictions on movie or TV show titles. Search for a title like *Notorious*, for example, and you might see the title listed with "More" instead of a broadcast date. "More" indicates that there are multiple TV show episodes and/or movies with the same title. Click More to display the episodes or movies to choose from (Figure 5.12). Make sure you select the show or movie you want.

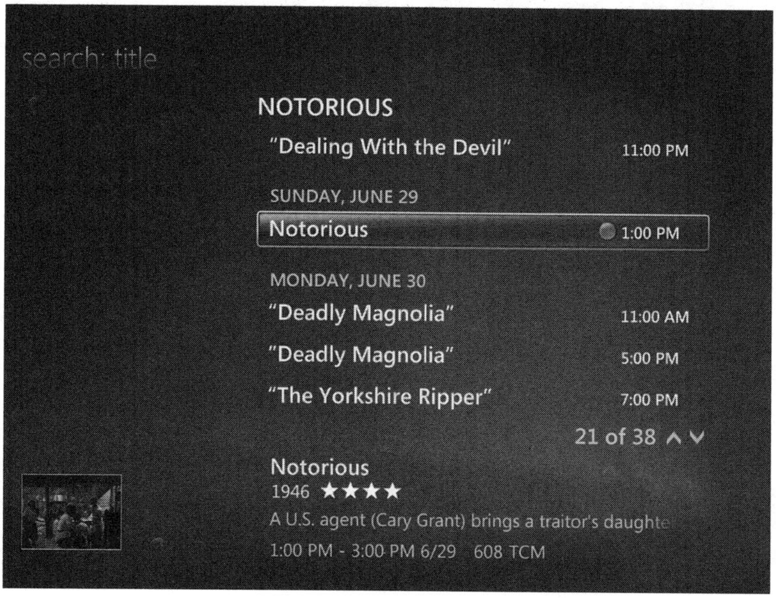

FIGURE 5.12

Select the exact TV show episode or movie you want to record when WMC indicates there is more than one episode or movie with a matching title.

Recording Movies

You can record movies from the Movies Guide in a variety of ways, which is perfect if you don't have time right now to watch your favorite films but don't want to miss them. You can use the On Later, Genres, and Top Rated menus as the starting points for recording, depending upon where your movie is listed.

Recording from the Movies Guide

To record a movie from the Movies Guide, select a movie using any of the menus, open the Movie Details menu for the movie, and select Record from the menu.

When you select a movie for recording, its Movie Details listing displays the message, "This program will record," and the movie listing displays the red dot icon WMC uses to indicate recording (see Figure 5.13).

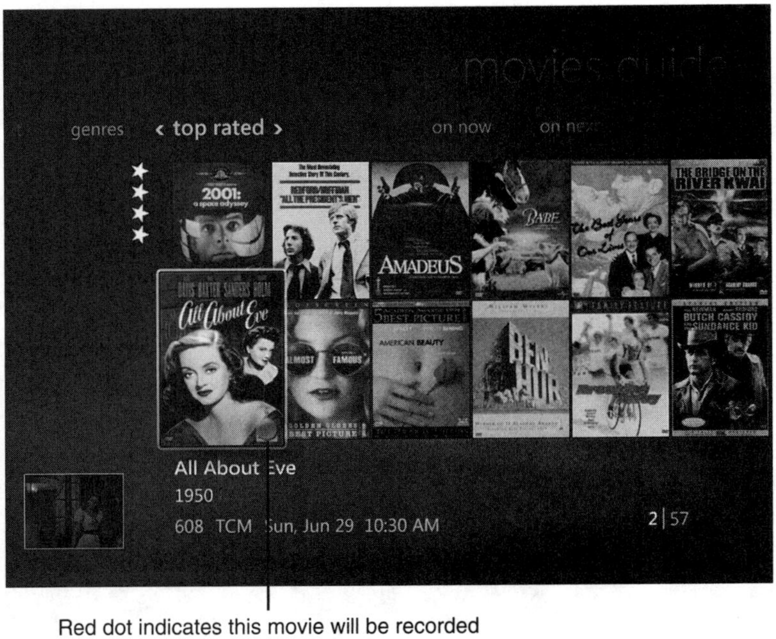

FIGURE 5.13

When you select a movie for recording, its Movies Guide listing indicates you've selected it for recording.

Recording Movies Not Listed in the Guide

What if you want to record a movie, but it's not available in the Movies Guide yet? Are you stuck checking the guide every day from now until...whenever? Thankfully, no.

From the Similar Movies menu (refer to Figure 5.6), you can select movies to record, even if they're not listed in the guide. When you select an unlisted movie to record in the future, the Movie Info dialog lists a Record in Future option (Figure 5.14 A). Select this option, and the movie will be automatically scheduled for recording the next time it appears in the Movies Guide (Figure 5.14 B), and the Movie Info dialog also reminds you the program will record (Figure 5.14 C).

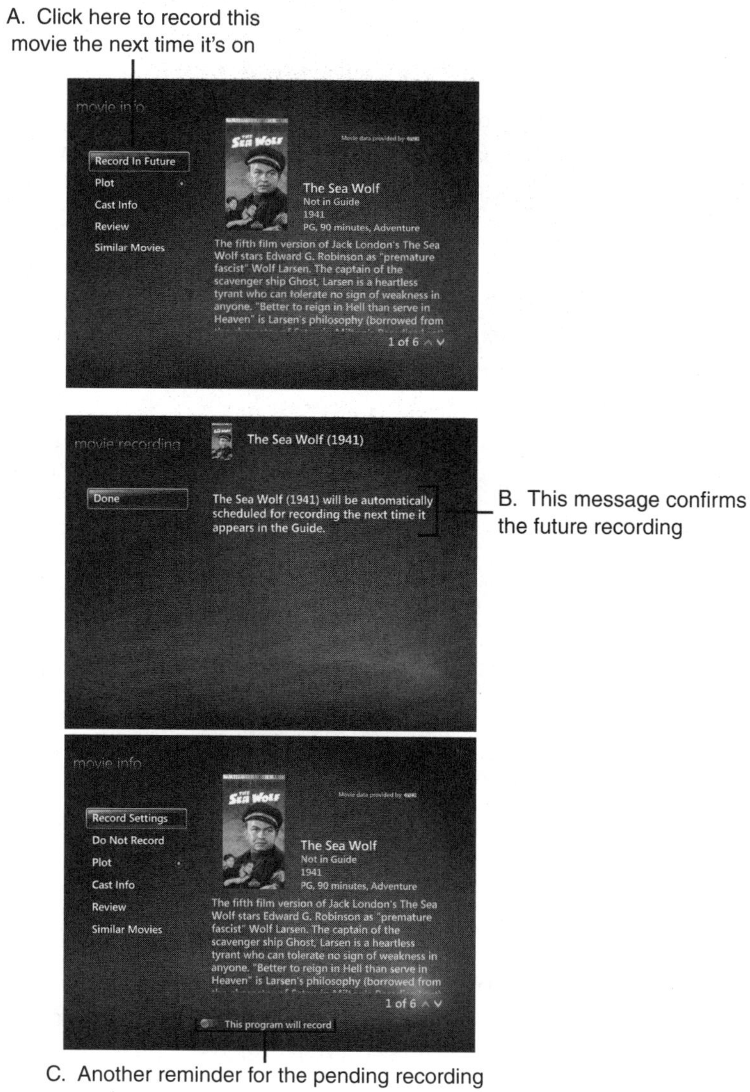

FIGURE 5.14

Selecting a non-Guide movie for recording (A), confirming the selection (B), and viewing the reminder (C).

You can also select a non-Guide movie from the Movies search shown in Figure 5.11 for future recording. Press the Record button on your WMC remote or right-click the movie and select Record from the menu.

caution There's no guarantee of when (or whether) a non-Guide movie you select for recording will appear in the Guide.

Recording from the Search Tool

The Search tool can be used for very fast selection of movies to record, especially if you know what you're looking for. When you search by title or keyword, highlight the movie you want to record and press the Record button on your remote. If you prefer, you can still open the Movie Details dialog and select Record instead.

Searching by category involves a couple of additional steps: First, you must select Movies and then select the genre you're interested in. Then you can record right from the title listing.

When you search by Movie Star or Director name, highlight the picture you want to record and press the Record button on your remote.

tip If you don't use a remote control, right-click the listing and select Record for fast recording.

Customizing Recording Options

The Movie Info dialog lists Record Settings or Advanced Recording as a menu option. Record Settings is displayed after you select the movie to record, while Advanced Recording is displayed for films you haven't yet selected for recording. Select either of these options to open the Record Settings dialog and view (or change) the settings that will be used to record the movie (Figure 5.15).

You can choose from three options in the Record Settings menu: Stop, Quality, and Keep. Here's what I suggest:

- **Stop:** Movies generally start and stop on time (unlike some types of sports events), so you should use the default Stop: On Time setting.
- **Quality:** If you are building a permanent WMC movie library, or if you plan to burn a DVD of your movie before deleting it, use the Quality: Best setting. For movies you are merely watching once, use lower quality settings, depending on how much disk space you want to use and how critical viewing quality is to your enjoyment. Note that if you have digital cable, broadcast TV, or satellite TV service, selecting lower-quality settings has no effect on quality or disk space used.

- **Keep:** If you are building a permanent WMC movie library, select Keep: Until I Delete. With this option, you're in charge of how long the recording stays on your system. If you have plenty of space but don't plan to keep the recording, use the default Until Space Needed setting. Want an incentive to watch your recordings right away? Choose After 1 Week. To automatically delete a movie after you watch it, choose Until I Watch.

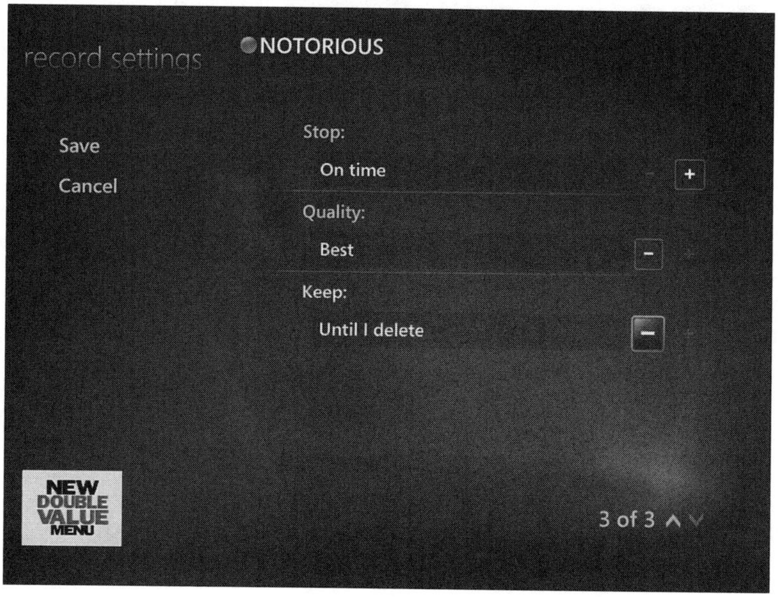

FIGURE 5.15
Adjusting recording settings for best quality and "permanent" storage.

Be sure to save your changes by clicking Save.

→ For more information about how much disk space is used by TV/movie recording, see "Crunching the Numbers: TV Recording" in Chapter 2, Equipping Your PC for Media Center," **p. 29**.

Canceling a Recording

Change your mind about recording a movie? Whether you realize that you selected the wrong movie, want to record a different showing to avoid a recording conflict, or just plain changed your mind, it's easy to cancel a recording.

You can look for films scheduled to be recorded by checking the Movies Guide or searching for the film title. The films that will be recorded show up with a red dot in the listing (refer to Figure 5.12) or have a red dot overlaying the thumbnail (refer to Figure 5.13). If you want to cancel a recording, open the Recorded TV menu, select View Scheduled, and scroll through the listing to the movie you want to drop from the schedule (Figure 5.16).

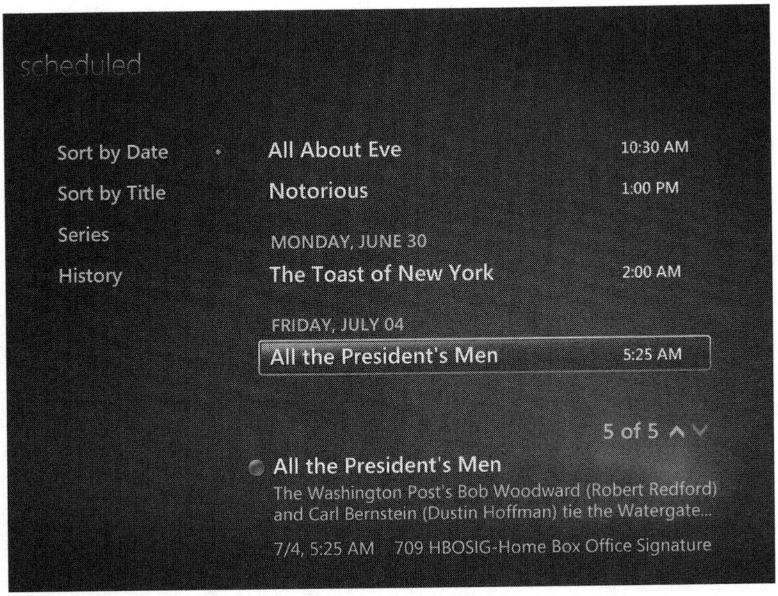

FIGURE 5.16

Use the Recorded TV menu to view scheduled recordings, and choose a picture to cancel from the recording schedule.

After you find the picture, open the Movies Info dialog and select Do Not Record (Figure 5.17). The movie is removed from the schedule.

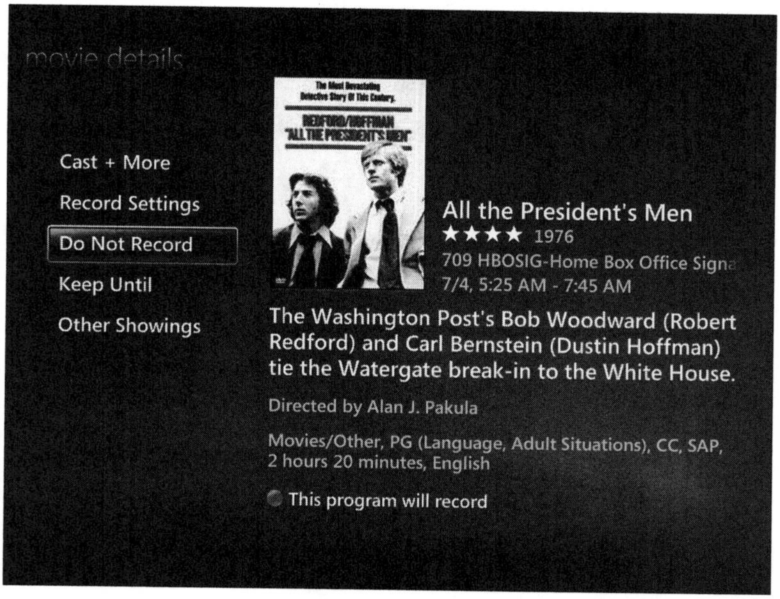

FIGURE 5.17

Using the Do Not Record option in the Movie Details menu to cancel recording.

Watching Recorded Movies

Once you've recorded your first movie, how do you watch it? To find your recorded movies, open the Recorded TV menu. The recordings of your movies are listed alongside TV and sports recordings. To play your movie, select it, and select Play from the Program Info menu (Figure 5.18).

Depending on the aspect ratio used by your movie and your display, you might need to adjust the aspect ratio used for playback.

➔ For more information about adjusting zoom settings for the best-quality playback, see "Selecting Zoom Settings," this chapter, **p. 156**.

5

FIGURE 5.18

After selecting a movie from the Recorded TV menu, click Play.

Resuming or Restarting Movie Playback

Don't have time to finish your movie? Press Stop on your remote or select Stop with your mouse. When you return to your movie, you will see two new options: Resume and Restart. Select Resume to play the movie where you stopped it and Restart to start it from the beginning (Figure 5.19).

tip If you're worried about not being able to finish the movie before it will be deleted, click the Keep Until link, and select the Until I Delete option.

➔ For more information about Keep Until options, see "Recording Defaults," Chapter 4, "Viewing and Recording Live TV," **p. 113**.

FIGURE 5.19

Preparing to resume playback of a recorded movie.

Saying "Goodbye" to Your Recording

You can delete a recording whenever you want. To delete a recording, select Delete from the Program Info menu. The disk space occupied by the recording is freed up, so you have room for new movie recordings.

Watching a DVD Movie

To watch a DVD movie from within WMC, insert the DVD into your computer's DVD drive, select the Play DVD option from the Movies + TV menu, and the DVD starts playing immediately.

For more options, press the More Info/Details button on your remote or right-click the screen to display the menu shown in Figure 5.20.

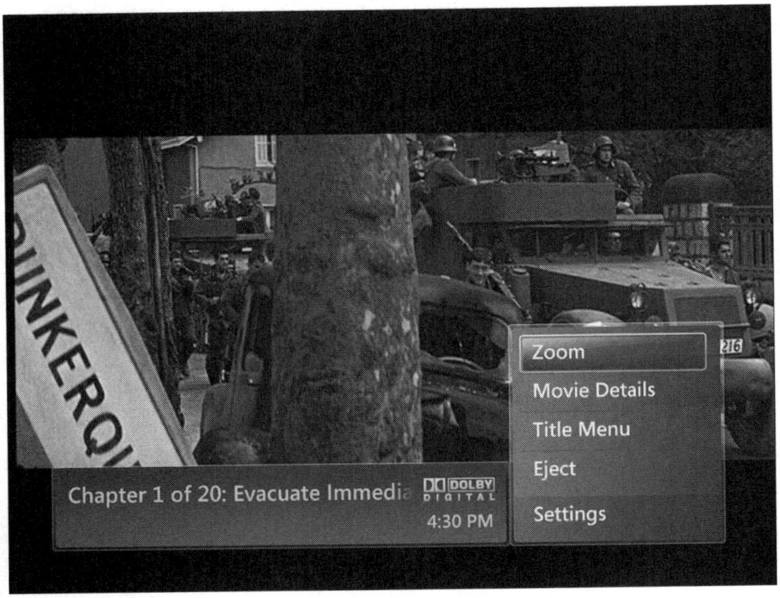

FIGURE 5.20
Opening the More Information menu while playing a DVD.

Selecting Zoom Settings

Because we live in a world where movies and TV shows might use any one of several aspect ratios, you might need to tweak the screen settings used for playback to avoid squashed or vertically stretched displays, even if you followed the procedure described in Chapter 3, "Setting Up Windows Media Center," for configuring your display.

> **note** Your ability to zoom the display is limited by the aspect ratio setting of your display if you're using an HDTV monitor with adjustable aspect ratio. For the best results, configure your HDTV to use Full aspect ratio and then use the Zoom control in Windows Media Center.

Use the Zoom setting on the DVD playback menu to help match your display and the aspect ratio used by your movie.

To toggle through zoom options, select Zoom from the Info menu and press the OK button on your remote or keep clicking Zoom in the Info menu with your mouse. The options include

- **Zoom option 1 (Normal):** The movie displays full-screen on displays with the same aspect ratio. Widescreen films will display letterbox black bars on standard displays; standard films will display black bars at the side on widescreen displays.

- **Zoom option 2 (Zoom):** The movie is zoomed to display full-screen; edges of the image will be cropped.
- **Zoom option 3 (Stretch):** The movie is stretched to fit the screen without cropping, but the image might be distorted horizontally (standard movie) or vertically (widescreen movie).
- **Zoom option 4 (Intelligent Zoom):** The movie is zoomed to display full-screen, but the edges are stretched more than the center.

> **tip** If you are not able to change the screen display by using the zoom controls shown in Figures 5.21 and 5.22, you probably don't have your display set for the correct resolution. Exit WMC, open the Appearance and Personalization menu in Control Panel, select Adjust Screen Resolution, select the display used by WMC, and use the Resolution slider to select the correct resolution. If the display is a PnP display, you will normally use the highest setting (right-most slider). If this setting doesn't work, experiment with lower resolutions.
>
> You might also need to download and install an updated driver for your graphics card or onboard graphics port. You can use the Update Driver feature in Device Manager, or manually download and install an updated driver. Some graphics card vendors also provide a special menu option that provides options for HDTV and other displays. See your graphics card's or motherboard vendor's website for details.

Which zoom option works the best? That depends on the aspect ratio of your display and of the movie itself. If the movie is in the same aspect ratio as the the display (for example, a widescreen movie on a widescreen HDTV or desktop display, or a classic movie on a standard TV or display), use the default, zoom level 1. However, if the movie and the display don't match, use one of the other zoom options if you want to fill the screen. I prefer to view films at their native aspect ratio and put up with letterbox borders, but if you don't, the Zoom menu is your friend.

Figures 5.21 and 5.22 compare zoom results when viewing a typical 1.85:1 widescreen comedy (Bill Murray's classic *Groundhog Day*) on a widescreen display.

FIGURE 5.21
Normal Zoom versus Zoom.

FIGURE 5.22
Stretch versus Intelligent Zoom.

Using Other Menu Options

The Movie Details option doesn't do much: Select it, and you get two choices—play the movie from its current position or restart it. WMC might crash when you use this option, so stay away from it.

You can restart a paused movie by pressing the Play button on your remote or by clicking the Play icon in the mouse menu, and you can restart a film from the beginning by selecting Title Menu and restarting the film from there.

Use the Settings selection to open the Settings menu.

Creating a DVD Library with My Movies 2

Although you can play your DVDs through WMC, if you want to create a true DVD library, whether you flip discs in and out of your system's DVD drive or copy discs you own to your hard disk, you'll need some third-party software.

> **note** My Movies 2 is freeware, but to unlock some advanced features, you must accumulate various levels of points. Points can be earned by making financial contributions to My Movies 2's developer, by adding information about DVDs or Blu-Ray discs not in the My Movies database, or by enhancing existing information for a movie. See the website for details.

One of the most popular choices among WMC users is the My Movies 2 program. Developed by Brian Binnerup, My Movies 2 enables you to more easily manage and enjoy your DVD or Blu-Ray movie collection in WMC. In the following sections, I'll provide some guidance for helping you use My Movies 2. However, for the most up-to-date information, be sure to see the My Movies 2 website at www.mymovies.dk.

Installing My Movies

My Movies 2 comes in two different versions, with separate downloads for 32-bit and 64-bit Vista. You must have the Server/Client edition installed on the system that is used for watching DVDs within WMC. Despite its name, it is installed on both networked and standalone systems. The Client version is installed on other Windows Vista (or XP) systems that connect to the system running Server/Client, enabling you to use remote systems to manage your collection.

tip If you have one system running WMC, install the Server/Client edition on that computer. If you later add a second system, install the Client edition on the new computer. For details, see http://www.mymovies.dk/documentation/multizone-connection.aspx.

The Server/Client edition is about 75MB and downloads as a ZIP file you decompress with Windows Explorer before installing; the Client edition is about 9MB and is a self-extracting .EXE file.

My Movies Server/Client edition includes SQL Server 2005 Express Edition, which is installed automatically during installation. After SQL Server 2005 Express Edition is installed, the installation process for My Movies begins. By default, the program installs to C:\Program Files\MCE\My Movies.

When you install My Movies, it creates a My Movies folder in the Start menu with the following shortcuts:

- Collection Management (run this first)
- Donate for My Movies (the program is free, but donations enable you to unlock advanced features)
- Frequently Asked Questions (a useful resource for learning how the program works)
- My Movies (the main program)
- Uninstall My Movies (the uninstaller)

note For frequently asked questions (FAQs) about using My Movies, see http://wiki.mymovies.dk/Frequently%20Asked%20Questions.ashx.

Getting Started

After you download and install My Movies 2 Server/Client, you must run its Connection Management program from the standard Windows desktop before you can use it within WMC.

Click the splash screen to configure your server. After the server is configured, you can start adding movies to your database, using a variety of methods:

- If you have already copied DVDs to your hard disk, open the File menu and select Folder Content. Point to the folder that contains your DVDs, and My Movies adds them to its database.
- To add movies on your shelf, select Add Titles, and choose By Barcode (you can type in the barcode or scan it in with a webcam), By Disc ID (insert your DVD and click Search), By Title, By Manual Typing (use this feature to add a movie that is not in the My Movies database), or by Upcoming Releases. When you add a movie, you can choose whether to catalog it as Online (stored on your hard disk) or Offline (run from your DVD drive), and you can categorize the movie thus:
  - Owned, For Keeps (the default)
  - Owned, For Sale
  - Owned, For Sale or Trade
  - Pre-Owned
  - Ordered
  - Wished
  - Rented
  - Pre-Rented

My Movies helps you keep track of your favorite films, whether you buy, borrow, or rent them.

When you add a movie, you might be prompted to add updated information from the My Movies 2 webservice. Select this option to get the most up-to-date information about the film.

note For additional information about using My Movies, including how to catalog series and box sets, see http://www.mymovies.dk/documentation/my-movies-2-quickguide.aspx.

Blu-Ray and HD-DVD Support

My Movies 2 includes support for these formats when you have a compatible decoder and appropriate hardware installed.

→ To learn more about using Blu-Ray movies in WMC and My Movies 2, see "Watching Blu-Ray Movies in WMC," this chapter, **p. 162**.

Adding My Movies to the WMC Interface

To add My Movies to the WMC interface, start WMC after you close the Connection Manager. You will be prompted where to place My Movies. You can add My Movies as an option to the TV + Movies strip or as a separate My Movies strip (the third option, as a menu option in the Program Library, doesn't work in Windows Vista). Select an option (Figure 5.23), and you will be prompted to restart Media Center to apply the change.

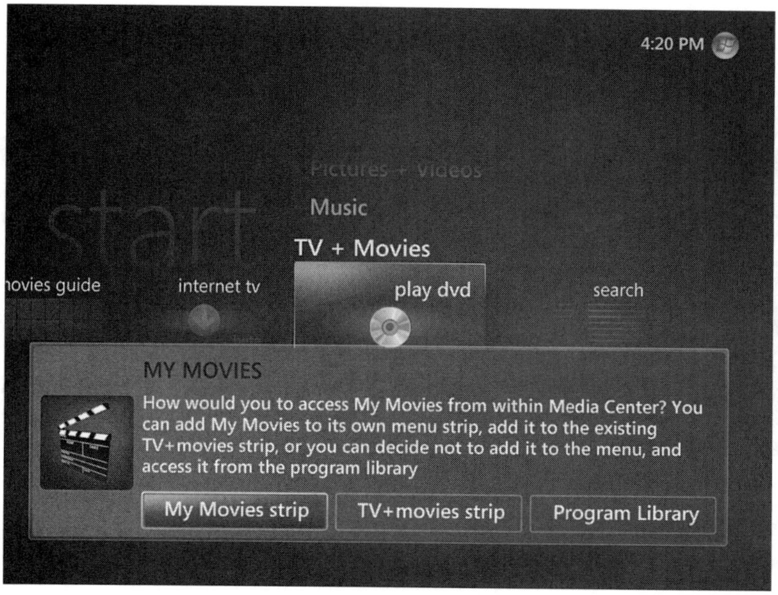

FIGURE 5.23

Selecting how to display My Movies in WMC.

Figure 5.24 illustrates these options.

If you want to change how My Movies is displayed in WMC, follow this procedure:

1. Exit WMC.
2. Restart Collection Management.
3. Open the Configure menu.
4. Select Media Center Interface.
5. On the Interface tab, click the Reset button next to Current Menu Program Interface.

6. Click OK on the confirming dialog.
7. Close the Media Center Interface tab.
8. Close the Collection Management program.
9. Restart WMC.
10. Select the view you prefer when prompted.
11. Click OK on the confirming dialog.
12. Close WMC.
13. Restart WMC.
14. My Movies will be placed in the WMC interface as desired.

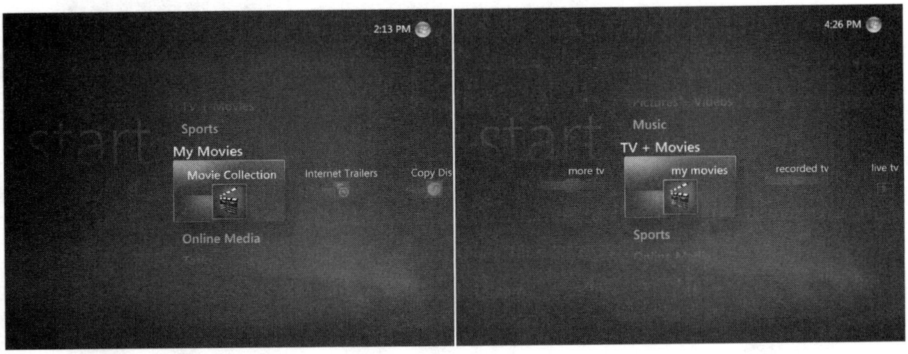

A. B.

FIGURE 5.24

My Movies in its own strip (A) compared to My Movies as a menu item in the TV + Movies strip (B).

The Settings Menu

The Settings Menu in My Movie 2's WMC interface provides options for configuring its user interface, the movie list (Views), parental control restrictions (this option requires that WMC's own Parental Controls option be enabled first), DVD playback and copying, and managing your DVD collection.

➔ For more information about using WMC's Parental Controls, see Chapter 4, **p. 85**.

Watching Blu-Ray Movies in WMC

If you've moved up to Blu-Ray HD movies, you're probably wondering, "OK, how can I enjoy this 1080p goodness in WMC?" The following sections show you exactly what you need.

Hardware

You'll need the following hardware in order to enjoy Blu-Ray movies with WMC:

- Blu-Ray read-only or Read/Write drive (these also support CD and DVD media)
- HDCP-enabled onboard or discrete graphics card
- HDCP-enabled HDTV or widescreen LCD panel

Software

You'll need the following software in order to enjoy Blu-Ray movies with WMC:

- Blu-Ray decoder that supports Windows Vista (minimum)
- Blu-Ray decoder that supports WMC (preferred)

Although Microsoft includes DVD decoding in Windows Vista (including Media Center), it does not include Blu-Ray decoding in Windows Vista. You can use a third-party DVD decoder, but if it doesn't include an WMC plug-in, you must exit or minimize WMC to run the decoder. Some Blu-Ray decoders for Windows Vista include

- CyberLink PowerDVD 8 Ultra—www.cyberlink.com (about $100; free trial available). Add WMC support by downloading and installing freeware Cyberlink/VMC plug-in version 1.6 or later (available at http://ourmediacenter.com/node/9).
- Blu-Ray/HD-DVD plugin for Nero 7 or Nero 8—www.nero.com (about $30; Nero 8 Ultra [required for use of plug-in] is about $80–100; free trial available).
- ArcSoft TotalMedia Theatre—www.arcsoft.com (about $90; free trial available). Incorporates WMC plug-in.

note My Movies 2 also supports Blu-Ray (as well as HD-DVD) movies if you have a compatible decoder installed. (The developer recommends ArcSoft TotalMedia Theatre.) Contribute or earn 2,500 points, and you can unlock My Movies 2's Blu-Ray and HD-DVD backup feature so you can copy your movies to hard disk for easier access. To learn more about My Movies 2's support for Blu-Ray and HD-DVD movies, go to http://wiki.mymovies.dk and search for Blu-Ray.

Which is the best solution for you? In reviewing comments from existing users of these products, the answer seems to be "it depends." Try the trial versions of the applications and plug-ins to see which ones work the best for you.

→ To learn more about My Movies 2, see "Creating a DVD Library with My Movies 2," this chapter, **p. 158**.

CHAPTER

6

Importing and Playing Audio

The core of many people's media collection is, not surprisingly, music, and Windows Media Center (WMC) is music-friendly—*very* music-friendly. WMC has no problem playing your existing digital music libraries (of course), but you can also use it to play and rip music CDs, create and play playlists based on various criteria, and even rate your favorites. You can also use WMC to play FM radio (if you have a TV tuner that also supports FM radio) and play online news and music sources. So let's get started!

IN THIS CHAPTER

- Overview of the Music Menu
- Using Existing Digital Music Libraries
- Playing and Ripping Music CDs
- Playing and Editing Individual Album Tracks
- Working with Albums
- Creating and Using a Queue
- Using and Managing Playlists
- Searching for Your Favorite Music
- Listening to FM Radio
- Listening to Internet Radio
- Synchronizing with Portable Players

Overview of the Music Menu

The Music menu (Figure 6.1) includes the following options:

- **More Music:** Click to enter the world of online audio sources.
- **Music Library:** Open this option to select the music you want from your music folders and shared music folders on other systems.

- **Play All:** Don't care what's playing as long as there's music in the background? This option plays every digital music file in reach of WMC.
- **Radio:** On systems with an FM radio tuner (a popular option on TV tuner cards), use this option to play (and pause) your favorite radio stations.
- **Search:** Use this option to track down music by name.

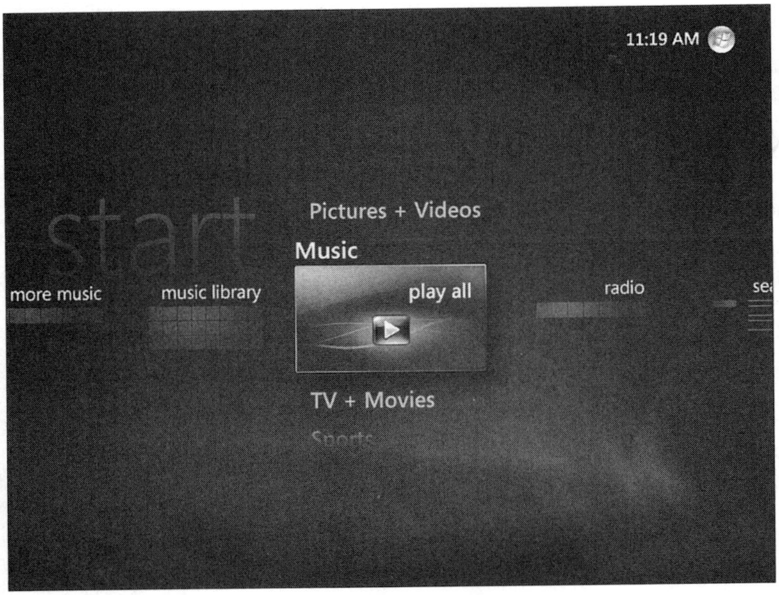

FIGURE 6.1

The Music menu.

Using Existing Digital Music Libraries

If you already have a digital music collection available to Windows Media Player, Windows Media Center uses it automatically. The first time you open the Music Library, it builds its music library from the music available to Windows Media Player and then prompts you to choose other folders to watch for media files (Figure 6.2). Click Yes to open Library Setup to choose the folders you want to keep an eye on. These folders can include

- External hard disks
- Other users' Music folders
- Network users' Music folders

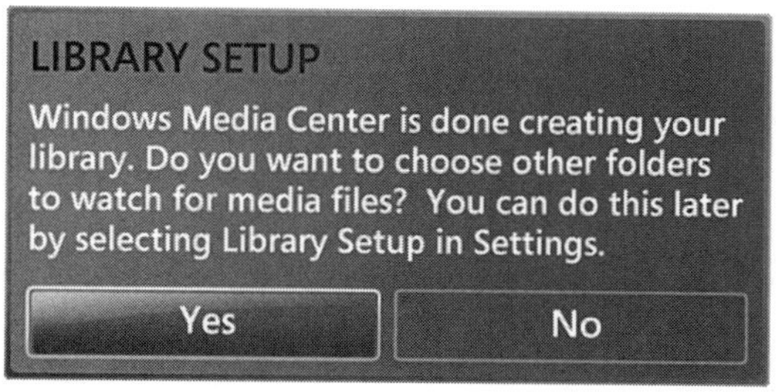

FIGURE 6.2

Preparing to choose other music folders after starting Music Library.

This process is the same as the Library Setup process discussed in Chapter 3, "Setting Up Windows Media Center."

➔ For details, see "Optional Setup: Music, Pictures, and Videos Library" in Chapter 3, **p. 74**.

Music from shared libraries as well as from your own music libraries is available in WMC's Music Library.

> **note** If you want to access the contents of media folders on systems using Windows XP or older Windows versions, these folders must be configured as shared.
>
> To share a folder in Windows XP, open Windows Explorer or My Computer, navigate to the folder location, right-click the folder, select Sharing and Security, and click the Share This Folder on the Network check box. To prevent media from being deleted or changed by other users, do *not* click the Allow Network Users to Change My Files check box. Click Apply and then OK.
>
> To share a folder in Windows Vista, open the Network and Sharing Center and turn on Media Sharing.

Playing and Ripping Music CDs

When you insert a music CD, WMC switches automatically to the Now Playing dialog (Figure 6.3). From this dialog, you can choose to

- Copy (rip) the CD to WMC's Music Library
- View the playback queue
- Run a visualization while playing the CD

- Play a slide show while playing the CD
- Shuffle the tracks on the CD
- Repeat playback
- Buy digital music

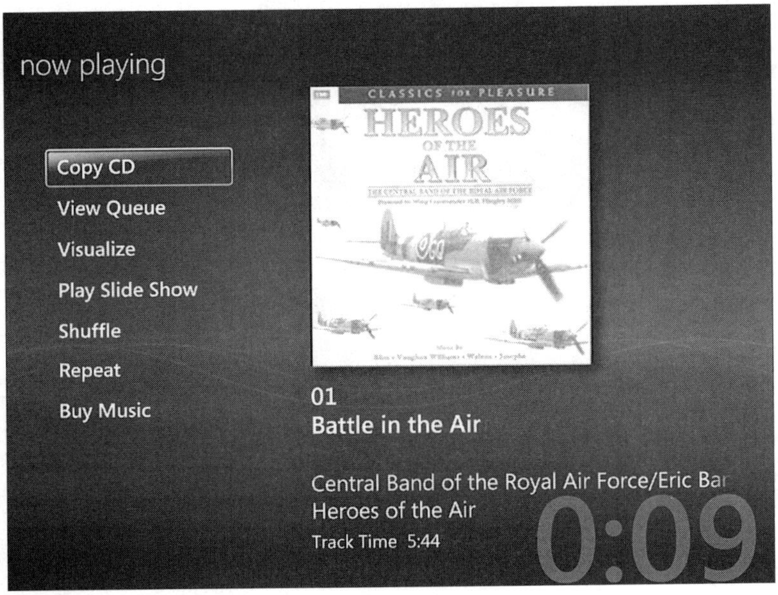

FIGURE 6.3
The Now Playing dialog with Shuffle enabled.

If you don't select any options, WMC will rip the music CD to your music library, using the music rip settings in Windows Media Player (format, bit rate, whether to eject the CD after ripping, and so on).

➔ For details, see the "Configuring Audio Ripping" section in Chapter 13, "Using Windows Media Player with Windows Media Center," **p. 376**.

> **note** Music you rip to your system with WMC is available to other computers running WMC or Windows Media Player *if* you select the option to share your media files in the Network and Sharing Center.

If you manually select the option to copy the CD, a Copy CD prompt appears; click Yes to continue.

When the Shuffle option is selected (Figure 6.4), the tracks are played in random order. A check mark indicates the tracks that have been copied, and an equalizer icon indicates the track currently being played.

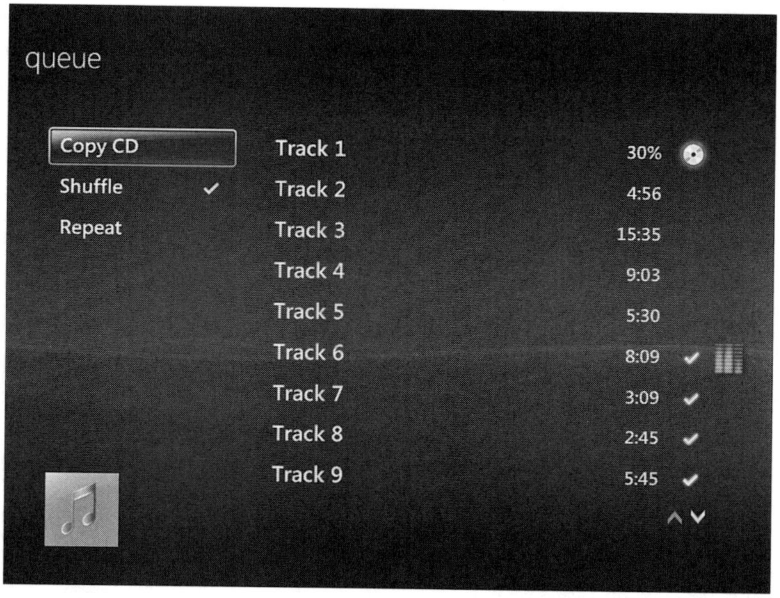

FIGURE 6.4

Copying a CD while playing it in Shuffle mode.

DEALING WITH MIXED-CONTENT CDS

Unfortunately, Windows Media Center (WMC) isn't very smart when it comes to dealing with mixed-content CDs, such as the Enhanced-CD format that combines CD audio tracks with other content, such as music videos or album art that is only visible on a PC. WMC obediently rips the CD audio tracks but ignores the rest of the CD. If you want to copy nonaudio track content from an Enhanced CD to your computer, you will need to exit WMC and use the Computer Explorer to grab the rest of the content.

6

Selecting a Visualization

If you prefer to see your display doing something while you pump music from WMC through your speakers, select Visualize from the Now Playing menu (refer to Figure 6.3). A visualization from

note To add more visualizations, open Windows Media Player and use its Visualization option to download additional visualizations.

the Windows Media Player library appears onscreen (Figure 6.5), and a banner displaying the current track appears for a few seconds. To cycle through visualizations, use the arrow keys or the channel up/down controls.

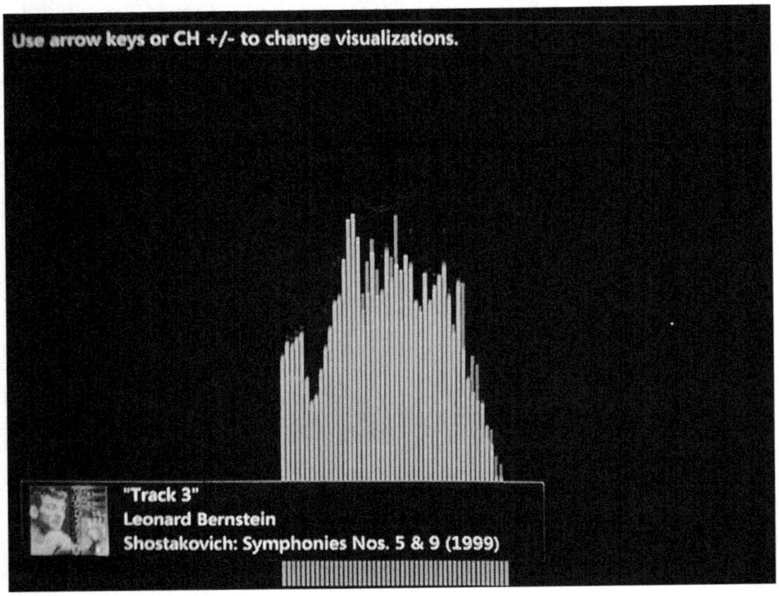

FIGURE 6.5
A visualization available in WMC.

To exit visualization, press the Enter key on your keyboard or the Back/Exit button on your remote control.

➔ For more information about adding visualizations, see "Downloading Visualizations" in Chapter 13, **p. 389**.

6

Working with Music as It Is Being Played

As you work with the Music Library (or other libraries), the currently playing media (music, TV, slide shows, and so forth) is shown as a thumbnail at the lower left-hand corner of the screen. Hover the mouse over the thumbnail for details (Figure 6.6).

To repeat the track, select a visualization, or perform other tasks, double-click the thumbnail to open the Now Playing menu.

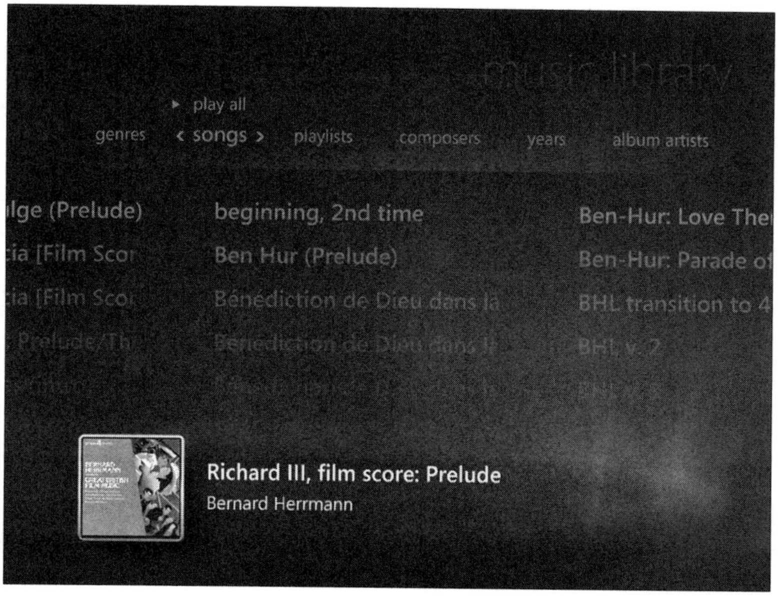

FIGURE 6.6

Viewing details of the current music track.

Playing and Editing Individual Album Tracks

You can play individual tracks from any album in a variety of ways:

- To choose a track from a particular album, select the album from the default Albums view or select the artist from the Artists view and then the album.
- If you prefer to select music by type (Rock, Jazz, Soundtrack, Classical, World, Folk, and so on), select the Genres view. You can select a track from the albums that contain tracks matching the genre, or select Songs to select the track by title (Figure 6.7). The details of the highlighted track are shown at the bottom of the dialog.
- If you know the name of the track, cut to the chase and select the Songs view. All audio tracks are listed in alphabetical order.
- Want to immerse yourself in the music of your favorite songwriter? Select the Composers view. Select the composer and then select the album or switch to the Songs view.

- Are you performer-driven in your music choices? Choose the Album Artists view. (You might also find some composers lurking in this view.) Select your favorite artist and then select the album that contains your favorite track—or switch to the Songs view.
- Want to re-create that special year in music? The Years view might do it for you—but keep in mind, it's based on the *release year* of the album, not the release date (or composing date) of the tracks it contains. As with other views, you can choose by album or song title.

note If you see duplicate track titles (as in Figure 6.7), there might be two or more folders in the library that contain the same music tracks or the same song title has been recorded by different artists or is on different albums. In such cases, use the Albums view to choose the preferred track.

Once you see the track you want, right-click it and select Play (Figure 6.8) to play it immediately or click Add to Queue to add it to the list of media being played.

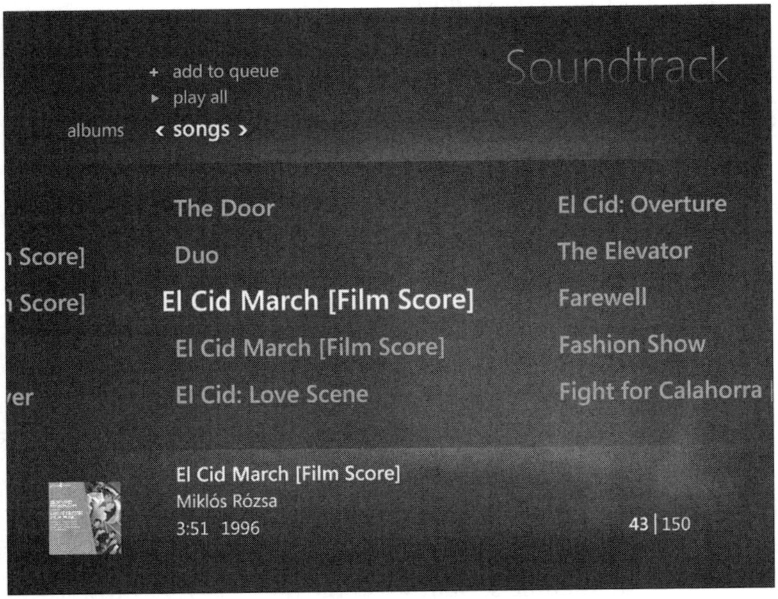

FIGURE 6.7

Selecting a track in the Soundtrack genre.

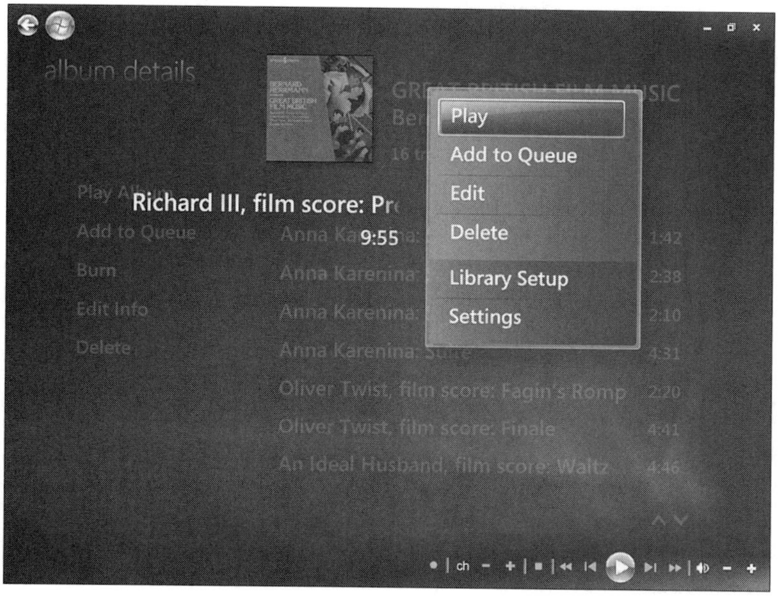

FIGURE 6.8

Preparing to play or queue up a selected track.

Editing Song and Rating Information

Although WMC usually chooses the correct album information for you, it might not always get the name of a track or artist right. To correct this information, select Edit from the right-click menu shown in Figure 6.8. The Edit menu (Figure 6.9) offers you the ability to edit the song title and the artist and add (or edit) the star rating.

You can use a keyboard or the keypad on your remote control to perform edits. Click Mode to remap the keypad to enter lowercase, uppercase, or special punctuation marks.

> **note** The star ratings you assign a song in WMC are also displayed when the song track is viewed in WMP, and vice versa.

After making changes, click Save to keep the changes or Cancel to discard them.

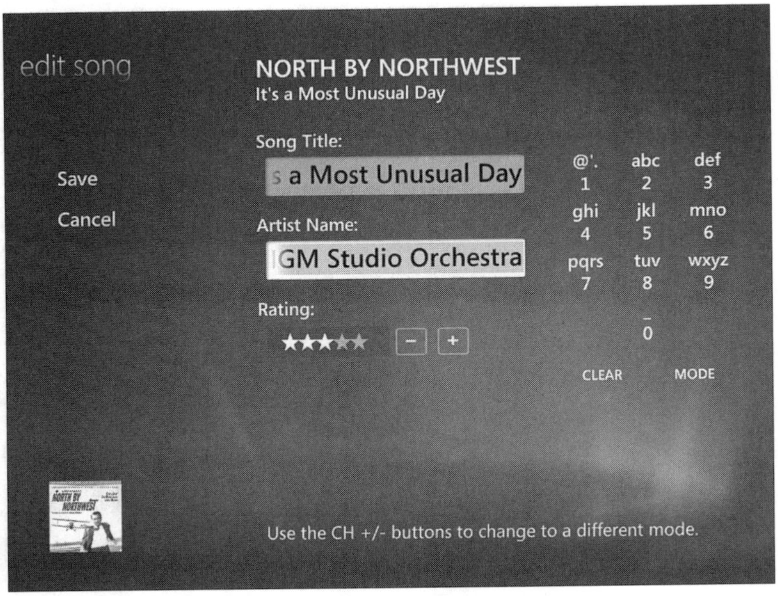

FIGURE 6.9

Editing song track information.

Working with Albums

If you prefer albums to mix-and-match tracks, the Albums view is the one you'll prefer. By default, the Albums view uses the Large album cover view shown in Figure 6.10, giving you a comfortable view of your digital music collection from your couch or easy chair. However, if you're tired of scrolling through a large collection, right-click any album and select View Small to see smaller-sized album art or View List to view albums by title.

The right-click menu shown in Figure 6.10 is also your pathway to playing an entire album (Play), adding the album's contents to a queue for upcoming playback (Queue), removing the album from the hard disk (Delete), changing album information (Edit), or copying the album to a CD (Burn). You can also access the library setup or settings menus from this menu.

➔ For more information about Library Setup, see "Optional Setup: Music, Pictures, and Videos Library" in Chapter 3, **p. 74**.

➔ For more information about Settings, see "Using Settings to Reconfigure Your System" in Chapter 3, **p. 77**.

➔ For more information about burning CDs, see "Creating Music CDs" in Chapter 10, "Creating CDs and DVDs," **p. 289**.

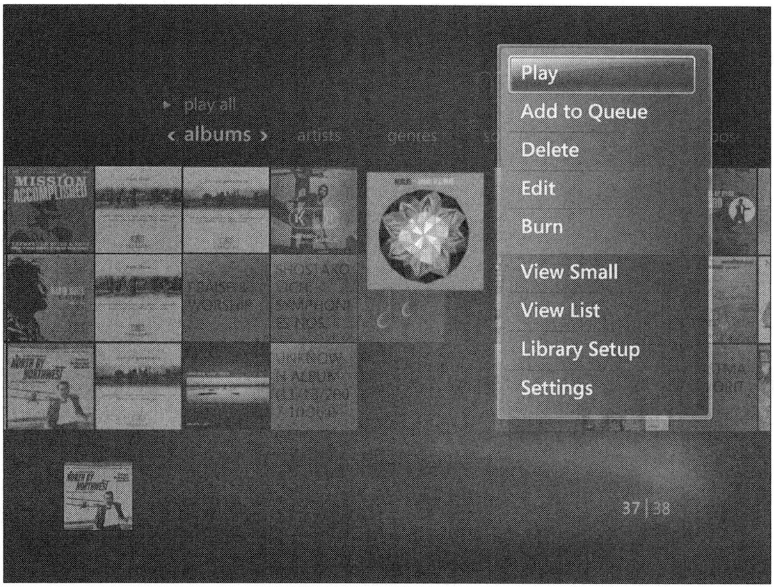

FIGURE 6.10
The right-click menu in Albums view.

Editing Album Information

If the album artist, genre, or title is incorrect, or you want to add more information, select Edit from the right-click menu shown in Figure 6.10. You can use a keyboard or the keypad on your remote control to change the album title or artist name. To select a different genre, click the + and – symbols next to the Genre name (see Figure 6.11).

If you need to add (or change) album art, use Windows Media Player.

➔ For more information about changing album art, see "Adding/Changing Album Art and Track Information" in Chapter 3, **p. 387**.

tip Although you can only choose from predefined genres when you edit album information, there's a workaround. Thanks to WMC's tight integration with Windows Media Player, any genre you assign to an album in Windows Media Player shows up in the list of genres you can choose from in WMC. So feel free to create your own genre classifications! How about Hip-Hop Bach?

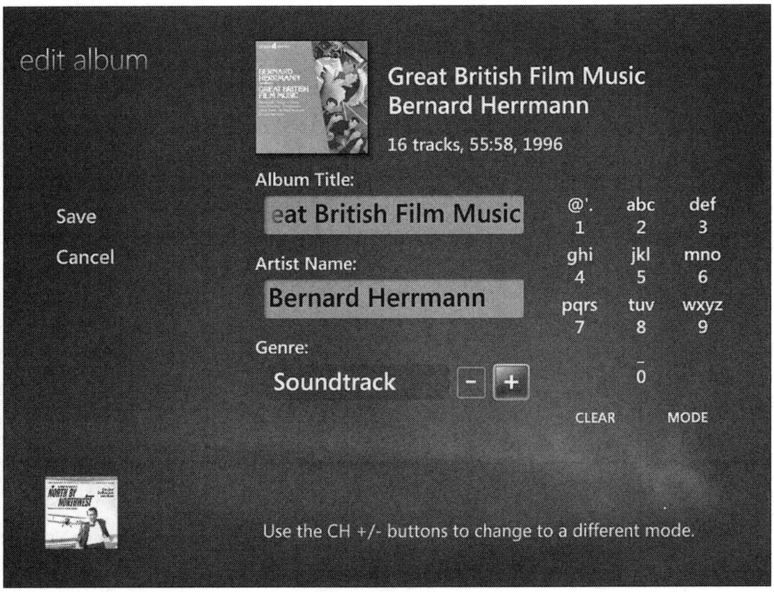

FIGURE 6.11
Editing album information.

Creating and Using a Queue

To add an individual song or an entire album to the list of music waiting to be played (the queue), right-click it and select Add to Queue. You also create a candidate for the world's longest queue if you select Play All from the Music menu shown in Figure 6.1.

You can view the contents of the queue in two ways:

- From WMC's Start (main) menu, click Now Playing + Queue. Select View Queue from the Now Playing menu.
- At any time, click the Now Playing thumbnail in the lower-left corner of the screen. Select View Queue from the Now Playing menu.

Use the Queue menu (Figure 6.12) to change the playback order or remove selected song tracks (Edit Queue), delete the entire queue (Clear Queue), create a playlist from the queue (Save as Playlist), randomly change playback order (Shuffle), play the queue again when you reach the end of the queue (Repeat), or copy the files to CD or DVD (Burn).

Click the up and down arrows at the bottom of the screen to move to the previous or next screen. The current song track is indicated with animated volume bars.

FIGURE 6.12
The Queue menu.

Editing the Queue

Use the Edit Queue menu (Figure 6.13) to change playback order or to delete songs from the queue. To move a song higher in the queue, click its up-arrow icon; to move it lower, click its down-arrow icon. To remove it from the queue, click the X. (Removing it from the queue does not delete the song track from the computer; rather, it just deletes it from the queue.) When you're finished rearranging the queue, click Done.

Creating a Playlist from a Queue

If you look at your queue and say to yourself, "Dude, that's a great mix," make a playlist out of it. It's simple. Click Save As Playlist from the Queue menu, use your remote control's keypad (or a keyboard) to enter the name (see Figure 6.14), and click Save. Your playlist shows up in both WMC and Windows Media Player.

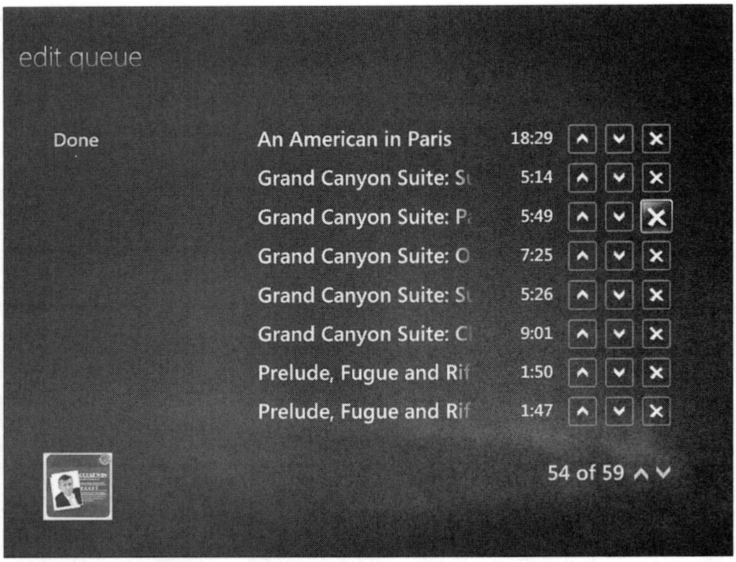

FIGURE 6.13
The Edit Queue menu.

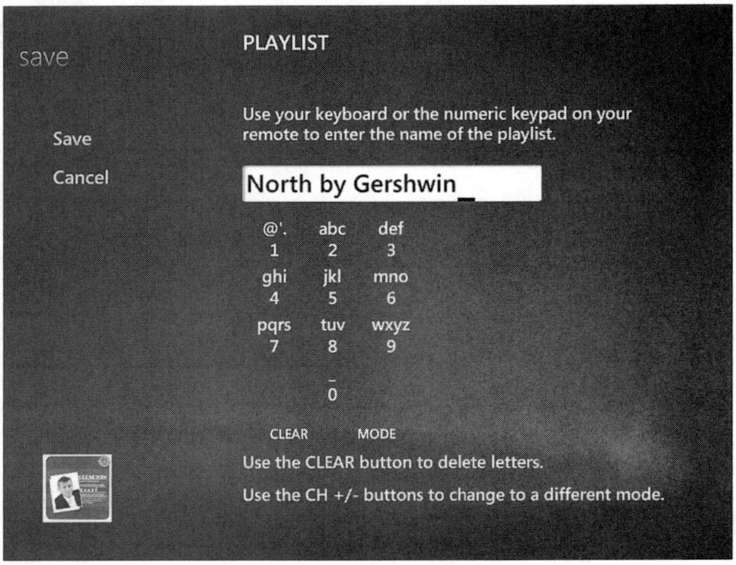

FIGURE 6.14
Saving the current queue as a playlist.

→ To learn how to burn your queue or playlist to a CD, see "Creating Music CDs" in Chapter 10, **p. 289**.

6

If you want to clear the queue and start over, I recommend saving the current queue as a playlist first.

Using and Managing Playlists

As you learned in the previous section, you can create a playlist from a queue in Windows Media Center. Want to play a playlist? Select Playlists in the Music Library (Figure 6.15).

FIGURE 6.15

Viewing current playlists.

Windows Media Center and Windows Media Player share both user-created and auto playlists (but I bet that doesn't surprise you). User-created playlists (like the "North by Gershwin" mash-up I created in Figure 6.14) show up under the heading "Playlists." Auto playlists are generated for you by the dynamic duo of WMC and WMP and include the following music categories:

- **All Music:** If you don't know what you want to listen to, this is the playlist for you. It plays all of your music—and I do mean *all*. If you have "orphan" tracks that lack album information, they're played first, followed by every song on all your albums.

- **Music Added in the Last Month:** Use this playlist to remind yourself what you've downloaded or ripped lately or what's new on the rip/download scene on other systems that share their media with you.
- **Music Auto Rated at 5 Stars:** Play a tune often enough, and Windows assigns it a five-star rating. If you're a big fan of "play it again," this playlist is one you'll love.
- **Music Played in the Last Month:** Sure, you might have ripped that album a couple of years ago (back when you were running Windows XP, for example), but if you played it in the last month, WMC knows it and serves it up to you—fresh.
- **Music Played the Most:** Back when LPs and 45s were the music distribution media of choice, you could literally wear out the grooves on your music by playing it too much. No worries here. This playlist contains your favorites—automatically.
- **Music Rated at 4 or 5 Stars:** You might play a mixture of "guilty favorites" (the bad music that everybody listens to on the radio anyway) and the tunes you prefer. Use either WMC or Windows Media Player to rate them as four-star or five-star, and you'll find them in this playlist.

→ For more information about editing or adding song ratings, see "Editing Song and Rating Information" in this chapter, **p. 173**.

Searching for Your Favorite Music

Rip more than a few CDs to your system or hit the download buffet at your favorite digital music online store, and sooner or later you're going to be drowning in music tracks. To make it easier to find just the tune you're looking for, scroll over to the Search option in the Music menu.

Use your remote control's keypad or computer keyboard to enter the name of an artist, song title, composer, album, or genre (Figure 6.16). Select a song, and you go directly to the Song Details menu. Choose an artist, composer, album, or genre, and you go to the Albums view, with the option to switch to the Songs view. Either way, it's a short distance between you and the music you prefer.

FIGURE 6.16

Using Search to track down your favorite music.

Listening to FM Radio

Quite a few internal and external TV tuners also include FM radio tuners. If your computer has one, you can use WMC to listen to your FM favorite news or music programs. To find out if you have an FM tuner, select Radio from the music menu. If you don't have a tuner, you'll see a "no services found" message. However, if you do have a tuner, you'll see FM Radio listed as a source (Figure 6.17).

Click FM Radio, and the display switches to the current station view shown in Figure 6.18. Use this view to tune the radio, create presets, and set up preset stations.

note If you tune into a station and still hear static, make sure you have connected the FM antenna to the TV tuner card or external device. It is often supplied as a small wire that connects to a dedicated FM coaxial connector. If you are trying to pick up a distant or low-power station in a brick or concrete building, you might need a stronger antenna.

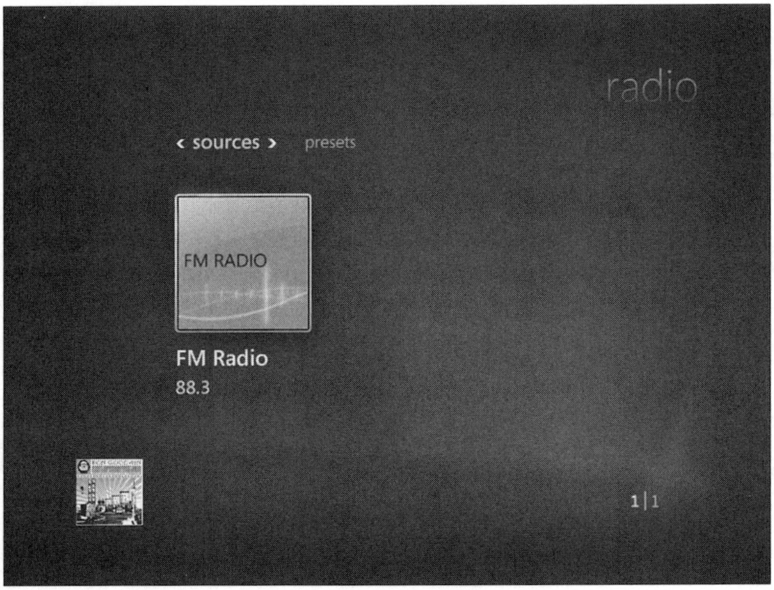

FIGURE 6.17

Preparing to play FM radio.

FIGURE 6.18

Playing FM radio.

Selecting Stations and Creating Presets

Click the Tune or Seek buttons below the station frequency display in Figure 6.18 to home in on your favorite rock, pop, folk, country, or talk stations. When you reach a station you want to store as a preset, click Save as Preset. The Edit Preset dialog shown in Figure 6.19 appears. Use your remote control's keypad or computer keyboard to enter a custom name for the preset. Click Save to save the preset, Cancel to stop the creation process, or Delete to remove a preset that's no longer a favorite.

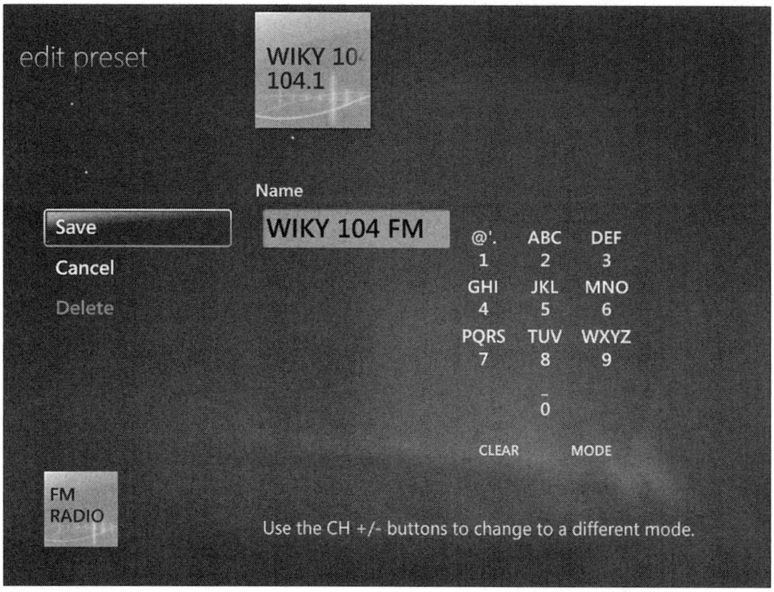

FIGURE 6.19

Creating a preset.

After you create presets, select the Presets option from the Radio menu, and you can select the preset for your preferred station (Figure 6.20).

Pausing and Recording FM Radio

Just as you can pause live TV to grab the phone or have a conversation, you can pause live radio broadcasts: Just click the Pause button on your remote control or the Pause icon on the mouse dialog in the lower-right corner of the screen. When you pause radio, a timeline appears at the bottom of your screen (Figure 6.21). The white bar indicates how long you've paused live playback. Press the Play button on your remote or the mouse dialog to start playing back the broadcast where you left off.

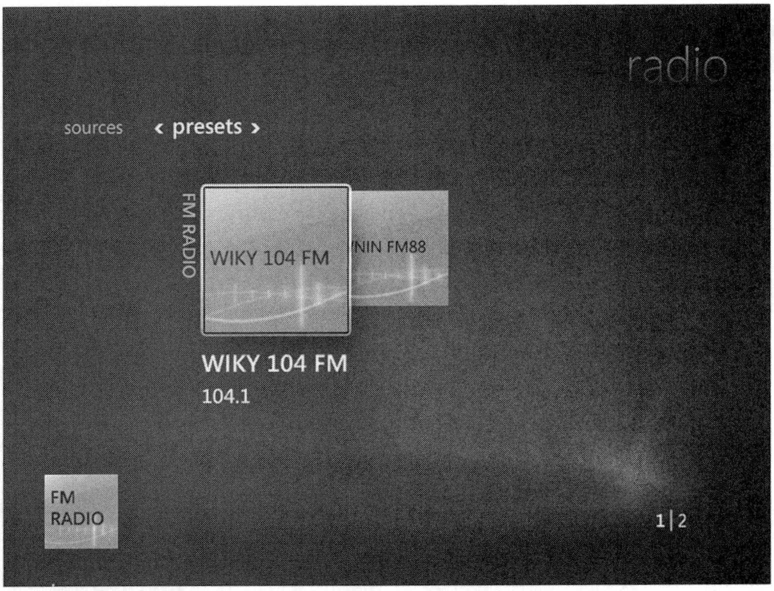

FIGURE 6.20
Selecting a preset station.

FIGURE 6.21
Pausing live radio.

While there's no built-in capability in WMC to record FM radio, you can purchase low-cost utilities to provide this capability. Some also support recording Internet radio.

→ For more information about recording FM radio, see Chapter 15, "Extending Media Center with Third-Party Apps."

Listening to Internet Radio

WMC features a variety of preselected Internet radio services, including NPR, Live365, and others. To view them, open More Music from the Music menu. Select the service you'd like to try, and it opens inside the WMC interface. Figure 6.22 illustrates some typical services.

Depending on the service you select, it might be necessary to install some ActiveX controls or other software to permit the service to run. Some services also open a web page for additional configuration.

> **note** Remember how I suggested you add a mouse and keyboard to your WMC PC configuration back in Chapter 2, "Equipping Your PC for Media Center"? These input devices make it easier to deal with third-party services you might want to add to your WMC system. You cannot click on a security warning using an IR remote—you *must* use a mouse (or a keyboard); similarly, you'll need a mouse (and maybe a keyboard as well) to navigate the web unless you install a WMC-optimized web browser. Learn more about WMC-optimized web browsers in Chapter 15.

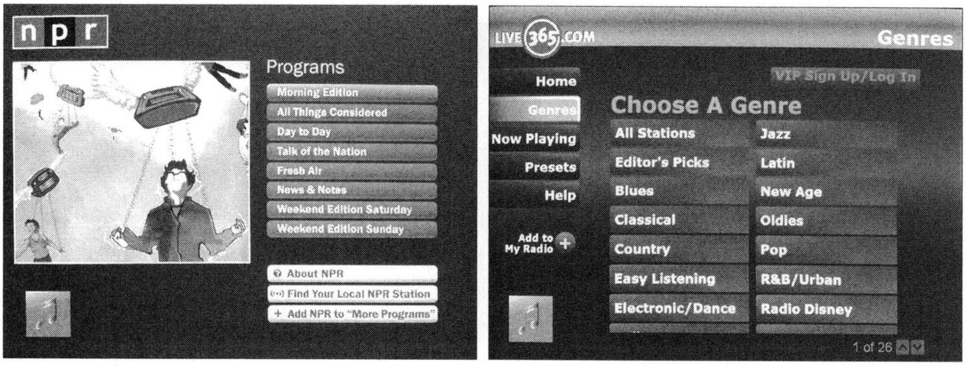

FIGURE 6.22

Some typical Internet radio services incorporated into WMC.

Synchronizing with Portable Players

So you've created some great playlists with Windows Media Center, but it's time to get off the couch and head off to work. No problem, just use WMC's ability to synchronize media with portable players.

To start the sync process for the first time, connect your portable media player to a USB port, go to WMC's Tasks menu, and select Sync. A Sync dialog similar to the one in Figure 6.23 appears. Select Yes to continue.

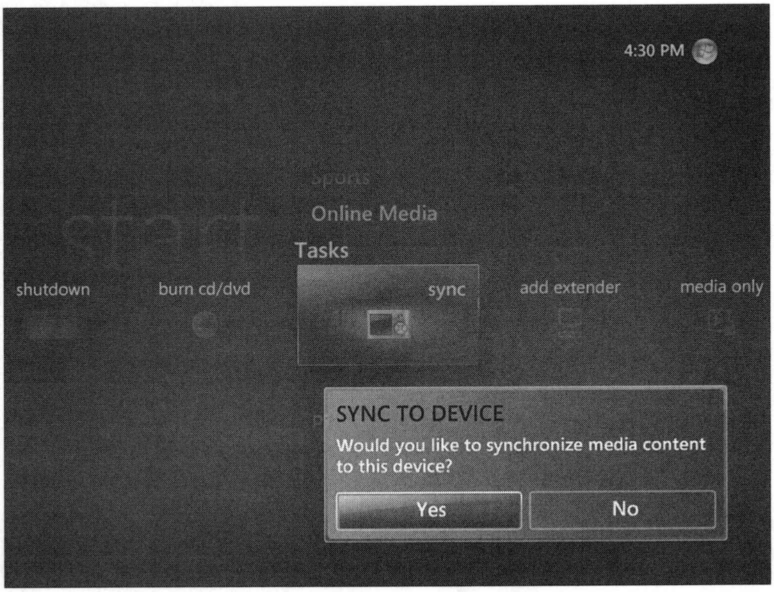

FIGURE 6.23
Preparing to sync to a portable device.

The system lists the auto playlist options appropriate for the device and the device's capacity. The playlists use the default order shown in Figure 6.24 from top to bottom. Click the up arrow for a particular option to move it higher in the list; click the down arrow to move it lower; click X to remove it from the list.

> **tip** Using Add More also shows you how many tunes will be transferred to your device (space permitting). As you point to each auto playlist in the Add More Music menu, the number of songs in that playlist is displayed.

If you have deleted an auto playlist you want to use, click Add More, select Music, choose the list(s) you want to use, and click Save. Click Start Sync to start the synchronization process.

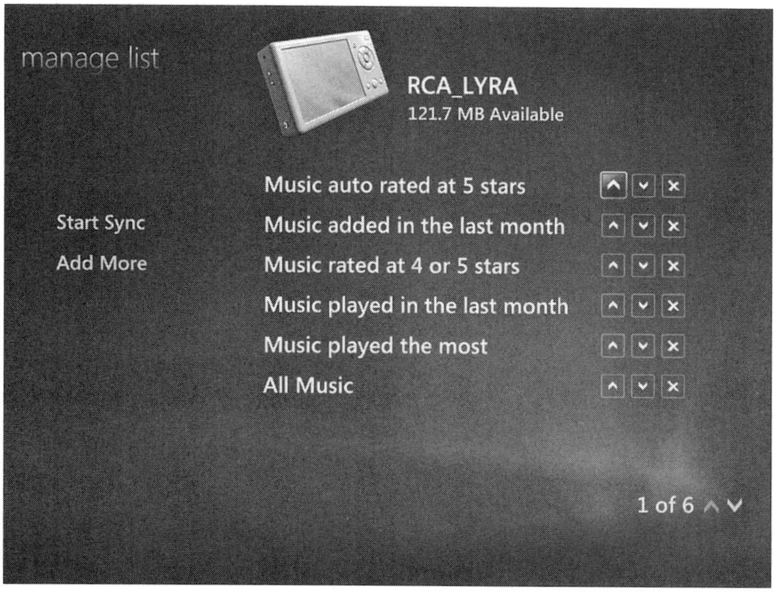

FIGURE 6.24

Auto playlists are used to sync the device.

The Sync Progress dialog appears (Figure 6.25 A) as the transfer process begins. Click OK to use WMC in other ways, Stop to stop the transfer process, or Edit Lists to add or remove auto playlists. At the end of the process, the Sync to Device dialog appears. Click View Results to see the percentage of each playlist synced to the device (Figure 6.25 B).

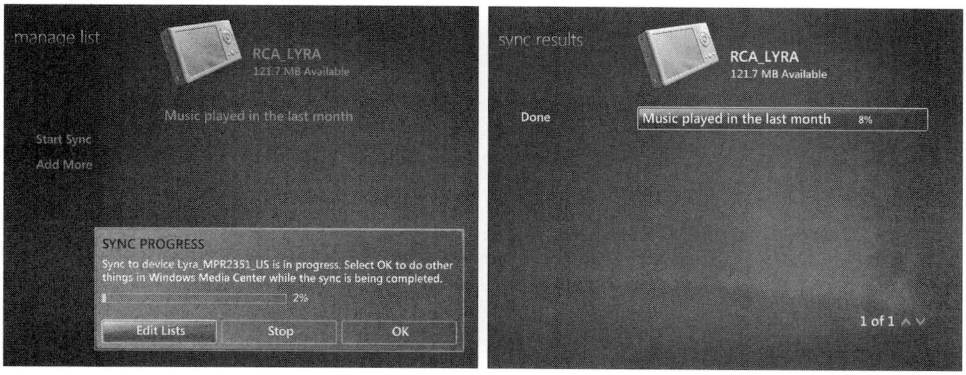

A. B.

FIGURE 6.25

Synchronizing music to a portable audio device.

CHAPTER

7

Importing and Viewing Photos

IN THIS CHAPTER

What's Cool about Photos with WMC

If you're tired of gathering the family around the computer screen to "Ooh," "Ahh," and (occasionally) "Grr" over your vacation photos, give your tiny PC display a rest, and take advantage of the big-screen picture viewing pizzazz available through Windows Media Center (WMC). Of course, WMC doesn't care whether you use it with your ordinary display or with the newest HDTV, but for viewing photos, whether for fun or play, it's hard to beat WMC's simple, yet powerful, interface.

To get started, select the Pictures + Videos menu (see Figure 7.1) and open the Picture Library.

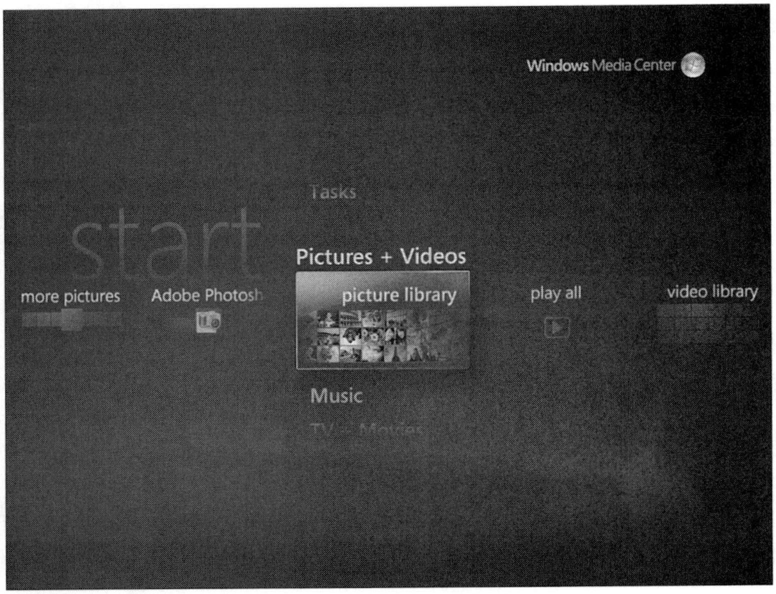

FIGURE 7.1

Windows Media Center uses the Pictures + Videos menu to display your photos.

Using the Picture Library

Picture Library displays photos stored in the current user's Pictures folder, subfolders of the current user's Pictures folder, and any other media folders monitored by WMC.

The Picture Library offers three ways to view photos:

- By folders (the default)
- By tags
- By date taken

Using the Folders View

In the default Folders view, pictures stored in the Pictures folder are displayed in thumbnail form. Move the selection box over a picture to enlarge it, to see the name of the photo, and the date last modified (see Figure 7.2).

7

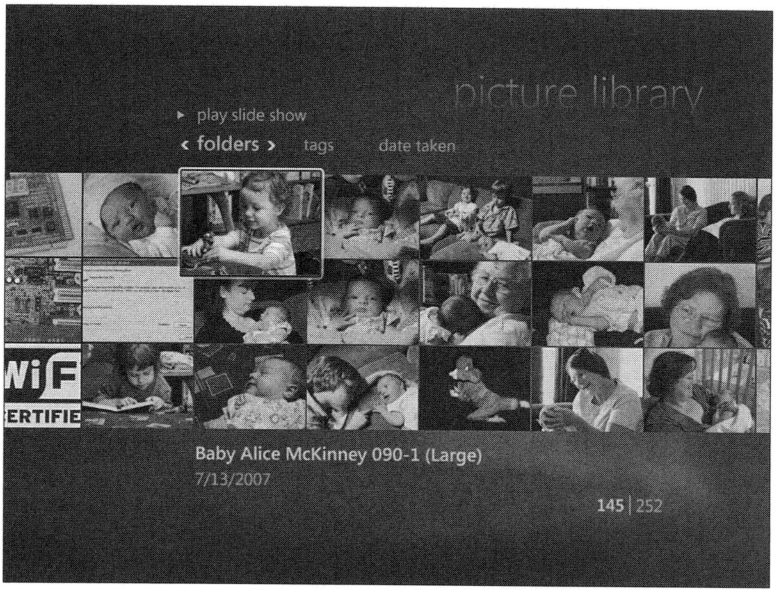

FIGURE 7.2

Viewing the name and date for a photo in Folders view.

What will you see if you use folders to organize your pictures? The Picture Library displays folders that contain pictures with thumbnails but lists the names only for folders that contain other folders (see Figure 7.3). In either case, the number of items in the selected folder and the date the folder was created are listed below the folder list.

To open a folder, click it, or use the Go button on your remote. After each photo's thumbnail is generated or retrieved, all of the photos in the folder are displayed (see Figure 7.4).

tip Use the Folders view to locate the photos you want to view or print (if you do not use tags to organize your photos or if you know that the photos you want to view or print are located in a particular folder).

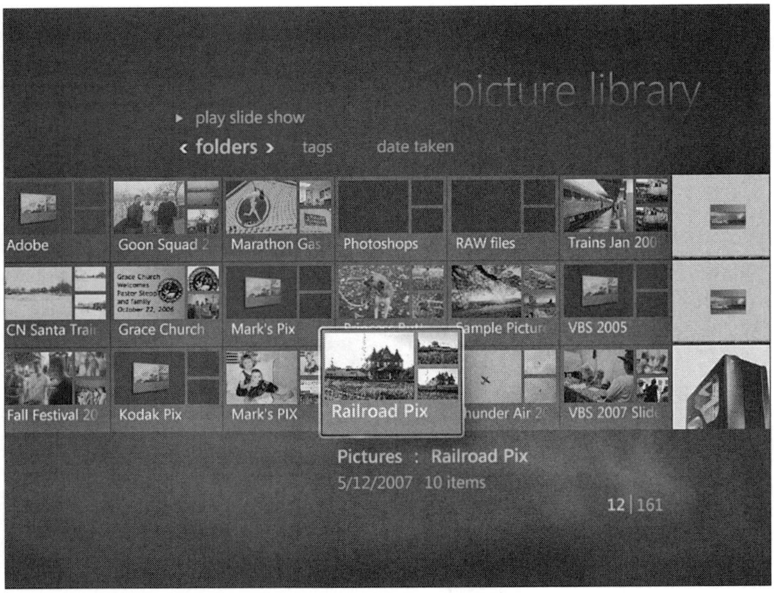

FIGURE 7.3

Displaying the number of photos in a folder in Folders view.

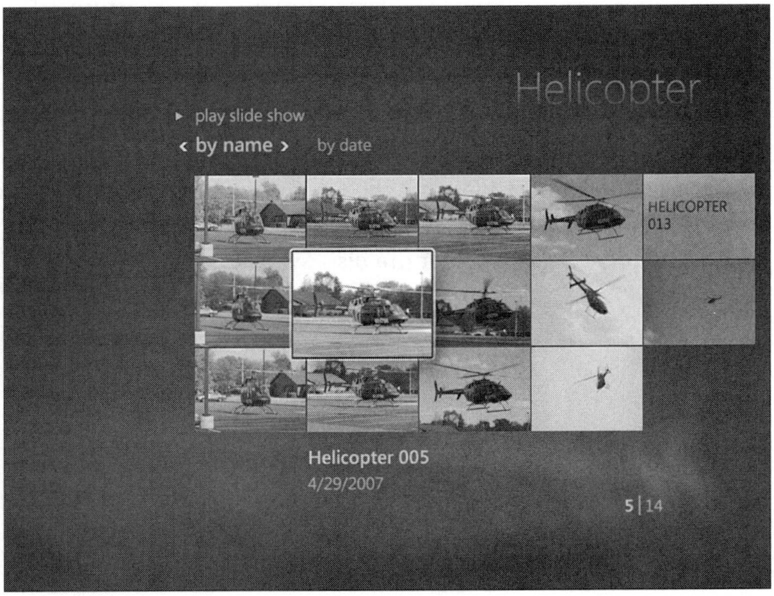

FIGURE 7.4

Selecting a photo in a folder. The folder name is listed in the top-right corner.

Using the Tags View

Windows Vista is the first version of Windows to integrate support for tags into its photo-handling applications. So, what is a *tag*? A tag is a word or phrase used to identify the subject of a photo or other significant information about a photo. You can use multiple tags to identify a single photo, and you can identify as many photos as you want with one or more tags. For example, let's say I want to view pictures of my granddaughter Vivian. I've taken a lot of pictures of her at different times and places. To name just a few...

- at her birth (December 2005)
- on vacation (summer 2006 and 2007)
- on visits with us (fall 2006 and spring 2007)
- at a wedding (summer 2006)

...and each event has its own folder or series of subfolders.

Finding all of my pictures of Vivian would be extraordinarily difficult if I had to scour each of the subfolders in my Pictures folder—and the odds are good that I might forget an occasion or two. But if I tag every picture she is in, I can find all of my pictures of her by opening the Picture Library in the Tags view (refer to Figure 7.5) and opening the Vivian thumbnail. Each tag is represented by a thumbnail of a photo that uses the tag listed.

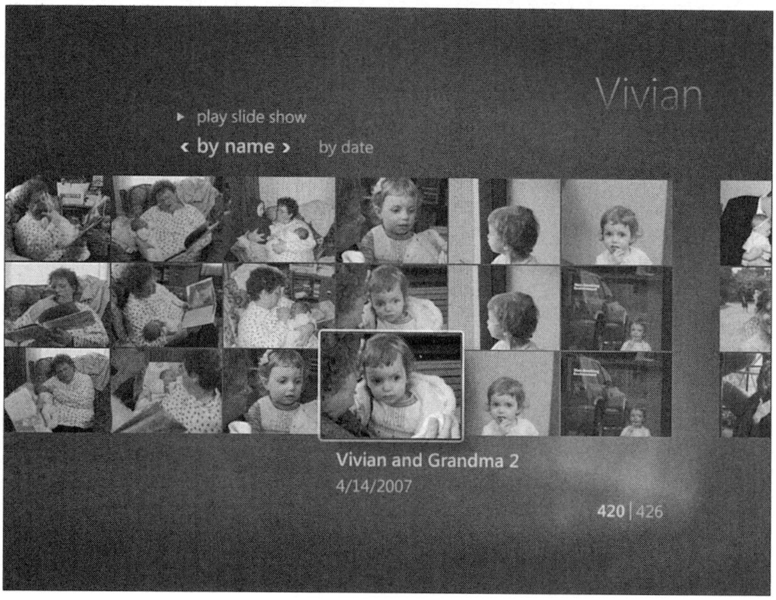

FIGURE 7.5
Using the Tags view to view pictures with a specified tag.

Tags are even more powerful when you understand that a picture can have multiple tags, making it easy to find the same picture in different ways. Figure 7.6 shows the same picture is listed in the "Cheryl" tag and the "Erin" tag.

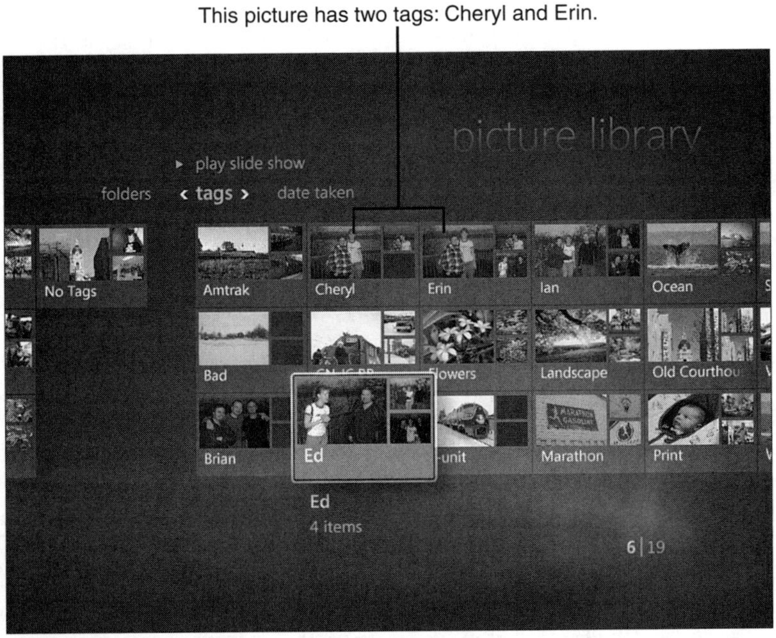

FIGURE 7.6

Assigning multiple tags to the same picture.

HOW TAGS ARE CREATED AND STORED

The tag or tags you assign to a picture are stored as metadata that is visible in WMC, Windows Photo Gallery, and other applications.

You can apply tags when you import pictures from your digital camera with Vista's Photo Import Wizard, from the properties sheet for a particular photo, or with Windows Vista's Photo Gallery.

When you import pictures with tags into a third-party photo editor's catalog or collection (such as Adobe Photoshop Elements' Organizer), the tags can also be imported. See the documentation for your photo editing program for details.

→ To learn more about using Photo Gallery and Windows Live Photo Gallery to improve your WMC experience, see "Windows Photo Gallery, Meet Windows *Live* Photo Gallery," Chapter 14, "Creating Photo and Video Content for Media Center," **p. 396**.

tip Make Photo Gallery and the Photo Import Wizard even better. Download Microsoft Windows Live Suite's Windows Live Photo Gallery. Get this application or the entire Windows Live Suite from http://get.live.com.

Using the Date Taken View

The Date Taken view displays images by the month and year they were originally photographed or scanned. Each month's icon contains thumbnails from the photos for that month, although it takes a few moments for WMC to display all thumbnails (see Figure 7.7).

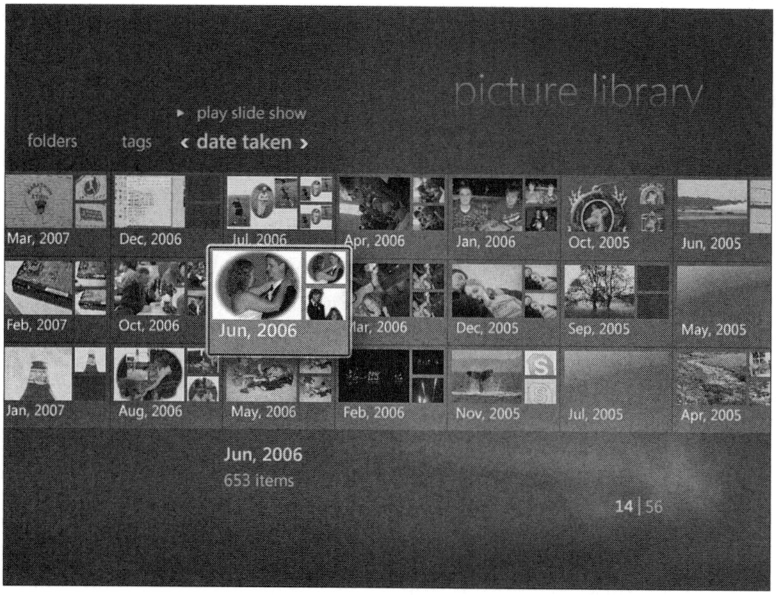

FIGURE 7.7

Displaying the number of photos taken in a specified month in Date Taken view.

The number of photos for the month is listed at bottom center. The numbers in the bottom-right corner refer to the timespan of the collection in months (in this example, 56), and the selected month (the 14th month).

"Date Taken"—What It Means and What It Doesn't

The Date Taken view is designed to help digital photographers track down their favorite photos by the dates they were taken. For this feature to work properly, your digital camera must have the proper date and time settings. And, no, I'm *not* referring to that annoying date and time stamp you find on some digital pictures.

Whenever you take a picture with a digital camera, the camera creates a file, just like a computer does (hence my favorite one-line explanation of what a digital camera is: "a computer that takes pictures"). Like any good computer, the digital camera stores the date and time (down to the second) when it saves the picture to flash memory, CD, DVD, or floppy disk. So how *does* the digital camera know what time it is?

When you first set up a digital camera, you're supposed to dutifully go through every setup menu listed on the display on the rear of the digital camera and adjust settings as desired. One of the most important settings is the date and time. If this information is not set correctly when you start using the camera, each and every photo you take will list the wrong date and time. I teach digital photography classes, and I find students in every opening class session whose cameras are set to the wrong date and time.

In addition to just forgetting to set this information, another common mistake digital camera newbies make is forgetting that digital cameras, like any other type of computer, use a 24-hour clock. Thus, if you're setting up a brand-new camera at 7:02PM, the correct time is *not* 7:02, but 19:02. (You add 12 hours to a time in AM to calculate the 24-hour clock equivalent.) What happens if you don't set the date and time information at all? The camera calculates the date and time from the manufacturer's internal default, which could be any date and time selected by the manufacturer. The one thing all digital cameras have in common as far as internal default date and time settings are concerned is that they're always in the past, and therefore, they're always *wrong*.

So, if you set the date and time when you first set up your camera, are you home free from now on? Unfortunately, no. Some digital cameras retain date and time information in a non-volatile RAM chip, so when you swap batteries, the date and time information is still correct. Others, unfortunately, revert to the manufacturer's default date until you reset the date and time manually. Some cameras display a warning on the rear LCD menu screen that the date and time need to be reset, but some might not. Not sure what your camera does? The next time you swap batteries, check the date and time menu after the battery swap to find out.

What if you edit a photo? Although the "date modified" information stored as part of the picture changes, the "date taken" information is not changed. A picture taken in May 2005, for example, will still be listed as being taken in

May 2005, even though you might have changed its tint, cropping, or other settings any number of times since.

If you also scan traditional photographs, negatives, or slides, keep in mind that the Date Taken for scanned photos is *not* the date the original film camera photographed the now-vanished world inside the photo, but is rather the date the photo was scanned to disk. Therefore, as far as Windows Vista is concerned, photographs of my family from 1963 were "taken" in August 2003—40 years later!

Viewing and Importing Pictures in WMC

Unless you installed Windows Vista on an existing PC containing photos, the odds are pretty good that you didn't have a lot of pictures on your system for WMC to play with. Naturally, WMC keeps an eye on your Pictures folder and any other local or network folder you told it to watch in Library Setup. Whether you import pictures from a digital camera on your system or a remote system being monitored by WMC, copy pictures from a CD, DVD, or USB drive, or download photos from an online photo service, as long as they're stored in a folder that WMC watches, they'll show up in WMC's Picture Library.

But you don't need to exit the comfortable WMC interface to import pictures. Just as you can import pictures from a digital camera, USB flash memory card, or another drive in Windows Vista, you can also import them from within WMC.

When you connect a digital camera, a USB flash memory drive, or a card reader containing photos, an AutoPlay dialog similar to the one in Figure 7.8 appears. The first time you connect the device, your options include

- Take no action (ignores the device)
- Import pictures and videos
- View pictures

> **tip** If your system is running third-party software for importing photos, such as the photo importers included with Adobe Photoshop Elements or other photo-editing programs, these programs might prevent WMC's AutoPlay menu from appearing.
>
> If the AutoPlay menu shown in Figure 7.8 does not appear after you connect a device, minimize WMC. If you want to use WMC to import your pictures, stop any other picture import program that's running and maximize WMC. WMC's AutoPlay menu should now appear.
>
> If you prefer to import photos with WMC, disable the other program's photo import feature; see the program help files or documentation for details.

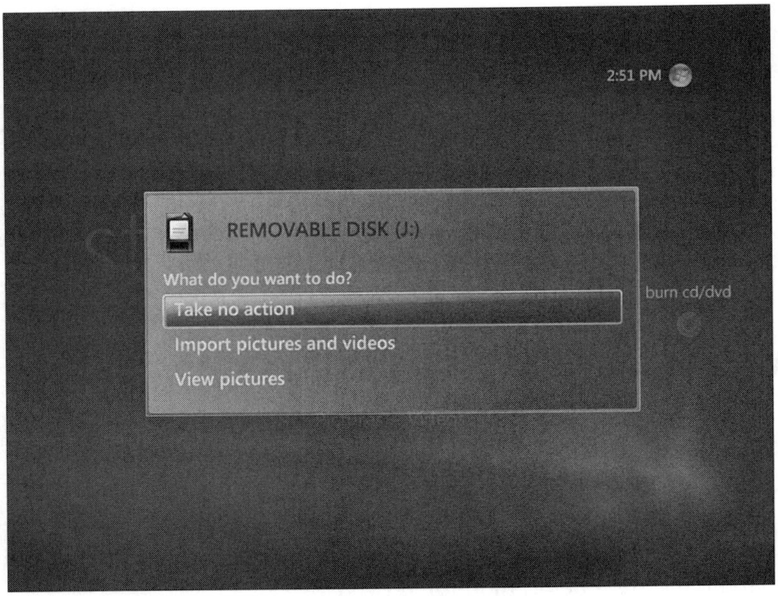

FIGURE 7.8
WMC displays an AutoPlay menu like this one when you connect a removable-media drive or a digital camera containing photos or videos to your computer.

A fourth option, Sync to a Device, appears if you connect the device to the computer after performing transfers from it.

Viewing Pictures Before Importing Them

Use the View Pictures option to see the pictures on your digital camera or media. Folders that contain at least one picture of a supported file type in the folder or subfolder display a photo icon, while folders without any supported picture types are blank (refer to Figure 7.9).

To navigate to a folder, highlight it, and click Go on your remote or click your mouse. To view a picture full-screen, highlight it, and click Go on your remote or click your mouse. The picture name and the date the picture was last modified appear in the upper-left corner of the screen.

Viewing your pictures before you import them is a useful way to determine if you want to import them to your system. If you don't want to wait for all of the photo thumbnails to appear, use the View Slide Show option to display your pictures in sequence.

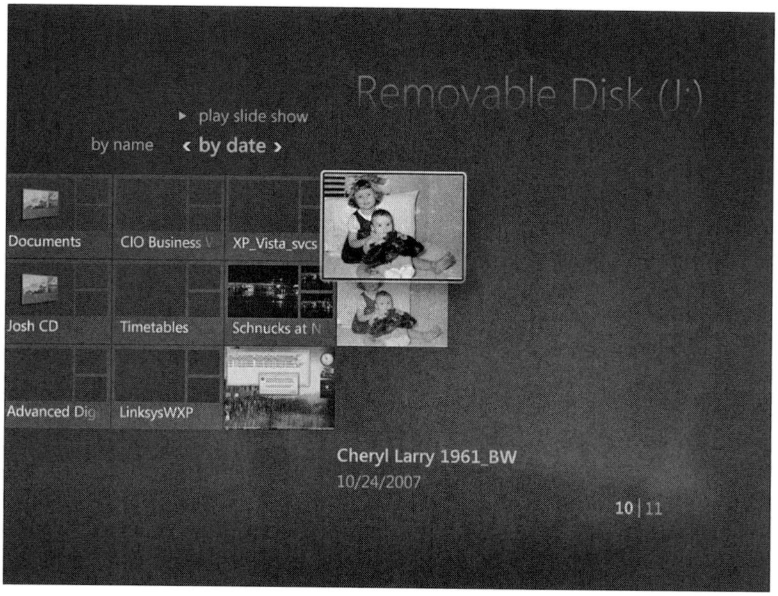

FIGURE 7.9

Viewing pictures files and other folders on a removable disk.

After you have finished viewing your photos, return to the main WMC (Start) menu.

To redisplay the AutoPlay menu, use the appropriate method:

- Turn off your digital camera, and turn it back on again.
- Remove the USB flash memory card from your card reader, and plug it in again.
- Disconnect the USB flash drive from the USB port, and plug it in again.

note If you prefer to use the Safely Remove Hardware dialog to stop your device before removing it, minimize WMC, select the dialog from the notification area, and follow the prompts. Safely Remove Hardware is not available within the WMC interface.

Importing Your Pictures and Videos

To import your digital photos from your digital camera, USB flash memory drive, or card reader, select Import Pictures and Videos from the AutoPlay menu. The Import dialog appears (see Figure 7.10).

7

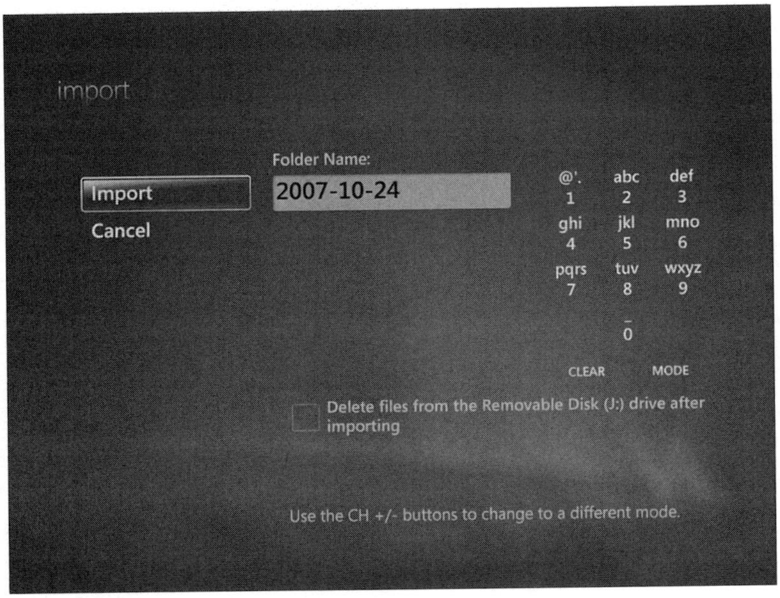

FIGURE 7.10

Creating a folder for imported pictures.

By default, the folder name used for imported pictures is the current date.

To rename the folder using a mouse or remote control:

1. Click Clear in the telephone-style pad to the right of the Folder Name: field to delete the default name.
2. Click the appropriate key until the letter or punctuation symbol you want appears. Click Mode to shift between lowercase letters, uppercase letters, and special punctuation (see Figure 7.11).
3. Repeat step 2 until you have spelled out the folder name.

caution Although WMC offers the option to delete your pictures after transfer (as most transfer utilities do), I don't recommend it if you are transferring pictures from a digital camera (either directly or via a card reader).

If you transfer only some of your photos, deleting only those photos creates gaps in the flash memory structure that will be reused by your camera for new photos. If you use an import utility that reads the media in order by physical location on the media, rather than by filename, some of your pictures will appear out of order during the review process (if you don't use WMC).

It's better to reform the card after transferring all pictures, using the camera's own format utility.

7

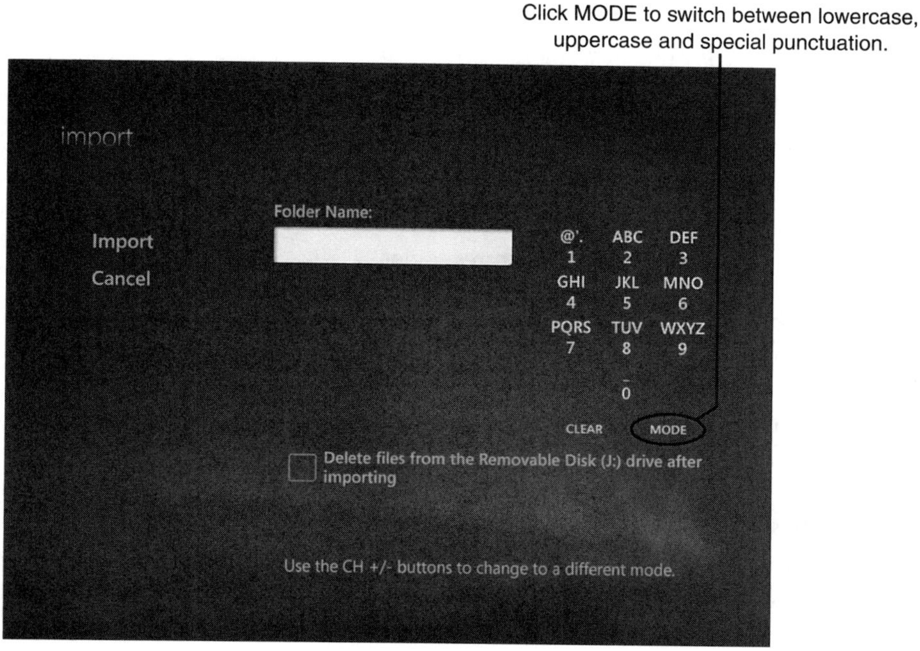

FIGURE 7.11

You can switch between lowercase, uppercase, and special punctuation by clicking MODE.

To perform the transfer:

1. If desired, rename the folder as described in the previous set of steps.
2. To delete your pictures from the removable drive or device after transfer, click the Delete Files checkbox.
3. To import the pictures, click Import. A progress dialog appears during the import process. Click OK to return to WMC while the import process continues. With today's large flash memory cards and high megapixel-rate cameras, it could take quite a while before the transfer is complete.

tip WMC's Import dialog imports all folders on your removable media drive, including those folders that do not include any photos. However, it does not import documents or other file types that are not supported by WMC.

When you transfer photos from your digital camera or from a digital camera's flash memory card, only the DCIM folder (the standard folder name for digital camera storage) and its subfolders are transferred.

To remove unwanted folders, minimize or close WMC and use Windows Explorer's Delete function.

4. At the end of the transfer, an Import complete pop-up message appears, listing the number of photos transferred. Click View Pictures to see your pictures or OK to return to WMC. The folder you created during the transfer process is located in your Pictures folder.

> **tip** How can you find out if a picture import is still in progress? Try to close WMC. If an import is still in progress, you will see an Import in Progress pop-up message telling you that the import will stop if you close WMC. Click Yes to close WMC (and stop the import process). Click No to keep WMC open (and the import process going).

After the import process is over, your removable-media drive or digital camera will show up in the Picture Library until you eject it or shut off your digital camera.

Viewing and Working with Individual Photos

The Folders, Tags, and Date Taken views make it easy to view groups of photos the way you prefer in WMC. From any view, click a picture to view it full-screen. The upper left corner notes the picture name and the date the picture was taken or scanned.

While you're viewing the picture full-screen, you can right-click it to bring up a menu of options (refer to Figure 7.12):

- **Picture Details:** Use this option to select options including rotation, printing, minor edits (touch ups), delete, or slide show. For details, see "Using the Picture Details Menu," **p. 204**, this chapter.
- **Rotate:** Rotates a picture to the correct orientation (handy for fans of vertical photos, which are often displayed sideways).
- **Burn:** Burns the picture to a CD or DVD.
- **Settings:** Opens the Settings menu. See "Using Settings to Reconfigure Your System," Chapter 3, "Setting Up Windows Media Center," **p. 77**, for details.

The options available when you right-click a picture from the Folders, Tags, or Date Taken views include the following (see Figure 7.13):

- **Picture Details:** For details, see "Using the Picture Details Menu," **p. 204**, this chapter.
- **Delete:** Dump bad photos immediately with this option.
- **View Small/View Large:** Toggles the thumbnail size (default is large). Use View Small to see more thumbnails at one time.

FIGURE 7.12

The right-click menu for a picture being viewed full-screen.

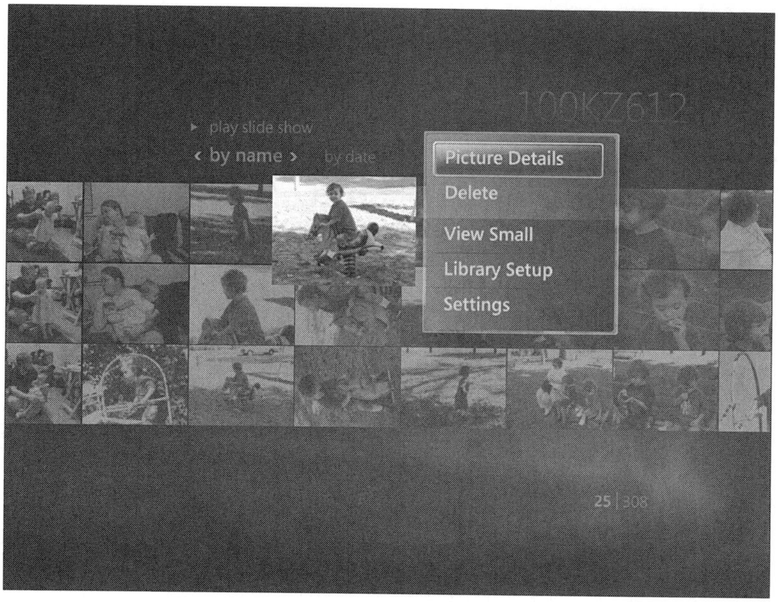

FIGURE 7.13

The right-click menu for a picture varies when it's viewed with other photos.

- **Library Setup:** Add folders to watch or stop watching folders on your local or remote systems. See "Optional Setup: Music, Pictures, and Videos Library," Chapter 3, **p. 74** for details.
- **Settings:** Opens the Settings menu.

Using the Picture Details Menu

The Picture Details menu (refer to Figure 7.14) provides a convenient one-stop shop for virtually all of the picture-handling features in WMC.

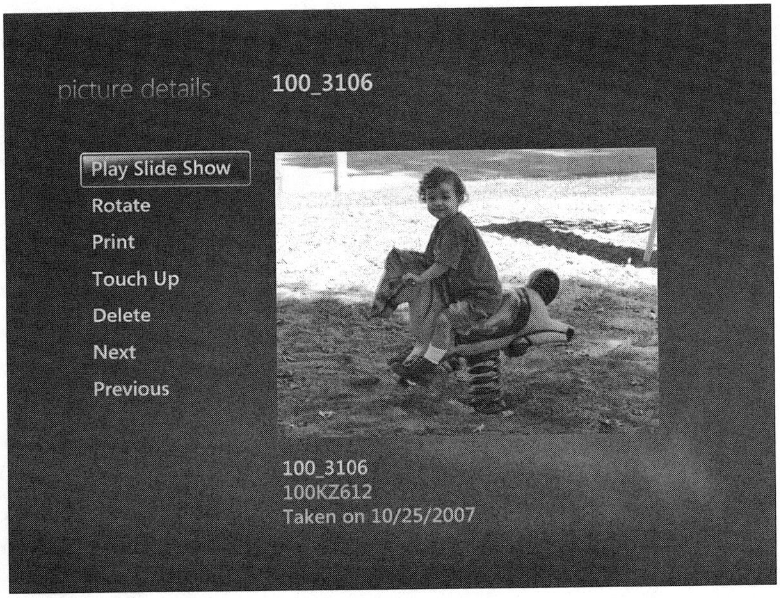

FIGURE 7.14
The Picture Details menu.

Want to see a slide show? Click Play Slide Show, and the show starts, using the current picture as picture number one. By default, WMC uses the "Ken Burns" pan and zoom effect.

> **tip** You can change how slide shows play with the Pictures portion of the Settings menu (see "Playing a Slide Show with WMC," this chapter, **p. 208**, for details).

Use the Rotate option to rotate a vertical photo to the correct orientation. See "Rotating Pictures," **p. 205**, this chapter, for details.

Use the Print button to send a full-page printout of the current picture to the default printer.

To crop, remove red eye, or adjust contrast, click Touch Up. See "Touching Up Photos," **p. 206**, this chapter, for details.

note To configure printer properties such as default printer, paper size, type, print quality, and so on, minimize WMC, and open Control Panel's Hardware and Sound category. Open the Printers link to view available printers.

To change the default printer, right-click the printer you want to use and select Set as Default Printer. To change other printer settings, right-click the default printer, and select Properties. After making changes, click Apply and then OK to save and use settings. Maximize WMC and print away!

Rotating Pictures

Although some digital cameras now rotate pictures automatically, many do not. If you shoot a lot of vertical pictures and your camera doesn't rotate the picture for you, you'll probably find the Rotate feature in WMC pretty handy.

To use it, select Rotate from the right-click menu or Picture Details menu. WMC rotates the picture 90 degrees to the right. If this is the wrong direction, repeat Rotate until the picture is properly oriented. The thumbnail view in WMC shows only the top portion of vertical pictures, but don't worry—your rotated pictures are intact.

note Although the Confirm Delete pop-up shown in Figure 7.16 suggests that the picture is gone from your system if you click Yes—it's not. Files you delete in WMC go to the Windows Vista Recycle Bin, and you can open Recycle Bin and restore them to their original locations.

Although holding down the shift key in a Windows Vista Explorer window when you press Delete does force the deletion of files, WMC's file "deletion" feature ignores the Shift key. If you are deleting files to free up space, instead of deleting them in WMC, count on going into the Recycle Bin to remove files or use Shift-Delete from the appropriate Explorer window to delete files and make the space available for new files.

Deleting Pictures

To delete a photo in WMC, select Delete from the right-click menu or Picture Details menu. Click Yes on the Confirm Delete pop-up box (see Figure 7.15), and the picture is deleted from your system.

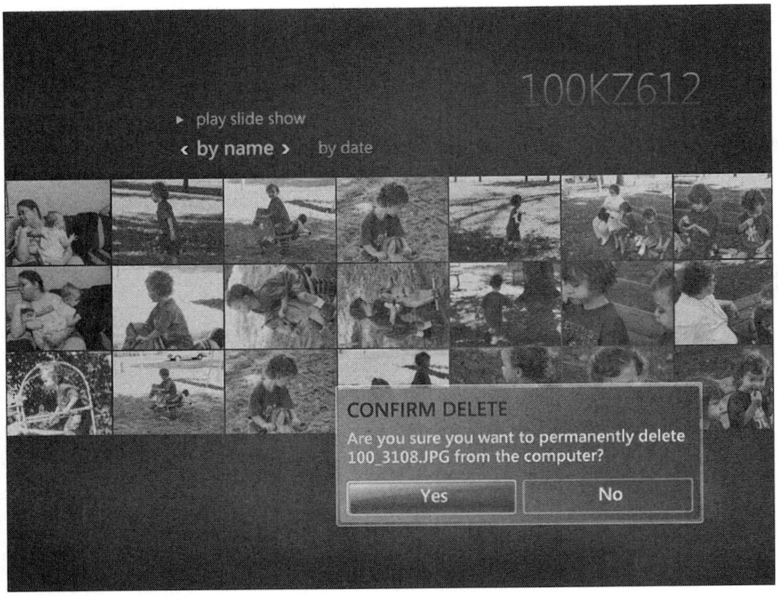

FIGURE 7.15
Confirming the deletion of a photo.

Touching Up Photos

WMC makes it easy to make simple edits to your photos. To edit a photo, select Touch Up from the Picture Details menu.

You can perform three types of edits from the Touch Up menu:

- Red Eye (removes red-eye)
- Contrast
- Crop

> **note** If you need to rotate a picture, you can perform this action from the Picture Details menu.

Select Contrast to adjust the contrast in your photo. This selection analyzes the photo and reduces or increases contrast automatically as needed to provide a full range of tones. Figure 7.16 compares a photo before and after the Contrast option is selected.

Select Crop to create a cropped version of your photo. Use the arrow controls to move the cropping frame around the picture. Use the magnifying glass controls to adjust the size of the cropping frame. The crop uses the same proportions (aspect ratio) as the original photo. To create a vertical crop, click the rotate frame button at the right of the cropping tools. Figure 7.17 compares horizontal and vertical cropping.

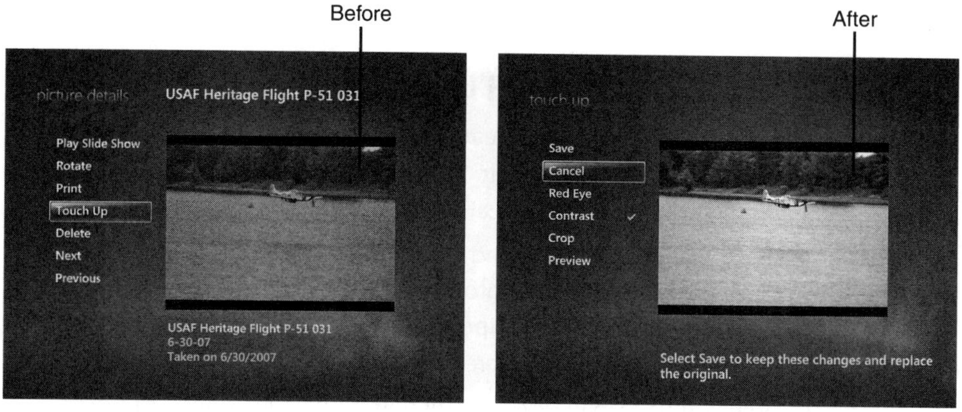

FIGURE 7.16

Changing the contrast of a picture using the Touch Up menu.

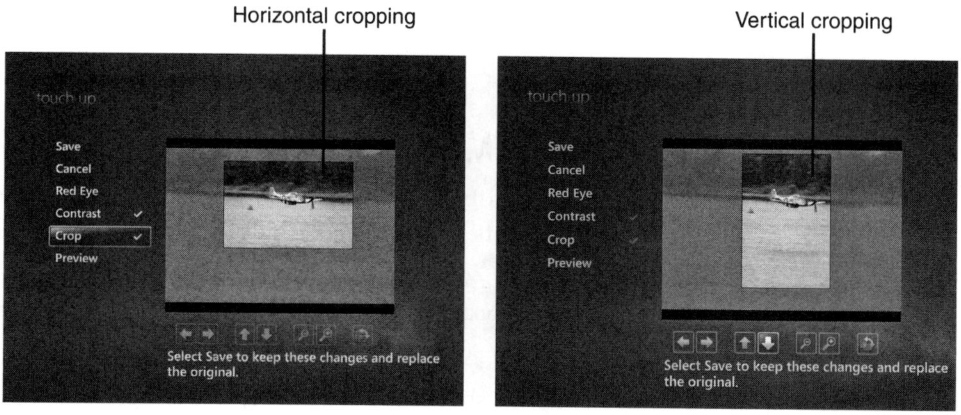

FIGURE 7.17

Comparing horizontal and vertical cropping in the Touch Up menu.

To preview the changes you've made in full screen, click Preview. Click Back or press Esc (Escape) on your keyboard to exit the Preview mode. To save changes (replaces the original photo), click Save. An Apply Changes dialog appears. To continue the save process, click Yes. To cancel, click No.

> **note** Forget what changes you've made to your picture? Checkmarks appear next to Red Eye, Contrast, and Crop as you use those features. Refer to Figure 7.16.

To cancel changes and return to the Picture Library, click Cancel.

BEFORE YOU TOUCH UP, PREPARE

If you're smart, you should treat each original digital photo like a "digital negative" and never alter it. So how do you "get smart" and still take advantage of the touch up features in WMC? In a word—backup.

Make sure you use the File and Folder Backup feature in Windows Vista to make backups of your photos before you edit them. A great time to make backups is after you import pictures from your digital camera or another computer—and *before* you make changes to those pictures.

If you use Touch Up in WMC or edit your photos in Windows Photo Gallery, Windows Live Photo Gallery, or a third-party program, you can retrieve the original from backup by viewing the photo's properties in Pictures Explorer and going to the Previous Versions tab. Previous Versions works only if you backup—so make sure you do!

Playing a Slide Show with WMC

You can display a slide show with WMC's built-in slide show player or, if you have Adobe Photoshop Elements 5 or greater, with its slide show player.

→ To learn more about using Adobe Photoshop Elements features within WMC, see "Supercharging Your Picture Viewing Capabilities with Photoshop Elements for Windows Media Center," this chapter, **p. 210**.

To play your pictures as a slide show within WMC, open your preferred view and navigate to the pictures you want to play. Click Play Slide Show, and the pictures in the current category begin playing in a full-screen slide show. By default, WMC uses the animated pan and zoom "Ken Burns" effect during the slide show.

To change how the slide show feature works, right-click a picture or any part of the screen, and select Settings. Open the Pictures submenu (see Figure 7.18) and make changes as desired (use the up and down arrows at the bottom right of your screen to scroll through all available choices—not all choices are shown in Figure 7.18):

- To play back pictures in random order, click the Show Pictures in Random Order checkbox.
- To display only the picture and not its filename, clear the Show Caption checkbox.
- If you use the Folder view and do not want to play pictures in a subfolder of the current folder, clear the Show Pictures in Subfolders checkbox.
- If you play music during the slide show (see "Music with Your Photos," **p. 210** for details), use the radio buttons to select how you want the song to be displayed: At Beginning and End of Song (default), Always, or Never.
- Select the transition type desired: Animated (default), Cross-fade, or None.
- Select the transition time desired: the default is 4 seconds, but options range from 2 seconds to 60 seconds.
- Select the background color: black (default), 50% gray, or white.

Click Save to save changes.

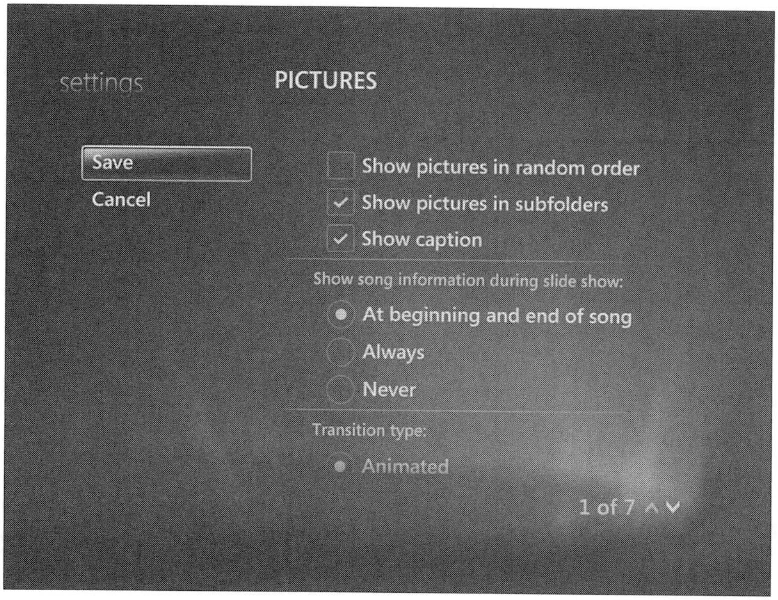

FIGURE 7.18

Use the Settings menu's Pictures submenu to configure slide show playback.

MUSIC WITH YOUR PHOTOS

If you prefer your WMC slide shows with a side of music, it's easy to do. Simply open the Music Library, place each song you want to accompany your photos into a queue, and play the music before you start your slide show.

If you want to precisely synchronize the music (or other audio) to specific slides, use Windows Movie Maker to build your slide show as discussed in Chapter 14.

If you use Adobe Photoshop Elements 5.0 or later, you can create slide shows that include additional transitions, a soundtrack, and variable slide length that can be viewed using WMC. See "Supercharging Your Picture Viewing Capabilities with Photoshop Elements for Windows Media Center" for details.

Supercharging Your Picture Viewing Capabilities with Photoshop Elements for Windows Media Center

Adobe Photoshop Elements provides photo-editing features that go way beyond those included in Windows Vista—or any other operating system, for that matter. If you save picture or image files in formats recognized by WMC, such as JPEG or TIFF, you can view your photo creations using the standard Picture Library.

However, if you use Photoshop Elements' powerful layer features, which enable you to place editable text in a photo, combine elements from multiple images together, adjust color or exposure in adjustment layers, and more, you will probably have a lot of images stored in Adobe's PSD file format, which supports layers. Unfortunately, PSD files are not supported by WMC or Windows Vista's Photo Gallery.

What to do? If you use Photoshop Elements 5 or above, you can view PSD files in WMC (as well as other photo file types) by selecting Adobe Photoshop from the Pictures + Videos menu (see Figure 7.19). This opens the Adobe Photoshop Elements for Windows Media Center (PSE-WMC), also known as Photoshop Elements for the Digital Home.

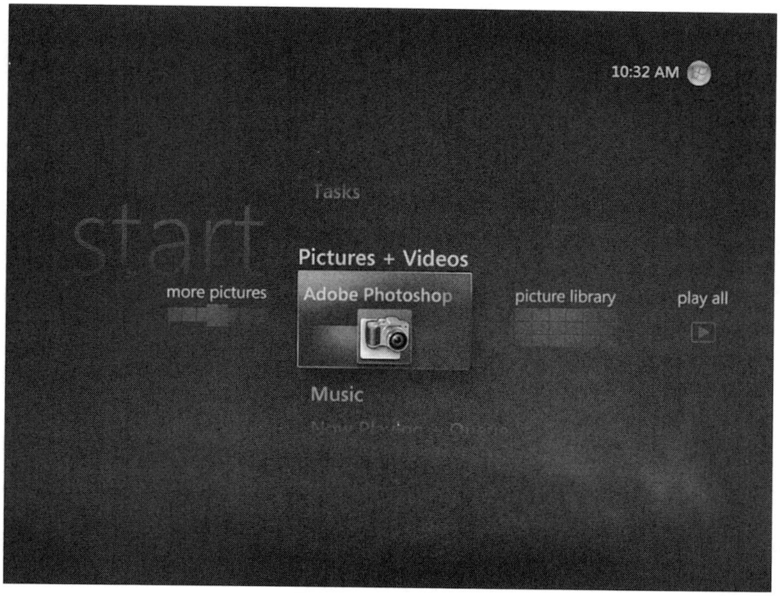

FIGURE 7.19

Use Adobe Photoshop to access content created by Adobe Photoshop Elements within WMC.

Before you start PSE-WMC, you need to use the Photoshop Elements Organizer to create a catalog of your digital photos. See Photoshop Elements' documentation for details.

When you open PSE-WMC, you can choose from the following options (shown in Figure 7.20):

- View Photos
- Slide Shows
- Settings

> **note** If you use Photoshop Elements 5 and you do not see Adobe Photoshop show up as an option in Pictures + Videos, download and install the Adobe Photoshop Elements 5.0.2 update from the Support page at Adobe.com: http://www.adobe.com/downloads/updates/. This update supports Windows Vista (32-bit versions). Photoshop Elements 6.0 has native support for Windows Vista.

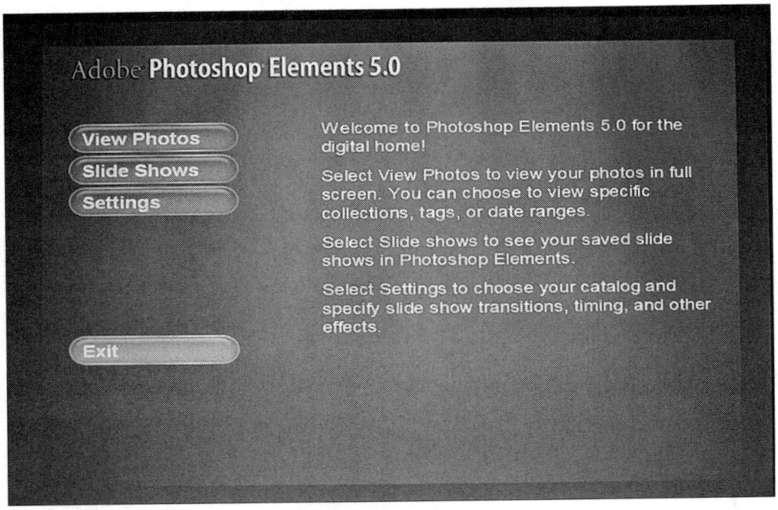

FIGURE 7.20

The main menu of the Adobe Photoshop for the Digital Home component running inside WMC.

Viewing Photos with Photoshop Elements for Windows Media Center

Select View Photos to view photos in full screen. You can choose photos by album, keyword tag, or date ranges.

> **note** When you create or recreate a Photoshop Elements catalog, it can import the tags you create with Windows Photo Gallery or Windows Live Photo Gallery. Use this option to view your photos by tag with either WMC's standard Picture Library or with PSE-WMC.

The View Photos menu defaults to displaying all photos in order from newest to oldest (see Figure 7.21). Use the up/down arrows at lower right to navigate through your picture collection.

If you have hundreds (or thousands!) of digital photos, slogging through them twelve at a time is going to get old after a while. So use the other options to zero in on your favorite pix:

- **By Date displays a calendar that shows the date(s) you took pictures or created other types of images.** Use the single forward and back arrows to navigate a month at a time or the double arrows to navigate 12 months at a time. Highlight the date, and click it to view the photos and images created on that date. To select a range of dates, click Date Range, select the first date, then select the last date, and click any date. Only the photos or images created on that date (or in that date range) appear (see Figure 7.22).

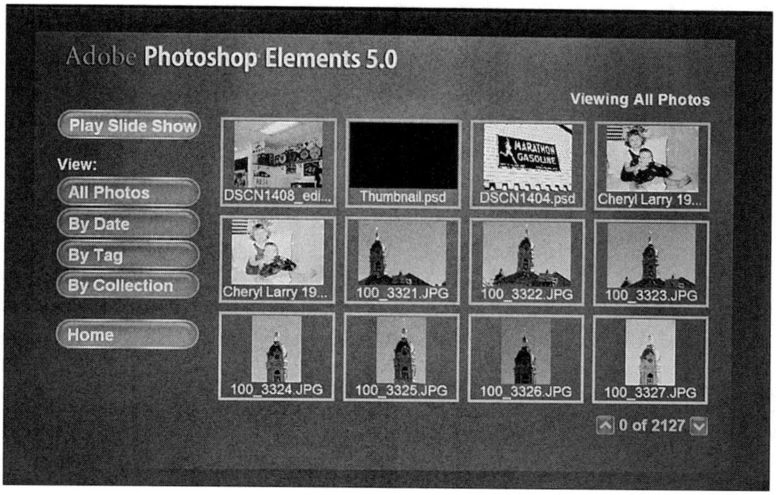

FIGURE 7.21
Viewing All Photos.

- **By Tag views photos by assigned tags.** Tags assigned in Photoshop Elements' Organizer module are shown first. If you tagged photos using Windows tools and then imported the tags when you created your Photoshop Elements catalog, click the Imported Keywords button to see those tags (see Figure 7.23). To display only pictures matching a tag or imported keyword, click the appropriate button. You can select multiple tags; the tags selected are shown in the right column. To reset the tag selection, click Clear Tags.

> **tip** Collections/albums and tags are complementary, not competing, methods for organizing photos. Use Collections or Albums to create a photo collection with a common theme, such as an event or a vacation. Use Tags to identify specific people or places in each photograph.

- **Choose by Collection or Album to view photos organized into collections (Photoshop Elements 5) or albums (Photoshop Elements 6) in Adobe Photoshop Elements' Organizer module (refer to Figure 7.24).** If you have no collections or albums in the current catalog, you will see an error message.

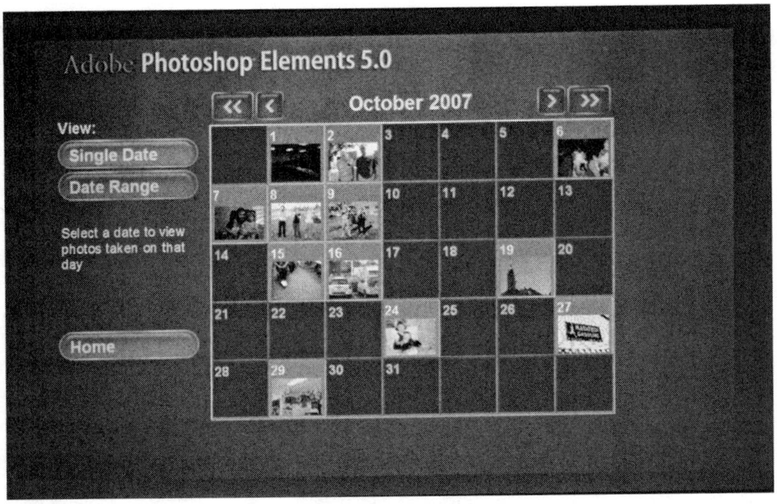

FIGURE 7.22

Selecting photos to view by date.

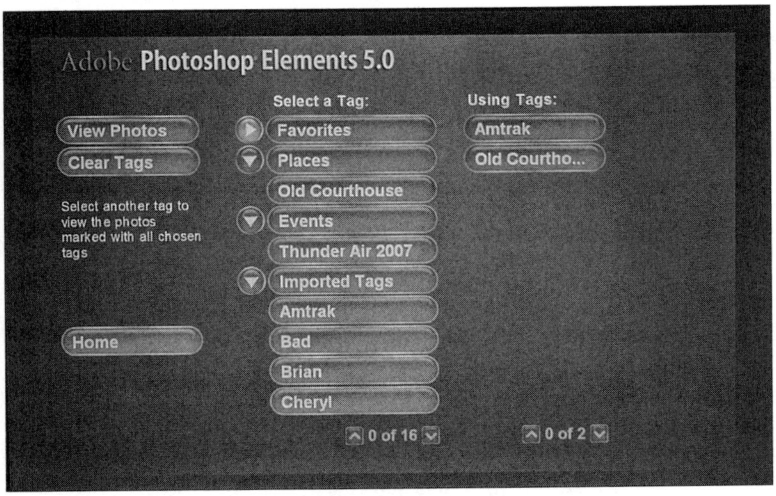

FIGURE 7.23

Selecting photos to view by tag or imported keyword (tags created outside of Adobe Photoshop Elements).

7

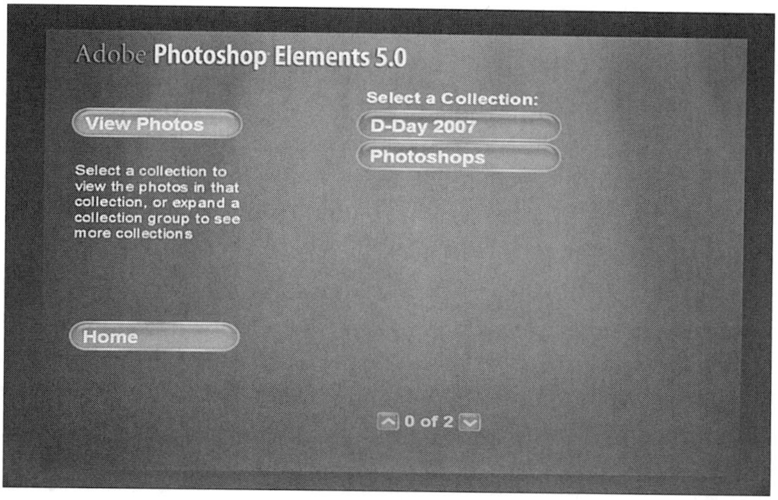

FIGURE 7.24

Selecting photos to view by collection in Photoshop Elements 5 (collections are known as albums in Photoshop Elements 6).

Note that you can jump from one view to another from any submenu. And as you view photos by album/collection, date, tag, or imported keyword, the Recently Viewed sidebar on the main menu changes show the latest items displayed. Scroll down to see more recently viewed items.

VIEWING CAMERA RAW FILES IN WMC

By default, WMC (and PSE-WMC) can display digital camera pictures stored in the popular JPEG (.JPG) file format. However, WMC does not support viewing camera RAW files. RAW files are favored by serious photographers because they provide higher quality and more powerful editing options. Even if you install the appropriate RAW codec to enable RAW files to be viewed in Windows Photo Gallery and Windows Live Photo Gallery, WMC displays folders containing RAW files as containing "no pictures."

PSE-WMC is not designed to display RAW files either; it displays a black rectangle instead of the photo. However, after you install the appropriate RAW codec to enable Windows Photo Gallery and Windows Live Photo Gallery to view RAW files, you can launch either of these programs from within WMC. See "Solving Codec Problems," in Chapter 16, **p. 495**, for more information.

Viewing Slide Shows Created in Photoshop Elements

If you have created slide shows in Photoshop Elements, view them in WMC by selecting Slide Shows from the opening menu of PSE-WMC. The Slide Shows menu displays the slide shows in the current collection. To select slide shows by date, click the By Date button and then select the slide show you want to view from the calendar.

When you see the slide show you want to play, click its thumbnail. The slide show starts automatically and plays in a window (see Figure 7.25); double-click the window to see the slide show play in full-screen mode. Slide shows created in Photoshop Elements' Organizer might include features such as pan and zoom, titles, and an audio track.

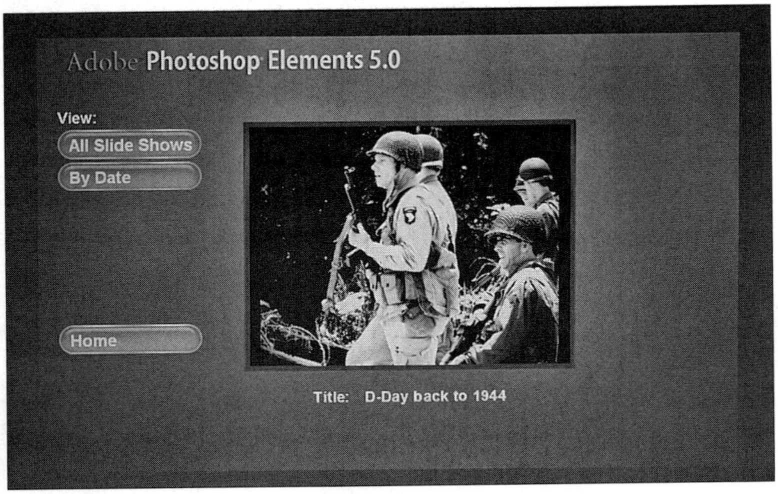

FIGURE 7.25

Playing a slide show created in Adobe Photoshop Elements in PSE-WMC.

The standard WMC control panel can be used to pause, continue, or stop playback in either windowed or full-screen playback; move your mouse, or click your remote to display the control panel.

To change how the slide show plays, edit the slide show in Photoshop Elements' Organizer.

note PSE-WMC might not list some of the slide shows you create in Photoshop Elements' Organizer.

To view a slide show that is not listed in PSE-WMC, open the slide show in Organizer and output it to a .WMV (Windows Media Video) file. To play the slide show, use WMC's Video Library.

Displaying Other Pictures as a Slide Show

From the View Photos menus, you can play any pictures you select using the built-in slide show features in PSE-WMC. To play all pictures, click Play Slide Show. To play only selected pictures, open the appropriate view (by Collection, by Date, or by Tag), select the pictures you want to view, and click Play Slide Show.

To adjust how PSE-WMC plays your pictures as a slide show, open the Settings menu.

Tweaking Photoshop Elements for Windows Media Center

Even before you view your first photo with PSE-WMC, you may prefer to open the Settings menu. The Settings menu has two submenus:

- **General:** Changes picture display options. This menu opens by default when you open the Settings menu (see Figure 7.26).
- **Slide Shows:** Changes display options when playing photos back as a slide show.

> **note** If you see blank thumbnails for some of your photos, this could be caused by several issues:
>
> - **The picture might no longer be in the location stored in the current catalog.** Use Adobe Photoshop Elements' Organizer to reconnect missing pictures to their current locations or to remove them from the catalog. Removing pictures from the catalog does not delete the pictures unless you specifically select the deletion option when prompted.
> - **The picture might be in a format not supported by PSE-WMC.** Install the latest updates to Photoshop Elements and keep in mind that some .TIFF formats (as well as RAW and some other less common formats) are not supported by PSE-WMC. Some complex .PSD images might not display properly in PSE-WMC.
> - **You might need to install an update or hotfix for Windows Vista.** Contact Adobe Technical Support for specific suggestions.

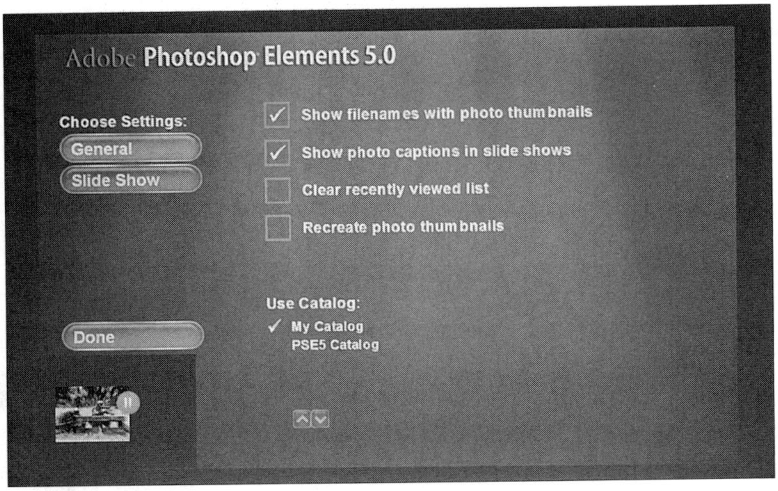

FIGURE 7.26

Configuring PSE-WMC's General settings.

The General menu has four options (see Figure 7.26), all of which are disabled by default:

> **note** The Slide Shows option has no effect on slide shows you created in Photoshop Elements' Organizer.

- **Show filenames with photo thumbnails.** Enable this option if you want to see the filename as you review your pictures in PSE-WMC. I use this option to help me determine which picture of a set of similar photos is the one I prefer.
- **Show photo captions in slide shows.** You can add captions to your pictures using Photoshop Elements' Organizer. Enable this option to make captions visible while a slide show plays.
- **Clear recently viewed list.** By default, PSE-WMC displays the pictures and slide shows you most recently viewed on its opening menu. Enable this option to clear the list. Clearing the list redisplays the opening message you saw the first time you ran PSE-WMC.
- **Recreate photo thumbnails.** Enable this option if some of your photos don't display properly in PSE-WMC.

By default, PSE-WMC uses My Catalog. However, if you have additional catalogs, use the up and down arrows to scroll through them to select the catalog you want to use. If you have multiple catalogs, some pictures or slide shows might be located in different catalogs.

The Slide Show menu (refer to Figure 7.27) has the following options:

- **Slide duration:** The default is 4 seconds, but other options range from 3 seconds to 15 seconds, or manual.
- **Transition speed:** The default is Medium, but Slow and Fast are also available.
- **Transition type:** You can choose from 18 transitions (including None). See Figure 7.28 for examples of the checkerboard, blinds, and wheel transitions.

caution If you are performing maintenance operations on a catalog in Adobe Photoshop Elements' Organizer while you are running WMC, such as adding photos or reconnecting pictures, you might not see any catalog listed, and you won't be able to view any pictures with PSE-WMC. Do not run PSE-WMC while you perform maintenance operations on your Photoshop Elements catalogs.

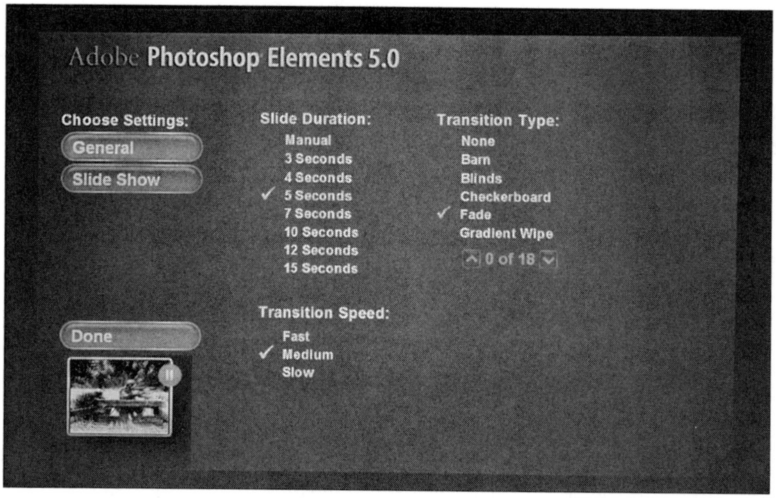

FIGURE 7.27

Configuring slide show settings for slide duration, transition speed, and transition type.

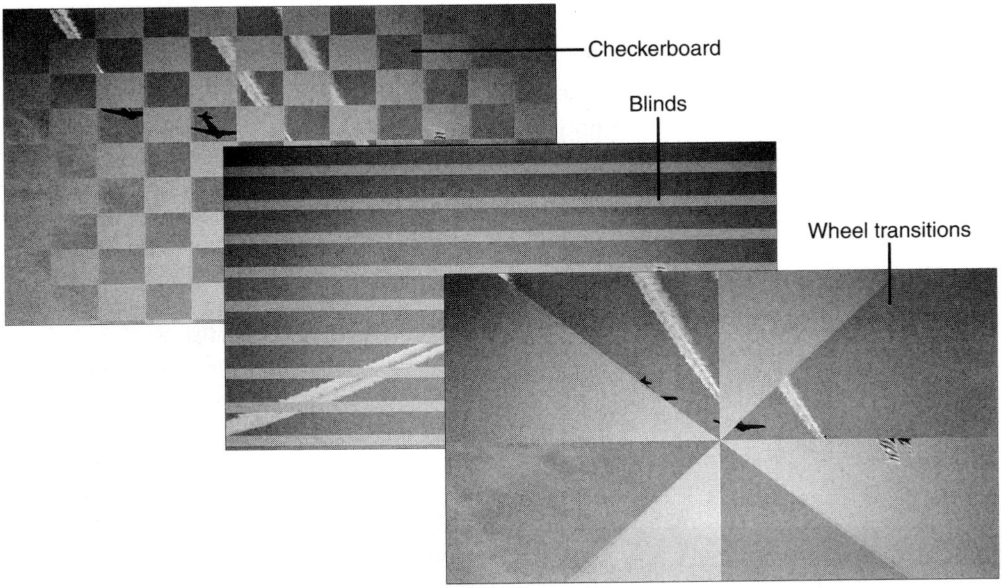

FIGURE 7.28
Checkerboard, blinds, and wheel transitions.

Using More Pictures

The More Pictures menu in Pictures + Videos provides a gateway for third-party digital photo service providers to offer you their wares. The contents of this menu change over time as the latest offers are brought to your WMC desktop via automatic updates.

To try a service offered by More Pictures, open the menu, and click the link. Follow the instructions to set up the service. You might need to install one or more ActiveX controls.

PART

III

Beyond the Basics of Windows Media Center

CHAPTER

8

Enjoying Sports with Windows Media Center

Windows Media Center (WMC) provides great ways to stay on top of your favorite sports. No matter what the season, the Sports menu in WMC (Figure 8.1) helps you keep track of games, scores, highlights, and news of your favorite pastimes—provided your WMC PC is connected to cable TV.

If you don't connect your WMC PC to a TV tuner, many of the Sports menu features won't function, so even if you prefer to do your primary TV watching on a standard or HD television, you'll want to pick up a TV tuner for your WMC rig.

→ For TV tuner selection tips, see Chapter 2, "Equipping Your PC for Media Center." For TV setup tips, see Chapter 3, "Setting Up Windows Media Center."

IN THIS CHAPTER

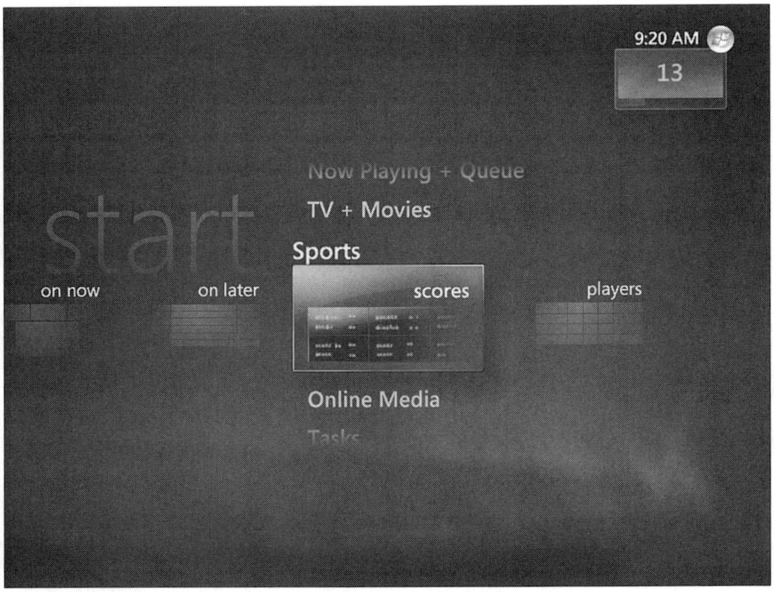

FIGURE 8.1
The Sports menu.

The On Now Menu

If you're a diehard sports fan, your first question is probably, "What's on now?" Click On Now to find out.

The On Now menu (Figure 8.2) gives you quick access to sports content brought to you via your cable or broadcast TV connection to your PC. The scrolling menu across the top of the screen shows you all of the sports TV currently available to you.

> **note** Not satisfied with the sports broadcasts available? Contact your cable TV provider for an upgrade to a better sports package.

The programs available in the On Now menu change throughout the day (and night) as sports-related programs come and go from networks such as the ESPN family, the Fox Sports family, the Big 10 network, and others, depending upon your local broadcast TV schedule or cable provider's offerings. To scroll through the list, hover your mouse over either the left edge or the right edge of the program list.

FIGURE 8.2
Viewing currently available TV sports programs from the On Now menu.

Remember, the On Now menu relies on selecting the correct cable TV program guide and broadcast TV channel configuration.

➔ For more information about configuring your TV channels, see Chapters 3 and 4.

Viewing Sports Programs and News

To view a program, click it. The program plays in the SportsLounge window (more about SportsLounge later in this chapter). To accommodate channel-surfing sports fans, the scrolling TV program window stays visible above the playback window (see Figure 8.3).

The Fox Sports news ticker appearing below the playback window provides instant access to sports stories. Click the headline to display the story in the main window; WMC keeps your TV program playing in the picture-in-picture thumbnail at the lower left (Figure 8.4).

➔ For more information about viewing sports stories in WMC, see "Hanging Out in the SportsLounge," **p. 230**, in this chapter.

8

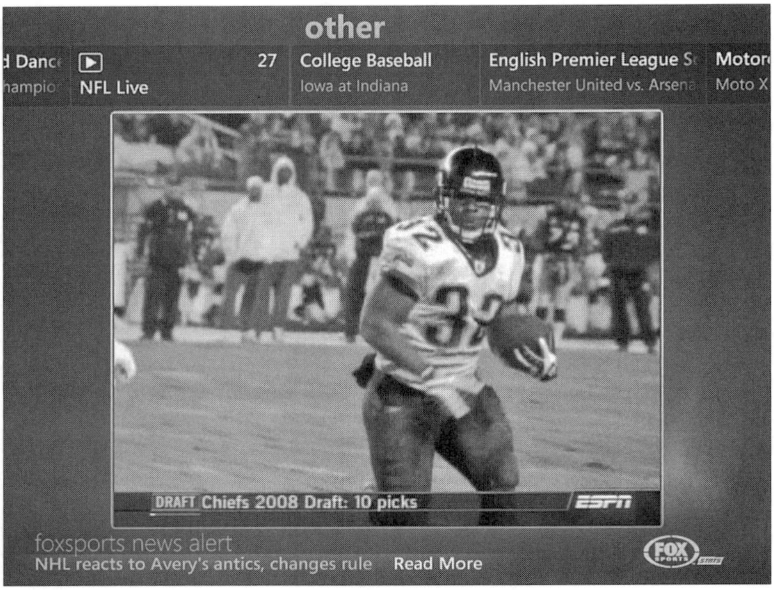

FIGURE 8.3
Checking out NFL Live.

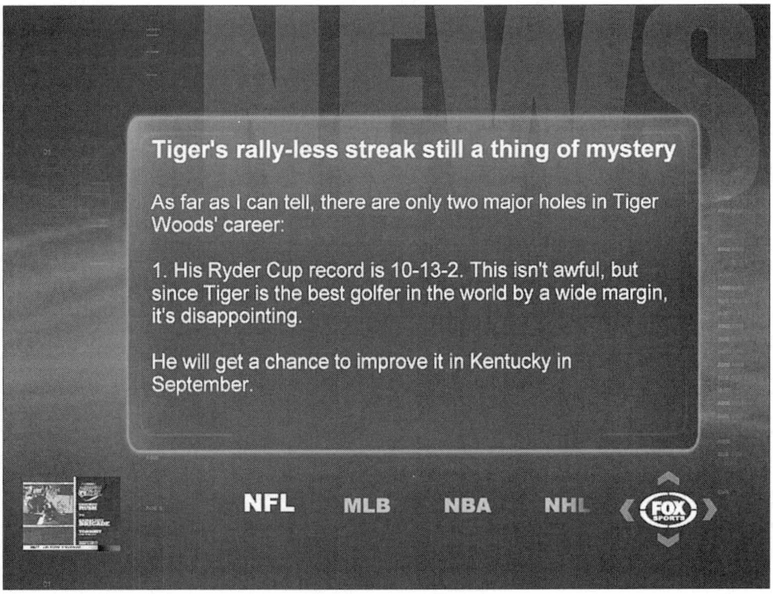

FIGURE 8.4
Viewing the Sports News ticker while your TV program continues to play.

If you click on the picture-in-picture playback window, your current sports TV program will play in full-screen. To return to the playback window with scrolling sports programs (see Figure 8.2), click the Back/Exit button on your remote control or click the back arrow icon with your mouse.

Pausing and Resuming Live Sports

> **note** If 30 minutes is just not enough time to get your long-winded brother-in-law off the phone or send an encyclopedia salesman away, you can increase the size of the live TV buffer by installing the freeware MCE Live TV Buffer Manager, available at www.dougknox.com/xpmce/utils/mce_livetvbuffermgr.htm.

One of the great features of WMC is its ability to pause live TV. If the phone or doorbell rings at the decisive moment in the big game, just click the Pause button on your remote or move your mouse to display the onscreen playback control and click the Pause icon. The default pause buffer is 30 minutes, giving you plenty of time to answer Nature's call (or somebody else's call, for that matter), while the maximum size of the Live TV buffer is determined by the amount of free space available on the hard disk used for TV recording.

When you pause a video in the SportsLounge window, there's no indication of how long the pause has been. However, you will see the Pause bar (Figure 8.5) when you are viewing sports (or other) TV in full-screen mode.

FIGURE 8.5
Pausing a sports TV program playing in full-screen mode.

8

Watching TV Sports on the WMC Desktop

If you need to perform other tasks within WMC while watching your favorite sport broadcast or video, click the WMC icon at the upper-left corner of the WMC desktop. Your televised game, program, or video clip will continue to play as you scroll through other WMC menus (Figure 8.6).

FIGURE 8.6

Viewing a baseball game while working with WMC menus.

The TV or video clip stops playing if you select music, photos, or other TV or video content to play, or when you exit WMC.

Recording Live Sports TV

Recording live sports TV from the SportsLounge menu is easy. If you're using a mouse to control WMC, move your mouse to display the playback control and click its red button.

If you prefer to use a WMC remote, highlight the playback window, click OK to switch to full-screen mode, and then press the Record button on your remote. To return to the normal playback window, click the Back/Exit button on your remote or click the back arrow icon with your mouse.

Unfortunately, the On Now playback window does not indicate that the current program is being recorded. To determine if you're recording what's currently on now, click the playback window to switch to full-screen view and click the Menu button on your remote or right-click the screen with your mouse. The channel indicator displays the red-circle recording icon if you're currently recording the channel (see Figure 8.7). To stop recording, select Stop Recording from the menu.

FIGURE 8.7

Checking the recording status of a sports program.

➔ For more information about configuring recording options for games, see "Watching and Recording Games with the On Later Menu," **p. 234**, in this chapter.

Recorded games are stored in your system's Public\Recorded TV folder and can be watched from within WMC, from a Media Center Extender, or with Windows Media Player 11. See "Viewing and Managing Sports Recordings," **p. 240**, in this chapter for details.

➔ For more information about configuring systems running WMC to enable systems running Windows XP to view TV recordings over the network, see Chapter 12, "Connecting with Windows Home Server and Other PCs."

➔ For more information about using Media Center Extenders with Windows Media Center, see Chapter 11, "Adding and Using Media Center Extenders."

Hanging Out in the SportsLounge

The SportsLounge window is also your connection to news stories, pictures, and videos. To access the sports news of the day, click the featured story on the news ticker (it's powered by Fox Sports) and then click the Fox Sports icon at the lower right to display the news menu. Figure 8.8 A shows a typical news story, while Figure 8.8 B shows the News menu.

> **note** If you don't have a TV tuner installed, you can access sports news stories from the Online Media menu's Showcase option instead. Select Fox Sports (or the sports provider available in your location). You can also access your sports provider by opening the More Sports icon in the Sports menu. For more information about Online Media, see Chapter 9, "Playing Games and Enjoying Online Resources."

A. *B.*

FIGURE 8.8

Using the SportsLounge window to access the top sports stories of the day.

Viewing News Stories and Photos

Click the News banner shown in Figure 8.8 B to display a numbered list of the leading news stories from all major sports (Figure 8.9), or select a league to see the list of top stories for that league only.

The story appears in a scrollable window in the center of the screen. To see related content, like photos (Figure 8.10 A), videos, and scores, select it from the scrolling menu at the bottom of the screen. To scroll through pictures, move the remote control or mouse pointer over the pointer arrows on the left or right edges of the screen (Figure 8.10 B).

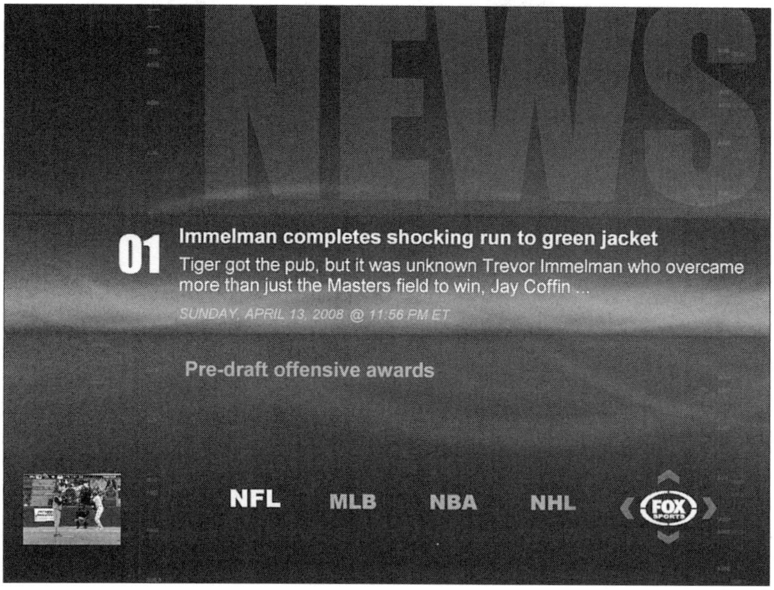

FIGURE 8.9
Reviewing the most important sports stories of the day.

A. *B.*

FIGURE 8.10
Selecting and viewing sports pictures.

Viewing Sports Videos

Videos are displayed in a vertically scrolling list, complete with a thumbnail and a brief description (Figure 8.11). Click the video, and it plays full-screen.

FIGURE 8.11

Selecting sports stories on video.

To replay the video, open the Now Playing menu and click Restart. You can also click Done if you are finished viewing the video. (WMC automatically deletes the video from your system.)

note Some of the videos may take a very long time to load, even over a 1Mbps or faster broadband connection. And they replace whatever sports TV or other WMC content you're playing.

Viewing Scores and Game Details

Select Scores to jump directly to a scrollable list of scores for the current day's games (Figure 8.12) in the currently selected league.

Click the selected game to go to the Summary page (Figure 8.13 A). From the Summary page, you can also view other information, such as team statistics (Figure 8.13 B), injuries, the depth report for each position, and individual stats.

FIGURE 8.12

Viewing baseball scores.

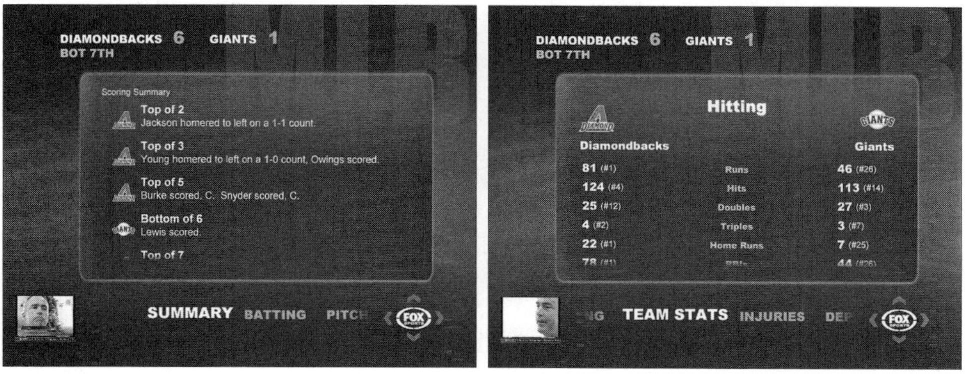

A. *B.*

FIGURE 8.13

Viewing the scoring summary (A) and team statistics (B) for a game.

8

Watching and Recording Games with the On Later Menu

You don't need to wade through the WMC Program Guide's "wasteland" of TV movies of the week, reality programs, and local news to find out what's coming in the world of TV sports. Just open the On Later menu to see upcoming major-league games (Figure 8.14).

note All times listed are in local time for your location; no need to convert Eastern to Central or Pacific to Mountain times!

FIGURE 8.14
Viewing information for upcoming MLB games.

When you select a game, you will see a recording menu (Figure 8.15 A). If the game has just started, you will also see Watch as an option (Figure 8.15 B). Note that the game will "fall off" the On Later menu right after it starts.

To schedule a recording, click Record. The game is recorded automatically using the current recording defaults. If the game is part of a series, click Record Series to set up recording for the series.

note "Series" in WMC-speak doesn't refer to "World Series" or "Playoff" series necessarily. Instead, it refers to any regularly scheduled series of games. For example, the games shown in Figure 8.15 are part of the continuing broadcast series on each network. Select Record Series, and you'll get every game—as long as you have enough hard disk space and there are no other scheduled recordings at the same time.

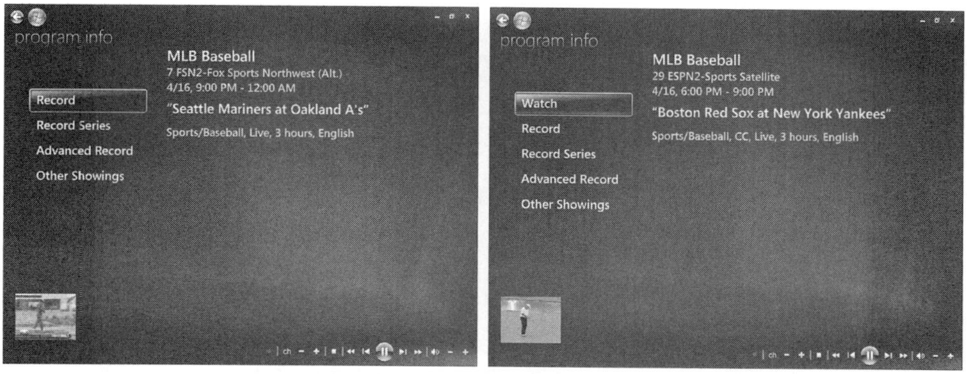

A. *B.*

FIGURE 8.15

The recording menu also includes a Watch option if the game has just started.

Dealing with Recording Conflicts

How many games can you record at a time? If you have only one TV tuner, you can record only one game or other TV show at a time. If you try to record a game that overlaps another recording, you will see a Conflict dialog similar to the one shown in Figure 8.16.

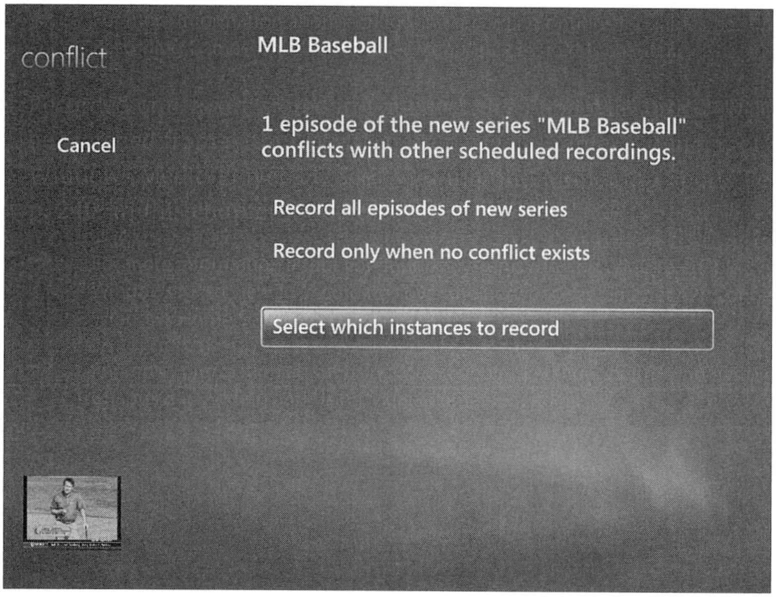

FIGURE 8.16

Uh-oh! There's a recording conflict to solve.

Your options include

- Record All Episodes of New Series, which will override your previous settings
- Record Only Where No Conflict Exists
- Select Which Instances to Record

I recommend the third option. Click it to see a list of existing recording settings. The exclamation mark (!) symbol shown in Figure 8.17 indicates a conflict.

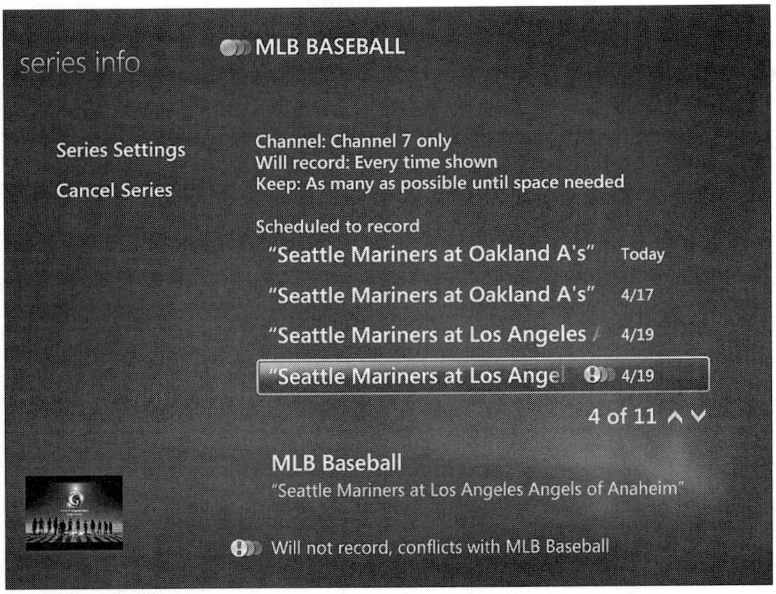

FIGURE 8.17
Highlighting the recording conflict.

Once you've viewed the recording conflict, you have a choice: You can resolve the conflict, or you can cancel recording the entire offending series. To stop the series from recording, click Cancel Series. To see other options, highlight the conflicting episode and press Menu on your remote or right-click the episode with your mouse. Now your options include

- **Program Info:** Displays more information about the game
- **Do Not Record:** Disables recording of the selected game only

- **Resolve Conflict:** Brings up a dialog (Figure 8.18) in which you can choose which game to record
- **Settings:** Opens the Settings dialog

Be sure to select Done to keep the setting you choose in the Resolve Conflict dialog.

tip If you're running into recording conflicts too often, or if you'd like to watch one show while recording another, you need a TV tuner card or USB device with a dual tuner. Dual-tuner cards and devices enable you to watch one show while recording another or record two games (or any two TV broadcasts) at the same time. A dual-tuner TV device is perfect for snuggling up with your sweetheart for a romantic movie on TV while recording the big game for viewing later. See Chapter 2 for some recommendations. If you have a spare USB 2.0 port, PCI slot, or PCI Express slot, you could also add a second TV tuner card. Either way, fewer watching or recording conflicts make for happy TV watching.

Setting Advanced Recording Options

As I discussed earlier in this book ("Recording Live TV," **p. 110**, in Chapter 3), TV recording takes a lot of disk space—a *huge* amount of disk space. And because many TV sporting events run two hours or longer, recording at Best quality can run you out of disk space in a hurry. For example, a three-hour baseball game recorded at Best quality uses more than 10.5GB of disk space.

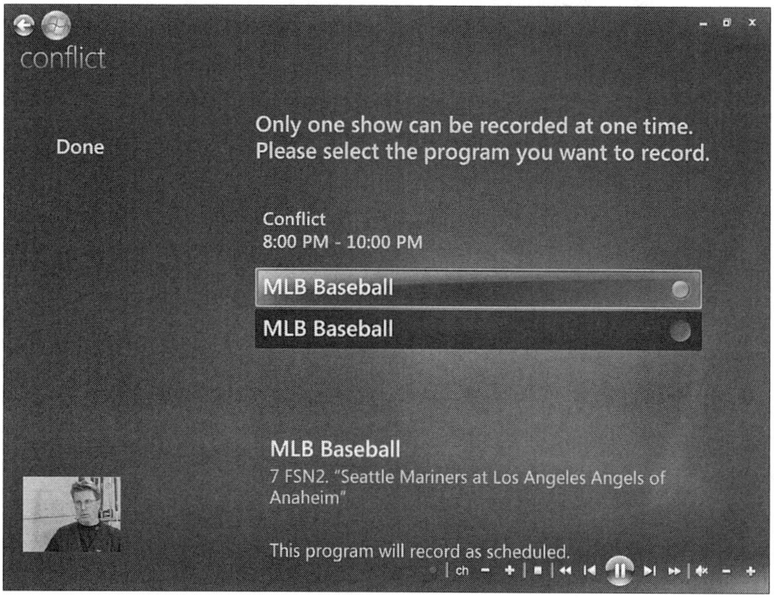

FIGURE 8.18

Selecting which game to record when a conflict exists.

If you set your system to record every game available in your favorite sport, you're probably going to be looking for a 1TB (terabyte) hard disk sooner rather than later, or if you share WMC, your family's going to be wondering why there's no space left on the hard disk for *their* favorite programs.

If you're not ready to run out and buy a 1TB hard disk, there's a cheaper way to solve the problem: Change your advanced recording options. From the Record menu shown in Figures 8.15 A or 8.15 B, select Advanced Record to open the menu shown in Figure 8.19.

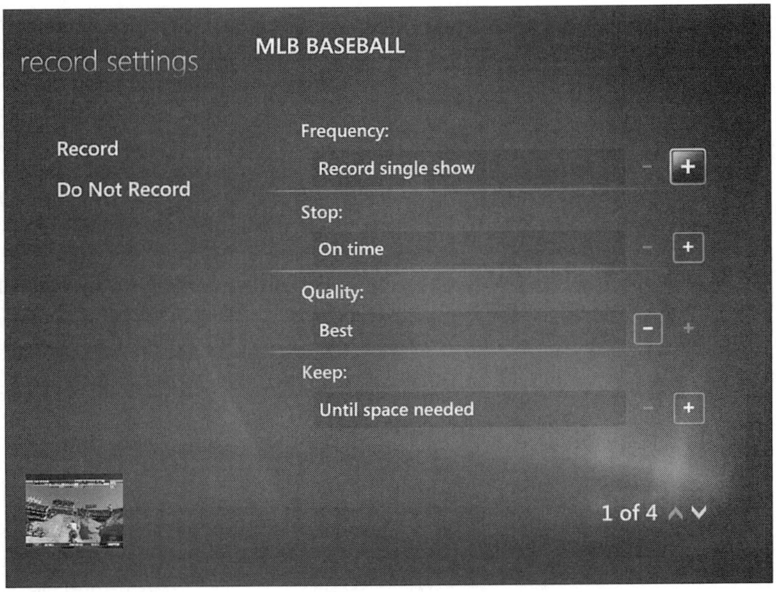

FIGURE 8.19
The Advanced Recording (Record Settings) menu.

Table 8.1 lists the default and other settings used in this menu.

Table 8.1 Advanced Recording Default and Alternative Settings

Option	Frequency	Stop Time	Quality	How Long to Keep
Defaults	Record single show	On time	Best	Until space needed
Alternative Settings	Record series	5, 10, 15, 30 minutes after; 1, 2, 3 hours after	Better, Good, Fair	For one week; Until I watch; Until I delete

So should you stick with the default settings? Not necessarily.

If the game or show you're recording is part of a series and you don't want to record each game or episode separately, select Record Series. Just keep in mind that you can use up a lot of disk space.

Adjusting Stop Time is a good idea, especially if you're recording a game; overtime, sudden death, playoff rounds, and penalty kicks wreak havoc with scheduled ending times. I'd select a stop time of at least 30 minutes after and maybe an hour or more. You can always edit the game recording to eliminate the start of the following program by using Windows Movie Maker.

Best quality uses the most disk space, while Fair uses the least. When I recorded some standard-quality test TV clips with all four settings, I didn't see much difference between Best, Better, and Good when I viewed the shows on a 19-inch monitor, but Fair displayed a lot of really obvious blockiness and loss of fine detail. The visual difference will be more significant with larger screens or if you're recording from a high-quality source. My advice? Try recording some half-hour or hour-long shows in each quality setting, play them, and see what *you* prefer. Keep in mind that you can always reduce the quality of a high-quality recording to save disk space, but you can never recover image quality lost during recording if you use lower-quality recording settings.

How long should you keep your recordings? WMC's Until Space Needed default is designed to keep you from hogging all the available space on a hard disk (WMC uses about two-thirds of the available system hard disk for recording.) With this setting, WMC starts dumping the oldest recordings overboard when there's no more space for newer recordings. As you can imagine, newer recordings start replacing older recordings more quickly on small (under 300GB) disks than on larger models. If you want an incentive to watch what you record, the For One Week setting should motivate you: Your recordings vanish after a week with this option enabled. If you're going to watch the game just once, choose the Until I Watch option. If you have plenty of disk space, are using an external hard disk as a dedicated location for video recordings, will edit your recordings into a more compact form, or just plan to watch your recordings when you're good and ready to do so and not before, choose Until I Delete. Those recordings aren't going anywhere until you say so!

➔ For more information about editing the MS-DVR recording format used by Windows Media Center into other, more compact file formats and eliminating unnecessary footage, see the "Converting WMC TV Recordings to Save Space" section in Chapter 14, "Creating Photo and Video Content for Media Center," **p. 431.**

➔ For more information about using a different hard disk for TV recording storage, see Chapter 4, "Viewing and Recording Live TV."

8

AVOID "HEIDI GAME" WOES BY ADDING RECORDING TIME

By adding time after the scheduled end of the game to your recording settings, you avoid the problem of creating your own version of the notorious *Heidi* pro football game. In late 1968, NBC had scheduled the Oakland Raiders-New York Jets football game to run three hours, immediately followed by a special broadcast of the then-new *Heidi* made-for-TV movie. NBC dutifully cut away from the game at 7 p.m. to broadcast *Heidi*, leaving football fans in most of the country wondering what happened in the last 65 seconds of the game. As it turned out, the seemingly victorious Jets lost their lead and the game during the time that *Heidi's* opening credits were running. After that, standard network policy changed—never again would fans ever miss the end of a game again, no matter how long the game took to play. By adding time to the end of your game recordings, you can avoid repeating the *Heidi* fiasco.

However, there's one situation in which you should *not* add recording time: if you are recording a program that starts immediately after another program that's also being recorded. For example, if you're recording a program (or game) that's scheduled to run from 2:00 p.m.–5:00 p.m. and another that's scheduled to run from 5:00 p.m. to 7:00 p.m. (even on the same channel), don't add time to the end of the first program, or else you'll have an overlap that will prevent recording of the second program.

Viewing and Managing Sports Recordings

When it's time to sit back, relax, and catch the "big game" you recorded, go to the TV+Movies menu and select Recorded TV (Figure 8.20 A). You can then select by date recorded (Figure 8.20 B) or by title.

When you select a recording, the Program Info menu appears (Figure 8.21). To play back your recording in full-screen, click Play, sit back, and enjoy.

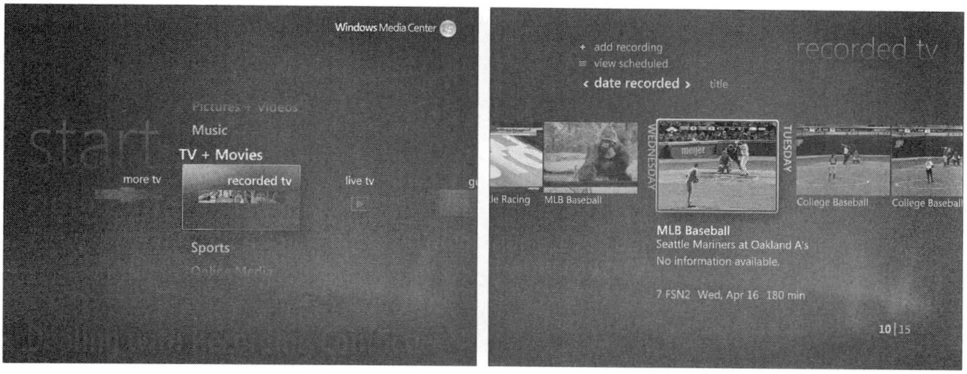

A. *B.*

FIGURE 8.20

Reviewing your list of recorded games and programs.

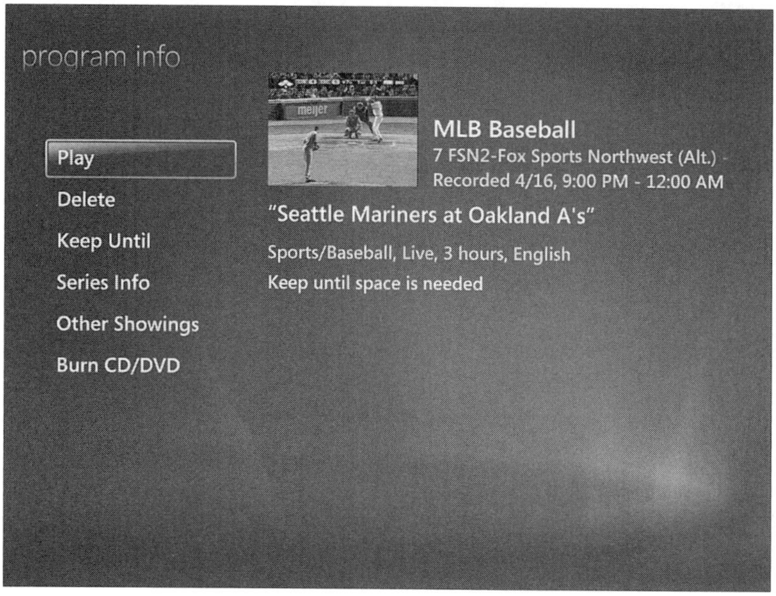

FIGURE 8.21

The Program Info menu for a recorded game.

You can do much more than play your sports recordings:

- **Delete:** Removes the recording from your system.
- **Keep Until:** Changes the current setting for how long the recording stays on your system. (The current setting is displayed below the preview window.)

8

- **Series Info:** Displays the recording settings.
- **Other Showings:** Displays other times the program will be available.
- **Burn CD/DVD:** Copies the recording to disc.

Viewing Your Recording Schedule

If you've forgotten exactly what games and programs (sports and otherwise) you've scheduled for recording, click the View Scheduled icon shown in Figure 8.20 B to see your recording schedule (Figure 8.22). Note that the number of shows and the number of hours is also listed.

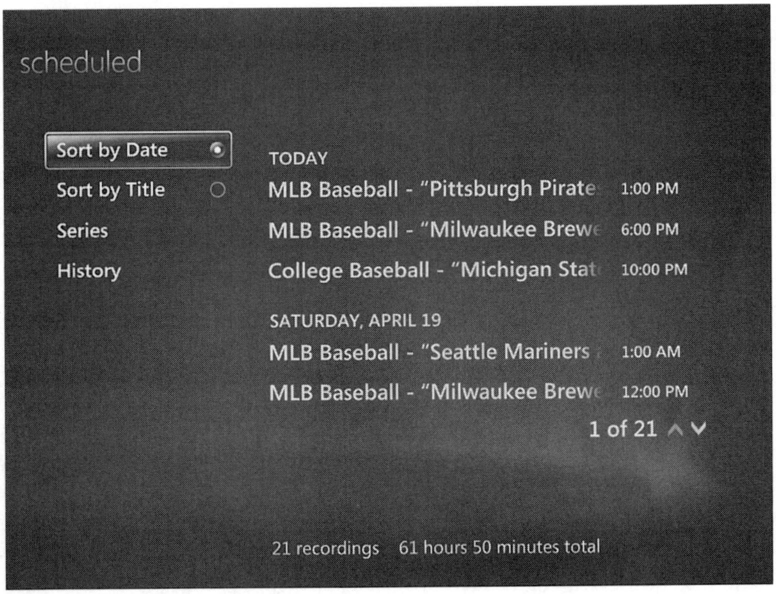

FIGURE 8.22

Viewing the list of scheduled recordings.

You can sort the list by date, title, or series.

Viewing Your Recording History

Click the History button shown in Figure 8.22 to see the details of what you have recorded in full, deleted, canceled, or recorded in part. You can sort this list by date, title, or status (Figure 8.23).

To delete the current recording history, click Clear History.

FIGURE 8.23

Reviewing recording history by title and status.

Managing Scheduled Series Recordings

If you want to adjust recording quality or other settings for the series you record or change the priority of different series, click Series from the Scheduled menu.

You can sort the Series menu (Figure 8.24) by priority (the default), name, or type. To change the settings for a particular series, click the series to open the Series Info menu.

The Series Info menu lists the upcoming games or other programs that will be recorded, the channel, and recording settings. To change those settings, click Series Settings to open the menu shown in Figure 8.25.

From this menu, you can change the recording stop time, quality, keep until settings, add or change channels, change airtime, and specify whether to record the show live, first-run, or first-run and rerun.

> **tip** Most games are broadcast only once on conventional channels but might be repeated frequently on premium sports packages or league-specific networks such as the NFL Network, NBA League Pass, and others. If you are recording a series that might be rerun, you'd better change the Show Type setting to Live Only to avoid using up disk space with recordings of the repeats. The only reason not to make this change is if the show or game might conflict with other recordings at its original time.

→ For more information about configuring recording settings, see Chapter 4.

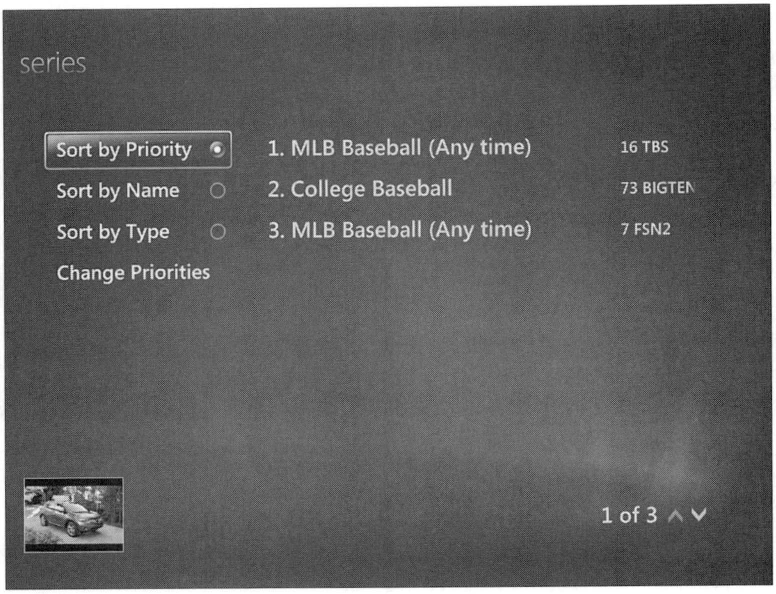

FIGURE 8.24

Use the Series menu to change recording priority or customize recording settings for different series.

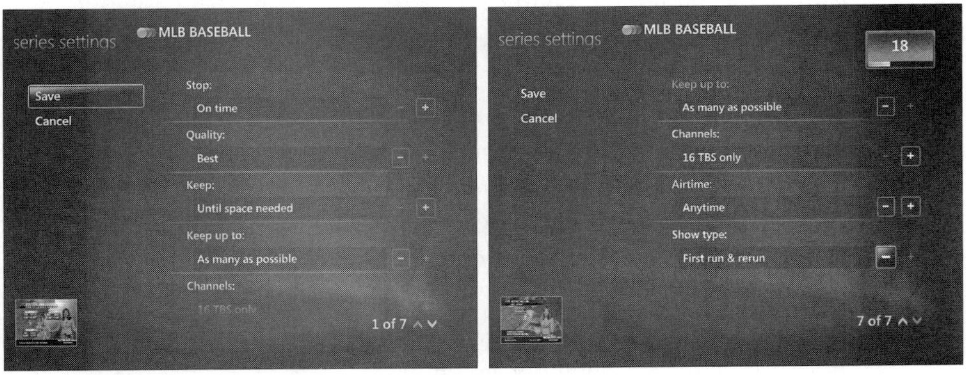

FIGURE 8.25

Configuring series recording settings.

If you are recording sports or other series, instead of just individual games and shows, you may run into situations in which you've asked Windows Media Center to record more shows at the same time than you have TV tuners. Don't bother with the traditional coin toss to figure out which series is the victor. Instead, open the Series menu and click Priority.

In the Priority menu (Figure 8.26), the series you've selected for recording are listed in priority order. The first series listed has the highest priority in case of conflicts, the second series listed has the next-highest priority, and so on. To move a series higher or lower in the list, click Change Priorities and use the up or down arrow icons to move around the series. Click Done when you are finished.

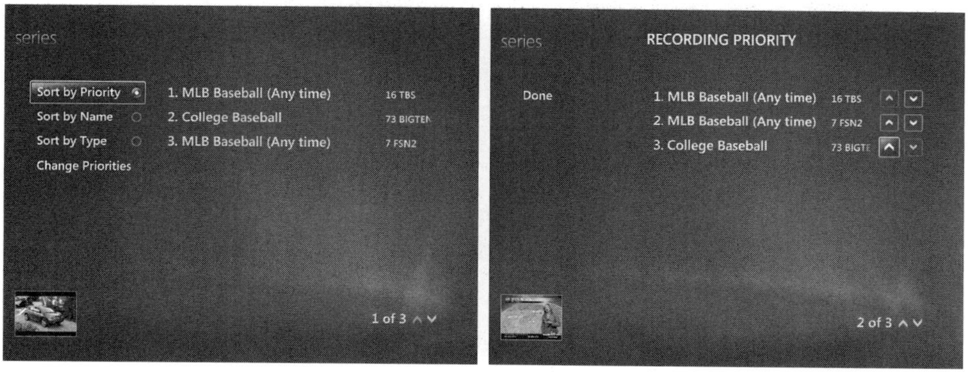

FIGURE 8.26

Changing series recording priority.

Burning DVDs of Your Favorite Games

You can burn a DVD of a recorded game or other program. This process is generally similar to the DVD burning process covered in "Burning a Recorded TV Data Disc" in Chapter 10, "Creating CDs and DVDs," **p. 299**. However, if you are trying to burn a video DVD of a recording that lasts longer than two hours (many baseball games and some other games fall into this category), you might see a Burn with Reduced Quality error message like the one in Figure 8.27 if you use a standard recordable or rewritable DVD.

If you click OK, you might be able to record the show at lower quality, but you might not like the results. A better move is to use a dual-layer recordable DVD if you are using a dual-layer (DL) compatible DVD drive.

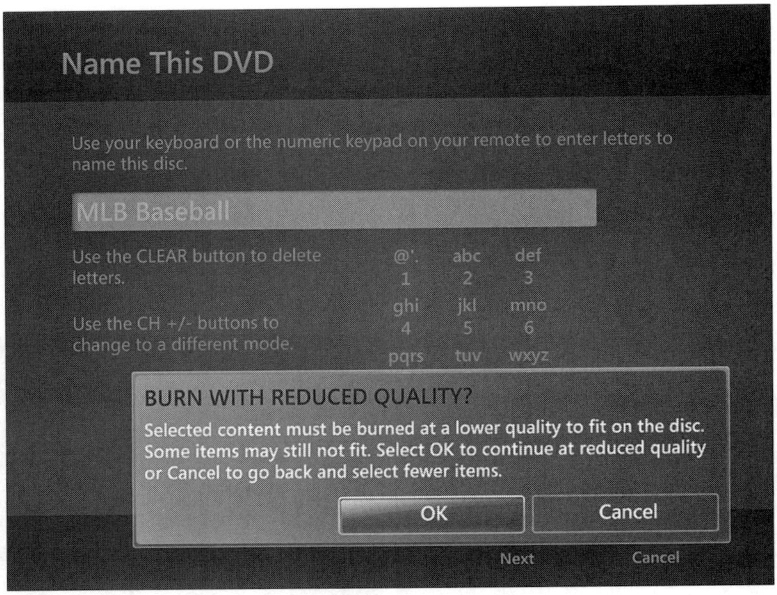

FIGURE 8.27

This error message appears when a TV recording is larger than the DVD can store at full quality.

A standard single-layer recordable DVD holds 4.7GB, while a dual-layer DVD holds almost twice as much (8.5GB). For games or other recordings that are three hours or longer, the only way you can record the show or game as a video DVD might be to use a dual-layer DVD. You might see the same error message as in Figure 8.27 even if you use a dual-layer DVD (depending upon the length of the recording), but the quality reduction necessary will be slight. If you click OK on the dialog when you are using a single-layer DVD disc and see the error message again, you *must* use a dual-layer DVD.

> **note** Some older DVD drives and some DVD set-top devices might have problems reading dual-layer DVD media. To improve compatibility, you might prefer to create a video DVD with a third-party program such as Nero, Roxio Easy Media Creator, or others that permit selection of different burn speeds. See Chapter 15, "Extending Media Center with Third-Party Apps," for Windows Media Center-compatible DVD burning applications from third-party vendors.

Keeping an Eye on Scores and Games

Get the latest scores and check the schedules for your favorite professional sport by going to the Scores menu (Figure 8.28). Select your favorite league and any game to see scores and highlights.

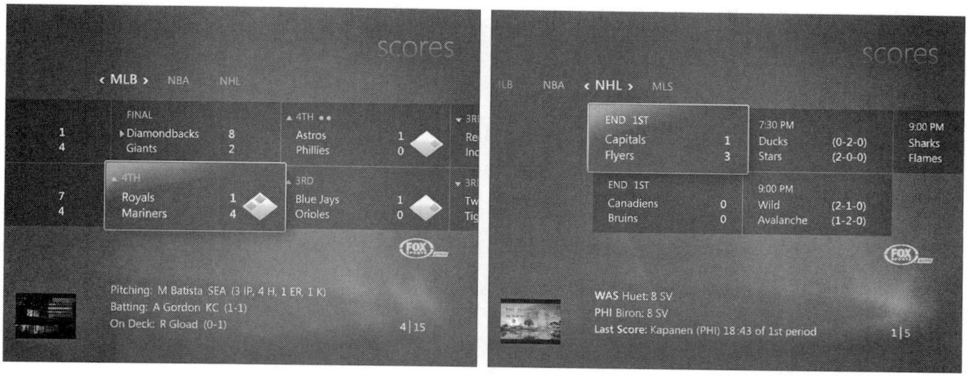

A. B.

FIGURE 8.28

Viewing major-league baseball (A) and NHL hockey (B) scores and highlights.

Click a completed game for a complete box score (Figure 8.29 A). Click the Fox Sports button to bring up a detailed summary of the game (Figure 8.29 B) as well as detailed statistics for each participating player.

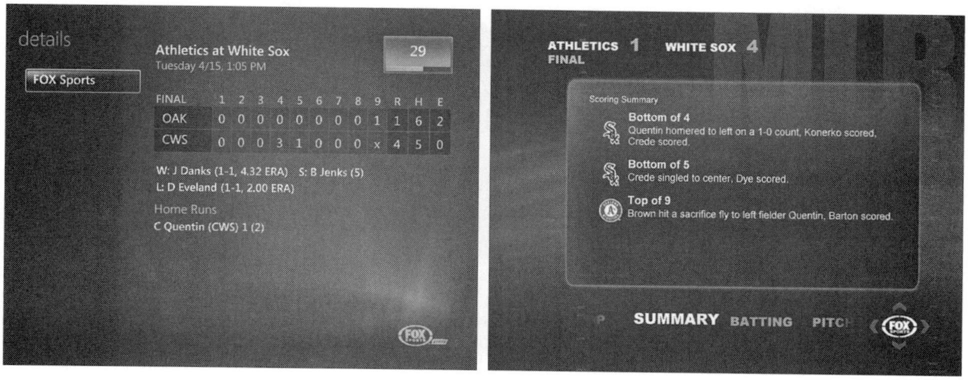

A. B.

FIGURE 8.29

Viewing the box score (A) and game highlights (B).

Click the Fox Sports icon at the bottom of the Summary and Statistics pages to go directly to the Fox Sports News roundup.

➔ For more information, see "Viewing News Stories and Photos" in this chapter, **p. 230**.

Adding Players to Your Fantasy Team with the Players Menu

Although you can display the game-day stats for any player on your favorite professional sports fantasy team with the Scores menu, there's a lot easier way to track your fantasy team members or your favorite professional players: Use Windows Media Center's Players menu.

To get started, click Add Players and then select the major league sport your fantasy league is based on (Figure 8.30)—it's like running your own major-league draft!

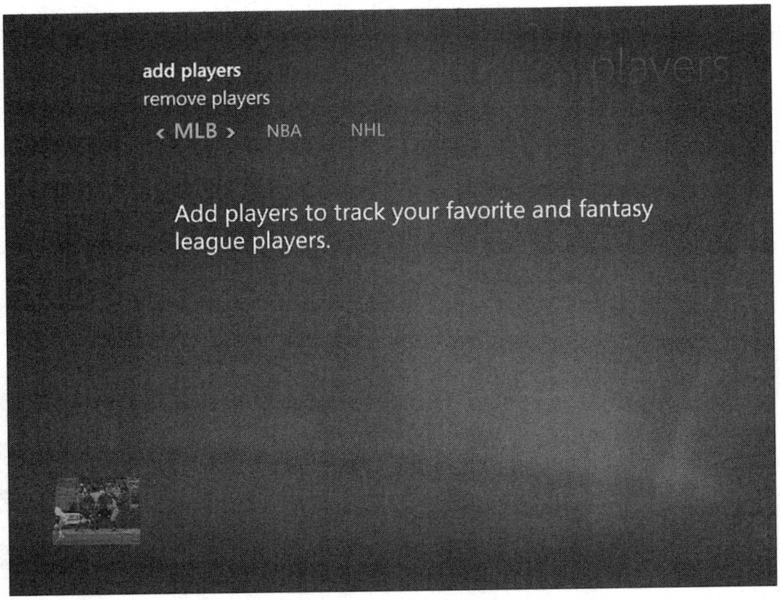

FIGURE 8.30
Getting started with fantasy team and favorite player selections.

Select a position and then select the player or players you want to track (Figure 8.31). After selecting the player(s) for a particular position, click Save.

After you've selected the player or players you want to track at each position in your chosen sport, their daily statistics are displayed (Figure 8.32).

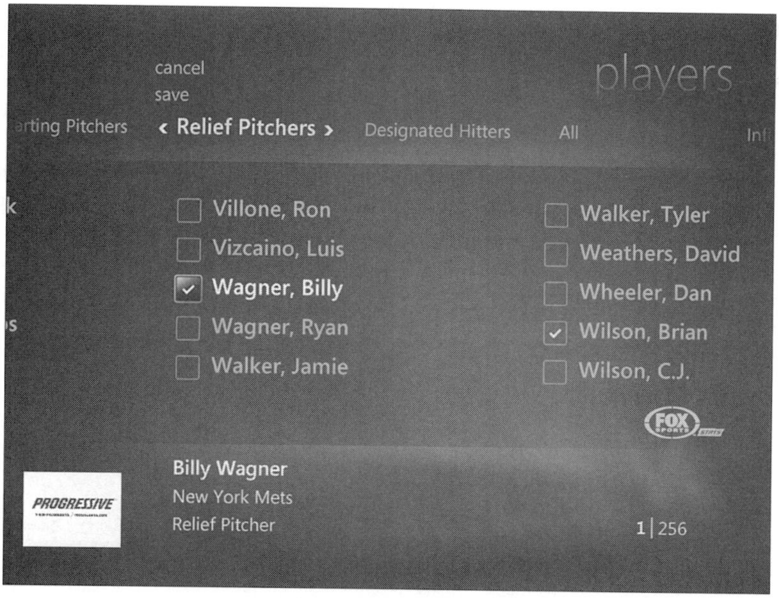

FIGURE 8.31

"Drafting" your players by position.

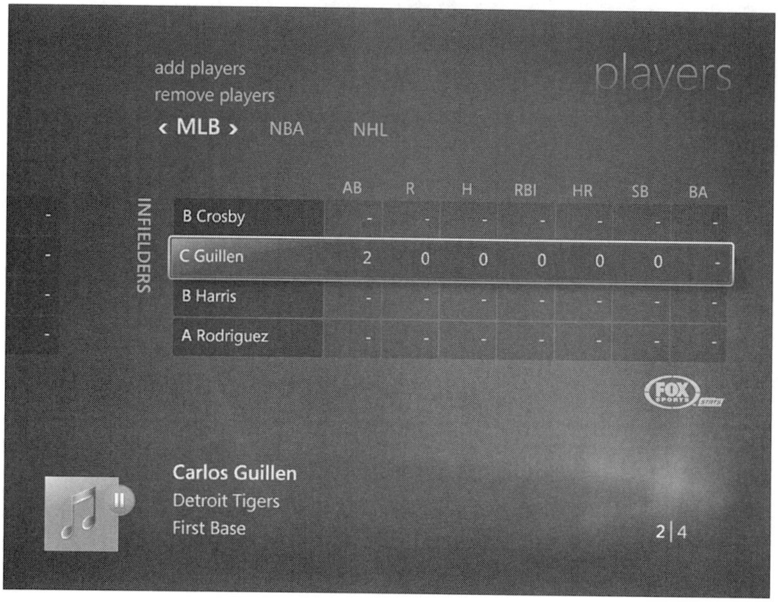

FIGURE 8.32

Viewing daily stats.

8

See More Sports Stories on Internet TV

> **note** Because the Players menu displays only daily stats for selected players, the best time to see how your fantasy team players are doing is late in the evening after the day's games are completed.

U.S. versions of Windows Media Center include Internet TV, which brings you an assortment of recent sports programs and clips brought to you by MSN Video. If you don't have a TV tuner, or if you missed a sports story, be sure to stop in and see what's playing.

Open the TV+Movies menu, scroll to Internet TV, select Sports, select your favorite category, and choose a video clip (Figure 8.33).

FIGURE 8.33

Viewing sports stories on Internet TV.

→ For more information on Internet TV, see the "Watching Internet TV" section in Chapter 4, **p. 129**.

CHAPTER

9

Playing Games and Enjoying Online Resources

IN THIS CHAPTER

- Tracking Down WMC's Games Menu
- MSN Games for Media Center
- EMUCenter
- Exploring Online Media

You don't need to leave the comfort of your favorite easy chair or couch to enjoy games or enjoy a world of online content on your Windows Media Center (WMC) PC. Just grab your remote and your favorite mouse, and you're ready to play.

Tracking Down WMC's Games Menu

You'll look in vain for a "Games" listing on the Windows Media Center menu—or its submenus, for that matter. WMC's selection of games is located in the Program Library submenu of the Online Media menu (Figure 9.1).

Open the Program Library, and the default Programs by Name view (Figure 9.2) lists the games available in WMC as well as any third-party programs you've installed.

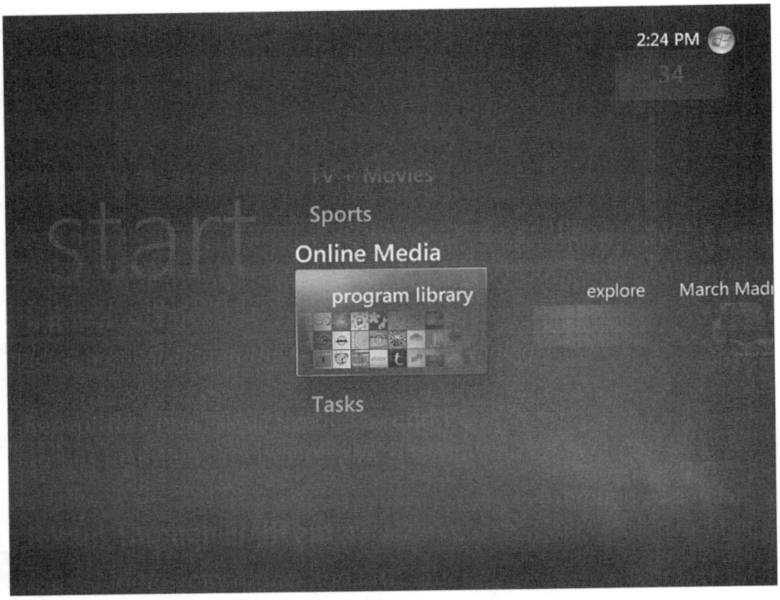

FIGURE 9.1

The Program Library is the gateway to gaming in WMC.

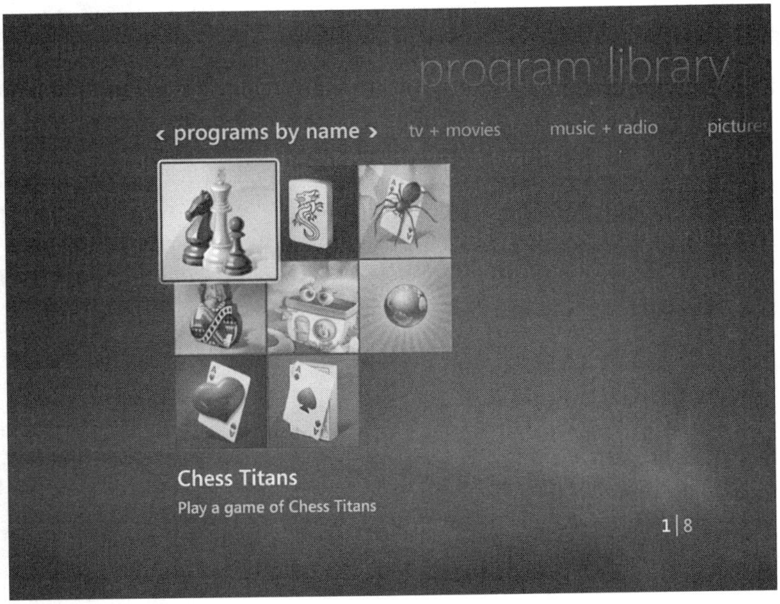

FIGURE 9.2

WMC includes many games preinstalled as part of Windows Vista.

Compatible Games

So what games can you choose from in WMC's Program Library menu?

- *Chess Titans 3D Chess*
- *FreeCell Solitaire*
- *Hearts*
- *Mahjong Titans 3D Mah-jong*
- *Standard Solitaire*
- *Spider Solitaire*
- *Purple Place Kids' Activities*

note As you add programs to the Program Library, the Programs by Name view will also contain a lot of non-game content. To find games, and only games, scroll to the Games view.

All these games are preinstalled as part of Windows Vista Home Premium and Ultimate. So you don't need to bail out of WMC to play a game. You don't need to get up off the couch to enjoy a relaxing game of solitaire or give the chess player in your family some competition. However, if you're looking for blood, guts, gore, and action, you won't find it in this collection. Don't panic, though. We have the solution.

Playing the Games

Although you can use your MCE remote to select the game, you won't be able to play the game with it. Once you select the game, put your remote away and get out your mouse. When you exit the game, you return immediately to Windows Vista Media Center.

See Chapter 2, "Equipping Your PC for Media Center," for suggestions on the best mice to use with Windows Vista Media Center.

Getting Access to More Games

In theory, you can get access to more games by clicking the More Tasks button in the Program Library menu. However, third-party media providers have been laggard at providing access to online games through More Tasks. However, there are plenty of places to get your hands on more games that work in Windows Vista Media Center.

MSN Games for Media Center

The MSN Games for Vista website (http://zone.msn.com/en/vistagames) offers a variety of downloadable games for Windows Vista that include Media Center integration. Here are some of those titles:

- *7 Wonders of the Ancient World*
- *Bliss Island*
- *Crystal Quest*
- Darwinia
- *Geometry Wars: Retro Evolved*
- *Jewel Quest II*
- *Luxor II*
- *Spinword*

note Although you can sample the games free, you must purchase the full versions to have Media Center integration.

Most of these games are aimed at the younger set, enabling you and the kids to enjoy gaming on the big (or not so big) screen connected to your WMC PC.

EMUCenter

Although the choices available at MSN Games add a bit more variety to the Media Center experience, hardcore gamers looking for hits like *Half-Life, World of Warcraft, Crysis,* and others won't be satisfied. Fortunately, there's a solution.

The best way I know of to add more gaming gusto to Vista Media Center is to use the free EMUCenter program available from http://www.push-a-button.com.au/products/mce/vista/emucenter/index.php.

EMUCenter was originally intended to enable you to play your favorite console and arcade games from within WMC, but it also supports most recent and older Windows-based games.

After EMUCenter is installed, it adds a picture of (what else?) an emu to your Games menu (Figure 9.3). However, before you can use EMUCenter to launch your favorite games, you'll need to leave WMC's "10-foot UI" and return to the standard Windows desktop for some configuration.

note If you plan to use EMUCenter to run emulated console games, you can find links to the most popular emulators on the EMUCenter download page. Note that you must own the original game ROMs to legally download ROM images for use with emulators. So don't be in too big a hurry to run that old console game and cartridges to the Salvation Army drop-off center!

FIGURE 9.3

EMUCenter adds its icon to the Games menu automatically.

Adding Your Favorite Games to EMUCenter

When you install EMUCenter, it adds a shortcut called Configure EMUCenter to the Start menu. Click this shortcut to open the Configure EMUCenter menu (Figure 9.4).

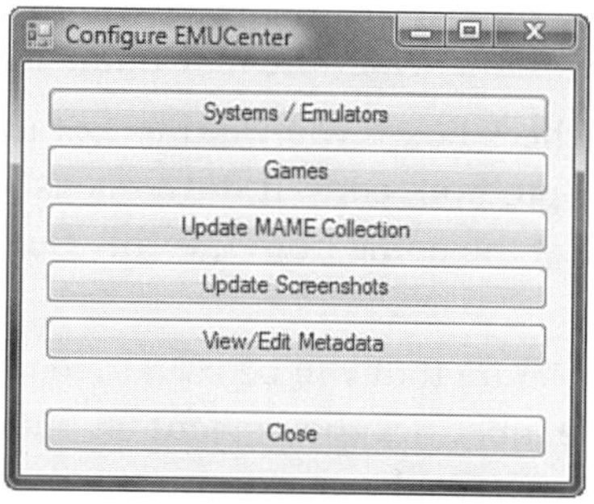

FIGURE 9.4

Starting the configuration process for EMUCenter.

To add a Windows-based game installed on your system to EMUCenter

1. Click Games. A blank Games Collection dialog appears. Click Add to continue.
2. Navigate to the location where the game executable is located, select it, and click Open (Figure 9.5).

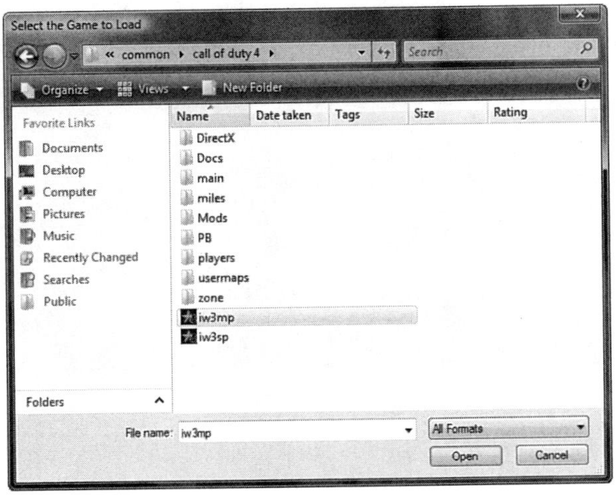

FIGURE 9.5

Selecting the game's executable file.

3. The GameV2 dialog displays the executable name, system type (Windows), and path to the executable (Figure 9.6). To change the name displayed in EMUCenter from the executable name to a more descriptive name, enter the new name in the Name field.
4. Click the check box if you want to exit the game and return to WMC before the program ends. If the game is based on another installed game, select the game from the This Game Is a Version Of drop-down menu.
5. To add a picture that will be used to identify the game in WMC, click the Picture tab. Click the navigation button next to the Title field to navigate to the folder containing a suitable image file. (Certain games include image files, but in some cases you might need to download one from an online source or scan the box art.)
6. Select the file and click Open (Figure 9.7 A). The Pictures Title field displays the path to the image (Figure 9.7 B).

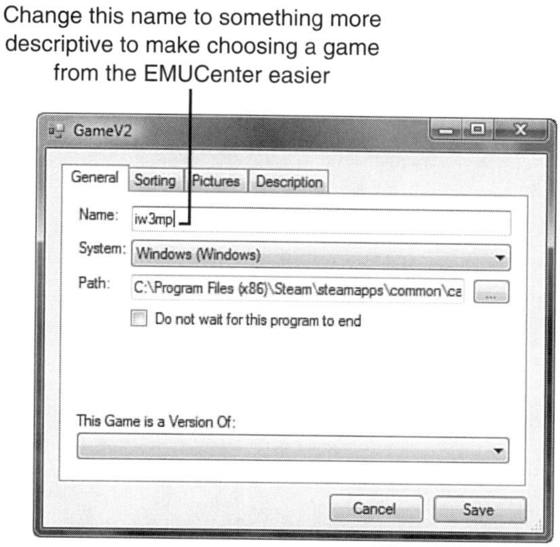

FIGURE 9.6

Configuring game settings and editing the game name.

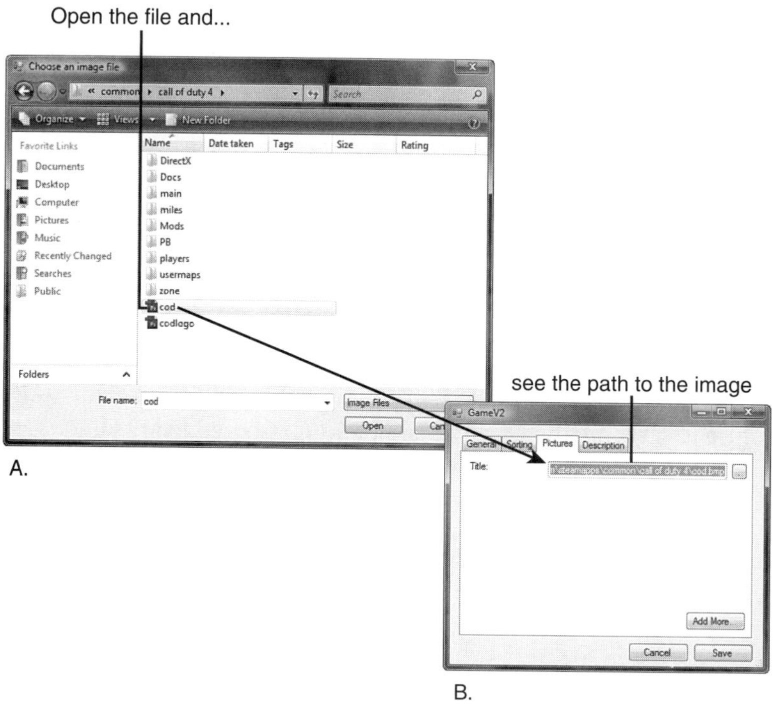

FIGURE 9.7

Selecting an image file to identify the game.

7. Click Save to save your changes. The Game Collection dialog lists your game (Figure 9.8).

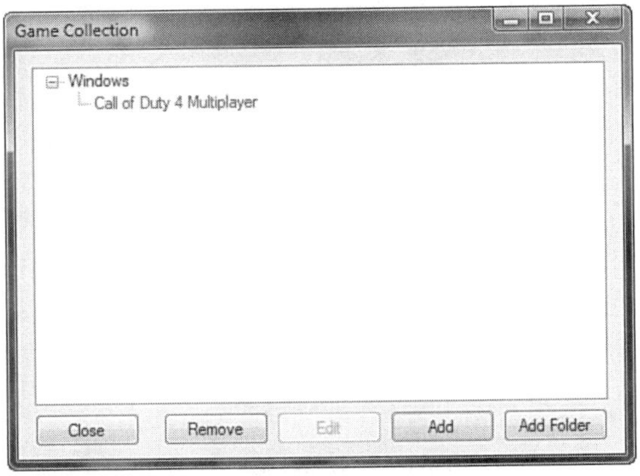

FIGURE 9.8
The completed game listing in the Game Collection dialog.

Repeat this process as needed to add PC games installed on your system.

> **note** To learn how to add games that play through an emulator or to learn how to add metadata such as the number of players, game type, and more, see the *Using EMUCenter – Configuration* page at http://www.push-a-button.com.au/products/mce/vista/emucenter/manualindex.php.

Playing Games Through EMUCenter

After adding your games to EMUCenter, restart WMC, navigate to the Online Media menu, open the Program Library menu, and select either the Program Library menu (Figure 9.2) or the Games menu (Figure 9.9). Click the EMU icon to continue.

The game(s) you added to EMUCenter are listed. If you didn't add a game picture to a game, the game uses a plain text-based icon like the one shown in Figure 9.10. Compare the icons shown in Figure 9.10, and you can see how much more fun it is to add pictures. (See the previous section for details.)

Click the game's icon to launch the game. It starts immediately. When you are done playing, quit the game, and you immediately return to EMUCenter within WMC.

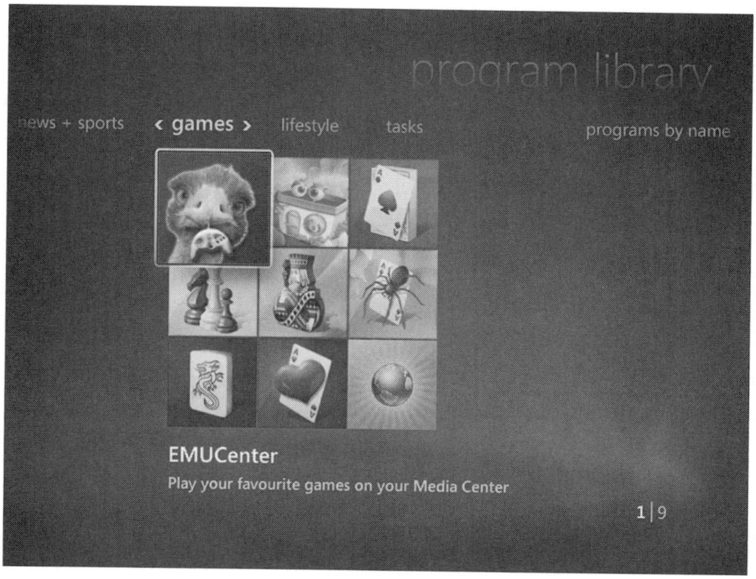

FIGURE 9.9

Launching EMUCenter from the Program Library's Games menu.

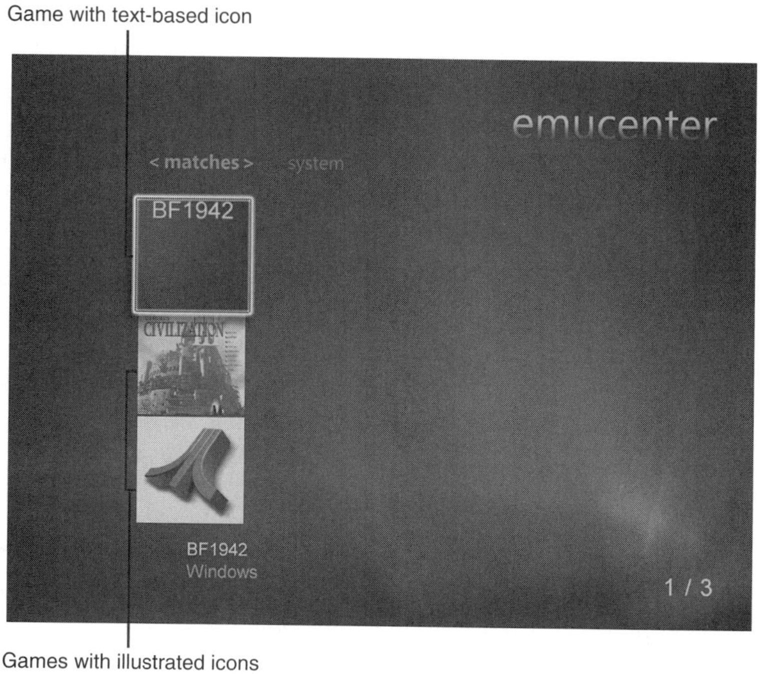

FIGURE 9.10

Typical examples of EMUCenter's game launching dialog.

9

GAME DESIGNERS, LISTEN UP! HERE'S HOW TO MAKE YOUR GAME WMC-FRIENDLY

While it's great that the clever designers at Push-a-Button Software have figured out how to help frustrated gamers add their games to WMC, how about adding WMC support to games as you create them?

If you use Nullsoft's NSIS Windows Installer for your games, Nullsoft has a free plug-in you can use to add the game to the Games section of WMC. (It also registers the game in Vista's Games Explorer menu.) NSIS Windows Installer is a free open-source installation program for Windows applications. Learn more at http://nsis.sourceforge.net/. (The Games plug-in is available at http://nisis.sourceforge.net/Games_plug-in.)

Exploring Online Media

Even if gaming with WMC doesn't grab you, there's plenty of other content in the Online Media menu to interest you. Select Explore to get started.

Online Media (Figure 9.11) is divided into five categories:

- **Showcase:** Everything that's currently available
- **TV + Movies:** TV series, on-demand movie services, home shopping, and more
- **Music + Radio:** From talk to pop, country to classical, the home of Internet and satellite radio services galore
- **News + Sports:** Online news and sports sources
- **Pictures:** Online photo services

note Because the "only constant is change" and because WMC online offerings vary in different locations, you might see other services than the ones discussed in this chapter in your location or at different times.

FOR BETTER ONLINE MEDIA, GET FASTER INTERNET SERVICE

Many of these services are designed to deliver high-bandwidth video content including, in some cases, 720p or higher-quality HDTV. If you currently have a 1Mbps or slower broadband connection, you might experience a lot of pauses and choppy playback and be spending a lot of time staring at the rotating ring symbol WMC uses when it's waiting for information.

For maximum enjoyment, upgrade to a faster broadband connection of at least 3Mbps. Most DSL providers offer 3Mbps speed as part of their product offerings, and most cable Internet services already exceed this speed.

If you can't get DSL or cable Internet, your options are more limited. The fastest satellite Internet speed available to most users is 1.5Mbps, offered by HughesNet, WildBlue, and StarBand. (HughesNet also offers a 2Mbps service priced and designed for commercial customers.) Terrestrial wireless plans using microwave transmission typically top out at 1.5Mbps maximum, although guaranteed throughput might be under 1Mbps. For more information about your Internet connection choices, see "Boosting Network and Internet Performance" in Chapter 12, "Connecting with Windows Home Server and Other PCs," **p. 355**.

You will also want the fastest possible network connections for your PCs and Media Center Extender devices to prevent a "last-mile" bottleneck: I recommend 802.11n dual-band wireless and Gigabit Ethernet wired networking. For details, see "Boosting Network and Internet Performance," Chapter 12, **p. 355**.

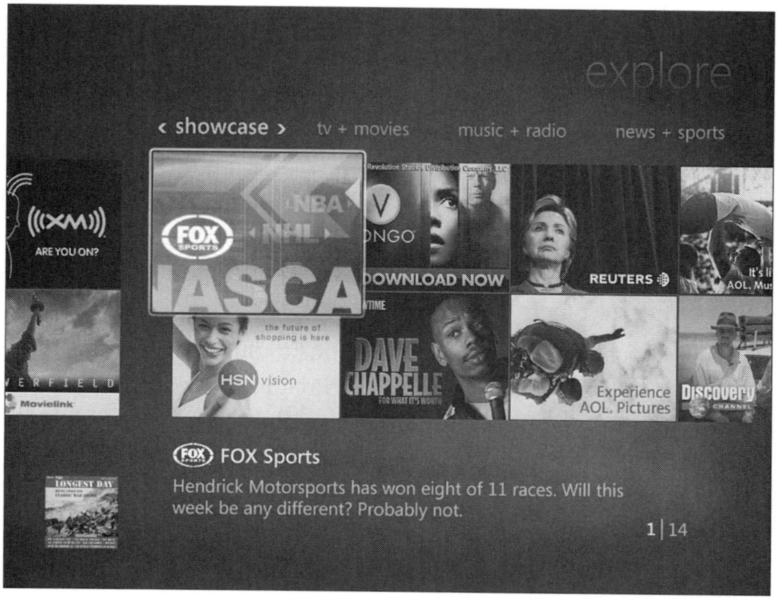

FIGURE 9.11
Exploring online media.

In the following sections, I'll provide a *Short Takes* segment at the end of each discussion summarizing what the service does and why you want it, offering installation notes, and addressing any potential concerns you might have.

tip When you select the option presented by some Online Media content to add the program to the More Programs (Program Library) menu, WMC launches the RegisterMCEApp.exe program. This program will pop up a User Account Control dialog asking for permission to run. You must click Allow and then click the Add Link button (and you might need to click Allow again) to complete this task.

Fox Sports

Fox Sports provides sports content that is also available through the Sports menu of WMC, including news stories, videos, and photos.

➔ For more information, see Chapter 8, "Enjoying Sports with Windows Media Center," **p. 223**.

note You can also access third-party services from the Program Library menu. To do so, click the globe-shaped More icon shown at the lower-right corner of Figure 9.3.

HSN Live

If you love the Home Shopping Network, you'll love HSN Live. It combines the live HSN broadcast in a central window along with on-demand videos of recent products and links to all products (Figure 9.12). Click the HSN Live button to open the live broadcast in full-screen mode.

To view products and shop by viewing on-demand channels, click the On Demand button on the left pane. The On Demand section offers products in various categories. Select a category in the left pane, a product in the right pane, and the presentation plays in the central pane (Figure 9.13). Click the Buy button to buy the item.

Rather choose from everything HSN has to offer? Click the All Products link shown in Figure 9.12 to open the All Products menu shown in Figure 9.14. HSN Live uses an effective drill-down method to take you from the top-level department to the category you're looking for.

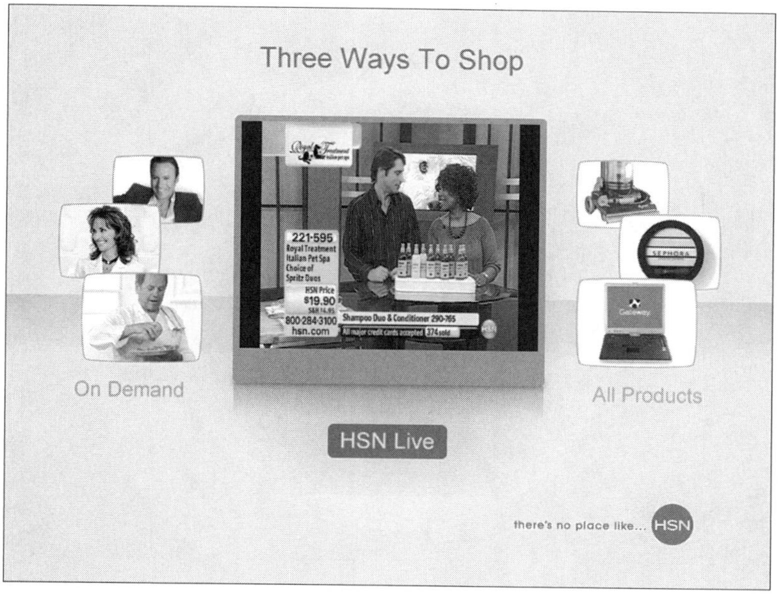

FIGURE 9.12

The HSN Live opening menu.

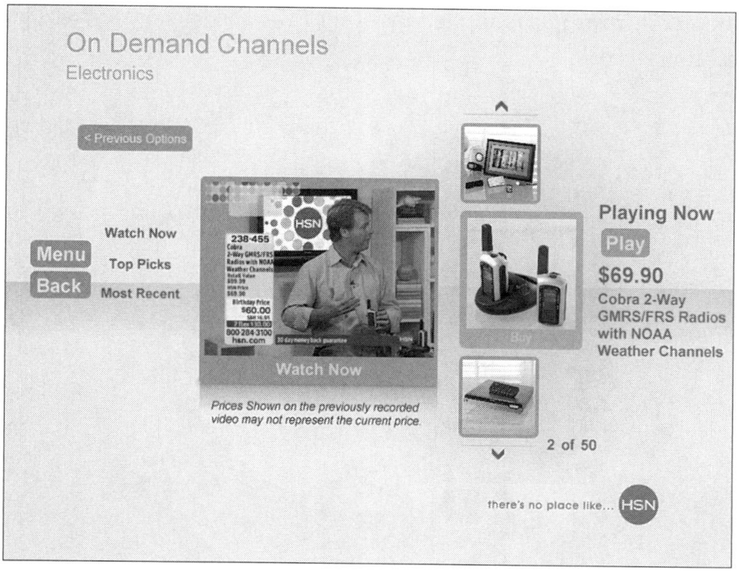

FIGURE 9.13

Shopping the On Demand channels.

FIGURE 9.14
Shopping the All Products menu.

As Figure 9.15 shows, you can filter your selections by price, brand, and other criteria. Star ratings (supplied by other HSN shoppers) can help you decide the best item to buy.

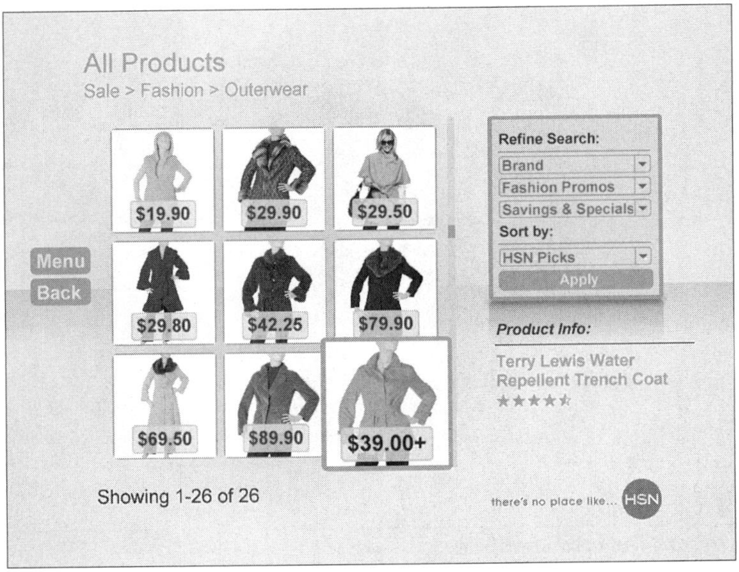

FIGURE 9.15
Using HSN product search to find the right product.

HSN LIVE SHORT TAKE

What it does: Live and prerecorded shopping offers from HSN.

Why you want it: Helps you buy from HSN with less pressure than the "buy it now" fever of live TV.

Installation notes: None.

Potential concerns: Before you can buy from HSN Live, you must set up an HSN account. Go to Set Up an HSN Account in the HSN Live Help Center for details.

AOL for Windows Media Center

AOL offers WMC users Internet radio, music performances on-demand, photo sharing, and Internet video services. When you start AOL Radio or AOL Pictures for the first time, you must install the AOL third-party services Media Center Extensibility Host application, and you must have an AOL screen name before you can access any AOL Services.

note Don't panic over the requirement to have an AOL screen name to use AOL services; if you're not already using AOL IM, AOL email, or other AOL services, getting an AOL screen name is as easy as visiting myAOL at http://my.aol.com, signing up for myAOL, and replying to the email AOL sends you after registration.

If you don't want to burden your memory with yet another screen name, you have the option to use your current email address (from any email provider) as your myAOL screen name. Once you reply to the Screen Name Service Registration Confirmation email, you can access AOL services through WMC.

Once you have installed the AOL software needed for some AOL services and obtained an AOL screen name, start AOL from any of the AOL links in the Online Media menu and select the AOL service you want to launch from the AOL menu (Figure 9.16). After you scroll to the service you want to launch, click the Start button displayed above the service description.

Log into the AOL service using the dialog shown in Figure 9.17.

tip Click the Abc icon next to the username and password fields, and you display an onscreen keyboard you can use to log in easily with your remote control.

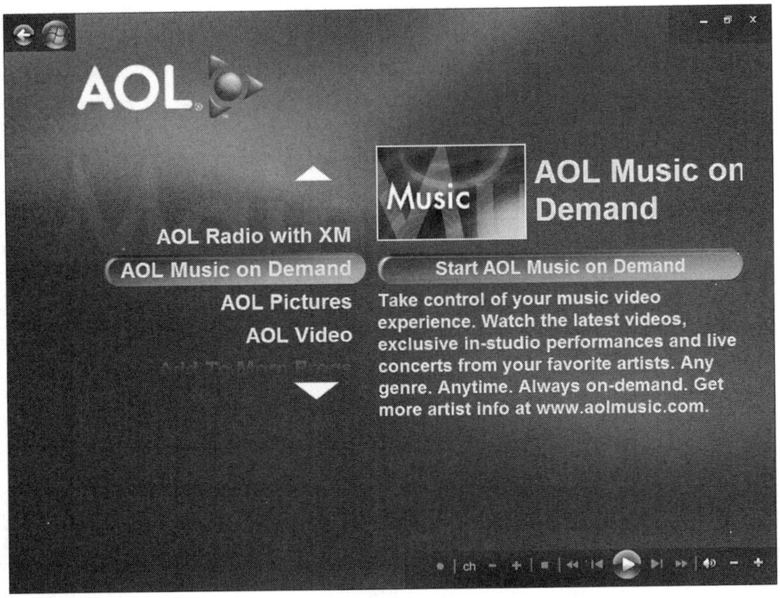

FIGURE 9.16

Launching AOL services for WMC from the AOL menu.

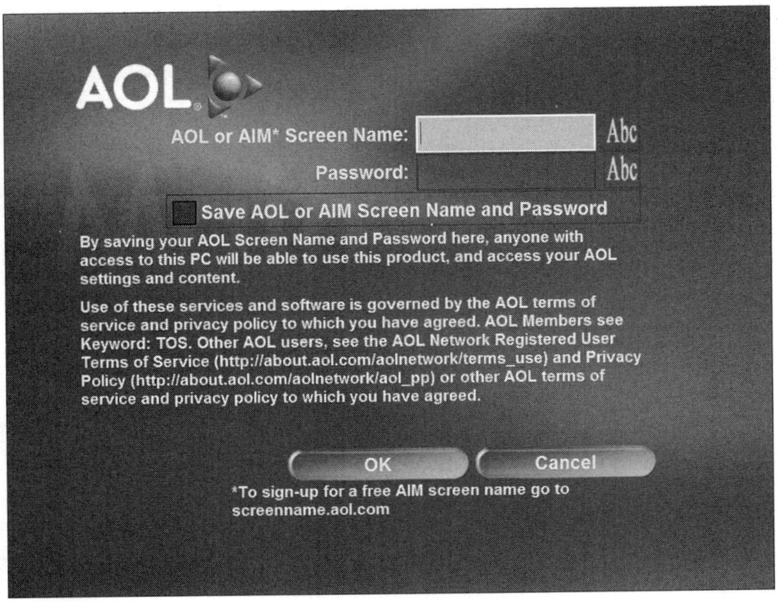

FIGURE 9.17

Logging into an AOL service for WMC.

AOL Music on Demand

AOL Music on Demand brings you dozens of music, recording studio, and concert videos in categories ranging from alternative to rock and featuring selected artists and AOL original studio recordings (Figure 9.18).

FIGURE 9.18

AOL Music on Demand features popular music genres and artists.

When you start AOL Music on Demand, it tests the speed of your Internet connection and selects one of three speeds: High (1Mbps cable), Medium (700Kbps DSL), and Low (500Kbps DSL). You can also select the speed you want (Figure 9.19). AOL Music on Demand uses the auto-detect or manual speed settings to configure video playback.

AOL MUSIC ON DEMAND

What it does: Provides access to music and concert videos from popular singers and groups.

Why you want it: Enjoy music videos without a trip to VH-1.

Installation notes: Requires you to have an AOL screen name before you can log into the service.

Potential concerns: Playback on Internet connections slower than 1Mbps may produce skips in video.

FIGURE 9.19

Use this screen to fine-tune connection speed and play back the video in your choice of windowed or full-screen modes.

AOL Pictures

AOL Pictures (http://pictures.aol.com) is a free photo storage and sharing website that also offers light photo editing (when you install a free tool available on the site). The AOL Pictures service in WMC makes it easy to upload pictures from your system to the AOL Pictures website and view the pictures already on the site.

To enable AOL Pictures to work with your pictures, select Pictures on My PC from the AOL Pictures menu and click Add New Folder (Figure 9.20). Navigate to the folder containing your photos and click OK.

To upload photos from that folder, press the zero (0) key on your remote or keyboard to bring up the Folder menu and select Upload from Folder. Select photos individually or click Select All to choose all photos in the folder. Each selected photo is check-marked. Click Upload to start the upload process (Figure 9.21).

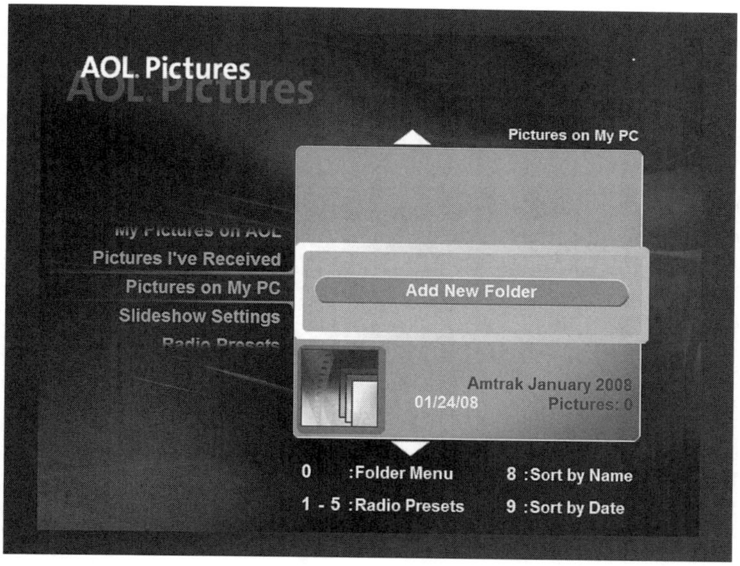

FIGURE 9.20

Selecting folders on your system for use by AOL Pictures.

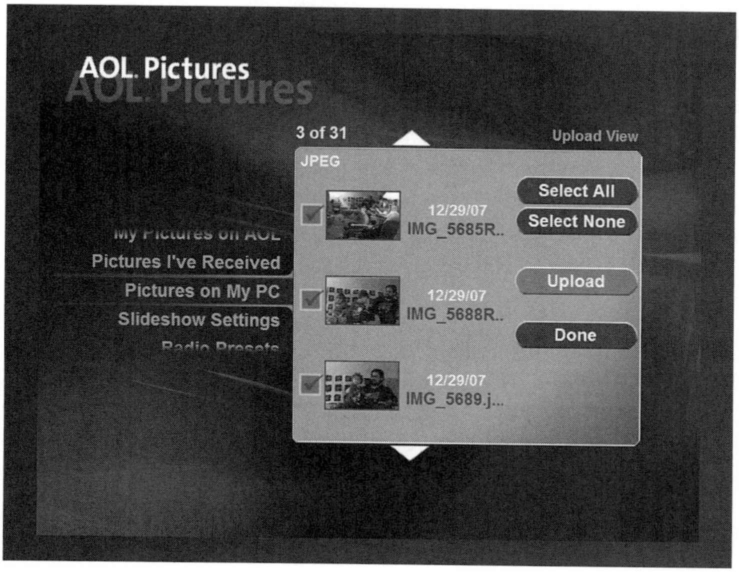

FIGURE 9.21

Preparing to upload pictures to your AOL Pictures web folder.

Pictures can be uploaded to an existing folder, or you can click the Create New Album button to create a new album for the pictures. Edit the name of the album (click the Abc icon if you need an onscreen keyboard), and click OK. During the upload process, a progress bar dialog appears.

To see your folders on AOL Pictures, select My Pictures on AOL from the menu. Navigate to the folder containing your pictures (Figure 9.22).

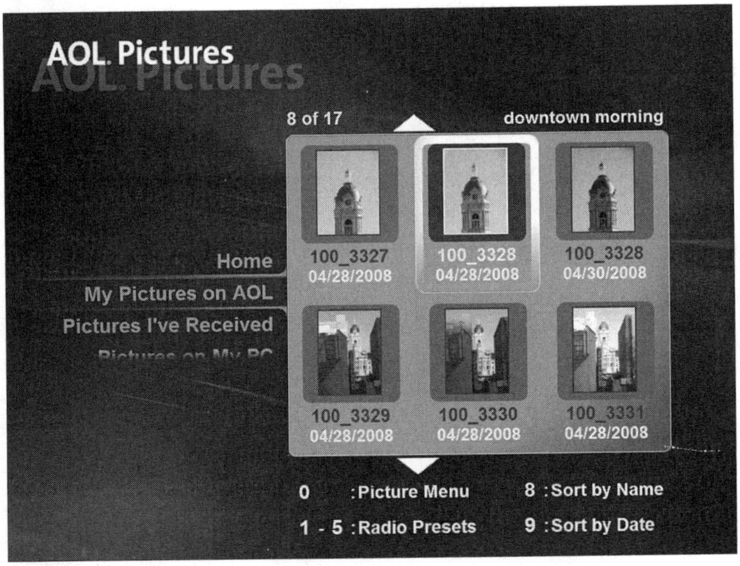

FIGURE 9.22

Viewing your web albums on AOL Pictures.

If you use the AOL Pictures web interface to receive photos from other users or to share an album as a public album, you can also view those pictures with AOL Pictures for WMC. AOL Pictures also lets you play any of your preset radio stations from AOL Radio.

AOL PICTURES

What it does: Convenient uploading to and viewing of your AOL Pictures web albums.

Why you want it: Free photo sharing and convenient printing.

Installation notes: Requires you to have an AOL screen name before you can log into the service; requires you to install the AOL third-party services Media Center Extensibility Host application.

Potential concerns: Slide show feature doesn't work with all JPEGS; doesn't support RAW files from digital SLR cameras.

WHAT HAPPENED TO AOL RADIO FEATURING XM?

Until April 2008, AOL also offered AOL Radio featuring 20 XM Satellite Radio channels as well as 200 other channels. This service was based on the browser-based AOL Radio service. However, AOL Radio is now powered by CBS Radio and no longer offers XM Satellite Radio channels. Thus, the AOL Radio Featuring XM link in WMC is no longer operative.

Showtime

The Showtime Interactive service enables you to preview upcoming shows on the premium cable network, purchase individual episodes or entire series for viewing on your PC, and sign up for Showtime as part of your cable service. When you install Showtime, you must open a browser window to register your account and unblock the Windows installer so it can accept incoming connections.

The What's Hot section provides previews of upcoming movies and series (Figure 9.23) as well as information on future airings.

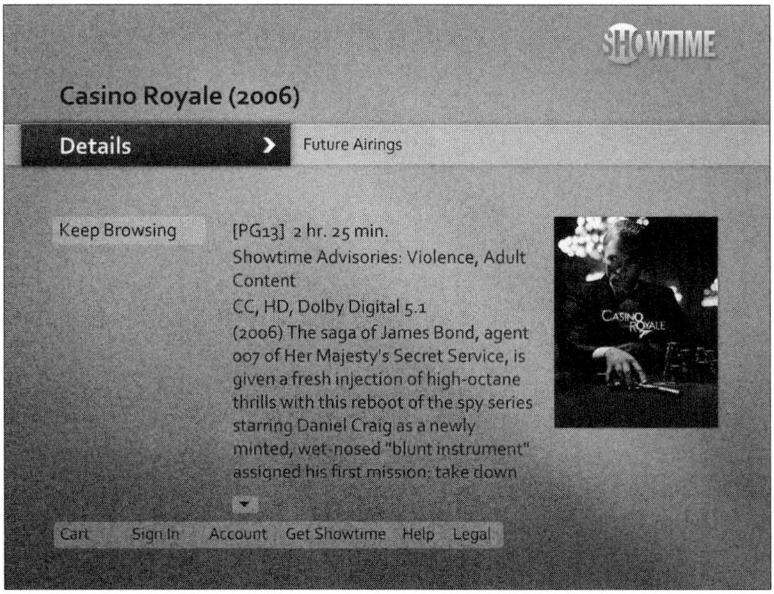

FIGURE 9.23

Getting more information for a popular recent film on Showtime.

To purchase episodes or entire seasons of selected series (Figure 9.24), you must log into the Showtime service. The login screen offers an onscreen keyboard to make logging in easier if you use a remote to navigate WMC.

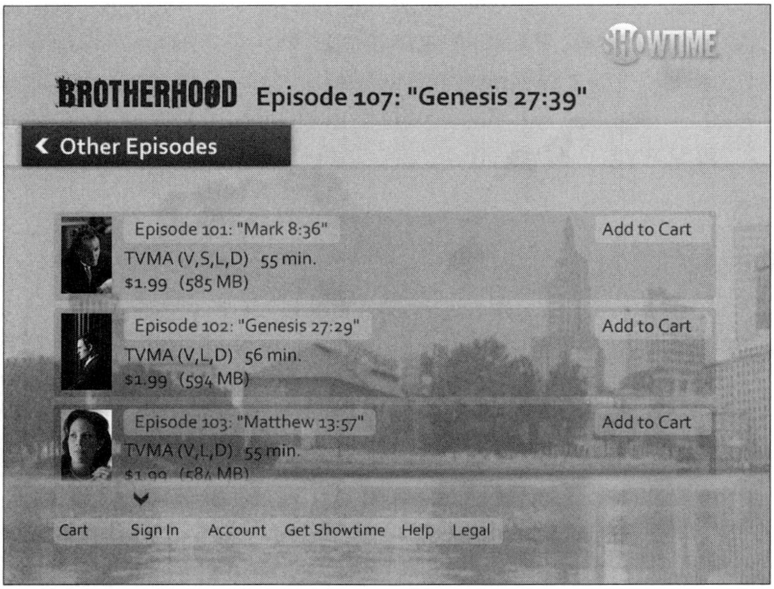

FIGURE 9.24
Selecting an episode for purchase from the Showtime store.

SHOWTIME INTERACTIVE

What it does: Program guide, preview of current content, offers series and episodes for purchase.

Why you want it: Easy way to see what's happening on Showtime and to purchase your favorite episodes.

Installation notes: Requires you to install software on your system via a web browser; must unblock the installer when prompted to complete installation.

Potential concerns: Playback on Internet connections slower than 1Mbps may produce skips in video.

Discovery Media Center

Discovery Media Center (Figure 9.25) provides previews of programs from Discovery Channel, Animal Planet, TLC, and Travel Channel. Select the channel, select the program, and you can view a preview of the show in the preview window.

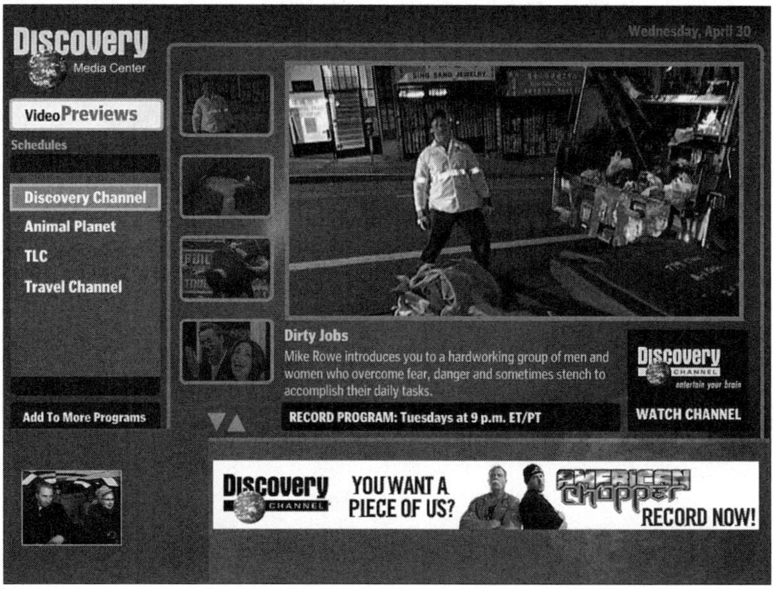

FIGURE 9.25

Using Discovery Media Center.

To jump directly to the channel, select it from the left menu and then click the Watch Channel button below the preview window's right corner. The current program plays in the thumbnail window at lower left. To see the current program in full-screen, just click the thumbnail window.

Use the Record Now and Record Program buttons below the preview window to schedule recordings of the show being previewed or offered in the Record Now banner. Note that you must, of course, have a TV tuner and have the selected channel on your cable TV lineup if you want to record the series. Follow the prompts onscreen to schedule the recording (Figure 9.26).

To view recordings of the show or to see its recording priority, open the Recorded TV menu in the TV + Movies menu.

➔ For more information about working with Recorded TV, see Chapter 4, "Viewing and Recording Live TV," **p. 85**.

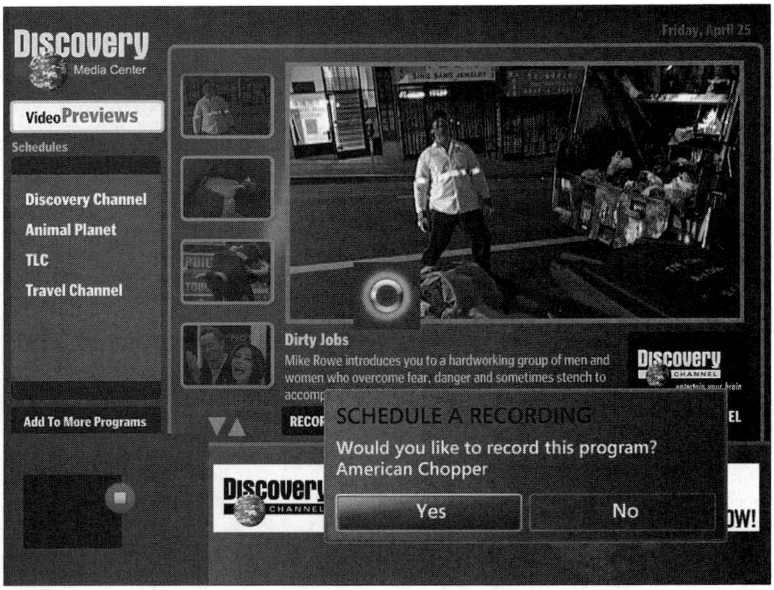

FIGURE 9.26

Selecting a Discovery Channel TV show for recording.

> ## DISCOVERY MEDIA CENTER
>
> **What it does:** Previews current shows for Discovery Channel, Animal Planet, TLC, and Travel Channel.
>
> **Why you want it:** Easy way to preview shows and set up recordings of your favorites.
>
> **Installation notes:** No installation necessary.
>
> **Potential concerns:** Playback on Internet connections slower than 1Mbps may produce skips in video.

Live365

Live365 (Figure 9.27) gives you free access to thousands of Internet radio stations and dozens of genres.

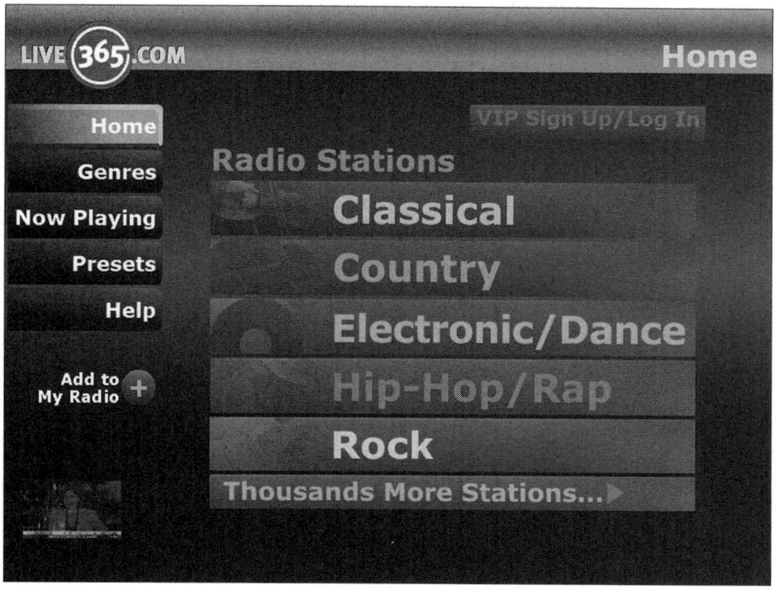

FIGURE 9.27
Live365's home page.

For a quick entry into Live365's world, select your favorite type of music or talk, and a scrolling list of stations appears. Click the Next and Prev buttons to move to the next group of stations in the same genre. To select a station, click the Listen icon. From the station listing (Figure 9.28), click the Listen icon again to hear the current track.

The Genre listing provided by Live365 in WMC only scratches the surface of the programming content available. To dig deeper, select All Stations from the Choose a Genre menu, scroll down each screen, and then click the Next button. As Figure 9.29 suggests, Live365 brings you an amazing variety of Internet radio.

note Occasionally, you might select a station that is "off the air" temporarily. You will hear a message that the station is not available at this time, and the message might be repeated until you select another station or other A/V content to play in WMC.

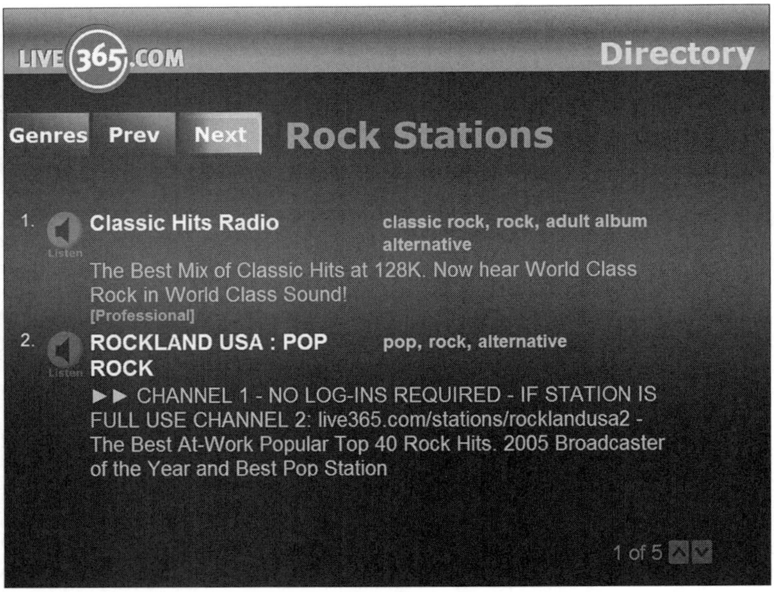

FIGURE 9.28

Listening to Rockland USA on Live365.

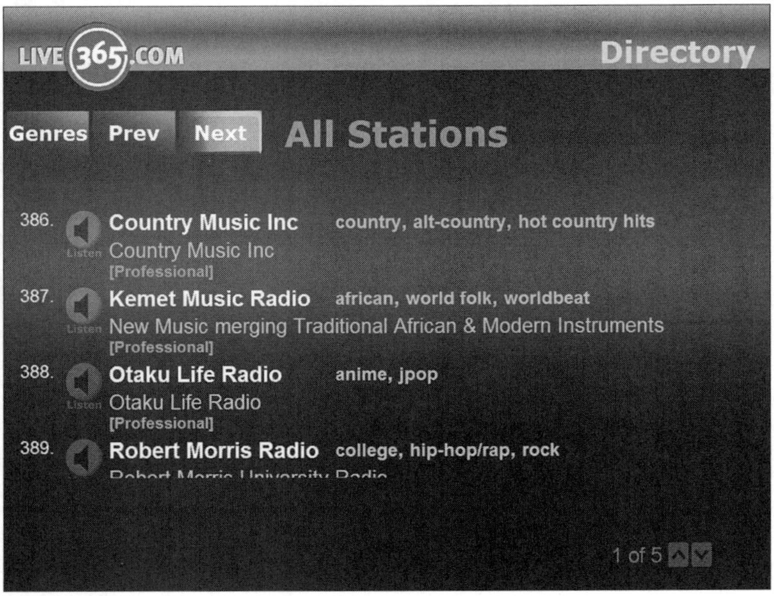

FIGURE 9.29

A sampling of the variety available on Live365.

Live365 stations can only accommodate a specified number of simultaneous listeners at a time. In some cases, you might not be able to connect to a particular station. To avoid "sold out" stations, receive higher-quality audio broadcasts, skip commercials, and gain access to VIP-only stations (indicated by a gold VIP speaker icon), you can purchase a VIP membership by clicking the link on the home page (refer to Figure 9.27).

LIVE365

What it does: Provides access to thousands of Internet radio stations with diverse genres.

Why you want it: Easy access to a variety of music and talk.

Installation notes: No installation necessary.

Potential concerns: VIP access is an extra-cost option.

TVTonic

TVTonic brings you a variety of Internet TV and video content, ranging from classic cartoons to video podcasts at resolutions up to HD-quality. It also supports QuickTime playback. (You must install the latest QuickTime player from Apple to enable QuickTime support.)

To get started, click the TVTonic icon in the Online Media Explore menu and then click Download TVTonic. If you want to install it right away, click the Open Website option. To create a link you can open later, click Save Link (see Figure 9.30). If you normally run WMC on a screen that does not display a high-quality standard Windows desktop, choose the latter option and install it later. The installation process requires several steps, followed by an Activation button you must click to turn on your account.

TVTonic automatically adds a button to the Program Library view of the Online Media menu and adds a menu option to the TV + Movies menu.

note If you don't already have QuickTime installed when you install TVTonic, you will be prompted to install QuickTime during the TVTonic installation process.

note The activation process is anonymous; however, TVTonic does track some channel subscriptions and advertising. (It's a free service, and somebody has to pay for it!)

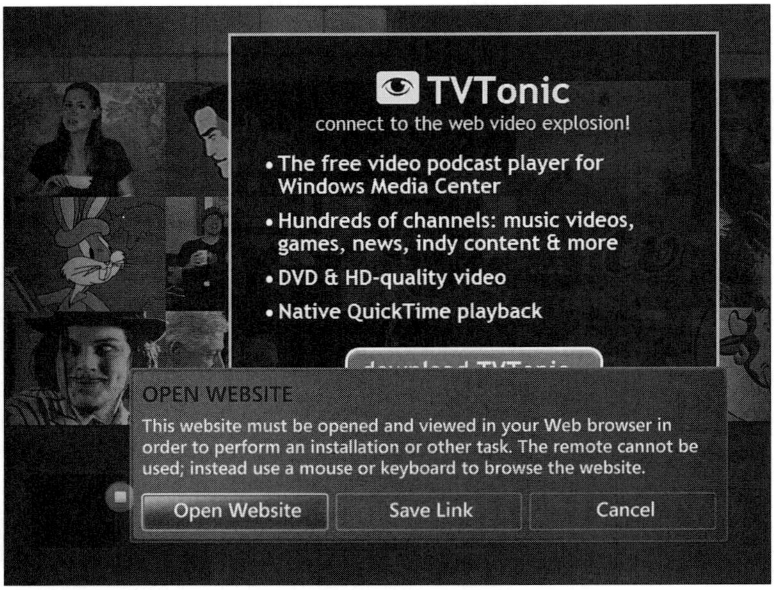

FIGURE 9.30

Starting the installation of TVTonic.

Viewing and Subscribing to Channels

When you start TVTonic, it opens to the TVTonic preview (Figure 9.31). To select other channels, select the Channel Guide and press the right arrow button on your remote or keyboard. (Use the left arrow button to return to the previous menu.) A list of channel categories appears. Note that the current video plays in the background as you select a new channel.

It's important to realize that TVTonic works best when you subscribe to the channels you want to see. There are two reasons for this:

- **Many channels use QuickTime, which cannot be streamed in WMC (refer to Figure 9.32):** The *only* way to view these channels in TVTonic's WMC interface is to subscribe to them.
- **TVTonic downloads channels in the background:** If you don't subscribe to channels with the content you want to see most, you will spend a lot more time watching the WMC rotating "hula hoop" icon while you wait for your program to begin playing.

To subscribe to a particular channel, click the Add to My Channels button.

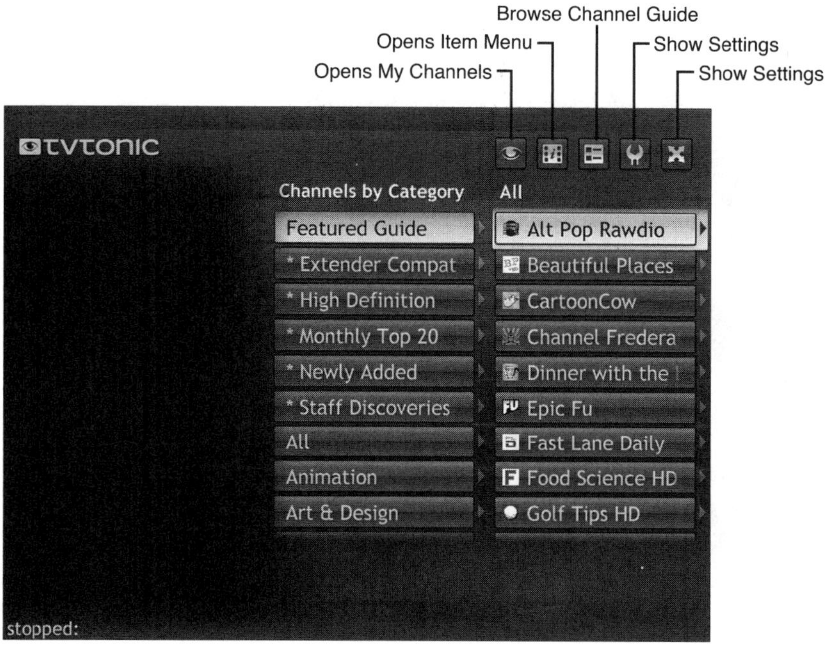

FIGURE 9.31

Working with the TVTonic channel guide.

> **note** Remember, the channel playing in the main window is the last channel you selected, not necessarily the channel you're subscribing to. To see information about the channel you're watching, hover your mouse over the TVTonic "eye" icon in the upper-right corner of the screen to return to the main menu (shown in Figure 9.31).

Because TVTonic downloads content for the channels you subscribe to, it can use up a lot of disk space in a hurry. Fortunately, you can control how much disk space TVTonic uses on a per-channel basis.

Click the Show Settings (wrench) icon and select Cache Settings. Select a channel from the Cache Settings menu (Figure 9.32).

Figure 9.33 shows the Cache Settings dialog. The light green area at right indicates the amount of space currently used by the channel, while the dark green area indicates unused space. To adjust the amount of space allocated, drag the thin red bar to the left (to decrease space) or to the right (to increase space). Click Save to save changes.

9

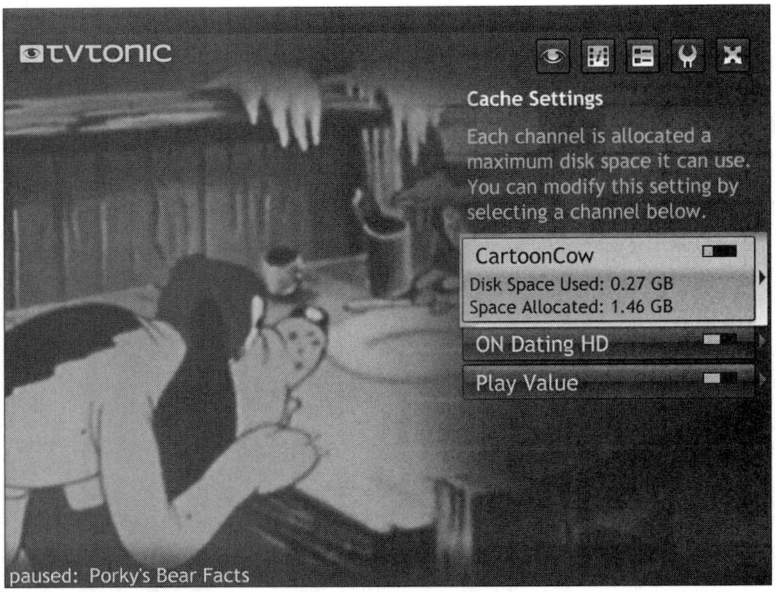

FIGURE 9.32
Viewing the disk cache usage for the user's current channels.

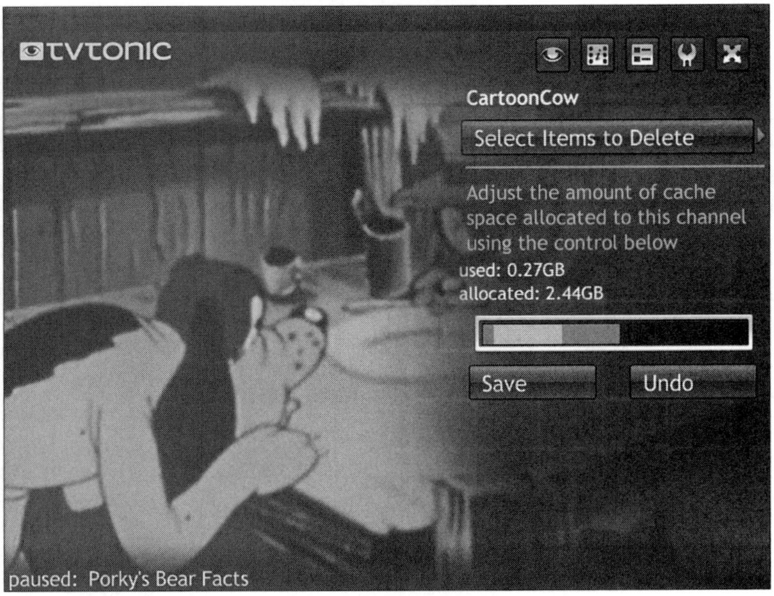

FIGURE 9.33
Adjusting disk cache (disk space) allocation for a channel.

Changing Viewing Modes

By default, TVTonic displays tips in the lower portion of the playback screen. To hide tips, open the Service Settings menu and click Hide Tool Tips. To restore tips, select Show Tool Tips.

To switch to full-screen playback from the Main Menu, press the left arrow control on your remote or mouse over the playback area. To restore the menu, hover the mouse over the translucent TVTonic "eye" icon that overlays the upper-right corner of the screen.

TVTONIC

What it does: Provides access to hundreds of Internet TV channels.

Why you want it: Broad range of Internet TV and video content, including QuickTime and HD-quality content.

Installation notes: Must install from browser interface.

Potential concerns: Very slow operation on less than a 2Mbps Internet connection, especially when sampling programs rather than watching already-downloaded subscriptions; can use a lot of disk space if you subscribe to many channels.

NPR

NPR brings the most popular National Public Radio news and information programs from the lower reaches of your FM and AM radio dial to WMC. Select the program you want to hear from the main menu (Figure 9.34), and you can scroll through that show's stories from the most recent broadcast.

From the show's menu, you can play the entire show, add the entire show to the playlist, play an individual segment, or add an individual segment to the playlist (Figure 9.35). Use this feature to create your own NPR custom Internet radio mix. A description of the highlighted segment appears above the selection window.

Select Show Archive to select from the past seven shows.

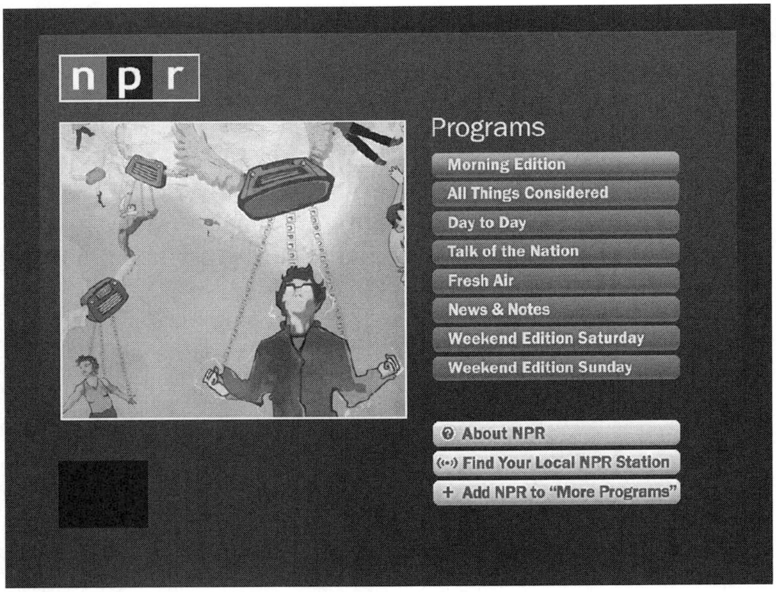

FIGURE 9.34

The NPR opening menu.

FIGURE 9.35

Preparing to listen to Morning Edition.

NPR

What it does: Provides access to NPR's leading news and information programs.

Why you want it: If you missed the show, you can hear all or selected portions later, even the same day.

Installation notes: No installation necessary.

Potential concerns: The Find Your Local NPR Station option on the main menu requires you to use a web browser, although you can also create a desktop shortcut for later viewing.

Movielink

Movielink (Figure 9.36) offers downloadable movie rentals and purchases.

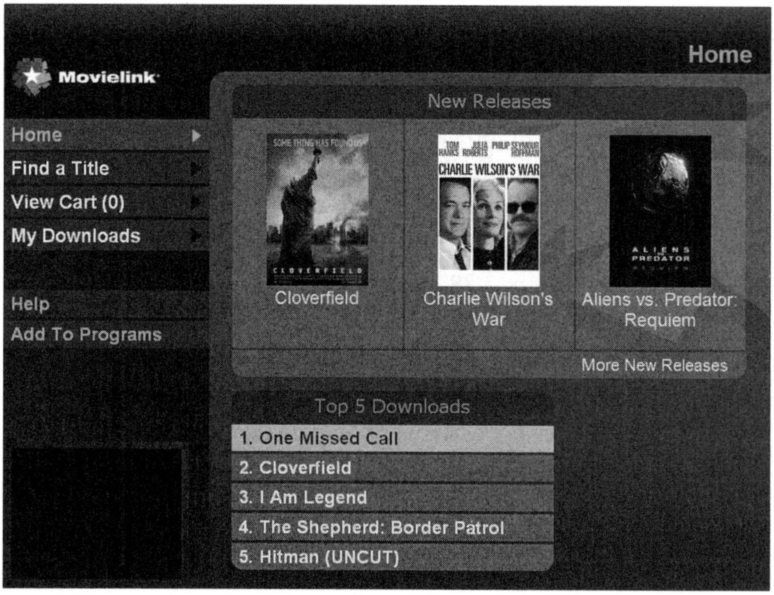

FIGURE 9.36
The Movielink home page.

You can browse the movie collection's over 30 categories or search by actor/actress, title, director, or keyword using an onscreen keyboard to make data entry easier (Figure 9.37). Note that you can search films available for rental only, for purchase only, or all films.

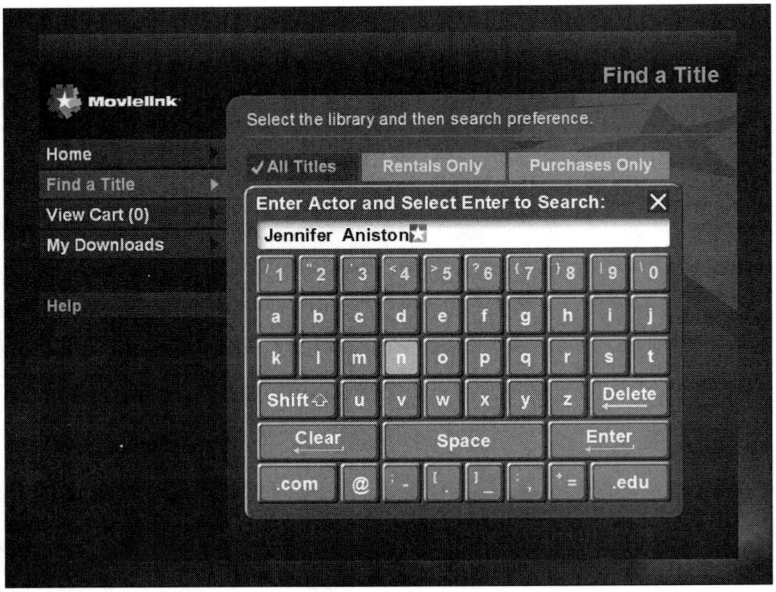

FIGURE 9.37
Searching for movies and TV shows by actor/actress.

When a trailer is available for a film (far too few Movielink offerings include a trailer, unfortunately), click the View Trailer link in the left column to play the trailer in the thumbnail window; click the window to play the trailer in full-screen.

Rented movies (Figure 9.38) can be stored for up to 30 days but must be viewed on your PC within 24 hours of first playback. There are no viewing-time restrictions on purchased movies, but purchased films can be viewed only on a PC.

Before you can rent or purchase films from Movielink, you must sign up for an account at the Movielink website (www.movielink.com).

MOVIELINK

What it does: Online rental and purchase of movies downloaded directly to your PC.

Why you want it: No need to travel to the video store; offers recent films, cult favorites, and classics in over 30 categories.

Installation notes: No installation necessary.

Potential concerns: No trailers available for most films; films can be played back only on a PC.

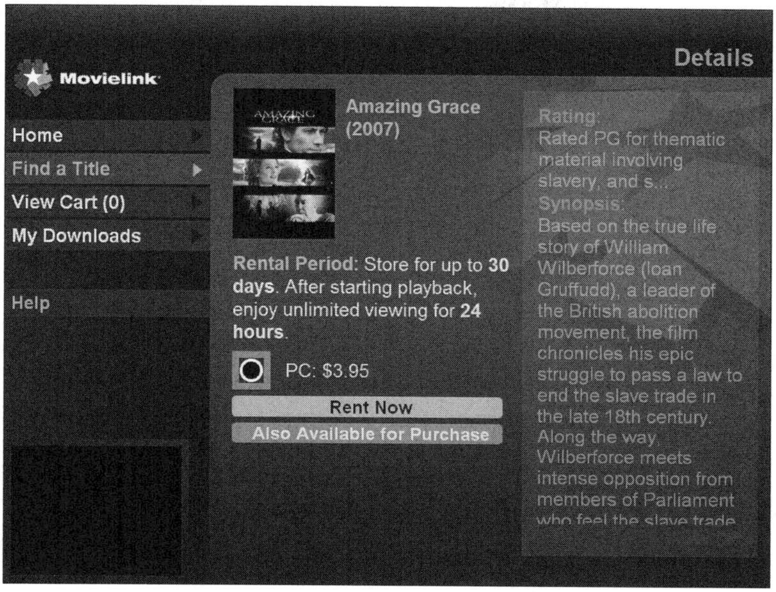

FIGURE 9.38

Movielink's rentals and purchases are available for playback only on your PC.

MSN TV Today

MSN TV Today, as the name implies, brings you hundreds of videos in a variety of genres, including news, entertainment, sports, and many more.

You can create a playlist of top videos with a single click of the Top Videos button. MSN TV Today shows a thumbnail of the next video while the current video is playing in a window.

As with other WMC video sources, you can switch to full-screen playback by clicking the default playback window. However, keep in mind that some of MSN TV Today's content is a repackaging of videos originally designed to play on the MSN website in a relatively small window. This content will not look very good when played full-screen. However, other video, such as movie trailers, looks good when played full-screen.

One of MSN TV Today's strengths is implied in its title: It is devoted to fresh content. With as many as 100 or more videos each in categories from a variety of networks, there's plenty to watch (Figure 9.39).

FIGURE 9.39
Enjoying selections from the Food Network on MSN TV Today.

MSN TV TODAY

What it does: Brings you lots of fresh video content in a variety of news, information, business, sports, and entertainment categories.

Why you want it: Frequent changes of content mean you're getting fresh content in every category.

Installation notes: No installation necessary.

Potential concerns: Some videos are repurposed from the MSN website, so they're not really sharp enough for full-screen playback.

CinemaNow

CinemaNow (Figure 9.40) offers downloadable movie rentals, purchases, and an unlimited "all you can watch" monthly subscription service.

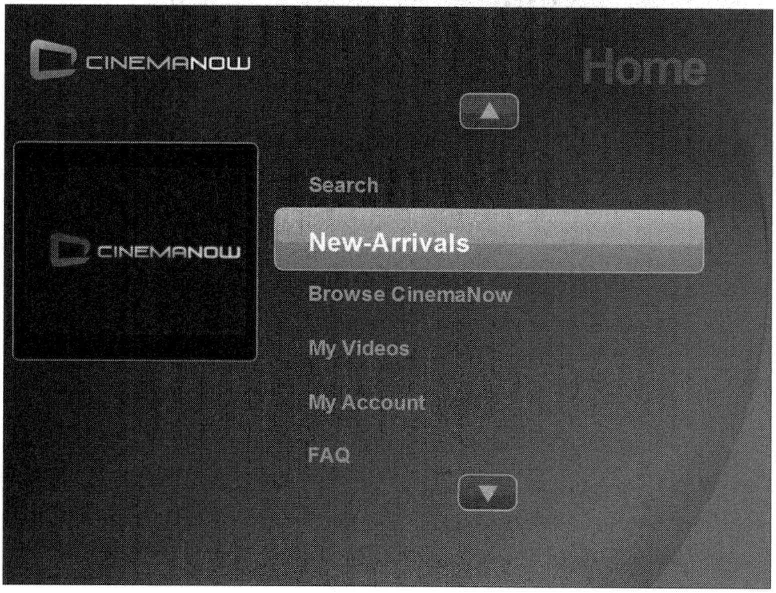

FIGURE 9.40
The CinemaNow home page.

CinemaNow offers movies in categories ranging from action to westerns, and you can play trailers in the playback window on the left side of the interface. The TV category offers classics, genres, reality TV, network series, and a "too hot for TV" category. CinemaNow groups all seasons of a TV series together, so click the View Seasons button to see what seasons are available. You can browse thousands of music videos by genre or artist. Looking for bargain-priced movie rentals or purchases? Click the Video Vault to find rentals for as little as $1.99 and low prices on purchases. The CinemaNow HD category offers HD-quality interviews and travelogues.

CinemaNow's unique feature is its Subscription category, which gives you unlimited access to a wide variety of movies, shorts, classic TV, and much more for $29.95/month.

Rented movies can be stored for up to 30 days but must be viewed on your PC within 24 hours of first playback. There are no viewing-time restrictions on purchased movies, but purchased films can only be viewed on a PC. Use the My Movies link to view the movies you have purchased or rented.

Parents, keep in mind that CinemaNow supports WMC's Parental Controls feature, enabling you to keep the kids from viewing adults-only material offered by CinemaNow.

Before you can rent or purchase films from CinemaNow, you must install the CinemaNow Media Manager; click My Videos to find the install link.

CINEMANOW

What it does: Online rental and purchase of movies downloaded directly to your PC. Subscriptions offer unlimited access to members-only subscription content.

Why you want it: No need to travel to the video store; offers recent films, cult favorites, TV shows, music videos, and classics in many categories.

Installation Notes: Must install CinemaNow Media Manager.

Potential Concerns: No trailers available for most films; films can only be played back on a PC.

Promotional Features and Limited-Time Offerings

Some of the Online Media offerings are basically promotions for commercial services, such as XM Satellite Radio and Napster. Although these services are offered through WMC's Online Media, they do not use the WMC interface once you register for the service.

Scroll to the right side of Program Library, and you will see a changing menu of media offerings brought to you by MSN Video. You don't need to install any special software to view this content.

NBC Nightly News, which brings you video highlights of current news, and Learn How, a video training series on WMC features, are media offerings you can expect to see over the long term, but expect most other offerings to change as events come and go.

CHAPTER

10

Creating CDs and DVDs

Windows Media Center (WMC) isn't just for playing back music, video, or photo CDs or DVDs. It can also be used to create CDs and DVDs, all from the comfort of your media room's recliner. Use this chapter to help you master the techniques you need to share your media discoveries and creations with others and to avoid problems along the way.

IN THIS CHAPTER

Creating Music CDs

You can burn individual songs or albums to CD with WMC in a variety of ways:

- Burn all of the songs in an album
- Select one or more individual songs for burning
- Burn all of the songs in a queue

To get started, switch to the Music task and open the Music Library.

Choosing Music or Data CDs

The Music Library contains music tracks you have ripped from music CDs or downloaded from online music libraries and stores. Music tracks compatible with WMC are stored in either WMA (Windows Media Audio) or MP3 digital music formats. When you burn media from your music collection, you must select the type of disc you are burning (see Figure 10.1):

- **Select Audio CD to convert each digital music track into a CD audio track.** An audio CD can be played in computers, in older music CD boom boxes, car audio players, set-top DVD players, and other devices compatible with music CD discs. Essentially, when you create an Audio CD, you're creating a disc that mimics a music CD fresh out of the shrink-wrap. The difference is that it's *your* music mix.

10

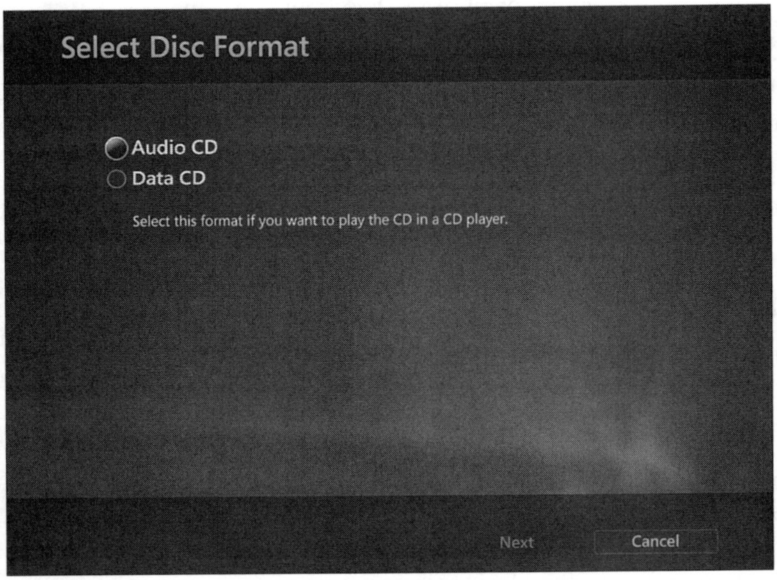

FIGURE 10.1
Selecting the type of CD to create.

- **Select Data CD to copy the digital music tracks as-is to the media.** A data CD can be played in computers and in other devices that are compatible with WMA or MP3 audio, such as recent music CD

note Not sure how smart the target device is? Insert CD-R media and select Audio CD to create a "universal" music CD that works on virtually any device that can play CDs.

boom boxes, set-top DVD players, and other devices. When you select this option, WMC creates a Windows Media Player playlist of your songs in the root folder and places the music into a subfolder on the CD called Music. The CD uses the Universal Disc Format (UDF) file system. If you use CD-RW media, you can write additional information to the disc or erase it. If you use CD-R media, the disc is read-only, and you can't erase it or write additional files to it. To store more information than a CD can hold, use a DVD. Keep in mind, though, that only computers and other devices designed to use DVDs can use a data DVD.

Burning an Album to CD

To burn an album to CD, switch to the Album view and right-click the Album you want to burn to CD. Select Burn from the right-click menu (refer to Figure 10.2). Insert CD media, and click Retry to continue.

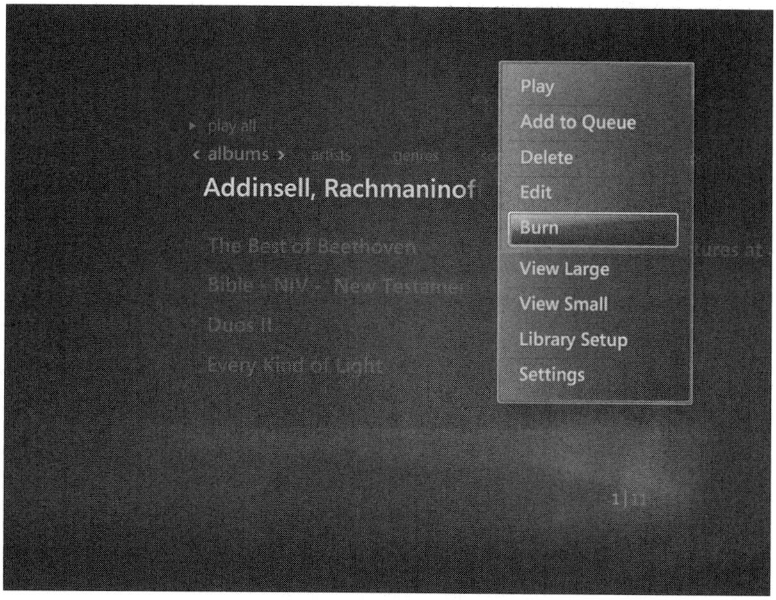

FIGURE 10.2
Burning an album to CD.

Choose the burn type (audio or data CD) when prompted. During the burn process, click OK to do something else while the burn takes place. WMC notifies you when the burn is complete and pops open the drive so you can remove your disc.

From the Completing Burn dialog, click Burn to make another copy or Done if you're finished. Insert new media when prompted if you're making multiple copies.

Burning Selected Tracks to CD

Working with digital music enables you to create your own music mix CDs. To build a mix CD with WMC, you can use the following methods:

- Create a playlist using Windows Media Player, and burn the contents of the playlist to CD.
- Burn the contents of a queue you create in WMC.

Burning a Playlist to CD

When you create a playlist in Windows Media Player, WMC can use it for music playback or for burning a CD. To view playlists in WMC, open Music, select Playlists, and you will see two sets of playlists:

- Custom playlists are playlists you've created in WMC (or in Windows Media Player).
- Auto playlists are created by WMC or Windows Media Player from your music, picture, and video collections (see Figure 10.3).

FIGURE 10.3
Choosing a playlist to burn to CD.

Auto playlists for music include

- All Music
- Music added in the last month
- Music auto rated at 5 stars
- Music played in the last month
- Music played the most
- Music rated at 4 or 5 stars

To burn the contents of any of these playlists, open one, and select Burn from the menu.

note Don't panic if you see a message that says, "We were unable to find music for the playlist." If you haven't played a lot of music lately or haven't rated your tracks, some auto playlists might not contain any music. You have the option to delete a playlist, but don't. As you use WMC (and Windows Media Player) more, auto playlists will be populated over time.

Selecting Tracks Manually for Burning

Use the Music Library's various categories (albums, artists, genres, songs, composers, years, album artists) to select songs. Navigate through the category until you see an option to Add to Queue (see Figure 10.4). If you select Add to Queue when more than one song or album is displayed, all song tracks are queued.

FIGURE 10.4
Adding music to the queue.

Continue this process until you have enough songs for your mix CD.

After adding songs to the queue, return to WMC's main menu, and go to Now Playing + Queue. Click the Music icon to open the Music queue. From the Now Playing menu, click View Queue to see the contents of your queue.

> **tip** For a shortcut, right-click an item in any category and select Add to Queue from the right-click menu. If the selection includes more than one song track, all tracks will be added to the Queue.

From the Queue menu (see Figure 10.5), choose Burn to burn the contents of the queue to disc.

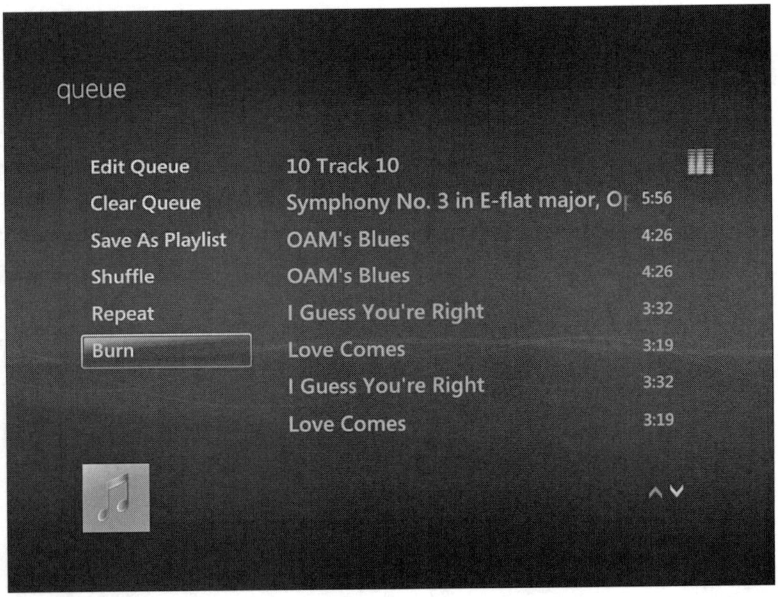

FIGURE 10.5
Preparing to burn a queue (list) to CD.

Before you burn the queue to CD or DVD, I recommend you use the option to save the queue as a playlist. By saving your queue as a playlist, you can reuse it for playback or burn a CD later.

> **tip** Watch out for duplicate entries in your queue. If you select music by using two or more methods to create a queue, such as selecting music by genre and by artist, duplicate entries are likely to happen.

Editing a Queue

You can delete tracks or change the order of tracks in a queue. Use these features to customize the contents of an audio CD you burn from a queue.

tip Be sure to make the desired changes to music and music order before you save your queue as a playlist. A playlist can't be edited from within WMC unless you add it to a queue and make changes to the queue.

To edit a music queue currently playing, open the Now Playing + Queue menu, and select Music. Click View Queue from the Now Playing menu to display the queue and then click Edit Queue from the Queue menu.

Use the up and down arrows next to each track to move a track higher or lower in the queue (shown in Figure 10.6). Each track selected for playback has an X in the right-most column. To remove a duplicate entry, click Edit Queue, and click the X (Delete) box next to the duplicate entry. After you make the changes desired, click Done.

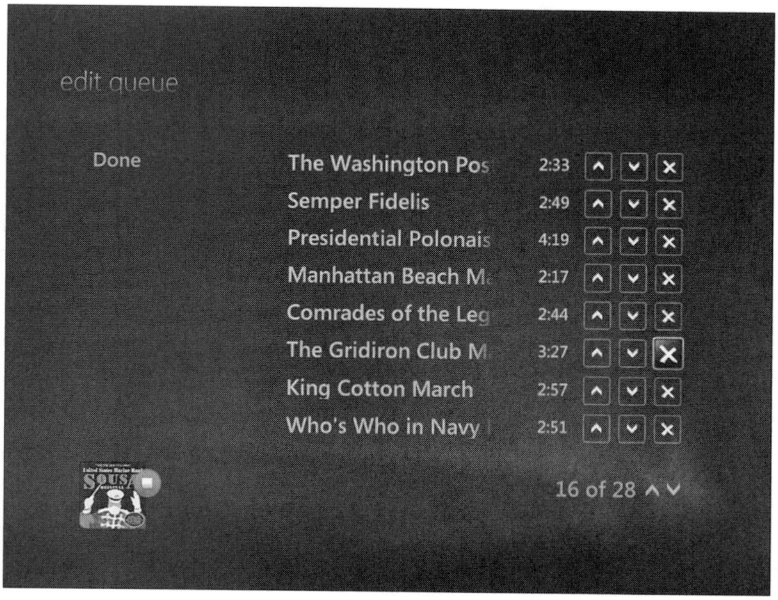

FIGURE 10.6
Editing a queue.

Transferring TV Recordings to DVD

As you learned in Chapter 4, "Viewing and Recording Live TV," WMC records from live TV, and you can use WMC's ability to burn CDs and DVDs to create an archive of your favorite TV shows.

You can create a video or data disc. Which should you choose?

Choose a data CD or DVD if you want to keep the program in an editable format. In other words, choose this option if you want to:

- Edit the program with Windows Movie Maker or another program.
- View or edit recorded TV on your computer or another computer.
- Create a video disc later.

Choose a video DVD if you want to create a disc you can play on a set-top DVD player.

Creating a Video DVD

To burn a TV show to DVD for use on a set-top DVD player:

1. Go to the TV + Movies menu, and select Recorded TV.
2. Select the program you want to burn to disc.
3. From the Program Info menu, select Burn CD/DVD.
4. If you have already inserted recordable media, go to step 5. Otherwise, insert writable media into the DVD recorder, and click Retry.
5. Select Video DVD from the Disc Format menu, and click Next.
6. Use your keyboard or remote control to rename the disc. (The default is the name shown in the Recorded TV listing.) See Figure 10.7. Click Next when finished.
7. The Review and Edit List appears. Click Add More to add more recordings to your list; click Clear All to remove all listed shows; or click Change Name to rename a program.
8. Click Burn DVD to burn the disc. Click Yes when prompted to start the burn.
9. A progress indicator appears during the disc burning process. Click OK to work with other WMC features while your disc is being burned.

If you select Add More (see Figure 10.8), you can choose from the current user's Recorded TV programs or from the Video Library. Select Video Library to browse all accessible TV programs and other media. Click Next to continue. Select one or more items, click Next, and WMC adds the selected items to the list.

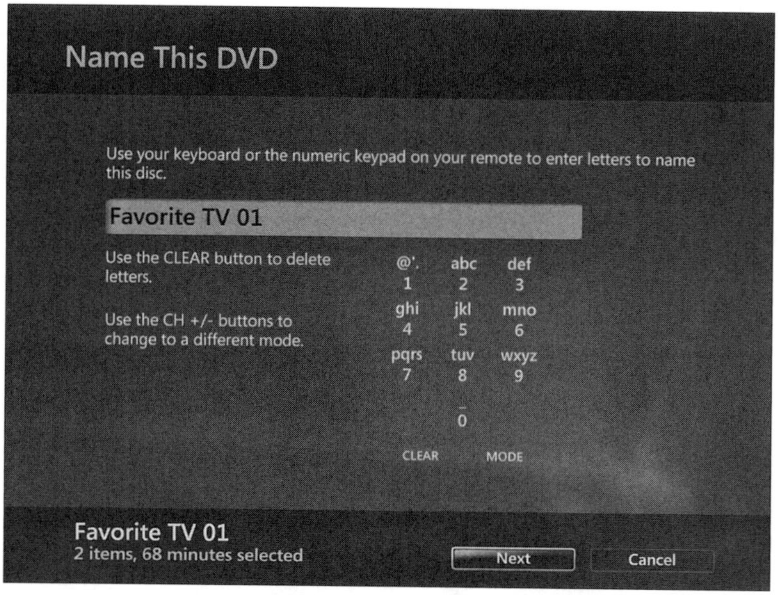

FIGURE 10.7

Naming your video DVD.

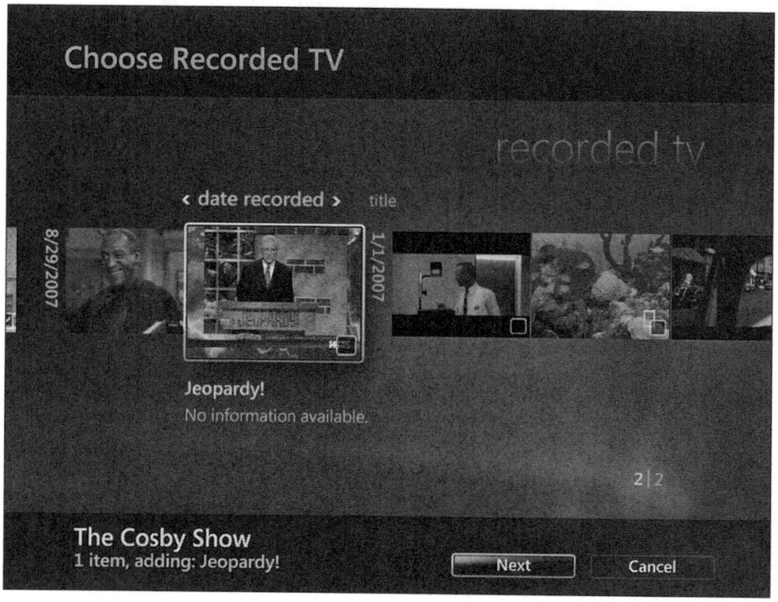

FIGURE 10.8

Selecting additional recordings to add to your video DVD.

Playing Your Video DVD

The video DVD you create with WMC will play on any DVD set-top player that is compatible with the DVD media you use; you can also play it back on any PC that has a DVD playback program (and uses a DVD drive compatible with your media), including Windows PCs running Windows Media Player 11. When you create a video DVD with WMC, WMC creates a DVD menu that resembles the one shown in Figure 10.9. The Windows Media Center logo is at the top-right side of the display with the disc name on the left side. Select a program by name or thumbnail. To view additional program names, highlight the down arrow at the bottom of the screen, and press OK on your remote. To return to a previous display, highlight the up arrow, and press OK on your remote.

tip Can't wait to play your new DVD? Insert it back into your system's DVD drive, and WMC will play it automatically. It appears in the Now Playing menu.

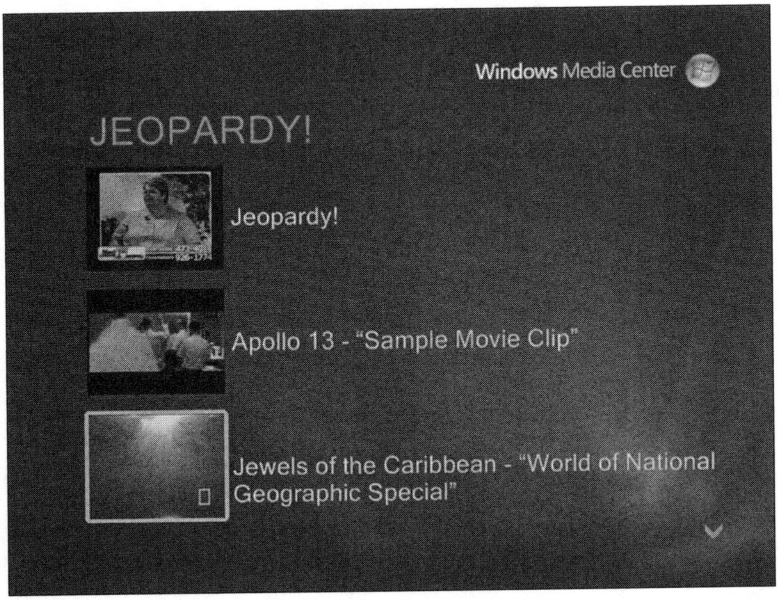

FIGURE 10.9
A typical menu from a video DVD created with WMC.

If you want to create a video DVD with different types of menus, chapter divisions, and other features, you can use Windows Movie Maker.

➔ To learn more about using Windows Movie Maker to enhance your WMC experience, see "Windows Movie Maker," in Chapter 14, "Creating Photo and Video Content for Media Center."

Burning a Recorded TV Data Disc

The process of burning a data CD or DVD is similar to the one used for creating a video DVD:

1. Go to the TV + Movies menu, and select Recorded TV.
2. Select the program you want to burn to disc.
3. From the Program Info menu, select Burn CD or DVD.
4. If you have already inserted recordable media, go to step 5. Otherwise, insert writable media into the CD or DVD recorder, and click Retry.
5. If you are using DVD media, select Data DVD from the Disc Format menu, and click Next. If you are using CD media, Data CD is the only option provided.
6. Use your keyboard or remote control to rename the disc. (The default is the name shown in the Recorded TV listing.) Click Next when finished.
7. The Review and Edit List appears. Click Add More to add more recordings to your list; click Clear All to remove all listed shows; or click Change Name to rename a program (see Figure 10.10.)
8. Click Burn DVD/CD to burn the disc. Click Yes when prompted to start the burn.
9. A progress indicator appears during the disc burning process. Click OK to work with other WMC features while your disc is being burned.

caution TV recordings made with WMC require a lot of disk space. For example, a 30-minute TV show recorded in highest quality requires about 2GB of disk space, compared to about 700MB of disk space on a CD-R disc. Consequently, if you want to use CDs rather than DVDs to store TV programs, you must reduce recording quality. Using Better rather than Best quality, for example, creates a recording a bit over half the size of a Best quality recording. However, with the near-universal availability of low-cost DVD drives and media, I recommend you use CDs for digital music and DVDs for storing TV recordings.

Remember, use the data CD/DVD feature to create a backup of your original TV recording. Although you can watch the files on a data CD or DVD from your PC or another PC (running Windows Media Player 11 or WMC), the discs cannot be viewed on a set-top DVD player.

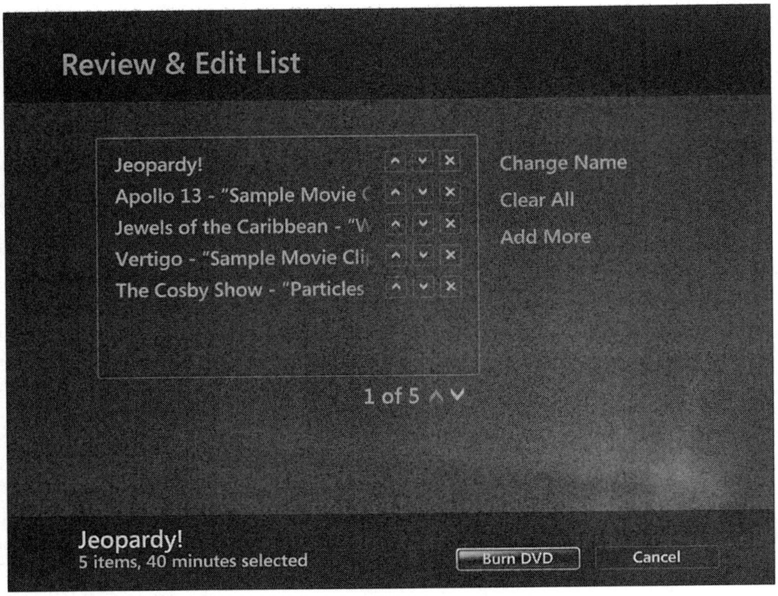

FIGURE 10.10

Reviewing a list of TV recording items to be burned.

Reclaiming Disk Space by Deleting Recordings

After you burn a disc of TV episodes, you can delete the recordings from your hard disk to save space. By default, recordings are kept until space is needed for newer recordings. However, you can also configure WMC to delete recordings at a particular time or after a particular condition is met.

Wondering if you're running low on TV recording space? Open the Tasks menu, select Settings, TV, Recorder, and open Recorder Storage. This dialog displays the current recording quality, the drive being used for TV recordings, the current recording quality, and the total recording time. If you have an additional hard disk attached to your system, use the plus (+) sign next to Record on Drive to specify that drive.

By default, WMC stores video recordings on the system drive, which is also used by Windows Vista for system files, program files, and other data files. Using a different drive for TV recordings provides you with much more space (compare Figures 10.11 A and 10.11 B).

> **tip** To change the default Keep Until setting for all recordings, open Tasks, Settings, TV, Recorder, Recording Defaults, and select the option desired. Click Save to keep your changes.

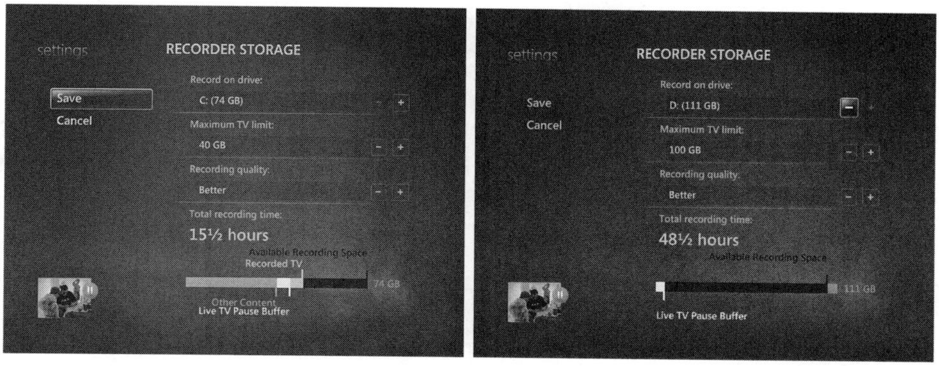

A. *Recording TV to the system drive uses the remaining space.*

B. *You can record many more hours of TV by using a non-system drive.*

FIGURE 10.11

Available recording time on the C: drive is limited by existing contents. Over three times as much TV can be recorded on the D: drive which is larger and contains no files.

To change automatic deletion settings for a particular recording, open the Keep Until menu for the recording, and select how long you'd like to keep a recording (see Figure 10.12). Options include

- Keep until space needed (the default)
- Keep for a week (the exact date is listed)
- Keep until watched
- Keep until deleted

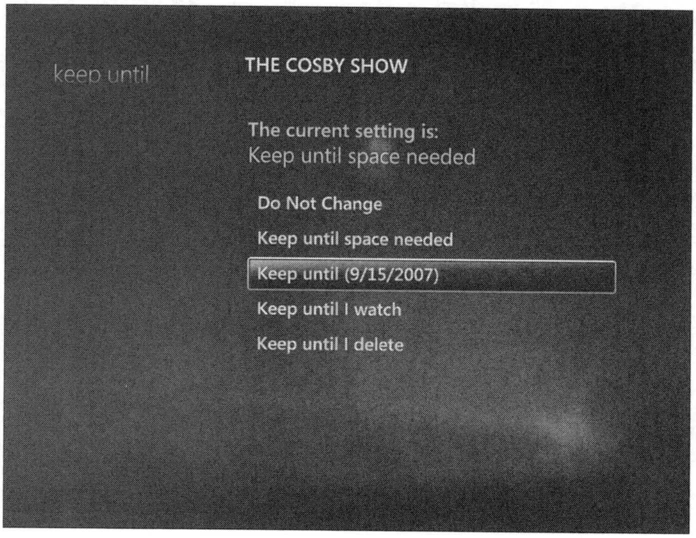

FIGURE 10.12

Selecting how long to keep a recording.

Unfortunately, there's no specific option to keep a recording until you burn it to disc.

To delete an episode manually, open the TV Recordings menu, select the recording, and select Delete from the menu. Click Yes on the Delete Recording prompt to remove the recording from your system and reclaim the disk space it used.

Burning a DVD Photo Slide Show

WMC makes it easy to share your favorite photos with your friends and family with its DVD slide show burning feature. To get started, open the Pictures + Videos menu, and go to the Picture Library.

You can create a DVD video slide show from an entire folder of pictures or from selected pictures in different folders, and you can add music to your show for extra enjoyment.

Creating a DVD Slide Show from a Folder

To create a video DVD of all the pictures in a particular folder:

1. Right-click the folder.
2. Select Burn from the right-click menu (see Figure 10.13).

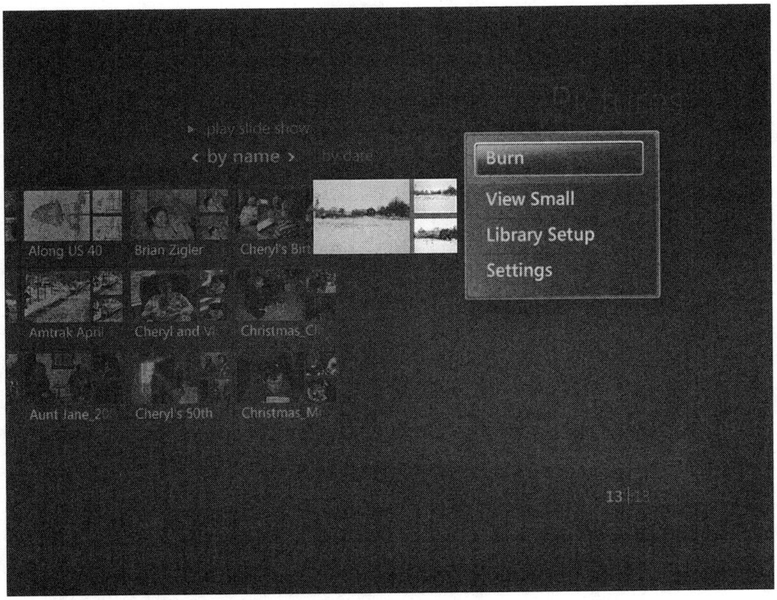

FIGURE 10.13
Preparing to burn a folder of photos to disc.

3. Select DVD Slide Show from the Select Disc Format menu, and click Next to continue.
4. Name the disc using the numeric keypad on your remote or your keyboard, and click Next to continue.
5. From the Review & Edit menu, click Burn DVD to burn the DVD.

➔ To edit your slide show before burning it, see "Editing the Slide Show," this chapter, **p. 304**.

tip If you plan to remove photos or reorder your slide show, use relatively short names for your photos. Although you can see the full name of the selected photo, file names longer than about 24 to 25 characters are not displayed fully in the Review & Edit List dialog.

Creating a DVD Slide Show from Various Folders

The easiest way to create a DVD slide show from various folders is to tag the photos that contain related content with Windows Photo Gallery or its successor, Windows Live Photo Gallery, and then use the Tags view of your Picture Library to display tagged items.

You can also use the Add More button in the Review & Edit menu. You can navigate to the folders in your picture library, and select photos for the slide show (refer to Figure 10.14).

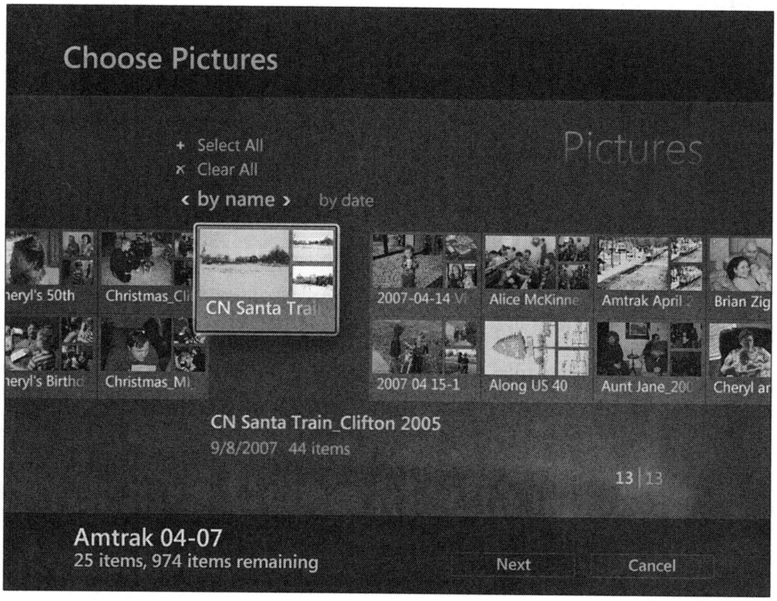

FIGURE 10.14
Browsing for additional photos.

To select all of the photos in a folder, click Select All and then Next. You can also select by date. To select individual photos, click a photo. If you have a keyboard, hold down the Ctrl key, and click additional photos.

When you select additional photos, the counter at the bottom of the display updates as each photo is added to the slide show.

When you return to the Review & Edit List dialog, the list of photos is not updated until all of the photos selected have been added. Repeat this process until you have selected all of the pictures you want—or until you run out of space on your disc.

➔ To learn more about using Windows Live Photo Gallery to enhance your WMC experience, see "Windows Live Photo Gallery," in Chapter 14.

note As you create your show, note that the Review & Edit menu and the Select Media menu list the number of photos in the show and the maximum number remaining. You can have up to 999 photos in your slide show.

note The counter at the bottom of the Review & Edit List menu can be misleading, especially if you are creating a DVD slide show from pictures taken with a 6MP or larger-resolution digital camera. This counter may show you have reached 999 items, even if the counter directly under the list of pictures shows you have far fewer pictures in your slide show. Basically, when the counter at the bottom of the screen shows 0 items remaining, you've run out of space on your DVD.

If you need to have more pictures on your DVD, you have a couple of options: You can store your pictures on a dual-layer (DL) DVD disc (but keep in mind that some DVD drives and set-top players might not be able to use the disc) or use the new Resize Image option available in Windows Live Photo Gallery (a free downloadable enhancement to the original Windows Photo Gallery, available from http://get.live.com) to create smaller versions of your pictures and use them in your slide show. (The originals are unchanged.)

Editing the Slide Show

After you have selected the pictures you want in your slide show, you can remove some items from the slide show or change the order of items from the Review & Edit list. Editing the list is performed the same way as editing a queue:

- Use the up and down arrows to move the selected item higher or lower in the playback order.
- Click the Delete (x) box to remove an item from the list.

Adding Music to Your Slide Show

Add extra enjoyment to your slide show by adding music. To add music to your show, click Add More from the Review & Edit List menu, and select Music Library as the location to browse for media. Select the songs you want to add to your slide show. When your slide show is played back from DVD, the music starts as soon as you start the show and plays as each photo is displayed.

note If you want to synchronize a particular music track to a particular photo or group of photos, create your DVD slide show with Windows Movie Maker.

➔ To learn more about using Windows Movie Maker to enhance your WMC experience, see "Windows Movie Maker," in Chapter 14.

Burning Data CDs or DVDs

To create a data CD or DVD of your photos, TV recordings, videos, or music, select Data CD or Data DVD when prompted. Navigate the appropriate library to select the items you want to store on the disc. Use the Add More option from the Review & Edit List menu to add additional files. When you have selected the items you want, click Burn to burn the list to your disc.

note You can add different types of files to your disc with this method or with the method described in the "Creating a Mixed-Content CD or DVD" section that follows. However, to make importing media into another system simpler, I recommend you select media from only one library type when you use this method.

Creating a Mixed-Content CD or DVD

If you insert a blank CD or DVD into your system while WMC is running, a Burn a CD or DVD dialog appears briefly onscreen (see Figure 10.15). Highlight the Burn button, and click OK with your remote (or click Burn with your mouse), and you can select the type of disc you want to burn.

Insert a DVD, and you can choose from:

- Data DVD
- Video DVD
- DVD Slide Show

Insert a CD, and you can choose from:

- Audio CD
- Data CD

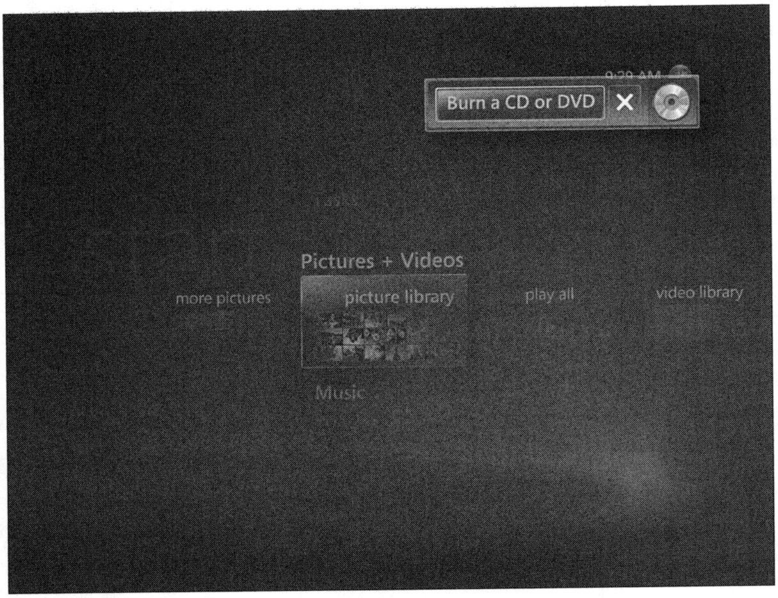

FIGURE 10.15
Starting the burn process by inserting a blank CD or DVD.

When you start the burn process this way, the disc's default name is "Untitled." Enter the name from your remote or keyboard, and click Next to continue.

If you are burning a data DVD or CD, you can choose from the following libraries:

- Recorded TV
- Music Library
- Picture Library
- Video Library

> **tip** Wondering what you've selected from the Recorded TV, Video Library, or Picture Library? Each selected item has a checkmark in the lower right corner.

Choose a library, select one or more items in that library, and click Next to continue.

After you select content from a library, the selected items are shown in the now-familiar Review & Edit List dialog. Click Add More to select more media from a library. As you select items, the counter at the bottom of the screen keeps track of the number of items and the amount of disc space remaining.

Click Burn CD/DVD to start the burn process. Because a data disc does not require encoding, the burn process is much faster than when you create a video DVD, DVD slide show, or audio CD.

Burning Tips and Tricks

Use the tips in this section to help you create the media you want more easily.

Make Two!

When you burn a data CD or DVD, the Completing Burn dialog gives you the opportunity to create another disc. To save time, insert another disc of the same type, and click Burn.

Make One Now, More Later

If you are creating an audio CD and don't want to burn more copies right away, create a playlist from your queue as described in "Burning a Playlist to CD," this chapter, **p. 292**. You can burn an audio CD from the playlist at any time.

Troubleshooting CD/DVD Burning

Use the following sections to help you solve the most common problems with making CDs and DVDs in WMC.

Drive Compatibility Issues

If Windows Vista properly recognizes your rewritable CD or DVD drive, WMC will have no problems using it. If you discover that Windows Vista does not recognize your drive, check the following:

- Make sure you have up-to-date drivers. This is particularly important for external drives.
- The most common type of internal rewritable CD or DVD drive connects to a 40-pin cable called the ATA/IDE or PATA cable. If the cable has 80 wires, make sure that the drive and any other device on the cable are both set to run in Cable Select mode using a jumper block on the rear of the drive. If the cable has 40 wires, one drive must be connected as master and one as slave.

You can replace a defective rewritable CD or DVD drive with a rewritable DVD drive for around $50-60 (internal) or around $90-100 (external), so don't waste a lot of time trying to solve problems with a balky drive.

Media Compatibility Issues

You can use any media type supported by your system's CD/DVD drive with WMC:

- Recordable CD (CD-R)
- Rewritable CD (CD-RW)
- Recordable DVD (DVD+R, DVD-R)
- Rewritable DVD (DVD+RW, DVD-RW, DVD-RAM)

Depending upon the media you choose, you could run into problems when you give your digital masterpieces to others. Follow these guidelines to avoid problems:

- **Use recordable, not rewritable, media for best results.** Rewritable media's biggest advantage is (can you guess?), it's reusable! This is great for projects in your own home or office. However, it can cause problems for other users. Old PCs and a lot of older CD boom boxes and DVD drives can't read rewritable media. (It has lower reflectivity than recordable media). To keep your recipients happy and yourself away from providing impromptu tech support, use CD-R, DVD-R, or DVD+R media as appropriate.
- **Use dual-layer (DL) DVD media only with recent devices.** Although virtually all recent rewritable DVD drives can use DL media, which holds 8.5GB (versus just 4.7GB for standard single-layer media), older DVD-ROM and recordable drives and many DVD players can't read it; the second layer confuses the device. Again, as with rewritable media, it's great for use in your own projects, but you're likely to spend a lot of time explaining to Uncle Louie why he can't view the family reunion photos until you put them on a different disc.
- **DVD-RAM is not very compatible with anything that's not a PC.** DVD-RAM media has its benefits: It's ready to perform drag-and-drop file copying on older versions of Windows without special drivers. So-called Super Multi DVD drives can use DVD-RAM as well as DVD+R/RW and DVD-R/RW, but very few non-PC devices can read it. (A few Panasonic DVD player-recorders come to mind, but that's about it.)
- **Giving a gift of photos? Give a DVD *and* a CD.** I've been using the DVD slide show features in Windows Vista and WMC to create DVDs that play on DVD players for my family the last few months—they love the memories, and they can use their big-screen TVs instead of small PC displays for playback. However, I also provide a CD of the same

pictures. Here's why: When you create a DVD slideshow, the DVD stores the pictures as a video, and the photo printing kiosks available at retail stores can't read video DVDs (and, if they use CD-ROM drives, they can't read data DVDs either). However, these kiosks have no problems using data CDs containing photos. Consider using a media case designed to handle two discs to make organization and gift-giving easier.

Error Messages

You may see errors during the CD/DVD burning process such as:

- Unable to Add File
- Invalid Application CD/DVD Writer
- CD/DVD Full

"Unable To Add File" Error

If you attempt to burn music that is license-protected, you will see an Unable to Add File error dialog similar to the one in Figure 10.16. You cannot burn license-protected music to a CD or DVD. Click OK.

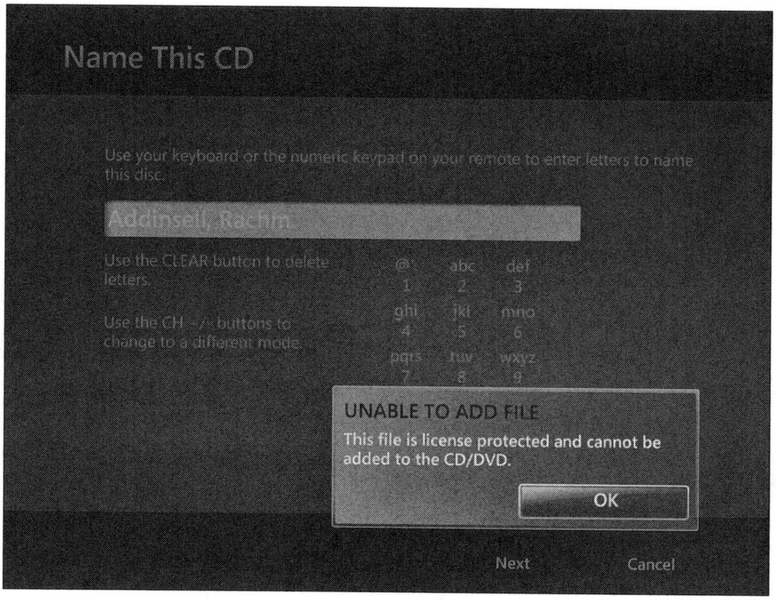

FIGURE 10.16

License protected music? No burn for you!

To avoid this problem, make sure you use the following types of music sources:

- **DRM-free music downloads.** Buy music from most online music stores, and your ability to burn or otherwise use "your" music is severely limited by digital rights management (DRM). To find out what you can do with "your" music, right-click the music track in Windows Media Player, select Properties, and click the Media Usage Rights tab. Figure 10.17 shows you a typical example of a file that cannot be burned. Some vendors, including Apple, Amazon.com, and Wal-Mart, now offer DRM-free MP3 audio. Apple calls its DRM-free offerings iTunes Plus. DRM-free music is often recorded at higher bit rates for better playback quality, which helps make up for the higher cost per track.
- **If you bought the CD, rip it yourself.** To avoid DRM woes, make sure you don't choose the "copy protect" option when you rip your CD.

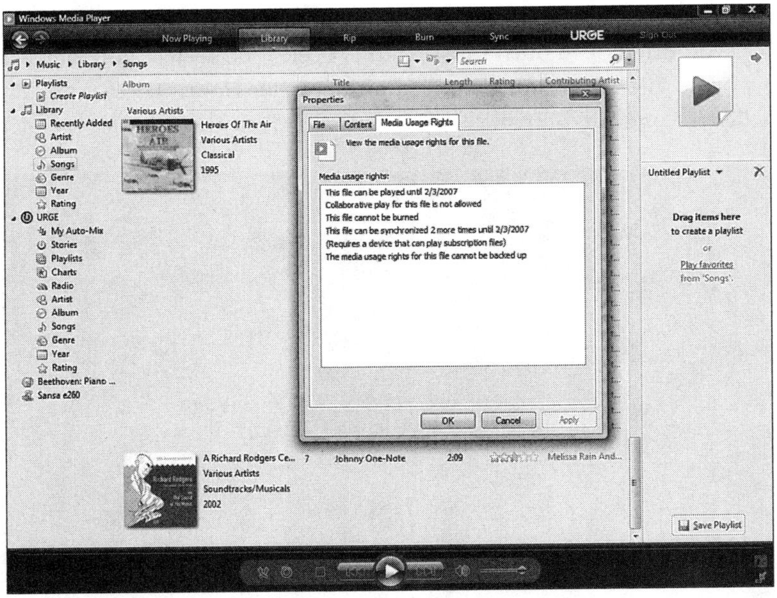

FIGURE 10.17

Not many "media usage rights" for this track.

➔ To learn more about ripping CDs you own into noncopy-protected tracks, see "Working with Music CDs," in Chapter 6, "Importing and Playing Audio."

"Invalid Application CD/DVD Writer" Error

If you see this error when you're trying to create a CD or DVD, there's probably a simple solution—and it's *not* the option offered ("disable the program"). Check the CD or DVD drive to see if there's some media in use already, such as a CD you forgot to remove after ripping or a DVD movie you forgot to put away after watching. Insert writeable media, click OK, try the operation again, and you should be all set to burn, baby, burn!

note WMC cannot determine how much space your selections take until you insert media, choose the type of disc to make, and select the audio tracks, photos, recordings, or videos you want to place on the disc. An audio CD can hold no more than the capacity of the CD in minutes (typically 80 minutes of music with standard CD-R discs; slightly less with CD-RW). However, a data CD can hold hundreds of minutes worth of music, depending upon the compression type and sampling rate used for ripping.

"CD/DVD Full" Error

If you see a CD/DVD Full error (refer to Figure 10.18), click OK to return to the list of items to burn. Clear selection boxes to remove items, and watch the bottom of the screen to determine the number of items and space remaining on the media.

Keep in mind that if you quit the burn process, your queue will be discarded unless you saved it as a playlist.

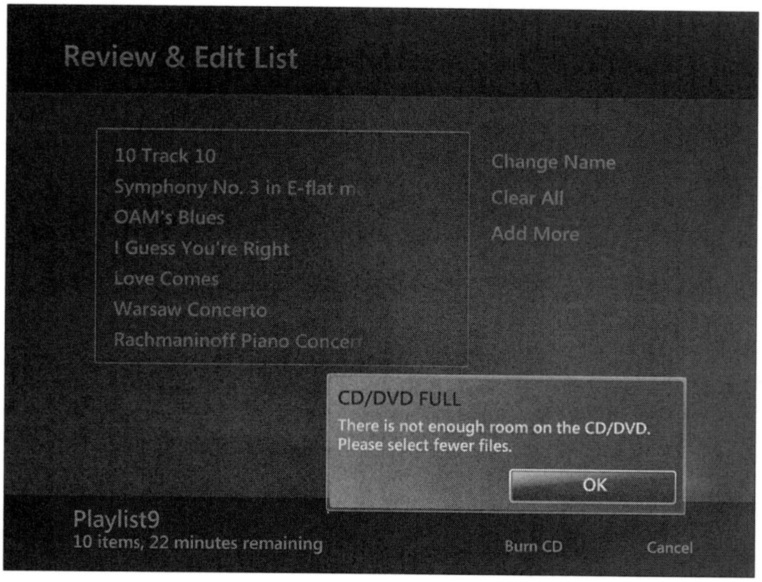

FIGURE 10.18

Out of space—time to delete some items from the list.

PART

IV

Adding Windows Vista Media Center to Your Home Network

CHAPTER

11

Adding and Using Media Center Extenders

IN THIS CHAPTER

You don't need to be sitting in front of a PC running Windows Vista Media Center to enjoy Media Center content. In fact, you don't need to be sitting in front of a PC at all. Thanks to Media Center Extenders, you can enjoy Media Center content on any TV, large or small.

In this chapter, you'll learn about the types of Media Center Extenders available, how to set up and use a Media Center Extender, and how to improve the performance of your Media Center Extender.

What Is a Media Center Extender?

A Media Center Extender (MCE) is a device that enables Windows Media Center (WMC) content to be played remotely on a TV or home theater system. An MCE uses a wired or wireless Ethernet connection to display the WMC desktop on your choice of standard or high- definition TVs. You can work with WMC from an extender just as you can when you are sitting at the keyboard and mouse (or remote control) connected to a PC running WMC.

An MCE can use WMC, even when the host computer is not running WMC, so you can perform your favorite work (or play) tasks at a Windows Vista Home Premium or Ultimate PC while other users enjoy digital music, photo, or video content hosted on that PC on TVs connected to MCEs. Essentially, an MCE is a special type of set-top box that plays WMC content.

Figure 11.1 shows how MCEs can be used to distribute WMC content throughout a typical home.

> **note** Windows Vista Media Center *cannot* use extenders built for earlier versions of Windows or WMC, except the Xbox 360 (which works with both Windows XP and Windows Vista). Windows Vista Home Premium and Ultimate include built-in support for using the Xbox 360 as an MCE, and for third-party devices that support Windows Vista Media Center.
>
> Devices made for Windows XP are Version 1 Extenders; devices made for Windows Vista are Version 2 Extenders.

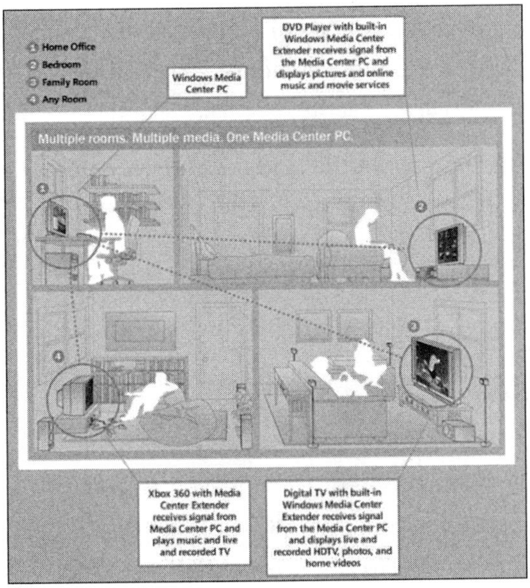

FIGURE 11.1

Media Center Extenders can be built into game systems (Xbox 360), HDTVs, or DVD players, or they can be self-contained devices.

Types of Media Center Extenders

As Figure 11.1 shows, MCE technology can be built into a variety of devices. Some MCEs are built strictly as extenders, with connections for various types of standard and HD video and audio outputs, but many also include other features.

Table 11.1 provides a representative sampling of different types of MCEs currently on the market, listed alphabetically by brand.

Table 11.1 Media Center Extenders for Windows Vista Media Center

Brand	Model	Network Support	Integrated Features
D-Link	MediaLounge DSM-750 HD Media Center Extender	Wireless N/G; 10/100 Ethernet	
HP	MediaSmart TV[1]	Wireless-A/B/G; 10-100 Ethernet	37-inch HDTV (720p/1080i)
HP	MediaSmart TV[1]	Wireless A/B/G/N; 10/100 Ethernet	42-inch or 47-inch HDTV (1080p)
HP	Mediasmart Receiver x280N	Wireless A/B/G/N; 10/100 Ethernet	HP Pocket Media Drive connection
Linksys	DMA2200	Wireless A/B/G/N; 10/100 Ethernet	Upscaling DVD player (720p, 1080i, 1080p)
Linksys	DMA2100	Wireless A/B/G/N; 10/100 Ethernet	
Microsoft	Xbox 360	10/100 Ethernet; Wireless A/B/G (optional)	Console game system with onboard DVD drive
Niveus	EDGE	10/100 Ethernet	Supports up to four tuners; supports CableCARD tuner; RS-232 (serial) port for integration with home automation products
Samsung	Home Digital Media Adapter (DMA)	10/100 Ethernet; Wireless A/B/G/N (optional)	Connects to certain Samsung HDTVs

[1]Requires PC running Windows Media Center to be updated to Vista SP1; might require free firmware upgrade for some TVs.

For additional products, see www.extenderforwindowsmediacenter.com.

Connecting a Media Center Extender to a TV

Although some MCEs, such as the HP MediaSmart TVs, incorporate an HDTV, most MCEs must be connected to a TV and home theater system.

Because an MCE works independently of the host PC's video and audio configuration, you should use the highest-quality connection supported by your TV and audio output device.

If you need to connect your MCE to an HDTV, use an HDMI cable if possible. An HDMI cable carries both high-quality digital audio and HDTV video signals between devices.

Your next best choice for HDTV is a component cable. A component cable uses the same RCA connector as stereo audio and composite video but uses three separate connectors for Red, Green, and Blue signals (the cable is also heavier-gauge than other RCA-connector AV cables). However, a component cable cannot carry audio: You must also use stereo audio or other audio connectors to connect your MCE to the speakers on the TV or a home theater system's amp.

If you are connecting an MCE to a standard TV, you'll have higher picture quality if you use an S-video connector, which separates brightness (luma) and color (chroma) signals, than if you use the composite connector (a single RCA jack, normally color-coded yellow).

Figure 11.2 illustrates these cables.

tip If the component cable and stereo cables are built as an assembly (as is usually the situation if you are using an Xbox 360 as an MCE), you might not be able to run the component cable to the HDTV and the stereo cables to a separate home theater amplifier. There are a couple of workarounds to consider:

1. If the HDTV has some type of audio-out connections, such as a stereo-out or HDMI-out, use the appropriate connector to run the audio from the HDTV to the amplifier.
2. If the HDTV does not have an appropriate audio-out connector, connect extension (RCA male/female) cables between the stereo cables and the stereo-in connectors on the amplifier.

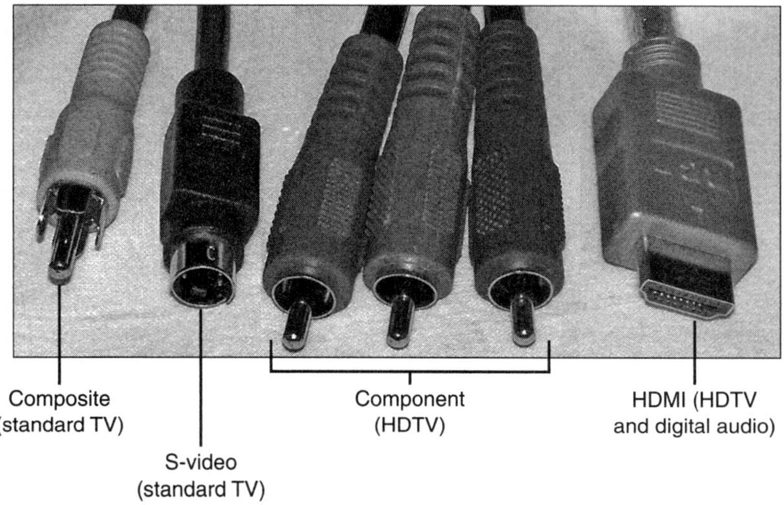

FIGURE 11.2
Video cable types used for connecting an MCE to a TV.

Connecting Your MCE to Your Home Network

Most MCEs offer a choice of wired or wireless Ethernet network connections for joining a home network. Although wireless Ethernet's the hot choice, it might not always be the fastest choice. If your wireless network supports Wireless-B (IEEE 802.11b, 11Mbps maximum), Wireless-G (IEEE 802.11g, 54Mbps maximum), or Wireless-A (IEEE 802.11a, 54Mbps maximum) but it's possible to connect your MCE to a 10/100Mbps wired Ethernet network, use the wir—it's faster.

However, if your wireless network supports Wireless-N (802.11n, up to 270Mbps maximum) and your MCE also supports Wireless-N, use it instead. It's generally faster than 10/100 Ethernet and is much faster than older wireless standards.

The Xbox 360 is a special case. It includes only 10/100 wired Ethernet, but Microsoft makes a Wireless-A/B/G gaming adapter that connects to the console's 10/100 Ethernet port. If you prefer the additional speed and range of Wireless-N, opt for a third-party device such as the Linksys WGA600N, which supports Wireless-N as well as Wireless-A/B/G.

Setting Up Windows Media Center to Work with an MCE

How does a PC running WMC find an MCE on the network? How does an MCE know which PC to "talk" to? It's up to you, the user, to "introduce" them. Here's how the process works.

1. Check the documentation for your MCE to determine how to display the Media Center setup key. This eight-digit (two groups of four digits each) key must be entered into the setup dialog on the PC running Windows Media Center.
2. After connecting your MCE to a TV, audio output source, and home network, start it up and follow the instructions for displaying the Media Center setup key. Figure 11.3 shows how the Xbox 360 displays the key.

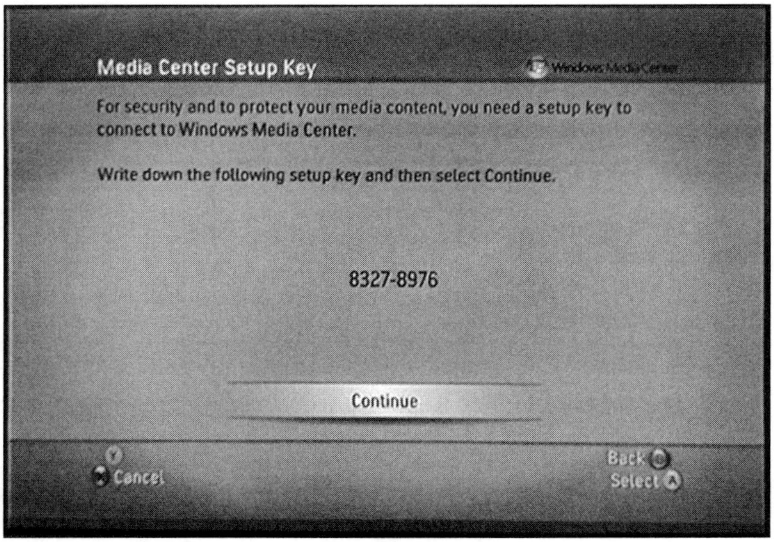

FIGURE 11.3
Displaying the Media Center setup key on the Xbox 360.

3. Record the setup key—you'll need it in Step 6. You can write it down or take a picture of the screen with a digital camera or camera phone.
4. Start up Windows Media Center on the PC you want to connect to the MCE. (The remainder of the steps are performed within Windows Media Center.)

5. Select the Tasks menu and open Add Extender (Figure 11.4). Click Next to continue.
6. Enter the setup key obtained from the Media Center Extender (Figure 11.5) and click Next to continue.
7. The next screen mentions that some firewall settings might need to be changed on the host PC to enable the connection to work. The Add Extender program makes these changes automatically for you (see Figure 11.6). Click Next to continue.

note You can also start the Add Extender task by clicking the MCE icon that is displayed in the notification area of the Windows Vista desktop. It appears after you start the configuration process on an MCE.

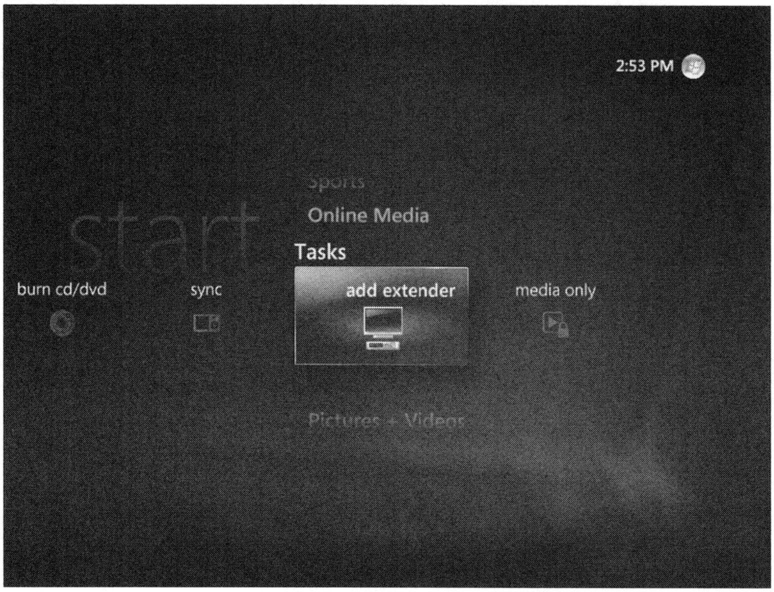

FIGURE 11.4

The Add Extender task in the Tasks menu.

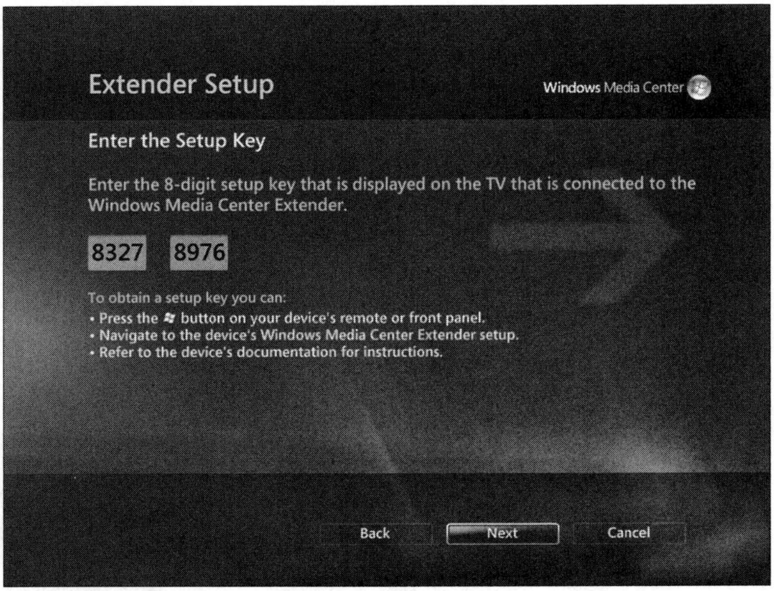

FIGURE 11.5

Entering the setup key from the MCE into the Add Extender dialog on the WMC PC.

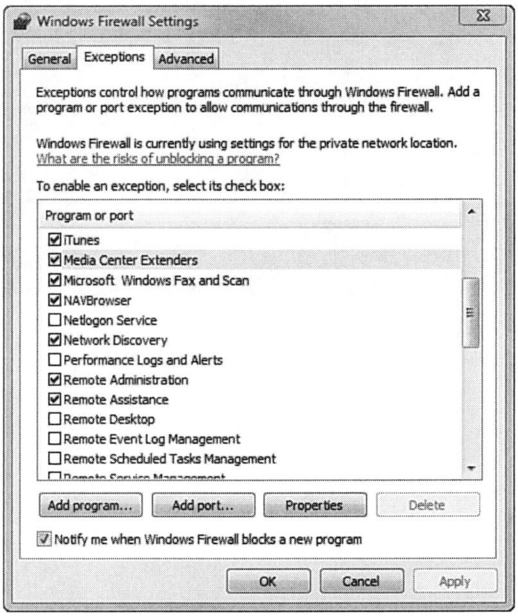

FIGURE 11.6

The Add Extender process automatically adds Media Center Extenders to the Windows Firewall Settings Exceptions list.

8. On the next dialog, you are asked if you want to copy your media folder settings (not the folders themselves, thankfully!) to your MCE. Click Next, and be sure to select Continue on the UAC prompt that follows.
9. The Configuring Your Extender and Computer screen appears (Figure 11.7). As each step is completed, it is checked off. If the process stops, see "Troubleshooting Media Center Extenders," this chapter, **p. 333**.
10. The Network Tuner dialog appears. You can run the Network Performance Tuner later, but I recommend you run it now. Click Yes and then Next to continue. On the next screen, a progress bar appears as the test is performed.

> **note** All MCEs display a setup key as part of the configuration process, and the setup key is used by the PC running Windows Media Center to locate the extender.
>
> If you must restart the MCE setup process, shut down the Xbox 360 or other MCE, wait a few moments, and restart it. A new setup key will be displayed the next time you view the extender's Media Center Setup Key dialog. You must enter the current session's key on your WMC PC to locate the extender.

11

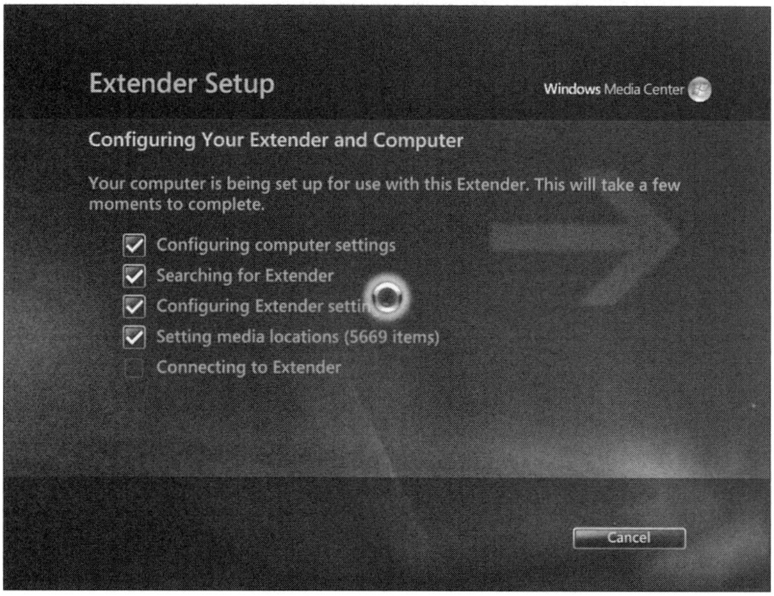

FIGURE 11.7

This checklist is completed automatically as Windows Media Center sets up a connection to an extender.

11. If the connection between your WMC PC and your MCE is fast enough, the process is finished. Click Exit. However, if you see the message "Marginal Network Performance," see the section "Improving Performance of MCEs" in this chapter, **p. 329**, for more information.

note If you use a third-party firewall program, you must make changes in its configuration manually. See the sidebar "Adjusting Your Firewall for MCE Use" for details.

ADJUSTING YOUR FIREWALL FOR MCE USE

According to Microsoft's article "Windows Vista: Firewalls and Media Center Extender," (www.microsoft.com/windows/products/winfamily/mediacenter/firewall.mspx), the Windows Firewall built into Windows Vista as well as the following add-on firewall programs work automatically with Media Center Extenders: Norton Internet Security 2007, Norton 360, McAfee Internet Security Suite 2007, and Windows Live OneCare 2.0.

However, Windows Live OneCare 2.0 might require manual configuration. This involves enabling the Connect My Xbox 360 or MCE to My Media Center PC option in the Firewall Connection Tool dialog and selecting Automatic as the Firewall setting. See the article just mentioned for details.

To enable third-party firewalls to permit connections between the WMC PC and a MCE, the following exceptions must be made to the default firewall configuration settings:

- The svchost.exe program needs UDP 1900 and TCP 3390 opened to the local subnet for inbound connections, and TCP/UDP 2177 opened for inbound and outbound connections to the local subnet.
- The System program needs TCP 10244 opened for inbound and outbound traffic to the local subnet.
- The ehshell.exe program needs the following ports opened for inbound and outbound traffic to the local subnet: TCP 554, 8554-8558; UDP 5004, 5005, 7777-7781, and 50004-500013.
- The mcx2prov.exe and mcrmgr.exe programs need random ports opened for inbound and outbound traffic to the Internet.

Before manually configuring your firewall, check with the firewall vendor to see if an updated version of it is available. An updated version might include a simplified configuration option for WMC.

Using a Media Center Extender

After the configuration process is complete, you can run WMC remotely from your MCE, using its remote control. (If you have an Xbox 360 set up as an MCE, you can also run WMC using a game controller.)

The MCE displays the same WMC desktop as the PC does when it runs WMC. You will see the Adding Media dialog displayed when you open WMC on your extender. Click OK to work with MCE while folders from your PC are being added to the MCE's view of your system.

There are very few limitations to running WMC via an extender:

- I don't recommend using an MCE to delete media files. Your connection will lock up when you delete WMC files via an MCE.
- Some third-party add-ons for WMC, such as AOL services, might not work. You will see a message to this effect if you attempt to run an unsupported service.

Otherwise, enjoy using the WMC interface to play your favorite videos, pictures, and music resources on your extender. It's not necessary to have WMC running on the host system.

Adding an Xbox 360 as an MCE

If you have an Xbox 360 video game console, you already have an MCE. It's just a matter of enabling the system running WMC to communicate with the Xbox 360.

If you're considering buying an Xbox 360 console to use as an MCE, the good news is that you don't need to specify a particular model. Any Xbox 360, from the stripped-down Core edition to the top-of-the-line Elite edition, can be used as an MCE.

Although any Xbox 360 can be used as an MCE, some console models might be better choices than others, depending on the TV and home theater setup you use for WMC enjoyment. While there are plenty of differences from a gamer's standpoint among different models, Table 11.2 discusses the differences that matter when you use an Xbox 360 as an MCE.

Table 11.2 Xbox 360 Models and Windows Media Center

Model	Video Output	Audio Output	Remote Control	Controllers
Core[1]	Composite (Component optional) (HDMI optional)[2]	Stereo (HDMI optional)	Optional	Wired (Wireless optional)
Arcade	Composite (Component optional) (HDMI optional)	Stereo (HDMI optional)	Optional	Wireless
Console (aka Pro or Premium)	Component Composite (HDMI optional)	Stereo (HDMI optional)	Optional	Wireless
Elite	HDMI[3] Component Composite	HDMI Stereo	Included	Wireless

[1]Discontinued but still available through appliance rental centers and used/refurbished outlets, including eBay.

[2]HDMI output supported on lot number 0728 and above only.

[3]The HDMI port is located next to the trapezoidal A/V port connector on the rear of the unit.

11

For other differences between Xbox 360 consoles, see the official Xbox 360 website at www.xbox.com.

➔ To learn more about upgrading the Xbox 360's video output, see "Upgrading the Xbox 360's Video Support" in this chapter, **p. 328**.

note To determine the lot number of a particular Xbox 360 console, look at the barcode label on the bottom of the unit. The lot number is shown above the upper right-hand barcode. See www.360drives.com/howto for illustrations of the lot number, the A/V port, and the HDMI port.

Configuring the Xbox 360 as a Media Center Extender

1. Turn on the Xbox 360.
2. Select the Media menu (Figure 11.8).
3. Select Media Center.
4. Write down the Media Center Setup Key displayed on the next dialog (refer back to Figure 11.3) and stop. (The Continue prompt shown is used when setting up a Windows XP Media Center Edition PC to communicate with the Xbox 360.)

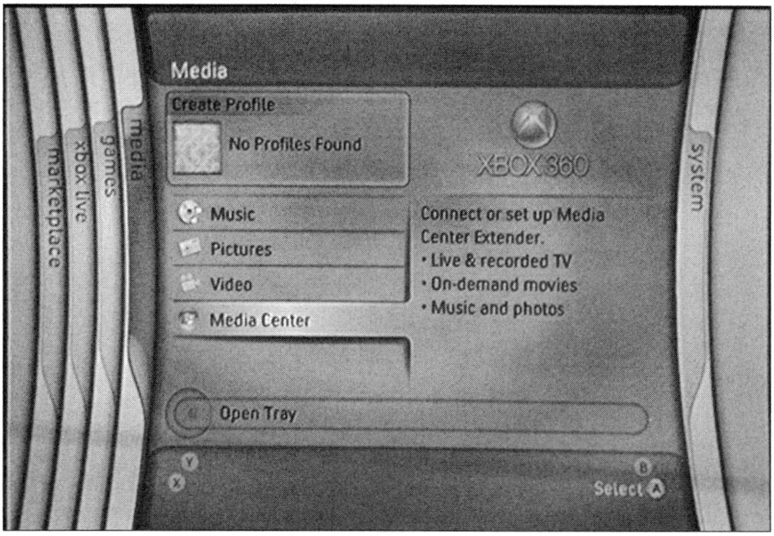

FIGURE 11.8
The Xbox 360's Media menu.

The remainder of the configuration process is performed on the PC running Windows Media Center.

➔ To learn more about setting up Windows Media Center to connect with an extender, see "Setting Up Windows Media Center to Work with an MCE" in this chapter, **p. 320**.

> **tip** If you plan to use the Xbox 360 primarily as an MCE, use the Console Settings menu's Startup blade to specify Media as the default startup dialog.

After the configuration process is complete, the Xbox 360's Media menu is used to start the MCE connection. When you select Media Center, the WMC interface appears after a few moments.

Adding a Remote Control

Although you can use your Xbox 360's standard wired or wireless remote as an MCE remote, it's kind of clumsy—and you just might get a yen to start up a new Halo 3 session when you're supposed to be reviewing the video of your daughter's dance recital. Seriously, though, adding a remote control to your Xbox 360 makes sense on a lot of levels. Not only does it make using the MCE feature a lot easier, but it makes using the Xbox 360 as a DVD player a lot easier as well.

Fortunately, you have a couple of choices in remote controls.

Xbox 360 Universal Media Remote

Microsoft's Xbox 360 Universal Media Remote, available for around $20 U.S., can be configured to control most TVs, supports WMC functionality, includes the ABXY buttons found on the game controller, and has a backlit keypad. It can be added to any Xbox 360 model that doesn't include a remote. As is typical for universal remotes, it uses TV brand codes that you enter through the keypad for configuration.

For more information, see www.xbox.com/hardware/x/xbox360universalremote/.

Logitech Harmony Advanced Universal Remote for Xbox 360

Although the Xbox 360 Universal Media Remote can control most TVs, if you have your TV connected to a home theater system, you still need a second remote to operate your receiver. If you need a single-controller solution that can be programmed through your PC, the Logitech Harmony Xbox 360 Remote is worth considering. It supports up to 12 devices, including most types of home automation (X10 and many others), and retails new for around $100 U.S. but can be purchased used for less from various outlets.

note WinSuperSite's Paul Thurrott offers a useful comparison of these remotes, emphasizing their support for Xbox 360 features, at www.winsupersite.com/reviews/xbox360_remotes.asp.

For more information and to check device compatibility, see www.logitech.com/index.cfm/remotes/universal_remotes/devices/375&cl=us,en.

Upgrading the Xbox 360's Video Support

The bad news is that the Xbox 360 uses a proprietary A/V cable connection. The good news is that both Microsoft and third-party vendors make replacement cables.

If you need to upgrade your Xbox 360 for better video, Microsoft offers a wide variety of cable upgrades, including HDMI, component, S-video, and VGA. All cable assemblies, except for HDMI, also include stereo audio cables. Prices range from around $30 to around $50 US. To order direct or for more information, see www.xbox.com/en-US/hardware/accessories/ and click the Xbox 360 Cables link.

caution Be sure to turn off the Xbox 360 and unplug it from AC power before swapping the cable module.

Third-party universal component cables are also available from several vendors. These cables typically support both the Xbox 360 and PlayStation 2, and some might also support the Nintendo Wii and are available for $10–30 US.

note If the Xbox 360 does not automatically switch to the higher-quality mode available when you connect an HDTV-compatible cable (HDMI or component), open the Console Settings menu, go to the Display tab, and select the appropriate display type.

Improving Performance of MCEs

During the Add Extender configuration process on your PC, you are given the option to run the Network Performance Tuner. Whether you run the Network Performance Tuner during the Add Extender process or start it from the Tasks menu, the Network Performance Tuner (Figure 11.9 A) checks your network to determine if its performance is fast enough for consistent delivery of HDTV or video content to your MCE.

If you see the Marginal Network Performance dialog shown in Figure 11.9 B, click Next to see details of your current performance and learn what you can do to improve throughput.

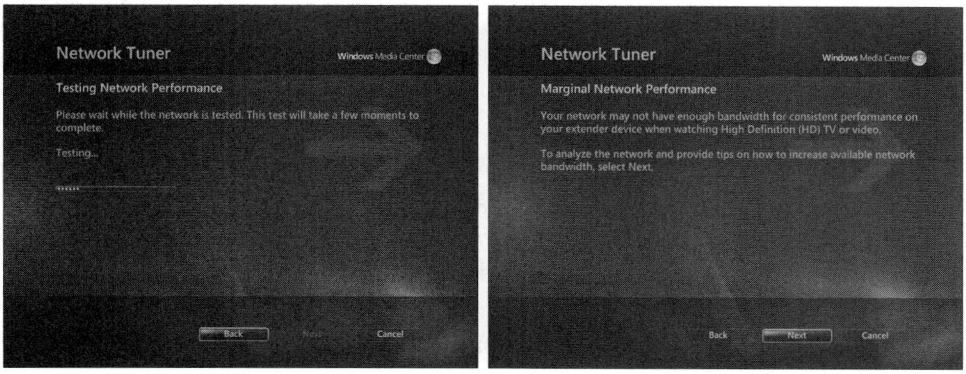

A. *B.*

FIGURE 11.9

Testing the connection between the MCE and your PC (A). If it is too slow, you are offered the chance to analyze the network and improve performance (B).

On the next screen, you can choose between a bar graph (Figure 11.10 A) and a line graph (Figure 11.10 B). During the test, if you use a wireless connection between the PC, the MCE, or both, move the wireless access point or extender or reduce obstructions.

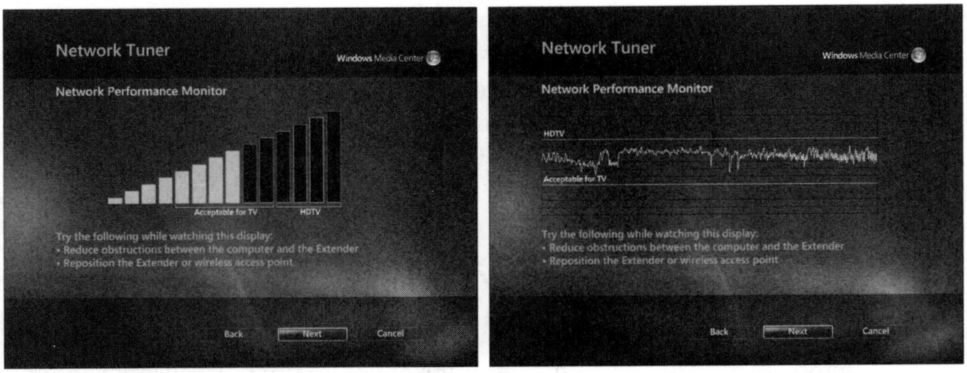

A. *B.*

FIGURE 11.10

The Network Tuner's bar graph (A) and line graph (B) options indicating a network connection too slow for video or HDTV viewing.

note If you cannot reposition the access point or extender, but your PC uses a USB-based wireless adapter or has a movable antenna, try moving the wireless adapter or antenna to see if the speed improves. If your access point or router has adjustable-position antennas, try moving them as well. Some access points and routers feature removable antennas that can be replaced with more powerful models.

At the end of the test, click Next to continue. The final dialog offers you the option to launch a web browser to view performance-boosting tips, create a desktop shortcut to the website, or simply exit the tuner.

So what else can you do to improve performance? The Windows Vista: Advanced Wireless Network Troubleshooting for Windows Media Center Extenders page at www.microsoft.com/windows/products/winfamily/mediacenter/troubleshooting.mspx has several suggestions, to which I've added some useful detail:

- **Upgrade the firmware in your wireless router or access point:** A firmware upgrade changes the "personality" of your router and might improve performance or features. Contact your router or access point vendor to see if a firmware upgrade is available and what features it supports.

- **Change wireless network channels:** Wireless-B, Wireless-G, and Wireless-N networks that use 2.4GHz signaling really only have three channels to choose from: 1, 6, and 11. (The others have too much overlap with other channels to work very well.) There are two ways to approach this problem: You can open the configuration dialog for your wireless router or access point and see what channel it's using (Figure 11.11 shows a typical example), or you can use a program such as Network Stumbler (Figure 11.12) to check for existing networks and their channel usage.

note Wireless-N networks that also support 5GHz signaling have many more channels to work with, and 5GHz network channels don't overlap with each other—every channel can be used without interference from other channels.

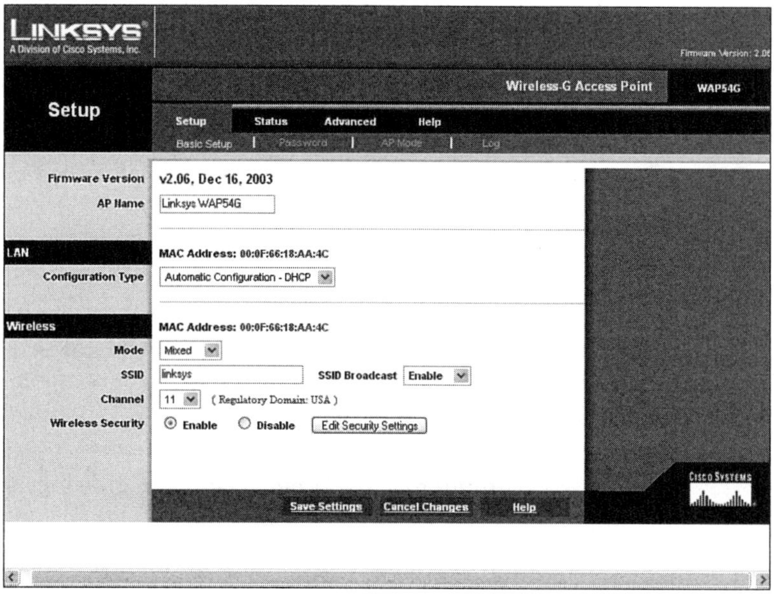

FIGURE 11.11

This Wireless-G router is using Channel 11; other workable choices include Channel 1 and Channel 6.

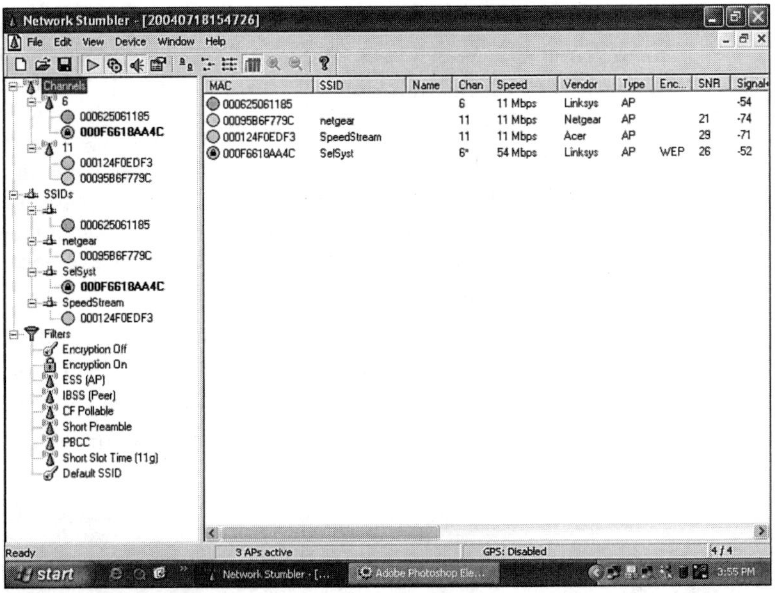

FIGURE 11.12

Network Stumbler (aka "NetStumbler") has found several nearby wireless networks using Channels 6 and 11; it's time to switch to Channel 1!

- **Connect the PC running WMC or the MCE to the router using an Ethernet cable rather than a wireless connection:** By using a wireless connection for only part of the connection, rather than the entire connection, you can improve performance over an all-wireless connection if you are not using Wireless-N networking.

note Network Stumbler can be downloaded from www.netstumbler.com/downloads/.

- **Record TV shows in WMC using lower-quality settings:** Lower-quality settings reduce the amount of data that must be transported between the PC running WMC and the MCE. You'll need to judge how low to reduce the quality before it becomes unacceptable.

➔ To learn how to reduce TV recording quality, see Chapters 4 and 8.

- **Watch out for other devices using 2.4GHz frequencies:** The 2.4GHz frequency band is an unlicensed radio band that's also used by microwave ovens; 2.4GHz cordless phones; and Bluetooth mice, keyboards, and other devices.

In addition to Microsoft's advice, I recommend you consider upgrading the wired and wireless portions of your network. For my suggestions, see Chapter 12, "Connecting with Windows Home Server and Other PCs."

Troubleshooting Media Center Extenders

If you're having problems setting up your MCE or using it, check the following solutions.

Can't Finish the Configuration Process

A configuration error message (Figure 11.13) during the setup process indicates something's gone wrong.

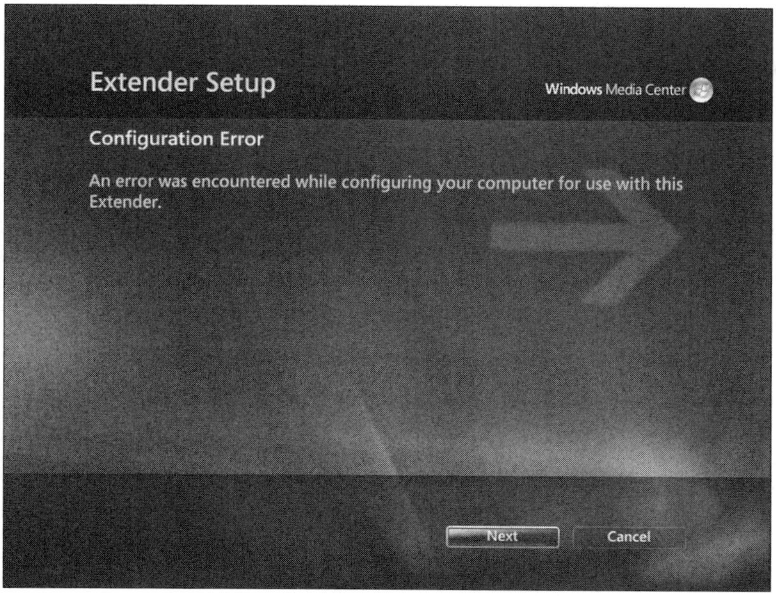

FIGURE 11.13

See a Configuration Error message like this one? You need to start the setup process over again.

Before you start over, check the following:

- Make sure you have installed the latest firmware updates for your MCE. See the vendor's documentation for details.
- Make sure the MCE can "see" the network. If you're not sure if the MCE is connecting with the network, check the wireless router or access point's configuration screens. Most routers and access points can

display a list of detected devices. If the wireless network is secured (which I strongly recommend), make sure the MCE has the proper SSID, encryption type, and encryption key value configured in its network configuration settings.

- If you are using a network cable between the MCE and the router, make sure it's plugged in correctly and plugged into the correct port on the router. Some routers and switches include an Uplink port as well as numbered ports for computers and devices such as MCEs. The Uplink port is for use only by switches or hubs, and if the Uplink port is in use, you typically cannot use the switch port next to it.
- Be sure to shut down the MCE, leave it off for a few seconds, and start it up again. You will need to get a new Media Center Setup Key before you can try the configuration process again.

Can't View Some Types of Content Through the MCE

An MCE has the same limitations as WMC itself, so if you can't view or listen to a particular type of media on your PC, you can't view or listen to it through an MCE either. For example, digital camera RAW files are not supported by WMC. However, if you convert the RAW files to JPEG, you can view the converted files on either your PC with WMC or with an MCE.

> **tip** MCEs are not designed to play back DVD movies. However, if you rip the DVD file to disc, you can convert it into a supported format, such as WMV, or you can use the methods listed on http://lifehacker.com/361470/play-back-ripped-dvds-in-vista-media-center to enable an MCE to play the DVD files remotely without conversion.

My MCE Has Stopped Working

Don't panic. Before you assume that something fiendishly complicated has happened, check the simple stuff first:

- Is your MCE plugged into a working power source? If it's plugged into a surge suppressor, make sure other devices plugged into the surge suppressor are still working. If nothing's working, the suppressor might need to be reset, or it might have given its silicon life to save your electronics. Replace it.
- Is the network cable between the MCE and the router plugged in correctly?

- Can the PC running WMC connect to the Internet and other devices? If not, you might need to run network diagnostics (see Chapter 16, "Troubleshooting Media Center," for details), or the router or access point might be unplugged.

My Picture Quality Is Not Acceptable

Make sure the MCE is configured for the HDTV type your HDTV is using or the connection type used for HD or regular TV. There are three resolutions used for HDTV: 720p, 1080i, and 1080p. 1080i is an interlaced resolution (refreshing half of the screen lines per pass), while the others refresh all of the screen lines per pass. Make sure you know the true resolution of your HDTV.

> **tip** If you have problems with resetting your Xbox 360's resolution, see the useful tutorial Reset Xbox 360 Resolution at http://cocaman.ch/wp/2006/12/reset-xbox360-resolution/

There's No Audio

Make sure the HDMI or stereo cables from the MCE are connected to the appropriate audio device and that the volume control is set correctly. If you are using a receiver, make sure the receiver is configured for the correct audio source and that the receiver is turned on.

CHAPTER

12

Connecting with Windows Home Server and Other PCs

IN THIS CHAPTER

- Configuring PC Shares for Media Sharing
- Setting Up Windows Home Server for Media Sharing
- Boosting Network and Internet Performance
- Choosing the Fastest Internet Connection
- Understanding Wi-Fi (Wireless Ethernet) Network Standards
- Using Gigabit Ethernet Instead of Fast Ethernet
- Upgrading Your Router

One of the benefits of Windows Media Center (WMC) is its ability to help you enjoy music, photos, and videos stored on other PCs on your home network. This won't happen, though, if you don't configure those PCs properly. However, configuring PCs for media sharing is more than setting up their operating systems properly. To get the best performance, especially with today's huge digital photo and HD video files, upgrading to faster wired and wireless network hardware might also be necessary.

This chapter helps you to assure that the computers on your home network can work together to bring your WMC PCs a full load of media goodness.

Configuring PC Shares for Media Sharing

If you have a home network, the PC running WMC probably isn't the only PC on the network with media you'd like to enjoy through WMC's "10-foot UI." You might have other Windows Vista–based systems with their own collections of photos, videos, and music, or you might have systems running Windows XP or older versions of Windows that include media assets you'd like to share. While the process of configuring WMC to use other PCs' shared folders was covered in Chapter 3, "Setting Up Windows Media Center," WMC can't find those folders if they're not shared properly. In the following sections, you'll learn just how to do it.

Configuring Windows XP for Media Sharing

If you have Windows XP, there are several ways to share media:

- You can run the Network Setup wizard to configure folders for media sharing.
- You can manually share folders containing media as read-only folders.
- After sharing the Shared Documents folder, you can place files and folders you want to share in that folder only.
- You can set up a separate computing running Windows Home Server and use it to share media.

Not all of these methods are created equal, as you will see in the coming sections.

Is Your Network Already Working? Skip the Network Setup Wizard!

The Network Setup Wizard (Figure 12.1) included in Windows XP should be used to set up a home network or to add a computer to an already-existing home network. If you run it on a system that is already on the home network and is working properly, you might change the existing computer name or workgroup name.

By default, the Network Setup Wizard uses MSHOME as the workgroup name. Windows XP uses WORKGROUP as the default name if you don't run the Network Setup Wizard or change the workgroup name manually. If the workgroup name is changed, the shared files on that computer will become inaccessible to other PCs. As you can see, the odds of this happening are pretty high if you're unfamiliar with the wizard.

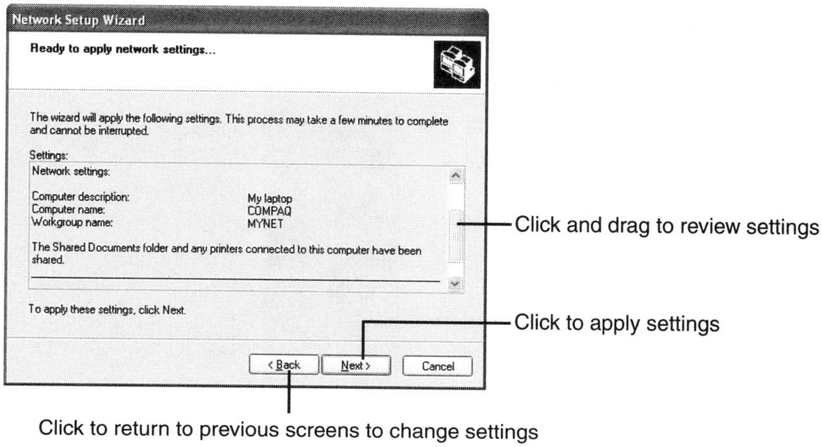

FIGURE 12.1

When you run the Network Setup Wizard on a system that is already configured for network sharing, changing the workgroup name causes existing shares to become inaccessible.

Another problem with the Network Setup Wizard is that it's designed to share the Shared Documents folder only; it's much more likely that the media files you want to share with WMC are found in other folders.

However, if you want to use the Network Setup Wizard on a Windows XP system that's new to your network to enable it to share folders, here's how to do it:

1. First, make sure you know the name of the home network (also known as the workgroup name). Go to a system that's already on the network to learn this information:
   - On a Windows XP system, open the System icon in Control Panel (available from Classic View or from the Performance and Maintenance category) and click the Computer Name tab (Figure 12.2).
   - On a Windows Vista system, open the System icon in the System and Maintenance category of Control Panel. It's listed in the Computer Name, Domain, and Workgroup Settings section (Figure 12.2).

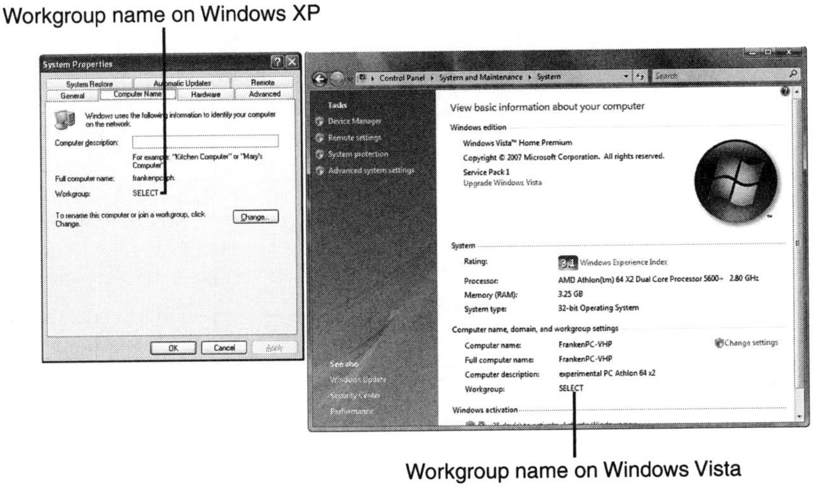

FIGURE 12.2

Viewing the workgroup (network name) information on a Windows XP or Windows Vista computer already added to the network.

2. Next, make sure the new computer has a working connection to the network. If the system uses a wired connection, make sure you have connected the network cable between the PC's network port and a switch or router on the network. If the system uses a wireless connection, make sure you have configured the PC with the SSID, encryption type (preferably WPA2 or WPA), and encryption key used by the wireless network.

3. Next, run the Network Setup Wizard. Select the option to connect to the Internet through another computer or a residential gateway (Select a Connection Method). If you have both a wired and wireless connection, select the connection you are configuring (Select the Connection to Bridge). When prompted for a computer name (Give This Computer a Description and Name), be sure to use a name that is not already in use on the home network. However, when

> **note** For a much more detailed examination of the processes of building and configuring a wired or wireless network with Windows XP, see my book *Absolute Beginner's Guide to Home Networking*, Que, 2005 (ISBN 0-7897-3205-X). For much more detailed information on networking Windows Vista, see *Networking with Windows Vista*, by Paul McFedries, Que, 2008 (ISBN 0-7897-3777-9).

prompted for the workgroup (Name Your Network), be sure to use the network name you discovered in the first step.

4. Next, at the end of the process, choose the option to Just Finish the Wizard. Reboot the system when prompted, and after the system reboots, its Shared Documents folder will be visible to other network users.
5. Now that your system has been configured to share folders, you can manually select other folders to share, such as the My Pictures or My Music folders. For details, see the next section.

Configuring Windows XP Manually for File Sharing

To manually share media folders, you must first have the File and Printer Sharing for Microsoft Networks service installed. If you previously ran the Network Setup Wizard on your system, it's already installed. However, if you didn't run the wizard, you must install File and Printer Sharing manually.

To determine if you have File and Printer Sharing installed (see Figure 12.3), take the following steps:

1. Click Start and open My Network Places.
2. Click View Network Connections in the Network Tasks pane.
3. Right-click your network connection and select Properties.
4. Review the list of components. If File and Printer Sharing for Microsoft Networks is listed, you're ready to share media folders.

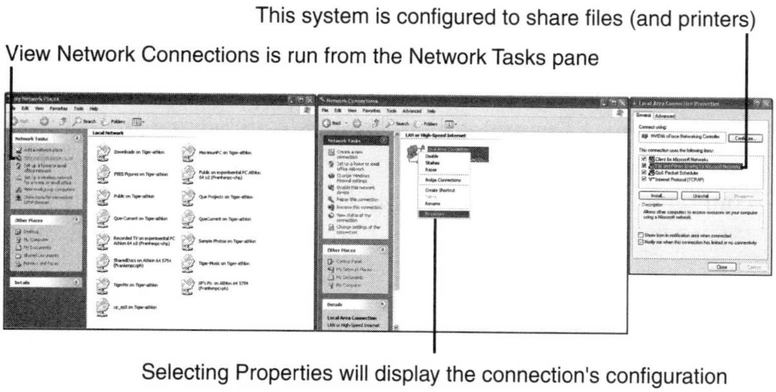

FIGURE 12.3
This system has File and Printer Sharing installed.

If File and Printer Sharing for Microsoft Networks is not listed, follow this procedure to install it (see Figure 12.4):

1. Click the Install button.
2. Select Service from the Select Network Component Type dialog and click Add.
3. Highlight File and Printer Sharing for Microsoft Networks in the Select Network Service dialog and click OK.
4. File and Printer Sharing for Microsoft Networks now appears in the list of network components (refer back to Figure 12.3). Click Close.

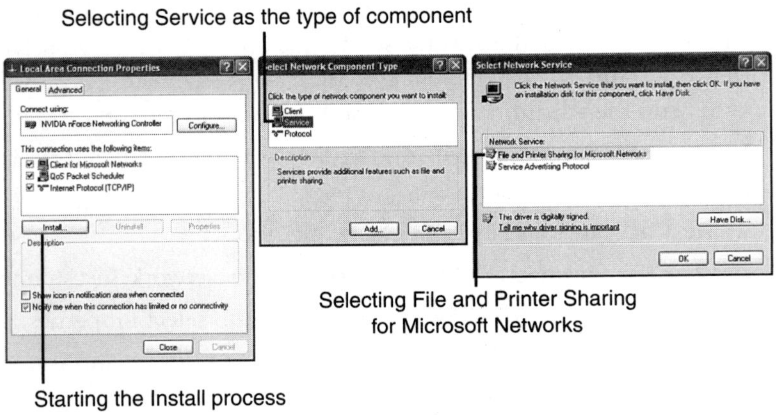

FIGURE 12.4

Installing File and Printer Sharing on a system running Windows XP.

Once you have File and Printer Sharing installed, it's time to figure out where your media files are installed. Don't laugh! Although Microsoft provides preconfigured folders for pictures (My Pictures), music (My Music), and videos (My Videos), there's no rule requiring third-party apps to use them. Some of the biggest offenders, in my experience, have been digital photo downloader programs supplied by camera vendors; these programs often store pictures in a subfolder of the application. Fortunately, it doesn't matter where your media files are stored. As long as you can find the folder on your system, you can share it.

Configuring Media Folder File Sharing

Windows XP editions support two types of file sharing on workgroup networks (the type of network used at home and in small businesses that don't use domains):

- Simple File Sharing
- Permissions-Based File Sharing

Simple File Sharing is the default (in fact, the only) method used by Windows XP Home Edition. It is also the default for Windows XP Professional and other Windows XP editions when the computer is connected to a workgroup. (Your home network is a workgroup, by the way.)

Simple File Sharing is exactly what the name implies: simple. You don't need to set up users or access permissions. The only option you have is to allow full access (network users can add, edit, or delete files) or read-only access (network users can read files but can't delete or change them). I recommend using the read-only access option for media sharing to ensure that the media files on your system don't get nuked by another user on the network.

To share a folder in Windows XP with Simple File Sharing enabled

1. Navigate to the parent folder of the folder containing the media you want to share. For example, My Pictures and My Music are subfolders of each user's My Documents folder. If you want to share either or both of these folders, navigate to My Documents.
2. Right-click the folder and select Sharing and Security (Figure 12.5). The Sharing tab of the folder's properties sheet opens.
3. Click the Share This Folder on the Network check box. Do *not* click the Allow Network Users to Change My Files check box unless other users need to add, delete, or edit files in the shared folder.
4. By default, the folder name is used for the share name. To avoid confusion, rename the share name with a descriptive name, such as the computer name plus the type of media being shared. (The actual folder name is not changed, but

note If you create a share name including more than 12 characters, you will see a warning that computers running old Windows versions such as NT 4.0, Millennium Edition, 98SE, or earlier can't access the share. Unless your network doubles as a computer museum, click Yes to use the share name anyway. If you have old Windows versions on your home network, click No and rename the share with a name containing no more than 12 characters.

12

network users will see the share name.) For example, instead of the default My Pictures name, I used XP-Office-Pictures (see Figure 12.5). Click Apply.

5. Click OK to close the dialog.

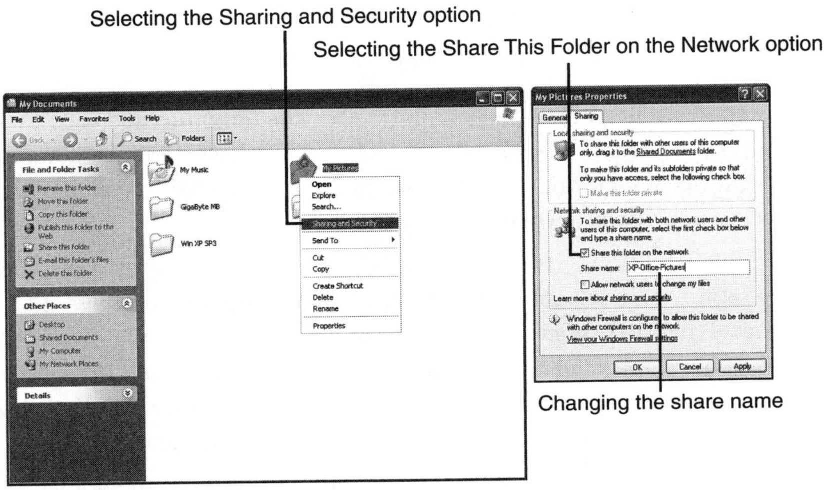

FIGURE 12.5

Sharing the user's My Pictures folder on a system running Windows XP with Simple File Sharing enabled.

When you view the contents of the folder containing a shared folder in Windows Explorer, each folder share has a hand icon indicating it's being shared (Figure 12.6).

When the folder is shared as a read-only folder, other users can view the contents of the folder but cannot change the folder's contents. This is the easiest method for sharing media—assuming that all of the media in the folder should be shared.

> **caution** Do *not* store confidential personal or work documents in a folder sbeing shared on the network. Remember, WMC and other network clients can see all of the videos and photos stored in a shared folder.

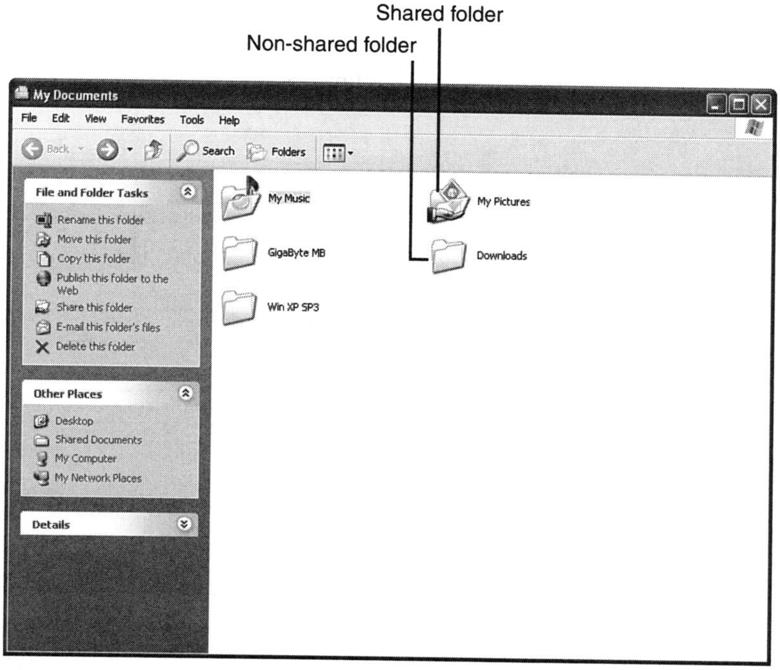

FIGURE 12.6

Shared and non-shared folders on a system running Windows XP.

If it is necessary to enable different levels of access for a shared folder on a drive that uses the NTFS file system, Simple File Sharing must be disabled. To disable it:

1. Open My Computer or Windows Explorer and click Tools, Folder Options.
2. Click the View tab and scroll down to Use Simple File Sharing (Recommended). Clear the check box (Figure 12.7).
3. Click Apply and then OK.

Once you disable Simple File Sharing, the Sharing dialog (Figure 12.7) looks very different. You can configure the number of simultaneous users that can share a folder (up to 10), and there are new dialogs for Permissions and for Caching.

note Most users of WMC will never need to use permissions–based networking to access a share on a Windows XP–based system. However, if you do, I recommend reading *Special Edition Using Windows XP Professional, Third Edition*, Que, 2005 (ISBN 0-7897-3280-7).

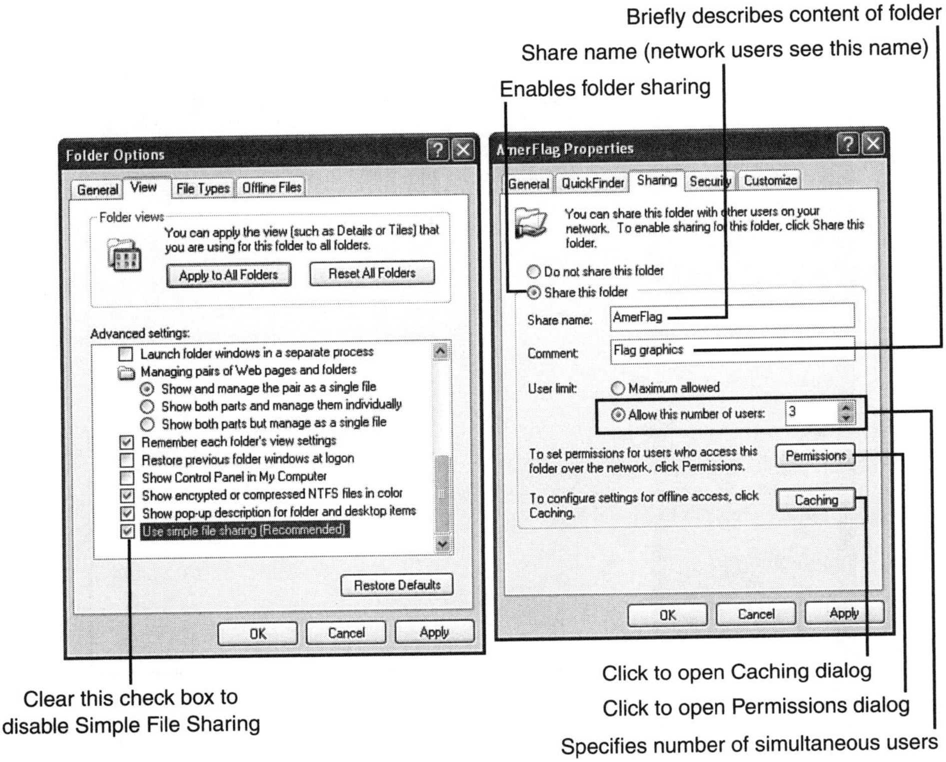

FIGURE 12.7

Disabling Simple File Sharing on Windows XP.

12

Before you can assign permissions to users, you must create user accounts for each user on your network that you want to allow to connect to a share, and then you must use the Permissions button shown in Figure 12.7 to configure each user.

IS PERMISSIONS-BASED MEDIA SHARING WORTH THE TROUBLE?

About the only reason to disable Simple File Sharing on a Window XP Professional system that's sharing media files with a Vista system running WMC is if you need to provide different levels of access to different users. This would be necessary, for example, in a home office environment where the Windows XP system is used to create and edit media files coming from that system and others. Because Windows XP does not include an option specifically for sharing media files the way that Windows Vista does, the only option available with Simple File Sharing, as you have seen, is to enable read-only or full access for all network users.

By disabling Simple File Sharing, you can set up lists of users with different levels of access. For example, a network user running WMC to review media on a big-screen TV could be granted read-only access to media folders, while a network user who creates files but does not make changes to existing files could be granted change-only access. A network user who needs to create, delete, and edit files would need to be granted full control of the media folders.

Using the Shared Documents Folder for Shared Media

If you don't want to provide unrestricted shared access to media files but don't want to mess around with the complexities of setting up permissions (and believe me, it *is* complicated if you're not a full-time network jockey), you might prefer to use a third approach: After sharing the Shared Documents folder, place files and folders you want to share in that folder.

The Shared Documents folder is automatically shared with the network when you run the Home Network Setup Wizard, or you can use the manual sharing method in the previous section to share the Shared Documents folder on the network. Thus, if you use that wizard to add a PC to your home network, you can copy media files to that folder, and they'll be shared with other users. It isn't necessary to share the media folders themselves.

Consider this approach if you want to keep most of your media files private but want to share some of them with other network users.

As you'll see in the next section, sharing media files on a Windows Vista machine is a lot easier and can be done from a single menu.

Configuring Windows Vista for Media Sharing

The Windows Vista Network and Sharing Center (Figure 12.8) is the one-stop-shop for configuring media sharing. To launch it, open Control Panel's Network and Internet category or select the link displayed in Network Explorer.

To enable read-only sharing of the contents of the Public folder (equivalent to Windows XP's Shared folders) and allow other systems to find your folders, enable Network Discovery, File Sharing, and Public Folder Sharing (Read-only), as shown in Figure 12.8.

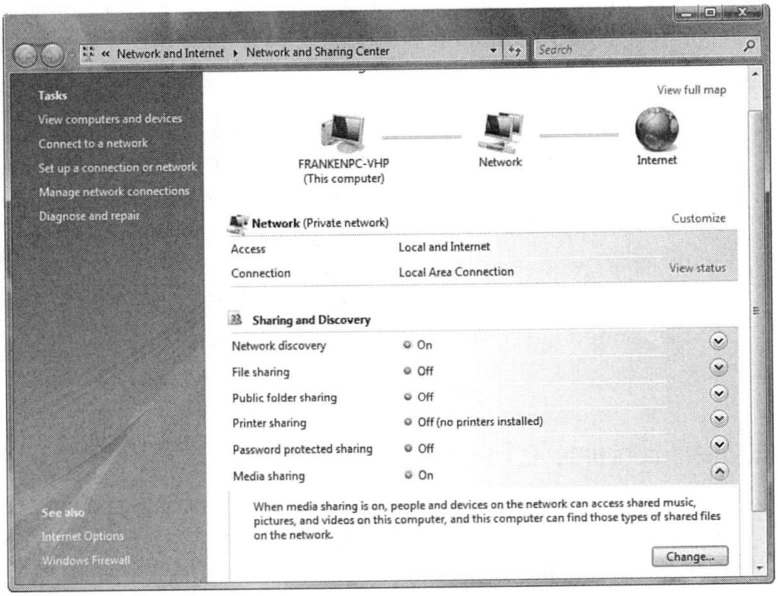

FIGURE 12.8

Configuring Windows Vista to share Public folders.

You can also enable Password Protected Sharing, but this is not necessary for home networks. If you enable this option, you must set up users and permissions.

Enabling Sharing of Media Folders

To enable sharing of media folders, open the Media Sharing portion of the Networking and Sharing menu, click Change, and make sure Share My Media To is checked. Click OK (see Figure 12.9).

From the next menu (Figure 12.9), select the PCs to which you want to permit access. You can do this by selecting each one and clicking Allow. If your system is never used outside a secure network, click Settings and then click the Allow New Devices and Computers Automatically check box (Figure 12.9). Computers and devices that are added to the network will automatically share media folders.

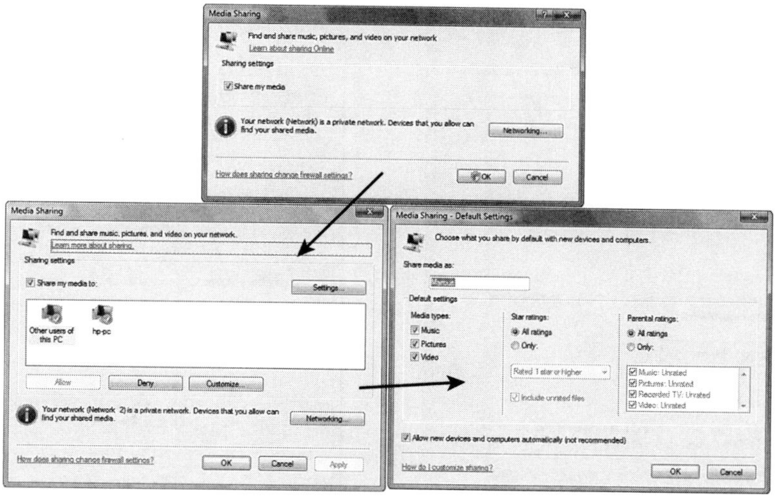

FIGURE 12.9

Configuring Windows Vista to allow new devices to connect to shared media folders automatically.

Note that you can also specify what types of media to share, what ratings to share, and what parental ratings to share. This last option is useful for preventing the kids from listening or viewing inappropriate material. Once other PCs are permitted to access shared folders, they are listed with check marks (refer back to Figure 12.9).

Note that you can also customize sharing with individual PCs or devices. To block a particular device, select it and click Deny. To change sharing settings for a particular device, select it and click Customize. Clear the Use Default Settings menu, and you can fine-tune what you share with a particular system or device.

> **note** If children in your family use a particular computer, the customization feature enables you to prevent their PCs from access to inappropriate material.

12

Sharing Media Folders

Now you're ready to share media folders. Open your user explorer, right-click the media folder you want to share, and select Share. From the Share menu (Figure 12.10), click Advanced Sharing and then click the Share This Folder checkbox on the Advanced Sharing dialog (Figure 12.10). Enter a new name for the share, click Apply, then OK to close this dialog, and then click Close.

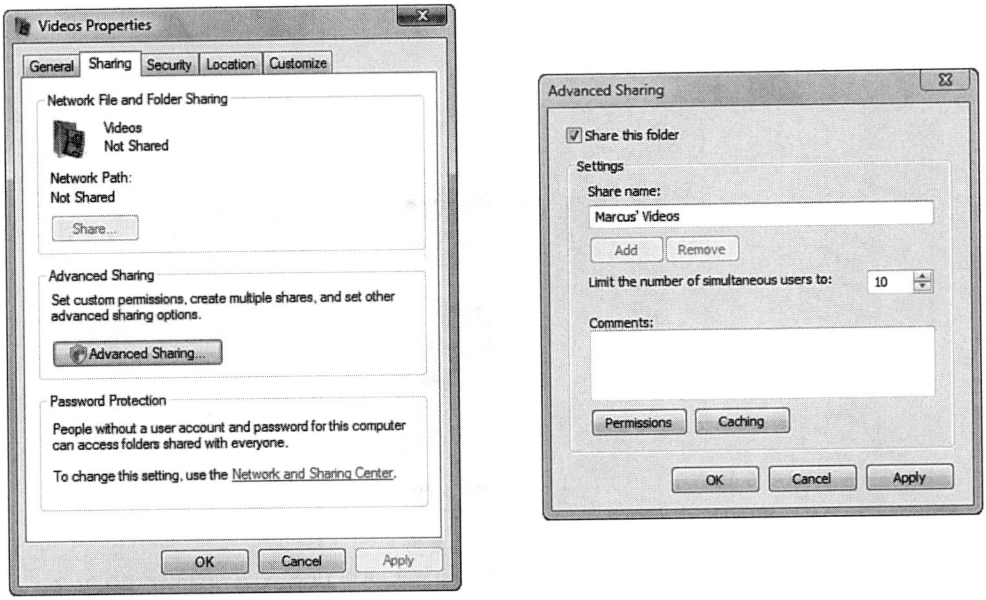

FIGURE 12.10

Sharing media folders in Explorer.

Other computers running WMC can then use the Library Setup menu to watch the newly shared folders for media (Figure 12.11).

➔ For more information on the Library Setup menu, see "Optional Setup: Music, Pictures, and Videos Library," Chapter 3, **p. 74**.

Configuring Other Operating Systems for Media Sharing

More and more users have MacOS or Linux systems on their networks. If your network includes MacOS or Linux computers with media files you'd like to view in WMC, this section will help you access media on these systems.

Accessing MacOS X Media Shares from Windows Vista

note For details, see the article, "Windows Vista File Sharing in Mac OS X Leopard," at http://pelz-sherman.net/blog/?p=46.

In MacOS X "Leopard" and newer versions, the user needs to configure file sharing to use SMB (which is not the default method) and might need to manually enter the IP address of the MacOS X computer in Windows Vista's Network Explorer. Media in the Mac's Public folder will then be available to Windows Vista (and other Windows versions on the network).

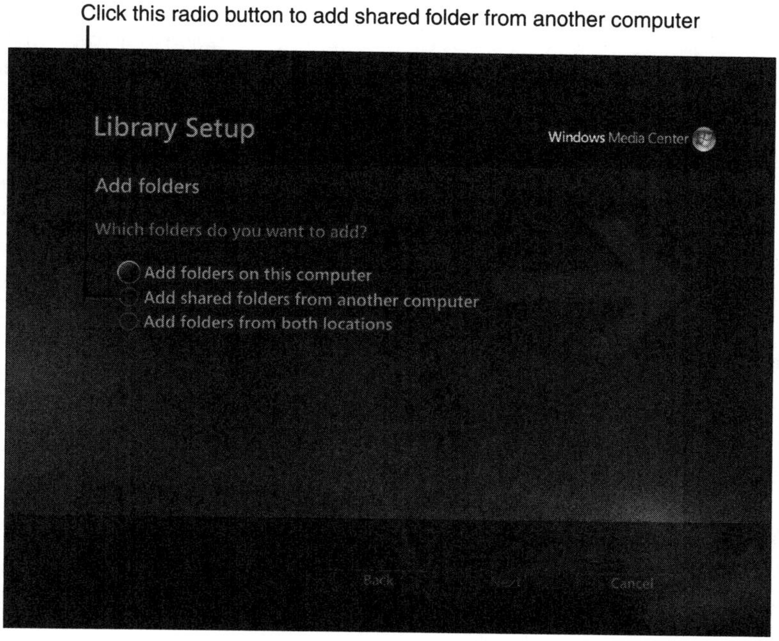

FIGURE 12.11

Using the Library Setup menu to watch shared folders on other systems.

Accessing Linux Media Shares from Windows Vista

To enable Windows Vista to view shared folders on a Linux system, you must install Samba version 3.0.22 or greater on the Linux system. This version of Samba supports the default password authentication method used by Windows Vista (NTLM version 2). You must also configure Samba with the name and password of the Vista user who will be accessing the share.

> **note** For details, see Ed Bott's article, "Vista Hands On #13: Connect to a shared folder on a Linux machine," at http://blogs.zdnet.com/Bott/?p=236.

Setting Up Windows Home Server for Media Sharing

The Windows Home Server operating system enables Windows home networks to have a centralized storehouse for media and other types of files and a centralized backup for valuable information. Windows Home Server (WHS) can provide media files for WMC and can back up media created or edited with WMC and complementary programs such as Windows Movie Maker and Windows Live Photo Gallery.

Windows Home Server is included in home servers from various vendors and is available separately for use on existing hardware. The following sections discuss how to use Windows Home Server in conjunction with WMC.

note For more information about Windows Home Server, read the documentation available from the Microsoft website (you can find a guide to most of this information at http://mswhs.com/documentation/, which is part of the excellent MS Windows Home Server blog) and the book *Microsoft Windows Home Server Unleashed* by Paul McFedries (Sams, 2008).

Storing Media on Windows Home Server

Windows Home Server has several preconfigured folders that can be used for sharing media (see Figure 12.12). These include

- Music
- Photos
- Videos

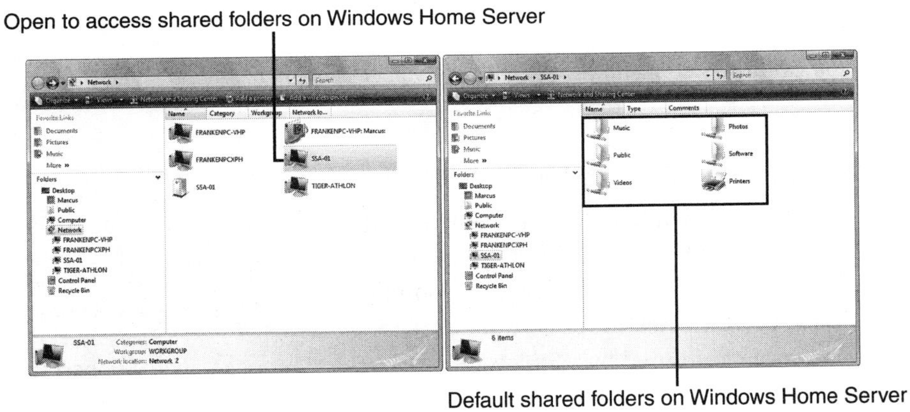

FIGURE 12.12

Windows Home Server as viewed in Windows Vista's Network Explorer.

Before you can store media in these folders, you must set up an account on Windows Home Server. You can either set up a user account that matches the username and password you use on the system connected to Windows Home

Server, or you can activate the Guest account, which requires no password and enables all systems on the network to access folder shares on WHS.

To enable the Guest account in WHS, log into the WHS Console and click the User Accounts icon. Click Enable Guest (Figure 12.13) and click OK to enable the Guest account.

After setting up a user account or a Guest account, you can close the Windows Home Server Console.

You can copy/paste or drag and drop media from your photo, video, or music folders into the corresponding folders on your server (Figure 12.14). After media is copied to a share in Windows Home Server, you view the share the same way you'd view any other shared or local folder (Figure 12.14).

note The Guest account is easier to use in a home network environment, but you should not use the Guest account unless you use a secure wireless network or a wired network.

A secure wireless network should use a non-standard SSID (the name of the wireless network) and should use WPA2 (or WPA if WPA2 is not supported by all hardware) security with a strong mixed-case alphanumeric key (capital and lowercase letters and numbers).

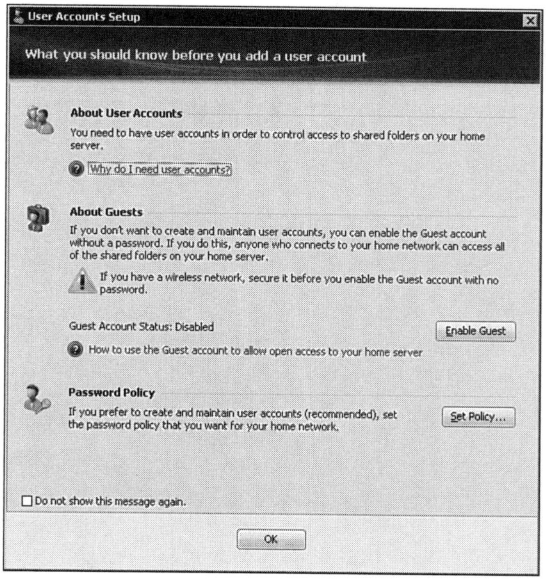

FIGURE 12.13

Enabling the Guest account on Windows Home Server.

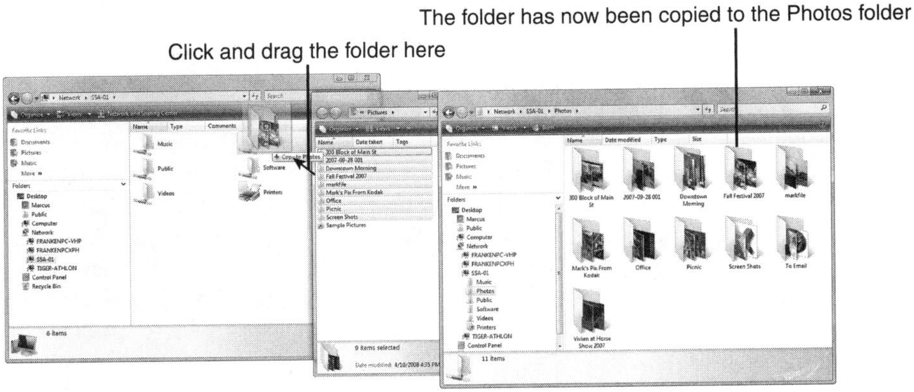

FIGURE 12.14

Using drag and drop to copy pictures to the Photos folders in Windows Home Server.

Accessing Media Stored on Windows Home Server

To access shared media stored on Windows Home Server from WMC, use Library Setup, specify the option Add Shared Folders from Another Computer, and select the folders you want to watch on the system running WHS (Figure 12.15).

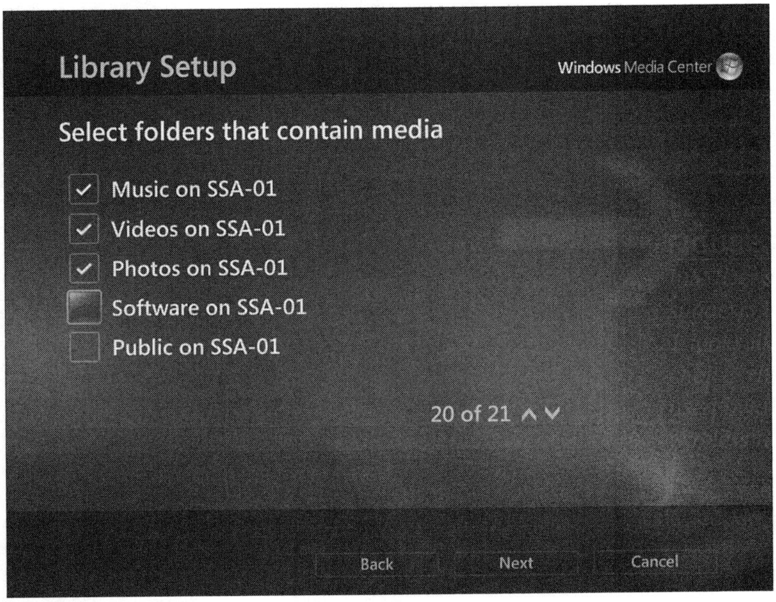

FIGURE 12.15

Adding folders from WHS to the folders to watch list in WMC.

You can work with the media stored in Windows Home Server shared folders the same way you would work with media stored in other shares on the network.

→ For details, see "Optional Setup: Music, Pictures, and Videos Library," Chapter 3, **p. 74**.

Boosting Network and Internet Performance

Whether you use WMC to view media shared by other PCs on your local network, Windows Home Server shares, or Internet video and TV content, the last thing you want to see is the WMC animated circle icon (WMC's replacement for the traditional Windows hourglass) telling you to wait. Although system performance has some impact on how fast WMC delivers network and Internet media to you, the choices you make in Internet and network connection types and configuration have a bigger effect on how fast—or how slow—you receive media. Faster is better, and the following sections will help you choose the fastest connection types and best configuration tricks for your hardware.

Choosing the Fastest Internet Connection

If you live in an area that has both cable and DSL broadband connections, keep in mind that it's no longer always the case that cable connections are faster than DSL. Many cable and DSL providers have switched from a single "one-size-fits-all" broadband package to various tiered services ranging in speed from 768Kbps down/384Kbps up to as much as 10Mbps down/1Mbps up or faster.

You might have four or more tiered packages to choose from, so how can you make sure you're getting the performance you need for enjoying the online media you crave? Skip the low-end packages and choose from the following:

- If you're mainly using the Internet for streaming music or web-quality (YouTube-style) video, a mid-range package offering download speeds of 1.5Mbps to 4Mbps will be sufficient.
- If you want to stream standard-quality video and web TV, opt for a 6Mbps to 8Mbps package.
- If you want to stream HD Video, or if your home network has multiple

tip You can save money by bundling multiple services, such as telephone, TV, or wireless on the same bill.

users who want to stream various types of media at the same time, opt for a 10Mbps or faster package.

If you're beyond the reach of cable or DSL connections, your choices are far more limited:

- Satellite Internet services such as HughesNet and StarBand offer maximum download speeds of 1.5Mbps, and downloading excessively large media files or other content can trigger significant download speed reductions under the terms of each company's Fair Access Policy.
- Point-to-point wireless broadband services are available in some rural areas. Generally, these services depend on a direct line-of-sight connection to the service provider's towers.

note HughesNet's Fair Access Policy is available at http://go.gethughesnet.com/faPolicy.cfm.

StarBand's Fair Access Policy is available at http://www.starband.com/acceptableuse.html#fairaccesspolicy.

HughesNet determines Fair Access on a daily usage basis, while StarBand uses a rolling seven-day window to determine Fair Access.

Understanding Wi-Fi (Wireless Ethernet) Network Standards

Although IEEE-802.11n (Wireless-N) networking is becoming the preferred network type for new home and small-business wireless networks, the vast majority of existing home wireless networks use the IEEE-802.11g (Wireless-G) standard, which is a faster version of the 802.11b standard. A few home and office networks use the 802.11a standard.

To help you get the most out of the following sections, it's useful to understand how the various flavors of 802.11-based wireless networks compare to each other. Table 12.1 provides that comparison.

Most wireless routers can connect with more than one 802.11-based standard, so you can have a mixture of devices on a wireless network. However, if all of the devices on your wireless network use the same standard, you can change your router's configuration to improve performance.

➔ For details, see "Changing Your Router's Configuration," this chapter, **p. 361**.

Table 12.1 802.11-Based Wireless Network Types

Wireless Ethernet (Wi-Fi) Standard	Radio Frequency Used	Maximum Speed	Number of Channels[1]	Also Known As	Connects With
802.11a	5GHz	54Mbps	12	Wireless-A	—[2]
802.11b	2.4GHz	11Mbps	3	Wireless-B	802.11g
802.11g	2.4GHz	54Mbps	3	Wireless-G	802.11b
802.11n[3]	2.4GHz & 5GHz[4]	130Mbps[5] 300Mbps[6]	3 (2.4GHz) 12 (5GHz)	Wireless-N	802.11b, g (2.4GHz) 802.11a (5GHz)

[1]Non-overlapping

[2]Requires dual-frequency hardware to connect to other standards

[3]802.11n is not yet a final standard; Wi-Fi Certified 802.11n products are currently certified as meeting Draft 2.0 (or later) pre-release specifications.

[4]5GHz support optional and not available on most 802.11n hardware

[5]Narrow (20MHz) channel; same channel width as used by 802.11a, b, and g

[6]Wide (40MHz) channel

The following sections provide tips and tricks to boost the performance of your network, many of which apply to more than one type of wireless network.

Boosting Signal Strength—Inexpensively

The speed of a wireless network is heavily influenced by the signal strength you receive. Most systems are configured to display a signal strength icon in the Windows notification area or system tray (directly to the left of the clock). If you are seeing only one or two bars, your system is getting a low signal and is probably not running as fast as it could. What can you do?

- If your wireless adapter has an adjustable antenna, move the antenna around to see if you can improve signal strength. Most PCI desktop adapters have a swivel antenna, as do some USB adapters for notebook or desktop computers (see Figures 12.16 and 12.17).
- If you use a compact USB adapter that has a fixed antenna, connect the adapter to the computer with a USB extender cable. You can then move the adapter around to see if you can find a stronger signal.

FIGURE 12.16
A D-Link 802.11g wireless network adapter for desktops (PCI slot). Photo courtesy of D-Link.

FIGURE 12.17
A Linksys 802.11g wireless network adapter for desktops or laptops (USB 2.0 port). Photo courtesy of Linksys, a division of Cisco Systems.

- If your wireless adapter is built into your notebook computer, move the computer to a different position or adjust the screen angle. (Most notebook computers with onboard adapters use an antenna that surrounds the LCD panel.)
- If your wireless router or desktop adapter has a removable antenna (or antennas), check with the vendor or a third-party source to see if a stronger antenna is available. Antennas are rated in dB gain: the higher the number, the more powerful the antenna.

caution There are several connector types used for removable router and desktop adapter antennas. The most common include RP-SMA, RP-TNC, and MC. If you decide to order a third-party antenna, you must be sure to specify the correct connector type. You can see examples of these and other connectors and the wireless routers and network adapters that use each connector type by visiting http://www.radiolabs.com/products/cables/cable.php?length=5#connector.

Checking for Interference from Other Wireless Networks

When you configured your 802.11g or other 2.4GHz wireless network, you might have read that you could choose from wireless channels ranging from 1–11. You can, but the dirty little secret of wireless networks that use signals in the 2.4GHz range is that only channels 1, 6, and 11 don't overlap with each other. In other words, instead of 11 channels, you have only three that are worth choosing.

Even though channels 1, 6, and 11 don't interfere with each other, if your wireless network uses the same channel as other nearby networks, interference from those networks can reduce the range of your wireless network and can cause your network to run at slower speeds.

So how can you find out what other networks are running in your neck of the woods—and the channels they're using? There are a couple of ways:

- If one or more of the PCs on your wireless network use proprietary client software instead of the standard Windows wireless network software, you can use the site survey feature found in most proprietary wireless network client programs to see the channels used by other networks. As shown in Figure 12.18, a site survey shows the name of the wireless network (its SSID), its channel, and other information.
- If you use only the standard Windows (XP or Vista) wireless network client software, you can download and run a third-party program to detect and display information about nearby wireless networks. I currently recommend Metageek's InSSIDer, available from www.metageek.net/products/inssider. Figure 12.19 shows how InSSIDer shows nearby networks.

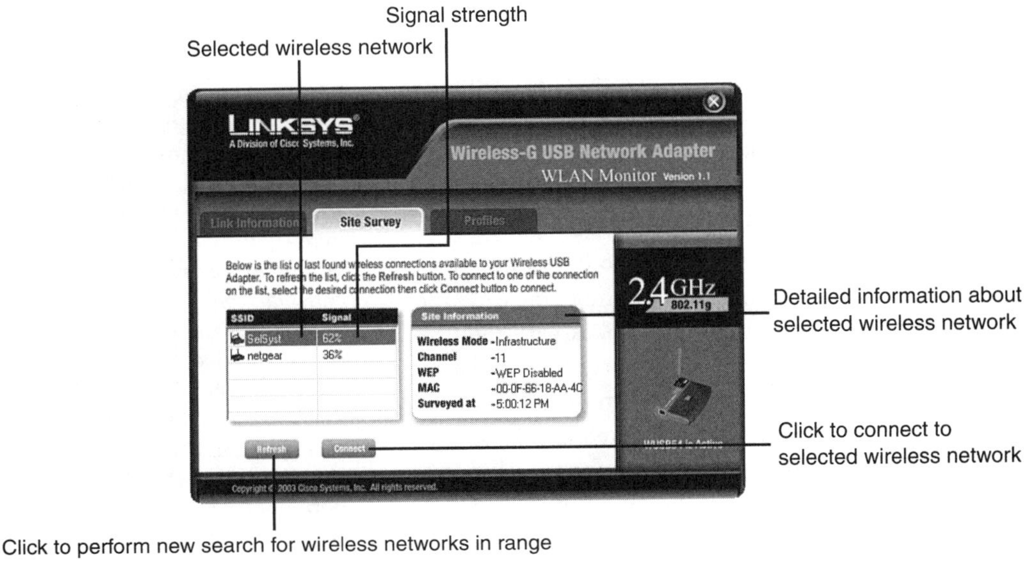

FIGURE 12.18

Using the Site Survey feature in the Linksys wireless network client to detect information about wireless networks in range.

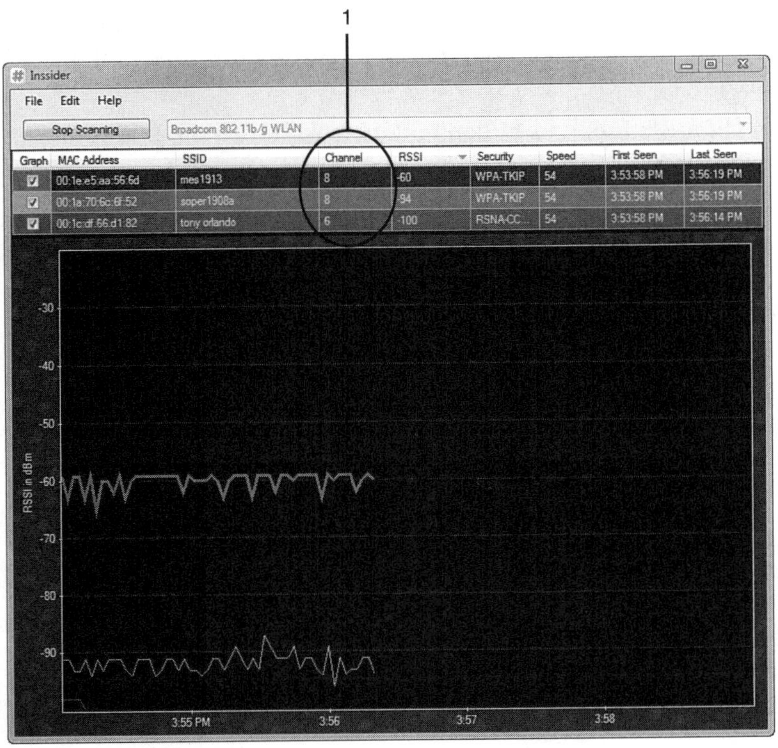

FIGURE 12.19

InSSIDer's survey suggests that channel 1 looks like a good choice. (It's not being used by any nearby wireless networks.)

12

If you find that one or more wireless networks use the same channel that you are using, you should reconfigure your router to use a channel that is not in use by other nearby networks. If that is not possible, use a channel that is used by weaker signals. (The lower the dB rating shown in InSSIDer, the weaker the signal.)

➔ To learn how to change the channel in your wireless router's configuration, see "Changing the Channel," this chapter, **p. 363**.

Finding Out What Wireless Standards Are on Your Network

Before you can determine whether (and how) to change your wireless network's configuration, you need to determine the types of wireless clients on your network. That is, you need to find out which computers have 802.11g, 802.11n, or other wireless adapters.

You can use each computer's Windows Device Manager to determine this information.

Follow this procedure to open the Device Manager in Windows XP:

1. Right-click My Computer.
2. Select Properties.
3. Click the Hardware tab.
4. Click the Device Manager button.

To open the Device Manager in Windows Vista, follow this procedure:

1. Right-click Computer.
2. Select Properties.
3. Click the Device Manager link in the Tasks menu.

Figure 12.20 shows the Device Manager from a laptop with an integrated 802.11b/g wireless adapter and an 802.11n dual-band USB wireless adapter.

Changing Your Router's Configuration

To change the channel used by your wireless router or to make other changes to your router's configuration, you need to log into your router's built-in configuration dialogs. Although some wireless network adapters include a proprietary wizard that can be used for changing some router settings, you're usually better off making the needed changes manually.

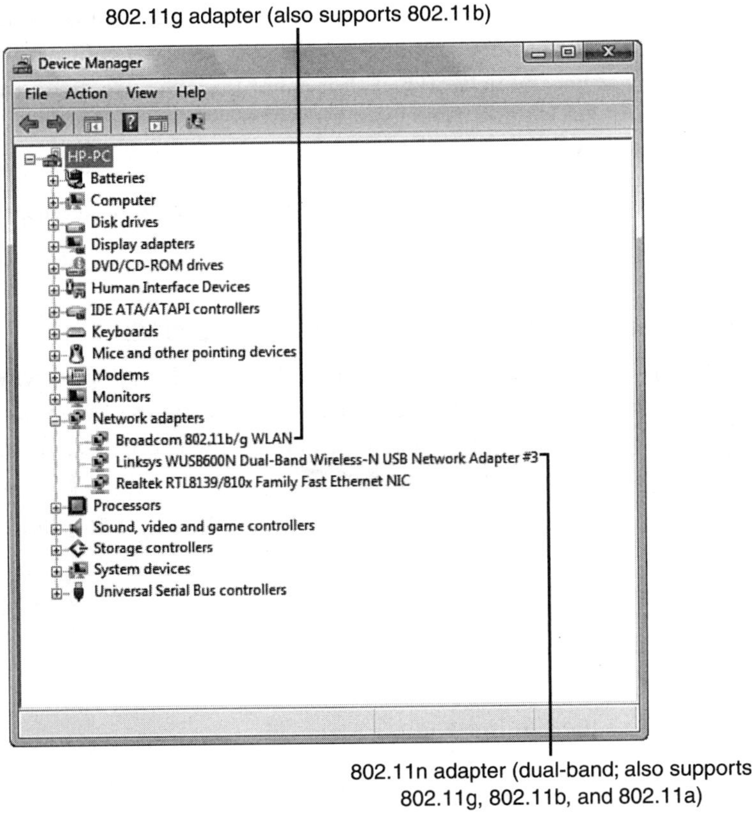

FIGURE 12.20

How 802.11g and 802.11n wireless adapters might appear in a typical Device Manager screen.

To log into the router manually, follow this basic procedure:

1. Connect a CAT5, 5e, or 6 UTP cable between your computer's Ethernet port and the LAN (not WAN) port on the router. Most routers include a multiport switch for wired clients, and you can use any available port.
2. Open your web browser and enter the IP address of the router into the address field. For example, if your router's IP address is 192.168.1.1, enter **http://192.168.1.1**.
3. Enter the username and password needed to open the configuration dialog.
4. The router's configuration dialog appears. Figure 12.21 shows a typical configuration dialog from a Linksys WAP54G wireless router.

tip To determine the IP address of your router, check the documentation for the router. If you don't have the documentation, look it up at the vendor's website. The website will also list the default username and password needed to access the configuration dialog.

Another way to determine the IP address of your router is to open a command prompt in Windows and enter the command **ipconfig**. The IP address listed for your network's Default Gateway is the router's IP address.

If you changed the default password or username when you set up your router, enter that information when prompted. Otherwise, enter the default values.

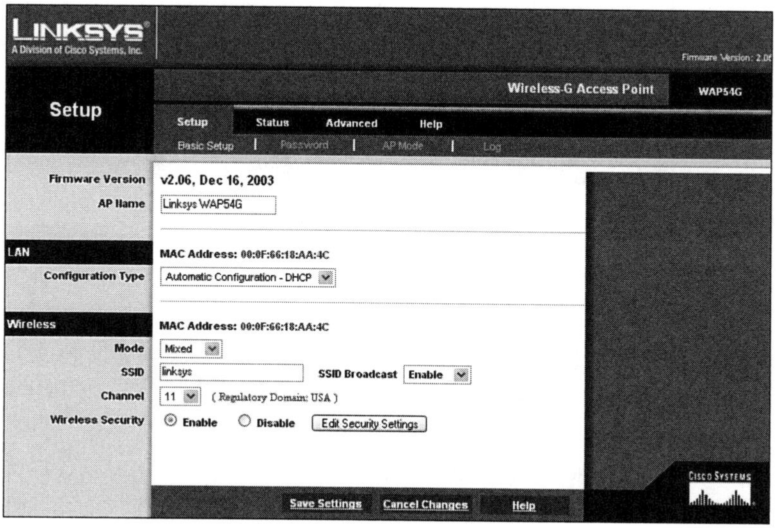

FIGURE 12.21

The basic wireless configuration dialog for a Linksys 802.11g router.

Changing the Channel

To change the channel, select a channel from the Channel menu (see Figure 12.22). Be sure to choose a channel that is not in use by nearby networks or a channel used by a low-powered network.

note Some 802.11n wireless routers use an Auto setting by default. When the Auto setting is used, the router determines the best channel to use and can change to a different channel when necessary.

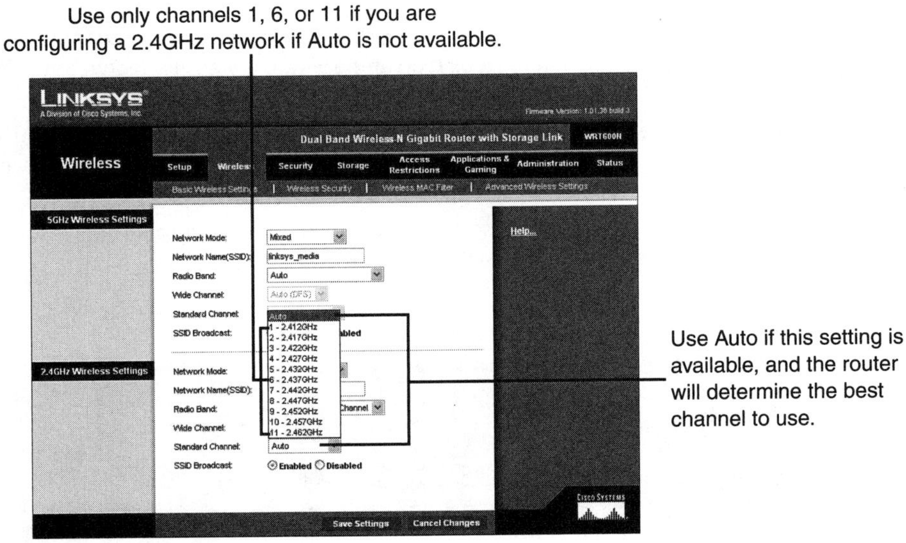

FIGURE 12.22

Selecting a channel on a 2.4GHz wireless network.

Using Wide Channel Settings (802.11n)

802.11n networks can provide faster performance than other 802.11-based wireless networks if wide channel settings are used. You can select this option from the basic wireless settings dialog. Available options include Standard (20MHz), Wide (40MHz), or Auto. Figure 12.23 shows you a typical example.

> **note** Use the Auto setting if there are other nearby wireless networks, as this setting enables the router to use the faster Wide setting when possible, and switch back to the default (and slower) Standard setting if Wide would interfere with other networks.
>
> If you select Standard or Wide, you must also select the appropriate channel to use.

Changing Network Mode Settings

802.11g and 802.11n-based routers are designed to work with other versions of the 802.11 family. To enable a router designed to support one version of the 802.11 standard to connect with other versions, use the Mixed setting in the Network Mode menu. (Mixed is the default setting in most routers.) However, using Mixed mode slows down the network and should be used only if the network has different types of 802.11-based clients. If all clients on the network use the same 802.11 standard, choose the appropriate standard from the Network Mode menu, as shown in Figure 12.24.

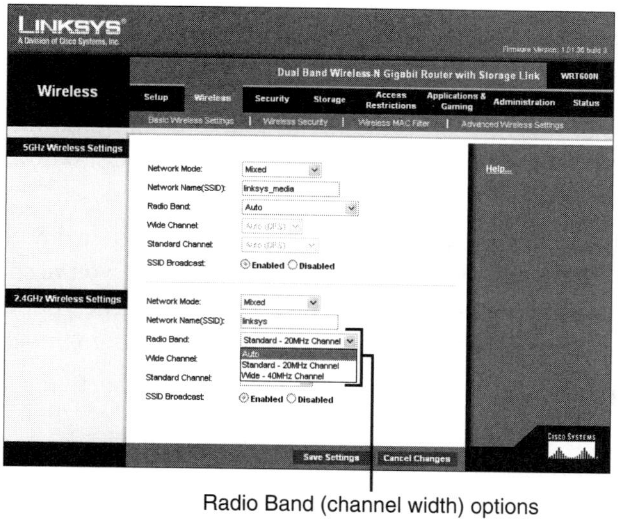

FIGURE 12.23

Choosing the Radio Band (channel width) setting on an 802.11n-based router.

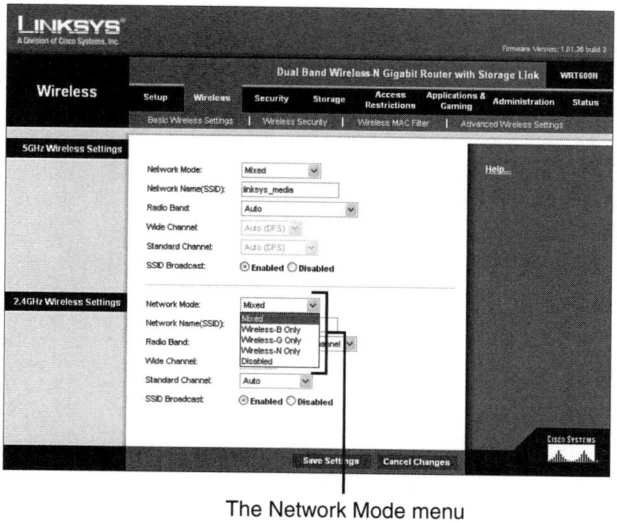

FIGURE 12.24

Choosing the appropriate Network Mode.

Using WPA or WPA2 Encryption Instead of WEP Encryption

Back when 802.11b (the first widely available version of wireless Ethernet networking) was new, the only way to secure the network was to use WEP encryption. Unfortunately, WEP encryption caused huge slowdowns in performance and wasn't very secure.

The only reason to keep using WEP encryption these days is if you have some old 802.11b devices on the network. If you don't, you need to switch to WPA or WPA2 encryption. (WPA2 is preferred.) These encryption standards have a relatively low effect on network performance and are much more secure.

To change to WPA or WPA2 encryption, you must change both the router and each client setting.

On the router (Figure 12.25)

1. Open the Wireless Security menu.
2. Select WPA Personal (also known as WPA-PSK) or WPA2 Personal (WPA2-PSK) encryption; WPA uses the TKIP algorithm, while WPA2 uses the AES algorithm.
3. Enter an alphanumeric shared security key.
4. Save the changes.

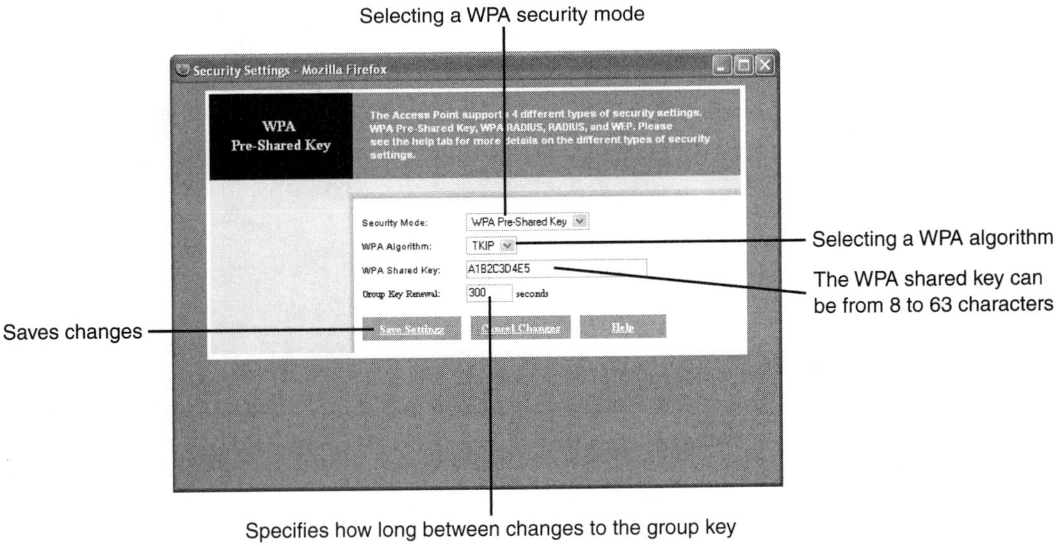

FIGURE 12.25

Configuring WPA encryption on a typical wireless router.

On a Windows XP client (Figure 12.26)

1. Open the Network Properties menu.
2. Click the Association tab.
3. If necessary, enter the SSID used by the wireless network.
4. Select/enter the options used on the router for encryption type, algorithm, and security key.
5. Click OK.

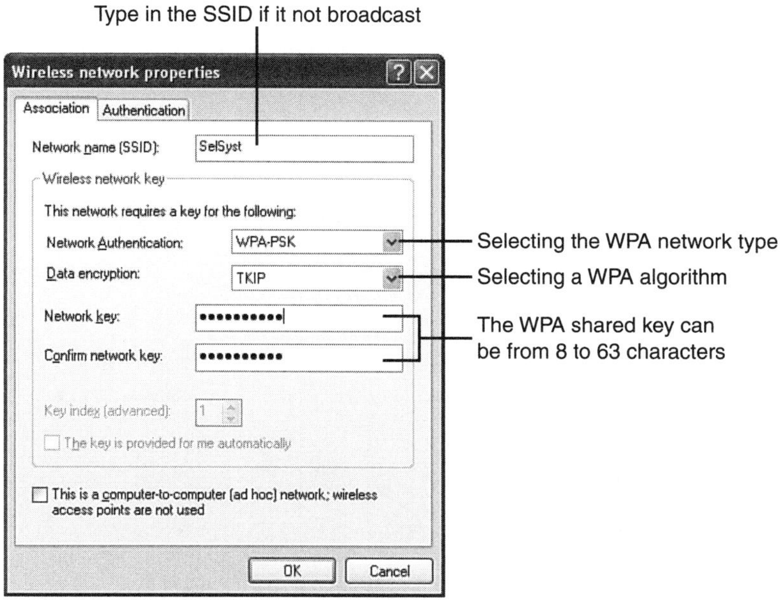

FIGURE 12.26

Configuring WPA encryption on a typical Windows XP client.

On a Windows Vista client when the wireless network is shown in the Connect to a Network dialog

1. Select the network to connect to.
2. When prompted, enter the encryption key (Figure 12.27). Vista will automatically determine the encryption settings for you.
3. Save the network settings when prompted.

If the wireless network is not displayed in the Connect to a Network dialog

1. Click Manually Connect to a Wireless Network.
2. Enter the SSID (Network Name), security type, encryption type, and encryption key using the same settings as those used on the router (Figure 12.27).
3. Check the Start This Connection Automatically and Connect Even If the Network Is Not Broadcasting check boxes.
4. The changes are saved for you.

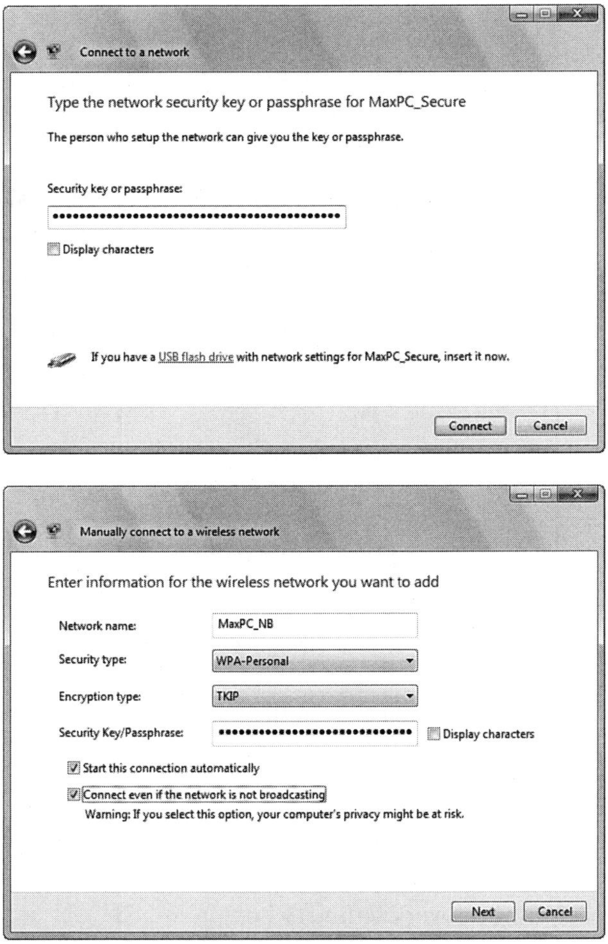

FIGURE 12.27

Configuring WPA encryption on a typical Windows Vista client.

caution As soon as you reconfigure the router to use a different type of wireless security, *no one can access the network (or the Internet) until each client is configured with the same settings*. Make sure nobody's using the network or the Internet when you start this process!

tip To generate a strong (e.g., hard to crack) encryption key, visit the Ultra High Security Password Generator page at Gibson Research Corporation: https://www.grc.com/passwords.htm. Every time you visit (or refresh) the page, new random passwords are generated.

To make it easy to configure your router and client PCs with the new encryption key, visit the page, highlight the key you want to use, and copy/paste the key into Notepad. Save the file.

When you configure the router, open the file you saved in Notepad, highlight the key, copy it, and paste it into the encryption field on the router's configuration dialog.

When you configure each client PC, use the same procedure to copy/paste the encryption key.

Using Gigabit Ethernet Instead of Fast Ethernet

Although wireless Ethernet (802.11 or Wi-Fi) networking is very popular, if you have PCs that are near your router, you can get even faster performance if the PC and the router support Gigabit Ethernet.

Gigabit Ethernet runs at 1000Mbps, which is several times faster than even the fastest wireless standard (802.11n), and it's also ten times faster than Fast Ethernet (100Mbps).

To determine if your router supports Gigabit Ethernet, check its documentation. You can also check your computer's documentation, but if you've added your own network adapter or your computer manual's lost in a drawer somewhere, you can also check the Windows Device Manager (Figure 12.28).

Although many recent PCs (both desktops and laptops) include Gigabit Ethernet adapters, many routers only support Fast Ethernet. (Gigabit Ethernet also supports Fast Ethernet.) If you want to use Gigabit Ethernet networking, you might need to upgrade your router.

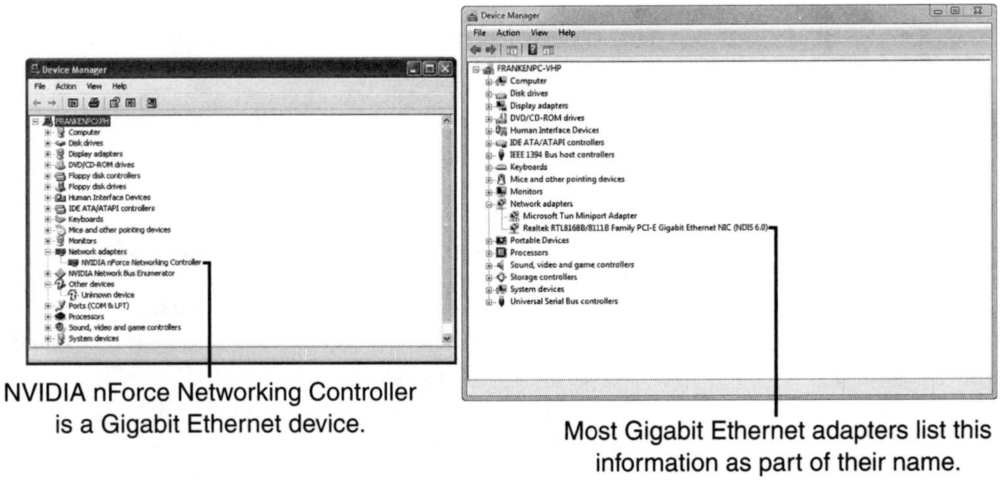

FIGURE 12.28

Some Gigabit Ethernet adapters as listed in Device Manager.

Upgrading Your Router

If the PCs on your home network have faster wired or wireless network adapters than the router supports, the router is slowing down your network and should be replaced. Here are some typical examples:

- Your computers have Gigabit Ethernet network adapters, but they connect to a router that supports only Fast Ethernet.
- Your computers have 802.11a or 5GHz versions of 802.11n wireless Ethernet adapters, but they connect to a router that supports only 2.4GHz 802.11n or 802.11g.
- Your computers have 2.4GHz 802.11n wireless Ethernet adapters but connect to a router that supports only 802.11g or 802.11b.

Before you replace your router, make sure you record

- The type of encryption used to secure the wireless network (WEP or preferably WPA or WPA2)
- The encryption algorithm used
- The encryption key used to secure the wireless network
- Channel, mode, and channel width settings

- The MAC (hardware) address of the router; by using the MAC address cloning feature found in most routers, you might be able to switch the router without needing to contact your Internet service provider (ISP)

> **note** If you are unable to connect to the Internet, contact your ISP. You might need to reregister your new router as an access device.

- Any other special settings, such as DMZ, port forwarding, MAC address filtering, and so on

After you unplug the old router from your broadband device (cable, DSL, or satellite modem) and plug in the new router, you must reconfigure the new router to use the same encryption type, algorithm, and encryption key used by the wireless devices on your network. You must also plug in any network cables from PCs into the switch ports on the new router. After the new router is configured, your systems should be able to reconnect to the Internet and to each other.

PART

V

Enhancing Windows Vista Media Center

CHAPTER

13

Using Windows Media Player with Windows Media Center

IN THIS CHAPTER

- Why WMP and WMC Are "Made for Each Other"
- Configuring Audio Ripping
- Creating Playlists
- Editing Track and Album Information
- Downloading Visualizations

Why WMP and WMC Are "Made for Each Other"

As you learned in Chapter 6, "Importing and Playing Audio," you can import your favorite music into Windows Media Player (WMP), rate it, and play it. However, if you want to have maximum control over your music collection, you'll probably want to use WMP to give Windows Media Center (WMC) a hand. Here's why they're "better together":

- WMP provides more control over the ripping process than WMC. In fact, to configure the audio format and quality settings that WMC uses to rip a CD, you must open WMP.
- You'll find it easier to edit and create genres and ratings in WMP than in WMC.
- You can add or edit album art after ripping an album in WMC by using WMP.

- If you want to enjoy additional visualizations in WMC, you must download them using WMP. And some optional visualizations make creating a slide show plus music very simple.
- WMC is fully compatible with WMP's genres, ratings, and other music features.

Configuring Audio Ripping

If you plan to use WMC to rip music from your CD collection, you need to configure Windows Media Player to do the heavy lifting for you; the options you set in WMP are used by both Windows Media Center and Windows Media Player. Even if you are using WMC strictly to enjoy music on other systems, it's useful to know what ripping options are available in Windows Media Player so you can choose the options you prefer to build the best-quality digital music collection you can.

You can configure audio ripping in Windows Media Player 11 in two ways:

- Open the Rip menu and select the digital music format from the Format menu and the bit rate from the Bit Rate menu (refer to Figure 13.1).
- Right-click the lower left-hand corner of the WMP screen, select Tools, Options, and open the Rip Music tab (refer to Figure 13.2).

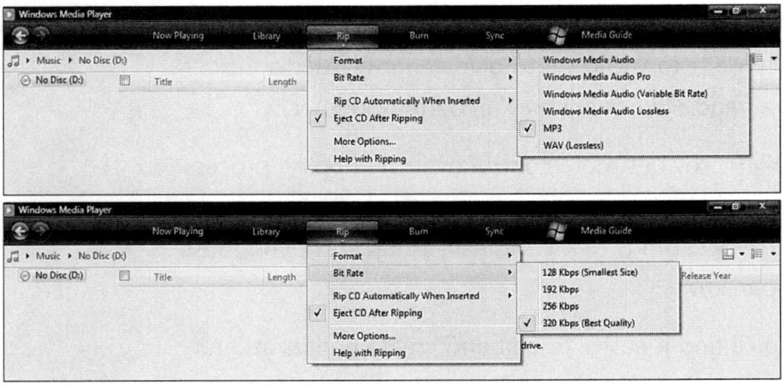

FIGURE 13.1

Configuring ripping format and bit rate using WMP's Rip menu.

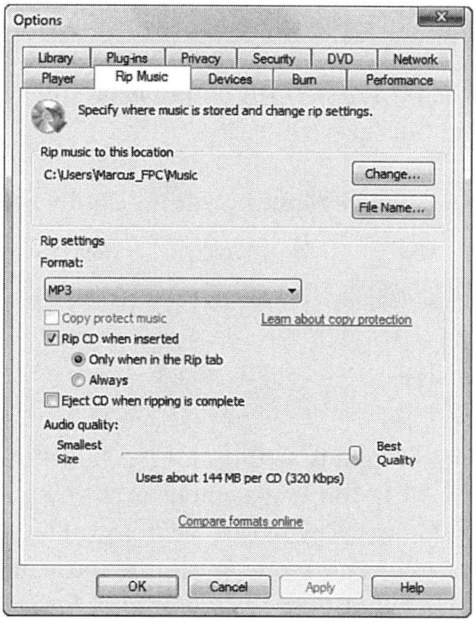

FIGURE 13.2

Configuring ripping format and bit rate using WMP's Rip Music options tab.

Format and Bit Rate Options

You can use WMP and WMC to rip music into either compressed (lossy) or uncompressed (full-quality) formats. Lossless formats include

- Windows Media Audio Lossless
- WAV

Lossy formats include

- Windows Media Audio
- Windows Media Audio Pro
- Windows Media Audio (variable bit rate)
- MP3

Which format should you choose for ripping your audio collection? That depends on what you want to do with it and how much storage space you have available for digital audio.

note A "lossy" format discards or reduces the precision of less audible audio data to reduce the size of the output file, while a lossless format faithfully stores all audio data in the original source, thereby creating a very large output file. The higher the bit rate used to encode music in a lossy format, the closer to the original (and the larger the output file).

Within WMP (but not WMC), you can always convert a lossless format to a lossy format to save space on a portable media player. (Use the Device Options dialog's Advanced settings to configure conversion settings.) Keep in mind that you can never restore the audio quality lost when you use lossy audio ripping.

I pulled a CD from my collection (PDQ Bach's *A Little Nightmare Music)* containing 41:48 minutes of music and ripped it into WAV and WMA lossless formats, as well as MP3 and WMA (variable bit rate) lossy formats. Table 13.1 shows the resulting rip sizes.

Table 13.1 *A Little Nightmare Music* in Various Digital Formats

Digital Music Format	WAV	WMA (lossless)	WMA (VBR: 240–355Kbps)	MP3 (320Kbps)
Size Per Album	421MB	157MB	77.6MB	95.7MB
Estimated Number of Albums per 50GB	114	318	649	521

I chose the highest-quality settings for the "lossy" formats in the comparison shown in Table 13.1, and they demonstrate why I use 320Kbps MP3 as my ripping format of choice. As you can see from Table 13.1, this format/bit rate combination uses less than one-fourth the space of a WAV file and about 40% less space than a WMA (lossless) file. It's not the smallest high-quality file (the Oscar for that category goes to WMA-VBR), but MP3 enables me to store hundreds of albums on a hard disk, and it has the advantage of being playable on virtually all digital media devices, including otherwise closed-in systems like the Apple iPod family that can't deal with WMA files.

No matter what your preferences are, you can set WMP to rip your music any way you please.

Use Table 13.2 as a quick reference for each recording format supported by WMP 11. The highest bit rate in each format provides the best quality but also the largest file size.

Table 13.2 WMP 11's Recording Formats

Recording Format	Extension	Supported Bit Rates	Notes
Windows Media Audio	WMA	48Kbps 64Kbps 96Kbps 128Kbps[1] 160Kbps 192Kbps	Uses higher bit rates for classical and symphonic music; uses lower bit rates for spoken word or to create smaller files

13

Table 13.2 Continued

Recording Format	Extension	Supported Bitrates	Notes
Windows Media Audio Pro	WMA	32Kbps 48Kbps 64Kbps[1] 96Kbps 128Kbps 160Kbps 192Kbps	Supports up to 5.1 surround audio; provides comparable quality to standard WMA at half the bit rate; also optimized for Windows-based smartphones
Windows Media Audio Variable Bit Rate (VBR)	WMA	40–75Kbps 50–95Kbps 85–145Kbps 135–215Kbps 240–355Kbps	Some older WMA-compatible players may not be able to handle VBR recordings
Windows Media Audio Lossless	WMA	470–940Kbps[2]	Performs no file compression for quality identical to original; creates very large music files
MP3	MP3	128Kbps 192Kbps 256Kbps 320Kbps	Works with players not compatible with WMA files
WAV	WAV	1411.2 Kbps[2]	Performs no file compression for quality identical to original; creates very large music files (larger than WMA lossless); best choice for audio that needs additional editing before use; also the choice of serious audiophiles

[1]Default bit rate

[2]Only bit rate for this format

13

Other Options

You can use the Rip Music tab to set other options for ripping music in both WMP and WMC. These include

- **Where to store music:** By default, the Music folder for the current user is the default destination. If you prefer to use a different drive or a network share folder, click the Change button to choose the location.

- **File name:** By default, each digital audio track name contains the track number and song title. Click File Name to choose additional or other options, such as the artist's name (Figure 13.3) and to choose a different separator character between options, such as an underscore character.
- **Whether to eject the music CD when you're done ripping:** This option is enabled by default.

FIGURE 13.3
Music track file naming options.

Creating Playlists

As you learned in Chapter 6, you can use playlists generated in either WMP or WMC to play your digital music favorites. You can create playlists manually using drag and drop or by using criteria to filter your collection into a playlist automatically.

Creating a Custom Playlist Manually

To create and save a custom playlist manually (see Figure 13.4):

1. Click Library, Create Playlist.
2. Select one or more songs from the Library pane.

3. Drag them to the Playlist pane.
4. Repeat steps 2 and 3 until you have finished your playlist.
5. Click Save Playlist and provide a name when prompted.

> **tip** If the Playlist pane isn't visible in WMP 11, click the left arrow next to the Search box at the upper right-hand corner of the WMP display.

FIGURE 13.4

Creating a custom playlist.

Filtering Your Collection to Create an Auto Playlist

To filter your collection to create a playlist automatically:

1. Click Library, Create Auto Playlist.
2. Enter a name for the playlist.
3. Click the plus (+) sign next to Music in My Library to continue.
4. Specify the first set of criteria (album, artist, bit rating, various date-related settings, ratings, how often the music has been played, and others).
5. Specify additional information as prompted.

6. Click the plus (+) sign under And Also Include or And Apply the Following Restrictions to the Auto Playlist to narrow the criteria.
7. When finished, click OK. Figure 13.5 shows the dialog after selecting criteria for composer and for duration.

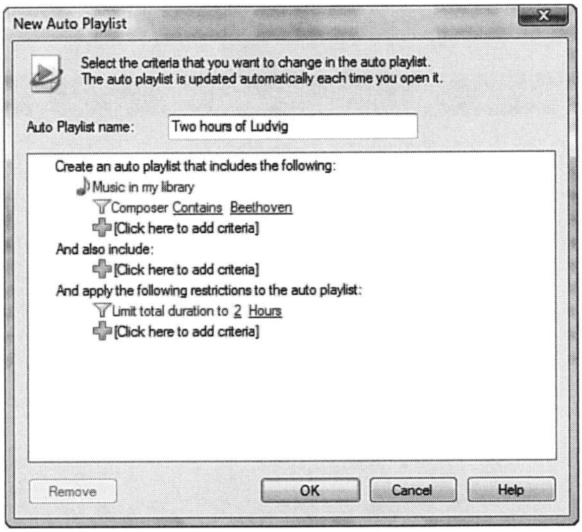

FIGURE 13.5
Creating an Auto Playlist.

Viewing and Editing Playlists

Your new playlists appear in the Playlists section of the left-hand pane in WMP (Figure 13.6). Custom playlists and auto playlists have distinctive icons.

To edit a custom playlist, double-click it to display its contents in the central pane. You can right-click any track and select from options such as move up or down or remove (see Figure 13.7). To use drag and drop to change the order, click the Edit in List Pane button. The playlist opens in the Playlist pane at the right.

To edit an auto playlist, right-click it and select Edit. The filtering criteria appear in the Edit Auto Playlist dialog.

13

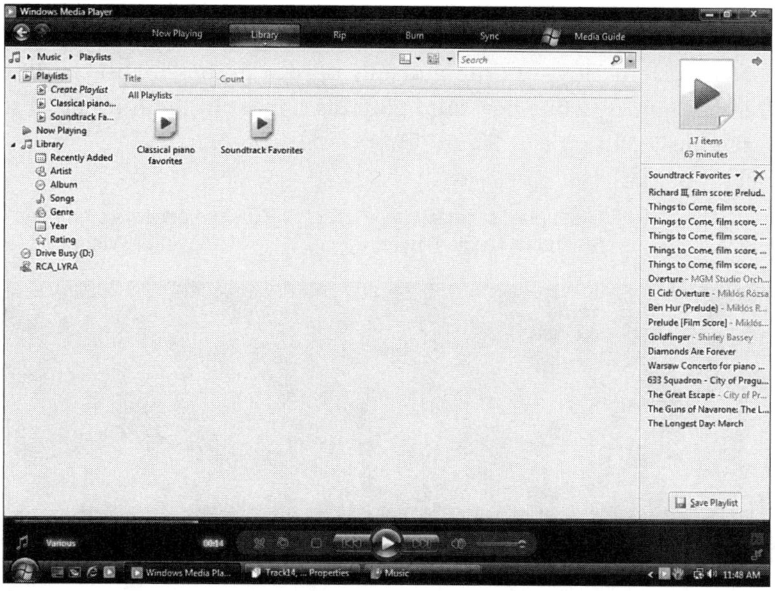

FIGURE 13.6

Custom and auto playlists.

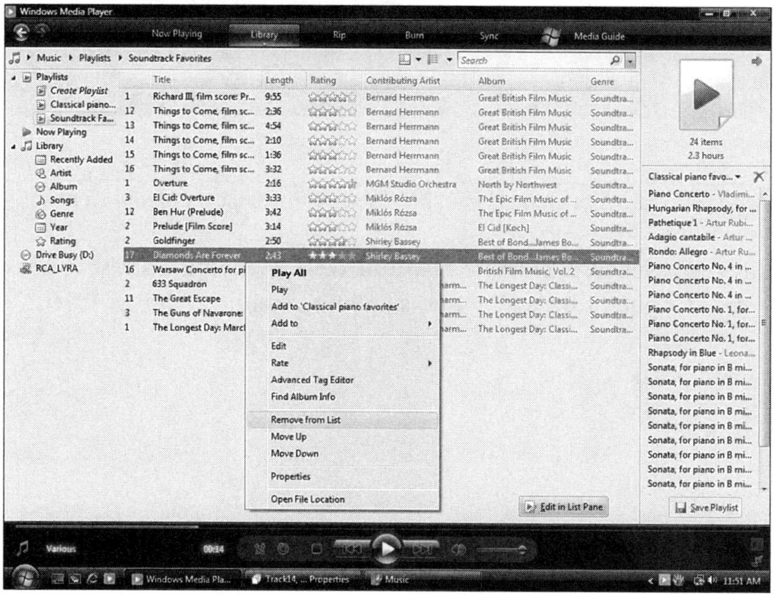

FIGURE 13.7

Editing a custom playlist.

Using New Playlists in Windows Media Center

New custom playlists automatically appear in the Playlists portion of the music library, while new auto playlists appear in the Auto Playlists portion of the music library (see Figure 13.8).

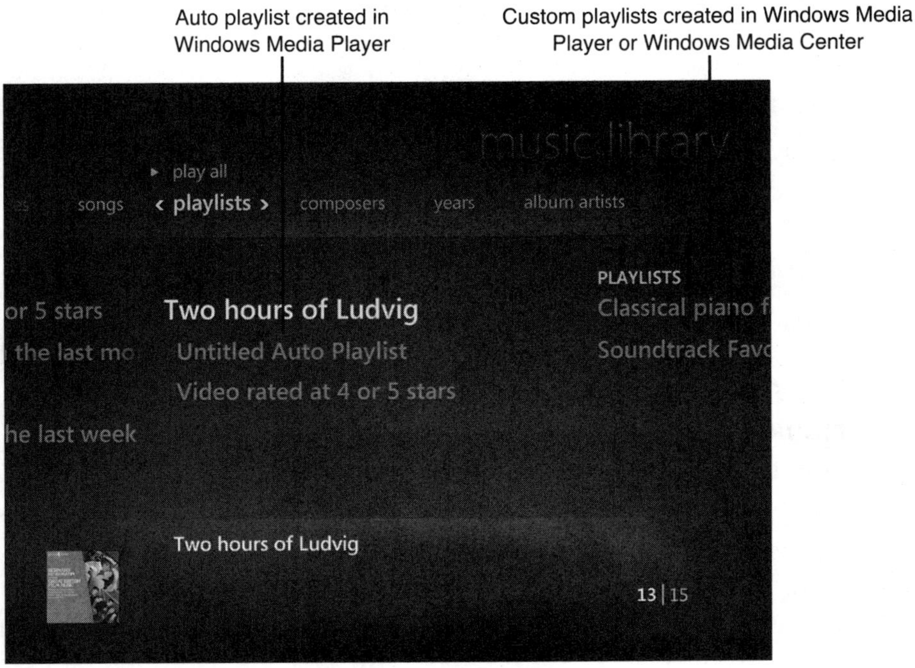

FIGURE 13.8
Custom and auto playlists created in WMP as seen in Windows Media Center.

If you delete a playlist from within WMC (see Figure 13.9), it is removed from the computer and will not be available in either WMP or WMC.

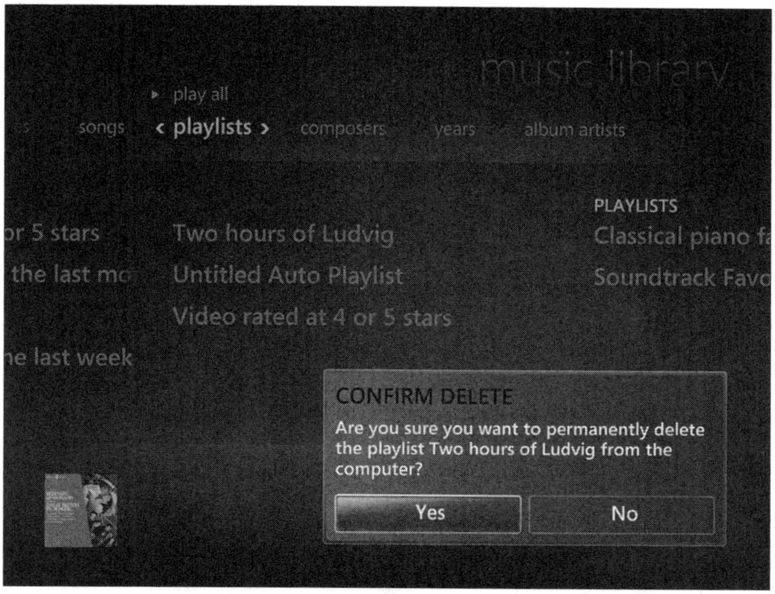

FIGURE 13.9

Preparing to delete an auto playlist from Windows Media Center.

Editing Track and Album Information

Windows Media Player is the perfect place to make changes to album and song ratings, album art, and genres. While some of these changes can be made in Windows Media Center, WMP makes these types of changes faster and easier.

Rating Audio

Windows Media Center and Windows Media Player automatically assign star ratings based on how frequently you listen to a song. (The greater the play frequency, the more stars are assigned.) However, you don't need to play your favorites incessantly to give them the rating they deserve.

13

While you can rate audio in Windows Media Center, its "10-foot UI" forces you to rate audio tracks one at a time. However, in Windows Media Player, you can rate a group of tracks quickly. Here's how:

1. Create (or edit) a custom playlist.
2. Open the playlist.
3. Drag the mouse across the stars next to each song in the playlist until you have highlighted the desired rating.
4. Click the mouse to lock in the rating. (WMP uses yellow stars for user-assigned ratings and white stars for automatically assigned ratings.)
5. Repeat steps 3 and 4 until all songs are rated as desired.

Figure 13.10 shows a playlist with a mixture of automatic and manual star ratings.

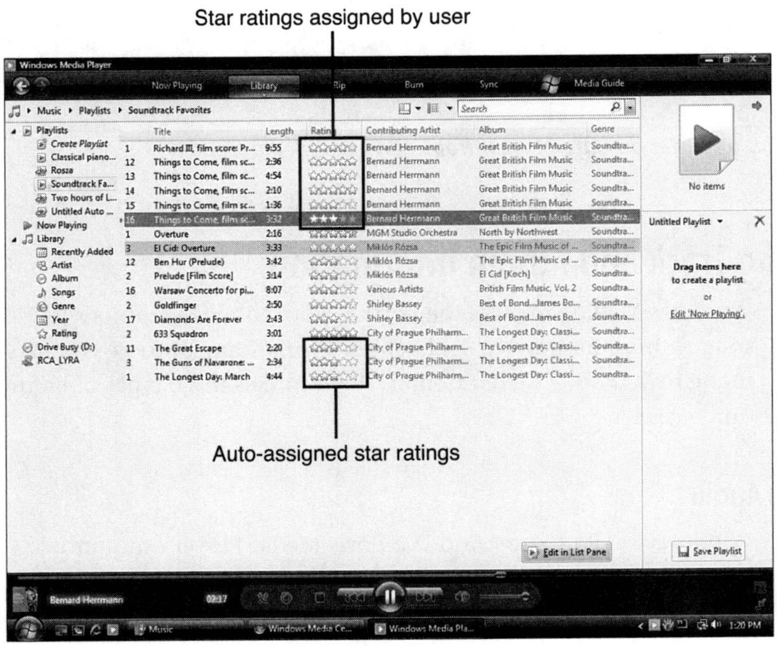

FIGURE 13.10

Assigning star ratings.

To rate all of the songs on an album with the same rating, right-click the album in Library view, select Rate, and select the rating desired (1–5 stars or unrated). You can also use this trick to change an individual song rating or to change a song (or album) to "unrated." To change an individual song rating, right-click the song track, select Rate, and select the rating desired.

Adding/Changing Album Art and Track Information

So you've been busy ripping some of your favorite CDs in Windows Media Center, and you notice that the album art's gone missing or is incorrect, or you might note that there's no artist, genre, or track information. These problems can be fixed in two ways:

- You can search for a matching album online.
- You can enter the information manually.

Before editing incomplete or incorrect information, right-click any track and select Find Album Info. An Album Info dialog appears that attempts to match what it knows about your selected track (from its tag information) to its own online music database.

> **note** The accuracy of the results you get from the Find Album Info feature really depends on having at least an accurate track title. It also helps to have the artist or album in place. Also keep in mind that if information in these fields is inaccurate, Windows Media Player will have a more difficult time tracking down the correct information in its online database.

If Windows Media Player has enough to work with, it's likely to come up with a short list of potential albums that includes the one for your track. If you find a match, simply select it and click Finish. Media Player will apply all known information about that album and its tracks to your music files, including the album's cover art (if available).

If you can't find a match, however, right-click the missing or incorrect information (album name, artist, composer, date, and so on) and type in the correct information from the CD liner notes or other source.

If you can find a picture of the album online or can scan the album yourself, you can fix the missing album artwork problem quite easily. Once you've obtained a copy of the album art:

1. Reduce the image to a size around 200×200 pixels.
2. Save the image as a JPEG (.jpg) or PNG (.png) file.
3. View the image file in Windows Photo Gallery or Windows Live Photo Gallery.

4. Verify that the file size is less than 20Kbps (see Figure 13.11). If not, return to step 2 and reduce the image quality when you save the file. (Use Save for Web or Resize for Email.)

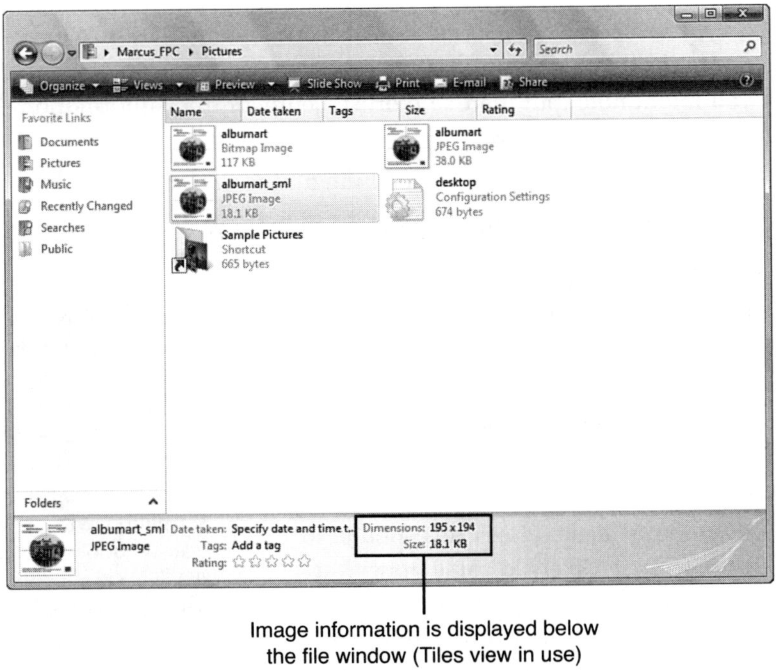

FIGURE 13.11

Selecting an album art file of suitable dimensions and file size.

5. Right-click the file and select Copy.
6. Open Windows Media Player and select a view that shows album art or the placeholder CD icon.
7. Right-click the album art or placeholder you want to update and select Paste Album Art (Figure 13.12).

13

Adding and Editing Genres

To add a genre in Windows Media Player, open the album in Library view, right-click the genre, and type in the replacement genre name. For example, instead of Classical, you can specify Classical Piano. Instead of rock, specify the type of rock (alternative rock, acid rock, pop-rock, and so on). By creating additional genre subdivisions, you can make a large and diverse music collection a whole lot easier to navigate.

Any genre you enter in Windows Media Player can then be selected in either WMP or Windows Media Center.

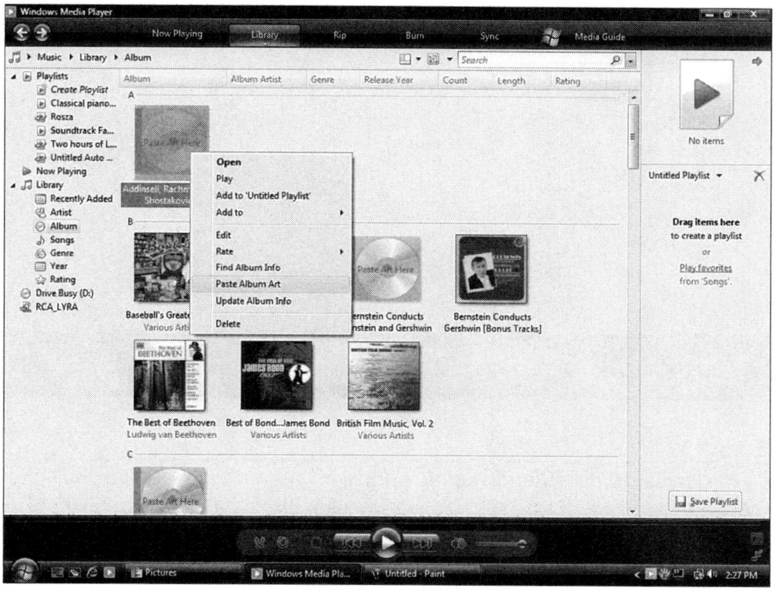

FIGURE 13.12

Pasting in the replacement album art.

Downloading Visualizations

Windows Media Player 11 includes a large number of visualizations that can be displayed onscreen when playing music in either WMP or Windows Media Center. However, if you want to get additional visualizations, they're easy to obtain. Click Now Playing, Visualizations, Download Visualizations (Figure 13.13).

The Microsoft Visualizations for Windows Media Player web page opens in your web browser. You can use visualizations made for Windows Media Player 10 or Windows Media Player 11. You can also make your own visualizations. To learn how, follow the link on the web page to the MSDN website.

Downloadable visualizations include adaptations from popular live-action and animated movies, slide show players with animated transitions, as well as abstract animations similar to those packaged with WMP 11.

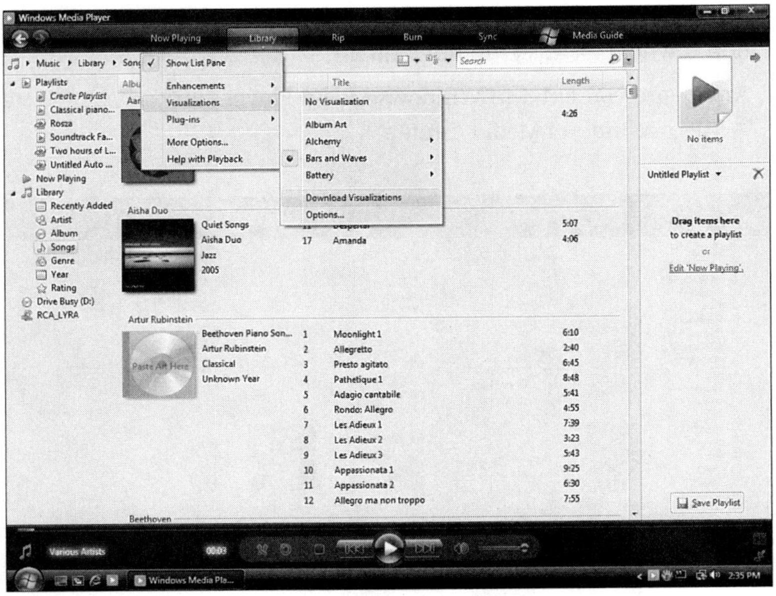

FIGURE 13.13

Preparing to download additional visualizations.

To use a visualization, click Download and follow the onscreen prompts to run or open the visualization file when prompted; you can also save the visualization and run it from the hard disk to install it. Provide administrator credentials if prompted by User Account Control.

You can use most visualizations within WMC immediately. However, if the visualization has configuration options, you can configure these by clicking Visualization, Options in Windows Media Player. This opens the Plug-Ins tab shown in Figure 13.14. From this tab, select the Visualizations category in the pane on the left, the visualization to configure in the pane on the right, and click Properties to open the properties sheet. Select the desired properties, click OK to save changes, and use the visualization in either WMP or Windows Media Center.

> **tip** Use Picture Viz I or II visualizations to make musical slide shows easy. With Picture Viz I, you must specify a single folder as the picture source. Picture Viz II lets you select a folder that contains subfolders (it uses the current user's Pictures folder as the default) and features new and improved animation transitions. Both support JPEG, BMP, PNG, TIFF, EXIF, and TGA image formats.

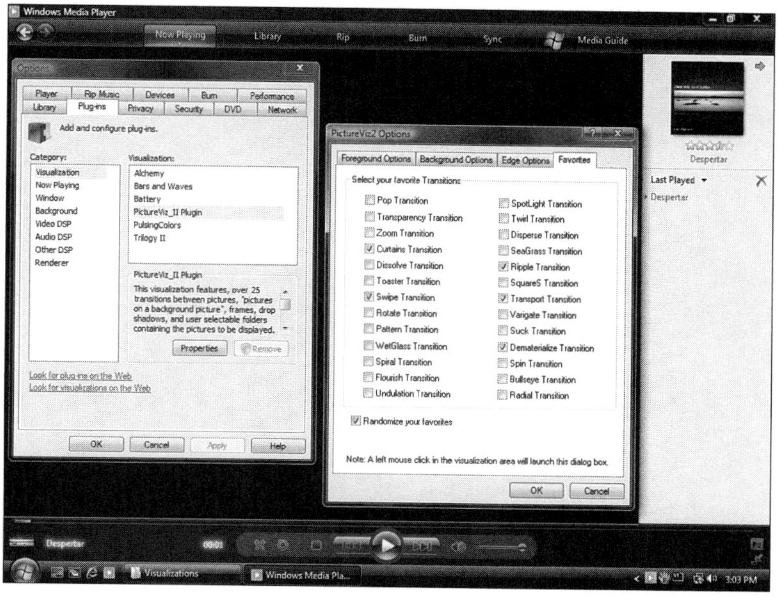

FIGURE 13.14

Configuring transition settings for the optional Picture Viz II visualization.

CHAPTER

14

Creating Photo and Video Content for Media Center

IN THIS CHAPTER

Using Other Vista Features to Make Media Center Even Better

As you've already learned, Media Center is an amazing feature in Windows Vista, but if you want to get the most out of it, you should use it in conjunction with other Windows Vista features such as Windows Photo Gallery or Windows Live Photo Gallery and Windows Movie Maker. Here's why:

- Although you can import digital photos directly into Windows Vista, you have much more control over the process if you use the import feature built into Windows Live Photo Gallery.
- You can crop pictures to match the 16:9 widescreen format of HDTV, fix color and exposure problems, and perform many other fixes by using Windows Photo Gallery or Windows Live Photo Gallery.
- You can tag pictures with Windows Photo Gallery or Windows Live Photo Gallery to make finding your favorite pictures easier.

- You can use Windows Movie Maker to create slide shows with synchronized audio.
- To save space in your recorded video library, you can also use Windows Movie Maker to convert your recordings of live TV or movies into more compact formats or to DVD.

As you can see, there are plenty of reasons to leave the WMC interface, head back to the Windows Vista desktop, and make your picture and video content even easier to enjoy.

tip If you use one system exclusively for WMC, remember that you can edit your pictures and videos with other systems running Windows Vista Home Premium, Ultimate, Business, and Enterprise. Although Business and Enterprise editions don't include WMC, they include Windows Photo Gallery and Windows Movie Maker and can be upgraded to Windows Live Photo Gallery.

Why Tag Your Photos?

If you like digital photography even half as much as I do, you're likely to be swimming in a sea of thousands of digital photos—and you need to get them organized. As you learned in Chapter 7, "Importing and Viewing Photos," Windows Media Center can navigate through your picture collection in three ways:

- By folders
- By date taken
- By tag

At first glance, you might think that navigating by folders is perfect. After all, you probably store pictures of your child's birthday in a folder called...well, maybe it's called Birthday, or maybe you called it Dan's Birthday or Dana's Birthday—or maybe you got creative and used the birth date as the folder name. Hey, they're your pictures, so you can store them any place you want.

Navigating by folder has the following advantages:

- You automatically create a folder when you transfer your pictures from your digital camera or flash memory card reader with most transfer programs.
- You control what goes into a particular folder, so you can create and use different folders for different subjects or events.
- You can browse your photo collection the same way you browse other types of documents and content.

The problem is that photos aren't exactly like other types of documents or content on your computer. The same photo could be classified by the event it portrays ("Jack and Jennie's Wedding"), the date ("June 24, 2006"), the location ("Frederick, Maryland"), the people in the photo ("Jack, Jennie, Edwin, Erica, Cathy, Hubert, Jerome"), or any number of choices. So, what folder do you want to use for a photo like that? And how do you find it later?

So what about option two, navigating by date? It also has a couple of advantages:

- You don't have to do anything—except set your camera's date and time—to use it. Every time you take a picture, your digital camera, like the specialized computer that it is, stores the date and time of creation along with the photo.
- Find the date—find every picture you took on that date.

Again, though, navigating by date isn't perfect. For one thing, if you set your digital camera's date and time incorrectly, every picture you take will be assigned the wrong date and time. I teach digital photography for both point-and-shoot and digital SLR users for a local community college, and in almost every class one or two students discover their cameras' date/time settings are wrong. (You can put this book down for a minute if you want to check your own camera's date and time setting; I'll be here when you get back.)

The second problem is that finding photos by date is a relatively low priority for most of us. Most photographers are more interested in locating picture subjects ("Quick, Vista: Show me every picture of Linus") than the dates the pictures were taken.

The third problem is that finding photos by date simply doesn't work for scanned photos. For example, if you scan a picture of your great-grandparents taken in 1922 in May 2008, the computer places this photo along with the rest of the May 2008 pictures.

So what's left? Tagging. Tagging the pictures you take with subject, location, and other information does take some effort (but not nearly as much as you think), but in the end, you *can* find every picture of Linus, no matter when you took them or how many folders contain Linus's distinctive smile. Figure 14.1 shows you how tagging makes it easy to find just the pictures you want.

So how can you tag your pictures? You'll need to leave the "10-foot UI" of WMC to do it, but it's easy to do with either Windows Photo Gallery or Windows Live Photo Gallery.

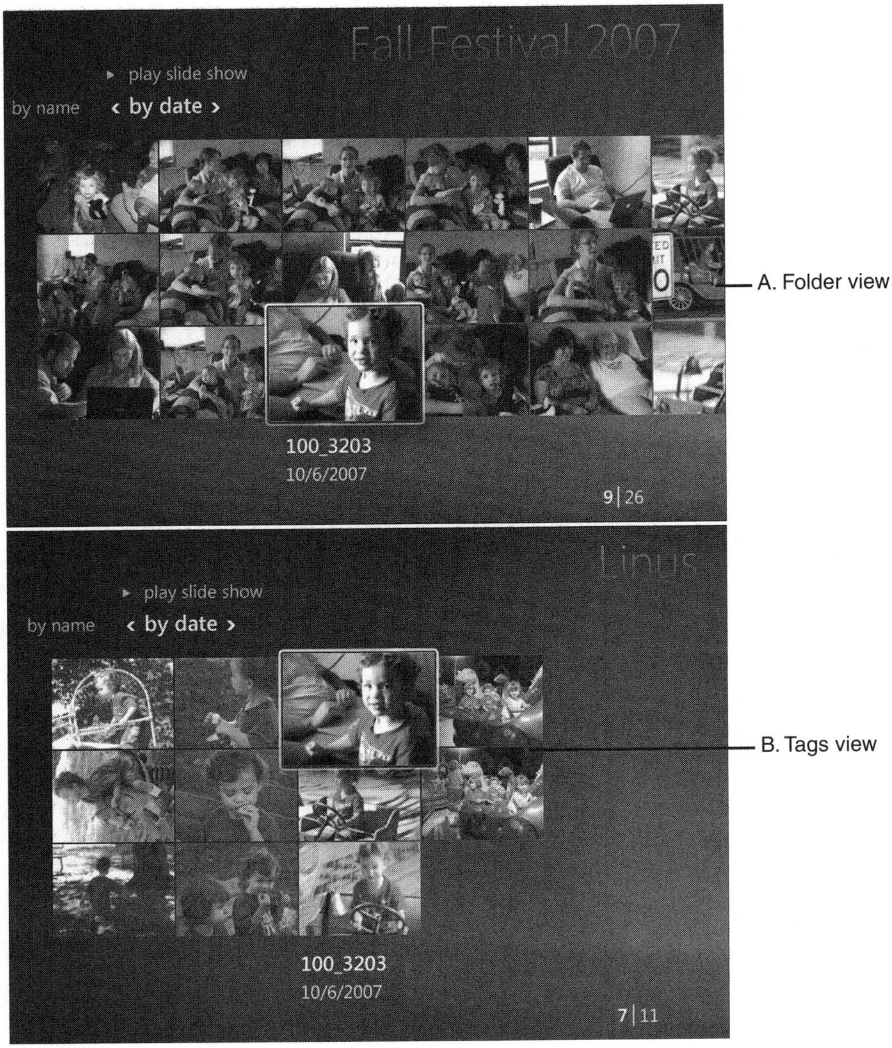

FIGURE 14.1

Using the Folder view (A), it's hard to find just who you're looking for. But if you tag your pictures, the Tags view (B) makes it easy to find the picture you want.

14

Windows Photo Gallery, Meet Windows *Live* Photo Gallery

Windows Vista contains a perfectly serviceable digital image manager called Windows Photo Gallery. Windows Photo Gallery can:

- Tag your pictures
- Perform simple color and exposure editing
- Remove red-eye
- Crop your pictures to a variety of sizes, including HDTV-friendly 16×9
- Make a movie from your photos (using Windows Movie Maker)

Nevertheless, I'm telling you to look Windows Photo Gallery straight in the eye, say "You're Fired!" and go to the http://get.live.com website for its free replacement—Windows Live Photo Gallery. Windows Live Photo Gallery can do everything that Windows Photo Gallery can do, along with lots of new features:

- More powerful photo importing, including grouping and tagging
- Better image editing features, including shadow and highlight controls, histogram adjustment, and image sharpening
- Publishing options to Flickr and other social-networking sites like MSN Soapbox and Windows Live Spaces

The most important features for enjoying your photos in WMC include importing, tagging, image editing, and cropping, so let's take a closer look at how Windows Live Photo Gallery makes WMC's photo viewing features even better.

> **tip** Windows Live Photo Gallery, like other Windows Live components, works with Windows XP SP2 and SP3 as well as Windows Vista.

Importing and Tagging Photos

With Windows Live Photo Gallery, you don't need to wait until your digital photos are stored on your computer to tag them. You can tag photos during the import process. As soon as you connect your digital camera or slide a flash memory card from your camera into a card reader, an AutoPlay menu similar to the one shown in Figure 14.2 appears. Select Import Pictures and Videos using Windows Live Photo Gallery.

Selecting Import Options

The next dialog (Figure 14.3) offers one of two options:

- Review, Organize, and Group Items to Import
- Import All New Items Now

FIGURE 14.2
Beginning the import process from the AutoPlay menu.

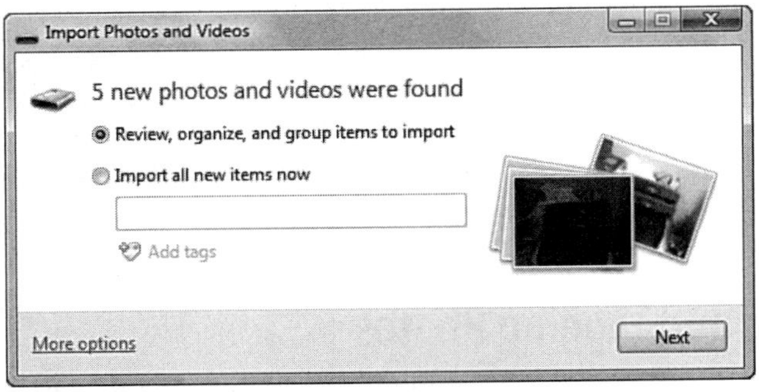

FIGURE 14.3
Selecting a transfer option.

To check or change how your pictures will be imported, click the More Options link visible in Figure 14.3. The Import Settings dialog (Figure 14.4) offers you the following options:

> **tip** The wizard transfers only new (never before imported) pictures in its number if you select Import All New Items Now. If you need to reimport pictures, choose the Review, Organize, and Group Items to Import option.

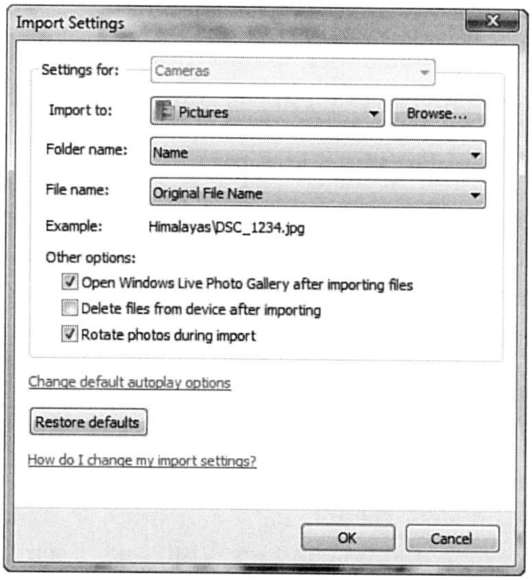

FIGURE 14.4

The Import Settings dialog controls how your pictures will be imported.

- **Import to:** By default, the current user's Pictures folder will be used for the destination folder. The pull-down menu offers Videos as an alternative, or you can use the Browse button to navigate to any other folder.
- **Folder name:** By default, a folder using the name you specify for the import will be created as the destination folder. Other options include Date Imported + Name; Date Taken + Name; Date Taken Range + Name; Name + Date Imported; Name + Date Taken; Name + Date Taken Range; or (None). Use (None) if you prefer to import pictures directly into the Import To folder rather than a subfolder.

> **tip** **To rename or not to rename?** At one time, I preferred to rename pictures from their original names during import. If you want to rename your pictures, you have plenty of options. However, I now find that the tagging feature in Windows Live Photo Gallery makes it even easier to find the pictures I'm looking for. Another advantage of using the original filename is that different brands of cameras use different naming schemes. If you use more than one digital camera, keeping the original filename during import makes it easy to figure out which camera took a particular picture when you view pictures later.
>
> **To rotate or not to rotate?** Leave rotation enabled if your digital camera does *not* rotate vertical pictures for you. However, if your camera rotates pictures for you, and you rotate them again during import, you're back where you started!

14

- **File Name:** By default, the original filename created by the digital camera is used. Other options include Name (the name you provide during import); Original File Name (preserve folders); Name + Date Taken; and Date Taken + Name.
- **Other Options:** Use check boxes to select whether to open Windows Live Photo Gallery after importing files (enabled by default); whether to delete photos after import (disabled by default); or whether to rotate photos during import (enabled by default).

Import All New Items Now

If you're in a hurry, or if all of the pictures have the same subject and you have not imported pictures from the media before, select Import All New Items Now and enter a name for the pictures. To add tags to all pictures, click the Add Tags icon and type in tags. Vista puts a semicolon (;) between tags. Click Import to import the pictures into your computer.

Review, Organize, and Group Items to Import

If the pictures include different subjects, were taken at different times, or were already imported (but you need to import them again), select Review, Organize, and Group Items to Import. Click Next to continue. On the next dialog, your pictures are divided into groups based on the date and time they were taken. As you can see in Figure 14.5, the import wizard uses Vista's picture-stacking feature to give you a preview of what's in each group. By default, all groups are selected for import. To prevent a group from being imported, clear the check box next to the group.

Before importing a group, click the Enter a Name link for each group and enter a name. By default, the name you enter for each group will be used as its destination folder. If you don't specify a name, the date will be used for the folder name. If there's more than one group of pictures on the same date, the first group is numbered 001, the second is numbered 002, and so on. To import all pictures, click Import.

To select photos within a group, or just to see every picture in a group, click the Expand All link at the bottom of the dialog. Figure 14.6 shows the expanded group view. To prevent a particular picture from being imported, clear the check box next to the picture. To return to the group-only view, click Collapse All. Click Clear All to unselect all pictures; Select All to select all pictures.

By default, the import wizard uses a four-hour window to determine groupings. Use the Adjust Groups slider at the bottom of the dialog window to adjust the timing. The minimum is 30 minutes (0.5 hours); the maximum is 30 days.

To add tags to all pictures in a group, click the Add Tags icon shown in Figures 14.5 or 14.6 and type in tags. Vista puts a semicolon (;) between tags. Click Import to import the pictures into your computer.

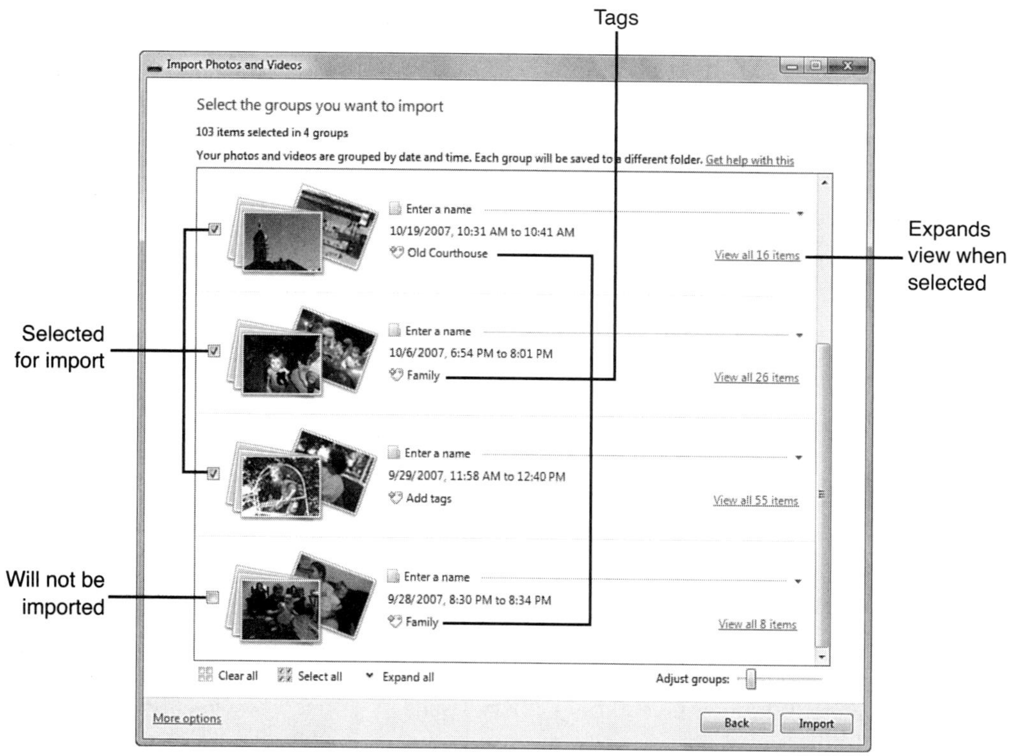

FIGURE 14.5

Selecting groups to import.

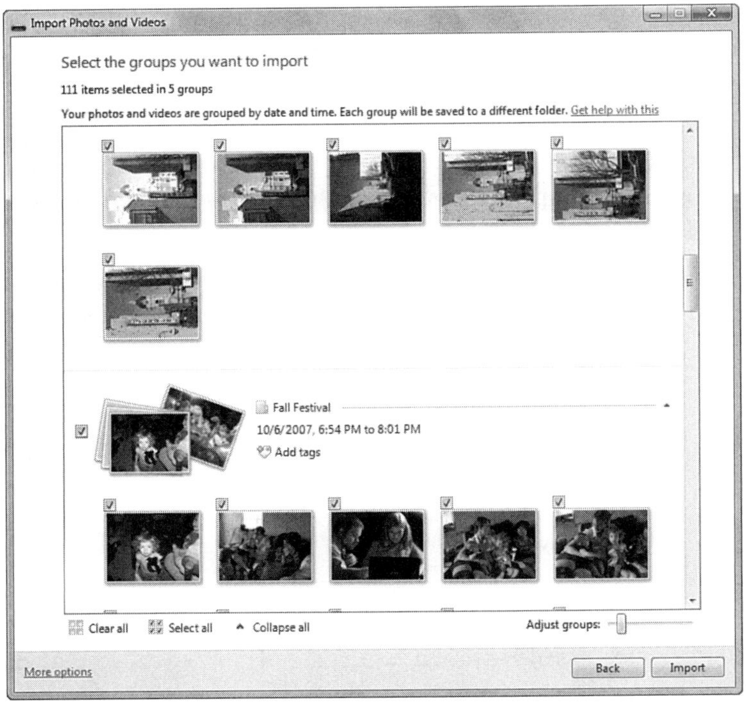

FIGURE 14.6
Using the expanded groups view.

Completing the Import Process

During the import process, a progress indicator appears and displays each picture. To delete the pictures from your camera or flash card, click the Erase After Importing check box. After the import process is complete, Windows Live Photo Gallery opens.

caution Although you can erase the pictures after the import is done, I don't recommend it. By keeping the pictures on your camera or flash card, you can import them into another computer or print them from a printer that supports direct printing from the camera or media. It is also usually better to clear your card by formatting it in the camera after you've transferred your pictures.

Using Gallery Mode

You don't need to wait until you have a camera full of digital pix to open Windows Live Photo Gallery in Gallery mode. There are a couple of other ways to open it:

- You can run Windows Live Photo Gallery from the Start menu; it's an option in the Windows Live folder.
- Right-click a picture and select Preview to open it in Windows Live Photo Gallery. Click Go to Gallery to open the Gallery view.

The left pane of Gallery mode provides you with the following ways to view your pictures:

- **Folder view:** Lists each folder in the current user's Pictures folder. The contents of the current folder are shown in the pane on the right (see Figure 14.7).
- **Date Taken view:** Click a year, month, and day to see the pictures taken that day.
- **Tags view:** Click a tag to see pictures matching that tag or click Not Tagged to see pictures without tags.

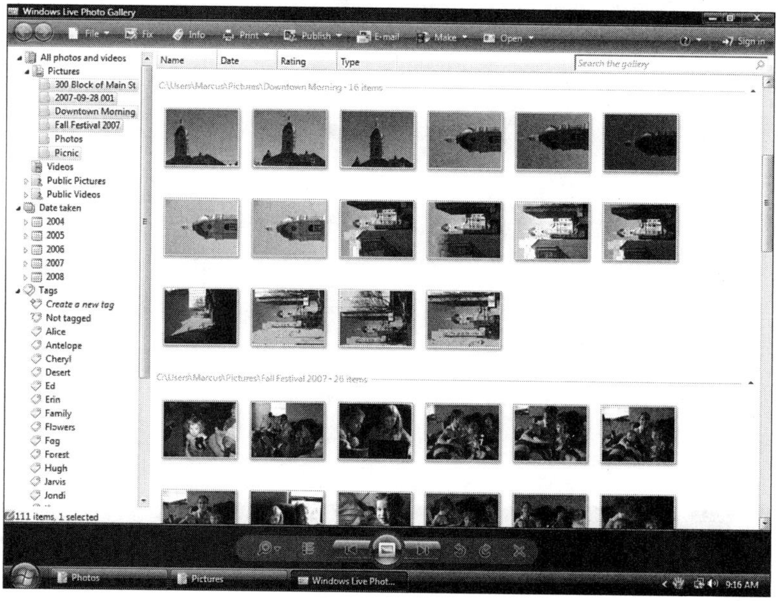

FIGURE 14.7

Windows Live Photo Gallery's Gallery view.

If you want to add tags to your untagged photos in a hurry or add additional tags to already-tagged pictures (for example, a picture of Joe and Josephine has the "Joe" tag but not the "Josephine" tag), Gallery's Tags view is the view for you.

Tagging Pictures in Gallery View

Although you can tag individual pictures in Windows Live Photo Gallery's Preview mode (discussed later in this chapter), it's faster to tag pictures in Gallery mode because you can drag pictures to the tag you want. Here's how:

1. Look at your current list of tags to determine if the tag you want has already been created. If not, click Create a New Tag and type in the tag text you want. Repeat this process until you have created the tags you need.
2. Select the photos you want to tag. Click the first photo, hold down either Ctrl key, and continue to click photos until you have selected all of the photos you want to tag. Selected photos have a contrasting-color border. If you can't see a picture clearly, hover the mouse over the picture and a larger version is displayed (Figure 14.8).

FIGURE 14.8

Hovering over a picture to see an enlarged preview.

3. After the pictures are selected, scroll the left window as needed to display the tag you want to apply.
4. To apply the tag, drag the selected pictures to the tag. The tag will display "Property *tagname*." See Figure 14.9.

FIGURE 14.9

Applying a tag to a group of pictures.

5. To apply an additional tag, repeat steps 1–4.
6. To view only pictures marked with a particular tag, click the tag.
7. To view pictures matching multiple tags, select each tag with Ctrl-click. Pictures matching each tag are grouped in the right-hand pane.

note You can use either Windows Photo Gallery or Windows Live Photo Gallery to apply tags in Gallery view. The process is the same in either program.

Creating a Panoramic Photo Montage

One of the new options in Windows Live Photo Gallery is the option to create a panoramic photo from two or more photos with overlapping edges. This is a great way to make your landscape and vacation photos work better on a 16:9 HDTV screen. Here's how to do it:

tip Need a reason to take a tripod with you on your next photo outing? You'll get better panoramic photo results if you use a tripod to hold your camera level and at the same height for each picture.

1. Select the photos you want to turn into a panoramic photo.
2. Click Make, Create Panoramic Photo. After analyzing the pictures, Windows Live Photo Gallery stitches them into a single image.
3. When prompted, enter a new name for the panoramic photo. By default, it is saved as the same image type and the same folder as the source photos. You can also select from TIFF and WMPhoto image types. Use the Browse button to select a different folder or drive. Click Save to complete the process.
4. The panoramic composite appears in Windows Live Photo Gallery's Preview mode (Figure 14.10).

note Never heard of the WMPhoto picture format before? The Windows Media Photo format is also known as HDPhoto, and Microsoft is pushing it as a higher-quality replacement for JPEG. Don't hold your breath waiting for that to happen, though. If you want to save your image with maximum quality, choose TIFF. If you want to save your image with maximum versatility for sending to family and friends or ordering prints, choose JPEG. WMPhoto isn't supported by very many programs at this time, so don't worry about it.

FIGURE 14.10
Creating a panoramic photo.

Using Preview Mode

Gallery mode is a little like working with the index prints you might have received when you used a film camera. Sure, all of the pictures are displayed there, but they're fairly hard to see. If you want to see your photos in a larger view, fix exposure or color problems, crop them, or make other fixes, it's time to switch to Preview mode.

To enter Preview mode from Gallery mode, double-click the picture. Figure 14.11 shows a picture opened in Preview mode.

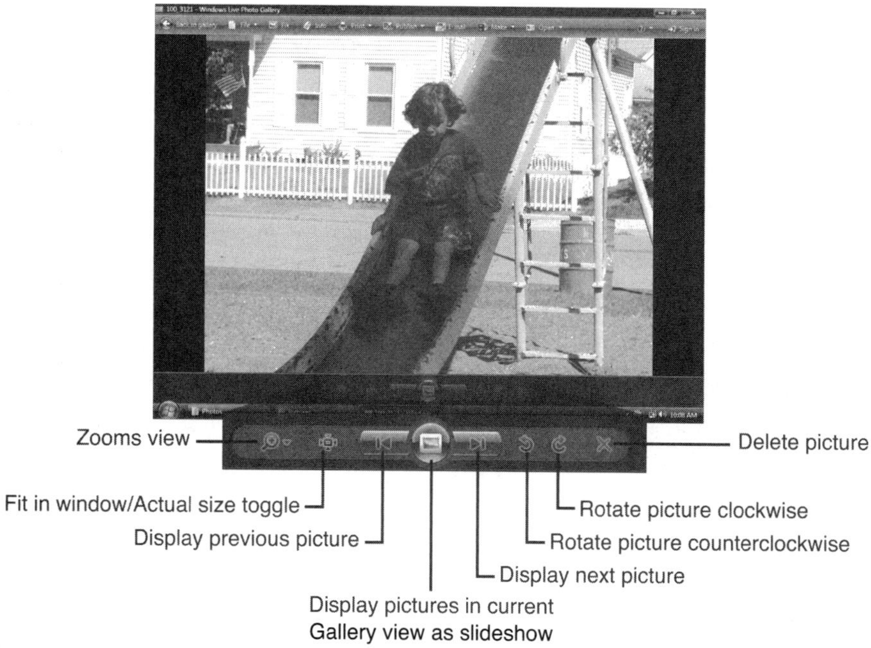

FIGURE 14.11

Windows Live Photo Gallery's Preview mode.

To see other pictures in the current folder, use the forward and back arrows at the bottom of the screen. To run a slide show of pictures in the current folder, click the slide show button between the arrows. The controls to the left of the slide show/playback buttons adjust the magnification level. The controls to the right are used to rotate the picture or to delete it.

If you're using Preview mode to improve a picture for viewing in WMC, you may need to make adjustments such as:

- Exposure
- Color-correction
- Cropping
- Red-eye removal

The following sections show you how to make these edits.

BEFORE YOU REPAIR, PREPARE

If you're smart, you should treat each original digital photo like a "digital negative" and keep an unaltered copy of it. The easy way to do this is to use the File and Folder Backup feature in Windows Vista to make backups of your photos before you edit them. A great time to make backups is after you import pictures from your digital camera or another computer—and *before* you make changes to those pictures.

Although you can reverse some changes you make to a picture with Windows Live Photo Gallery (and Windows Photo Gallery), you're still better off making a backup first—especially if you plan to use a third-party program to edit your photos. After you edit a picture, you can retrieve the original from backup by viewing the photo's properties in Pictures Explorer and going to the Previous Versions tab—if (and only if) you ran backup first.

➔ For more information on using Backup and Previous Versions, see Chapter 16, "Troubleshooting Media Center."

Windows Live Photo Gallery provides a mixture of basic tools (inherited from Windows Photo Gallery) and new advanced tools to enable you to correct pictures that are too dark or too light. To access these tools, click the Fix button at the top of the Preview dialog.

note When you use any of the tools in the Fix menu, Windows Live Photo Gallery and Windows Photo Gallery automatically save your changes. You can use the Undo menu to reverse selected or all changes, but for maximum security, be sure to make a backup first.

Using Auto Adjust

Auto Adjust is the easy way to fix a picture that is too dark, too light, or off-color. It analyzes the picture and makes changes for you. Figure 14.12 compares before and after versions of a severely underexposed (very dark) photo fixed with Auto Adjust.

tip Auto Adjust works best with photos that are overall very dark and have no bright areas. To fix problems with photos that have both light and dark areas, use other tools in the Adjust Exposure or Adjust Color menus.

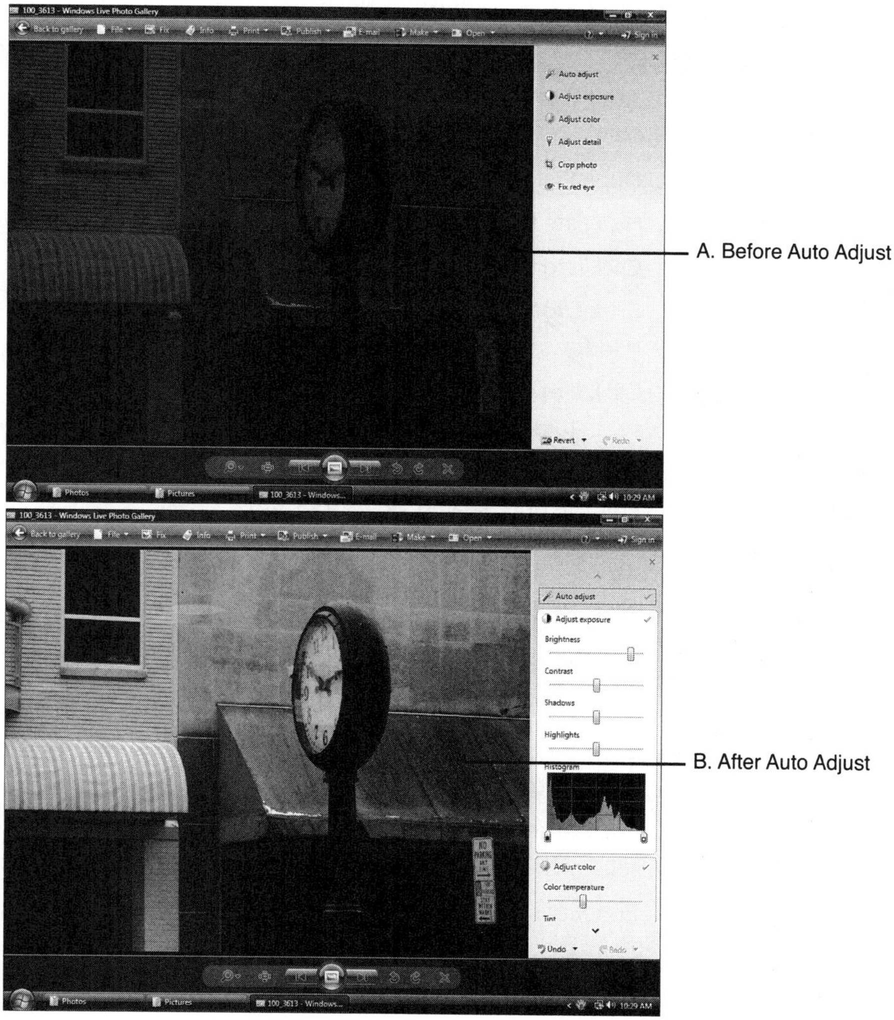

FIGURE 14.12

Using Auto Adjust to fix a very dark (underexposed) photo.

CREATING COPIES OF ORIGINAL PHOTOS BEFORE YOU EDIT

Although running File and Folder Backup before you edit your photos keeps the originals safely tucked away, you might want to be able to compare the originals and edited versions in beautiful WMC big-screen glory. To do that, you need a way to save your original as well as your edited version in separate files. Here are a couple of ways to do it. Method 1 is a good choice if you are planning to edit most (or all) of the pictures in a particular folder. Method 2 is a better choice if you want to edit only a few pictures.

Method 1:

1. Open Picture Explorer.
2. Navigate to the folder containing pictures you will be editing.
3. Click Organize, Select All to select all pictures in the folder.
4. Click Organize, Copy to copy all pictures in the folder to the Windows Clipboard.
5. Click Organize, Paste to paste all pictures in the folder into the same folder. Each picture has –Copy appended to the original name.
6. Edit the original versions as desired.

Method 2:

1. Open Picture Explorer.
2. Navigate to the folder containing pictures you will be editing.
3. Select the picture you want to edit.
4. Click Organize, Copy to copy the picture to the Windows Clipboard.
5. Click Organize, Paste to paste a copy of the picture into the same folder. The copy has –Copy appended to the original name.
6. Repeat as needed for any other pictures you want to edit.
7. Edit the original versions as desired.

Using Adjust Exposure

Windows Photo Gallery offers brightness and contrast adjustments in its Adjust Exposure menu. Windows Live Photo Gallery offers three additional tools:

- **Shadows:** Lightens or darkens dark areas only
- **Highlights:** Lightens or darkens bright areas only
- **Histogram:** Sets black-and-white points in an image and displays a visual map of exposure data

These new tools make it much easier to solve problems with your photos.

Picture too dark or too light overall: Adjust the black point (left-side) and white point (right-side) sliders at the bottom of the Histogram control to match the ends of the exposure data (represented by a mountain-shaped graph). Compare Figures 14.13 A and 14.13 B.

Subject is too dark. Adjust the Histogram control as needed to ensure that the black-and-white points match the ends of the data. Then move the Shadows control to the right to lighten the subject.

Subject is too light. Adjust the Histogram control as needed to ensure that the black-and-white points match the ends of the data. Then move the Highlights control to the left to darken the subject.

Subject is too dark, and the background is too light. Adjust the Histogram control as needed to ensure that the black-and-white points match the ends of the data. Then move the Highlights control to the left to darken the background. Move the Shadows control to the right to lighten the subject.

Subject is too light and the background is too dark. Adjust the Histogram control as needed to ensure that the black-and-white points match the ends of the data. Then move the Highlights control to the left to darken the subject. Move the Shadows control to the right to lighten the background (see Figure 14.14).

In Windows Live Photo Gallery, the new exposure adjustment controls enable you to convert even marginal images into useful photos.

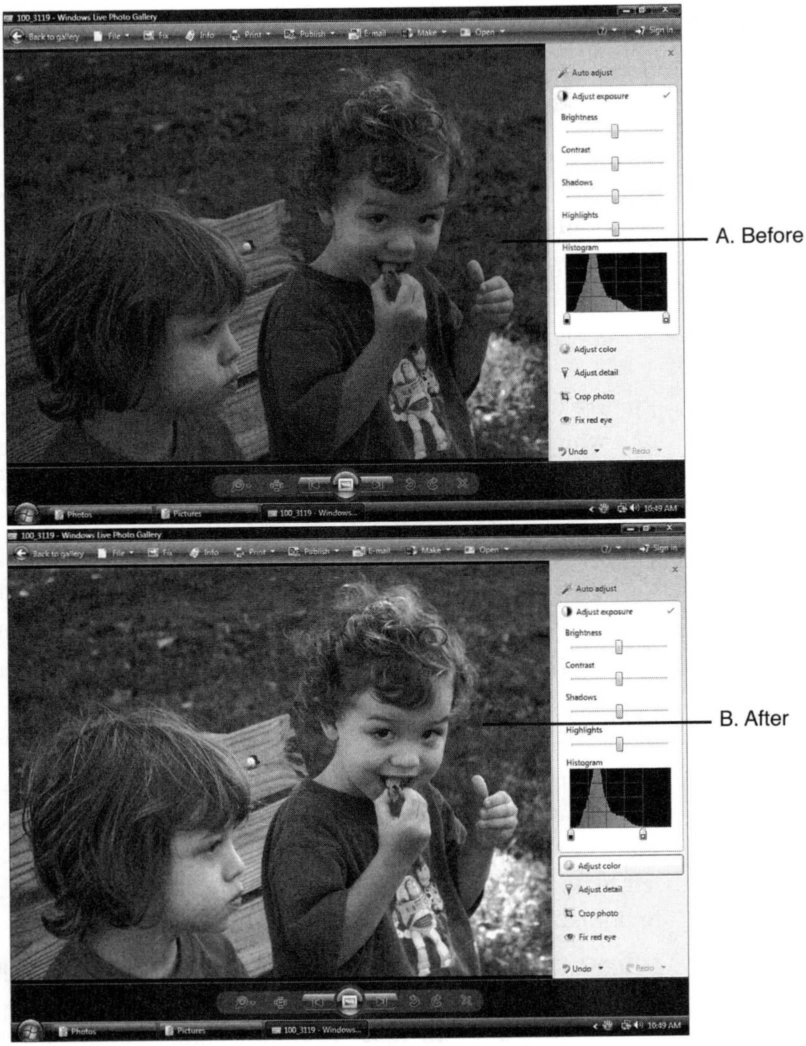

FIGURE 14.13

Using Histogram to lighten a dark photo.

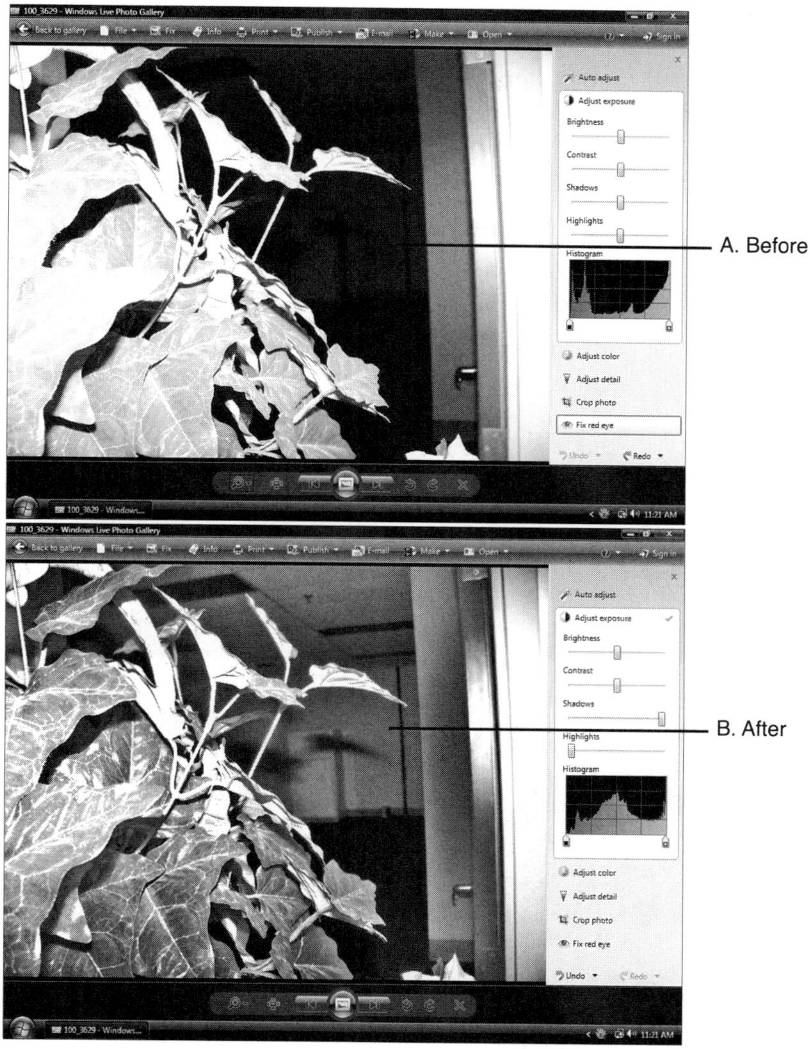

FIGURE 14.14

Using Shadows and Highlights controls to rebalance a photo.

Using Adjust Color

Despite auto color and white-balance features in digital cameras and easy color restoration features in image scanners, you might still need to fix off-color photos. The Adjust Color menu in both Windows Photo Gallery and Windows Live Photo Gallery provides three tools you can use:

- **Color Temperature:** Adjusts problems with white balance
- **Tint:** Adjusts problems caused by off-color lighting or color shifting in scanned photos
- **Saturation:** Intensifies faded colors or reduces overly vivid colors

> **tip** Before using the Adjust Color menu, be sure to adjust pictures that are too light or too dark by using the Adjust Exposure menu.

To scroll up or down to other menus, use the up arrow and down arrow controls at the ends of the menu pane. Figure 14.15 shows these controls.

FIGURE 14.15

Fixing color, tint, and saturation problems in a scan of an old family photo.

CREATING A BLACK-AND-WHITE IMAGE FROM A COLOR PICTURE

If some of your photos would look better in black and white than in full color, you can perform the conversion in Windows Live Photo Gallery. Here's how:

1. Open the Adjust Color menu and slide the Saturation slider all the way to the left. This removes all color from the image.
2. Adjust the Color Temperature and Tint sliders as desired to adjust tones in the picture.
3. Open the Adjust Exposure menu and adjust the controls until you reach the best appearance.

Cropping Your Photos for HDTV Viewing and More

The Crop Photo tool in both Windows Photo Gallery and Windows Live Photo Gallery supports a wide variety of traditional picture sizes as well as the 16:9 format used by HDTVs and widescreen LCD monitors.

Keep in mind this simple fact: You don't need to crop your pictures for playback on an HDTV. If you run a slide show in WMC with uncropped pictures on your HDTV, what's the worst that can happen? Black bars on the sides of your pictures (because the pictures don't match the 16:9 screen ratio of your TV). It's not a big deal, really (although you can now buy digital cameras that offer a 16:9 picture format as an option).

So should you crop some of your pictures? Maybe. Consider the following:

- By cropping your photo, you can eliminate extraneous detail and make a photo more interesting.
- Some subjects, such as mountain and desert vistas, trains, and large group photos, benefit from being cropped to 16:9 format.
- You can create both cropped and uncropped versions of your favorite photos by using the trick I discussed in the sidebar, "Creating Copies of Original Photos Before You Edit" (this chapter, **p. 410**).

So what's not to like? Here's how to crop your pictures to 16:9 with either Windows Live Photo Gallery or Windows Photo Gallery:

1. Open the Crop Photo menu.
2. Select 16×9 from the Proportion menu.
3. Use the adjustment points on the corners of the cropping frame to adjust the cropping area (see Figure 14.16).
4. When you're satisfied, click Apply to crop the photo.

To crop a picture to a different size, select a different size in step 2.

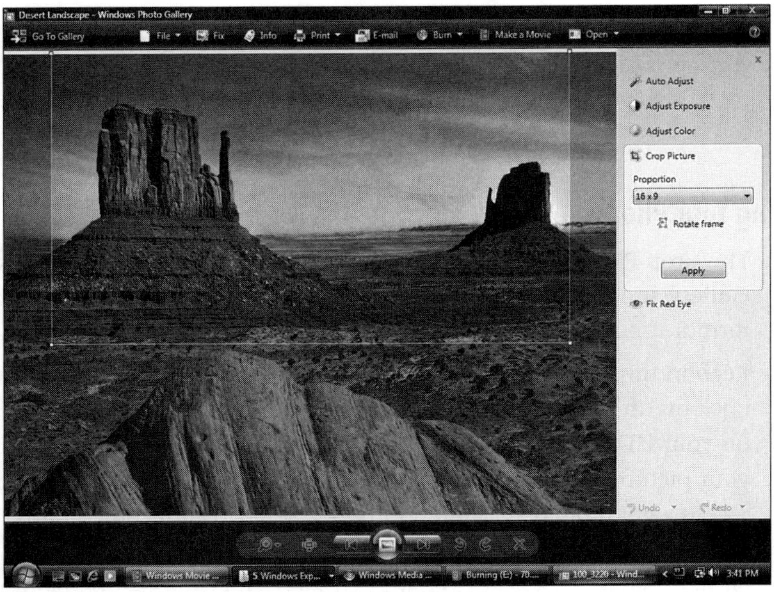

FIGURE 14.16

Cropping a desert landscape to 16:9 proportions for HDTV viewing without the black bars.

As you can see from Figure 14.16, cropping enables you to eliminate extraneous subject matter and, if you crop for 16:9 HDTV format, you can emphasize the horizontal.

Other Fixes

Windows Live Photo Gallery also offers additional photo repair tools:

- Use the Adjust Detail tool to sharpen fuzzy photographs, particularly those that are out of focus. (It doesn't do much for camera shake.)
- Use the Fix Red-Eye tool to remove red-eye from pictures.

As soon as you make the changes you want with Windows Live Photo Gallery (or Windows Photo Gallery), you can immediately enjoy the improvements in Windows Media Center.

Using Windows Movie Maker

In Windows Vista, Windows Movie Maker has become a much more powerful and versatile video-editing and production tool than in previous Windows versions. In this section, you'll learn how to:

- Create slide shows with synchronized audio from your favorite photos. The slide show is stored as a video file you can view with Windows Media Center or Windows Media Player.
- Use Windows Movie Maker (WMM) to reduce the size of your WMC DVR recordings by recording them to another format you can view in Windows Media Center or Windows Media Player.
- Record your videos to DVD for playback in WMC (and on DVD players).

caution If you are unable to run the version of Windows Movie Maker included in Windows Vista (version 6.0), I have bad news for you: It means that your video card does not support Windows Display Driver Model (WDDM), the video card driver format standard in Windows Vista. WDDM changes how display drivers work to provide more stability and features than with older designs. Instead, your video card is using the older Windows XP Driver Model (XDDM), which does not support Windows Movie Maker 6.0.

If you can't upgrade your video card, you can download Windows Movie Maker 2.6, which is essentially the same as Windows Movie Maker in Windows XP. Unfortunately, you will also wave goodbye to MS-DVR conversion, new special effects, better clip creation, and other new WMM features. However, you can still create slide shows with transitions manually or with AutoMovie.

Download WMM 2.6 from www.microsoft.com/downloads/details.aspx?familyid=d6ba5972-328e-4df7-8f9d-068fc0f80cfc&displaylang=en.

Creating Slide Shows Quickly with AutoMovie

Although WMC includes a simple slide-show viewing capability (as you learned in Chapter 7, it does not support audio/video synchronization, dissolves, or other special effects. You can start playing your favorite music before you start a slide show, but you might have some awkward juxtapositions of music and images.

note An AutoMovie is the term that WMM uses for any video or slide show that is automatically assembled by WMM. AutoMovies can be edited. WMM considers all types of finished output a movie, even if it includes only still photos.

If you want more control over your slide shows, WMM is the way to go. You can add narration, adjust how long each picture is displayed onscreen, control transitions between pictures, and much more. You can start from scratch, or if you're in a hurry, you can create an AutoMovie and edit it as desired.

Creating an AutoMovie from Your Photos

The Make a Movie menu option in Windows Live Photo Gallery or Windows Photo Gallery is the fastest (and easiest) way to start creating a slide show from your favorite photos. Here's how to do it:

1. Select the photos you want in your slide show. After you select the first one, hold down the Ctrl key as you click additional photos.
2. Open the Make menu and select Make a Movie (Figure 14.17).

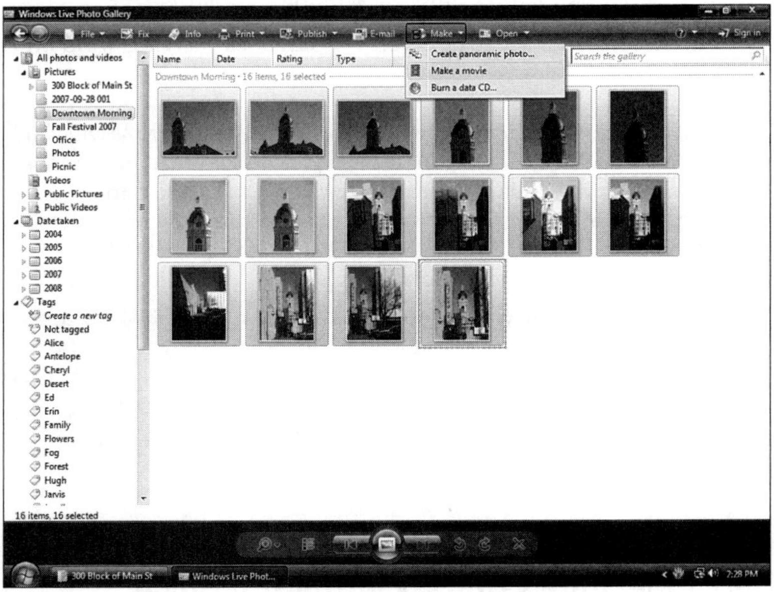

FIGURE 14.17

Selecting pictures for a slide show movie in Windows Live Photo Gallery.

3. WMM imports your pictures. It automatically sequences your pictures by date/time stamps and adds them to its timeline (Figure 14.18).
4. Click the Play button to preview your slide show.

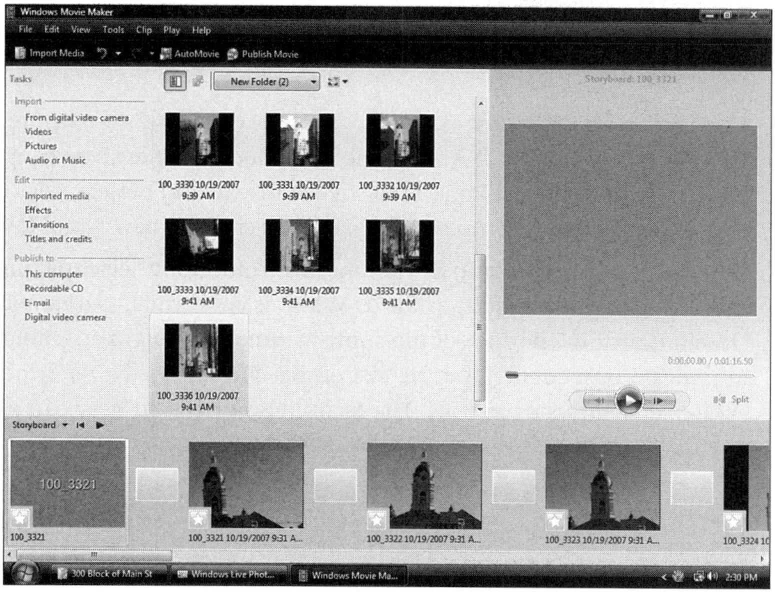

FIGURE 14.18

An AutoMovie project created by Windows Movie Maker.

Selecting an AutoMovie Style

An AutoMovie uses the name of the first photo as the title for the slide show, and by default uses the Fade and Reveal transition types between pictures. Each picture is displayed for four seconds. Here are the styles available for AutoMovies:

- **Fade and Reveal (default):** Fade and Reveal transitions between photos or video clips
- **Flip and Slide:** Flip, Slide, Reveal, and Page Curl transitions
- **Highlights Movie:** Cuts, fades, adds title and credits
- **Music Video:** Adjusts the speed of edits to match the music

note If you start the movie-making process from within Windows Live Photo Gallery, each time you select photos, they will be added to a different folder in WMM's Imported Media menu. The first is called New Folder, the second is called New Folder (1), and so on. You do not need to import the same pictures more than once, so if you don't see your pictures in WMM's Imported Files window, open the folder menu (it's directly above the thumbnails of imported media) and select a different folder.

- **Old Movie:** Applies the film age effect to photos/videos
- **Sports Highlights:** Selects action clips and adds score overlays and credits

To try a different style of AutoMovie or to create a slide show completely from scratch, click File, New Project. To save your existing project, click Yes and provide a name when prompted. You can now create a new AutoMovie.

Whether you use the AutoMovie process or manually select pictures for a slide show in WMM, the result, as far as WMM is concerned, is a movie, even if the "moving picture" portion of the show is transitions between photos or scrolling titles. Consequently, for the rest of this chapter, I'll be referring to your WMM slide shows as movies. The techniques discussed here can also be used to enhance video clips you bring into WMM.

Saving Your Movie Project

To save your movie project, click File, Save Project As. By default, the project will be saved to the current user's Videos folder. Click Browse Folders if you want to save the project to a different folder. Enter a name for the project and click Save to save the project.

> **tip** If you want to collaborate with others on your movie project, make sure you save it to a folder that others can access, such as the Shared Videos folder in the Public folder.

Adding Audio to Your Movie

When you start the movie-making process from within Windows Photo Live Gallery or Windows Photo Gallery, the wizard doesn't provide the opportunity to add music or an audio track. Don't let that bother you. After your pictures are imported into WMM, you can add audio and create a movie that incorporates it.

To import prerecorded music or audio, click Audio or Video in the Import menu. Navigate to the folder containing your audio, select the files you want to import, and click Import. The audio files are listed after your picture files in the list of imported media.

If you are creating an AutoMovie, open the AutoMovie menu, select the style of AutoMovie you want, and then click Select Audio or Background Music. Select the music you want from the pull-down menu (which lists imported tracks) or click Browse to locate other audio sources (see Figure 14.19).

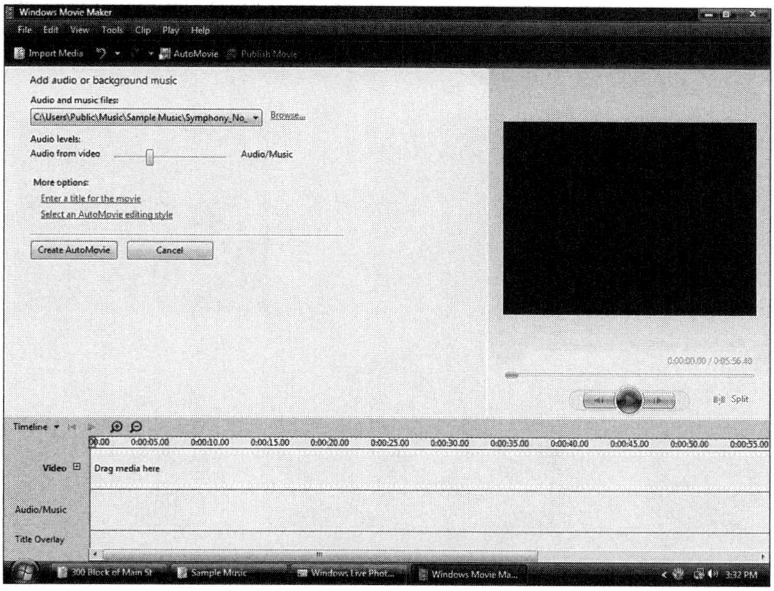

FIGURE 14.19

Adding audio to an AutoMovie project.

Adding and Editing the Title

To add a title of your choice, click Enter a Title for the Movie. Enter the text desired. Use the links to go back and select a style or audio or click Create AutoMovie. Don't like the title appearance? Don't worry—you can change it.

1. From the default Storyboard view, double-click the title slide to edit it. The Enter Text for Title dialog contains two text-entry window. The top window is used for the main title; the lower window is used for the subtitle (if any). You can return to this dialog from other title-edit dialogs by clicking Edit the Title Text.
2. Click Change the Title Animation to choose from numerous animated effects. Choose an effect, and the preview window displays it. Scroll up or down to choose from effects for single-line titles, two-line titles, and credits.
3. Click Change the Text Font and Color to select the font (Microsoft Sans Serif is the default), text color, transparency, size, alignment (position), and attributes such as Italic, Bold, and Underline. You can also change the background color (Figure 14.20).
4. Click Add Title to save the changes as part of your project.

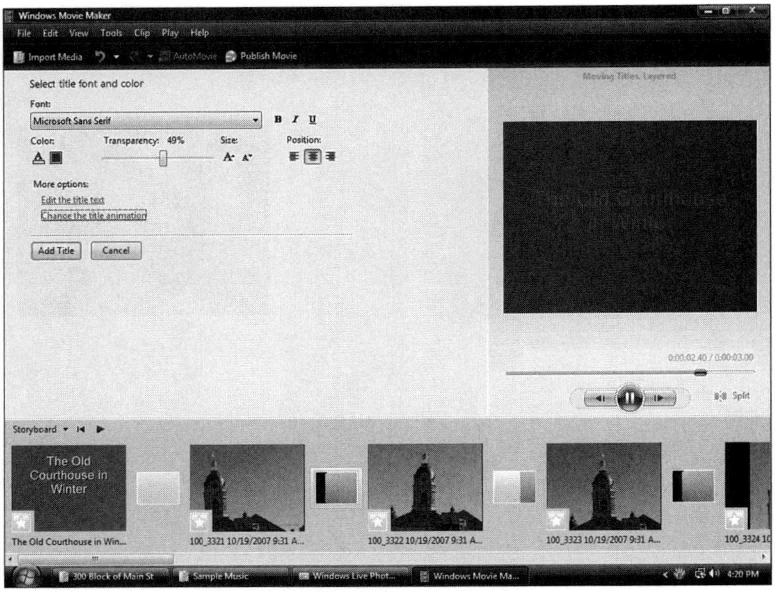

FIGURE 14.20

An AutoMovie project created by Windows Movie Maker.

Editing Transitions

By default, WMM adds a transition between each photo or video clip when you make an AutoMovie. To see the transition in use, hover the mouse over the small Transitions box between photos or video clips in the default Storyboard view.

To use a different transition, select Transitions from the Tasks pane, select a transition, and drag it to the transitions box you want to change. To preview the transition, click the photo or video clip before the transition and click the Play button on the preview window.

Working with Timeline View

The Timeline view shows components of a movie that are normally not visible in the default Storyboard view as separate tracks and adds a time scale to the top of the tracks. To switch to Timeline view, select it from the menu at the bottom left.

The Audio/Music track lists any music that's part of the show, and, after narration is added, narration. The Title Overlay track shows titles that overlay the video (standard opening and closing titles are part of the Video track). Click the plus (+) sign on the Video track to open separate tracks for Transitions between photos or video clips and Audio for narration (see Figure 14.21).

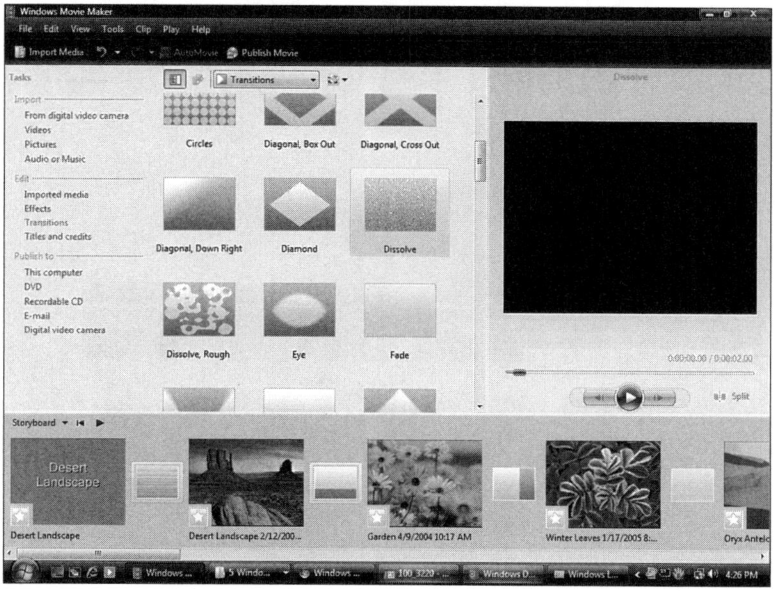

FIGURE 14.21

Selecting the Dissolve transition from the Transitions menu.

The Timeline view might occupy only a portion of the screen width. To zoom in for more detail, click the Zoom Timeline In magnifying glass icon, or press the Page Down key. Each click or Page Down press increases the magnification. A horizontal scrollbar appears below the Timeline view when the entire timeline no longer fits onscreen. To zoom back, click the Zoom Timeline Out icon or press Page Up. Figure 14.22 compares the default Timeline view with a zoomed out view after adding music and expanding the Transitions track.

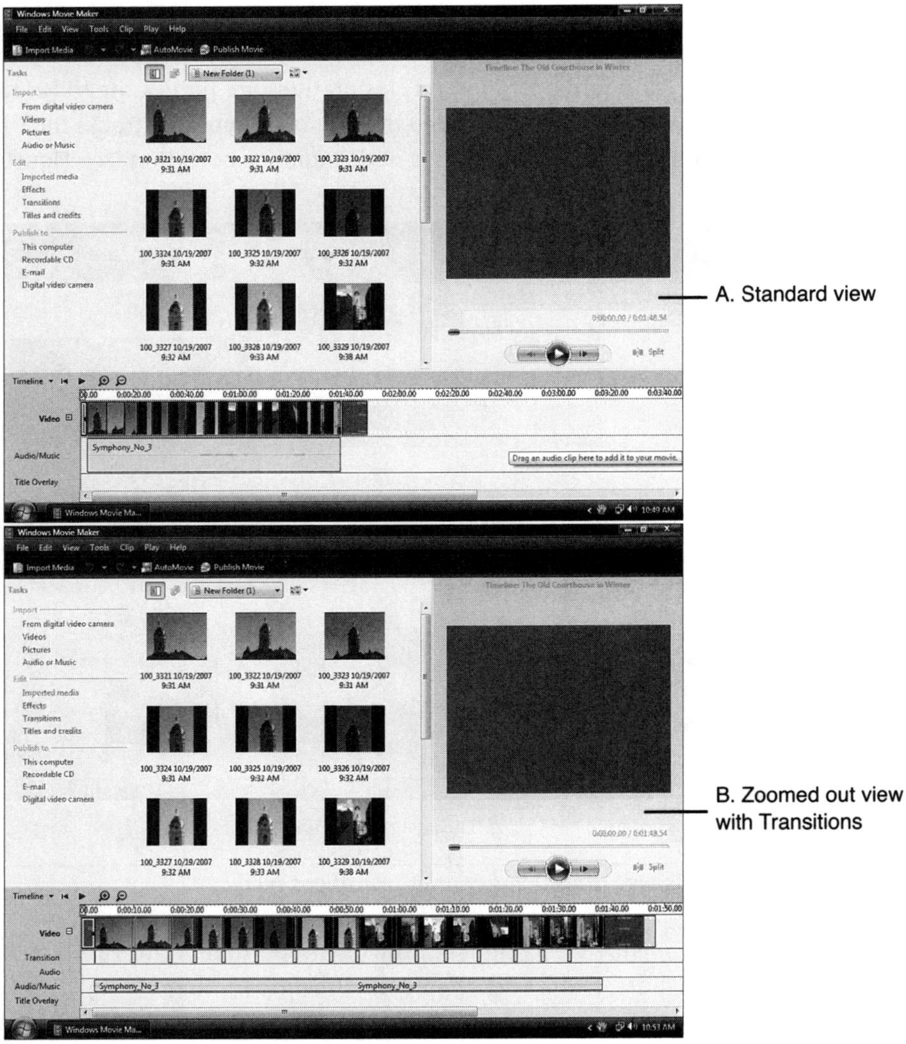

FIGURE 14.22
The Timeline view.

Adding Narration to Your Movie

To add narration, select Narrate Timeline from the bottom-left menu. WMM automatically switches to Timeline view and displays a pop-up message chiding you for not switching to Timeline view yourself first. Click OK to close it.

The upper-left side of the dialog now displays a Narrate Timeline dialog. Make sure your microphone is plugged into the correct jack on your sound card or onboard audio (it's marked with a pink jack on most recent models) and that it's not muted. Click Start Narration, and the slide show starts (see Figure 14.23). Begin speaking into the microphone to narrate the show.

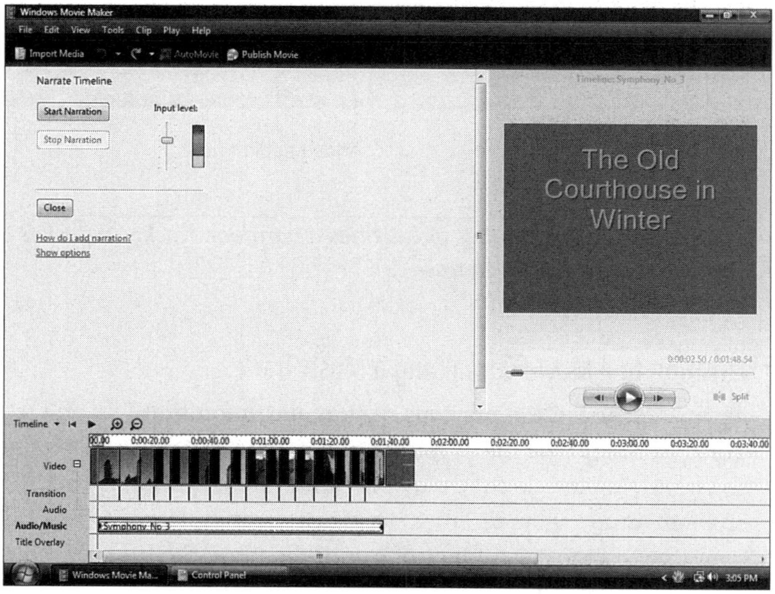

FIGURE 14.23

Creating a narration track.

When you're done narrating, click Stop Narration. A Save dialog appears. By default, WMM stores your narration in the Narration subfolder of the Videos folder, using the name ***Movie* Narration**, where ***Movie*** is the name of your show. Click Save to save the narration as a Windows Media Audio (WMA) file.

When you add narration to a slide show that contains a music track, the narration displaces the music in the audio track. Similarly, if you add music to a slide show that already contains a narration track, the music displaces the narration. In either case, the audio you added first is pushed down the timeline so it will not play until after the newly added audio plays (see Figure 14.24). This brings up an interesting question. Can you use WMM to create a slide show that includes both music and narration overlaid on each other? Yes, you can.

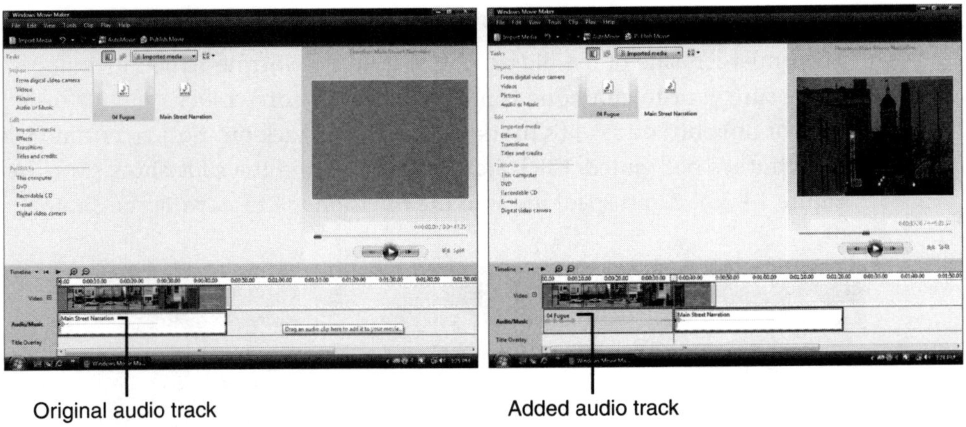

FIGURE 14.24

Adding a music track to a movie that already has a narration track (A) pushes the existing audio track behind the newly added track (B).

Adding Narration to a Movie Containing a Music Track

As you learned in the previous section, narration that you add to a movie is stored as a separate file by WMM and pushes any music clips in the movie down the timeline so they play only after the narration is over. To solve this problem, drag the audio track over the narration track. A blue triangle forms. Continue to drag the audio track until the tip of the triangle reaches the point of the show when you want it to start (Figure 14.25).

Don't drag it too far, or the audio track will simply change places with the narration track. When you preview the movie now, you should hear both the narration and the music tracks.

If you find that one or the other audio source is too loud, use the Undo button (left arrow) to undo the overlay, select the audio track you want to adjust, right-click it, and select Volume. Use the Audio Clip Volume slider to adjust the volume. Other right-click options enable you to fade in, fade out, or mute the clip, copy it, or remove it. Drag the clips back into place and preview the movie again.

> **tip** For more Windows Movie Maker tips, see the Windows Movie Maker website at www.windowsmoviemakers.net/Tutorials/. Although many of the tips listed are specific to Windows Movie Maker 2, most work with Windows Vista's version as well.

FIGURE 14.25

Overlaying a music track on a narration track.

Creating and Editing a Slide Show Manually

If you'd rather create your own slide show from start to finish, the overall process works like this:

1. Click File, New Project. If you want to keep your existing project, save it when prompted. (WMM can work on only one project at a time.)
2. Click Import Media, navigate to the folder containing the pictures you want to use, select the pictures you want to add to the slide show, and click Import.
3. Drag each picture to the storyboard and place it in the appropriate location (Figure 14.26).
4. To add transitions between pictures, select Transitions from the Edit menu in the left pane, select a transition, and drag it to the small transition placeholder between each picture placeholder on the storyboard.
5. To add an effect to a picture, select Effects from the Edit menu, select an effect, and drag it to the picture.

FIGURE 14.26
Dragging a picture to the Storyboard.

6. To add music, switch to Timeline view, click Audio or Music in the Import menu, select the audio or music files you want to use, and click Import. Drag each music or audio file to the appropriate spot on the timeline.

> **tip** If the music is too long for the slide show, click the end of the track in Timeline view and drag it to the end of the pictures.

7. To add titles and credits, click Titles and Credits in the Edit menu, select the style (title at beginning, before selected clip, after selected clip, or credits at end), enter the text, and click Add Title.
8. When you're finished, save the project.

Publishing Your Movie for Use with WMC

Before you can enjoy your new and improved movie (slide show) in WMC, you must publish it (WMM's term for outputting the project into a viewable format). Before starting the process, make sure you've saved your project.

To start the publishing process, click Publish Movie. You can choose from five different targets:

- This Computer
- DVD

- Recordable CD
- E-Mail
- Digital Video Camera (better known as DV-Camcorder)

Use the default, This Computer. Click Next to continue.

Enter a name for your movie and select a folder. By default, your movie will be published to your Videos folder. If you have selected this folder for media sharing, others on your network can also enjoy this slide show.

Next, you need to select output options for your movie. The default setting, Best Quality for Playback on My Computer, creates a Windows Media Video (WMV) file that works well on traditional TVs or standard aspect ratio monitors. However, WMM also offers several HD options. Choose one of these if you plan to view your movie on widescreen displays. Table 14.1 gives you a rundown of the available settings.

note In addition to the standard sizes listed in Table 14.1, you can compress your video to a specified size in MB or KB, which is useful primarily for crunching your movie down to a size suitable for a portable device.

Table 14.1 WMM Movie Publishing Options

Name	File Type	Bit Rate	Display Resolution	Aspect Ratio	Frames Per Second	Relative File Size
Best Quality for Playback on My Computer	WMV	Variable	640×480	4:3	30	Small to Medium
DV-AVI	AVI	28.6Mbps	720×480	4:3	30	Largest
WM Portable Device	WMV	1.0Mbps	640×480	4:3	30	Small
WM DVD Quality	WMV	3.0Mbps	720×480	4:3	30	Medium
WM DVD Quality Widescreen	WMV	3.0Mbps	720×480	16:9	30	Medium
WM HD 720p	WMV	5.9Mbps	1280×720	16:9	30	Large
WM HD Xbox 360	WMV	6.9Mbps	1280×720	16:9	30	Large
WM HD 1080p	WMV	7.8Mbp	1440×1080	16:9	30	Very Large
WM Low Bandwidth	WMV	117Kbps	320×240	4:3	15	Smallest
WM VHS Quality	WMV	1.0Mbps	640×480	4:3	30	Small

As you can see from Table 14.1, the default Best Quality for Playback on My Computer option is probably *not* the best option if you are going to be viewing your video on an HDTV, either with a direct connection to your WMC PC or via a WMC extender. Another problem with the Best Quality for Playback option is that you have no idea how large the final version will be. So what's best for you?

- Use Best Quality for Playback on My Computer when you are primarily concerned about creating content for use on your PC and disk space is not an issue.
- Use the appropriate DVD Quality setting to create a movie you can burn to a DVD using Windows. If your content uses the traditional 4:3 ratio, select the standard DVD option. For widescreen (16:9) content, select the Widescreen DVD option.
- If you use HDTVs to view content through WMC, choose the appropriate HDTV option.

To create your movie, select the appropriate option and then click Publish. WMM renders the movie and displays a progress bar onscreen during the procedure. Click Finish when the process is complete. By default, your new movie opens in Windows Media Player.

To enjoy your movie in Windows Media Center, open the Pictures + Video section and find it in the Video Library (Figure 14.27).

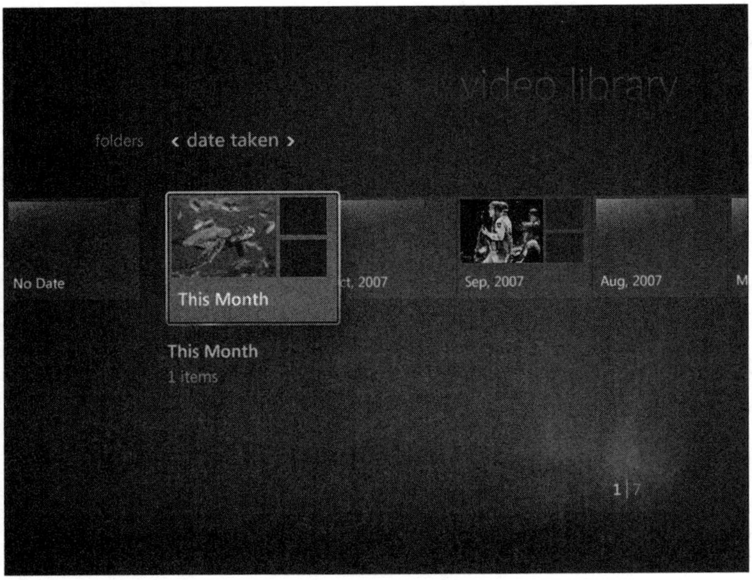

FIGURE 14.27

WMC's Video Library includes slide show movies produced with WMM.

14

Converting WMC TV Recordings to Save Space

Windows Movie Maker has another way to make your Windows Media Center experience better: It can put your WMC TV recordings on a diet! Windows Media Center uses the MS-DVR format to store recorded TV, and it creates whoppingly huge files. How big? At high quality, a recording of a one-hour TV show on standard broadcast or cable TV occupies over 3.5GB of hard disk space. Record just 20 hours of TV, and you'll use up over 70GB of hard disk space! The amounts per hour are even higher if you're recording HDTV.

You can see that using WMC as a DVR can use up a lot of disk space in a hurry, especially if you record at best quality. However, by using Windows Movie Maker to rerecord your videos into a different format and then deleting the original recordings, you can recover a significant amount of disk space without loss of visible quality. You can save your video to a different recording format or to a DVD.

Publishing Your TV Recording to a Different Format

Choose this option if you want to keep your TV recordings on your system.

1. Start WMM.
2. Select File, New Project. Save your existing project when prompted.
3. Click Import Media. Navigate to the Public, Recorded TV folder and import the recordings you want to convert.
4. Drag a video to the Storyboard or Timeline.
5. Click Publish Movie.
6. Select This Computer as the target. Click Next to continue.
7. Enter a name and select a location for the video. Click Next.
8. Select the best-quality option for the video depending on the original TV broadcast quality and what you plan to do with the recording. The default Best Quality for Playback on My Computer can save the most space. However, if you plan to use the video for another purpose, choose another option (see Table 14.1). For example, if you are recording a show from standard broadcast or cable TV in 4:3 ratio and you may want to make a DVD from the recording later, select DVD Quality. If the show was broadcast in widescreen, select DVD Quality (Widescreen). For a show recorded from HDTV, select the appropriate HDTV setting.
9. Click Publish to convert your movie.
10. After the movie is created, view it briefly and then delete the original MS-DVR file.

By selecting Windows Media DVD Quality as the publishing option, I reduced the size of the recording from 3.5GB to 1.8GB, a savings of almost 50%. Keep in mind that it takes about 1.5 times the original recording time to convert it to another format. My advice? Don't wait until the end of the season to convert your recordings!

Publishing Your TV Recording to a DVD

If you'd prefer to create an off-system archive of your favorite TV shows, you can use WMM to record them directly to a DVD.

1. Start WMM.
2. Select File, New Project. Save your existing project when prompted.
3. Click Import Media. Navigate to the Public, Recorded TV folder and import the recordings you want to convert.
4. Drag a video to the Storyboard or Timeline.
5. Click Publish Movie.
6. Select DVD as the target. Click Next.
7. Click OK to continue.
8. Save your project when prompted. WMM closes.
9. Windows DVD Maker starts and adds your video to the DVD layout.
10. Click Options to change the aspect ratio, DVD playback options, or other settings (see Figure 14.28). Make any changes desired, and then click OK to return to the main DVD Maker dialog.
11. Click Next and select a Menu Style. Use the Preview option to see how your video will appear. Use the Menu Text, and Customize Menu options as desired.
12. When you're satisfied, Click Burn to create your DVD (Figure 14.29). Insert media when prompted and sit back and relax.
13. Once the recording is done (it can take an hour or longer), Windows DVD maker ejects the disc. You can preview your new disc using Windows Media Center, Windows Media Player, or by sticking it into a DVD player hooked to your TV. Check the recording, and if you're satisfied, you can then delete the original MS-DVR file if you don't need it for anything else.

> **tip** To save even more space before you convert your recording to another format or a DVD, use Windows Movie Maker's Trim feature to cut away extraneous footage before the actual program starts. For details, see Windows Movie Maker Help.

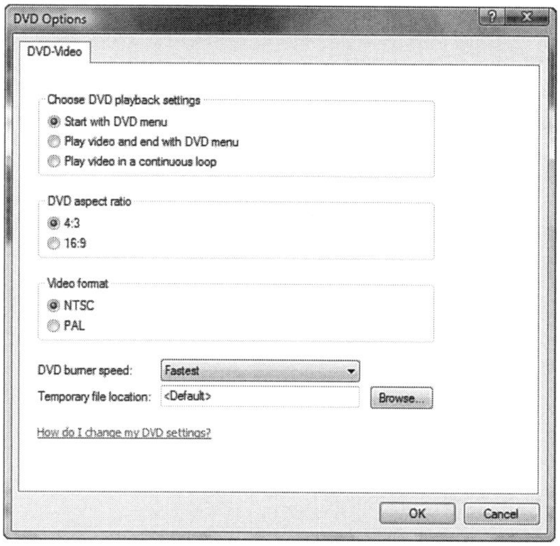

FIGURE 14.28

Options for recording a DVD with Windows DVD Maker.

FIGURE 14.29

Options for recording a DVD with Windows DVD Maker.

CHAPTER

15

Extending Media Center with Third-Party Apps

Windows Media Center (WMC) by itself is a powerful reason to use Windows Vista, but what if you could make WMC even better? You can!

In this chapter, you'll learn where to track down free and low-cost utilities that make WMC work harder, work smarter, and do more for you.

IN THIS CHAPTER

A Word of Introduction

The programs in this chapter have the ability to bring new features and capabilities to your WMC installation, but they also have the potential to frustrate and madden you. Why? Most of the programs cited in this chapter are utilities built by small companies or individuals to add features to WMC or solve problems in WMC. The following sections will help you to cope with some of the issues you might encounter as you try add-on programs.

15

Codecs 101

To enable some add-on programs to run, you might need to download and install additional programs or codecs first. What's a codec? A codec (short for "coder-decoder") is a file that enables a multimedia program to decode (view) or code (create) audio or video content. WMC, like other Windows Vista multimedia components, uses a codec library included in Windows Vista. However, the codecs provided by Microsoft are only a small fraction of the codecs available and are often not the most efficient or might not support certain types of content. If your system doesn't have the correct codec needed for a particular media file, it cannot play the file.

For these reasons, many of the programs in this chapter recommend or require that you first install codecs from other sources before installing the main program. Some of the most popular choices include

> **note** Once you install a particular codec required or recommended for an application, you do not need to install it again.

- **AC3Filter:** Audio codec; available from http://ac3filter.net/
- **Cyberlink PowerDVD 7 or higher:** Commercial program with integrated audio and video codecs; information and free trial available from http://www.cyberlink.com
- **FFDShow:** Video codec; available from http://www.free-codecs.com/download/FFDShow.htm; for more information about FFDShow, see http://en.wikipedia.org/wiki/Ffdshow

Working with Converted Files

Several of the utilities highlighted in the following sections can convert the MS-DVR files used by WMC to store recorded TV and movies into other formats. MS-DVR is a notorious space hog, as I've pointed out elsewhere in this book. However, before you go "hog-wild" converting files to other formats, consider these potential drawbacks:

- **Possible quality reductions:** Some programs offer conversion from MS-DVR to WMV (Windows Media Video) format. WMV files are much smaller but don't have the same visual quality. However, convert the MS-DVR to an MPEG-2 file, and you'll see little to no loss of visual quality.
- **Loss of metadata information:** In Chapters 4 and 5, you saw how WMC displays information (metadata) about recorded TV shows and

movies, including cast, year of release, and even cover art from the DVD. If you convert the original MS-DVR recording to another format, such as MPEG-2 (comparable quality to MS-DVR) or WMV (lower quality) and delete the MS-DVR recording, wave goodbye to the metadata! The WMV and MPEG-2 file formats just store the audio and video from the source file, with none of the metadata information that helps you enjoy your collection. So it's your choice: more information = more space; less space = less information.

- **Playback issues:** By default, WMC uses the Recorded TV menu in the TV + Movies stripe to play and manage recordings of TV and movies. However, if you convert an MS-DVR file to another format, you won't see the converted file listed there, regardless of the folder you store it in. If you convert the recording to WMV, you can find it in the Video Library. But no matter where you look in WMC, you won't find videos converted to MPEG-2.

WMC has no problems playing MPEG-2 videos, but the problem is that by default, Windows uses WMC's desktop stablemate, Windows Media Player, as the default application for MPEG-2 videos. If you prefer to use WMC to play MPEG-2 videos, though, here's how you do it:

1. Make sure the WMC Library watches the folder you use to store converted MPEG-2 videos, as discussed in Chapter 3, "Setting Up Windows Media Center."
2. Exit WMC.
3. Navigate to the folder containing your MPEG-2 videos.
4. To determine which videos are MPEG-2 (.mpg) videos, compare the icons used for the different video types in Figure 15.1. Videos with the white triangle icon are played by default by Windows Media Player (WMP), while videos with the green WMC button are played by default by WMC. Windows Media Video (WMV) videos use the WMV video icon, and on some systems, MPEG videos use a similar MPEG icon.
5. To determine if a file that uses WMP for playback is an MPEG file, right-click it and select Properties. The General tab indicates the file type. If the file is an MPEG file, you can configure Windows to use WMC as the default playback program on this computer. To get started, click the Change button on the General tab.

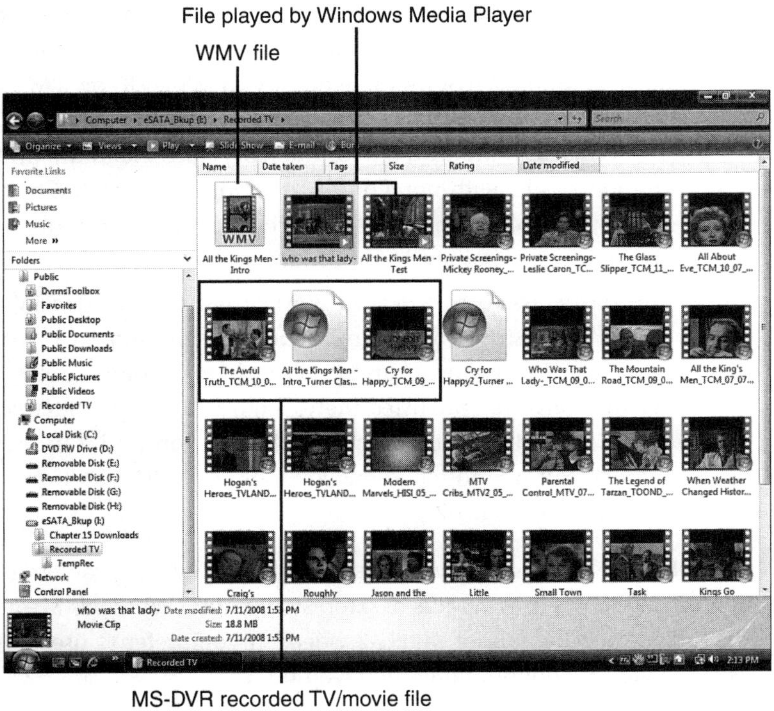

FIGURE 15.1

Determining video file types.

6. The Open With menu opens. Click Browse to locate the executable file used by WMC.
7. Navigate to C:\Windows\ehome\, select the ehshell application (it is one of a few programs in this folder to use the WMC "green button" icon), and click Open.
8. Make sure Media Center is highlighted in the Open with Other Programs menu and click OK (Figure 15.2).

> **tip** If you decide you want to view an MPEG-2 file in Windows Media Player after making this change, navigate to the folder containing the file, right-click it, and select Play with Windows Media Player. On some systems, the file might start playing without opening the WMP window. To open Windows Media Player, click Start, All Programs, Windows Media Player, and restart playback if necessary.

9. You can now play MPEG-2 videos in WMC. To find them, go to the Pictures + Videos strip, open the Video Library menu, and navigate to the No Date submenu.

FIGURE 15.2

Selecting WMC as the default application for playing MPEG-2 files.

Software Installation Notes

Almost all of the programs covered in this chapter are distributed as downloadable files. Some might be MSI (.msi) files that are used by the Microsoft Installer, while others might be EXE (.exe) files that include their own installers.

Many of the programs in this chapter are provided in the ZIP (.zip) compressed file archive format, which must be uncompressed before the MSI or EXE files they contain can be used to start the installation process. To unzip a ZIP file, right-click it and select Extract All. By default, the file is extracted to the current folder.

Before you start the installation program for a WMC plug-in, close WMC. In some cases, the changes you make with an installation program aren't registered until you exit WMC and restart it, so it saves time to install programs while WMC is closed.

Unless you have disabled Vista's User Account Control feature, when you start an installation program, you might see the UAC dialog. To continue, provide the credentials requested.

If you are installing a program from the command prompt, you might need to use an elevated command prompt to ensure that the program installs properly. To open an elevated command-prompt window, click Start, All Programs,

Accessories, right-click Command Prompt, and select Run as Administrator. Provide UAC credentials as prompted.

Before restarting WMC, check the Windows Start menu to determine if you need to run a configuration or set-up program first.

Find It Useful? Donations Welcome!

Most of the applications and utilities in this chapter are freeware, so you don't need to pay a dime for them. However, you can help the developer fix bugs, develop new features, and feel better about his or her work by making a donation. Look for the PayPal or other donation button—and use it if you find the program saves you time and effort.

Getting More Help

Because most of the programs discussed in this chapter originate with small development companies or individual developers, official documentation is not always easy to find. While I've added usage tips and screenshots to some program descriptions to help get you started, please don't mistake these write-ups for a full-blown instruction manual.

If you can't find instructions on the vendor's website, use a search engine such as Google (www.google.com) or search engine aggregator like Dogpile (www.dogpile.com) to track down instructions, tips, blog entries, and other help. Enjoy!

TV, Video, and Movies

Use the programs discussed in this section to help you record, manage, view, and convert TV and video recordings or your favorite movies on DVD, Blu-Ray, or hard disk.

clipShow

Description: Creates playlists from your video files and recorded TV shows and plays them on demand.

Available from: http://www.codeplex.com/mceclipShow.

Cost: Free.

Requirements: MS-DVR recordings created with WMC or other types of video files compatible with WMC.

Usage Notes: When you install clipShow, it adds the clipShow Playlist Creator icon to the Online Media strip's Program Library menu (Figure 15.3).

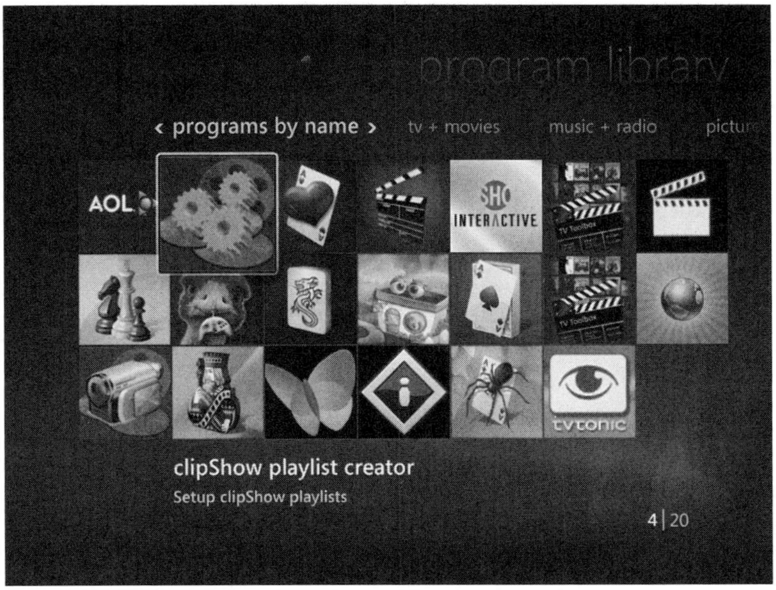

FIGURE 15.3
Start clipShow from the Program Library menu.

The playlist creator wizard prompts you to name the playlist and then to browse the folders that contain video clips. Select the videos you want to add to the playlist, and then save the playlist.

To play your playlist, start clipShow from the Pictures + Videos menu. Select a playlist from the top-level menu. Video clips will play in a window, while recorded TV plays in the "Now Playing" menu.

DVRMSToolbox

Description: An extensible toolbox for editing, converting, and skipping commercials in MS-DVR files. Originally command-line driven, it now includes a GUI (Figure 15.4) so you can run it easily without doing a lot of typing.

Available from: http://babgvant.com.

Cost: Free.

Requirements: MS-DVR recordings created with WMC.

15

Usage Tips: DVRMSToolbox runs from the standard Windows desktop, not from within WMC. If your WMC system is dedicated exclusively to WMC, consider installing DVRMSToolbox on another system on your network that has full access to the Recorded TV folder(s) on the WMC system.

For additional information, see http://babgvant.com/Wiki/view.aspx/DVRMSToolbox for brief instructions or http://onlydarksets.wordpress.com/dvrmstoolbox-users-guide/ for a much more detailed look at the program. It offers many options, but I was very satisfied with the results I received with default settings.

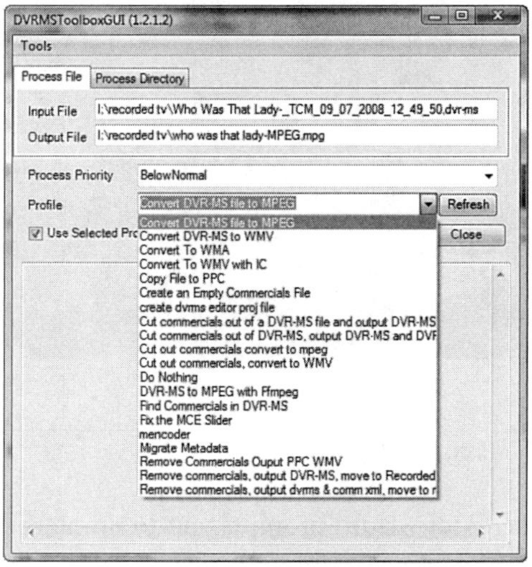

FIGURE 15.4

DVRMSToolbox offers a variety of conversion options, including options to remove commercials.

In the Movies SE for MCE

Description: Find out what's playing in U.S. and Canadian movie theaters. Also supports Xbox 360 MCE.

Available from: http://mcezone.com/products.php.

Cost: $5.99.

Requirements: Internet connection.

Usage Tips: Provide your Zip or postal code when prompted to receive localized information. See website for screenshots.

15

Joost.com http://www.mytvgenie.com/

Description: Free Internet TV.

Available from: http://www.joost.com.

Cost: Free.

Requirements: Broadband Internet connection.

Usage Notes: If you use a firewall, you must unblock Joost, or it cannot work. (Windows Firewall will prompt you to unblock Joost; for others, see their documentation.) The first time you start Joost, you must get a Joost name.

Figure 15.5 illustrates the Joost channel selection menu. Note that some Joost channels are recommended for adults over 18 only. To control access to Joost's adult content, use the Advanced Settings menu to set up a minimum age and a PIN number. The Advanced Settings menu also specifies whether to run Joost in full-screen or windowed mode and whether to leave it in standby or close it when you're not watching it.

FIGURE 15.5

Joost offers a variety of Internet TV content.

To view Joost from within WMC, install the WMC plug-in available at http://www.tv0.nl/Downloads.htm. The WMC plug-in adds a Joost icon to the TV + Movies strip. Click it, and it launches Joost from the Windows desktop and minimizes WMC.

Lifextender

Description: Provides automatic commercial removal from MS-DVR files and replaces the original file with the commercial-free version.

Available from: http://www.lifextender.com/.

Cost: Free.

Requirements: MS-DVR recordings created with WMC; optional WMC plug-in.

Usage Notes: See http://www.lifextender.com/screens.aspx for plenty of screen shots demonstrating its operation. See other parts of the website for documentation, FAQ, and other information.

MCEBuddy

Description: Provides automatic commercial removal from MS-DVR files and converts the file into the more compact WMV, DivX, or H.264 video formats.

Available from: http://mcebuddy.com/.

Cost: Free.

Requirements: MS-DVR recordings created with WMC; requires FFDShow (32-bit Vista versions) or VistaCodecx64 (64-bit Vista versions) if you want to play back DivX or H.264 recordings in WMC. Links are provided for these and other optional components.

Usage Notes: See http://mcebuddy.com/blogs/ for links to official and third-party information and documentation sites. Note that Version 1.x operates only from the Windows desktop; version 2.x includes a WMC interface.

Movie Collector MCE

Description: Catalog your movie discs from the Windows desktop; browse and launch movies from the WMC desktop.

Available from: http://www.collectorz.com/movie/windows-media-center-mce.php.

Cost: $24.95 and up; free trial available.

Requirements: Movies and TV shows on DVD, Blu-Ray, or HD DVD media.

MSN Remote Record

Description: Enables remote TV recording from a web browser.

Available from: http://tv.msn.com/tv/rr/rrsetup.aspx.

Cost: Free.

Requirements: TV tuner on PC running WMC; always-on Internet connection on WMC TV; Internet Explorer 6 or above on client PC; Windows Passport (MSN or Hotmail e-mail address)

Usage Tips: Install MSN Remote Record on the PC running WMC. To record remotely, log into the MSN TV website http://tv.msn.com and select the TV listings tab.

Click an episode listing to open the Program Details box and click Record Show to record the show. Figure 15.6 shows the program details box with program listings in the background.

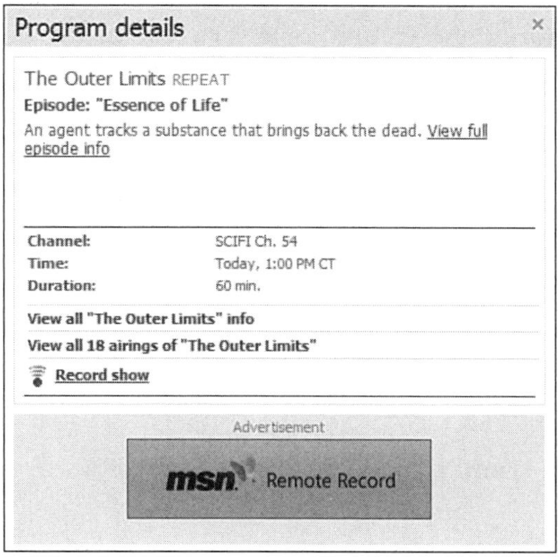

FIGURE 15.6
Preparing to record a program remotely with MSN Remote Record.

A confirming dialog indicates the recording has been scheduled. You must log into MSN TV before you can download MSN Remote Record to your WMC system or before you can use it remotely to schedule TV programs.

Learn more at http://thegreenbutton.com/forums/thread/163921.aspx.

My Blockbuster

Description: Manages your Blockbuster Total Access queue, browses movies, views trailers.

Available from: http://www.permanence.com/MCE/.

Cost: Free.

Requirements: Blockbuster Total Access membership.

My Trailers SE for MCE

Description: View trailers for current and forthcoming movies on your WMC system and Xbox 360 MCE.

Available from: http://mcezone.com/products.php.

Cost: $5.99.

Requirements: Internet connection.

Usage Tips: See website for screenshots.

My TV to Go

Description: Converts and copies TV recordings to portable devices such as iPod, PSP, smartphone, Zune, Pocket PC.

Available from: http://www.mytvtogo.com/.

Cost: $29.99.

Requirements: MS-DVR files recorded with WMC; supported video player; see http://www.mytvtogo.com/site/products.htm.

MyNetflix

Description: Manage your Netflix queue and view "watch now" movies from within WMC.

Available from: http://www.anpark.com/Software.aspx.

Cost: Free.

Requirements: Netflix subscription.

MyTV Genie http://www.mytvgenie.com/

Description: Automatically records TV shows based on your ratings.

Available from: http://mytvgenie.com.

Cost: $19.99.

Requirements: TV tuner.

Recorded TV Manager

Description: Enables networks that include Windows Vista or XP Media Center and Windows Home Server to record, store, play back, and manage recordings of TV series.

Available from: http://www.fjdrasch.com/.

Cost: $24.95.

Requirements: WMC with TV tuner on same network with Windows Home Server. For Windows Vista Media Center playback, download free MCECollections.

Usage Notes: See http://www.wegotserved.co.uk/2008/02/01/add-in-review-recorded-tv-manager/ for features and a product review.

Recording Broker

Description: Distributes TV recording requests to other networked computers running WMC with TV tuners to avoid recording conflicts.

Available from: http://babgvant.com/files/folders/recbrocker/entry3374.aspx.

Cost: Free.

Requirements: Two or more networked computers with TV tuners that run WMC that also have TV tuners.

TV Manager

Description: Automatically copies TV recordings from a WMC PC to Windows Home Server; provides collection management features.

Available from: https://brentf.homeserver.com/blog/technology/windows-home-server/tv-manager/.

Cost: Free.

Requirements: WMC with TV tuner on same network with Windows Home Server.

Usage Notes: See http://www.wegotserved.co.uk/2008/07/02/add-in-tv-manager-beta-released/ for screenshots and more information.

TV Toolbox

Description: Edit and convert recorded TV shows from within WMC.

Available from: http://www.mcedev.com.

Cost: Free.

Requirements: MS-DVR recordings created with WMC.

Usage Tips: When you install TV Toolbox, it installs into the Online Media strip's Program Library. Use its Settings menu to configure it to run in its own strip.

Use your remote to select a start and finish time for each scene you want to keep in a recording (Figure 15.7). You can use this to remove extraneous material before a movie starts, remove commercials, or remove scenes that aren't family-friendly.

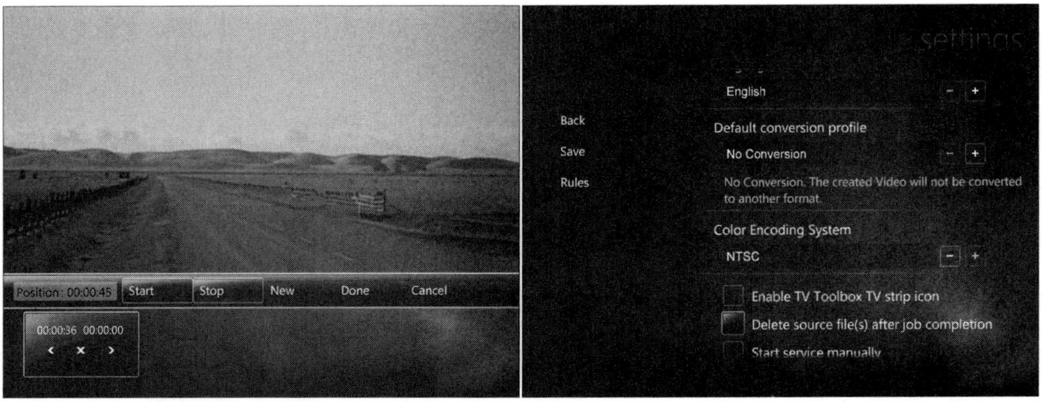

FIGURE 15.7

Selecting scenes with TV Toolbox and configuring TV Toolbox.

Each recording you process is stored in a queue. To create the new recordings from the queue, open the Queue menu and start the processing. During processing, TV Toolbox can also transcode audio and video, or audio only, into WMA or WMV formats. Use the Settings menu (Figure 15.7) to add it to the TV + Movies strip (click Add Link when prompted) and to configure other settings, particularly this one: By default, it uses the European PAL color encoding system: North American users will want to select NTSC instead as shown in Figure 15.7.

Video Browser for mce

Description: Browses your recorded TV shows and movies ripped to hard disk.

Available from: http://code.google.com/p/videobrowser/downloads.

Cost: Free.

Requirements: MS-DVR recordings created with WMC; DVD movies stored on hard disk.

Usage Notes: See http://www.samsaffron.com/downloads/1 for screen shots, sources for TV and movie metadata, and other help. For the official forum, visit http://bbs.wasnotwas.com/.

WebGuide

Description: Remote viewing and playback of live TV, recordings, and other media from a web browser, Pocket PC, or smartphone.

Available from: http://www.asciiexpress.com/webguide/.

Cost: Free.

Requirements: Broadband Internet connection; TV tuner to record or view live TV.

Usage Notes: Install WebGuide on your WMC PC. If you use a firewall, you must unblock WebGuide, or it cannot work. (Windows Firewall will prompt you to unblock WebGuide; for others, see their documentation.) The WebGuide Configuration program starts as soon as the installation is completed.

The WebGuide Configuration program has two tabs. Use the Configuration tab to configure general program operation, users (you must create at least one user), network configuration, media sharing, language, and groups of computers that can share WebGuide (Prism). The Cyberlink Power DVD video decoder and AC3Filter audio decoder are recommended for use with WebGuide's transcoding feature (in Media Sharing's Live/Recorded TV streaming settings menu); get them from http://www.asciiexpress.com/webguide/download.aspx. Note that Cyberlink is a commercial program (however, you can try it for 30 days). The Network Address tab displays the URL to use to access WebGuide from a web browser. You might need to configure the port forwarding option in your browser to get this feature to work. (Go to http://www.portforward.com for details.) Here's a sample URL:

http://*yourcomputername:52970*

To access WebGuide remotely, enter the URL into your web browser and provide the username and password you set up on the Users tab. To view a recorded program, select it from the menu and click Stream Program (Figure 15.8). You can also download the program or delete it.

Select a profile for streaming (aspect ratio and speed) and click Start Stream to view it. You also have the option to open the recording directly into Windows Media Player. The default bandwidth setting is quite conservative; choose a speed that is close to the maximum bandwidth available for the best viewing quality.

Use the Guide to view live TV or to set up recordings on your remote WMC system. Basically, WebGuide enables you to enjoy virtually any content available to your WMC PC from another system.

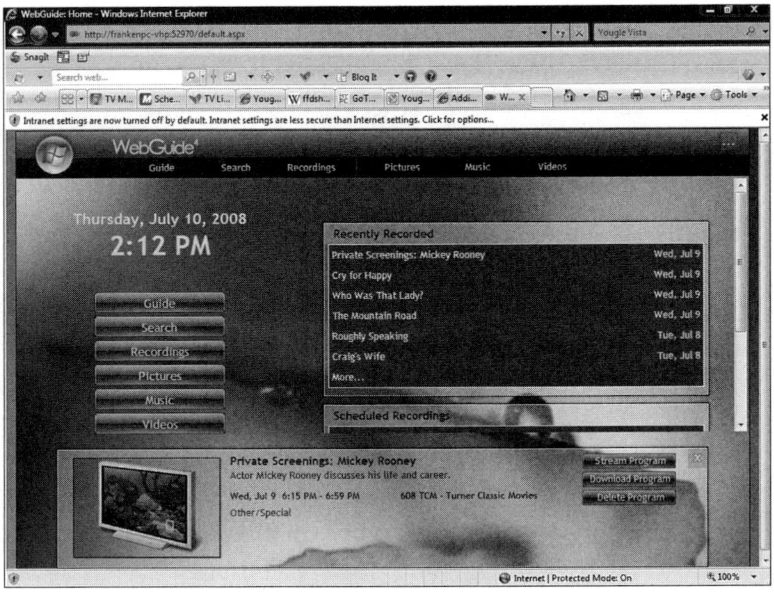

FIGURE 15.8

Preparing to view a WMC recording remotely with WebGuide.

Yougle

Description: Watch community video sources such as MSN Soapbox, YouTube, Google Video; pictures from Flickr and ICanHasCheezburger; other TV and video sources.

Available from: http://www.push-a-button.com.au/products/mce/vista/youglevista/.

Cost: Free.

Requirements: Install the FFDShow codec first. You must register (free) with Push-a-Button.com.au before you can download Yougle.

Usage Tips: Install Yougle Vista on the PC running WMC. It automatically adds itself to the Start menu as a separate strip (Figure 15.9).

To get started, select a media type. Depending on the media type you select, a media source might already be loaded. To get more sources, click the plus (+) Get More Sources button and choose the source you want. Once you have added the sources you want, click the source to find the media you want. A search tool with onscreen keyboard (see Figure 15.9) is provided when needed.

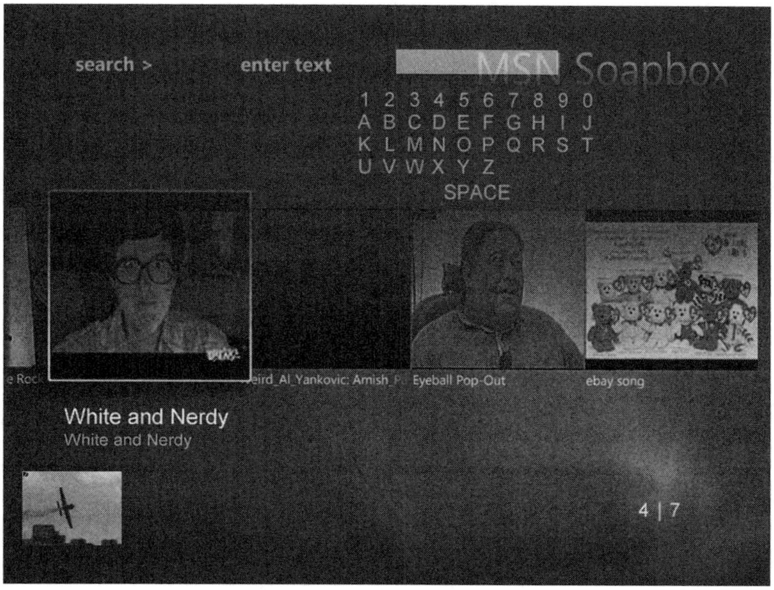

FIGURE 15.9

Selecting video content to view with Yougle.

Music

Use the programs in this section to enable WMC to play music from more sources and to manage your collection.

MCE Tunes

MCE Tunes enables you to enjoy various types of iTunes media within WMC, including audio, movies, and TV shows.

Available from: http://www.mcetunes.com/.

Cost: $14.99 (MCE Tunes); $29.99 (MCE Tunes Pro); free trial available.

Requirements: iTunes subscription and media. Pro version required for playback of protected audio as well as video and TV.

Usage Notes: Compare versions by feature at http://www.mcetunes.com/download.htm.

15

RadioTime

Description: Free access to Internet and local radio stations via Windows desktop and optional WMC plug-in.

Available from: http://www.radiotime.com/.

Cost: Free; optional RedButton software (http://www.radiotime.com/redbutton) for pausing, timeshifting, and recording of live radio is $29 (free trial available).

Requirements: RadioTime subscription (free); FM radio tuner for tuning into local FM radio stations.

Usage Notes: To install the WMC plug-in, close WMC, go to http://mce.radiotime.com/mcl.aspx, and save the RadioTime.mcl plug-in to a folder. Select the plug-in and open it, and the RadioTime WMC interface opens within WMC. Click Add to More Programs and click Add Link to add a link to WMC's Program Library (available in the Online Media strip). Figure 15.10 shows a portion of the RadioTime program guide.

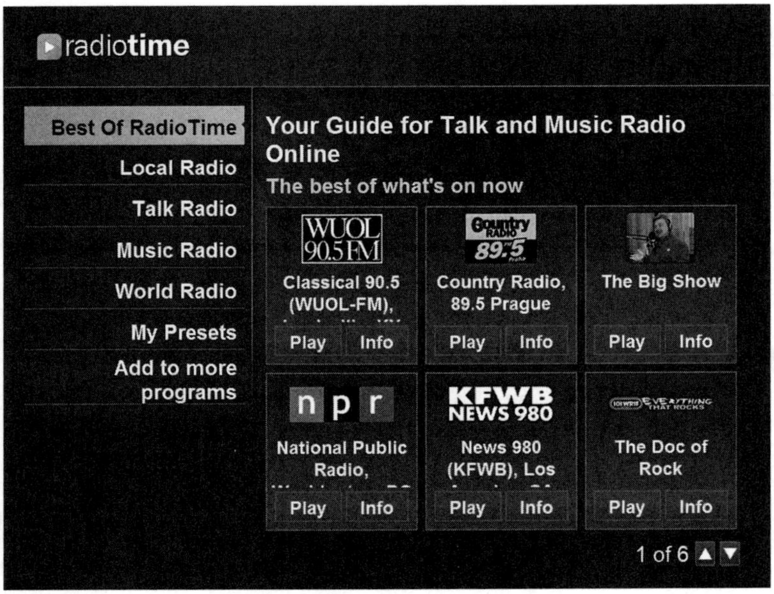

FIGURE 15.10

Using the RadioTime program guide.

For FAQs and troubleshooting, visit http://wiki.radiotime.com/doku.php?id=help:faqs:mce. Installing RedButton automatically installs the WMC plug-in.

Music Player

Enables WMC to browse folders for recorded music.

Available from: http://www.th-haandbold.dk/musicplayer/.

Cost: Free.

Requirements: MP3 files.

Usage Notes: To uncompress this plug-in, you will need an uncompressing utility compatible with RAR (.rar) files, such as WinRAR (http://www.win-rar.com/) or UltimateZip (http://www.ultimatezip.com/).

Web Media for Windows Vista Media Center

Description: Adds your favorite Internet radio and TV stations to customized WMC menus.

Available from: http://www.mcesoft.nl.

Cost: Free (registration required).

Usage Tips: See website for screenshots.

Photography

WMC already does a great job of displaying pictures on your TV, but you can make it even smarter with the add-ons in this section.

Big Screen Photos 2

Description: Displays Flickr-hosted photos on WMC.

Available from: http://bigscreenglobal.com/bgproduct.aspx?PID=BSPV2.

Cost: $24.95 (free trial available).

Requirements: Internet access to Flickr.com.

Usage Notes: Supports up to five Media Center Extenders, each with custom device settings. When you install the program, you must start it for the first time from the Windows Start menu. A configuration wizard guides you through language selection and activation. After activation, you can launch Big Screen Photos 2 from an icon in the Pictures + Videos strip.

Big Screen Photos 2 supports most Flickr functions, including picture selection by set (Figure 15.11), by user, by tags, by geotags, and more.

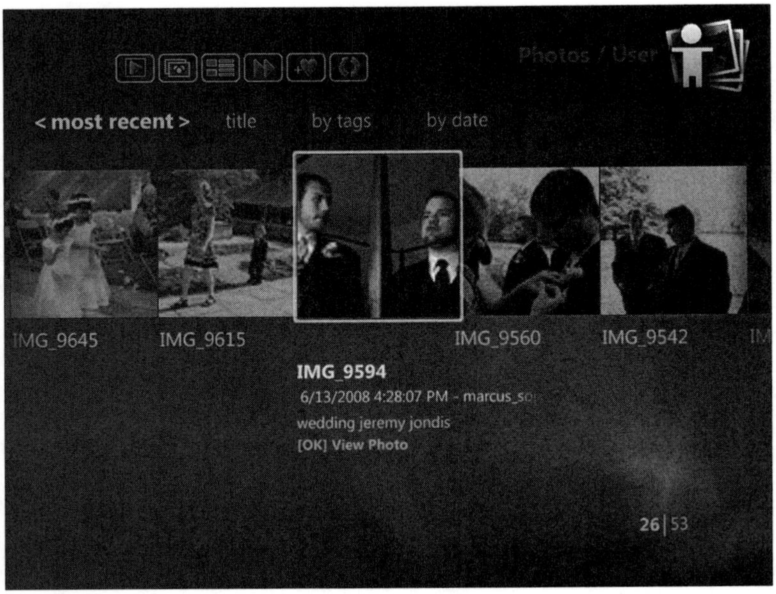

FIGURE 15.11
Viewing some of the author's Flickr-hosted photos with Big Screen Photos 2.

Photato

Description: Displays Facebook-hosted photos on WMC.

Available from: http://www.armchairware.com/.

Cost: Free.

Requirements: Internet access to Facebook.com; Facebook account.

Mapping

Whether you use online maps to plan your next road trip, vacation, or to make your children (or yourself) smarter about geography, you can use WMC to make the map-viewing process more fun.

Google Maps for Media Center

Description: Browse Google maps from within WMC. Features scrolling and zooming options.

Available from: http://savage.org.za/mediacenter.htm.

Cost: Free "Postcardware" (send a postcard to the developer as requested in the install program).

Requirements: Internet connection.

Usage Tips: Program installs into the Online Media stripe's Program Library. You can add the Moon and Mars add-ins when you start the application. Press 1 for road map; 2 for satellite image; 3 for hybrid road map/satellite image; 4 for terrain. Zoom with Channel up/down (in/out). Pan with arrow keys. Figure 15.12 shows a typical map display.

FIGURE 15.12

Viewing Indiana and nearby states with Google Maps for Media Center.

My Mapquest for MCE

Description: Get driving directions from Mapquest within WMC.

Available from: http://mcezone.com/products.php.

Cost: Free; free registration required.

Requirements: Internet connection.

Usage Tips: See website for screenshots.

System Utilities

As you've already seen, WMC enables you to customize your media experience. With the applications in this section, you can also customize the operation of WMC itself.

FrontView for Windows MCE

Description: Controls LCD and VFD information and status displays found on some Home Theater PC (HTPC) computers.

Available from: http://www.mediacentermagic.com/products.asp.

Cost: Free (free version); Basic version ($19.95); and Advanced ($29.95), which adds additional features.

Requirements: Supported LCD display and chassis. See http://www.mediacentermagic.com/frontview_documentation.asp for details.

Usage Tips: For additional help in using FrontView, see http://thegreenbutton.com/search/SearchResults.aspx?q=FrontView. Check with the developer for add-ins that extend support to more devices.

MCE Customizer

Description: Customizes features of WMC's appearance, menus, electronic program guide, recording, DVD playback, and more.

Available from: http://www.mcedev.com/.

Cost: Free.

Usage Tips: Start from Program Library in Online Media strip. Figure 15.13 illustrates the MCE Customizer main menu.

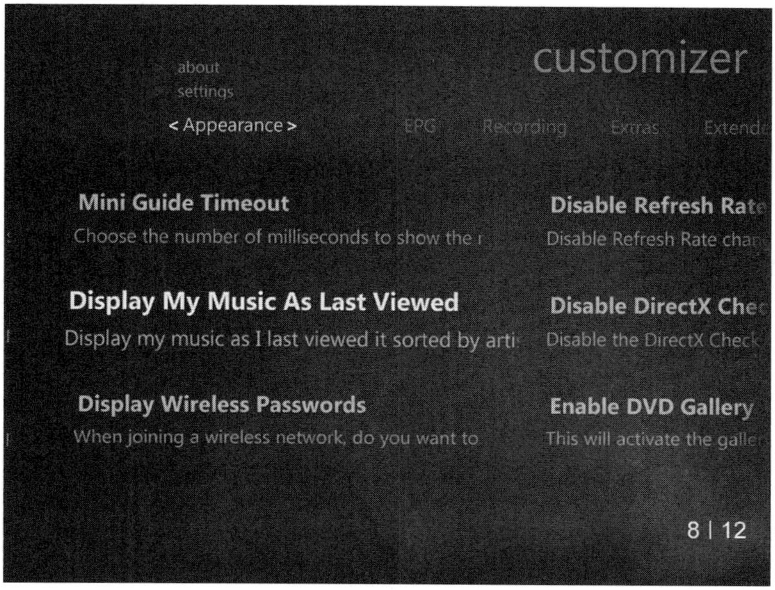

FIGURE 15.13

The MCE Customizer main menu.

MC Menu Customizer

Description: Add programs from the Program Library to the WMC strip menus with a simple drag-and-drop interface.

Available from: http://www.xpmediacentre.com.au/community/vista-plug-ins-addons/25714-new-util-mc-menu-customiser.html.

Cost: Free.

Requirements: Free registration at http://www.xpmediacentre.com.au/.

Usage Tips: Runs from the Windows desktop. You can add programs to a custom strip or to a strip added by a third-party program (see Figure 15.14).

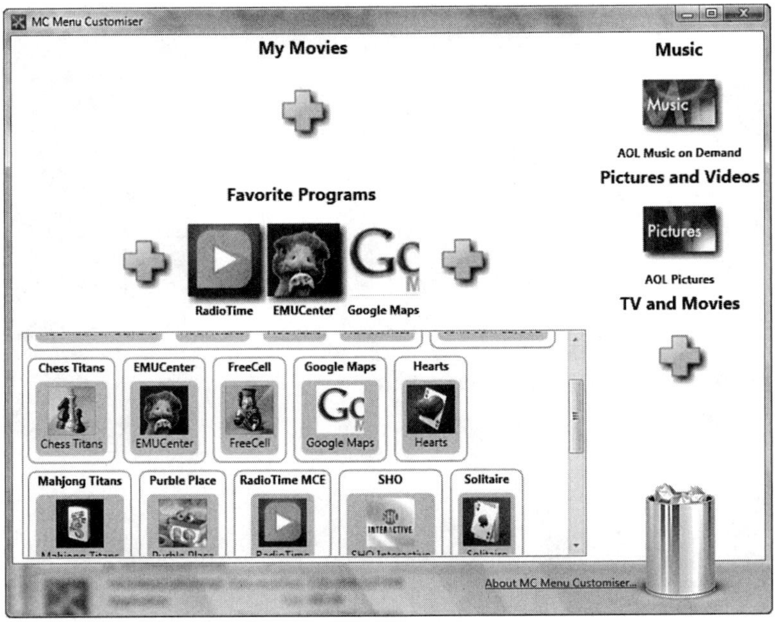

FIGURE 15.14

Creating a customized WMC "My Favorite Programs" menu with MC Menu Customiser.

Media Center Communicator

Description: Voice-activated control of WMC features including music, video photos, Skype VoIP, TV, and movies.

Available from: http://www.sayittoplayit.com/mcc.html.

Cost: $69.99 (free trial available); bundles with various microphone models also available at additional cost.

Requirements: Microphone.

Usage Tips: Can be used with Xbox 360; can create custom commands. See http://www.sayittoplayit.com/support.html for documentation.

Media Center Health Monitor

Description: Monitors health of one or more WMC-based systems from your Windows desktop, WMC desktop, or the web.

Available from: http://health.thedigitallifestyle.com/.

Cost: Free (registration required).

Requirements: Internet connection.

System Monitor for Vista

Description: Displays system stats such as voltage, fan speed, and internal temperatures for case, processor, and hard disk within WMC, using information gathered by Windows-based Speedfan utility. See Figure 15.15.

Available from: http://www.mcesoft.nl.

Cost: Free (free registration required).

Requirements: Requires Speedfan utility, available from http://www.almico.com/speedfan.php.

Usage Tips: Install Speedfan first and then System Monitor for Vista. See the System Monitor website for Speedfan configuration settings necessary for use with System Monitor for Vista. To change Speedfan labels, click the name of each label and replace it with the desired text, such as CPU, Fan speed, and so on. (See the Speedfan website for documentation.)

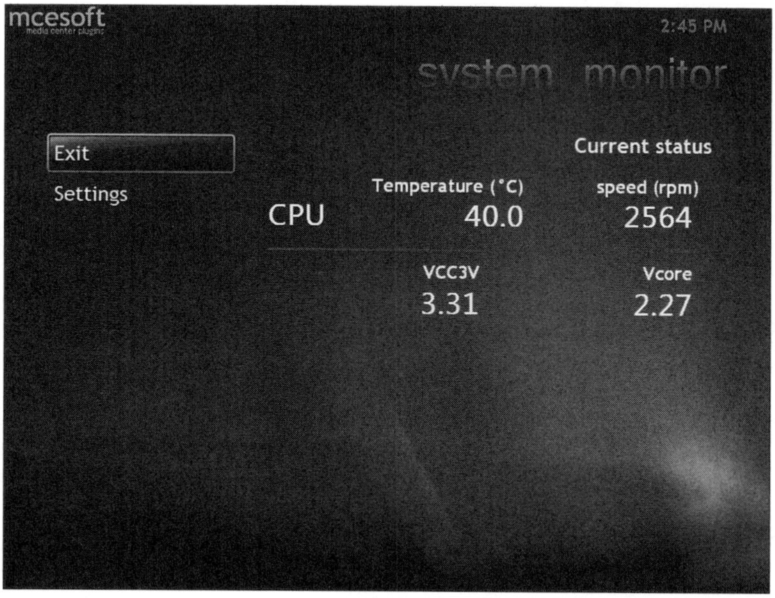

FIGURE 15.15

Using System Monitor for Vista to display system stats gathered by Speedfan.

Gaming

Although WMC is not designed as a hardcore gaming environment, you can play a variety of casual, family-friendly games within its "10-foot UI." If you're looking for additional game resources beyond those provided in Chapter 9, "Playing Games and Enjoying Online Resources," you've come to the right place.

Accedo Broadband Funspot

Description: Enjoy 15 card, puzzle, and strategy games you can play with your WMC remote or a mouse.

Available from: http://www.funspot.tv/portal/index.jsp?platform=microsoftmediacenter&page=start.

Cost: Free.

Usage Tips: To install, click the Get Funspot for Vista Media Center button. Installs an icon into the Program Library in the Online Media strip. Figure 15.16 illustrates the Funspot game menu.

FIGURE 15.16

Funspot delivers a variety of family-friendly casual games to your WMC PC.

GameEx

Description: Graphical front-end for MAME and other arcade emulators; can be run from within WMC.

Available from: http://www.gameex.net.

Cost: Free; donation ($14 or more) provides enhanced features and automatic updates.

Requirements: Windows Vista or older editions that include Windows Media Player 9 or later and a graphics card with DirectX 9 or later support.

Usage Tips: See http://www.gameex.net/Support/tabid/60/Default.aspx for screen shots, walkthroughs, and how to get arcade emulators.

MCEJoy

Description: Configures Windows-compatible game controller to act as a remote control for use with WMC.

Available from: http://www.spesoft.com/products.asp.

Cost: Free.

Requirements: Windows-compatible game controller.

Usage Tips: Run MCEJoy from Windows desktop.

Business and Information

WMC isn't just for fun. With the applications featured in the following sections, you can also use it to organize your life.

Big Screen Contacts 2

Displays Windows Vista contacts within WMC. Supports importing contacts from Microsoft Office Outlook and other apps, contacts stored on network drives, and can be used with Media Center Extenders.

Available from: http://bigscreenglobal.com/bgproduct.aspx?PID=BSCV2.

Cost: $14.95 (free trial available).

Usage Notes: Supports triple-tap text entry from your WMC remote (or you can use a keyboard). See website for screenshots and documentation.

Big Screen Headlines 2

Description: Displays RSS feeds, blog reading, podcasts, and photocasts within WMC; autosynchronizes with MCEs.

Available from: http://bigscreenglobal.com/bgproduct.aspx?PID=BSHV2.

Cost: $24.95 (free trial available).

Requirements: Internet access.

Usage Notes: Includes hundreds of preconfigured RSS feeds and supports Internet Explorer 7's Subscriber Feed system. See website for screenshots and documentation.

Big Screen Weather 2

Description: Displays weather forecasts for over 3,000 forecast locations; works with MCEs.

Available from: http://bigscreenglobal.com/bgproduct.aspx?PID=BSWV2.

Cost: $19.95 (free trial available).

Requirements: Internet access.

Usage Notes: Provides satellite imagery, maps, charts, and other supplementary weather information where available. See website for screenshots and documentation.

mceContacts

Description: Contact manager for WMC; works with same developer's mcePhone for Skype; support MS Outlook, Windows Address Book, or Skype contacts.

Available from: http://www.scendix.com/mcecontacts/index.php.

Cost: $24 (approximate; priced in Euros; free trial available).

Usage Tips: See website for screenshots.

mcePhone for Skype

Description: WMC interface for Skype phone calls and voice mail.

Available from: http://www.scendix.com/mcephone/.

Cost: $24 (approximate; priced in Euros; free trial available).

Requirements: Skype-compatible phone hardware and Skype phone account.

Usage Tips: See website for screenshots.

mceTapiRex

Description: WMC interface for TapiRex—TapiRex tracks incoming phone calls.

Available from: http://www.scendix.com/mcephone/.

Cost: Free.

Requirements: TapiRex (http://www.scendix.com/tapirex/index.php; about $27).

Usage Tips: See website for screenshots.

mceWeather

Description: Check the weather for your region.

Available from: http://www.scendix.com/mceweather/.

Cost: Free.

Requirements: Internet connection.

Usage Tips: See website for screenshots.

My Tracker for MCE

Description: Track UPS or FedEx shipments within WMC.

Available from: http://mcezone.com/products.php.

Cost: Free (free registration required).

Requirements: Internet connection; FedEx or UPS tracking number for package shipments.

Usage Tips: See website for screenshots and tips.

Remind Me for MCE

Description: Displays pop-up reminders of important tasks; compatible with Outlook 2003, Outlook 2007.

Available from: http://mcezone.com/products.php.

Cost: Free (free registration required).

Usage Tips: Enter reminder text manually from keyboard or WMC remote or import from Outlook 2003 or Outlook 2007. See website for screenshots and tips.

Vista Media Center Outlook

Description: Access Outlook emails, calendars, contacts, tasks, and notes within WMC.

Available from: http://vistamcoutlook.oabsoftware.nl/index.php.

Cost: Free; activation required.

Requirements: Microsoft Outlook.

Usage Tips: Run configuration program from the Windows desktop; program runs from Accessories strip; see http://vistamcoutlook.oabsoftware.nl/body-manual.htm for details and screenshots.

Vista Media Center Email

Description: Access emails from POP3 email servers within WMC.

Available from: http://vistamcmail.oabsoftware.nl/index.php.

Cost: Free; activation required.

Requirements: POP3-compatible email program; Internet access.

Usage Tips: Run configuration program from the Windows desktop; program runs from Accessories strip; see http://vistamcmail.oabsoftware.nl/body-manual.htm for details and screenshots.

Vista Media Center RSS Reader

Description: Access RSS feeds, podcasts, or video blogs within WMC.

Available from: http://vistamcrssreader.oabsoftware.nl/index.php.

Cost: Free; activation required.

Requirements: Subscriptions to one or more RSS feeds.

Usage Tips: Subscribe using web browser from Windows desktop; program runs from Accessories strip; see http://vistamcrssreader.oabsoftware.nl/body-manual.htm for details and screenshots.

Vista Media Center Video Phone

Description: Make and receive SIP video phone calls within WMC.

Available from: http://vistamcvideophone.oabsoftware.nl/index.php.

Cost: Free; activation required.

Requirements: SIP Phone VoIP account; available from http://www.sipphone.com/. Webcam for videophone/videoconferencing.

Usage Tips: Program runs from Accessories strip; unblock application with Windows Firewall or third-party firewalls; must be configured from Windows desktop; see http://vistamcvideophone.oabsoftware.nl/body-manual.htm for details and screenshots.

Vista Caller ID

Description: See caller ID information within WMC.

Available from: http://vistamccallerid.oabsoftware.nl/index.php.

Cost: Free; activation required.

Requirements: PC connected to phone and network (runs Vista Caller ID server); one or more PCs running WMC on a network (runs Vista Caller ID client).

Usage Tips: Program runs from Accessories strip; unblock application with Windows Firewall or third-party firewalls; must be configured from Windows desktop; see http://vistamccallerid.oabsoftware.nl/body-manual.htm for details and screenshots.

Home Automation

Want to control your home's lighting, HVAC, and security from your easy chair? It's easier than ever if you combine your existing home automation system with the WMC addons discussed in this chapter.

HAI Home Control for WMC

Description: Enables control of HAI home automation systems via WMC.

Available from: http://www.homeauto.com/products/software/mce.asp.

Cost: $110 (approximate cost).

Requirements: Supported HAI home control modules: HAI Omni LT, Omni, Omni II, Omni IIe, OmniPro, OmniPro II, Lumina, or Lumina Pro controller with 1.8 firmware or later. Controller must be connected to the PC running WMC.

Usage Tips: If the controller uses an RS-232 or RS-485 interface and your PC doesn't have an RS-232 (serial) interface, you can use a RS-232 to USB adapter; an RS-232 to RS-485 adapter is used to connect to RS-485-based systems. Configuration is performed within the WMC interface. See the website for documentation and screenshots.

Life|Ware

Description: Professionally installed home automation and entertainment system incorporating WMC and home automation hardware

Available from: http://www.exceptionalinnovation.com/.

Cost: Contact website or Life|Ware dealer.

Requirements: Life|Ware home automation system.

Usage Tips: See website for features, dealers, and more information.

mControl

Description: Enables WMC to control a wide range of home automation products, including user-installed solutions.

Available from: http://www.embeddedautomation.com/EAHAmControl.htm.

Cost: $100; free trial available.

Requirements: One or more of the home automation, security systems, cameras, climate control, AV, irrigation, voice control, and third-party automation systems supported. See website for details.

Usage Tips: To add mControl to WMC, start the mControl for MCE program from the Windows Start menu. See the website for slideshows of features, program screens, and documentation.

Hobbies and Special Interests

WMC makes it easy to enjoy your hobbies, whatever they are, as this sampling of special-interest plug-ins proves.

New Rides for MCE

Description: View information about the newest vehicles from major auto manufacturers.

Available from: http://mcezone.com/products.php.

Cost: Free (free registration required).

Requirements: Internet connection.

Usage Tips: See website for screenshots and tips.

Lottery Results SE for MCE

Description: Get lottery results for most U.S. states in WMC or on the Xbox 360 MCE.

Available from: http://mcezone.com/products.php.

Cost: Free (free registration required).

Requirements: Internet connection.

Usage Tips: See website for screenshots and tips.

mceAuction

Description: Watch, bid, and buy on eBay within WMC; supports My eBay; pop-up notifications of auctions ending.

Available from: http://www.scendix.com/mceauction/index.php.

Cost: Free.

Requirements: Internet connection; eBay account.

Usage Tips: See website for screenshots and tips.

Tracking Down Additional WMC Add-Ons

There are many more add-ons available for WMC than the ones discussed here. To find more, I recommend spending time at the following websites, listed in no particular order:

- **MCEWorld:** Blog that covers WMC-related software and hardware; http://mymce.wordpress.com/.
- **The Green Button:** From software to forums, this might be the most useful WMC website anywhere. Microsoft agrees, considering it purchased The Green Button in July 2008; http://thegreenbutton.com.
- **We Got Served:** This is actually a site devoted to Windows Home Server, which enables Windows XP and Vista systems to connect to a dedicated home server, but it's also a great place to find out about products that enable WMC and Windows Home Server to work together; http://www.wegotserved.co.uk.
- **Media Center:** Chris Lanier's Blog—"News, Analysis, and Opinion on Microsoft Digital Media Technologies"; http://msmvps.com/blogs/chrisl/default.aspx.

- **The Digital Lifestyle:** This website is the home of The Media Center Show, providing podcasts, video shows, forums, and blogs to help you get up to speed; http://thedigitallifestyle.com/cs/.
- **Australian Media Center Community:** A great destination for forums, news, and WMC applications for Vista as well as XP Media Center users; http://www.xpmediacentre.com.au/.
- **Lifehacker:** Includes helpful coverage of WMC software, hardware, tips, and tricks; also covers other computer topics; http://lifehacker.com.
- **Windows Vista Community:** Microsoft's community forum for all things Vista; http://windowshelp.microsoft.com/windows/en-US/community/default.mspx.
- **MarkESoper.com:** My personal website, covering Windows Vista tips and tricks, Media Center features and add-ins, imaging, and related subjects; http://www.markesoper.com.

CHAPTER

16

Troubleshooting Media Center

If you use Windows Media Center (WMC) as the primary (or sole) Windows task on your WMC PC, keeping your system working well is even more important than with a regular PC. After all, your WMC PC might be the primary or sole repository of family pictures, videos, and your CD and DVD collection, or you might use it as the main way to enjoy your digital entertainment assets. If you use it with a TV tuner, it might be your digital video recorder.

However you use WMC, keeping the system or systems where you use WMC running properly will help you enjoy glitch-free media. Use this chapter to learn how.

IN THIS CHAPTER

- Solving Performance Problems
- Optimizing Power Management
- Improving Disk Management
- Optimizing Screen Display Settings
- Solving Network and Internet Problems
- Solving HDTV Viewing Problems
- Solving TV Tuning Problems
- Solving TV Recording Problems
- Solving Audio and Music Playback Problems
- Solving Codec Problems
- Useful Troubleshooting Resources

Solving Performance Problems

> **note** The tasks in most of the following sections are performed from the Windows desktop; close or minimize WMC to access the Windows desktop.

WMC is a CPU-intensive application, which is why we recommend using it on a fast dual-core or multi-core processor. However, making sure that other computer settings that affect CPU performance are also set properly can have a big effect on overall system performance, especially when you change between live TV and the Guide, encode a DVD, burn a CD or DVD, or other tasks.

Optimizing Power Management

WMC needs every bit of performance available from your system's processor. However, default settings in Windows can rob you of maximum performance. Use the following tips to restore your system to full performance.

Enable High Performance Power Plan

By default, both desktop and notebook/portable computers running Windows Vista use the Balanced power management scheme. Balanced drops CPU performance to 5% of maximum performance during idle periods, which can reduce heat and fan noise. Unfortunately, switching from 5% to maximum performance can cause lags and glitches in WMC performance.

To reduce or eliminate lag, use High Performance, which never changes the processor speed. You can switch to High Performance through the Power Plan icon in the notification area of the Windows Desktop (Figure 16.1).

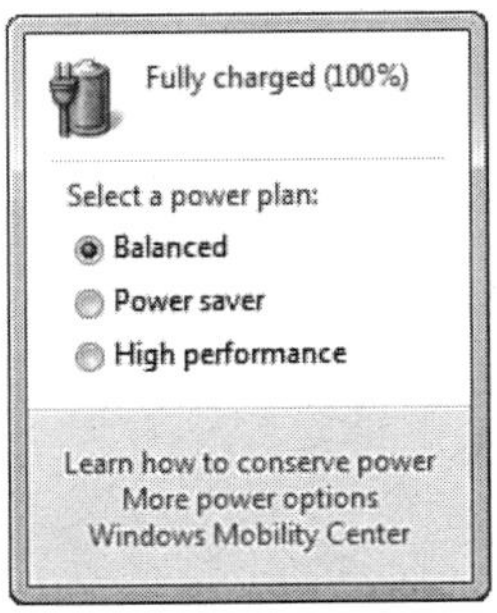

FIGURE 16.1
Switch from Balanced to High Performance power plan to improve WMC responsiveness and cut lag time when changing channels or performing other tasks.

Improving Performance in Balanced Power Plan

If your system is too noisy when you use High Performance continually and you have a fast dual-core system, you might prefer to set a higher minimum for the processor state in the Balanced Power Plan.

> **note** Not all systems include the Processor Power Management category in the Balanced Power Plan.

Here's how:

1. Open Control Panel.
2. Open the Hardware and Sound category.
3. Select Power Options.
4. Click Change Plan Settings under the Balanced power plan (Figure 16.2) selection.

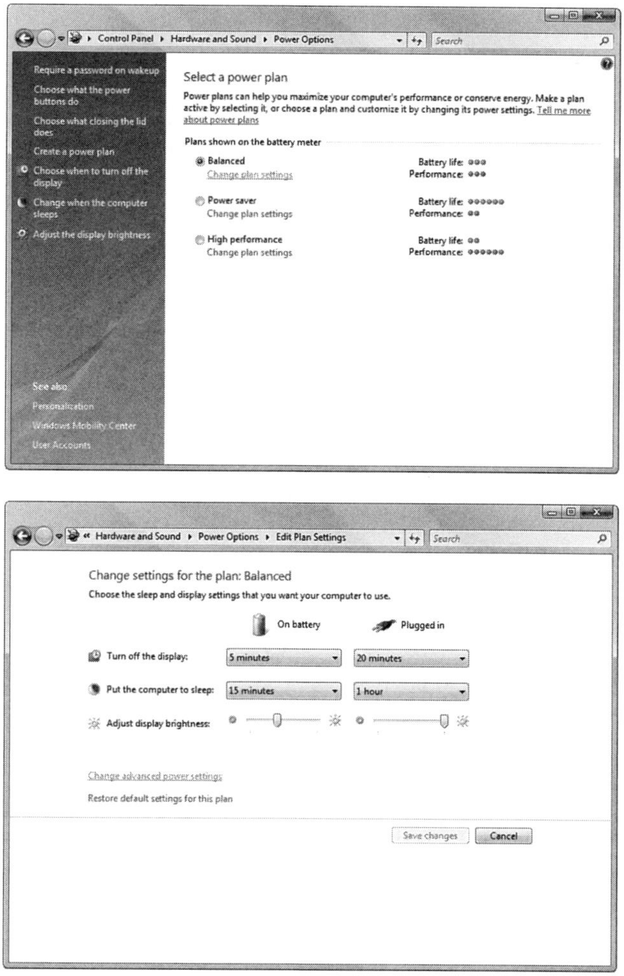

FIGURE 16.2

Starting the process of changing settings for the Balanced power plan.

5. Select Change Advanced Power Settings in the Edit Plan Settings dialog (Figure 16.2).
6. Expand the Processor Power Management category in the Power Options dialog (refer to Figure 16.3).
7. Expand the Minimum Processor State category, and change the value when plugged in from 5% to 50% (Figure 16.3).
8. Click Apply and then OK to save changes.

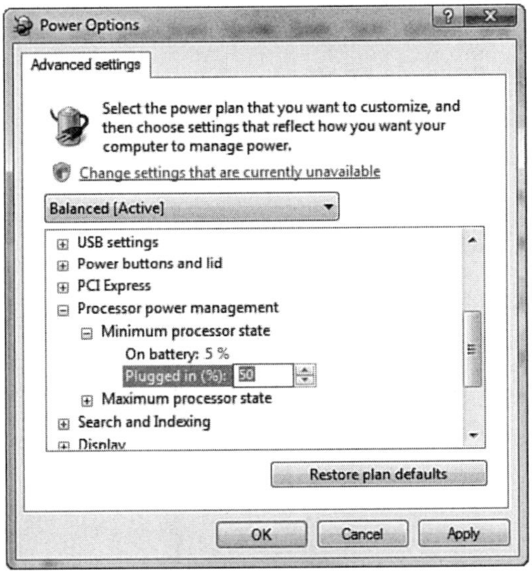

FIGURE 16.3

Increasing minimum processor performance for the Balanced power plan.

Improving Disk Management

As noted in other chapters, systems running WMC need lots of disk space, especially if they are used for TV recording or other types of video storage. Use the tips in this section to maximize disk space and drive performance.

Freeing Up Space on Your System Drive

If you record TV and delete recordings frequently, your hard disk's available space will become fragmented over time. The result? The system has to work harder to store TV recordings and other information, and you could wind up with choppy recordings. To stay out of trouble, make sure you keep at least 20% of your system drive free for defragmentation and for temporary file creation. On a 250GB hard disk, for example, you should keep at least 50GB free for these purposes.

To find out how much of your hard disk is currently in use

1. Open Computer.
2. Right-click your system drive (C:) and select Properties.
3. The blue section is the area in use, while the magenta section is the unused space (Figure 16.4).

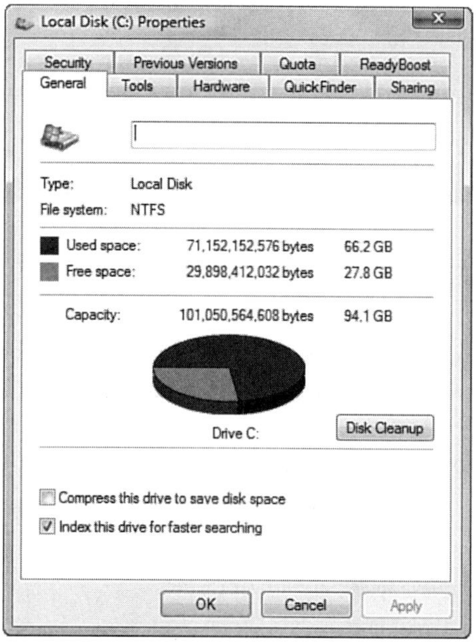

FIGURE 16.4
Checking available space on the system drive.

To free up additional space, click the Disk Cleanup button and specify whether you want to clean up files for all users (provide UAC credentials as prompted) or only for yourself. After the wizard checks for various types of files, it displays file types that can be removed. Files that can be removed without affecting the operation of your system are checked (Figure 16.5).

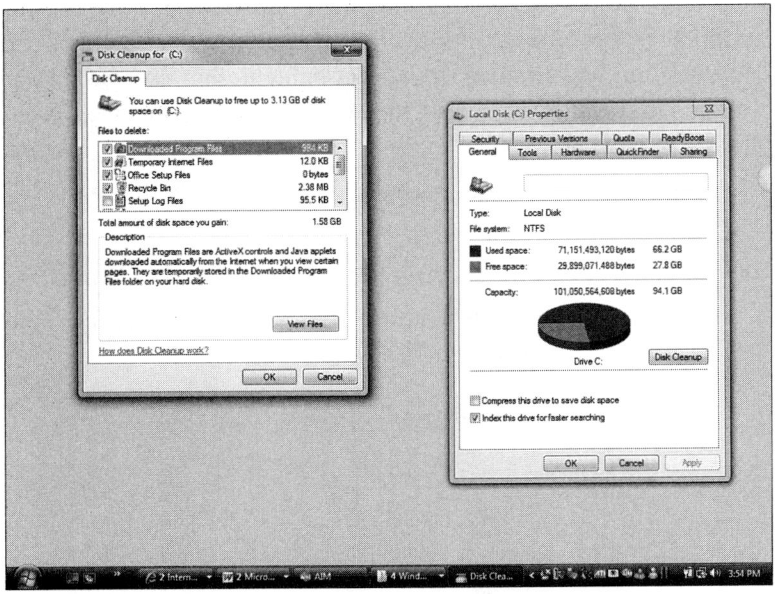

FIGURE 16.5
Selecting files to delete with Disk Cleanup.

Other types of files can also be selected if you don't need them around anymore. If you're not sure what to do, take a look at Table 16.1.

Table 16.1 File Types That Can Be Deleted by Disk Cleanup

File Type	Used For	When to Delete Safely
Downloaded Program Files	Programs used by your browser, such as Java applets and ActiveX controls	Anytime
Temporary Internet Files	HTML files, images, and other web page contents	Anytime
Office Setup Files	Temporary log and setup files used by Microsoft Office	Anytime
Recycle Bin	Files removed from normal folders with Delete but not yet removed from system	After checking to be sure you don't need these files anymore
Setup Log Files	Files logging Windows Vista installation	After Vista is installed and is working properly
Temporary Files	Files used as temporary workspace for applications and installers	After you close all other open applications; do not delete if you use applications that store information for future processing in the Temp folder

File Type	Used For	When to Delete Safely
Thumbnails	Displays thumbnails of image and other files in Windows Explorer in Extra Large, Large, and Medium Icons views	Only if you don't use these views
Per User Archived Windows Error Reports	Error reports for individual users already sent to Microsoft using the Problems and Solutions applet in Control Panel	After reviewing reported problems and solutions
Per User Queued Windows Error Reports	Error reports waiting to be sent to Microsoft	Only if you don't want to send the reports
System Archived Windows Error Reports	Systemwide error reports already sent to Microsoft using the Problems and Solutions applet in Control Panel	After reviewing reported problems and solutions

After selecting the files you want to delete, click OK and then click Delete Files on the confirming dialog. A progress dialog appears as the files are deleted. Click the Close button on the Disk properties sheet to complete the process.

Defragging Your System on the Right Schedule

Windows Vista's disk defragmenter helps improve the performance of your system by putting files and unused disk space into contiguous allocation units ("clusters"). To schedule defragmentation for a time that you normally aren't using your WMC computer (including times you normally aren't recording TV programs)

1. Open Control Panel.
2. Select System and Maintenance.
3. Select the Defragment Your Drive task under the Administrative Tools section.
4. Provide administrator-level credentials if prompted by User Account Control.
5. The Disk Defragmenter dialog (Figure 16.6) displays the current settings. By default, all connected hard disks are defragmented at the same time weekly.
6. To change the current schedule, click Modify Schedule and select the preferred frequency (daily, weekly, monthly), day of the week, and time desired (Figure 16.7). Click OK to close the dialog.

7. To add or remove volumes (drive letters), click Select Volumes (refer to Figure 16.6). Checked drives will be defragmented. Make any changes desired and click OK to close the dialog.

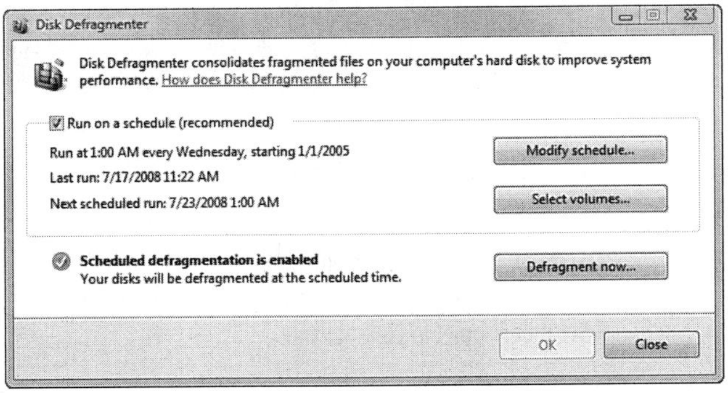

FIGURE 16.6

Viewing current defragmentation settings.

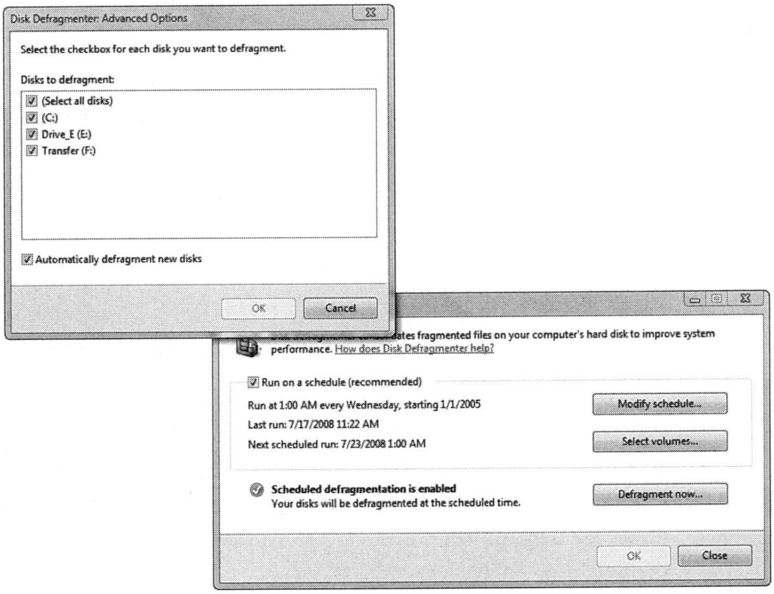

FIGURE 16.7

Changing the list of drives to be defragmented.

8. To defragment now, click Defragment Now. Defragmentation will run as a background task.
9. After reviewing current settings on the main dialog or making changes, click OK and then Close to close the Disk Defragmenter dialog.

> **note**
>
> ally operate
> hours. Howe
> watch (or re
> find that other times of the day are "vast wastelands" of TV viewing, choose a time when you don't usually watch or record TV. Weekly defragmentation is recommended for best performance.

Optimizing Screen Display Settings

WMC, especially when you are using it to watch TV, movies, or videos, is very display-intensive. Use the tips in the following sections to improve display performance.

Switch to the Vista Basic Color Scheme

Almost all Windows Vista systems running WMC are configured to use the Windows Aero 3D desktop scheme. While Aero's see-though overlapping windows and 3D task switching are great benefits for standard Windows users, if you're spending most (or all) of your time looking at WMC, you're losing about 5% of CPU time to the Desktop Window Manager (dwm.exe). To get back lost CPU performance, switch to Vista Basic. Here's how:

1. Right-click an empty section of the Windows desktop and select Personalize or open Control Panel, select Appearance and Personalization, and click Personalize.
2. From the Personalization menu, click Windows Color and Appearance.
3. From the Window Color and Appearance menu, click the Classic Appearance Properties link (Figure 16.8).
4. Select Vista Basic from the Appearance Settings tab.
5. To change the color of the desktop, click Advanced and select the desired color from the Desktop color palette (Figure 16.9).
6. To accept changes, click Apply and then OK.

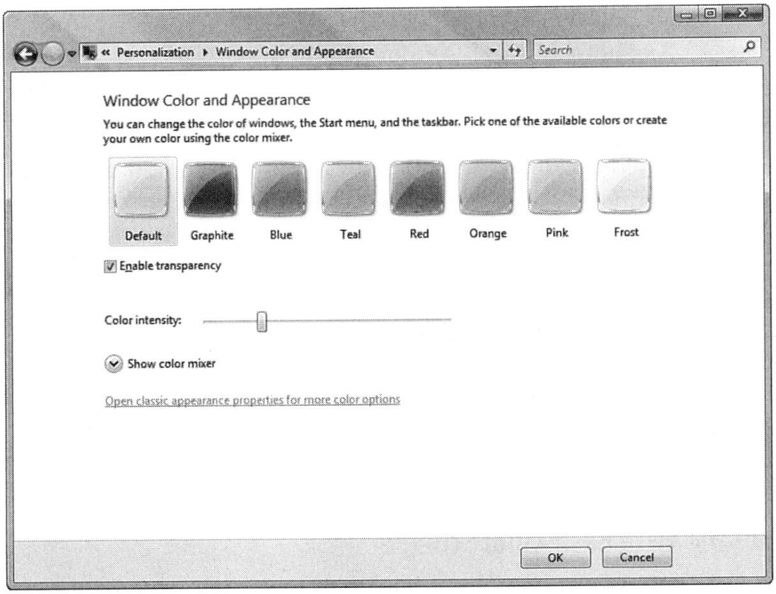

FIGURE 16.8

Accessing the Classic Appearance Properties menu.

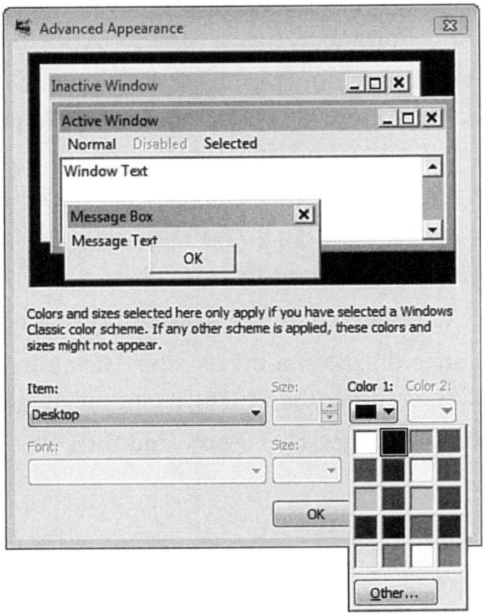

FIGURE 16.9

Choosing the preferred desktop background color.

Disabling Windows Sidebar

Windows Sidebar (Figure 16.10) is another productivity booster in Windows Vista that has no function once you leave the standard Windows desktop for the "10-foot UI" of WMC. When Windows Sidebar is running, it consumes about 12MB of RAM and uses some processor time.

FIGURE 16.10

Windows Sidebar's useful gadgets aren't visible from within WMC.

Closing Sidebar doesn't free up the resources it uses. However, you can stop Sidebar from starting by using this procedure:

1. Right-click the Windows Sidebar icon in the notification area and select Exit. The Windows Sidebar dialog opens.

> **note** You can restart Windows Sidebar from the Start Menu's Accessories menu. To enable it to run automatically when Windows starts, select Properties from the right-click menu and click the Start Sidebar when Windows Starts check box.

2. Clear the Start Sidebar when Windows Starts check box (Figure 16.11).
3. Click Exit. The Sidebar closes.

FIGURE 16.11
Preventing the Sidebar from starting up when the system restarts.

Solving Network and Internet Problems

Some symptoms of network or Internet problems include

- You can't connect to the Internet to update Guide listings (Figure 16.12).
- You see a prompt to Set Up an Internet Connection Before Trying to Update the Guide.
- You can't view other computers' shared folders in Library Setup's Add Folders wizard.

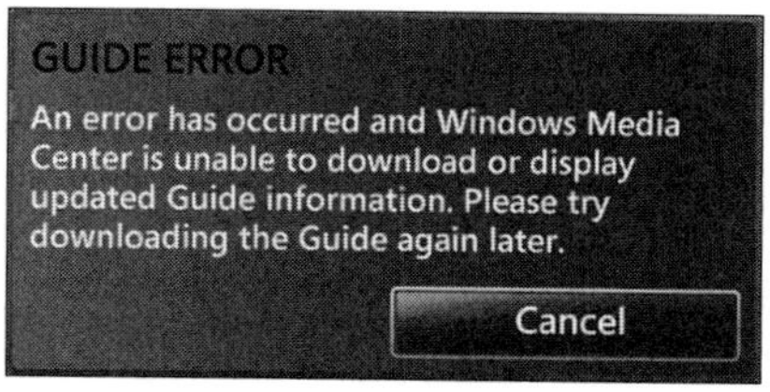

FIGURE 16.12
Errors like this indicate a problem with your network or Internet connection.

If you see an error message like the one in Figure 16.12, but retrying the connection works, try the following:

- Update the drivers for your network card or internal adapter. If your WMC computer uses a removable network adapter, check with the adapter vendor for an updated driver. If your WMC computer has a built-in network adapter, check with the computer vendor for an updated driver. Note that you can use the Update Driver option in the network adapter's properties sheet in Device Manager (Figure 16.13) to look for a driver update.
- If your wireless network adapter or wireless router has a movable antenna, try adjusting the antenna position. If your wireless network adapter plugs directly into the USB port, use an extension cable to move the adapter away from your PC. Try different positions until you find a location with the most reliable (and fastest) connection. More bars equals a better connection.
- If the problem is sporadic, you might be encountering interference from other devices that use the same frequency as your wireless network. 2.4GHz phones, microwave ovens, and other wireless networks can interfere with the operation of 802.11g, 802.11b, and most 802.11n networks.

To avoid interference, upgrade to 5.8GHz or 6GHz wireless phones, or use 5GHz 802.11n wireless network hardware. Microwave ovens can interfere with 2.4GHz wireless networks, especially those that use channel 11. Other wireless networks near yours can also interfere with your wireless network if they use the same channel. To avoid interference from other wireless networks, configure your wireless router to automatically select the channel, or use a program like InSSIDer to determine the channels being used by other nearby wireless networks.

→ For more information about InSSIDer, see "Checking for Interference from Other Wireless Networks," in Chapter 12, "Connecting with Windows Home Server and Other PCs."

→ To learn more about using InSSIDer to find the best channel to use for 2.4GHz networks, see "Checking for Interference from Other Wireless Networks," in Chapter 12, **p. 359**.

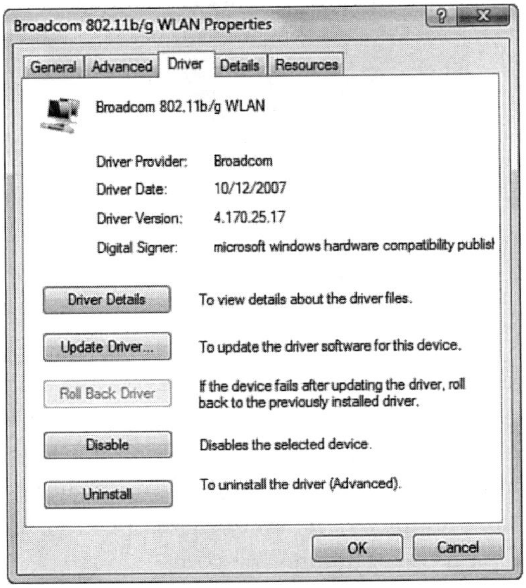

FIGURE 16.13
Preparing to use Device Manager's Update Driver wizard.

If you see a "No connection was detected" error message along with a prompt to "Set up an Internet Connection" message, it could mean that your computer is not connected to a network or that the network adapter is not working or is not connected to the computer. Check the simple stuff first:

- If you use a wireless adapter that plugs into a USB port, make sure the adapter is plugged into a working USB port—Move the adapter to a different port.
- If the adapter plugs into a USB cable, or if you use a wired network, replace the cable. A bad cable prevents the computer from detecting any device connected to it.

tip If you are somewhat familiar with home networking but need more help in understanding how networking works in Windows Vista, see my book *Maximum PC Microsoft Windows Vista Exposed* (Que Publishing, 2007). For a more in-depth treatment of networking, see *Networking with Microsoft Windows Vista: Your Guide to Easy and Secure Windows Vista Networking* (by Paul McFedries, Que Publishing, 2008).

- Check the Network and Sharing Center in Control Panel to see the status of your network (Figure 16.14). An X over the connection between the router and the Internet indicates a router connection problem, while an X over the connection between your PC and the router indicates a PC connection problem. Click the X to diagnose the problem. Keep in mind that a problem between the router and the Internet usually indicates a problem such as a loose or missing cable between your broadband modem and router or a configuration problem in the router.

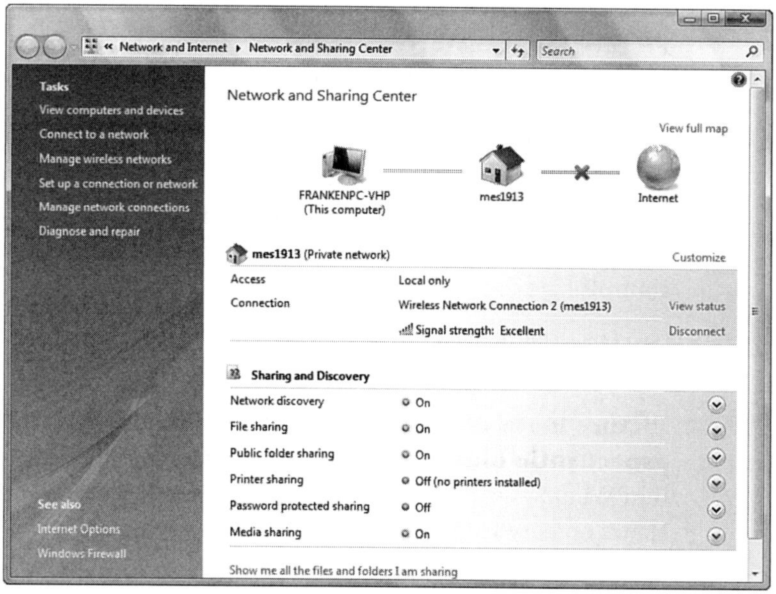

FIGURE 16.14

Network and Sharing Center shows this computer lacks a working Internet connection.

Solving HDTV Viewing Problems

If you use an HDTV to display WMC, its dual nature (TV and monitor) can cause some interesting problems. Use this list of common problems and solutions to get your WMC viewing back to normal.

- **Can't see any picture (Windows Desktop or WMC desktop):** The HDTV has probably been switched to a different input than the one needed for your computer. Most HDTVs have two or more digital (HDMI) inputs and several types of analog (composite, S-video, and component) inputs. Select the appropriate connection from the HDTV's onscreen menu. If you still don't see any picture after selecting the correct input, your WMC system might be running in a power-saving mode. Wake up the system by moving the mouse, tapping the keyboard, or pressing the WMC green button on your WMC remote.

> **tip** To prevent the screen saver from turning on, open the Personalization menu in Control Panel, select Screen Saver, and choose (None) as the screen saver type.
>
> To prevent the screen from blanking, open the Power Plan menu in Control Panel, click the Change Plan Settings link, and change the Turn Off Display option to Never.

16

- **Picture looks distorted:** As discussed in Chapter 5, "Watching and Recording Movies," the best way to handle different aspect ratios for TV and movies in WMC is to set your display to use Full aspect ratio and to adjust for other aspect ratios using the Zoom control. If you see distorted aspect ratios when viewing TV and movies in WMC, make sure your HDTV is configured to use Full aspect ratio using its onscreen controls.

➔ To learn how to use the Zoom control in WMC, see "Selecting Zoom Settings," Chapter 5, **p. 156**.

- **Picture looks distorted, even after adjusting HDTV to Full aspect ratio and using all Zoom options:** This usually indicates that Windows is not using the correct screen resolution for the display. Here's an easy way to check the screen resolution: Minimize WMC and display the Windows Sidebar. Add a round gadget, such as the CPU meter or the Clock, to the Sidebar. If a round gadget looks oval, your display is not configured properly.

TROUBLESHOOTING DISPLAY SETTINGS

If objects that are supposed to be round on the Windows desktop look oval, your display is not configured properly.

To select a different resolution, right-click an empty part of the Windows desktop, select Personalize, and select Display Settings. Select the display you use for WMC and adjust its resolution to the appropriate setting.

If you are using a standard or widescreen monitor, look up the documentation for the monitor to determine the correct setting to use. If you are using an HDTV, you might need to select the HD standard it supports (720p, 1080i, or 1080p) or choose a resolution that supports the aspect ratio and resolution of the display. For example, to drive my JVC 720p HDTV, I use a resolution of 1280×720 pixels. After choosing a different resolution, click Apply and then Yes on the confirming dialog to use a new resolution. Click OK to close the Display Settings dialog.

With some display adapters and driver versions, you might run a proprietary display setup utility in addition to, or instead of, the Windows Display Settings dialog.

Solving TV Tuning Problems

WMC enables you to watch and record TV, but if you're having problems, the following sections will help you solve the problem and get back to your favorite TV show.

tip If you're having a hard time finding the right display settings for your HDTV or widescreen monitor, download driver updates for your display card. You can use the Update Driver option in the Device Manager properties sheet for your display card, or you can visit the vendor's website.

If your display adapter is built into the motherboard, visit the motherboard vendor's website for an updated driver.

Troubleshooting Basic Cable TV Problems

If you don't use a set-top box to receive cable TV, you have what I refer to in this book as "basic" cable TV (although your provider probably has another name for it). In basic cable TV, the TV tuner in your PC tunes in the channel. Use the following checklist to find your problem and its solution:

- **Can't receive TV channels:** First, rerun TV setup in WMC. If TV setup doesn't detect a cable TV signal, check the connection between the wall jack and the TV tuner. Replace the coaxial cable if necessary. Use a TV set to verify that the jack is working correctly. After making the necessary changes, rerun TV setup. If you have more than one coaxial connection on your TV tuner, make sure you use the one intended for cable TV.

- **Some TV channels are fuzzy:** You might not be getting a full-power video signal. If you are using a splitter to split the signal between your PC and a TV, try replacing the splitter with one that has lower signal loss or attach a signal booster to the connection before splitting the signal. If the cable is damaged, replace the cable. Rerun TV setup in WMC.
- **Some TV channels in the Guide can't be viewed:** First, rerun TV setup and make sure you have selected the correct cable TV provider and service type. Some cable TV providers have more than one level of basic cable TV service. In such cases, the Guide might list TV channels that are not part of your service package. Edit your guide listing to show only the channels your service provides.
- **The Guide listing doesn't match the actual program being shown:** This problem can be caused by selecting the wrong cable TV provider or by having an incorrect date/time setting in your computer's clock. Check your computer's date and time by opening the Date and Time applet in the Windows desktop's notification area. Be sure to check the time zone setting as well.

➔ To learn how to edit channel listings in WMC, see "Editing Channel Listings" in Chapter 4, "Viewing and Recording Live TV," **p. 107**.

➔ To learn how to set up your TV signal in WMC, see "Setting Up Your TV Signal," Chapter 4, **p. 91**.

Troubleshooting Set-Top Box Problems

If you use the TV tuner on your system to receive output from a cable or satellite TV set-top box, an IR blaster from your PC is used to send channel-control signals to the set-top box. Check these problems and solutions:

- **Can't change channels:** First, replace the batteries in the remote. Then check the position of the IR blaster emitter. If the emitter is not over the IR receiver in the set-top box, the set-top box will not receive signals. If the emitter appears to be properly positioned, make sure the IR blaster is connected properly to the appropriate jack on your WMC remote control receiver or your PC's integrated IR blaster jack. If it is connected properly, use the remote control provided by your cable company to change channels. If you are unable to change channels with the set-top box remote, the set-top box might be defective.

- **Can't detect set-top box:** If you can watch TV using a standard or HDTV, but WMC can't detect the set-top box, check the connection between the set-top box and your PC's TV tuner. Make sure the cable is connected to the correct connection on the PC's TV tuner and the set-top box. Tighten the cable and rerun TV setup. If WMC still can't detect the set-top box, replace the cable between the set-top box and the TV tuner.
- **Channel changing is erratic:** Rerun the TV setup and make sure to select set-top box as the signal type. Be sure to run the channel changing and remote control configuration tests provided.
- **Some channels in your service pack aren't listed:** Rerun TV setup and make sure you selected the appropriate service provider. Note that if you have digital cable TV, you should choose the digital service provided by your provider.
- **Some channels listed in the Guide are not available:** Many providers offer multiple levels of service. Use the Edit Channels feature to remove channels that are not part of your TV package.

➔ To learn how to configure your system for use with a set-top box, see "Digital Cable TV," Chapter 4, **p. 88**.

➔ To learn how to set up your TV signal in WMC, see "Setting Up Your TV Signal," Chapter 4, **p. 91**.

Troubleshooting Set-Top Box and Remote Not Recognized Problems

WMC can recognize lots of set-top boxes and the remote control codes they use. However, it's possible that you might have an oddball that WMC can't recognize. Don't panic! Here's what to do.

- **WMC doesn't recognize your set-top box:** If WMC does not recognize your set-top box during TV setup, you will be asked to choose your set-top box brand (Figure 16.15) and then choose the remote control code to use. During this process, you will be asked to test the code by changing channels. If you are unable to change channels with the first code selected, choose another and repeat the process until you find a code that works.
- **WMC doesn't recognize your set-top box's remote:** If WMC isn't able to identify your remote (Figure 16.16), you can train WMC to "learn" the codes used by your set-top box's remote control.

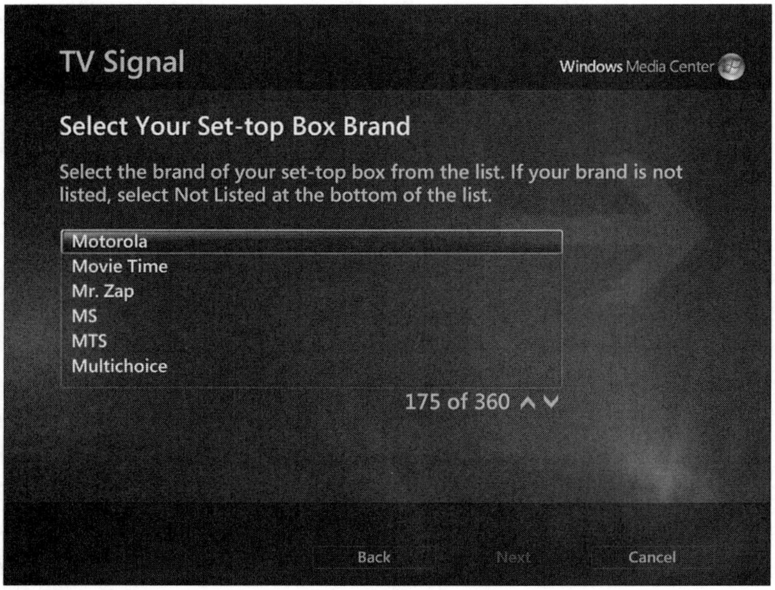

FIGURE 16.15
Manually selecting your set-top box.

FIGURE 16.16
Selecting the option to "train" WMC to recognize the codes used by your set-top box's remote.

First, you are prompted to point the set-top box's remote directly at the IR receiver used by your WMC remote control and to move the remote so it is almost touching the receiver window. Next, follow the prompts to identify the remote's buttons (numbers, channel up, down, and so forth), as shown in Figure 16.17.

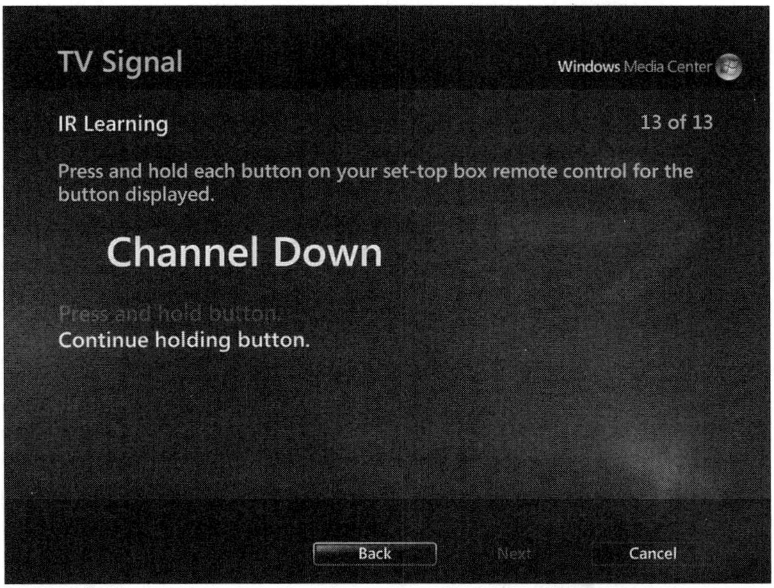

FIGURE 16.17
Training WMC's IR receiver to "learn" from the set-top box's remote.

After set-top box codes are set up successfully, you must then test the IR signal speed by changing channels with your WMC remote (Figure 16.18). Once you find the correct speed, the process is complete.

Troubleshooting Broadcast TV

Broadcast TV uses an antenna connection to the standard TV/cable TV connection on your TV tuner. See the following list of problems and solutions to help you get your standard TV connection working properly.

> **note** You can learn more about making the switch to digital TV (if you are using an antenna to receive your television signal) from Que's *Switching to Digital TV: Everything You Need to Know* by Michael Miller.

- **You can't receive any TV channels:** If you are in the U.S., check the calendar. If the date is

February 18, 2009, or later, time's up for virtually all broadcast TV signals. Starting at midnight on February 17, 2009, basically all analog TV broadcasting in the United States will be replaced by digital (ATSC) broadcast TV. Until then, check the connection between your TV antenna and your TV tuner. Make sure you are using the standard TV/cable TV connector on your TV tuner. Rerun TV setup in WMC.

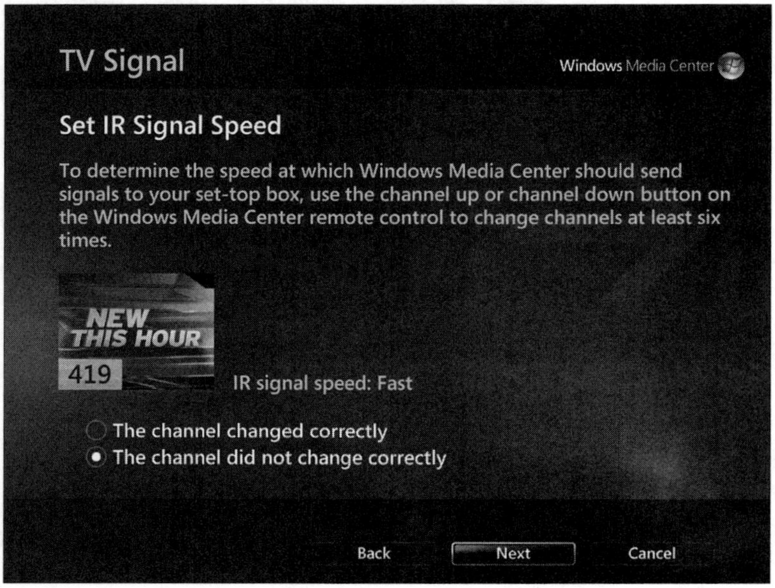

FIGURE 16.18
Testing channel changing speeds.

- **You can't pick up some TV channels:** Check the position of your antenna. If the antenna is powered, make sure the antenna is turned on. Change the position of the antenna.
- **Some TV channels in the Guide can't be picked up, or some channels you can pick up aren't in the Guide:** Edit the channel listings to match the channels you can receive.

Troubleshooting Digital Broadcast (ATSC) TV

ATSC (digital broadcast TV) will replace traditional NTSC broadcast TV in virtually every market in the U.S. starting February 18, 2009. While you can use the same types of antennas that are used for traditional broadcast TV, to pick up ATSC signals, you must use a TV tuner designed for ATSC signals. If you're having problems, use this list of problems and solutions to help you see your favorite crisp, clear ATSC TV channels again.

- **You can't receive ATSC TV channels:** First, check your TV tuner. Is it designed to pick up ATSC TV signals? If not, replace it. If it is, make sure the antenna lead is connected to the correct lead on the TV tuner. On most tuners, a separate lead is provided for ATSC TV signals. Next, rerun the WMC TV setup program. Make sure TV setup detects ATSC signals. If you are unable to pick up ATSC TV channels, make sure you are using a powered antenna, preferably a directional antenna.
- **You can't pick up all of the ATSC channels listed for your area:** This is normal, especially if you use an indoor antenna. Rerun TV setup and use the ATSC signal strength wizard to run through available ATSC channels. Adjust the antenna for each channel, and delete any channels that display no signal or a minimal (red lined) signal.
- **The TV picture freezes or audio/video becomes desynchronized:** Digital TV looks better than traditional broadcast TV, but it's an on/off signal. A weak signal will cause the picture to freeze or will cause video and audio to become desynchronized. Make sure the antenna is properly positioned and is turned on.

> **tip** If the antenna you use for ATSC (or traditional broadcast TV) can store different positions and settings for each channel, use this feature to store and recall the best setting for each channel.

➔ To learn how to configure your system for ATSC broadcast TV, see "Digital Broadcast TV (ATSC)," Chapter 4, **p. 87**.

➔ To learn how to use the ATSC signal strength wizard in WMC, see "Checking ATSC Channel Signal Strength," Chapter 4, **p. 102**.

Solving TV Recording Problems

If you use WMC to watch TV, you probably use it to record TV as well. Use this list of common problems and solutions to make your TV recording hassle-free.

- **Already-recorded programs in Recorded TV are labeled with an exclamation mark (!):** WMC uses the ! symbol as a general alert to tell you all is not well in Recordingland. To find out what this means, click one of the marked recordings. As you can see from Figure 16.19, the symbol indicates that the recording will be deleted on the day listed to make room for new recordings. If you want to keep the recording longer, change the Keep Until setting.

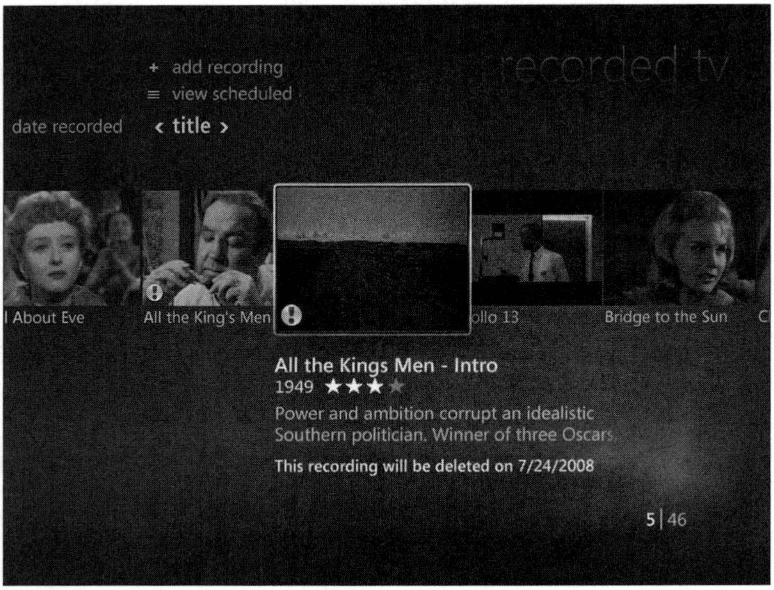

FIGURE 16.19

Recordings marked with the (!) symbol will be deleted soon—unless you change the Keep Until setting for each recording.

→ To learn more about Keep Until settings in WMC, see "Customizing Recording Options," Chapter 5, **p. 150**.

→ To learn how to change Keep Until settings for existing recordings, see "The Recorded TV Menu," Chapter 4, **p. 122**.

- **Already-scheduled movies and TV shows now display an (!) symbol:** WMC will not let you schedule a movie to record if there's not enough space, so if the Scheduled recordings dialog suddenly displays warning messages (Figure 16.20), and the Movie Details dialog indicates there's not enough space to record the movie, something has happened to available space. Open the Recorder Storage menu to see how much available space is listed. If you used an additional drive for recorded TV but it is no longer listed, you need to find out why the drive is no longer visible. Once you get the drive working again, you will need to go back to the Recorder Storage menu and reconfigure it to use the additional hard disk.

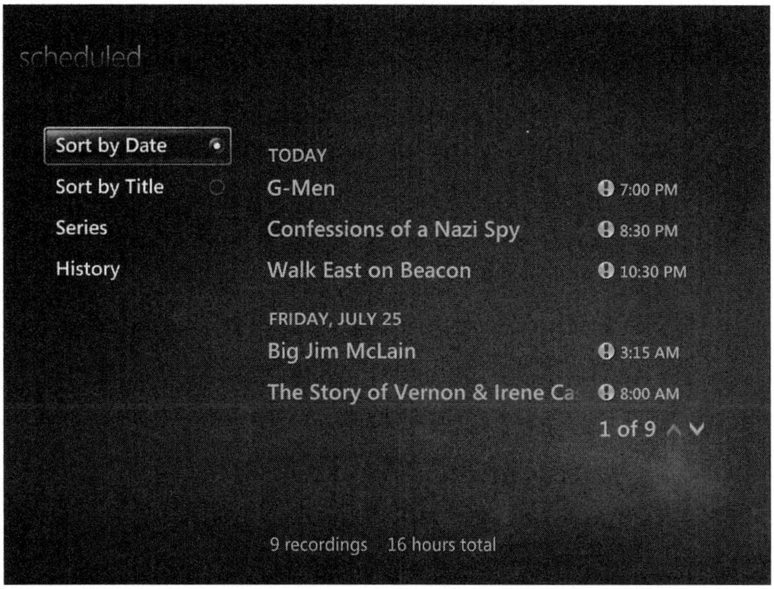

FIGURE 16.20

WMC warns you of a problem with scheduled recordings.

➔ To learn more about Recorder Storage settings in WMC, see "Recorder Storage," Chapter 4, **p. 110**.

TROUBLESHOOTING HARD DISK DRIVES

If you use a hard disk other than the system drive for storing Recorded TV, and it disappears from the Recorder Storage menu, it might have failed or gone offline.

Some external drives connected to USB or other interfaces might go offline if the system shuts down and restarts. Minimize or close WMC, disconnect and reconnect the drive, and use Windows Explorer to see if the drive reappears. To prevent power failures from taking down your WMC PC and external storage, plug the WMC PC, your set-top box (if you use one), and your external hard disk drives into a suitably sized battery backup (UPS) unit. For help in choosing the appropriate capacity for a UPS unit, check the websites of battery backup manufacturers.

If the drive is internal, it might have failed, but more likely causes of problems are loose data or power cables, or, in the case of PATA drives, incorrect master/slave jumpering. If you have recently installed system upgrades or opened the system for cleaning or maintenance, you might have accidentally jostled a cable or removed it for access and forgotten to reconnect it. Before checking the interior of the system, shut down Windows and either unplug the system's power supply or turn off the power supply (if it has its own power switch). For drive power and cable connection details, or for PATA jumper settings, see the drive vendor's website.

After you reconnect loose or dangling cables, be sure to close up the system and turn on the power supply (or reconnect its AC power cord) before starting the system. After the system boots, use Windows Explorer to verify that the drive is now visible to Windows.

After the "missing" drive reappears, you can reconfigure WMC to use it for TV recording.

Solving Audio and Music Playback Problems

Music, TV, movie, and video content you enjoy in WMC should include some type of an audio track. If you're not hearing anything, that's bad. Before you start shopping for a hearing aid, use the checklist in this section to fix audio playback problems.

- **You can't hear audio from the PC's speakers:** First, press the mute button on your WMC remote (or press the Mute icon on the mouse panel) to toggle audio on and off. (When audio is muted, you will see a Mute display appear briefly in the upper-right corner of your WMC display.) If the system isn't muted, use the volume control on your WMC remote (or mouse panel) to raise the volume to an audible level. If nothing happens, check the speaker connection to the computer and make sure the speakers are turned on and are receiving power. If you have a sound card as well as integrated audio, plug the speaker into whichever audio device you actually use.
- **You can't hear audio from a home theater system connected to your PC:** Before checking mute and volume controls on the PC as

in the previous suggestion, make sure the amplifier is turned on and that it is configured to receive audio from the PC. For example, if the PC is plugged into jacks marked "Video" on the amplifier, the amplifier must be set to "Video," or the PC's audio will not be received.

- **You can't hear digital (SPDIF or coaxial) audio from your PC, either through its own speakers or a home theater system:** By default, your PC uses analog mini-jack connections for audio output. If you want to use SPDIF fiber optic or coaxial digital output, you must select this option in the audio mixer. You can access the audio mixer through the Hardware and Sound category of Control Panel.

> **note** Almost all desktop systems follow the PC99 color coding system for audio jacks. Pink is used for microphones; light blue for line in; lime green for stereo speaker or headphones; orange for subwoofers. On systems that support 5.1 or 7.1 surround audio with mini-jack (analog) speakers, use the lime green jack next to the pink jack for stereo speakers.

Solving Codec Problems

As you learned in previous chapters, a codec is a program that encodes and decodes various types of digital media. Although Windows Vista includes codecs for playing back and creating digital music, video, and photo files, you can have a variety of problems caused by codec issues, such as

- **Can't play some types of media files in WMC:** Windows Vista doesn't support some types of video files, such as DivX, or it might not include the codecs used to create some files in file types it can normally use.
- **Can't burn video DVDs from WMC or from Vista's DVD Maker:** If you install third-party DVD burning software but decide to use Vista's own burning programs afterward, you might encounter this problem. It typically manifests itself by the encoding process quitting with an error long before the actual burning process begins. Although third-party DVD burning software offers many additional features over the built-in components in Windows Vista, I sometimes prefer to use Vista's own burning programs.

To solve these problems, I recommend downloading and installing the freeware Vista Codec Package available at http://shark007.net. The Vista Codec package enables Vista to recover from problems caused by third-party DVD burning programs and enables WMC to work with a wider variety of media types.

note If you have other playback problems, be sure to see the extensive help provided on the Vista Codec Package website for solutions.

Although you can install codecs provided by camera vendors to enable Windows Photo Gallery and its replacement, Windows Live Photo Gallery, to display RAW file types in Windows Vista, WMC does not support RAW files.

However, if you want to view RAW files from within WMC, here's a workaround: use the EMUCenter program discussed in Chapter 9, "Playing Games and Enjoying Online Resources," to set up Windows Photo Gallery or Windows Live Photo Gallery as a "Windows game." You can then launch either of these programs from within WMC and return automatically to WMC when you are finished.

- Windows Photo Gallery is located here on a typical system: C:\Program Files\Windows Photo Gallery\WindowsPhotoGallery.exe
- Windows Live Photo Gallery is located here on a typical system: C:\Program Files\Windows Live\Photo Gallery\WLXPhotoGallery.exe

➔ To learn more about EMUCenter, see "EMUCenter," Chapter 9, **p. 254**.

➔ To learn more about Windows Photo Gallery and Windows Live Photo Gallery, see "Windows Photo Gallery, Meet Windows *Live* Photo Gallery" in Chapter 14, "Creating Photo and Video Content for Media Center," **p. 396**.

tip Be sure to run Windows Update at least once a week. (I run it daily using the default automatic setting.) Windows Update delivers updates for all parts of Windows Vista, including Windows Media Center.

Useful Troubleshooting Resources

Some of the tips in this chapter were suggested by the following resources:

- Andrew Grant's Shiny Things blog (www.andrewgrant.org) covers WMC and Windows Home Server.
- Office Watch (http://news.office-watch.com) covers Microsoft Office and Windows + Office interactions.
- The How-To Geek (www.howtogeek.com) offers several tutorials for Windows Vista.
- Paul Thurrott's Windows Supersite (www.winsupersite.com) is a must-read for Windows Vista users or for users of older Windows versions who are moving to Vista and to Vista's WMC.

PART

VI

Appendices

APPENDIX

A

Using Windows Anytime Upgrade to Get WMC Features and More

IN THIS APPENDIX

- The Benefits of Windows Anytime Upgrade
- The Windows Anytime Upgrade Process

The Benefits of Windows Anytime Upgrade

With previous Windows versions, the only way to upgrade from one edition to the other in the same product family was to go back to the store, purchase the upgrade edition, and go through an upgrade installation. It was an expensive and time-consuming process, and for nonretail versions of Windows, such as Windows XP Media Center Edition or Windows XP Tablet Edition, no upgrades to a better version were available.

Windows Vista changes all that. One of the new features of Windows Vista is that all retail DVDs (both full and upgrade versions) include all Windows Vista editions sold in that country. The product key on the disc package must match the edition you purchase, of course, but by purchasing an upgrade, you can use the Windows Vista Home Basic DVD to upgrade to Windows Vista Home Premium. Or, you can use the Windows Vista Home Basic, Home Premium, or Business DVD to upgrade to Windows Vista Ultimate.

By upgrading from Windows Vista Home Basic to Windows Vista Home Premium, for example, you can enjoy Windows Media Center (the subject of this book) and create movies in HD with Windows Movie Maker. Windows Vista Business users can add Windows Media Center, DVD Maker, and Windows Movie Maker HD features by upgrading to Windows Vista Ultimate. Windows Vista Home Premium users can add full-system protection with Complete PC Backup and Restore and Bit-Locker full-disk encryption by moving up to Windows Vista Ultimate.

To compare features, see the Windows Vista: Compare Editions website at http://www.microsoft.com/windows/products/windowsvista/editions/choose.mspx.

The Windows Anytime Upgrade Process

You can start the Windows Anytime Upgrade process in one of two ways:

- To run Windows Anytime Upgrade from your existing copy of Windows Vista, open Control Panel, select System and Maintenance, and select Windows Anytime Upgrade.
- To run Windows Anytime Upgrade from a web browser, open the Windows Vista: Windows Anytime Upgrade: Overview page at http://www.microsoft.com/windows/products/windowsvista/editions/choose.mspx.

Either method enables you to choose an upgrade, purchase it, and use your existing Windows Vista DVD as a source for upgrade files. If you are using your Windows Vista DVD as a Windows Anytime Upgrade disc, you can upgrade by clicking Upgrade Now from the purchase page or from the link in the email message.

If you don't have a Windows Vista DVD or a Windows Anytime Upgrade disc (for example, if you are using a preinstalled version of Windows Vista), U.S. customers can buy one for $7 (prices vary elsewhere) during the Anytime Upgrade process. If you currently use a 64-bit version of Windows Vista, be sure to specify that you need a 64-bit version of the Anytime Upgrade disc. If you order a Windows Anytime Upgrade disk, start the upgrade process after you receive the disc.

note For more information about the Windows Anytime Upgrade process, see the Installation Overview and FAQ page at http://www.microsoft.com/windows/products/windowsvista/buyorupgrade/windowsanytimeupgrade/faq.mspx.

Control Panel Versus Website Anytime Upgrade

Why provide two ways to run Windows Anytime Upgrade?

One advantage of the Control Panel method is that you can view a feature comparison that highlights exactly what features are common to your current Windows Vista version and the upgrade you are purchasing.

However, if you are not sure whether your system is ready for a better version of Windows Vista, you can easily run the Windows Vista Upgrade Advisor from the Windows Anytime Upgrade website before starting the upgrade process.

Checking Your System with the Windows Vista Upgrade Advisor

The Windows Vista Upgrade Advisor can run from the Windows Anytime Upgrade website, or directly from http://www.microsoft.com/windows/products/windowsvista/buyorupgrade/upgradeadvisor.mspx.

This tool takes just a few minutes to survey your system to determine if you need to upgrade memory, video card, or other components before upgrading to a better version of Windows Vista. It also determines if you need to download updated drivers for any of your hardware, and if you are running software that may need to be upgraded.

After you verify that your computer's ready for a better version of Windows Vista, start the Windows Anytime Upgrade process as described above.

Other Preparations to Make Before Upgrading

Although Windows Anytime Upgrade preserves your existing documents, programs, and program settings, Microsoft recommends that you back up your system before running Windows Anytime Upgrade.

With Home Basic or Home Premium editions, back up all users' documents and settings with File and Folder Backup before running Windows Anytime Upgrade. With the Business edition, run a Complete PC Backup, followed by File and Folder Backup before running Windows Anytime Upgrade.

APPENDIX

B

Moving from Windows XP Media Center Editions to Windows Vista Media Center

IN THIS APPENDIX

- So, What's New In Windows Media Center for Vista?
- Can Your XP MCE System Run Vista?
- Everybody *Can* Upgrade, but not Everybody *Should* Perform an Upgrade Installation

If you're currently using Windows XP Home Edition or Professional, moving to Windows Vista Home Premium or Ultimate editions brings you into a whole new world of digital media excitement. However, if your current system is running Windows XP Media Center Edition, the move to Windows Vista Home Premium or Ultimate (both of which include Vista's version of Windows Media Center [WMC]) brings both the opportunity for new functionality and possible difficulties. Here's how you can make sure your upgrade goes smoothly.

So, What's New In Windows Media Center for Vista?

Quite a bit, actually:

- Support for digital TV tuners, including dual-tuner cards; Vista Media Center TV Pack also adds support for Clear QAM, DVB-S, and DVB-T European digital TV standards

- Support for up to four TV tuners in the United States or two TV tuners in other locations; on systems that include the Vista Media Center TV Pack, Windows Vista Home Premium supports up to six tuners, and Windows Vista Ultimate Edition supports up to 12 tuners
- Integrated DVD and MPEG-2 playback
- Internet TV (U.S.)
- Movies menu
- Tasks menu
- Automatic detection of ATSC (over-the-air HDTV) subchannels
- Sports menu (U.S.)
- Redesigned user interface for better use of the additional horizontal screen space of HDTV and widescreen displays
- Live TV and video overlays for some menus so you can browse while watching TV

note Microsoft released the Vista Media Center TV Pack to OEMs in July 2008. It also replaces the MS-DVR file format with a new WTV format, pools TV tuners to avoid duplicate recordings of TV episodes in HD and Standard TV formats, and recording priority. Vista Media Center TV Pack may be officially released to existing Vista users at a later date. Currently, it must be installed to a clean install of Windows Vista Home Premium or Ultimate SP1. See this forum thread on The Green Button website for details: http://thegreenbutton.com/forums/1/281532/ShowThread.aspx.

The Vista version of WMC is ready for the HD and digital TV and video future.

Can Your XP MCE System Run Vista?

To determine if your system can run Windows Vista adequately, start by visiting www.microsoft.com/windows/products/windowsvista/buyorupgrade/upgradeadvisor.mspx and downloading the Windows Vista Upgrade Advisor. This free utility analyzes your Windows XP system (including any MCE edition) and evaluates your system's hardware and application software to determine the following:

- Whether your system can run Windows Vista
- What edition(s) of Windows Vista your system can run
- Whether you need to perform any tasks before installing Windows Vista, such as downloading updated drivers, updating software, or uninstalling software

Figure B.1 shows portions of a typical report on a system that needs some upgrades and other tasks performed before being upgraded to Windows Vista Home Premium or Ultimate editions.

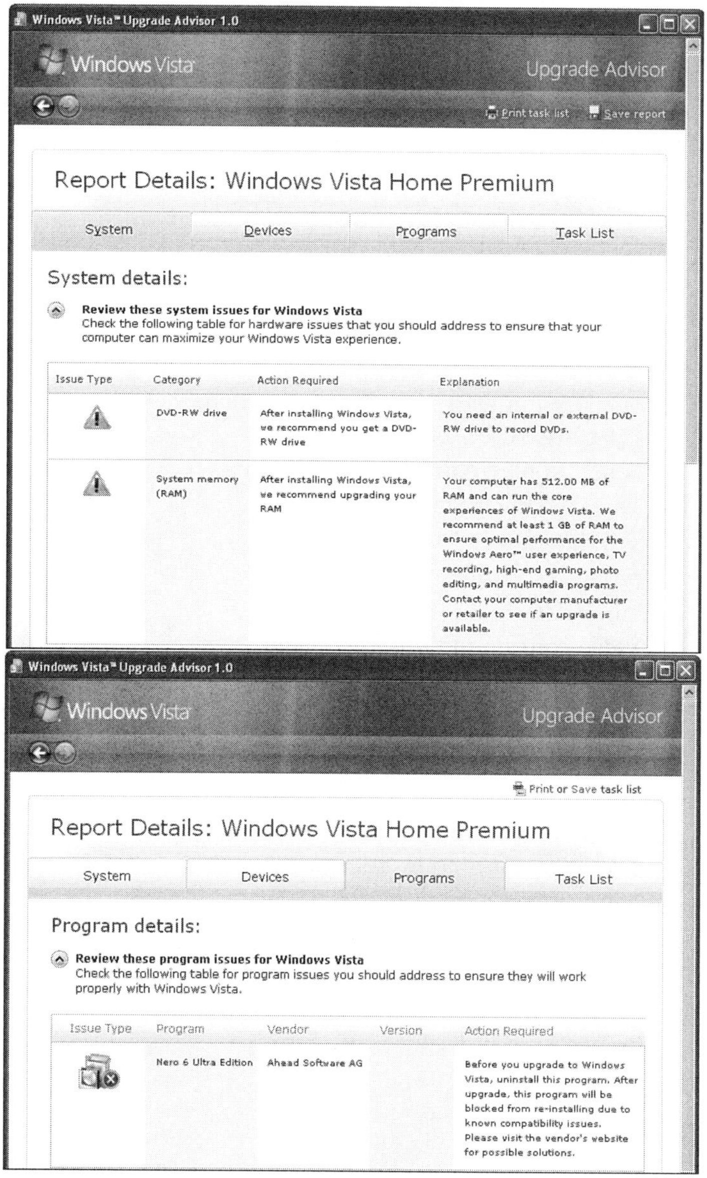

FIGURE B.1

This system needs a memory (RAM) upgrade, a rewritable DVD drive, and changes to application software before upgrading to Windows Vista Home Premium.

If Windows Vista Upgrade Advisor reports problems with your system, be sure to print the list of tasks (see the Task List tab) and perform those tasks as recommended.

> **note** If your system does not have version 2.0 of the .NET Framework installed, you'll be prompted to install it along with necessary upgrades before you can run the advisor.

Because Windows Vista Home Premium requires higher minimum and recommended hardware standards than Windows XP Media Center Edition, you might find multiple issues with an existing system. In particular, watch for

- **System RAM below 1GB:** I recommend at least 2GB, especially if you have integrated graphics that use part of system memory, if you use an Xbox 360 as a Media Center Extender, or plan to use Media Center Extenders with your Vista-based Media Center PC.
- **Video card issues:** If you want to view HDTV on Vista Media Center, you need at least 128MB of video memory with a 128-bit memory interface. Also, your video card must support Windows Vista Display Driver Model (WDDM) as well as support DirectX 9 or higher with Pixel Shader 2.0 to be able to run WMC. Some older DirectX 9 video cards found in some Media Center PCs might not meet these requirements.
- **Lack of free hard disk space:** Although Windows Vista Upgrade Advisor looks only for sufficient hard disk space to install Windows Vista, if you plan to record HDTV, you will need more disk space than in Windows XP MCE. HDTV uses 8GB per hour, meaning that 120GB of free hard disk space can store only 15 hours of programming, compared to 44 hours at Best quality standard TV, or as much as 99 hours of programming at the lowest-quality Fair setting.

> **note** How much should you spend on upgrades before replacing your PC? If you need to install several upgrades, such as a new video card, a new TV tuner, more RAM, a rewritable DVD drive, and a new remote control (just to name some typical examples), you might be looking at as much as $500 or more in upgrades. That sounds like a lot of money, but if you are happy with your system's features otherwise, it's still a lot cheaper than buying a brand new PC tricked out for Vista Media Center, which can run you $1000–3000 or more, depending on features.
>
> Still wondering what to do? Use the 50% rule: If it costs 50% or more of the cost of a new system to upgrade the old system to provide comparable features and performance, go for the new system.

B

- **TV tuner issues:** If your existing TV tuner doesn't have Vista-compatible drivers or doesn't support MPEG2 encoding in hardware, upgrade it.
- **Remote control issues:** Some remote controls made for some Windows XP Media Center editions don't work with Vista Media Center.

Whether you are planning to perform an upgrade installation or a clean install, be sure to download every driver update recommended by Windows Vista Upgrade Advisor before you start the upgrade/installation process. Contact the vendor of your system or the component vendors used to build a customized Home Theater PC (HTPC) for upgraded drivers. Windows Vista can recognize driver files, even for drivers required for booting the system (such as hard disk host adapter or RAID drivers) stored on a USB thumb drive or a recordable/rewritable CD or DVD—you no longer need to copy driver files to a floppy disk.

Everybody *Can* Upgrade, but not Everybody *Should* Perform an Upgrade Installation

If you have any edition of Windows XP Media Center, from the pre-Cambrian MCE 2002 to the latest MCE 2005, you can use the Windows Vista Home Premium or Ultimate edition upgrade editions and perform an "in-place upgrade," which preserves your existing software and settings, while replacing Windows XP MCE with Windows Vista. So why *not* upgrade? There are several reasons:

- An upgrade installation can take much longer than a clean install (even considering reinstallation of key applications).
- Your system might have a lot of legacy hardware or software that's not supported by Windows Vista.
- Your system might not be powerful enough to run Windows Vista, especially if you're wanting to work with digital video, high-resolution digital photos, HDTV, or stream HDTV/video content to a Media Center Extender.

If you decide to perform a clean install instead of an upgrade installation, I recommend you use the Windows Vista Transfer Wizard to back up media and other files and settings from your existing XP MCE PC to an external hard disk or network share folder, remove your old hard disk, install a new hard disk (at least 250GB or larger), and use it for the installation. After the installation is complete, use the Windows Vista Transfer Wizard to restore your media and other files and settings. This way, you have your entire Windows XP MCE installation tucked safely away on your original hard disk if you need to access it again for any reason.

note For more information about the installation process, including how to perform a clean install of Windows Vista Home Premium or Ultimate editions with an upgrade DVD, see my book *Maximum PC Microsoft Windows Vista Exposed*, Que, 2007.

After you are sure that you don't need it anymore, you can connect the hard disk containing the Windows XP MCE installation to your original system that is now running Windows Vista and use Vista's Disk Management to delete the contents. You can then use the drive for additional storage space for digital video as described in Chapter 4, "Viewing and Recording Live TV."

Index

Numerics

A

B

D

E

F

J–K

L

M

N

O

S

T

U

V

W

X–Z